마더텅 영문법 3800제 2 INTERMEDIATE 학습진도표

CHAPTER 1 문장의 기초

PSS		체크	학습날짜
PSS 1	1-1	☐	/
	1-2	☐	/
	1-3	☐	/
	1-4	☐	/
	1-5	☐	/
	1-6	☐	/
	1-7	☐	/
	1-8	☐	/
PSS 2	2-1	☐	/
	2-2	☐	/
	2-3	☐	/
	2-4	☐	/
	2-5	☐	/
	2-6	☐	/
Chapter Review Test		☐	/

CHAPTER 2 시제

PSS		체크	학습날짜
PSS 1	1-1	☐	/
	1-2	☐	/
	1-3	☐	/
	1-4	☐	/
PSS 2	2-1	☐	/
	2-2	☐	/
	2-3	☐	/
	2-4	☐	/
PSS 3		☐	/
PSS 4	4-1	☐	/
	4-2	☐	/
PSS 5	5-1	☐	/
	5-2	☐	/
	5-3	☐	/
	5-4	☐	/
	5-5	☐	/
Chapter Review Test		☐	/

CHAPTER 3 조동사

PSS		체크	학습날짜
PSS 1		☐	/
PSS 2		☐	/
PSS 3		☐	/
PSS 4	4-1	☐	/
	4-2	☐	/
	4-3	☐	/
	4-4	☐	/
	4-5	☐	/
	4-6	☐	/
	4-7	☐	/
	4-8	☐	/
	4-9	☐	/
Chapter Review Test		☐	/

CHAPTER 4 수동태

PSS	체크	학습날짜
PSS 1	☐	/
PSS 2	☐	/
PSS 3	☐	/
PSS 4	☐	/
PSS 5	☐	/
PSS 6	☐	/
PSS 7	☐	/
Chapter Review Test	☐	/

CHAPTER 5 명사와 관사

PSS		체크	학습날짜
PSS 1	1-1	☐	/
	1-2	☐	/
	1-3	☐	/
PSS 2	2-1	☐	/
	2-2	☐	/
	2-3	☐	/
	2-4	☐	/
	2-5	☐	/
	2-6	☐	/
	2-7	☐	/
PSS 3	3-1	☐	/
	3-2	☐	/
PSS 4	4-1	☐	/
	4-2	☐	/
	4-3	☐	/
PSS 5		☐	/
Chapter Review Test		☐	/

CHAPTER 6 대명사

PSS		체크	학습날짜
PSS 1	1-1	☐	/
	1-2	☐	/
	1-3	☐	/
PSS 2	2-1	☐	/
	2-2	☐	/
	2-3	☐	/
PSS 3	3-1	☐	/
	3-2	☐	/
PSS 4	4-1	☐	/
	4-2	☐	/
	4-3	☐	/
	4-4	☐	/
	4-5	☐	/
	4-6	☐	/
PSS 5	5-1	☐	/
	5-2	☐	/
Chapter Review Test		☐	/

CHAPTER 7 부정사

PSS		체크	학습날짜
PSS 1	1-1	☐	/
	1-2	☐	/
	1-3	☐	/
	1-4	☐	/
PSS 2		☐	/
PSS 3	3-1	☐	/
	3-2	☐	/
PSS 4		☐	/
PSS 5		☐	/
PSS 6		☐	/
Chapter Review Test		☐	/

CHAPTER 8 동명사

PSS		체크	학습날짜
PSS 1		☐	/
PSS 2	2-1	☐	/
	2-2	☐	/
	2-3	☐	/
PSS 3		☐	/
PSS 4		☐	/
Chapter Review Test		☐	/

CHAPTER 9 분사

PSS		체크	학습날짜
PSS 1		☐	/
PSS 2	2-1	☐	/
	2-2	☐	/
PSS 3		☐	/
PSS 4		☐	/
PSS 5	5-1	☐	/
	5-2	☐	/
Chapter Review Test		☐	/

마더텅 영문법 3800제 2 INTERMEDIATE 학습진도표

CHAPTER 10 형용사

PSS		체크	학습날짜
PSS 1		☐	/
PSS 2		☐	/
PSS 3		☐	/
PSS 4		☐	/
PSS 5	5-1	☐	/
	5-2	☐	/
	5-3	☐	/
	5-4	☐	/
PSS 6	6-1	☐	/
	6-2	☐	/
	6-3	☐	/
Chapter Review Test		☐	/

CHAPTER 11 부사

PSS		체크	학습날짜
PSS 1	1-1	☐	/
	1-2	☐	/
	1-3	☐	/
	1-4	☐	/
PSS 2	2-1	☐	/
	2-2	☐	/
	2-3	☐	/
	2-4	☐	/
	2-5	☐	/
	2-6	☐	/
	2-7	☐	/
Chapter Review Test		☐	/

CHAPTER 12 가정법

PSS		체크	학습날짜
PSS 1		☐	/
PSS 2	2-1	☐	/
	2-2	☐	/
	2-3	☐	/
PSS 3	3-1	☐	/
	3-2	☐	/
	3-3	☐	/
Chapter Review Test		☐	/

CHAPTER 15 접속사

PSS	체크	학습날짜
PSS 1	☐	/
PSS 2	☐	/
PSS 3	☐	/
PSS 4	☐	/
PSS 5	☐	/
PSS 6	☐	/
PSS 7	☐	/
PSS 8	☐	/
PSS 9	☐	/
PSS 10	☐	/
Chapter Review Test	☐	/

CHAPTER 13 비교구문

PSS		체크	학습날짜
PSS 1	1-1	☐	/
	1-2	☐	/
	1-3	☐	/
	1-4	☐	/
PSS 2	2-1	☐	/
	2-2	☐	/
PSS 3	3-1	☐	/
	3-2	☐	/
	3-3	☐	/
	3-4	☐	/
	3-5	☐	/
	3-6	☐	/
PSS 4	4-1	☐	/
	4-2	☐	/
	4-3	☐	/
Chapter Review Test		☐	/

CHAPTER 14 관계사

PSS		체크	학습날짜
PSS 1	1-1	☐	/
	1-2	☐	/
	1-3	☐	/
	1-4	☐	/
	1-5	☐	/
	1-6	☐	/
PSS 2	2-1	☐	/
	2-2	☐	/
Chapter Review Test		☐	/

CHAPTER 16 전치사

PSS		체크	학습날짜
PSS 1	1-1	☐	/
	1-2	☐	/
	1-3	☐	/
	1-4	☐	/
	1-5	☐	/
	1-6	☐	/
PSS 2	2-1	☐	/
	2-2	☐	/
	2-3	☐	/
	2-4	☐	/
	2-5	☐	/
	2-6	☐	/
	2-7	☐	/
	2-8	☐	/
PSS 3	3-1	☐	/
	3-2	☐	/
	3-3	☐	/
	3-4	☐	/
Chapter Review Test		☐	/

CHAPTER 17 일치·도치·화법&속담

PSS		체크	학습날짜
PSS 1	1-1	☐	/
	1-2	☐	/
PSS 2		☐	/
PSS 3		☐	/
PSS 4		☐	/
PSS 5		☐	/
PSS 6		☐	/
Chapter Review Test		☐	/

PROBLEM SOLVING SKILL

www.toptutor.co.kr

수동태의 형태 CHAPTER 4 PSS 2

형태 : 주어 + be동사 (not) + 과거분사 + by + 목적격.

They built this house.

This house was built by them.

	능동태	수동태
현재	Minho plants trees.	Trees **are planted** by Minho.
과거	Minho planted trees.	Trees **were planted** by Minho.
미래	Minho will plant trees.	Trees **will be planted** by Minho.
현재완료	Minho has planted trees.	Trees **have been planted** by Minho.

외워야 할 수동태 표현 CHAPTER 4 PSS 7

be made of	~로 만들어지다	be filled with	~로 가득 차 있다
be interested in	~에 흥미가 있다	be covered with	~로 덮여 있다
be surprised at	~에 놀라다	be known to	~에게 알려져 있다
be pleased with[about]	~에 기뻐하다	be satisfied with	~에 만족하다
be excited about	~에 흥분해 있다	be worried about	~에 대해 걱정하다

명사의 종류 CHAPTER 5 PSS 2-1

셀 수 있는 명사	a(n)을 붙이거나 복수형으로 쓸 수 있고, many, (a) few, some, any, no처럼 수를 나타내는 형용사와 함께 쓸 수 있다.	
	보통명사	bag, student, book, pencil, computer, tree, dish, animal
	집합명사	class, family, team, audience
셀 수 없는 명사	a(n)을 붙이거나 복수형으로 쓸 수 없고, 물질명사와 추상명사는 much, (a) little, some, any, no처럼 양을 나타내는 형용사와 함께 쓸 수 있다.	
	고유명사	David, Insuk, Korea, Chicago, Monday, Christmas
	물질명사	water, salt, money, juice, air, milk, ice, bread, gold, sugar
	추상명사	love, peace, knowledge, beauty, health, honesty, information, news, happiness, hope, kindness, advice

부정사/동명사를 목적어로 가지는 동사 CHAPTER 7 PSS 1-2 & CHAPTER 8 PSS 2-1~2-3

1. to부정사를 목적어로 가지는 동사

want, wish, decide, promise, would like, would love, plan, expect, refuse, hope, need, learn, agree

2. 동명사를 목적어로 가지는 동사

enjoy, mind, finish, stop, give up, practice, put off, deny, imagine, quit, suggest, dislike

3. 둘 다를 목적어로 가지는 동사

like, love, hate, begin, start, continue, intend, prefer

4. 둘 다를 목적어로 가지지만 뜻이 달라지는 동사

try, remember, forget

- I **tried calling** Bob yesterday. 나는 어제 Bob에게 **전화를 해봤다.**
- I **tried to call** Bob yesterday. 나는 어제 Bob에게 **전화하려고 노력했다.**

외워야 할 주요 접속사, 접속부사 CHAPTER 15

접속사	뜻	예문
and (명령문 + and)	~와, 그리고, ~하고 나서 (~해라, 그러면)	• I went back home **and** (I) studied for the exam. • Wake up now, **and** you'll catch the bus.
or (명령문 + or)	또는, 아니면 (~해라, 그렇지 않으면)	• Have you been to New York **or** Chicago? • Wake up now, **or** you'll miss the bus.
both A and B	A와 B 둘 다	• **Both** Jim **and** Sue like mathematics the best.
not only A but also B	A뿐만 아니라 B도	• Jim is good at **not only** singing **but also** studying.
either A or B	A와 B 중 어느 하나	• **Either** Jim **or** Sue likes mathematics the best.
neither A nor B	A도 B도 ~아닌	• **Neither** Jim **nor** Sue likes mathematics the best.
because	~ 때문에	• Linda often goes to concerts **because** she likes music.
so	그래서	• Linda likes music, **so** she often goes to concerts.

마더텅 영문법 3800제 2 INTERMEDIATE 핵심 문법 사항 암기표

핵심 문법 사항을 알기 쉽게 정리한 비법 노트

불규칙 변화 동사의 과거형 CHAPTER 2 PSS 2-4

원형	과거형	과거분사형	원형	과거형	과거분사형
beat	beat	beaten	ring	rang	rung
cut	cut	cut	rise	rose	risen
draw	drew	drawn	run	ran	run
dream	dreamed/dreamt	dreamed/dreamt	see	saw	seen
fly	flew	flown	sink	sank	sunk
hide	hid	hidden	spread	spread	spread
lay	laid	laid	stand	stood	stood
lead	led	led	steal	stole	stolen
lie (눕다/놓여 있다)	lay	lain	sweep	swept	swept
mean	meant	meant	teach	taught	taught
ride	rode	ridden	think	thought	thought

*교재 45~46쪽 나머지 동사의 변화형도 꼭 외우자!

현재완료의 형태와 용법 CHAPTER 2 PSS 5-1, 2

형태 : 주어 + **have/has (not)** + 과거분사
예문 : I have lost my puppy.

용법	예문
완료	I **have just planted** 10 trees. 나는 방금 열 그루의 나무를 심었다.
경험	**Have** you **ever tried** potato chips? 감자칩을 먹어본 적이 있니?
결과	She **has lost** her bag. 그녀는 가방을 잃어버렸다.
계속	I **have lived** here **since** March. 나는 3월부터 여기에서 살았다.

접속사	뜻	예문
if	~한다면	• **If** you read the book, you can do your homework.
so that ~	~하기 위해서, ~할 수 있도록	• I studied hard **so that** I could enter the university.
even though [although/ though]	비록 ~일지라도, 비록 ~에도 불구하고	• **Even though[Although, Though]** it was raining, I went shopping.
시간을 나타내는 접속사		
when	~할 때	• **When** I was a child, my family lived in Busan.
as	~하고 있을 때, ~하면서	• Ann sometimes listens to music **as** she studies.
before	~하기 전에	• I take off my shoes **before** I enter a room.
after	~한 후에	• Let's go for a walk **after** you finish your dinner.
until	~할 때까지	• My sister didn't go to bed **until** I got home.
while	~하는 동안	• **While** I was waiting for the bus, I read a book.
as soon as	~하자마자	• He got a job **as soon as** he finished school.
접속부사		
for example	예를 들면	• Mina does a lot of things for her family. **For example**, she helps her mom cook.
however	그러나	• Everyone agreed with Mark. **However**, I had a different idea.
therefore	그러므로	• I have an English quiz tomorrow, but I haven't studied. **Therefore**, I have to study hard tonight.
in addition [besides]	게다가	• I like the restaurant. The food is very delicious. **In addition[Besides]**, the service is very good.
finally	결국	• Sena was interested in law. **Finally**, she became a lawyer.

탄탄한 영어 실력을 위한 영문법의 시작

마더텅 영문법 3800제

토익·토플 TEPS 공무원영어 대비

INTERMEDIATE 2

발행 초판 1쇄 (2023년 4월 7일) **발행인** 문숙영 **발행처** 마더텅(Mother Tongue Co., Ltd.) **교재 개발 책임** 서은숙
교재 개발 진행 김현수, 최은조, 박상우, 신준기 **문제편 집필** 김석화(수원 수원여고) 선생님, 소피아(김규은 경기 분당) 선생님, 남현정, 서연서, 이윤정, 이옥현, 양진희, 김미경(서울 서초) 선생님, 하은옥, 홍성경, 고미라(서울 상경중) 선생님, 김현, 박혜미, 김다영, 박상우
교사용 검토 김경미(강남 대치) 선생님, 윤미선(서울 가양) 선생님, 문명기(서울 강동) 선생님, 김석화(수원 수원여고) 선생님, 김미경(서울 동작) 선생님, 최민제(서울 강동) 선생님, 이은혜(경기 일산) 선생님, 소피아(김규은 경기 분당) 선생님, 양원석(서울 서초) 선생님
교정 김경미, 김현수, 최은조, 정은주, 김다영, 유지원, 홍지민, 신진실, 도예원, 조수성, 서연서, 이윤정, 윤수경, 양진희, 성은혜, 홍성경, 오정훈, 하은옥, 이은영 **영문 감수** Kathryn O' Handley **단어장 녹음** 손정은, Janet Lee, 최석환 **녹음 편집** 와이알 미디어
디자인 김연실, 양은선 **삽화** 이혜승, 정제욱, 백승헌, 이유진, 이순웅, 정재환 **인디자인 편집** 박경아 **제작** 이주영
주소 서울시 금천구 가마산로 96, 708호(가산동, 대륭테크노타운 8차) **홈페이지** www.toptutor.co.kr **등록번호** 제 1-2423호

* 이 책에 실린 모든 내용에 대한 저작권은 (주)마더텅에 있으므로 적법한 허락 없이는 어떠한 형태나 수단으로도 전재, 복사할 수 없습니다.
* 잘못 만들어진 책은 바꾸어 드립니다.

Problem Solving Skill

차례

CHAPTER 1 | 문장의 기초 Introduction to Sentences

PSS 1 의문문과 감탄문
- PSS 1-1 Yes/No 의문문 ········ 6
- PSS 1-2 의문사로 시작하는 의문문 ········ 8
- PSS 1-3 부가의문문 Ⅰ ········ 10
- PSS 1-4 부가의문문 Ⅱ ········ 10
- PSS 1-5 선택의문문 ········ 11
- PSS 1-6 간접의문문 Ⅰ ········ 13
- PSS 1-7 간접의문문 Ⅱ ········ 14
- PSS 1-8 감탄문 ········ 15

PSS 2 문장의 5형식
- PSS 2-1 문장의 5형식 ········ 16
- PSS 2-2 주격 보어를 필요로 하는 동사 Ⅰ ········ 17
- PSS 2-3 주격 보어를 필요로 하는 동사 Ⅱ ········ 18
- PSS 2-4 두 개의 목적어를 필요로 하는 동사 ········ 19
- PSS 2-5 목적격 보어를 필요로 하는 동사 Ⅰ ········ 21
- PSS 2-6 목적격 보어를 필요로 하는 동사 Ⅱ ········ 22

Chapter Review Test ········ 24

CHAPTER 2 | 시제 Tense

PSS 1 현재시제
- PSS 1-1 동사의 3인칭 현재 단수형 ········ 36
- PSS 1-2 동사의 3인칭 현재 단수형의 발음 ········ 38
- PSS 1-3 현재시제의 쓰임 Ⅰ ········ 39
- PSS 1-4 현재시제의 쓰임 Ⅱ ········ 40

PSS 2 과거시제
- PSS 2-1 be동사의 과거형 ········ 41
- PSS 2-2 규칙 변화 동사의 과거형 ········ 42
- PSS 2-3 규칙 변화 동사 과거형의 발음 ········ 44
- PSS 2-4 불규칙 변화 동사의 과거형 ········ 45

PSS 3 미래시제 ········ 49

PSS 4 진행시제
- PSS 4-1 동사의 -ing형 ········ 50
- PSS 4-2 과거진행시제와 현재진행시제 ········ 53

PSS 5 현재완료
- PSS 5-1 현재완료의 형태 ········ 55
- PSS 5-2 현재완료의 용법 ········ 56
- PSS 5-3 for와 since ········ 57
- PSS 5-4 현재완료시제와 과거시제 ········ 59
- PSS 5-5 현재완료 진행시제 ········ 61

Chapter Review Test ········ 63

CHAPTER 3 | 조동사 Modals

PSS 1 조동사의 쓰임 ········ 72
PSS 2 조동사의 부정 ········ 73
PSS 3 조동사로 시작하는 의문문 ········ 75
PSS 4 조동사의 종류
- PSS 4-1 must Ⅰ ········ 76
- PSS 4-2 must Ⅱ ········ 77
- PSS 4-3 can, could Ⅰ ········ 79
- PSS 4-4 can, could Ⅱ ········ 80
- PSS 4-5 do ········ 81
- PSS 4-6 should, had better ········ 82
- PSS 4-7 will, would ········ 84
- PSS 4-8 may, might ········ 85
- PSS 4-9 used to, would ········ 86

Chapter Review Test ········ 89

CHAPTER 4 | 수동태 Passive Voice

PSS 1 수동태에 많이 쓰이는 불규칙 동사 ········ 96
PSS 2 수동태 문장 만드는 법 ········ 97
PSS 3 수동태의 부정문과 의문문 ········ 99
PSS 4 수동태의 시제 ········ 100
PSS 5 조동사가 있는 수동태 ········ 102
PSS 6 주의해야 할 수동태 ········ 103
PSS 7 수동태의 관용 표현 ········ 105

Chapter Review Test ········ 108

CHAPTER 5 | 명사와 관사 Nouns and Articles

PSS 1 명사의 복수형
- PSS 1-1 명사의 복수형 Ⅰ ········ 116
- PSS 1-2 명사의 복수형 Ⅱ ········ 117
- PSS 1-3 명사의 복수형 Ⅲ ········ 118

PSS 2 명사의 쓰임
- PSS 2-1 명사의 종류 ········ 119
- PSS 2-2 셀 수 있는 명사 ········ 120
- PSS 2-3 셀 수 없는 명사 ········ 122
- PSS 2-4 물질명사의 쓰임 ········ 124
- PSS 2-5 주의해야 할 명사의 수 ········ 126
- PSS 2-6 명사의 소유격 ········ 127
- PSS 2-7 동격 ········ 128

PSS 3 부정관사 a, an
- PSS 3-1 a, an의 쓰임 ········ 130
- PSS 3-2 a, an의 의미 ········ 131

PSS 4 정관사 the
- PSS 4-1 the의 쓰임 Ⅰ ········ 133
- PSS 4-2 the의 쓰임 Ⅱ ········ 134
- PSS 4-3 the의 쓰임 Ⅲ ········ 136

PSS 5 관사를 쓰지 않는 경우 ········ 137

Chapter Review Test ········ 140

CHAPTER 6 | 대명사 Pronouns

PSS 1 인칭대명사
- PSS 1-1 주격, 목적격 ········ 146
- PSS 1-2 소유격, 소유대명사 ········ 147
- PSS 1-3 재귀대명사 ········ 149

CONTENTS

PSS 2	it의 쓰임
PSS 2-1	비인칭주어 it ... 150
PSS 2-2	it의 특별 용법 ... 151
PSS 2-3	가주어 it / 가목적어 it ... 152

PSS 3	지시대명사
PSS 3-1	this, that ... 153
PSS 3-2	that/those의 특별 용법 ... 155

PSS 4	부정대명사
PSS 4-1	one ... 156
PSS 4-2	other, another ... 157
PSS 4-3	관용 표현 ... 159
PSS 4-4	each, every ... 160
PSS 4-5	all, both, rest ... 162
PSS 4-6	some-, any- ... 164

PSS 5	의문대명사
PSS 5-1	who ... 166
PSS 5-2	which, what ... 167

Chapter Review Test ... 169

CHAPTER 7 | 부정사 Infinitives

PSS 1	명사적 용법
PSS 1-1	주어와 주격 보어로 쓰이는 to부정사 ... 178
PSS 1-2	목적어로 쓰이는 to부정사 ... 179
PSS 1-3	목적격 보어로 쓰이는 to부정사 ... 180
PSS 1-4	의문사+to부정사 ... 182

PSS 2	형용사적 용법 ... 183

PSS 3	부사적 용법
PSS 3-1	목적을 나타내는 to부정사 ... 184
PSS 3-2	형용사 수식, 결과를 나타내는 to부정사 ... 187

PSS 4	to부정사의 의미상의 주어 ... 188
PSS 5	too ~ to, enough to ... 189
PSS 6	원형부정사 ... 191

Chapter Review Test ... 193

CHAPTER 8 | 동명사 Gerunds

PSS 1	주어와 보어로 쓰이는 동명사 ... 204

PSS 2	동사의 목적어로 쓰이는 동명사
PSS 2-1	동사+동명사 ... 205
PSS 2-2	동사+동명사/to부정사 Ⅰ ... 206
PSS 2-3	동사+동명사/to부정사 Ⅱ ... 207

PSS 3	전치사의 목적어로 쓰이는 동명사 ... 209
PSS 4	동명사의 관용 표현 ... 211

Chapter Review Test ... 213

CHAPTER 9 | 분사 Participles

PSS 1	분사의 종류 ... 222

PSS 2	분사의 역할
PSS 2-1	명사를 수식하는 분사 ... 223
PSS 2-2	보어로 쓰이는 분사 ... 224

PSS 3	현재분사와 동명사 ... 226
PSS 4	감정을 나타내는 분사 ... 227

PSS 5	분사구문
PSS 5-1	분사구문 만드는 법 ... 229
PSS 5-2	with+명사+분사 ... 231

Chapter Review Test ... 233

CHAPTER 10 | 형용사 Adjectives

PSS 1	형용사의 쓰임 ... 242
PSS 2	-thing, -one, -body+형용사 ... 244
PSS 3	주의해야 할 형용사의 용법 ... 244
PSS 4	형용사의 어순 ... 247

PSS 5	수나 양을 나타내는 형용사
PSS 5-1	many, much ... 248
PSS 5-2	few, little ... 250
PSS 5-3	a few, a little ... 251
PSS 5-4	some, any ... 253

PSS 6	수사
PSS 6-1	분수와 소수 ... 255
PSS 6-2	연도와 날짜 ... 256
PSS 6-3	배수사 ... 257

Chapter Review Test ... 258

CHAPTER 11 | 부사 Adverbs

PSS 1	부사의 형태
PSS 1-1	형용사를 부사로 만드는 법 Ⅰ ... 266
PSS 1-2	형용사를 부사로 만드는 법 Ⅱ ... 267
PSS 1-3	형용사와 형태가 같은 부사 ... 268
PSS 1-4	형용사 형태의 부사에 '-ly'를 붙이면 다른 뜻이 되는 부사 ... 270

PSS 2	여러 가지 부사의 용법
PSS 2-1	빈도부사의 위치 ... 272
PSS 2-2	already, yet, still ... 274
PSS 2-3	too, either ... 276
PSS 2-4	very, much ... 277
PSS 2-5	else, even ... 278
PSS 2-6	「타동사+부사」의 어순 ... 280
PSS 2-7	의문부사 ... 282

Chapter Review Test ... 284

CHAPTER 12 | 가정법 Conditionals

PSS 1	조건을 나타내는 if ... 292

PSS 2	가정법 과거
PSS 2-1	if+가정법 과거 ... 293
PSS 2-2	I wish+가정법 과거 ... 295
PSS 2-3	동사의 현재형+as if+가정법 과거 ... 296

PSS 3	가정법 과거완료
PSS 3-1	if+가정법 과거완료 ... 297
PSS 3-2	I wish+가정법 과거완료 ... 298
PSS 3-3	동사의 현재형+as if+가정법 과거완료 ... 299

Chapter Review Test ... 301

Problem Solving Skill

CHAPTER 13 | 비교구문 Comparisons

PSS 1 비교급과 최상급 만드는 법
- PSS 1-1 규칙 변화 I ········ 306
- PSS 1-2 규칙 변화 II ········ 306
- PSS 1-3 규칙 변화 III ········ 307
- PSS 1-4 불규칙 변화 ········ 309

PSS 2 원급을 이용한 비교
- PSS 2-1 as+원급+as ········ 311
- PSS 2-2 as+원급+as+주어+can[could] ········ 313

PSS 3 비교급을 이용한 비교
- PSS 3-1 비교급+than ········ 315
- PSS 3-2 비교급 강조 ········ 317
- PSS 3-3 less+원급+than ········ 318
- PSS 3-4 the+비교급, the+비교급 ········ 319
- PSS 3-5 There is nothing ~ 비교급+than … ········ 320
- PSS 3-6 비교급+and+비교급 ········ 322

PSS 4 최상급을 이용한 비교
- PSS 4-1 the+최상급 ········ 322
- PSS 4-2 one of+the+최상급+복수 명사 ········ 324
- PSS 4-3 최상급의 다른 표현 ········ 325

Chapter Review Test ········ 327

CHAPTER 14 | 관계사 Relatives

PSS 1 관계대명사
- PSS 1-1 who ········ 336
- PSS 1-2 which ········ 338
- PSS 1-3 that ········ 339
- PSS 1-4 what ········ 341
- PSS 1-5 관계대명사의 생략 ········ 342
- PSS 1-6 계속적 용법 ········ 343

PSS 2 관계부사
- PSS 2-1 관계부사의 종류 ········ 344
- PSS 2-2 관계부사의 주의해야 할 용법 ········ 345

Chapter Review Test ········ 347

CHAPTER 15 | 접속사 Conjunctions

- PSS 1 and, but, or ········ 356
- PSS 2 명령문+and/or ········ 357
- PSS 3 상관접속사 ········ 358
- PSS 4 because, so ········ 359
- PSS 5 if ········ 361
- PSS 6 so that ~, so ~ that … ········ 363
- PSS 7 명사절을 이끄는 that ········ 364
- PSS 8 시간을 나타내는 접속사 ········ 366
- PSS 9 even though, although, though ········ 367
- PSS 10 접속부사 ········ 368

Chapter Review Test ········ 370

CHAPTER 16 | 전치사 Prepositions

PSS 1 시간을 나타내는 전치사
- PSS 1-1 at, on, in I ········ 382
- PSS 1-2 at, on, in II ········ 383
- PSS 1-3 from, since ········ 385
- PSS 1-4 by, until ········ 386
- PSS 1-5 before, after ········ 387
- PSS 1-6 for, during ········ 389

PSS 2 장소, 방향을 나타내는 전치사
- PSS 2-1 at, in, on I ········ 391
- PSS 2-2 at, in, on II ········ 392
- PSS 2-3 above, below, over, under ········ 394
- PSS 2-4 up, down, into, out of ········ 395
- PSS 2-5 across, along, through, around ········ 397
- PSS 2-6 by, in front of, behind ········ 398
- PSS 2-7 between, among ········ 400
- PSS 2-8 to, for ········ 401

PSS 3 그 밖의 전치사
- PSS 3-1 with, about, like ········ 402
- PSS 3-2 by, as, in ········ 403
- PSS 3-3 형용사・분사와 함께 쓰이는 전치사 ········ 405
- PSS 3-4 동사와 함께 쓰이는 전치사 ········ 406

Chapter Review Test ········ 410

CHAPTER 17 | 일치・도치・화법 & 속담 Agreement・Inversion・Narration & Proverbs

PSS 1 시제의 일치
- PSS 1-1 시제 일치의 원칙 ········ 424
- PSS 1-2 시제 일치의 예외 ········ 425

PSS 2 도치 ········ 426

PSS 3 평서문의 화법 전환 ········ 428

PSS 4 의문문의 화법 전환 ········ 430

PSS 5 명령문의 화법 전환 ········ 432

PSS 6 속담 ········ 433

Chapter Review Test ········ 436

CHAPTER 1
문장의 기초

성취도 자기 평가 활용법

구분	평가 기준
Excellent	문법 내용을 모두 이해하고, 문제를 모두 맞힘.
Very good	문법 내용은 충분히 이해했으나 실수로 1~2문제 틀림.
Good	문법 내용이 조금 어려워 3~4문제 틀림.
needs **R**eview	문법 내용 이해가 어렵고, 5문제 이상 틀림, 복습 필요.

PSS 1 의문문과 감탄문	페이지	학습날짜	성취도 자기평가 E V G R	학습체크
PSS 1-1 Yes/No 의문문	6	/		☐
PSS 1-2 의문사로 시작하는 의문문	8	/		☐
PSS 1-3 부가의문문 I	10	/		☐
PSS 1-4 부가의문문 II	10	/		☐
PSS 1-5 선택의문문	11	/		☐
PSS 1-6 간접의문문 I	13	/		☐
PSS 1-7 간접의문문 II	14	/		☐
PSS 1-8 감탄문	15	/		☐

PSS 2 문장의 5형식	페이지	학습날짜	성취도 자기평가 E V G R	학습체크
PSS 2-1 문장의 5형식	16	/		☐
PSS 2-2 주격 보어를 필요로 하는 동사 I	17	/		☐
PSS 2-3 주격 보어를 필요로 하는 동사 II	18	/		☐
PSS 2-4 두 개의 목적어를 필요로 하는 동사	19	/		☐
PSS 2-5 목적격 보어를 필요로 하는 동사 I	21	/		☐
PSS 2-6 목적격 보어를 필요로 하는 동사 II	22	/		☐
Chapter Review Test	24	/		☐

의문문과 감탄문

PSS 1-1 Yes/No 의문문

Be동사가 있는 의문문	Be동사+주어 ~?
일반동사가 있는 의문문	Do[Does, Did]+주어+동사원형 ~?
조동사가 있는 의문문	조동사+주어+동사원형 ~?

1. 의문사로 시작되지 않는 의문문은 Yes나 No로 대답한다.

    Are you a student? 너는 학생이니?
    – **Yes**, I am. (= Yes, I am a student.) 네, 그렇습니다.
    – **No**, I'm not. (= No, I'm not a student.) 아니오, 그렇지 않습니다.

    Did they finish their homework? 그들은 숙제를 끝냈니?
    – **Yes**, they did. (= Yes, they finished their homework.) 네, 끝냈습니다.
    – **No**, they didn't. (= No, they didn't finish their homework.) 아니오, 끝내지 않았습니다.

    Will you come to my house? 너 우리집에 올래?
    – **Yes**, I will. (= Yes, I'll come to your house.) 네, 가겠습니다.
    – **No**, I won't. (= No, I won't come to your house.) 아니오, 가지 않겠습니다.

2. 부정어로 시작하는 의문문에 대한 대답은 질문과 상관없이 대답의 내용이 긍정이면 Yes, 부정이면 No로 답한다. 단, 우리말 해석은 반대로 한다.

    Isn't she kind? 그녀는 친절하지 않니?
    – **Yes**, she is. (= Yes, she is kind.) 아니오, 친절합니다.
    – **No**, she isn't. (= No, she isn't kind.) 네, 친절하지 않습니다.

    Didn't you meet Mr. Jones? 너는 Jones 씨를 만나지 않았니?
    – **Yes**, I did. (= Yes, I met him.) 아니오, 만났습니다.
    – **No**, I didn't. (= No, I didn't meet him.) 네, 만나지 않았습니다.

    Can't you play soccer? 넌 축구를 할 수 없니?
    – **Yes**, I can. (= Yes, I can play soccer.) 아니오, 할 수 있습니다.
    – **No**, I can't. (= No, I can't play soccer.) 네, 못합니다.

PRACTICE 1

〈보기〉와 같이 주어진 문장을 의문문으로 바꾸어 쓰세요.

보 기	Jack has a nice car.
	➡ Does Jack have a nice car?

1 She can get there on time.
   ➡ _____

2 Those gloves aren't yours.
   ➡ _____

3 He doesn't go to church on Sundays.
   ➡ _____

4 Your mom is angry at you.
   ➡ _____

5 David was drawing a picture.
   ➡ _____

6 This can be true.
   ➡ _____

7 Many people make plans for the New Year.
   ➡ _____

8 Your brother didn't win the race.
   ➡ _____

PRACTICE 2

〈보기〉와 같이 주어진 질문에 대한 알맞은 대답을 쓰세요.

보 기	You don't have a sister.
	A: Do you have a sister?
	B: No, I don't.

1 Ted likes swimming in summer.
   A: Does Ted like swimming in summer?
   B: _____

2 They don't have a small car.
   A: Don't they have a small car?
   B: _____

3 You felt cold outside.
   A: Didn't you feel cold outside?
   B: _____

4 He wasn't playing tennis at 5.
   A: Was he playing tennis at 5?
   B: _____

5 You were hungry during the meeting.
   A: Weren't you hungry during the meeting?
   B: _____

6 Cats can see well even in dark places.
   A: Can cats see well even in dark places?
   B: _____

7 He studies hard for the exam.
   A: Doesn't he study hard for the exam?
   B: _____

8 Linda isn't good at sports.
   A: Isn't Linda good at sports?
   B: _____

PSS 1-2 의문사로 시작하는 의문문

의문사로 시작하는 의문문은 Yes나 No로 대답하지 않는다.

Who is your English teacher? — **Mr. Kim.**
네 영어 선생님은 누구시니? 김 선생님이셔.

When did she arrive? — **At 9 o'clock.**
그녀는 언제 도착했니? 9시에.

Where does he live? — **He lives in Seoul.**
그는 어디에 사니? 그는 서울에 살아.

What are you watching? — **I'm watching the news.**
넌 무엇을 보고 있니? 난 뉴스를 보고 있어.

How was your weekend? — **It was great. I went to the aquarium with Ted.**
주말 어떻게 보냈니? 아주 좋았어. 나는 Ted와 수족관에 갔었어.

Why are you running? — **I'm running because I need to exercise.**
넌 왜 뛰고 있니? 운동을 할 필요가 있기 때문에 나는 뛰고 있어.

When can we meet again? — **Maybe next Tuesday.**
우리 언제 다시 만날 수 있을까? 아마도 다음 주 화요일쯤.

정답 p.2

PRACTICE 3

우리말과 일치하도록 괄호 안에 주어진 단어를 바르게 배열하세요.

1 식당에서 누구를 만났니?
➡ _____ (you, did, meet, who, at the restaurant)

2 Kelly는 오늘 왜 그렇게 바쁘니?
➡ _____ (Kelly, so busy, is, why, today)

3 그가 너한테 뭐라고 말했니?
➡ _____ (he, did, say, to you, what)

4 그 열쇠를 어디에서 찾았니?
➡ _____ (where, you, did, find, the key)

5 언제 그가 여행에서 돌아올까?
➡ _____ (return, from the trip, when, he, will)

6 (제가) 이 기계를 어떻게 사용하죠?
➡ _____ (how, I, do, this machine, use)

7 넌 어떻게 지내고 있니?
➡ _____ (everything, how, with, is, you)

PRACTICE 4

Becky의 대답을 보고, Tony의 질문을 완성하세요.

1	__Who is__ your best friend?	My best friend is Carrie.
2	_____ your birthday?	My birthday is August 10th.
3	_____ the concert?	It was great.
4	_____ you buy those shoes?	I bought them at a department store.
5	_____ you late for work today?	I got up late this morning.
6	_____ your favorite soccer player?	My favorite soccer player is Son Heung-min.
7	_____ you do last night?	I studied English.
8	_____ you want to visit next summer?	I want to visit Hawaii.
9	_____ the boss leave the office?	He left 30 minutes ago.
10	_____ you call him?	I called him to get his address.

Tony

PSS 1-3 부가의문문 I

부가의문문은 우리말에서와 마찬가지로 문장의 끝에서 '그렇지?', '그렇지 않니?'처럼 자신의 말에 확신하며 상대방의 동의를 구하는 표현이다. 평서문이나 명령문 뒤에 「동사＋주어?」의 형태로 쓴다.

1. 주어＋동사의 긍정형 ~, be/do/조동사의 부정 축약형＋인칭대명사?

    You **are** hungry, **aren't you?** 넌 배고프지, 그렇지 않니?
    Jina **likes** chocolate, **doesn't she?** 지나는 초콜릿을 좋아해, 그렇지 않니?
    You **can** go there without me, **can't you?** 너는 나 없이도 그곳에 갈 수 있어, 그렇지 않니?
    This movie **was** exciting, **wasn't it?** 이 영화는 흥미진진했어, 그렇지 않니?
    cf. 주어에 this나 that이 포함되어 사물을 가리킬 때, 부가의문문의 인칭대명사는 it을 쓴다.

2. 주어＋동사의 부정형 ~, be/do/조동사의 긍정형＋인칭대명사?

    It **isn't** a good idea, **is it?** 그것은 좋은 생각이 아니야, 그렇지?
    You **won't** go out now, **will you?** 넌 지금 나가지 않을 거야, 그렇지?
    The students **didn't** go on a picnic, **did they?** 그 학생들은 소풍을 가지 않았어, 그렇지?
    Those bananas **aren't** fresh, **are they?** 저 바나나들은 신선하지 않아, 그렇지?
    cf. 주어에 these나 those가 포함되어 있을 때, 부가의문문의 인칭대명사는 they를 쓴다.

PRACTICE 5

정답 p.2

다음 문장의 빈칸에 알맞은 부가의문문을 쓰세요.

1 You aren't a good swimmer, _____?
2 It's very sunny today, _____?
3 Mina didn't like the idea, _____?
4 This cake tastes really good, _____?
5 Peter could get the prize, _____?
6 That was a great party, _____?
7 Those guys don't work here, _____?
8 The children were so noisy, _____?
9 These aren't your notebooks, _____?
10 Sena won't write to us, _____?
11 She reads many books, _____?
12 He read many books, _____?

PSS 1-4 부가의문문 II

1. Let's ~, shall we?

    Let's have dinner now, **shall we?** 지금 저녁을 먹자, 어때?
    Let's not play computer games, **shall we?** 컴퓨터 게임을 하지 말자, 어때?

2. 명령문, will you?

긍정명령문에서는 어조에 따라 'will you?' 또는 'won't you?'를 쓸 수 있다.
즉, 명령조로 말할 때는 will you?, 정중하게 권할 때는 won't you?를 쓴다.
Pass me the sugar, **will you?** 설탕 좀 건네줘, 알겠니? – 명령
Pass me the sugar, **won't you?** 설탕 좀 건네주세요, 그러지 않으시겠어요? – 권유
Don't be late again, **will you?** 다시는 늦지 마라, 알겠니?
cf. 부정명령문에서는 will you?만 쓰인다.

3. I am ~, am I not[aren't I]?

I'm your friend, **am I not?** 난 너의 친구야, 그렇지 않니?
= **I'm** your friend, **aren't I?**
cf. 구어체에서는 aren't I?가 더 많이 쓰인다.

정답 p.2

PRACTICE 6

다음 문장의 빈칸에 알맞은 부가의문문을 쓰세요.

1 Don't enter the room, _____?

2 I look so tired, _____?

3 This movie is famous, _____?

4 Let's take a break now, _____?

5 Tom lived there for many years, _____?

6 Those puppies weren't very healthy, _____?

7 Let's not go for a movie, _____?

8 I'm your teacher, _____?

9 Call me tonight, _____?

10 Alex and Cathy can't play the flute, _____?

PSS 1-5 선택의문문

선택의문문은 or를 사용하여 선택의 대상을 묻는 의문문으로, 둘 중 하나를 선택하여 대답해야 하므로 Yes나 No로 대답하지 않는다.

How would you like to pay, **cash or credit card**? – **Cash.**
현금과 신용카드 중 어느 것으로 계산하시겠어요?   현금이요.

> Which is longer, **the Nile or the Mississippi**?
> 나일강과 미시시피강 중 어느 것이 더 깁니까?
>
> – **The Nile is longer than the Mississippi.**
> 나일강이 미시시피강보다 더 깁니다.
>
> Did you **make them or buy them**?
> 당신은 그것들을 만들었나요, 아니면 샀나요?
>
> – **I made them.**
> 나는 그것들을 만들었습니다.
>
> Is it **green or blue**?
> 그건 초록색인가요, 아니면 파란색인가요?
>
> – **It's blue.**
> 파란색입니다.

정답 p.2

PRACTICE 7

그림을 보고, 대화의 빈칸에 알맞은 말을 쓰세요.

1    2    3

4    5    6

1 A: What would you like to eat, steak or spaghetti?
    B: _____, please.

2 A: Is he playing soccer or baseball?
    B: He is playing _____.

3 A: Which do you wear more often, a skirt or pants?
    B: I wear _____ more often.

4 A: Are they eating hamburgers or noodles?
    B: They are eating _____.

5 A: Who gave the book to you, your father or mother?
    B: _____ gave me the book.

6 A: How would you like to go there, by bus or by train?
    B: I would like to go there _____.

PSS 1-6 간접의문문 I

한 문장 안에서 의문사가 이끄는 절이 그 문장의 일부로 쓰이는 경우, 의문사가 이끄는 절을 간접의문문이라고 한다.

1. 의문사가 있는 경우 - 의문사 + 주어 + 동사 ~

    I don't know. + What is her name?
    ➡ I don't know **what her name is**. 저는 그녀의 이름이 무엇인지 모릅니다.

    Can you tell me? + Why did she cancel the meeting?
    ➡ Can you tell me **why she cancelled the meeting**?
    당신은 왜 그녀가 회의를 취소했는지 나에게 말해줄 수 있나요?

    cf. 간접의문문에서 의문사가 주어로 쓰인 경우에는 직접의문의 어순을 그대로 쓴다.
    Do you know? + Who helped her?
    ➡ Do you know **who helped her**? 당신은 누가 그녀를 도왔는지 아십니까?

    Does anyone know? + Who said that?
    ➡ Does anyone know **who said that**? 누가 그걸 말했는지 누군가 아십니까?

2. 의문사가 없는 경우 - if[whether] + 주어 + 동사 ~

    I wonder. + Is she one of our clients?
    ➡ I wonder **if[whether] she is one of our clients**.
    저는 그녀가 우리의 고객 중 한 명인지 궁금합니다.

    I don't know. + Does she like you?
    ➡ I don't know **if[whether] she likes you**. 나는 그녀가 당신을 좋아하는지 모릅니다.

정답 p.3

PRACTICE 8

다음 직접의문문을 간접의문문으로 바꾸어 쓰세요.

1 What does that mean?   ➡ Do you know _____?
2 Is it important?   ➡ I wonder _____.
3 How can I get to the subway station? ➡ Can you tell me _____?
4 Who broke the window?   ➡ I don't know _____.
5 Did you pass the exam?   ➡ Please tell me _____.
6 Do you love Mike?   ➡ I wonder _____.
7 Can she swim?   ➡ Could you tell me _____?
8 Was Kate seeing him?   ➡ Do you know _____?

9   Where does she live?   ➡ I don't know _____.

10 Did Max buy a new car?   ➡ I wonder _____.

11 How much does this book cost?   ➡ Do you know _____?

PSS 1-7 간접의문문 Ⅱ

간접의문문이 포함된 문장에서 think, believe, suppose, guess와 같이 생각이나 추측을 나타내는 동사가 있으면 의문사를 문장 맨 앞에 쓴다.

Do you **think**? + **What** is she doing now?
➡ **What** do you **think** she is doing now? 너는 그녀가 지금 무엇을 하고 있다고 생각하니?

Do you **believe**? + **Who** will win?
➡ **Who** do you **believe** will win? 너는 누가 이길 것이라고 믿니?

Do you **suppose**? + **When** will the copy machine be repaired?
➡ **When** do you **suppose** the copy machine will be repaired?
너는 복사기가 언제 수리될 거라고 생각하니?

Do you **guess**? + **What** was her answer?
➡ **What** do you **guess** her answer was? 너는 그녀의 대답이 뭐였다고 생각하니?

cf. 'Can you guess?'의 경우는 의문사가 문두로 나가지 않는다.
Can you guess? + **What** did I buy? ➡ Can you guess **what** I bought?

정답 p.3

PRACTICE 9

다음 두 문장을 한 문장으로 연결하세요.

1 Do you think? + What is he making?
   ➡ _____

2 Do you know? + When did he arrive?
   ➡ _____

3 Do you believe? + Who is right?
   ➡ _____

4 Do you think? + Why should we learn English?
   ➡ _____

5 I don't know. + Does Susan have feelings for me?
   ➡ _____

6 Do you believe? + When will he come?
➡ _____

7 Do you guess? + What will happen next?
➡ _____

8 Can you tell me? + Are there bookstores near here?
➡ _____

9 Do you think? + How can we solve this problem?
➡ _____

10 I wonder. + How old is your brother?
➡ _____

11 Do you believe? + Where did you lose it?
➡ _____

12 Do you suppose? + Why is he so upset?
➡ _____

PSS 1-8 감탄문

1. What(+a[an])+형용사+명사+주어+동사!

   He is a very kind man. ➡ **What** a kind man he is!
   그는 매우 친절한 사람이다. 그는 정말 친절한 사람이구나!

   They are very good teachers. ➡ **What** good teachers they are!
   그들은 매우 좋은 선생님들이다. 그들은 정말 좋은 선생님들이구나!

2. How+형용사[부사]+주어+동사!

   You are very creative. ➡ **How** creative you are!
   너는 매우 창의적이다. 너는 정말 창의적이구나!

   A cheetah runs very fast. ➡ **How** fast a cheetah runs!
   치타는 매우 빨리 달린다. 치타는 정말 빨리 달리는구나!

   cf. 감탄문에서의 「주어+동사」는 생략할 수도 있다.

PRACTICE 10

다음 문장을 감탄문으로 바꾸어 쓰세요.

1 You are very patient.   ➡ _____

2 It is very hot and humid. ➡ _____
3 She is a very well-known writer. ➡ _____
4 That is a very excellent painting. ➡ _____
5 They were very angry. ➡ _____
6 This journey is very exciting. ➡ _____
7 They were very terrible players. ➡ _____
8 She is a very friendly teacher. ➡ _____
9 He was very polite. ➡ _____
10 These are very beautiful songs. ➡ _____

PSS 2 문장의 5형식

PSS 2-1 문장의 5형식

1. **목적어를 필요로 하지 않는 동사**

   ① 주어+동사 – 1형식
   He **walked**. 그는 걸었다.
   He **walked** to the parking lot. 그는 주차장까지 걸어갔다.
   cf. 「주어+동사」 뒤에는 부사(구)와 같은 수식어가 올 수 있지만 문장의 형식에는 영향을 주지 않는다.

   ② 주어+동사+주격 보어 – 2형식
   You **look good** today. 너 오늘 좋아 보인다.
   cf. 주격 보어로는 형용사나 명사가 온다.

2. **목적어를 필요로 하는 동사**

   ① 주어+동사+목적어 – 3형식
   I **bought a car** last month. 나는 지난 달에 차를 샀다.

   ② 주어+동사+간접목적어+직접목적어 – 4형식
   She **gave me some advice**. 그녀는 내게 약간의 충고를 해 주었다.

   ③ 주어+동사+목적어+목적격 보어 – 5형식
   My puppy **makes me happy**. 내 강아지는 날 행복하게 한다.

PRACTICE 11

밑줄 친 단어/구의 문장 성분을 〈보기〉에서 찾아 각각에 해당하는 번호를 쓰세요.

보 기	① 주어 ② 동사 ③ 목적어 ④ 간접목적어 ⑤ 직접목적어 ⑥ 주격 보어 ⑦ 목적격 보어 ⑧ 부사(구)

1 I like hiphop music very much.
2 I went to school on foot.
3 He gave me a bunch of flowers.
4 The pie tastes good with honey.
5 I found the book very useful.
6 She lives in a great apartment.
7 The people looked active and lively.
8 I made her delicious cookies.
9 We have a computer in our living room.
10 Everyone calls him Mr. Funny.
11 He became a doctor to make a difference.
12 She dances very well.
13 Sunny days make me happy.
14 She asked me a couple of questions.
15 He loves his parents very much.
16 We swam in the sea under the hot sun.
17 This restaurant offers its customers free drinks.
18 These bananas went bad in a very short time.

PSS 2-2 주격 보어를 필요로 하는 동사 I

다음 동사의 보어 자리에는 형용사나 명사가 온다.

1. '~이다, (~ 상태에) 있다' – be, stay, keep, remain

   Mr. Kim's class **is interesting**. 김 선생님의 수업은 흥미롭다.
   You should **stay healthy**. 너는 건강을 유지해야 한다.
   Babies should **keep warm**. 아기들은 몸을 따뜻하게 유지해야 한다.
   cf. stay, keep, remain 등의 동사 다음에는 보어로 주로 형용사가 온다.

2. '~되다' – become, get, go, turn, grow, run

   Bob **became a teacher**. Bob은 선생님이 되었다.
   Suddenly the students **got quiet**. 갑자기 학생들이 조용해졌다.
   The milk will **go bad** in three days. 우유는 3일이 지나면 상할 것이다.
   Her face **turned red**. 그녀의 얼굴이 빨개졌다.
   The players **grew tired**. 그 선수들은 피곤해졌다.
   This well **ran dry**. 이 우물은 말랐다.
   cf. get, go, turn, grow, run 등의 동사 다음에는 보어로 주로 형용사가 온다.

PRACTICE 12

〈보기〉에서 알맞은 단어를 골라 빈칸에 쓰세요.

보 기	popular healthy tired late quiet cold black bored

1 I was _____ for the meeting this morning.
2 You should stay _____ for the next match.
3 The weather turned _____. You have to wear a jacket.
4 The soccer player became _____ in Europe. Many soccer fans want to watch him play.
5 Jinsu felt _____ during the vacation. He didn't do anything special.
6 You should keep _____ here. Don't say anything.
7 I got _____ after the long trip to Australia. I needed a rest.
8 The sky grew _____ with the clouds.

PSS 2-3 주격 보어를 필요로 하는 동사 Ⅱ

다음 동사의 보어 자리에는 형용사가 온다.

1. 감각을 나타내는 동사 – sound '~하게 들리다', smell '~한 냄새가 나다', taste '~한 맛이 나다', feel '~한 느낌이 들다'

   That **sounds** **strange**. 그것은 이상하게 들린다.
   The food **smells** **bad**. 그 음식은 냄새가 나쁘다.
   It **tastes** **great**. 그것은 맛이 좋다.
   I **feel** **good** today. 나는 오늘 기분이 좋다.

2. '~해 보이다' – look, seem, appear

   You **look** **tired**. 너 피곤해 보인다.
   The box **seems** **heavy** to carry. 그 상자는 옮기기에 무거워 보인다.
   Becky **appears** **rich**. Becky는 부유해 보인다.
   cf. 「감각동사 like+명사」 '~처럼 …하다'
      He **looks like** **a famous movie star**. 그는 유명한 영화배우처럼 보인다.
      It **sounds like** **a good idea**. 그것은 좋은 생각처럼 들린다.
      This candy **tastes like** **apples**. 이 사탕은 사과처럼 맛이 난다.

PRACTICE 13

괄호 안에 주어진 단어 중 알맞은 것을 고르세요.

1 Sora looks (happy, happily) today.

2 Linda felt (terrible, terribly) about the news.

3 They treated me (nice, nicely).

4 I want to (look, look like) a famous star.

5 I don't speak English (good, well).

6 The mushroom soup tasted (salty, saltily).

7 That sounds (good, well) to me.

8 Jack appeared (sad, sadly).

9 You can solve this math problem (easy, easily).

10 This apple smells so (sweet, sweetly).

11 It seems a little (strange, strangely).

12 That (sounds, sounds like) a good plan.

13 The skin of an elephant (feels, feels like) tough.

14 The lady in white danced (beautiful, beautifully).

PSS 2-4 두 개의 목적어를 필요로 하는 동사

'~에게 …을 주다'라는 의미의 동사를 수여동사라고 하고, 수여동사는 두 개의 목적어가 필요하다. 두 개의 목적어를 필요로 하는 동사를 사용한 4형식 문장은 동사에 따라 to, for, of 의 전치사를 이용하여 3형식 문장으로 바꿀 수 있다.

1. give lend pay send tell show teach sell write + 간접목적어 [~에게] + 직접목적어 [~을/를] — 4형식

⇩

give lend pay send tell show teach sell write + 직접목적어 + to + 간접목적어 — 3형식

He **gave** her a blue box. ➡ He **gave** a blue box **to** her. 그는 그녀에게 파란 상자를 주었다.

My sister **sent** me a letter. ➡ My sister **sent** a letter **to** me. 언니가 내게 편지를 보냈다.

I **taught** students history. ➡ I **taught** history **to** students. 나는 학생들에게 역사를 가르쳤다.

2. buy cook get make find + 간접목적어 + 직접목적어 - 4형식
　　↓
buy cook get make find + 직접목적어 + for + 간접목적어 - 3형식

I **bought** my father a tie. ➡ I **bought** a tie **for** my father. 나는 아버지께 넥타이를 사 드렸다.
My mom **made** me a bag. ➡ My mom **made** a bag **for** me.
우리 엄마는 내게 가방을 만들어 주셨다.

3. ask + 간접목적어 + 직접목적어 - 4형식
　　↓
ask + 직접목적어 + of + 간접목적어 - 3형식

Can I **ask** you a question? ➡ Can I **ask** a question **of** you?
당신에게 질문을 하나 해도 될까요?

PRACTICE 14

정답 p.4

괄호 안에 주어진 단어를 바르게 배열하세요.

1 (me, lent, uncle, the bike, my)
➡ _____

2 (will, Mark, a pretty doll, me, buy)
➡ _____

3 (told, a surprising story, she, me)
➡ _____

4 (I'll, give, a birthday gift, you)
➡ _____

5 (they, us, some food, got)
➡ _____

6 (some cheesecake, us, made, she)
➡ _____

7 (asked, him, I, of the house, the price)
➡ _____

8 (me, show, why don't you, the picture)
➡ _____

37 다음 중 대화 내용이 어색한 것은?

① A: Why don't we have pizza for lunch?
　 B: Sure, I'd love to.
② A: Where did you see the ad?
　 B: I saw it on TV.
③ A: How do you go to work?
　 B: I go there by bus.
④ A: Which one is more boring?
　 B: The second one.
⑤ A: Is Brian shorter than Tom?
　 B: No, he doesn't.

38 빈칸에 들어갈 말끼리 알맞게 짝지어진 것은?

> • I heard a man _____ last night.
> • She let the bird _____ free.

① to scream – to go
② to scream – going
③ screamed – go
④ screaming – go
⑤ screaming – going

39 다음 빈칸에 들어갈 말로 알맞은 것은?

> I saw my mom _____ delicious cookies.

① baked　　② to bake　　③ is baking
④ baking　　⑤ have baked

40 다음 중 밑줄 친 부분이 잘못 쓰인 것은?

① The girl looks lovely.
② The restaurant's dishes taste bad.
③ I'm sure my dog feels hungry now.
④ The cookies smell good.
⑤ That sounds nicely.

41 다음 주어진 간접의문문을 지닌 문장을 두 문장으로 나눌 때 빈칸에 들어갈 알맞은 문장을 쓰세요.

(1) I wonder why he chose to come back.
　➡ I wonder. + _____

(2) What do you guess she said?
　➡ Do you guess? + _____

42 빈칸 (가), (나)에 들어갈 말로 바르게 짝지어진 것은?

> My friend, Alexa likes to post her selfies on her SNS. Her selfies look ___(가)___ when she uses filters. But sometimes I think her selfies don't look ___(나)___ her.

	(가)	(나)
①	well	at
②	good	at
③	well	like
④	good	like
⑤	goodly	like

30 빈칸에 들어갈 말로 알맞지 않은 것은?

(가) We should keep ____①____ so as not to catch a cold.
(나) Help me shift this table, ____②____?
(다) True marriage asks us ____③____ trust and loyalty.
(라) Can you find a hotel ____④____?
(마) At this moment, I don't know what my decision ____⑤____ be.

① warm ② will you ③ to show
④ to me ⑤ will

31 괄호 안의 우리말과 같은 뜻이 되도록 빈칸에 알맞은 부가의문문을 쓰세요.

A: Why are you laughing, Kate?
B: This book has a lot of funny pictures.
A: Show me one, ____ ____?
(하나만 보여 줘, 그럴래?)

32 우리말에 맞게 주어진 단어를 바르게 배열하여 문장을 완성하세요.

(1) 넌 우리의 문제가 뭐라고 생각하니?
(do, think, what, our, is, you, problem)
➡ _____?

(2) 넌 누가 그 편지를 썼다고 생각하니?
(do, suppose, who, the, wrote, letter, you)
➡ _____?

33 다음 대화의 빈칸에 들어갈 단어로 알맞은 것은?

A: How do you feel today?
B: I feel very _____.

① lonely ② sadly ③ happily
④ likely ⑤ terribly

34 다음 빈칸에 공통으로 들어갈 단어는?

• Stop talking, _____ you?
• Pick me up at 7, _____ you?

① do ② aren't ③ are
④ will ⑤ shall

35 다음 대화의 빈칸에 들어갈 단어로 알맞은 것은?

A: You look _____. What happened?
B: I lost the baseball game.

① sadly ② sadness ③ to sad
④ sad ⑤ like sad

36 다음 대화의 빈칸에 들어갈 말로 적절하지 않은 것은?

A: _____
B: I'm a doctor.

① What's your job?
② What do you do?
③ What's your occupation?
④ What do you want to be?
⑤ What do you do for a living?

25 다음 중 우리말을 바르게 옮긴 것은?

① 너 유럽에 가 본 적 있지, 그렇지 않니?
　→ You have been to Europe, have you?
② 넌 누가 그 게임에서 이길 거라고 생각해?
　→ Who do you think will win the game?
③ 이 초콜릿은 쓴 맛이 나.
　→ This chocolate tastes bitterly.
④ Jason이 자기 엄마에게 꽃을 드렸어.
　→ Jason gave to his mom flowers.
⑤ 내가 그의 생일 선물 고르는 걸 도와줄게.
　→ I'll help you to choosing his birthday present.

26 다음 질문에 대한 답으로 알맞지 않은 것은?

A: Do you know what her favorite color is?
B: _____

① Yes, I do.
② Yes. I think this is her favorite color.
③ No, I didn't know that.
④ No, I don't.
⑤ Yes. Red is.

27 다음 빈칸에 들어갈 말로 올바르지 않은 것은?

A: James left for the States.
B: _____
A: Yes. I am sure.

① Really?
② Are you certain about that?
③ Are you all right?
④ Is that true?
⑤ Are you sure?

28 다음은 Grease 뮤지컬의 후기이다. 밑줄 친 ⓐ ~ ⓔ 중 어법상 잘못된 것은?

Grease The Musical

Write a review

What people are saying

James　108 Reviews | 105 Followers

My wife and I went ⓐto see the musical. Our daughter ⓑgave tickets to us to celebrate our wedding anniversary. It was amazing!

Kevin　205 Reviews | 550 Followers

ⓒWhat a perfect show! It's one of the best musicals I've ever seen.

Clare　155 Reviews | 98 Followers

I still can't forget it! The performance ⓓmade me joyfully.

Mina　970 Reviews | 1550 Followers

I want all of you guys to see this musical. ⓔHow sentimental the songs are!

① ⓐ　② ⓑ　③ ⓒ　④ ⓓ　⑤ ⓔ

29 다음 대화의 빈칸에 들어갈 알맞은 말을 모두 고르세요.

A: What is Mike doing?
B: He is helping his father _____ the house.

① cleans
② cleaned
③ clean
④ cleaning
⑤ to clean

19 다음 제시된 〈조건〉을 반드시 지켜 주어진 우리말을 바르게 영작하시오.

그 경찰관은 나로 하여금 나의 차를 세우게 했다.

조건
- police officer, make, stop, car를 사용할 것 (필요할 경우 단어의 형태를 바꾸어 쓸 것)
- 8단어로 쓸 것

➡ _____

20 다음 중 의도하는 바가 나머지와 <u>다른</u> 것은?

① Let's go to the park.
② Shall we go to the park?
③ How do we go to the park?
④ How about going to the park?
⑤ Why don't we go to the park?

21 다음 빈칸에 들어갈 말로 알맞은 것은?

Zack told me _____ a number between one and ten.

① choose   ② choosing   ③ chosen
④ to choose   ⑤ chose

22 다음 대화의 빈칸에 들어갈 말로 알맞은 것은?

Jinny : James runs very fast.
Minsu: Yes, we _____ "Bullet Man."

① called he   ② call them   ③ call she
④ call him   ⑤ call to him

23 다음 대화의 빈칸에 들어갈 알맞은 표현은?

A: I went to my grandparents' house in the country and had to stay there for two months.
B: For two months? _____, did you?
A: No, I didn't. But now I miss being there.

① You didn't come back
② You liked the country
③ You didn't like the country
④ You didn't stay there
⑤ You liked your grandparents

24 다음 중 어법상 알맞은 문장은?

① I made his excited.
② Books make him to be sleepy.
③ He made me angrily.
④ Make your hands warmly.
⑤ My son makes me happy.

13 다음 빈칸에 들어갈 말로 올바른 것은?

> _____
> He was a famous American inventor.
> He was born in Milan, Ohio, in 1847. He
> invented a lot of things including a light bulb,
> a radio, a typewriter, and a phonograph.
> He also invented a toaster and an iron.

① Do you know whom is Thomas A. Edison?
② Who do you know is Thomas A. Edison?
③ Who do you know Thomas A. Edison is?
④ Do you know who Thomas A. Edison is?
⑤ Do you know who is Thomas A. Edison?

14 다음 중 어법상 어색한 문장은?

① Did you see the baby smile at me?
② I felt the house shake.
③ I watched them play games.
④ I heard the rain fell on the ground.
⑤ He noticed a bird sitting on the tree.

15 주어진 단어를 활용하여 다음 우리말을 7단어로 영작하세요. (단, 필요한 경우 단어를 추가하거나, 어형을 바꿀 것.)

> • 그 영화는 그녀를 웃고 울게 만들었다.
>   (laugh, cry, make)

➡ _____

16 다음 문장을 감탄문으로 올바르게 바꾼 것은?

> The dancer moves very fast.

① How the dancer moves fast!
② How fast does the dancer move!
③ How fast the dancer moves!
④ What a fast the dancer moves!
⑤ What the dancer fast moves!

17 다음 중 어법상 어색한 문장은?

① Everyone seems busy.
② They look like teachers.
③ He seems like tired.
④ Her advice sounded pretty good.
⑤ It sounds like a very interesting idea.

18 다음 글의 밑줄 친 두 문장을 간접의문문을 사용하여 한 문장으로 바꿔 쓰세요.

> February 28th
> I went shopping today. At the mall, a woman asked me the way to a restaurant in English. I told her the way, but she didn't look like a foreigner. <u>I wonder. Was she practicing English?</u> It was a little strange.

➡ _____
_____

7 다음 중 밑줄 친 what의 쓰임이 나머지 넷과 다른 것은?

① I have what you want.
② Tell me what her name is.
③ I wonder what the answer is.
④ She asked me what happened to James.
⑤ He doesn't know what she studied in America.

8 어법상 옳은 문장을 모두 고르세요.

① How many legs do a spider have?
② Who are your favorite singer?
③ When did you came home?
④ What do you do for a living?
⑤ Why didn't you show up yesterday?

9 다음 주어진 문장을 영어로 바르게 옮긴 것은?

> 그들은 정말 친절한 사람들이구나!

① What nice people they are!
② What a nice people they are!
③ What nice people are they!
④ How nice people they are!
⑤ How they are nice people!

10 밑줄 친 우리말과 같은 뜻이 되도록 괄호 안의 주어진 단어를 이용하여 영작하세요.

> Melissa read a book to her son. It was an adventure story about a bear called *Brown*. After reading the book, she asked her son, "다음에는 무슨 일이 일어날 거라고 생각하니?"
> (what, think, happen, next)

➡ _____

11 다음 중 어법상 올바르지 않은 문장은?

① What a handsome guy he is!
② How cold it is!
③ What a pretty girl she is!
④ What beautiful flowers it is!
⑤ How friendly they are!

12 다음 글을 읽고 어법상 올바른 문장의 개수를 고르세요.

> ⓐ I'm worried about my little sister, Lucy. ⓑ She has a bad stomachache because I let her to eat all the candies and chocolates. ⓒ She has been crying all day long. ⓓ I can't make her to stop crying. ⓔ What should I do?

① 없음 ② 1개 ③ 2개 ④ 3개 ⑤ 4개

Chapter Review Test

CHAPTER 1 문장의 기초

정답 p.5

1 다음 빈칸에 알맞은 단어끼리 바르게 짝지어진 것은?

- He asked me _____ had told me that information.
- She asked me _____ I was all right.

① what - that ② who - that
③ what - if ④ who - if
⑤ why - that

2 대화의 빈칸에 들어갈 말로 가장 알맞은 것은?

A: _____
B: No, I haven't. Have you?
A: Yes, I have. I was impressed by its story.

① Do you have this book?
② What have you been doing?
③ Are you interested in writing?
④ Have you ever read this book?
⑤ Do you have to read this book?

3 밑줄 친 부분의 쓰임이 잘못된 것은?

① Lily is interested in soccer, isn't she?
② John lost his bike yesterday, doesn't he?
③ They don't have any plans, do they?
④ Close the door, will you?
⑤ He can't go there, can he?

4 다음 중 밑줄 친 부분이 어법상 틀린 것의 개수를 고르세요.

There are various types of students in my class. Yunjin is kind and she makes her classmates ⓐ feeling happy. Jiho is ⓑ friendly and nicely. He makes us ⓒ laugh. Subin is picky, and she often makes us ⓓ uncomfortably.

① 1개 ② 2개 ③ 3개 ④ 4개 ⑤ 없음

5 다음 중 빈칸에 들어갈 말로 적절하지 않은 것은?

I _____ her to do the dishes.

① made ② wanted ③ told
④ helped ⑤ asked

6 다음 글의 밑줄 친 (A)~(E) 중 어법상 틀린 것은?

Pablo Picasso, a founder of cubism, was one of the most influential (A) artists of the twentieth century. He was born in Malaga, Spain (B) in 1881 and started to paint at the age of 14. What made Picasso (C) famous? Along with other artists, he developed a new form of painting called "cubism." One of Picasso's famous paintings (D) was his mural of the Guernica bombing. (E) How a unique painting it is! *cubism: 입체파 **mural: 벽화

① (A) ② (B) ③ (C) ④ (D) ⑤ (E)

2. 지각동사 - feel, see, hear, watch

I **felt** the table **shake**. 나는 탁자가 흔들리는 것을 느꼈다.
Did you **see** my son **ride** a bike? 내 아들이 자전거를 타는 것을 보았니?
I **heard** Mary **play** the violin. 나는 Mary가 바이올린을 연주하는 것을 들었다.
Let's **watch** Hana **swim** in the pool. 하나가 수영장에서 수영하는 것을 보자.

cf. 동작이 진행 중인 것을 강조할 때는 지각동사의 목적격 보어로 동사원형 대신 -ing형이 올 수도 있다.

I **saw** my students **playing** soccer in the playground.
나는 나의 학생들이 운동장에서 축구를 하고 있는 것을 보았다.
Did you **hear** the dog **barking**? 개가 짖고 있는 것을 들었니?

정답 p.4

PRACTICE 17

괄호 안에 주어진 말 중 알맞은 것을 고르세요.

1   Mina saw a man (to bake, baking) delicious cakes.
2   I'll let you (go, to go) when it is finished.
3   I heard the children (sing, to sing) all together.
4   Sarah had me (stay, to stay) with her baby yesterday.
5   James told me (considering, to consider) my options.
6   He always makes me (laugh, to laugh).
7   I heard people (to shout, shouting) in the cafe.
8   It will help you (remembering, remember) the rule.
9   Her parents didn't want her (marry, to marry) him.
10 Did you have them (come, to come) here?
11 How did you get him (pose, to pose) for this picture?
12 She allows the children (watch, to watch) television only on weekends.
13 I felt something (touching, to touch) my arm.
14 The professor advised me (study, to study) abroad.
15 Did you see Mary (plant, to plant) those trees?
16 I watched an ant (carrying, to carry) a little bit of bread.
17 The police officer asked us (tell, to tell) about the accident.

2. want, tell, ask, get, allow, advise – 목적격 보어로 to부정사가 온다.

I **want** you **to meet** Dave. 나는 네가 Dave를 만나기를 원한다.
Mom **told** me **to stay** home. 엄마는 내게 집에 있으라고 말씀하셨다.
He **asked** me **to write** about Korea. 그는 내게 한국에 대해 쓰라고 요구했다.
You have to **get** her **to wake** up early. 너는 그녀가 일찍 일어나게 해야 한다.
Dad **allowed** me **to go** fishing. 아빠는 내가 낚시하러 가는 걸 허락하셨다.
I **advised** him **to go** home. 나는 그에게 집에 갈 것을 권했다.

PRACTICE 16

괄호 안에 주어진 말 중 알맞은 것을 고르세요.

1 I made my friend (angry, angrily).

2 The high temperature turned the milk (sour, sourly).

3 They asked her (come, to come) back to work.

4 I want you (leave, to leave) right now.

5 He told me (clean, to clean) the room.

6 I found the bag (heavy, heavily).

7 Her doctor advised her (rest, to rest).

8 Why don't you keep the kids (quiet, quietly)?

9 I got Danielle (to come, come) to the party.

10 Her dimple makes her (more attractive, attractively).

11 He allowed me (use, to use) his photographs.

PSS 2-6 목적격 보어를 필요로 하는 동사 II

사역동사와 지각동사의 목적격 보어 자리에는 동사원형이 온다.

1. 사역동사 – let, make, have

I'll **let** you **know** how it works. 그것이 어떻게 작동하는지 내가 알려줄게요.
I can't **make** her **stop** crying. 나는 그녀가 우는 것을 멈추게 할 수 없다.
She **had** me **come** home early. 그녀는 내가 집에 일찍 오도록 시켰다.

cf. help는 준사역동사로 목적격 보어 자리에 동사원형 또는 to부정사가 올 수 있다.
These tips will **help** you **(to) work** effectively.
이 조언들이 네가 효과적으로 일할 수 있도록 도와줄 것이다.

9 (cooked, mother, a nice dinner, them)
➡ _____

10 (we, our grandmother, send, every year, a postcard)
➡ _____

정답 p.4

PRACTICE 15

〈보기〉와 같이 4형식 문장을 3형식 문장으로 바꾸어 쓰세요.

보 기	Could you send me your e-mail address? ➡ Could you send your e-mail address to me?

1 I cooked my son some soup. ➡ _____

2 The interviewer asked me a difficult question. ➡ _____

3 Jinho bought her a present. ➡ _____

4 She sent me some pictures of her son. ➡ _____

5 I wrote my cousin a letter. ➡ _____

6 They showed me their car. ➡ _____

7 He made her a cup of hot chocolate. ➡ _____

8 Mr. Smith teaches us English. ➡ _____

9 Can you get me a Coke? ➡ _____

10 I didn't lend her my bicycle. ➡ _____

PSS 2-5 목적격 보어를 필요로 하는 동사 I

1. keep, find, call, make, turn – 목적격 보어로 명사나 형용사가 온다.

You should **keep** it **cool**. 너는 그것을 차갑게 유지해야 한다.
Suji **found** the question **difficult**. 수지는 그 문제가 어렵다는 것을 알게 되었다.
We **called** her **Jen**. 우리는 그녀를 Jen이라고 불렀다.
Exercising regularly **makes** you **healthy**. 규칙적으로 운동하는 것은 당신을 건강하게 만든다.
Time **turned** my dad's hair **gray**. 시간은 나의 아빠의 머리를 희게 했다.
Living without a friend can **make** you **more depressed**.
친구 없이 사는 건 당신을 더욱 우울하게 할 수 있다.

43 다음 밑줄 친 우리말을 영어로 바르게 옮긴 것은?

> A: You won't be late again, will you?
> B: 네, 안 그럴게요.

① Yes, I will.   ② Yes, I won't.
③ Yes, I do.   ④ No, I don't.
⑤ No, I won't.

44 다음 대화의 빈칸에 들어갈 말로 알맞은 것은?

> A: Where is your bicycle?
> B: _____ Minji borrowed it from me this morning.

① I'd like to, but I can't.
② Don't you remember?
③ Here is your bicycle.
④ Yes, it is.
⑤ No, I don't.

45 다음 대화의 (A) ~ (C)에 들어갈 말이 바르게 연결된 것은?

> Mom   : What are you doing, sweetie?
> Angelina: I'm making some soup for you.
> Mom   : Wow, it smells __(A)__. Do you want me __(B)__ you?
> Angelina: No, thanks. Do you want to taste it?
> Mom   : OK. (tastes the soup)
> Angelina: It tastes good, __(C)__?
> Mom   : Well, I think it's too salty.

	(A)	(B)	(C)
①	well	to help	does it
②	good	to help	doesn't it
③	better	help	doesn't it
④	good	to help	does it
⑤	best	helping	doesn't it

46 다음 빈칸에 들어갈 말로 알맞은 것은?

> • I don't _____ play computer games.
> = 나는 그가 컴퓨터 게임을 하는 것을 원하지 않아.

① want him to   ② him want to
③ want he to   ④ he want to
⑤ to want he

47 다음 대화의 빈칸에 들어갈 말로 알맞은 것을 모두 고르세요.

> A: I heard my dog _____.
> B: Really? Are you sure?
> A: Yes, I am sure.

① crying   ② to cry   ③ cried
④ be crying ⑤ cry

48 다음 문장을 How로 시작하는 감탄문으로 고쳐 쓰세요.

> • Her new house is very nice.
> ➡ _____

49 다음 중 밑줄 친 부가의문문의 쓰임이 올바른 것은?

① She isn't ready, isn't she?
② He's already finished dinner, didn't he?
③ Mike and Ted are coming to the party, aren't they?
④ Let's not go out, will you?
⑤ You can tell me, can you?

50 다음 빈칸에 들어갈 단어로 알맞은 것은?

- I will make you some spaghetti.
  = I will make some spaghetti _____ you.

① of ② for ③ with
④ to ⑤ by

51 다음 빈칸에 들어갈 수 <u>없는</u> 것은?

That lady looks very _____.

① happy ② friendly ③ sadly
④ healthy ⑤ lovely

52 다음 대화의 빈칸에 들어갈 말로 알맞은 것은?

A: Let's go on a picnic this weekend, _____?
B: I'm sorry, but I can't. I've got to go to my uncle's place.

① will we ② won't we
③ shall we ④ will you
⑤ don't you

53 괄호 안에 주어진 단어들을 알맞게 배열하여 대화를 완성하세요.

Minho: Hey, Patrick, do you know who invented Hangeul?
Patrick: Yes, I learned that King Sejong invented it.
Minho: Do you know _____?
(Hangeul, how, letters, has, many)

54 다음 중 어법상 올바른 문장은?

① The milk went sourly.
② All the students grows tired.
③ He never stays angry for long.
④ Billy becomes a doctor last year.
⑤ The store stays openness until late on Thursdays.

55 다음 질문에 대한 답으로 알맞은 것은?

A: Which do you like better, pop or jazz?
B: _____

① Yes, I do. ② It's really good.
③ Do you think so? ④ I like jazz better.
⑤ I don't think so.

56 다음 세 문장의 빈칸에 공통으로 들어갈 수 있는 단어를 쓰세요.

- We _____ a good time yesterday.
- I _____ my daughter write a letter.
- They _____ a nice dinner last night.

57 다음 중 어법상 어색한 문장은?

① She wants you to stay home.
② I will give it to your brother.
③ Jake saw a bus came around the corner.
④ Draw a dog on the paper, will you?
⑤ They live in the cold weather, don't they?

58 그림을 보고, 〈보기〉에서 알맞은 말을 골라 Jamie에 대한 문장을 완성하세요.

(1)

(2)

| 보기 | happily   cute   prettily   healthy |

(1) Exercising makes Jamie _____.
(2) Jamie found the puppy _____.

59 다음 글을 읽고, 괄호 안의 단어를 배열하여 질문에 대한 답을 완성하세요.

Date: 12 December 2022
From: LindaHamilton1234@gmail.com
To: Kevinbrown11@gmail.com
Subject: Order No. 1002948 – request valid address

Dear Sir,
We thank you for your purchase (order no. 1002948). In the process of packaging the product you ordered, we found that you only wrote down the city name, Seoul, and didn't include the street address. So, I am writing this email to request your specific address including the ZIP code. Once your valid address is confirmed, we'll resume your delivery ASAP.
Thanks for your order. I await your reply.

Sincerely,
Linda Hamilton, K Clothing

Q: What does Linda want?
A: She wants the customer to _____ _____.

(her, a, address, to, specific, send)

60 우리말과 같은 뜻이 되도록 주어진 단어를 올바르게 배열하세요.

• 우리는 누군가를 기분 좋게 하려고 거짓말을 한다.
= We tell a lie to _____.
(good, make, feel, someone)

61 다음 빈칸에 알맞은 단어끼리 바르게 짝지어진 것은?

- Mark found the necklace _____ me.
- Can I ask a favor _____ you?

① for – of ② for – to ③ to – of
④ to – for ⑤ of – to

62 다음 중 4형식 문장의 3형식 전환이 어법상 어색한 것은?

① People gave me a big hand.
= People gave a big hand to me.
② The boy sent his friend a doll.
= The boy sent a doll to his friend.
③ She asked me a question.
= She asked a question to me.
④ Can you find me my bag?
= Can you find my bag for me?
⑤ I lent him my bicycle.
= I lent my bicycle to him.

63 주어진 우리말과 같은 뜻이 되도록 형식에 맞게 영작하세요.

Amy는 나에게 책 한 권을 보냈다.

4형식: _____
3형식: _____

[64 - 66] 다음 글을 읽고, 물음에 답하세요.

My favorite hobby is gardening. I started gardening when I was twenty. I dig the land, sow the seeds, and ⓐ water the plants in my garden. I feel refreshed and ⓑ cheerfully. Every afternoon I work for an hour in my garden. I watch the buds ⓒ come up and the branches nod in the breeze. It (A) makes me relaxed. My garden also serves as a grocery store. By using my garden's vegetables, I often cook dinner ⓓ to my family. The vegetables I grow ⓔ taste much better than the ones from the market. My hobby is a source of pleasure. I want to know (B) 너의 취미는 무엇인지.

64 다음 중 윗글의 밑줄 친 (A) makes와 쓰임이 같은 것은?

① She makes pasta for her guests.
② Three plus three makes six.
③ This makes no sense.
④ Music makes me happy.
⑤ He makes a living by working as a cook.

65 괄호 안에 주어진 말을 바르게 배열하여 밑줄 친 (B)의 우리말을 영어로 완성하세요.

➡ I want to know _____.
 (is, what, hobby, your)

66 다음 밑줄 친 ⓐ~ⓔ 중 틀린 것을 두 개 찾아 기호를 쓰고, 고쳐 쓰세요.

➡ ( ) _____ ( ) _____

CHAPTER 2
시제

성취도 자기 평가 활용법

구분	평가 기준
Excellent	문법 내용을 모두 이해하고, 문제를 모두 맞힘.
Very good	문법 내용은 충분히 이해했으나 실수로 1~2문제 틀림.
Good	문법 내용이 조금 어려워 3~4문제 틀림.
needs **R**eview	문법 내용 이해가 어렵고, 5문제 이상 틀림, 복습 필요.

PSS 1 현재시제	페이지	학습날짜	성취도 자기평가 E V G R	학습체크
PSS 1-1 동사의 3인칭 현재 단수형	36	/		☐
PSS 1-2 동사의 3인칭 현재 단수형의 발음	38	/		☐
PSS 1-3 현재시제의 쓰임 Ⅰ	39	/		☐
PSS 1-4 현재시제의 쓰임 Ⅱ	40	/		☐
PSS 2 과거시제	페이지	학습날짜	성취도 자기평가 E V G R	학습체크
PSS 2-1 be동사의 과거형	41	/		☐
PSS 2-2 규칙 변화 동사의 과거형	42	/		☐
PSS 2-3 규칙 변화 동사 과거형의 발음	44	/		☐
PSS 2-4 불규칙 변화 동사의 과거형	45	/		☐
PSS 3 미래시제	49	/		☐
PSS 4 진행시제	페이지	학습날짜	성취도 자기평가 E V G R	학습체크
PSS 4-1 동사의 -ing형	50	/		☐
PSS 4-2 과거진행시제와 현재진행시제	53	/		☐
PSS 5 현재완료	페이지	학습날짜	성취도 자기평가 E V G R	학습체크
PSS 5-1 현재완료의 형태	55	/		☐
PSS 5-2 현재완료의 용법	56	/		☐
PSS 5-3 for와 since	57	/		☐
PSS 5-4 현재완료시제와 과거시제	59	/		☐
PSS 5-5 현재완료 진행시제	61	/		☐
Chapter Review Test	63	/		☐

현재시제

PSS 1-1 동사의 3인칭 현재 단수형

일반적인 경우	동사원형+s	work – work**s** say – say**s** see – see**s**	leave – leave**s** grow – grow**s** put – put**s**
-o, -s, -x, -ch, -sh로 끝나는 경우	동사원형+es	do – do**es** relax – relax**es** wash – wash**es**	pass – pass**es** teach – teach**es**
자음+y로 끝나는 경우	자음+i+es	study – stud**ies** try – tr**ies** *cf.* 모음+y로 끝나는 경우 ➡ 동사원형+s play – play**s**	cry – cr**ies** copy – cop**ies** pay – pay**s**

정답 p.8

PRACTICE 1

다음 동사들의 3인칭 현재 단수형을 쓰세요.

1 depart   – _____
2 reward   – _____
3 bite   – _____
4 answer   – _____
5 use   – _____
6 sing   – _____
7 breathe – _____
8 open   – _____
9 destroy – _____
10 close   – _____
11 change   – _____
12 prove   – _____
13 make   – _____
14 cry   – _____
15 draw   – _____
16 reduce   – _____
17 tell   – _____
18 miss   – _____
19 mix   – _____
20 complain – _____
21 leave   – _____
22 raise   – _____
23 shoot   – _____
24 lift   – _____
25 like   – _____
26 bear   – _____

27 take – _____	28 elect – _____
29 recycle – _____	30 recommend – _____
31 stop – _____	32 want – _____
33 exchange – _____	34 interview – _____
35 allow – _____	36 keep – _____
37 marry – _____	38 pray – _____
39 act – _____	40 enjoy – _____
41 rescue – _____	42 start – _____
43 vow – _____	44 mention – _____
45 imagine – _____	46 bring – _____
47 do – _____	48 lead – _____
49 find – _____	50 fight – _____
51 wrap – _____	52 flow – _____
53 argue – _____	54 travel – _____
55 produce – _____	56 seem – _____
57 serve – _____	58 give – _____
59 follow – _____	60 finish – _____
61 add – _____	62 borrow – _____
63 copy – _____	64 discover – _____
65 admire – _____	66 sink – _____
67 understand – _____	68 worry – _____
69 remember – _____	70 quit – _____
71 stretch – _____	72 knock – _____
73 hope – _____	74 wake – _____
75 report – _____	76 introduce – _____
77 appear – _____	78 save – _____
79 suppose – _____	80 agree – _____
81 beat – _____	82 hatch – _____
83 become – _____	84 describe – _____
85 wonder – _____	86 try – _____

PSS 1-2 동사의 3인칭 현재 단수형의 발음

발음	용례
[s]	[s, ʃ, tʃ]음을 제외한 무성음으로 끝나는 동사 stops, departs, picks, laughs
[z]	[z, dʒ]음을 제외한 유성음으로 끝나는 동사 robs, digs, drives, breathes, becomes, runs, bears, vows
[iz]	[s, z, ʃ, tʃ, dʒ]음으로 끝나는 동사 passes, raises, pushes, reaches, exchanges

PRACTICE 2

<보기>와 같이 주어진 단어의 밑줄 친 부분의 발음으로 알맞은 것을 [s], [z], [iz] 중에서 골라 쓰세요.

| 보 기 | makes [s] | complains [z] | mixes [iz] |

1. shoots [ ]   2. leaves [ ]   3. rewards [ ]
4. answers [ ]   5. cries [ ]   6. bites [ ]
7. lifts [ ]   8. bears [ ]   9. uses [ ]
10. prays [ ]   11. starts [ ]   12. enjoys [ ]
13. brings [ ]   14. hatches [ ] 15. finds [ ]
16. spills [ ]   17. sinks [ ]   18. admires [ ]
19. publishes [ ] 20. selects [ ] 21. understands [ ]
22. supposes [ ] 23. remembers [ ] 24. washes [ ]
25. dictates [ ] 26. seems [ ]   27. consists [ ]
28. sets [ ]   29. loses [ ]   30. runs [ ]
31. relaxes [ ] 32. drops [ ]   33. wishes [ ]
34. walks [ ]   35. carries [ ] 36. waits [ ]
37. studies [ ] 38. fixes [ ]   39. forgets [ ]
40. teases [ ]   41. hurts [ ]   42. teaches [ ]
43. cuts [ ]   44. plans [ ]   45. invents [ ]

PSS 1-3 현재시제의 쓰임 I

1. 현재의 사실이나 상태를 나타낼 때 쓴다.

    I **am** a nurse. 나는 간호사이다.
    My dad **works** at the bank. 우리 아빠는 은행에서 일하신다.

2. 현재의 습관이나 반복적인 동작을 나타낼 때 쓴다.

    I **eat** lunch at one o'clock every day. 나는 매일 1시에 점심을 먹는다.
    John **reads** books before he **goes** to bed. John은 잠자리에 들기 전에 책을 읽는다.

3. 불변의 진리나 격언, 과학적 사실을 나타낼 때 쓴다.

    The Sun **rises** in the east. 해는 동쪽에서 뜬다.
    A friend in need **is** a friend indeed. 어려울 때 친구가 진정한 친구다.

PRACTICE 3

정답 p.9

그림을 보고, 〈보기〉에 주어진 단어를 알맞은 형태로 바꾸어 빈칸에 쓰세요.
(단, 한 번씩만 쓸 수 있습니다.)

| 보 기 | move   sleep   teach   go   play   be |

1
2
3
4
5
6

1 She __teaches__ music in high school.
2 He _____ tennis after work.
3 Bears _____ during the winter.
4 Jack _____ a great doctor.
5 The Earth _____ around the Sun.
6 I _____ to bed at 10 o'clock every day.

PSS 1-4 현재시제의 쓰임 II

1. 눈앞에서 진행되고 있는 일을 나타낼 때 쓴다.

   Here comes the bus. 버스가 온다.

2. 왕래발착동사(leave, go, depart, start, arrive, come, reach)가 미래를 나타내는 부사구와 함께 쓰일 때는 현재시제로 미래를 나타낼 수 있다.

   He **comes** back home **tomorrow evening**. 그는 내일 저녁에 집에 돌아온다.
   My sister **leaves** Busan **next week**. 나의 여동생은 다음 주에 부산을 떠난다.

3. 시간과 조건의 부사절에서는 현재시제로 미래를 나타낸다.

   Call me **when** you **arrive** home. 집에 도착하면 내게 전화해.
   I will go out **if** the weather **is** fine tomorrow. 내일 날씨가 맑으면, 나는 밖에 나갈 거야.
   I'll call you **as soon as** I **meet** him. 그를 만나자마자 너에게 전화할게.

정답 p.9

PRACTICE 4

괄호 안의 단어를 현재시제의 쓰임에 맞게 바꾸어 빈칸에 쓰세요.

1 There he ___goes___ with his son. (go)
2 My daughter _____ in London next Monday. (arrive)
3 Come to my house before you _____ lunch. (have)
4 Sam _____ for Seoul tomorrow. (leave)
5 Here _____ Mr. Smith. (come)
6 A bad workman always _____ his tools. (blame)
7 Jessie will be surprised when she _____ the news. (hear)
8 Hana _____ her aunt every Sunday. (visit)
9 Tom _____ until late at night every day. (study)
10 Come back home before it _____ dark. (get)
11 Our ship _____ the island next month. (reach)
12 She will go on vacation after she _____ this project. (complete)
13 I will call you when I _____ home. (arrive)

 과거시제

PSS 2-1 be동사의 과거형

과거시제는 과거에 일어난 동작이나 상태, 역사적 사실과 같이 과거에 이미 끝난 일을 나타낸다.

주어	현재형	과거형
I	am	was
you	are	were
he / she / it	is	was
we / you / they	are	were

Hangul **was** created by King Sejong. 한글은 세종대왕에 의해 만들어졌다.
We **were** at the library with Jina. 우리는 지나와 함께 도서관에 있었다.

정답 p.9

PRACTICE 5

다음 문장의 빈칸에 알맞은 be동사를 쓰세요.

1 He ___was___ a student last year, but he ___is___ a teacher now.
2 It is sunny today, but it _____ cloudy yesterday.
3 Tony, where _____ you now?
4 They _____ at the bank two hours ago.
5 Those pants _____ very expensive. I can't buy them.
6 Susan is my friend. She _____ also Jenny's friend.
7 My grandfather _____ 85 years old this year. He is still very healthy.
8 Namsu and I _____ at home last night. We watched a movie.
9 John _____ very sick yesterday.
10 I know Liz. She _____ my classmate before.

PRACTICE 6

다음은 Tony와 Becky의 대화입니다. 빈칸에 알맞은 be동사를 쓰세요.

1. Were you tall when you _____ a kid? — Yes, I _____ very tall.
2. _____ your brother good at football? — No, he _____. And he didn't like it.
3. _____ your sister a teacher? — Yes, she _____. She teaches math.
4. How _____ your travel last week? — It _____ wonderful. I'll never forget it.
5. How _____ business doing? — It _____ doing great. Sales are increasing.

PSS 2-2 규칙 변화 동사의 과거형

일반적인 경우	동사원형+ed	open – open**ed** start – start**ed** wash – wash**ed**	look – look**ed** pull – pull**ed** talk – talk**ed**
-e로 끝나는 경우	동사원형+d	decide – decide**d** live – live**d** use – use**d**	promise – promise**d** hate – hate**d** hope – hope**d**
자음+y로 끝나는 경우	자음+i+ed	study – stud**ied** worry – worr**ied** *cf.* 모음+y로 끝나는 경우 ➡ 동사원형+ed 　enjoy – enjoy**ed**　stay – stay**ed** 　play – play**ed**　delay – delay**ed**	reply – repl**ied** try – tr**ied**
단모음+단자음으로 끝나는 1음절과 뒤에 강세가 오는 2음절의 경우	동사원형 +마지막 자음 +ed	drop – drop**ped** pop – pop**ped** *cf.* 강세가 앞에 오는 2음절 동사 ➡ 동사원형+ed 　visit – visit**ed**　offer – offer**ed** 　enter – enter**ed**	stop – stop**ped** prefer – prefer**red**

PRACTICE 7

다음 동사의 과거형을 쓰세요.

#	Verb		#	Verb	
1	stay	— _____	2	rip	— _____
3	smell	— _____	4	cause	— _____
5	worry	— _____	6	destroy	— _____
7	die	— _____	8	bow	— _____
9	prefer	— _____	10	apply	— _____
11	judge	— _____	12	waste	— _____
13	control	— _____	14	play	— _____
15	watch	— _____	16	delay	— _____
17	invite	— _____	18	hurry	— _____
19	copy	— _____	20	hope	— _____
21	shop	— _____	22	expect	— _____
23	disappear	— _____	24	observe	— _____
25	study	— _____	26	fix	— _____
27	chat	— _____	28	carry	— _____
29	smile	— _____	30	jog	— _____
31	pop	— _____	32	notice	— _____
33	dance	— _____	34	try	— _____
35	stop	— _____	36	rush	— _____
37	enjoy	— _____	38	marry	— _____
39	plan	— _____	40	wait	— _____
41	reply	— _____	42	practice	— _____
43	pick	— _____	44	drop	— _____
45	agree	— _____	46	decide	— _____
47	fry	— _____	48	grab	— _____
49	clap	— _____	50	clean	— _____
51	save	— _____	52	cry	— _____
53	wrap	— _____	54	dry	— _____

PSS 2-3 규칙 변화 동사 과거형의 발음

발음	용례
[t]	[t]음을 제외한 무성음으로 끝나는 동사 pick**ed**, ripp**ed**, lik**ed**, rush**ed**, laugh**ed**
[d]	[d]음을 제외한 유성음으로 끝나는 동사 cri**ed**, believ**ed**, pull**ed**, us**ed**, hurri**ed**
[id]	[t, d]음으로 끝나는 동사 paint**ed**, invit**ed**, want**ed**, plant**ed**, need**ed**

PRACTICE 8

〈보기〉와 같이 주어진 단어의 밑줄 친 부분의 발음으로 알맞은 것을 [t], [d], [id] 중에서 골라 쓰세요.

| 보기 | pick<u>ed</u> [t] smil<u>ed</u> [d] hat<u>ed</u> [id] |

1 arriv<u>ed</u> [ ]	2 play<u>ed</u> [ ]	3 decid<u>ed</u> [ ]
4 lik<u>ed</u> [ ]	5 di<u>ed</u> [ ]	6 us<u>ed</u> [ ]
7 want<u>ed</u> [ ]	8 realiz<u>ed</u> [ ]	9 watch<u>ed</u> [ ]
10 talk<u>ed</u> [ ]	11 invit<u>ed</u> [ ]	12 popp<u>ed</u> [ ]
13 agree<u>d</u> [ ]	14 chang<u>ed</u> [ ]	15 ripp<u>ed</u> [ ]
16 plant<u>ed</u> [ ]	17 delay<u>ed</u> [ ]	18 look<u>ed</u> [ ]
19 stay<u>ed</u> [ ]	20 paint<u>ed</u> [ ]	21 work<u>ed</u> [ ]
22 wast<u>ed</u> [ ]	23 collect<u>ed</u> [ ]	24 form<u>ed</u> [ ]
25 bak<u>ed</u> [ ]	26 hurri<u>ed</u> [ ]	27 protect<u>ed</u> [ ]
28 tri<u>ed</u> [ ]	29 dropp<u>ed</u> [ ]	30 guid<u>ed</u> [ ]
31 kick<u>ed</u> [ ]	32 call<u>ed</u> [ ]	33 prov<u>ed</u> [ ]
34 repli<u>ed</u> [ ]	35 wait<u>ed</u> [ ]	36 publish<u>ed</u> [ ]
37 cri<u>ed</u> [ ]	38 mix<u>ed</u> [ ]	39 consist<u>ed</u> [ ]
40 clean<u>ed</u> [ ]	41 hop<u>ed</u> [ ]	42 report<u>ed</u> [ ]
43 wrapp<u>ed</u> [ ]	44 describ<u>ed</u> [ ]	45 appreciat<u>ed</u> [ ]

PSS 2-4 불규칙 변화 동사의 과거형

원형	과거형	과거분사형	원형	과거형	과거분사형
be	was, were	been	bear	bore	borne/born
beat	beat	beaten	become	became	become
begin	began	begun	blow	blew	blown
bring	brought	brought	build	built	built
buy	bought	bought	choose	chose	chosen
come	came	come	cost	cost	cost
cut	cut	cut	do	did	done
draw	drew	drawn	dream	dreamed/dreamt	dreamed/dreamt
drink	drank	drunk	drive	drove	driven
eat	ate	eaten	fall	fell	fallen
feel	felt	felt	fight	fought	fought
find	found	found	fly	flew	flown
forget	forgot	forgotten	get	got	got(ten)
give	gave	given	go	went	gone
grow	grew	grown	have	had	had
hear	heard	heard	hide	hid	hidden
hit	hit	hit	hold	held	held
hurt	hurt	hurt	keep	kept	kept
know	knew	known	lay	laid	laid
lead	led	led	leave	left	left
let	let	let	lie (눕다, 놓여 있다)	lay	lain
lose	lost	lost	make	made	made
mean	meant	meant	meet	met	met
overcome	overcame	overcome	pay	paid	paid
put	put	put	read	read	read
ride	rode	ridden	ring	rang	rung
rise	rose	risen	run	ran	run
say	said	said	see	saw	seen
sell	sold	sold	send	sent	sent

원형	과거형	과거분사형	원형	과거형	과거분사형
set	set	set	shut	shut	shut
sing	sang	sung	sink	sank	sunk
sit	sat	sat	sleep	slept	slept
smell	smelled/smelt	smelled/smelt	speak	spoke	spoken
spend	spent	spent	spread	spread	spread
stand	stood	stood	steal	stole	stolen
sweep	swept	swept	swim	swam	swum
take	took	taken	teach	taught	taught
tell	told	told	think	thought	thought
throw	threw	thrown	understand	understood	understood
wake	woke	woken	wear	wore	worn
win	won	won	write	wrote	written

PRACTICE 9

다음 동사의 과거형과 과거분사형을 쓰세요.

1 choose – _____ – _____
2 lay – _____ – _____
3 meet – _____ – _____
4 fall – _____ – _____
5 ring – _____ – _____
6 run – _____ – _____
7 spend – _____ – _____
8 take – _____ – _____
9 give – _____ – _____
10 keep – _____ – _____
11 hear – _____ – _____
12 sit – _____ – _____
13 bear – _____ – _____
14 teach – _____ – _____
15 sing – _____ – _____
16 cost – _____ – _____
17 think – _____ – _____
18 fly – _____ – _____
19 wear – _____ – _____
20 hurt – _____ – _____
21 read – _____ – _____
22 tell – _____ – _____
23 make – _____ – _____
24 fight – _____ – _____
25 see – _____ – _____
26 go – _____ – _____

27	bring	– _____ – _____	28	pay	– _____ – _____
29	draw	– _____ – _____	30	find	– _____ – _____
31	hit	– _____ – _____	32	buy	– _____ – _____
33	speak	– _____ – _____	34	begin	– _____ – _____
35	understand	– _____ – _____	36	lie(눕다)	– _____ – _____
37	steal	– _____ – _____	38	put	– _____ – _____
39	hold	– _____ – _____	40	sink	– _____ – _____
41	wake	– _____ – _____	42	write	– _____ – _____
43	overcome	– _____ – _____	44	lead	– _____ – _____
45	know	– _____ – _____	46	leave	– _____ – _____
47	set	– _____ – _____	48	rise	– _____ – _____
49	sweep	– _____ – _____	50	smell	– _____ – _____
51	eat	– _____ – _____	52	forget	– _____ – _____
53	have	– _____ – _____	54	become	– _____ – _____
55	sleep	– _____ – _____	56	let	– _____ – _____
57	spread	– _____ – _____	58	dream	– _____ – _____
59	send	– _____ – _____	60	beat	– _____ – _____
61	stand	– _____ – _____	62	drink	– _____ – _____
63	come	– _____ – _____	64	say	– _____ – _____
65	feel	– _____ – _____	66	mean	– _____ – _____
67	grow	– _____ – _____	68	build	– _____ – _____
69	cut	– _____ – _____	70	swim	– _____ – _____
71	throw	– _____ – _____	72	be	– _____ – _____
73	lose	– _____ – _____	74	blow	– _____ – _____
75	drive	– _____ – _____	76	do	– _____ – _____
77	hide	– _____ – _____	78	get	– _____ – _____
79	win	– _____ – _____	80	ride	– _____ – _____
81	sell	– _____ – _____	82	shut	– _____ – _____

PRACTICE 10

괄호 안의 단어를 알맞은 형태로 바꾸어 빈칸에 쓰세요.

1. My aunt _____ me a gift from L.A. last week. (send)

2. Sujin _____ born in Gwangju in 2005. (be)

3. I _____ a lot of time in front of my computer these days. (spend)

4. The oranges looked very sour, so I _____ _____ them. (not, eat)

5. Mark _____ up late and hurried to school. (wake)

6. Kate _____ _____ anything last night. (not, hear)

7. My daughter accidentally _____ a bowl and said she was sorry. (break)

8. The car _____ the dog and broke its legs. (hit)

9. Tony _____ down on the street and hurt his arm. (fall)

10. I _____ _____ the flute when I was young. (not, play)

11. The bank _____ at 4 o'clock on weekdays. (close)

12. Yumi _____ down on her bed and got some rest. (lie)

13. Peter _____ the newspaper after he finished his lunch. (read)

14. Sally _____ some cakes for the party yesterday. (bring)

15. I _____ Mr. Smith at the job fair last month. (see)

16. Hana _____ breakfast yesterday. (eat)

17. I _____ this picture three years ago. (draw)

18. His family _____ to Korea in 2001. (come)

19. Why _____ you _____ to work yesterday? (not, come)

20. My plane _____ at 8 o'clock tomorrow morning. (leave)

21. The movie ended at 10 last night, and I _____ straight home. (drive)

22. She felt the cold wind blowing, so she _____ the window. (shut)

23. On Hanna's birthday, we _____ Happy Birthday to her. She was very happy with it. (sing)

미래시제

will + 동사원형	1. 미래에 일어날 동작이나 상태를 예측한다. It **will be** very sunny this Friday. 이번 금요일은 매우 화창할 것이다. = It **is going to be** very sunny this Friday. *cf.* be going to와 바꾸어 쓸 수 있다. 2. 미래에 일어날 일에 대해 '~하겠다'는 의지를 나타낸다. Your bags look very heavy. I **will help** you. 네 가방들이 매우 무거워 보이는구나. 내가 널 도와줄게.
be going to + 동사원형	미래에 일어날 일이 미리 계획되거나 예정되어 있음을 나타낸다. Jack **is going to play** tennis with Sam this weekend. Jack은 이번 주말에 Sam과 테니스를 칠 것이다. They **are going to arrive** here at 6 o'clock. 그들은 6시에 여기에 도착할 것이다.

PRACTICE 11

괄호 안에 주어진 말 중 알맞은 것을 고르세요.

1. In this video clip, you (will, is, be) see some famous paintings.
2. (Will, Are, Be) you going to have a birthday party soon?
3. My team will (go, going, going to go) to the mountain next week.
4. We (will, be, are) going to play basketball this weekend.
5. I'm (going, go, will go) to teach at a middle school.
6. Susan (will join, joins, joining) us for lunch tomorrow.
7. I'm not (go, going, will go) to do the housework.
8. My grandfather (is, is going, will) be here during summer vacation.
9. Tomorrow I (am, will, be) going to leave for Incheon.
10. I (will, am, be) open the door for you.

PRACTICE 12

그림을 보고, 괄호 안의 단어와 be going to를 사용하여 문장을 완성하세요.

1 I <u>am going to stay</u> at home and watch TV. (stay)
2 _____ you _____ those shoes? (buy)
3 Ms. Baker _____ her daughter a pet on her birthday. (give)
4 Yoonhee and Jiho _____ until midnight. (study)
5 It _____ tomorrow. (rain)
6 Ted _____ his house. (paint)

 진행시제

PSS 4-1 동사의 -ing형

일반적인 경우	동사원형+ing	watch – watch**ing** hold – hold**ing**	follow – follow**ing** learn – learn**ing**
발음되지 않는 -e로 끝나는 경우	e를 빼고 ing	face – fac**ing** take – tak**ing**	smile – smil**ing** date – dat**ing**
발음되는 -e로 끝나는 경우	동사원형+ing	agree – agree**ing**	see – see**ing**
ie로 끝나는 경우	ie를 y로 고치고 ing	die – dy**ing**	lie – ly**ing**

단모음+단자음으로 끝나는 1음절과 뒤에 강세가 오는 2음절의 경우	동사원형 +마지막 자음 +ing	run – run**ning**　　plan – plan**ning** get – get**ting**　　sit – sit**ting** *cf.* 강세가 앞에 오는 2음절 동사 ➡ 동사원형+ing visit – visit**ing**　　enter – enter**ing**

정답 p.11

PRACTICE 13

다음 동사의 -ing형을 쓰세요.

1	plant	– _____		2	take	– _____
3	get	– _____		4	play	– _____
5	smile	– _____		6	bow	– _____
7	become	– _____		8	see	– _____
9	lose	– _____		10	breathe	– _____
11	stand	– _____		12	open	– _____
13	argue	– _____		14	tumble	– _____
15	worry	– _____		16	bite	– _____
17	teach	– _____		18	wrap	– _____
19	swim	– _____		20	copy	– _____
21	sing	– _____		22	bake	– _____
23	die	– _____		24	return	– _____
25	plan	– _____		26	operate	– _____
27	serve	– _____		28	join	– _____
29	carry	– _____		30	climb	– _____
31	go	– _____		32	set	– _____
33	study	– _____		34	clean	– _____
35	date	– _____		36	encourage	– _____
37	pull	– _____		38	burn	– _____
39	use	– _____		40	stay	– _____
41	come	– _____		42	act	– _____

#	verb		#	verb	
43	win	– _____	44	produce	– _____
45	celebrate	– _____	46	write	– _____
47	deny	– _____	48	repeat	– _____
49	enter	– _____	50	eat	– _____
51	make	– _____	52	hit	– _____
53	run	– _____	54	marry	– _____
55	shine	– _____	56	beat	– _____
57	enjoy	– _____	58	cause	– _____
59	move	– _____	60	solve	– _____
61	face	– _____	62	destroy	– _____
63	fight	– _____	64	roll	– _____
65	wash	– _____	66	say	– _____
67	stop	– _____	68	shake	– _____
69	introduce	– _____	70	happen	– _____
71	fly	– _____	72	hold	– _____
73	save	– _____	74	share	– _____
75	visit	– _____	76	put	– _____
77	lie	– _____	78	talk	– _____
79	ride	– _____	80	collect	– _____
81	dream	– _____	82	control	– _____
83	try	– _____	84	drive	– _____
85	hurt	– _____	86	fill	– _____
87	pay	– _____	88	wear	– _____
89	agree	– _____	90	cheat	– _____
91	cut	– _____	92	sell	– _____
93	form	– _____	94	fix	– _____
95	remove	– _____	96	turn	– _____
97	mention	– _____	98	increase	– _____
99	wait	– _____	100	pick	– _____

5 The hen's eggs _____ _____ . (hatch)

6 Mr. Smith _____ _____ his job. (lose)

7 _____ you ever _____ Korea, Cathy? (visit) → Yes, I _____ .

8 The plants _____ _____ no water for a week. (get)

9 They _____ _____ up places to live in. (set)

10 They _____ _____ the boy several books. (buy)

11 The singer's latest song _____ _____ successful in USA. (be)

12 I _____ _____ how to use a computer. (not, learn)

13 _____ you ever _____ to Singapore? (be) → No, I _____ .

14 Seoul _____ _____ my second home. (become)

15 This area _____ _____ so much. (change)

16 We _____ _____ potatoes since then. (not, eat)

17 _____ you _____ all of the six kids? (see) → Yes, I _____ .

18 She _____ _____ swimming a lot. (practice)

19 Almost everyone _____ _____ the fables because they are interesting. (read)

20 I _____ _____ your brother for a long time. (not, see)

PSS 5-2 현재완료의 용법

용법	예문	주로 함께 쓰이는 단어
완료	He **has already finished** his presentation. 그는 이미 그의 발표를 끝냈다. I **have just planted** 10 trees. 나는 방금 10그루의 나무를 심었다. *cf.* just는 완료시제와 함께 쓰이지만 just now는 '방금 전에, 조금 전에'의 의미로 과거시제와 함께 쓰인다. She **hasn't arrived** in Seoul **yet**. 그녀는 아직 서울에 도착하지 않았다.	already, yet, just *cf.* already와 just는 주로 have와 과거분사 사이에 위치하고 yet은 문장의 끝에 위치한다.

 **현재완료**

PSS 5-1 현재완료의 형태

현재완료는 「have/has + 과거분사」의 형태로 과거에 일어난 사건의 발생 시점을 나타내는 것이 아니라 과거의 그 사건이 현재와 관련이 있음을 나타낼 때 쓰인다.

Jerry forgot my name. He still can't remember it.
Jerry는 내 이름을 잊어버렸다. 그는 여전히 그것을 기억할 수 없다.
➡ Jerry **has forgotten** my name. Jerry는 내 이름을 잊어버렸다.
I lost my puppy. I still can't find it. 나는 강아지를 잃어버렸다. 나는 여전히 그것을 찾을 수 없다.
➡ I **have lost** my puppy. 나는 강아지를 잃어버렸다.

주어	have/has	과거분사
I/We/You/They	have (not)	been studied done ~ gone found
He/She/It	has (not)	

현재완료의 의문문은 주어 앞에 Have/Has를 쓰며, 긍정일 때는 「Yes, 주어+have/has」, 부정일 때는 「No, 주어+haven't/hasn't」로 답한다.

Have you finished your lunch? 너 점심 다 먹었니?
Yes, I have. 응, 다 먹었어. / **No, I haven't.** 아니, 다 먹지 않았어.

PRACTICE 16

괄호 안에 주어진 단어를 이용하여 현재완료시제의 문장을 완성하고, 의문문의 경우 대답을 완성하세요.

1 __Have__ you ever __heard__ of this actor? (hear) → Yes, I __have__.
2 My mother's parents _____ _____ away. (pass)
3 _____ you _____ about your future? (think) → No, I _____.
4 I _____ _____ your cake. (not, touch)

1 At 07:40 ➡ He ___was___ ___taking___ a shower.
2 At 08:25 ➡ He _____ _____ breakfast.
3 At 08:55 ➡ He _____ _____ a newspaper.
4 At 09:50 ➡ He _____ _____ the living room.
5 At 10:30 ➡ He _____ _____ TV.
6 At 11:40 ➡ He _____ _____ a book.

정답 p.12

PRACTICE 15

괄호 안에 주어진 단어를 이용하여 진행시제의 문장을 완성하세요.

1 The sky was blue and the birds ___were___ ___singing___. (sing)
2 He is in the kitchen now. He _____ _____ a cake. (bake)
3 They _____ _____ about the rule a few minutes ago. (argue)
4 When I saw her, she _____ _____ a bicycle. (ride)
5 You should be quiet. The baby _____ _____. (sleep)
6 The weather is hot now. He _____ _____ his tie and jacket. (remove)
7 What time _____ you _____ tomorrow? (leave)
8 Jina can't answer the phone right now. She _____ _____. (cook)
9 I saw you at the police station this morning. What _____ you _____ there? (do)
10 Sora and I _____ _____ bowling after work. Would you like to join us? (go)
11 Let's go shopping tomorrow. I _____ _____ _____ then. (not, work)
12 I saw Minsu on my way home. He _____ _____ at the bus stop. (stand)
13 At two o'clock yesterday, I _____ _____ lunch. (have)
14 Tom _____ _____ _____ his bike this afternoon. You can take it if you need it. (not, use)
15 I can't go out now. I _____ _____ cookies for my husband. (make)

PSS 4-2 과거진행시제와 현재진행시제

1. 과거진행 「was/were+-ing」 – 과거의 한 시점에 진행되고 있던 동작을 나타낸다.

   I **was having** lunch **an hour ago**. 나는 1시간 전에 점심을 먹고 있었다.

2. 현재진행 「am/are/is+-ing」 – 말하고 있는 시점에 진행되고 있는 동작을 나타낸다.

   I **am taking** a walk **now**. 나는 지금 산책을 하고 있는 중이다.

3. 가까운 미래에 있을 일이 미리 계획된 일인 경우에는 미래시제 대신 현재진행시제를 쓸 수 있다.

   We **are going** on a business trip to New York **tomorrow**.
   우리는 내일 뉴욕으로 출장을 갈 것이다.
   What **are** you **doing** this Sunday? 너는 이번 일요일에 무엇을 할 거니?

PRACTICE 14

다음은 Mike가 오늘 아침에 한 일입니다. 그림을 보고, 진행시제의 문장을 완성하세요.

1
07:30 - 08:00

2
08:00 - 08:30

3
08:30 - 09:30

4
09:30 - 10:00

5
10:00 - 11:00

6
11:00 - 12:00

경험	Have you **ever tried** potato chips? 감자칩을 먹어본 적이 있니? **cf.** ever는 의문문에서 '지금까지, 여태껏'이라는 의미로 have와 과거분사 사이에 위치한다. I**'ve been** to London **once**. 나는 런던에 가본 적이 한 번 있다. I**'ve never read** the book **before**. 나는 전에 그 책을 읽어본 적이 없다.	ever, never, before, once, often
결과	She **has lost** her bag. 그녀는 가방을 잃어버렸다. (그래서 지금 가방이 없다.) They **have gone** to New York. 그들은 뉴욕으로 갔다. (그래서 지금 여기에 없다.) **cf.** have been to: ~에 가본 적이 있다 (경험) have gone to: ~에 갔다 (그래서 지금 여기에 없다.)	go, come, leave, lose, buy
계속	Rachel **has worked** here **for** 6 years. Rachel은 여기에서 6년 동안 일했다. I **have lived** here **since** March. 나는 3월부터 여기에서 살았다.	for, since

정답 p.12

PRACTICE 17

주어진 단어를 이용하여 현재완료 문장을 완성하고, 괄호 안에 각 문장의 용법을 쓰세요.

1 __She has met__ Mr. Kim before. (she, meet) [경험]
2 _____ to Paris. (my father, go) [   ]
3 _____ the laundry. (I, already, do) [   ]
4 _____ for two years. (she, stay, in Korea) [   ]
5 _____ once. (he, be, to India) [   ]
6 _____ their lunch. (they, just, finish) [   ]

PSS 5-3 for와 since

for – '~ 동안'의 뜻으로, 사건이 일어나 지속된 시간의 길이를 나타낸다.

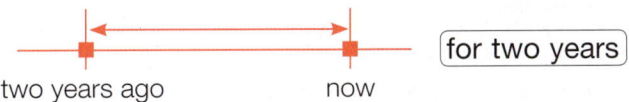

two years ago   now   for two years

She started to play the violin two years ago. She still plays the violin.
그녀는 2년 전에 바이올린을 연주하기 시작했다. 그녀는 아직도 바이올린을 연주한다.
➡ She **has played** the violin **for** two years. 그녀는 2년 동안 바이올린을 연주해 왔다.

> since - '~ 이후로'의 뜻으로, 사건이 시작된 시점을 나타낸다.
>
> 2012 ――― now   since 2012
>
> I bought a car in 2012. I still have the car.
> 나는 2012년에 차를 샀다. 나는 아직도 그 차를 가지고 있다.
> ➡ I **have had** the car **since** 2012. 나는 2012년 이후로 그 차를 가지고 있다.

PRACTICE 18

정답 p.12

다음 문장의 빈칸에 for나 since 중 알맞은 것을 쓰세요.

1 He hasn't had any food _____ a week.
2 She has lived here _____ a long time.
3 I have worked here _____ last year.
4 He has enjoyed soccer _____ three years.
5 We have raised apple trees _____ 2016.
6 They have been in the States _____ ten months.
7 Soccer has been very popular _____ then.
8 Jina has been sick _____ last Friday.
9 They have been married _____ many years.
10 My grandma has been happily married for 50 years, _____ the age of 22.

PRACTICE 19

정답 p.12

〈보기〉와 같이 괄호 안에 주어진 단어를 이용하여 두 문장을 한 문장으로 연결하세요.

> 보기
> I started to work here a month ago. I still work here.
> ➡ I have worked here for a month. (for)
> I started to work here in 2018. I still work here.
> ➡ I have worked here since 2018. (since)

1 Jack arrived here four days ago. He's still here now.
   ➡ _____ (for)

2 I began to teach students fifteen years ago. I still teach students.
→ _____ (for)

3 Liz started to study Japanese two years ago. She still studies it.
→ _____ (for)

4 My mom bought the house last year. She still has it.
→ _____ (since)

5 Kate first met Dave last April. She still dates him.
→ _____ (since)

6 Mark started to play tennis in 2015. He still plays tennis.
→ _____ (since)

PSS 5-4 현재완료시제와 과거시제

현재완료	과거
1. 과거에 시작되어 현재까지 계속되는 동작이나 상태를 나타낸다. I **have stayed** in London for two weeks. (I'm still in London.) 나는 2주 동안 런던에 머물러왔다. (나는 아직도 런던에 있다.)	1. 과거에 시작되어 과거에 종료된 동작이나 상태를 나타낸다. I **stayed** in London for two weeks. (I'm not in London anymore.) 나는 2주 동안 런던에 머물렀다. (나는 더 이상 런던에 있지 않다.)
2. 과거의 불특정한 시점에 일어난 동작이나 상태를 나타낸다. 과거의 특정한 때를 나타내는 부사(구)와 함께 쓰지 않는다. She **has lost** her purse. 그녀는 지갑을 잃어버렸다.	2. last year, yesterday, four weeks ago와 같이 과거의 특정한 때를 나타내는 부사(구)와 함께 쓰여 그 동작이나 상태가 일어난 구체적인 시점을 나타낸다. She **lost** her purse **last night**. 그녀는 지난 밤에 지갑을 잃어버렸다.

정답 p.12

PRACTICE 20

괄호 안의 단어를 알맞은 형태로 바꾸어 빈칸에 쓰세요.

1 A: Have you seen Mary lately?
B: Yes, I have. I _____ her last night at the mall near her house. (see)

2 A: What do you think of the novel *Pride and Prejudice*?
   B: I don't know. I _____ _____ _____ it. (never, read)

3 A: How's your sister doing in London?
   B: I'm not sure. I _____ _____ with her recently. (not, talk)

4 A: Did you pass the exam?
   B: Of course. I _____ good grades. (get)

5 A: How's the weather there?
   B: It _____ a lot this morning, but it has stopped now. (snow)

6 A: Are you nervous?
   B: Yes, I am. I _____ _____ _____ a truck before. (never, drive)

7 A: Have you finished your report?
   B: Yes. I _____ _____ _____ it. (just, finish)

8 A: Your kitchen is very clean.
   B: Thank you. I _____ it yesterday. (clean)

9 A: Are you hungry?
   B: Yes. I _____ _____ anything since this morning. (not, eat)

10 A: Why did you walk there?
   B: I _____ there because I missed the bus. (walk)

PRACTICE 21

정답 p.13

밑줄 친 부분 중 잘못된 곳이 있으면 올바르게 고치세요.

1 Yesterday, we <u>have had</u> the first snow of the winter.   _____

2 Doctors <u>have found</u> that this is very useful.   _____

3 It <u>has rained</u> heavily last night.   _____

4 My friend <u>has lost</u> his job lately.   _____

5 Yumi <u>has been</u> born in Gwangju.   _____

6 I <u>have bought</u> this car in 2013.   _____

7 She <u>has just gone</u> out to have dinner.   _____

8 I <u>have finished</u> the work two hours ago.   _____

9 He <u>has already seen</u> the movie.   _____

10 My dad <u>has got</u> a new job last month.   _____

PRACTICE 22

괄호 안의 단어와 과거시제 또는 현재완료시제 중 알맞은 것을 사용하여 문장을 완성하세요.

1 (I / not / read / the newspaper / yesterday). So, I didn't know what happened in London.
➡ I didn't[did not] read the newspaper yesterday.

2 (Mike / play soccer / for three hours). Now he is tired and needs a rest.
➡ _____

3 I don't remember what year they started working at this company.
(they / work / here / since 2010)?
➡ _____

4 (the train / arrive / at the station / five minutes ago). But I missed it by a second.
➡ _____

5 Did you say forty thousand dollars? (How / you / earn / so much / last year)?
➡ _____

6 (Eva / not / see / her sister / for a long time). She is going to the Philippines to meet her.
➡ _____

PSS 5-5 현재완료 진행시제

현재완료 진행시제는 과거에 시작된 어떤 동작이 현재까지 계속될 때 쓴다. 계속의 의미를 나타내므로 for, since와 함께 쓰이는 경우가 많다.

> have/has+been+-ing

Jake started playing the piano an hour ago. He is still playing the piano now.
Jake는 한 시간 전에 피아노를 치기 시작했다. 그는 지금도 아직 피아노를 치고 있다.

➡ Jake **has been playing** the piano for an hour.
Jake는 한 시간 동안 피아노를 치고 있다.

cf. 현재완료시제는 과거의 한 사건이 현재와 관련이 있을 때 쓰인다. 반면, 현재완료 진행시제는 과거에 시작한 어떤 동작이 현재까지도 계속 진행 중인 것을 강조한다.

I **have taught** her.
나는 그녀를 가르쳤다 (→ 뜻이 분명하지 않음. 현재완료의 '계속', '완료', '경험'으로 해석 가능)

I **have been teaching** her.
나는 그녀를 가르치고 있다. (→ 과거부터 지금까지 계속 가르치고 있는 상황)

PRACTICE 23

괄호 안에 주어진 동사를 이용하여 현재완료 진행시제 문장을 완성하세요.

1   I _____ English for ten years. (study)
2   My friends and I _____ basketball for three hours. (play)
3   How long _____ he _____ in his room? (sleep)
4   She _____ for this company since she was 28 years old. (work)
5   _____ you _____ this magazine for two hours? (read)
6   The engineer _____ the air-conditioner in the living room. (repair)
7   They _____ for you since 2 o'clock in the afternoon. (wait)
8   Amy _____ to her friend on the phone for one hour. (talk)
9   _____ Daniel _____ an apple pie in the kitchen? (bake)
10 She _____ TV for two hours. (watch)

PRACTICE 24

주어진 두 문장을 for나 since 중 알맞은 것을 사용하여 현재완료 진행시제 문장으로 바꿔 쓰세요. (단, 밑줄 친 단어를 주어로 사용하세요.)

1   I got my glasses in March. I still wear them.
    ➡ I have been wearing glasses since March.

2   Seyeon turned on her laptop two hours ago. She is still using it.
    ➡ _____

3   Two people started playing tennis at 4 o'clock. They are still playing tennis.
    ➡ _____

4   Mike began making lunch at noon. He is still making lunch.
    ➡ _____

5   Jisu and Minji began building a sand castle an hour ago. They are still building it.
    ➡ _____

6   It began to rain this morning. It is still raining.
    ➡ _____

Chapter Review Test

CHAPTER 2 시제
정답 p.13

1 다음 문장에서 어법상 적절하지 <u>않은</u> 것은?

> If you ①will take that flight now, ②what ③time ④will you ⑤arrive?

2 다음 밑줄 친 말 중 어색한 것을 고르세요.

> A: Look! ⓐ <u>There's</u> a dog on the bench.
> B: I know that dog. ⓑ <u>I had seen</u> it here since last month.
> A: Have you? Doesn't it have a home?
> B: ⓒ <u>It is</u>, but it waits here for its owner until he ⓓ <u>comes</u> home every day.
> A: The owner must be happy.
> B: You can say that again. I think the dog ⓔ <u>is waiting</u> for its owner now.

① ⓐ, ⓒ ② ⓑ, ⓒ ③ ⓑ, ⓓ
④ ⓐ, ⓒ, ⓔ ⑤ ⓑ, ⓓ, ⓔ

3 다음 중 주어진 문장과 현재완료의 용법이 같은 것은?

> I have been to Europe before.

① My son has lost his watch.
② He has just returned from a trip to Japan.
③ Have you ever seen this movie?
④ Mother has worked there since last year.
⑤ Has she lived in this house since then?

4 다음 중 밑줄 친 부분의 쓰임이 잘못된 것은?

① Mina has studied English <u>for</u> two years.
② I have slept <u>for</u> ten hours.
③ My uncle has lived there <u>for</u> last month.
④ I have had this book <u>since</u> 2001.
⑤ She has been sick <u>since</u> last night.

5 주어진 문장과 뜻이 같도록 빈칸을 채우세요.

> • My sister and I will go climbing this Saturday.
> = My sister and I _____ _____ _____ go climbing this Saturday.

6 다음 중 어법상 올바른 문장을 고르세요.

① My brother leaves for Gyeongju tomorrow.
② Ed studies English for the finals yesterday.
③ I was playing the violin next Sunday.
④ Was your parents angry at you?
⑤ You doesn't want to learn Chinese.

7 다음 두 문장을 현재완료를 이용해서 한 문장으로 만드세요.

> • My uncle and aunt moved to Washington D.C. three years ago.
> • They still live there now.

→ My uncle and aunt _____ _____ _____ Washington D.C. for three years.

8 다음 밑줄 친 우리말과 같은 뜻이 되도록 괄호 안의 주어진 말을 이용하여 영작하세요.

> A: What are you going to do during the vacation?
> B: I'm going to visit my cousin in London.
> A: What are you going to eat there?
> B: I'm going to eat fish and chips there.
> A: Sounds fantastic.
>   <u>나는 그것을 먹어본 적이 없어.</u> (never, eat)
> B: I'll take some pictures and send them to you.
> A: That would be nice.

➡ _____

9 다음 두 문장을 현재완료를 이용하여 한 문장으로 바꿔 쓰세요.

> • They started to serve free meals two years ago.
> • They still do.

➡ _____

10 다음 중 빈칸에 들어갈 말이 나머지 넷과 <u>다른</u> 것은?

① A: _____ you really go there last night?
  B: Yes, I was invited.
② A: _____ it snow this morning?
  B: No, it just rained.
③ A: _____ he wash the dishes?
  B: Yes, he did.
④ A: _____ you ever been to Seoul?
  B: No, I haven't.
⑤ A: When _____ you clean your room?
  B: Well, about an hour ago.

11 다음 중 밑줄 친 부분의 쓰임이 <u>잘못된</u> 것의 개수를 고르세요.

> Have you ever ⓐ <u>trying</u> Pho? Pho is one of ⓑ <u>the most popular foods</u> in Vietnam. It is a beef soup with rice noodles. I ⓒ <u>have tried</u> it when I visited Vietnam last year. It ⓓ <u>was</u> one of my favorite dishes ever since. Some people hate it ⓔ <u>because of</u> the herbs in it, but I have been enjoying it since I first tasted it.

① 2개 ② 3개 ③ 4개 ④ 5개 ⑤ 없음

12 우리말과 뜻이 같도록 빈칸에 알맞은 말끼리 바르게 짝지은 것은?

> • 우리 엄마는 전에 인도에 다녀오신 적이 있다.
>   ➡ My mom _____ India before.
> • 내 남동생이 막 숙제를 끝냈다.
>   ➡ My brother _____ his homework.

① has been to – just finishes
② has been to – is finished
③ has gone to – has just finishing
④ has been to – has just finished
⑤ has gone to – finishes

13 다음 중 어법상 올바른 문장의 개수로 알맞은 것은?

> ⓐ I have met my boyfriend in 2020.
> ⓑ We depart from the hotel this evening.
> ⓒ He swum in the river with them last week.
> ⓓ I have worked here since 2001.
> ⓔ They are arriving on the 9 o'clock flight.
> ⓕ My father was reading a newspaper when dinner was ready.

① 1개 ② 2개 ③ 3개 ④ 4개 ⑤ 5개

14 다음 문장의 밑줄 친 부분과 쓰임이 같은 것은?

> She has lived in Australia since 2003.

① I have learned Chinese for two years.
② Jenny has read the story twice.
③ She has lost her wallet.
④ I have met her before.
⑤ Kevin has been to America.

15 다음 대화에서 틀린 문장을 찾아 바르게 고치세요.

> A: ⓐ Have you finished packing your bag yesterday?
> B: Yes, I did. ⓑ I have been looking forward to the trip.
> A: How are you feeling?
> B: ⓒ I'm really excited. I don't think I will be able to sleep tonight.
> A: Well, ⓓ if you don't sleep, you'll be tired tomorrow.

➡ _____

16 다음 빈칸에 들어갈 말로 알맞은 것은?

> The captain of the boat checks everything. When something _____, he will take care of it.

① happen   ② happens   ③ will happen
④ happening   ⑤ to happen

17 주어진 문장의 밑줄 친 부분과 용법이 같은 것은?

> Have you ever heard of the yellow bird in this town?

① We have lived here for six months.
② I have never seen a rainbow.
③ Julie has just broken the vase.
④ He has gone to Europe.
⑤ I have stayed in Korea since 1996.

18 다음 밑줄 친 부분 중 어법상 틀린 것을 고르세요.

① They chose the boy for the team last week.
② The sleeping babies lied on the bed.
③ He hurt his back playing tennis yesterday.
④ We drank a whole bottle of orange juice.
⑤ I read the book to the children last night.

19 그림의 내용과 일치하도록 주어진 단어를 사용하여 알맞은 말을 쓰세요.

A: What is he doing in the yard?
B: He _____. (wash)

20 다음 괄호 안에 주어진 각각의 단어를 알맞은 형태로 고쳐 쓰세요.

> • I have just _____ the project. (finish)
> • My mom _____ to America last year. (go)

21 다음 우리말을 참고하여 빈칸에 들어갈 알맞은 말을 <u>모두</u> 고르세요.

- Bob은 매주 일요일마다 축구를 한다.
  = Bob plays soccer _____.

① next Sunday   ② last Sunday
③ this Sunday   ④ on Sundays
⑤ every Sunday

22 다음 ⓐ~ⓔ 중 어법상 <u>틀린</u> 것을 고르세요.

There was an honest lumberjack in the town. One day, as he was cutting down a tree, his axe slipped and ⓐ <u>fell</u> into the pond. Then a god ⓑ <u>appeared</u> with a gold axe and a silver axe. He asked, "Is one of these axes ⓒ <u>yours</u>?" The lumberjack said, "No, the one ⓓ <u>I've just drop</u> is an old iron axe." The god, ⓔ <u>impressed by</u> his honesty, gave both axes to the lumberjack.

① ⓐ   ② ⓑ   ③ ⓒ   ④ ⓓ   ⑤ ⓔ

23 다음 밑줄 친 우리말을 영어로 바르게 옮긴 것은?

Tom: Hong Kong is full of beautiful buildings. <u>너 홍콩에 가본 적 있니?</u>
Sue: Yes. I went there three years ago.

① Did you ever went to Hong Kong?
② Did you ever been to Hong Kong?
③ Have you ever went to Hong Kong?
④ Have you ever gone to Hong Kong?
⑤ Have you ever been to Hong Kong?

24 Alex와 Samantha가 어제 한 일을 적은 표를 보고, 바른 것을 <u>모두</u> 고르세요.

Time	Alex	Samantha
10 a.m.~11 a.m.	cleaned a room	took a shower
12 p.m.~1 p.m.	had lunch	made spaghetti
2 p.m.~3 p.m.	took a nap	took care of her little brother
4 p.m.~5 p.m.	listened to the radio	played the cello
6 p.m.~7 p.m.	played a computer game	wrote a letter to her dad
8 p.m.~9 p.m.	read a novel	talked to her friend on the phone

① Alex was cleaning the kitchen at 10:30 a.m.
② Samantha was taking care of her little brother when Alex was taking a nap.
③ Samantha was taking a shower at 12:20 p.m.
④ Alex was listening to the radio when Samantha was writing a letter to her dad.
⑤ Alex was reading a novel when Samantha was talking to her friend on the phone.

25 다음 대화의 빈칸에 공통으로 알맞은 것은?

Tom: Where have you _____, Julia?
Julia: I have _____ to China.

① gone   ② were   ③ been
④ went   ⑤ be

26 다음 빈칸에 들어갈 말로 알맞은 것은?

Your son _____ arrive here next Monday.

① is being   ② is going   ③ was
④ will be   ⑤ is going to

27 다음 밑줄 친 부분 중 올바르지 않은 것은?

> The first seed ① shook its head. "I don't want to go out. I want to stay here." The second seed ② said, "But it's not winter anymore. I want to see the bright sun." The second seed ③ tried to go out of the earth. It ④ grow and grow, and soon its bud ⑤ opened.

28 다음 문장의 현재완료와 용법이 같은 것을 모두 고르세요.

> Karen has never lost her mobile phone.

① I have read the magazine before.
② My father's hair has already turned gray.
③ My sister has met him twice.
④ I have just washed my car.
⑤ I have lived in Busan for a year.

29 현재완료 진행시제를 이용하여 다음 대화의 마지막 말을 완성하세요.

> A: Hey, what are you doing now?
> B: I'm reading a comic book.
> A: Weren't you reading that comic book this morning?
> B: Yes, I was.
> A: So, you _____ _____ _____ it _____ this morning.

30 다음 밑줄 친 부분 중 어법상 어색한 것은?

> Many people ① stood around the man. He ② kept ③ saying, "I'm not a thief. I haven't ④ stole ⑤ anything."

31 다음 중 어법상 틀린 문장만 짝지은 것은?

> ⓐ Have you ever emailed your friends?
> ⓑ My sister has visited London last year.
> ⓒ They arrived at the hotel yesterday.
> ⓓ Sam has lived in Seoul in 2018.
> ⓔ I saw the movie six months ago.

① ⓐ, ⓒ　　② ⓐ, ⓔ　　③ ⓑ, ⓒ
④ ⓑ, ⓓ　　⑤ ⓓ, ⓔ

32 다음 밑줄 친 부분의 올바른 형태끼리 바르게 짝지어진 것은?

> A little boy was playing on an escalator in a department store. He went up and down the escalator. Suddenly he fall on the escalator and his finger be bleeding. He cried out for help.

① falls – is　　② fallen – was
③ falls – was　　④ fell – is
⑤ fell – was

33 다음 중 어법상 옳은 문장을 모두 고른 것은?

> ⓐ James has been struggled with the problem lately.
> ⓑ My daughter has stayed in Italy for a year.
> ⓒ The number of immigrants in India have been declining since 1960.
> ⓓ He has been absent from school since last Thursday.
> ⓔ I haven't already read the book.
> ⓕ I have met him four days ago.
> ⓖ The woman has played many famous roles in several musicals since 2002.

① ⓐ, ⓓ, ⓖ ② ⓑ, ⓓ, ⓖ ③ ⓑ, ⓔ, ⓖ
④ ⓒ, ⓓ, ⓕ ⑤ ⓓ, ⓔ, ⓖ

34 다음 밑줄 친 ⓐ~ⓕ 중 어법상 잘못된 것을 골라 그 기호를 쓰고 문장을 바르게 고쳐 쓰세요.

> Seth: Alice, what are you going to do this weekend?
> Alice: I'm going to visit my grandma. ⓐ She lives in the country.
> Seth: I thought she lived in your neighborhood.
> Alice: She moved. ⓑ She has lived there since last year.
> Seth: I see. ⓒ Do you go there often?
> Alice: I want to, but ⓓ I have been not there since two months.
> Seth: Why is that?
> Alice: ⓔ I have been busy studying for the final exam. ⓕ It will be over tomorrow.

➡ _____

35 다음 중 어법상 올바른 문장은?

① They have gone to New York last winter.
② When have you taught him?
③ She has met him yesterday.
④ He has worn glasses since he was a kid.
⑤ They have been happy a week ago.

36 다음 밑줄 친 부분 중 will로 바꾸어 쓸 수 없는 것은?

① I am going to ask him about this.
② Jane is going to the library.
③ Matthew is going to go back to Canada.
④ The kids are going to go on a picnic.
⑤ My brothers are going to fly to Japan.

37 다음 두 문장을 한 문장으로 표현하려고 할 때, 가장 올바른 것은?

> • Alice began to work with us two years ago.
> • Alice still works with us.

① Alice has worked with us for two years.
② Alice has worked with us for two years ago.
③ Alice has worked with us two years ago.
④ Alice has begun to work with us for two years ago.
⑤ Alice has begun to work with us two years ago.

38 다음 글의 (A), (B), (C)에 알맞은 것끼리 바르게 연결된 것은?

I (A) [was reading / am reading] books in my room when a thief (B) [broke into / has broken into] our house last week. I was very surprised but I called 911 calmly. I've never had an experience like this (C) [since / for] I was born. Five minutes later, a police officer came to our house and arrested the thief.

	(A)	(B)	(C)
①	was reading	has broken into	since
②	was reading	broke into	since
③	am reading	broke into	for
④	was reading	broke into	for
⑤	am reading	has broken into	for

39 다음 중 흐름이 어색한 대화는?

① A: Have you ever thought about making a movie?
   B: No, I haven't. Why?
② A: Has he done his work well?
   B: Yes, he did.
③ A: Who has had lunch already?
   B: I don't know. Maybe Dongsu has.
④ A: I have never been to Japan.
   B: Really? I hope you will visit there someday.
⑤ A: Have we met before?
   B: No, we have never met before.

40 다음 그림을 보고 빈칸에 들어갈 알맞은 말을 쓰세요.

It started snowing at 3 o'clock in the afternoon.

It is still snowing now.

➡ It _____ _____ _____ since 3 o'clock in the afternoon.

41 다음은 Andy의 일기입니다. 〈보기〉의 표현에 단어를 추가, 변형하여 밑줄 친 부분의 뜻에 맞게 한 문장으로 영작하세요.

Andy's Diary Aug 17
Today is the last day of my part-time summer job at the library. 나는 도서관에서 일하기 시작했던 이래로 즐거운 시간을 보내왔다.

보기
have a great time, start to work at the library

➡ _____
_____
_____

42 다음 대화의 빈칸 (A), (B)에 들어갈 말로 가장 적절한 것은?

A: I'm so excited to try out this recipe!
B: Emily, what are you trying to make?
A: Oh! I'm trying to make a strawberry tart.
B: I love tart! My mom has made it for me (A) _____ I was a little boy.
A: You're so lucky. I've never (B) _____ a tart before.
B: Really? Then, this one would be your very first tart.
A: I know! I hope I can make it look as good as the one in this picture.

	(A)	(B)		(A)	(B)
①	since	eat	②	when	eaten
③	since	eaten	④	since	ate
⑤	when	ate			

43 수지와 지호가 경험해 본 것들을 표시한 표를 보고 〈보기〉와 같이 현재완료 문장을 완성하세요.

경험한 내용	Suji	Jiho
• eat Thai food	o	x
(1) visit Brazil once	o	o
(2) win a prize in the piano competition	x	x
(3) read Anna Karenina	o	x

보기
• Suji has eaten Thai food, but Jiho has not eaten Thai food.

(1) Suji and Jiho _____
_____.

(2) Suji and Jiho _____
_____.

(3) Suji _____,
but Jiho _____.

44 다음 빈칸에 들어갈 알맞은 말은?

A: I have been in Korea for almost three years now.
B: Wow! That is amazing. Then, have you ever been to Haeundae in Busan?
A: No, _____.

① I have never been there
② I have been there for a week
③ I went there last Friday
④ I didn't like the place very much
⑤ I have been there since last month

45 다음 여행 계획표 (A)를 참고하여 〈보기〉에서 알맞은 표현을 골라 블로그 게시글 (B)의 빈칸을 완성하세요. (단, 중복하여 사용할 수 있습니다.)

보기 | will   have been   am

(A) My Travel Plan

Day 1	see the Statue of Liberty
Day 2	go to Times Square
Day 3	go on a picnic in Central Park

(B) My Blog

I _____ going to visit New York this summer. I started to plan the trip a week ago, and I'm still planning it. So I _____ planning the trip for a week. On the first day, I _____ see the Statue of Liberty. On the second day, I _____ go to Times Square and enjoy a famous musical. On the third day, I _____ go on a picnic in Central Park.

CHAPTER 3
조동사

성취도 자기 평가 활용법

구분	평가 기준
Excellent	문법 내용을 모두 이해하고, 문제를 모두 맞힘.
Very good	문법 내용은 충분히 이해했으나 실수로 1~2문제 틀림.
Good	문법 내용이 조금 어려워 3~4문제 틀림.
needs **R**eview	문법 내용 이해가 어렵고, 5문제 이상 틀림, 복습 필요.

Problem Solving Skill	페이지	학습날짜	성취도 자기평가 E V G R	학습체크
PSS 1 조동사의 쓰임	72	/		☐
PSS 2 조동사의 부정	73	/		☐
PSS 3 조동사로 시작하는 의문문	75	/		☐
PSS 4 조동사의 종류	페이지	학습날짜	성취도 자기평가 E V G R	학습체크
PSS 4-1 must Ⅰ	76	/		☐
PSS 4-2 must Ⅱ	77	/		☐
PSS 4-3 can, could Ⅰ	79	/		☐
PSS 4-4 can, could Ⅱ	80	/		☐
PSS 4-5 do	81	/		☐
PSS 4-6 should, had better	82	/		☐
PSS 4-7 will, would	84	/		☐
PSS 4-8 may, might	85	/		☐
PSS 4-9 used to, would	86	/		☐
Chapter Review Test	89	/		☐

조동사의 쓰임

조동사는 동사 앞에서 의무, 추측, 가능, 요청, 허가, 제안 등의 의미를 더하는 동사로 조동사 뒤에는 동사원형이 온다.

조동사	뜻	예문
must	의무 ~해야 한다	You **must work** together as a team. 너희는 한팀으로 함께 일해야 한다.
can	능력 ~할 수 있다	I **can swim** in the sea. 나는 바다에서 수영을 할 수 있다.
could	능력(과거형) ~할 수 있었다	We **could plant** more trees. 우리는 더 많은 나무들을 심을 수 있었다.
do	강조의 do 정말로[확실히, 꼭] ~하다	She **does show** a talent in math. 그녀는 정말로 수학에 재능이 있다.
should	의무 ~해야 한다	We **should listen** to what he is saying. 우리는 그가 말하고 있는 것을 들어야 한다.
had better	충고, 권유 ~하는 것이 낫다	You **had better take** your umbrella with you today. 너는 오늘 우산을 가지고 가는 게 낫다.
will	미래(의지) ~할 것이다	I **will run** a marathon next Saturday. 나는 다음 주 토요일에 마라톤을 할 것이다.
would	미래(의지) 과거형 ~할 것이다	I **would shake** hands with him. 나는 그와 악수를 할 것이다.
may	추측 ~할지도 모른다	Scientists **may discover** a new planet. 과학자들은 새로운 행성을 발견할지도 모른다.
might	추측 ~할지도 모른다	She **might get** caught in the rain. 그녀는 비를 맞을지도 모른다.
used to	과거의 반복적 행위 ~하곤 했다	He **used to play** computer games all night. 그는 밤새도록 컴퓨터 게임을 하곤 했다.

정답 p.16

PRACTICE 1

빈칸에 들어갈 말로 알맞은 것을 고르세요.

1 Your sister must _____ me for the cakes.   ① pay   ② pays   ③ paying
2 When we go abroad, we can _____ English.   ① to use   ② use   ③ used
3 You should _____ off your shoes in the room.   ① take   ② to take   ③ took
4 Jina _____ to go for a walk in the evening.   ① like   ② likes   ③ liking
5 I used to _____ in a small house.   ① lived   ② live   ③ living
6 You had better _____ a doctor right now.   ① see   ② to see   ③ saw

#				
7	She may _____ us the answer.	① gave	② gives	③ give
8	That would _____ very nice.	① is	② being	③ be
9	I _____ watching TV two weeks ago.	① stopped	② stop	③ stops
10	Paul must _____ his report by tomorrow.	① finishes	② finish	③ finishing
11	We could _____ hiking next week.	① went	② to go	③ go
12	She might _____ this horror movie.	① hated	② hate	③ hates
13	I will _____ a taxi to the train station.	① took	② taking	③ take
14	My mom does _____ brown hair.	① having	② have	③ has
15	Mark always _____ to tell the truth.	① trying	② tries	③ try

PSS 2 조동사의 부정

조동사+not	축약형	예문
must not	**mustn't**	You **mustn't** jump into the pond. 너는 연못에 뛰어들면 안 된다.
cannot	**can't**	They **cannot[can't]** buy anything to eat. 그들은 먹을 것을 살 수 없다.
could not	**couldn't**	He **couldn't** take his eyes off her. 그는 그녀에게 눈을 뗄 수가 없었다.
do not	**don't**	I **don't** understand. 나는 이해를 못한다.
should not	**shouldn't**	You **shouldn't** touch the artworks. 당신은 그 예술작품들을 만지면 안 된다.
had better not	**'d better not**	You**'d better not** park here. 너는 여기에 주차하지 않는 게 낫다.
will not	**won't**	I **won't** forget you. 나는 너를 잊지 않을 것이다.
would not	**wouldn't**	I **wouldn't** worry about it. 난 그것에 대해 걱정하지 않을 것이다.
may not	-	He **may not** get an invitation. 그는 초대장을 받지 못할지도 모른다.
might not	**mightn't**	She **mightn't** join the speech contest. 그녀는 말하기 대회에 참가하지 않을지도 모른다.
did not use to (used to의 부정)	**didn't use to**	I **didn't use to[used not to]** like mushrooms, but now I love them. 나는 버섯을 좋아하지 않곤 했지만, 지금은 아주 좋아한다.

PRACTICE 2

다음 문장의 밑줄 친 부분을 부정형으로 바꾸어 쓰세요.

1 Ms. Kelly goes to church.
➡ Ms. Kelly does not[doesn't] go to church.

2 I can wait to meet them.
➡ _____

3 You may play the computer game now.
➡ _____

4 You must break your promise.
➡ _____

5 You had better go on a diet.
➡ _____

6 It might be safe to do so.
➡ _____

7 I could get to the office early.
➡ _____

8 You'd better bring your kids.
➡ _____

9 I will bring it to you.
➡ _____

10 You should hang it on the wall.
➡ _____

11 I used to play the guitar.
➡ _____

12 She could finish the work on time.
➡ _____

13 Denny will be fourteen years old soon.
➡ _____

14 We should listen to the teacher.
➡ _____

15 You must cross the street now.
➡ _____

조동사로 시작하는 의문문

조동사로 시작하는 의문문은 「조동사+주어+동사원형 ~?」의 어순으로 나타낸다.

조동사	주어	동사원형		
Can	you	join	our club?	너 우리 클럽에 가입할 수 있니?
Will	they	leave	here?	그들이 이곳을 떠날까?
Should	I	bring	an umbrella?	내가 우산을 가져와야 하니?

PRACTICE 3

다음 문장을 주어진 조동사로 시작하는 의문문으로 바꾸어 쓰세요.

1 You fix the computer. (can)
➡ Can you fix the computer?

2 Dave plays basketball. (will)
➡ _____

3 Jihye takes the first train. (should)
➡ _____

4 He drives a car. (can)
➡ _____

5 I give him my notebook. (should)
➡ _____

6 He teaches English at a middle school. (will)
➡ _____

7 Mike speaks five languages. (can)
➡ _____

8 She takes art classes in Italy. (will)
➡ _____

9 I order some food. (can)
➡ _____

10 They make Chinese dishes. (can)
➡ _____

 조동사의 종류

PSS 4-1 must I

의무 (~해야 한다)	과거	We **had to** buy boots and gloves yesterday. 우리는 어제 부츠와 장갑을 사야 했다.
	현재	We **must** buy boots and gloves. 우리는 부츠와 장갑을 사야 한다. = We **have to** buy boots and gloves.
	미래	We **will have to** buy boots and gloves when we get there. 우리는 그곳에 도착하면 부츠와 장갑을 사야 할 것이다. = We **must** buy boots and gloves when we get there. = We **have to** buy boots and gloves when we get there. ***cf.*** 조동사끼리는 나란히 쓰일 수 없다. 　　We **will must** buy boots and gloves when we get there. (×)

cf. must, have to, should는 모두 '~해야 한다'는 의미를 가지지만 강제성 강도와 뉘앙스가 다르다. 강제성의 강도는 must > have to > should의 순서이며 must는 '반드시 해야 한다'는 의미로 법이나 규제로 정해진 내용을 나타낼 때 쓴다. have to는 일상적인 '~해야 한다'는 의미로 개인적인 책임이나 의무 또는 필요를 나타낸다. should는 '~하는 게 좋을 거야'는 의미로 추천이나 제안할 때 주로 사용한다.

정답 p.16

PRACTICE 4

괄호 안에 주어진 단어 중 알맞은 것을 고르세요.

1　Did you (must, have, had) to leave the party so early?

2　Mary (must, has, had) go home and get some rest.

3　I (must, have, had) go to the station to meet him.

4　We (must, have, had) to find the exit now.

5　You will (must, have, had) to fix it by tomorrow.

6　You (must, have, had) take off your shoes to enter this room.

7　If Junho wants to be a lawyer, he will (must, have, has) to study hard.

8　The sun is too strong. I (must, have, had) buy sunglasses.

9　You (must, have, had) to wait for me last night.

10　Minji (must, have, has) to go to the airport to pick up her parents.

PRACTICE 5

have to를 알맞은 형태로 바꾸어 빈칸을 채우세요.

1. They are very weak. You _____ treat them very carefully.
2. Kelly _____ learn Chinese when she was young.
3. I'll have a test next week. I _____ study very hard.
4. I want to go shopping with Jane, but I _____ clean the house now.
5. He _____ stay there for the next three weeks.
6. Last Friday my dad _____ work until 10 p.m.
7. Jennifer needs money now. She _____ go to the bank.
8. My friend Jihoon _____ move to Chicago in two months.
9. I _____ reformat my computer yesterday because of a virus.
10. You _____ feed your dog twice a day. And walk him every morning.

PSS 4-2 must II

추측 (~임에 틀림없다)		She **must** be very sick. 그녀는 몹시 아픈 게 틀림없다. ↔ She **can't** be very sick. 그녀는 몹시 아플 리가 없다. *cf.* 「can't+동사원형」은 '~일 리가 없다'의 뜻도 지닌다.
부정	금지 (~해서는 안 된다)	You **must not** park there. 너는 거기에 주차를 해서는 안 된다. You **must not** take a photo here. 너는 여기에서 사진을 찍으면 안 된다.
	불필요 (~할 필요가 없다)	He **doesn't have to** carry those books. 그는 그 책들을 가지고 다닐 필요가 없다. = He **need not** carry those books.

PRACTICE 6

괄호 안에 주어진 단어 중 알맞은 것을 고르세요.

1. Mark got the highest grade again. He (must, can't) be very smart.

2   I can't believe the news. It (must, can't) be true.

3   Mary watches a movie every weekend. She (must, can't) like movies.

4   Suji was on the plane for 10 hours. She (must, can't) be very tired.

5   All of her friends came to her party. She (must, can't) be sad.

6   Bob has never learned Korean. He (must, can't) speak Korean.

7   She didn't eat anything. She (must, can't) be very hungry now.

8   Mr. Lee is a new teacher. He (must, can't) know all of the students.

9   Andy is always late for work. He (must, can't) be lazy.

10 I just saw Cathy on the street. She (must, can't) be home now.

PRACTICE 7

정답 p.17

그림을 보고, must not 또는 don't/doesn't have to 중 빈칸에 알맞은 것을 쓰세요.

1   A: Why don't we sit there?
    B: It's for the elderly. We _____ sit there.

2   A: I'm worried about tomorrow's quiz.
    B: You _____ worry about that. It won't be difficult.

3   A: He is off today.
    B: Good. He _____ wake up early then.

4   A: You _____ tell this to anyone.
    B: Of course not. I'll keep it secret.

5   A: You _____ stay late. You can go home.
    B: Thanks. See you tomorrow.

6 A: You _____ wear shoes here.
B: I see. I'm going to take them off.

PSS 4-3 can, could I

능력/가능 (~할 수 있다)	과거	She **could** do it without your help. 그녀는 너의 도움 없이 그것을 할 수 있었다. = She **was able to** do it without your help.
	현재	I **can** speak with them in English. 나는 그들과 영어로 이야기할 수 있다. = I **am able to** speak with them in English.
	미래	Daniel **can** go to London next summer. Daniel은 다음 여름에 런던에 갈 수 있다. = Daniel **will be able to** go to London next summer. = Daniel **is able to** go to London next summer.

정답 p.17

PRACTICE 8

be able to를 이용하여 짝지어진 두 문장의 의미가 같도록 빈칸을 채우세요.

1 The players can't win the game if they break the rules.
= The players _aren't able to_ win the game if they break the rules.

2 We could watch the dolphin show in the zoo.
= We _____ watch the dolphin show in the zoo.

3 I don't know if I can do it well.
= I don't know if I _____ do it well.

4 Kevin couldn't meet my sister last night.
= Kevin _____ meet my sister last night.

5 Can't you speak Chinese well?
= _____ you _____ speak Chinese well?

6 Ben can't go to university next year.
= Ben _____ go to university next year.

7 I could run faster when I was young.

= I _____ run faster when I was young.

8 They couldn't get there by bus.

= They _____ get there by bus.

9 We can go on a picnic next month.

= We _____ go on a picnic next month.

10 Mom is a great cook. She can make very good Chinese dishes.

= Mom is a great cook. She _____ make very good Chinese dishes.

PSS 4-4 can, could Ⅱ

요청	~해 주시겠어요?	**Can you** show me how to make it? 그것을 어떻게 만드는지 보여줄래? **Could you** open the door? 문 좀 열어주시겠어요? *cf.* Could you ~?는 Can you ~?보다 공손한 표현이다.
허가	~해도 될까요?	**Can I** speak to Mr. Kim? 김 선생님과 통화할 수 있을까? **Could I** borrow some money from you? 당신에게 돈 좀 빌려도 될까요? *cf.* Could I ~?는 Can I ~?보다 공손한 표현이다.
추측	~일 리가 없다. ~일 수 있다.	It **can't** be true. 그게 사실일 리가 없다. (강한 의심) I **could** be right. 내가 맞을 수도 있다. (can보다 약한 추측)

PRACTICE 9

정답 p.17

다음 문장에서 밑줄 친 단어가 어떤 의미를 나타내는지 고르세요.

1 <u>Could</u> you do me a favor? (요청 / 허가)

2 That <u>couldn't</u> be my cap. Mine is red, but that one is yellow. (추측 / 요청)

3 I've been playing football since I <u>could</u> walk. (요청 / 능력)

4 I <u>can't</u> find my purse. Where is it? (능력 / 추측)

5 It's unbelievable. She <u>can't</u> do such a bad thing. (허가 / 추측)

6 Could you turn on the radio? (허가 / 요청)

7 I couldn't play the violin well before I took the lesson last year. (허가 / 능력)

8 Could you stop by next week? (요청 / 추측)

9 Could I borrow your umbrella? I'll give it back to you tomorrow. (추측 / 허가)

10 There is a box office near the elevator. We can buy tickets there. (요청 / 능력)

PSS 4-5 do

1. **일반동사의 의문문과 부정문에 쓰이는 do**

   Do you remember his birthday? 넌 그의 생일을 기억하니?
   The airplane **did** not arrive on time. 그 비행기는 제 시간에 도착하지 않았다.

2. **동사를 강조하는 do**

   I **do have** good memories about my friends. 나는 내 친구들에 대해 좋은 기억을 정말 가지고 있다.
   She **does like** pizza. 그녀는 피자를 정말 좋아한다.
   We **did meet** him in the stadium. 우리는 그를 경기장 안에서 정말 만났다.

3. **동사(구)의 반복을 피하는 대동사 do**

   Who won the game? – She **did**. (= She won the game.)
   누가 그 경기를 이겼니? 그녀가 이겼어.

정답 p.17

PRACTICE 10

do를 알맞은 형태로 바꾸어 빈칸을 채우세요.

1 _____ you like baseball? – Yes, I do.

2 She _____ have blue eyes.

3 Brian plays the piano better than Sue _____.

4 My mom _____ live in the city two years ago.

5 I'm certain that my son has a bright future. – Yes, he really _____.

6 _____ your brothers go to school in Tokyo? – Yes. They go to Tokyo University.

7 Luke _____ not speak Spanish very well, so he's taking a Spanish lesson.

8 Kate and I _____ like to go to the movies. We watch a movie twice a week.

9 Do they find the idea interesting? – No, they _____.

10 I _____ clean my room yesterday.

PRACTICE 11
정답 p.18

우리말과 같은 뜻이 되도록 알맞은 조동사와 괄호 안의 단어를 사용하여 빈칸을 채우세요.

1 그것은 매우 지루한 게 틀림없다. (be)
   ➡ It _____ very boring.

2 그녀는 그에게 그 돈을 줄 필요가 없다. (give)
   ➡ She _____ him the money.

3 너는 버스를 타야 할 것이다. (take)
   ➡ You _____ a bus.

4 내 남동생은 수영하는 것을 정말 좋아한다. (like)
   ➡ My brother _____ swimming.

5 그는 똑똑하다. 그가 시험을 망칠 리가 없다. (fail)
   ➡ He is smart. He _____ the exam.

PSS 4-6 should, had better

should	의무, 추천, 제안 (~해야 한다/ ~하는 게 좋다)	You **should** wash your hands often to avoid catching a cold. 너는 감기에 걸리지 않기 위해서 손을 자주 씻어야 한다. **Should** I apologize to her? 제가 그녀에게 사과해야 하나요? You **shouldn't** do that again. 넌 다시는 그렇게 해서는 안 된다.
had better	충고, 권유 (~하는 게 낫다)	should보다 더 강한 뜻을 내포하며, 축약형인 'd better의 형태로 주로 쓰인다. You**'d better** go to bed right now. 너는 지금 당장 자러 가는 게 낫다. We**'d better** leave now, or we'll miss the train. 우리는 지금 출발하는 게 낫겠어, 안 그러면 기차를 놓칠 거야. You**'d better not** make a noise. 넌 시끄럽게 하지 않는 게 낫다.

PRACTICE 12

우리말과 같은 뜻이 되도록 주어진 단어를 바르게 배열하세요.

1 너는 너의 부모님께 그렇게 말해서는 안 된다. (to your parents, like that, should, talk, not, you)
   ➡ _____

2 제가 그곳에 다시 가야 하나요? (I, there, again, should, go)
   ➡ _____

3 너는 취침 시간 전에 너의 스마트폰 사용을 중단해야 한다.
   (using, stop, smartphone, your, bedtime, before, should, you)
   ➡ _____

4 Jenny는 그 사실을 잊어서는 안 된다. (Jenny, not, forget, the truth, should)
   ➡ _____

5 나는 그녀에게 사과해야 한다. (apologize, I, should, to her)
   ➡ _____

PRACTICE 13

그림을 보고, 괄호 안의 단어와 had better를 이용하여 대화를 완성하세요.

1 A: I have a sore throat.
   B: _You'd better see_ a doctor. (see)

2 A: My brother studied until late last night. He looks very tired.
   B: _____ some rest. (get)

3 A: It's going to rain this afternoon.
   B: _____ an umbrella when we go out. (take)

4 A: I have midterms next week.
   B: _____ hard. (study)

5 A: I had a car accident yesterday.
   B: _____ too fast. (not, drive)

PSS 4-7 will, would

Will[Would] you ~?	~해 주시겠습니까?	**Will you** introduce yourself? 자기 소개를 해 주시겠어요? **Would you** introduce yourself? 자기 소개를 해 주시겠습니까? *cf.* Would you ~?는 Will you ~?보다 공손한 표현이다.
would like +명사	~을 원하다	**I'd like** some bread. 저는 빵을 좀 원해요. = I **want** some bread.
would like to +동사원형	~을 하고 싶다	**I'd like to** have dinner with you. 나는 너와 함께 저녁식사를 하고 싶어. = I **want to** have dinner with you.

정답 p.18

PRACTICE 14

괄호 안에 주어진 조동사 중 알맞은 것을 고르세요.

1. (Will, Would) you like some oranges?
2. (Will, Should) you do me a favor?
3. (Will, Would) you like to play soccer tomorrow?
4. (Would, Can) I have some juice?
5. (Will, Would) you like to go fishing?
6. (Can, Will) I speak to Mr. Smith?
7. (Will, Must) you pass me the sugar, please?
8. (Will, Would) you like to go to the party?
9. (Could, Do) you bring it to me?
10. (Do, Will) you like your new car?
11. (Will, Would) you like an ice cream?
12. (Will, Could) I get your address, please?
13. (Will, Should) you open the door for me?
14. (Will, Would) you like some sugar in your coffee?
15. (Will, Do) you give it to your sister for me?

PSS 4-8 may, might

추측	~일지도 모른다, 아마 ~일 것이다	Mr. Lee **may** be sick. Lee 씨는 아플지도 모른다. She **may** not know your name yet. 그녀는 아마 아직 네 이름을 알지 못할 것이다. It **might** take more than two weeks. 2주 이상 걸릴지도 모른다. ***cf.*** might는 may보다 불확실한 추측을 나타낸다.
허가	~해도 좋다	You **may** go home now. 너는 지금 집에 가도 좋다. **May** I see your ID card? 제가 당신의 신분증을 봐도 될까요? – Yes, you **may**. 네, 그래도 돼요. – No, you **may not**. 아니오, 그럴 수 없어요. – No, you **must not**. 아니오, 그러면 안됩니다. ***cf.*** must not이 may not보다 더 강한 금지의 표현이다.

정답 p.18

PRACTICE 15

〈보기〉에서 알맞은 단어를 골라 may를 포함하는 문장을 완성하세요. (단, 필요한 경우 부정문으로 쓰세요.)

보기	know come go work feel want

1. A: Where are you going for your holidays?
   B: I'm not sure. I _____may go_____ to Busan.

2. A: Why does Sally look so sad these days?
   B: I'm not sure. She _____ lonely.

3. A: Why doesn't Minsu call my name?
   B: I'm not sure. He _____ your name.

4. A: When is Jina coming to see us?
   B: I'm not sure. She _____ on Saturday.

5. A: Why doesn't Tom answer the phone?
   B: I'm not sure. He _____ to talk to anyone.

6. A: What does Sam do for a living?
   B: I'm not sure. He _____ at a bank.

PRACTICE 16

괄호 안에 주어진 조동사 중 알맞은 것을 고르세요.

1 (May, Will) I take your order?

2 Jane (might, had better) be sick. I'm worried about her.

3 (Will, May) you turn down the volume?

4 Believe me. He (do, did) solve the problem by himself.

5 May I use your camera? – No, you (must not, might not).

6 (Can, May) you come to my office at 7?

7 You (might, have to) be careful driving on rainy days.

8 (Would, Will) you like to have dinner with me?

9 I will (can, be able to) finish it by tomorrow.

10 (May, Will) I speak to June?

11 (Would, Could) you like some tea?

PSS 4-9　used to, would

1. 과거에 반복적으로 일어났던 행위를 나타낼 때는 '~하곤 했다'의 의미를 가진 used to 또는 would를 쓸 수 있다.

   I went swimming every morning before, but I don't go swimming anymore.
   나는 전에는 매일 아침 수영하러 갔지만, 더 이상 수영하러 가지 않는다.
   ➡ I **used to** go swimming every morning. 나는 매일 아침 수영하러 가곤 했다.
   ➡ I **would** go swimming every morning. 나는 매일 아침 수영하러 가곤 했다.

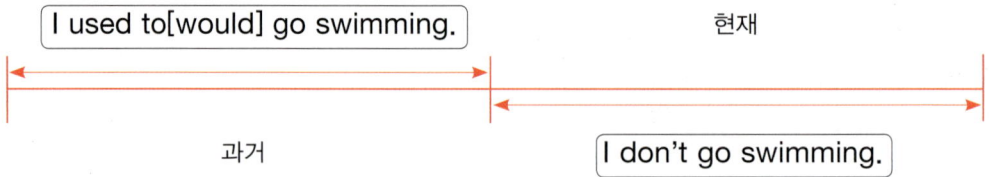

2. 과거에 있었던 행위가 아닌 상태를 나타낼 때는 would를 쓸 수 없다.

   Ben had a car before, but he sold it. Ben은 전에 차가 있었지만 팔았다.
   ➡ Ben **used to** have a car. Ben은 차가 있었다.
   ➡ Ben **would** have a car. (×)

3. used to(~ 하곤 했다)와 형태가 비슷하지만 전혀 다른 의미를 지닌 아래의 표현들을 혼동하지 말아야 한다.

used to+동사원형 : (과거에) ~ 하곤 했다	I **used to play** the piano. 나는 피아노를 연주하곤 했다. (지금은 연주하지 않는다.)
be used to+동사원형 : ~ 하기 위해 사용되다	Flour **is used to make** a cake. 밀가루는 케이크를 만들기 위해 사용된다.
be used to+~ing : ~에 (이미) 익숙하다	My brother **is used to playing** the piano. 내 남동생은 피아노를 연주하는 데 익숙하다.

정답 p.19

PRACTICE 17

그림을 보고, 괄호 안의 단어와 used to나 would를 이용하여 문장을 완성하세요.

1. There ____used to be____ a tree in the park. (be)

2. He _____ dark hair. (have)

3. My family _____ a dog. (raise)

4. He _____ soccer when he was young. (play)

5. I _____ a bike to school. (ride)

6 Sujin _____ in a city. (live)

BEFORE → NOW

정답 p.19

PRACTICE 18

우리말과 같은 뜻이 되도록 〈주어진 표현〉과 괄호 안의 단어를 사용하여 문장을 완성하세요.

| 주어진 표현 | used to+동사원형 / be used to+동사원형 / be used to+~ing |

1 나는 아침에 요가하는 것에 익숙하다. (do)
➡ I _____ in the morning.

2 그 기금은 나무들을 심는 데 사용되었다. (plant)
➡ The funds _____ trees.

3 난 오후 9시에 잠자리에 들곤 했다. (go)
➡ I _____ at 9 p.m.

4 많은 구급차들이 부상자들을 실어 나르기 위해 사용되었다. (carry)
➡ Many ambulances _____ the injured.

5 Mike는 차를 운전하는 데 아직 익숙하지 않다. (drive)
➡ Mike _____ a car yet.

6 우리는 유기견들을 위해 자원봉사를 하는 것에 익숙하다. (volunteer)
➡ We _____ for abandoned dogs.

7 카카오는 초콜릿을 만드는 데 사용된다. (make)
➡ Cacao _____ .

8 Jessica는 어렸을 때 통통했었다. (chubby)
➡ Jessica _____ when she was young.

9 내 딸은 아침에 일찍 일어나는 것에 익숙하다. (wake)
➡ My daughter _____ early in the morning.

10 나의 여동생은 거미를 무서워하곤 했다. (afraid)
➡ My sister _____ spiders.

Chapter Review Test

정답 p.19

CHAPTER 3
조동사

1 다음 중 짝지어진 대화가 자연스럽지 <u>않은</u> 것은?

① A: Could I borrow your pen for a minute?
   B: Yes, of course.
② A: May I use the toilet?
   B: No, you may not.
③ A: Will I need my jacket there?
   B: I think you won't need it.
④ A: Shouldn't you be studying for the exam?
   B: Yes, you should. You are out of time.
⑤ A: Can you give me a hand?
   B: Of course, what should I do?

2 다음 우리말과 같은 뜻이 되도록 빈칸에 들어갈 알맞은 말은?

• 저한테 100달러를 빌려주시겠어요?
  = _____ me 100 dollars?

① Should you lent
② Would you lend
③ Can you borrow
④ May I lend
⑤ Do you have to borrow

3 다음 문장의 밑줄 친 부분과 뜻이 같은 것은?

Helping her grandmother every day <u>must</u> be difficult for her, but she always smiles.

① You <u>must</u> turn left here.
② You <u>must</u> clean the window.
③ You stayed up late last night, so you <u>must</u> be tired.
④ You <u>must</u> be careful when you cross the street.
⑤ You <u>must</u> do your best to win the game.

4 밑줄 친 부분 중 어법상 알맞은 것은?

Here ⓐ <u>are</u> Donna's plan for this Saturday. In the morning, she will clean the house. She will vacuum the floor and ⓑ <u>wipes</u> all the windows. Then, she will go to the community center for her volunteer work. She takes care of kids there, and they always want her ⓒ <u>spending</u> more time with them. If it ⓓ <u>will be</u> sunny, she ⓔ <u>will go</u> on a short picnic with them.

① ⓐ　② ⓑ　③ ⓒ　④ ⓓ　⑤ ⓔ

5 다음 중 어법상 오류가 있는 문장은 몇 개인가?

ⓐ I used to living in China when I was little.
ⓑ She is the actress was on the TV show.
ⓒ Do you know if your brother came home late last night?
ⓓ The girl musts be very smart and bright.
ⓔ Penny hates to see her dentist regularly.
ⓕ You need to stop making excuses.
ⓖ Mr. Shang wanted me attend the meeting instead of him.

① 1개　② 2개　③ 3개　④ 4개　⑤ 5개

6 다음 빈칸에 들어갈 말로 가장 알맞은 것은?

Mickey can't run fast now, but he _____ run fast before.

① could
② couldn't
③ can
④ can't
⑤ is able to

7 다음 중 어법상 옳은 문장을 모두 고르세요.

① Bricks are used to make the building.
② I used to playing soccer on the weekends.
③ James is used to eat meat, but now he doesn't eat it.
④ Four colors are used to painting the national flag.
⑤ She is not used to speaking in public.

8 다음 밑줄 친 (a)~(e) 중에서 어법상 옳지 않은 것은?

Heather: Hey, Genie! I have this serious problem with my friend, Dana. You know, I always had long hair, but I decided (a) to cut my hair short. All my friends said that it looked good on me. And guess what? Dana cut her hair (b) short the next day. I was kind of angry and I didn't want us to look the same, so I dyed my hair brown. And she also dyed her hair brown the next day. Why is she copying me? I'm so (c) stressed out.

Genie: I know how you feel. I also had this friend who used to (d) copying everything that I did. At first, I was really stressed out and I even told her to stop copying me. The reason why Dana is copying you is because she doesn't know (e) what she likes yet. Just let her copy you until she finds what is right for her. Maybe she will thank you later.

① (a)   ② (b)   ③ (c)   ④ (d)   ⑤ (e)

9 다음 중 어법상 어색한 문장은?

① He doesn't must read it.
② Jane must get there on time.
③ You have to follow the rules.
④ We must not get up late.
⑤ They had to study for the test.

10 다음 문장의 밑줄 친 부분과 그 쓰임이 다른 것은?

> Experience really does make you a better man.

① I do like swimming in the river in the summer.
② I did some part-time jobs when I was at school.
③ He did love his pet, Moppy.
④ Jane does hate her cousin, David.
⑤ They do want to learn Japanese in Tokyo, Japan.

11 다음 중 어법상 올바르지 않은 문장은?

① You didn't do well on the test.
② I did nothing for them.
③ She does have your key.
④ He did look tired.
⑤ Mr. Kim does knows the truth.

12 다음 빈칸에 들어갈 말로 알맞은 것은?

> You _____ drink coffee a lot because you can't sleep well at night.

① must   ② should   ③ can
④ should not   ⑤ could not

13 우리말과 같은 뜻이 되도록 주어진 단어를 사용하여 9단어로 영작하세요.

> 이 문제를 해결할 다른 방법이 있는 게 틀림없다.
> (way, solve, problem)
> = _____
>   _____

14 다음 빈칸에 들어갈 말로 가장 적절한 것은?

> _____ you have to wear a uniform when you were in middle school?

① Do ② Should ③ Must
④ Don't ⑤ Did

15 대화의 흐름상 가장 어색한 것은?

> A: Hey, do you have any plans for the summer vacation?
> B: Yes. ⓐ I'm going to go on a trip.
> A: Really? ⓑ Where are you going to go?
> B: ⓒ To Jeju Island.
> A: Oh, I've been there before. ⓓ You shouldn't try horse-riding.
> B: That sounds like fun. ⓔ I will definitely try it.

① ⓐ ② ⓑ ③ ⓒ ④ ⓓ ⑤ ⓔ

16 주어진 문장의 밑줄 친 부분과 그 쓰임이 같은 것은?

> I do have a lot of memories about them.

① She doesn't have anything to do.
② I do like her very much.
③ The boy smiles as you do.
④ Do you remember me?
⑤ I do not have to do it.

17 우리말과 같은 뜻이 되도록 괄호 안의 말을 바르게 배열하여 문장을 완성하세요.

> • 나는 스무 살 때 우리 집 근처의 식당에서 일하곤 했다.
> = When I was 20 years old, _____
>   _____.
> (used to, my house, at, work, I, near, a restaurant)

18 다음 짝지어진 두 문장의 의미가 서로 <u>다른</u> 것은?

① You don't have to worry about it.
 = You need not worry about it.
② I used to go hiking every Sunday.
 = I would go hiking every Sunday.
③ You'd better ask him about fixing your car.
 = You would like to ask him about fixing your car.
④ We can solve the problem without your help.
 = We are able to solve the problem without your help.
⑤ Would you open the window for me?
 = Could you open the window for me?

19 다음 대화의 빈칸에 들어갈 말로 알맞지 <u>않은</u> 것은?

> *Mom*: Don't you see the sign? We _____ sit here.
> *Son* : Oh, I see. It is for disabled people.
> *Mom*: Right.

① should not
② must not
③ cannot
④ are not allowed to
⑤ don't have to

20 밑줄 친 ⓐ~ⓔ 중에서 빈칸에 들어갈 조동사가 나머지 넷과 <u>다른</u> 것은?

> If you like to ride a bicycle, there are some rules you should follow. First, you ____ⓐ____ always wear a safety helmet. Second, you ____ⓑ____ never violate the traffic signs. Third, you ____ⓒ____ turn on the lights at night. Finally, you ____ⓓ____ never use a cellphone while riding a bicycle. Breaking these rules ____ⓔ____ lead you to an accident. Keep these safety rules and be safe!

① ⓐ   ② ⓑ   ③ ⓒ   ④ ⓓ   ⑤ ⓔ

21 다음 빈칸에 들어갈 말로 알맞은 것은?

> The mother koala takes good care of her baby. The mother koala holds tight to the tree because the baby koala is on her back. When the baby koala gets lost, it cries as a little kid _____.

① are   ② is   ③ do
④ does   ⑤ did

22 괄호 안에 주어진 단어와 had better를 사용해 대화의 빈칸에 알맞은 충고의 문장을 쓰세요.

(1) A: I have a headache.
    B: _____
       _____
       (you, take, some medicine)

(2) A: I often feel sleepy in class.
    B: _____
       _____
       (you, go to bed, earlier)

(3) A: My sister has lost her cell phone on the subway.
    B: _____
       _____
       (she, check, the Lost and Found)

23 다음 밑줄 친 부분 중 어법상 알맞은 것은?

> ① <u>Do you like read books?</u> ② <u>Would you like to having a discussion</u> with your friends about the books you read? Then, come and join the book club. ③ <u>We might looks like a quiet club</u> that only reads books, but we are more than that! This is a place ④ <u>where you can talk about the book and watching the film version of the book as well.</u> Also, we make short films critiquing books. ⑤ <u>So, why don't you join our club where you will be able to indulge in books?</u>

24 우리말과 같은 뜻이 되도록 괄호 안에 주어진 단어를 바르게 배열하세요.

• 너는 오늘 밤에 밖에 안 나가는 게 좋겠다.
= _____
   (not, had, go, you, tonight, better, out)

25 다음 대화의 빈칸에 들어갈 말로 알맞지 <u>않은</u> 것은?

> A: Can I park here?
> B: No, _____.
>   The sign says "No parking."

① you can't park here
② you must not park here
③ you shouldn't park here
④ you don't have to park here
⑤ you're not allowed to park here

26 다음 밑줄 친 did를 대신해서 쓸 수 있는 말로 알맞은 것은?

> A: Who finished the work last night?
> B: Mina <u>did</u>.

① has not finished the work yet
② finished the work last night
③ didn't finish the work last night
④ didn't want to finish the work last night
⑤ worked with me last night

27 다음 질문에 대한 대답으로 바르지 <u>않은</u> 것을 <u>모두</u> 고르세요.

> Q: May I take a photo here?
> A: _____.

① Yes, you may.　　② Yes, you may not.
③ No, you may.　　④ No, you may not.
⑤ No, you can't.

28 다음 문장의 밑줄 친 부분과 바꿔 쓸 수 있는 말은?

> I <u>want to</u> thank you for helping me finish the project today.

① like　　② would like to　　③ would like
④ want　　⑤ had like to

29 문맥상 다음 빈칸에 공통으로 들어갈 표현으로 알맞은 것은?

> • You _____ watch TV so late.
> • You _____ forget to take an umbrella when you go out.
> • You _____ tell a lie to your friends.

① should not　　② might not
③ have to　　　④ want not
⑤ have not

30 다음 빈칸에 들어갈 말로 알맞은 것은?

> I'm very happy because I am _____ hear from you again.

① can　　② able　　③ able to
④ should　　⑤ will

31 대화의 흐름상 빈칸에 들어갈 문장으로 알맞지 않은 것을 두 개 고르세요.

> A: Honey, our family trip is only a week away.
> B: Oh, time has flown by! Have we booked our flight tickets?
> A: Not yet. Could you help me book the flight tickets?
> B: _____

① We should check if there are any flights with special fares.
② Sure. Let me look on the airline website.
③ Yes. We'd better take a night flight.
④ Why don't you travel alone?
⑤ You must not waste valuable time.

32 다음 중 어법상 올바른 문장만 짝지은 것은?

> ⓐ I'd not better go shopping today.
> ⓑ I'd better not eat them.
> ⓒ You'd better to answer him now.
> ⓓ You'd better not to bring the bag.
> ⓔ You'd better wash your clothes.

① ⓐ, ⓑ   ② ⓐ, ⓓ   ③ ⓑ, ⓔ
④ ⓒ, ⓓ   ⑤ ⓓ, ⓔ

33 다음 표를 보고 세 사람이 어렸을 때 할 수 있었던 것과 할 수 없었던 것에 대한 문장을 완성하세요.

	cook ramen	run errands
Amanda at age six	×	○
Travis at age ten	○	○
Jennifer at age ten	×	○

(1) Amanda _____ _____ _____
_____ cook ramen at age six.

(2) Travis and Jennifer _____ _____
_____ run errands at age ten.

34 그림을 보고, 주어진 우리말과 같은 뜻이 되도록 빈칸에 알맞은 말을 쓰세요.

- Jessica wants to win a prize in the violin competition.
- She practices playing the violin every day.

⬇

- She _____ _____ _____
_____ win a prize in the violin competition.
= 그녀는 바이올린 경연대회에서 상을 받을 수 있게 될 것이다.

35 괄호 안의 단어를 이용하여 다음 표지판이 나타내는 주의사항을 완성하세요.

➡ You _____ _____
_____ _____ here. (should, turn)

CHAPTER 4
수동태

성취도 자기 평가 활용법

구분	평가 기준
Excellent	문법 내용을 모두 이해하고, 문제를 모두 맞힘.
Very good	문법 내용은 충분히 이해했으나 실수로 1~2문제 틀림.
Good	문법 내용이 조금 어려워 3~4문제 틀림.
needs **R**eview	문법 내용 이해가 어렵고, 5문제 이상 틀림. 복습 필요.

Problem Solving Skill	페이지	학습날짜	성취도 자기평가 E V G R	학습체크
PSS 1 수동태에 많이 쓰이는 불규칙 동사	96	/		☐
PSS 2 수동태 문장 만드는 법	97	/		☐
PSS 3 수동태의 부정문과 의문문	99	/		☐
PSS 4 수동태의 시제	100	/		☐
PSS 5 조동사가 있는 수동태	102	/		☐
PSS 6 주의해야 할 수동태	103	/		☐
PSS 7 수동태의 관용 표현	105	/		☐
Chapter Review Test	108	/		☐

수동태에 많이 쓰이는 불규칙 동사

원형	과거형	과거분사형	원형	과거형	과거분사형
be	was, were	been	lend	lent	lent
bear	bore	borne/born	make	made	made
break	broke	broken	pay	paid	paid
bring	brought	brought	put	put	put
build	built	built	read	read	read
buy	bought	bought	say	said	said
catch	caught	caught	see	saw	seen
choose	chose	chosen	send	sent	sent
cut	cut	cut	sing	sang	sung
do	did	done	speak	spoke	spoken
draw	drew	drawn	steal	stole	stolen
eat	ate	eaten	take	took	taken
find	found	found	teach	taught	taught
give	gave	given	tell	told	told
hold	held	held	think	thought	thought
hurt	hurt	hurt	throw	threw	thrown
keep	kept	kept	understand	understood	understood
know	knew	known	write	wrote	written

cf. 수동태로 쓸 수 없는 동사
1) 타동사 일부: have(가지다), resemble(닮다), fit/become/suit(어울리다), cost(비용이 들다)
2) 자동사 전체: happen(일어나다), exist(존재하다), disappear(사라지다), occur(발생하다)

정답 p.21

PRACTICE 1

괄호 안의 단어를 알맞은 형태로 바꾸어 빈칸에 쓰세요.

1 Jenny was ___born___ on July 2nd, 1990. (bear)

2 This newspaper is _____ by many people. (read)

3 The picture was _____ yesterday. (steal)

4 That song was _____ by David Smith in 1995. (sing)

5 These toys are _____ by Mr. Han. (make)

6 The chair was _____ by my younger brother. (break)

7 The elephants were _____ by the people. (catch)

8 I was _____ how to fish by my grandfather. (teach)

9 This book was _____ by Thomas Hardy. (write)

10 English is _____ in New Zealand. (speak)

11 Coffee is _____ in Brazil. (grow)

12 My dog is _____ twice a day. (feed)

13 These photos were _____ at the beach. (take)

14 Eggs are _____ in the refrigerator. (keep)

PSS 2 수동태 문장 만드는 법

1. **능동태와 수동태의 차이**

    능동태: 주어가 동사의 동작을 하는 경우에 쓴다. (~가 …한다)
    My grandfather built this house. 우리 할아버지께서 이 집을 지으셨다.

    수동태: 주어가 동사의 동작을 받을 때 쓴다. (~가 …되어진다)
    This house was built by my grandfather. 이 집은 우리 할아버지에 의해 지어졌다.

2. **수동태 문장 만들기**

    ① 능동태 문장의 목적어를 수동태 문장의 주어로 한다.
    I made **them**. 내가 그것들을 만들었다.
    ➡ **They**

    ② 능동태 문장의 동사를 「be동사+과거분사」의 형태로 바꾼다.
    I **made** them.
    ➡ They **were made**

    ③ 능동태 문장의 주어를 「by+목적격」으로 바꾼다.
    I made them.
    ➡ They were made **by me**. 그것들은 나에 의해 만들어졌다.

PRACTICE 2

다음 문장을 수동태로 바꾸어 쓰세요.

1 Susie cleans the room.
➡ _The room is cleaned by Susie._

2 My friends love me.
➡ _____

3 Leonardo da Vinci painted *the Mona Lisa*.
➡ _____

4 They recycle plastic bottles.
➡ _____

5 I bought those black pants.
➡ _____

6 My mom made those cookies.
➡ _____

7 He reads a lot of books.
➡ _____

8 Jason invited all the classmates to the party.
➡ _____

9 The police catch thieves.
➡ _____

10 Harry reported the news.
➡ _____

11 Mrs. Lopez collects stamps and coins.
➡ _____

12 The hunter killed two black bears.
➡ _____

13 The police officer stopped the bus.
➡ _____

14 Mr. Kim held the meeting.
➡ _____

15 The president changed the rules of the meeting.
➡ _____

수동태의 부정문과 의문문

수동태의 부정문은 다음과 같은 어순으로 쓴다.

주어 + be동사 + not + 과거분사 + by + 목적격.

Jinhee **doesn't clean** the room. 진희는 방을 청소하지 않는다.
➡ The room **isn't cleaned** by Jinhee. 방은 진희에 의해 청소되지 않는다.

Jason **didn't draw** this picture. Jason은 이 그림을 그리지 않았다.
➡ This picture **wasn't drawn** by Jason. 이 그림은 Jason에 의해 그려지지 않았다.

수동태의 의문문은 다음과 같은 어순으로 쓴다.

Be동사 + 주어 + 과거분사 + by + 목적격?

Park Guell **was built by** Gaudi. Guell 공원은 Gaudi에 의해 지어졌다.
➡ **Was** Park Guell **built** by Gaudi? Guell 공원은 Gaudi에 의해 지어졌나요?

Our car **was washed by** my mom. 우리 차는 나의 엄마에 의해 세차되었어.
➡ **Was** our car **washed** by my mom? 우리 차가 나의 엄마에 의해 세차되었니?

PRACTICE 3

괄호 안의 지시에 맞게 주어진 문장을 바꾸어 쓰세요.

1 The picture wasn't drawn by me.
 ➡ _I didn't draw the picture._ (능동태)

2 My mother didn't make the cake.
 ➡ _____ (수동태)

3 Some people in Japan don't speak English.
 ➡ _____ (수동태)

4 He was invited to Jane's birthday party.
 ➡ _____ (의문문)

5 That book was written by him.
 ➡ _____ (의문문)

6 That play was not written by Shakespeare.
 ➡ _____ (능동태)

7 Lily's restaurant doesn't sell bibimbap.
➡ _____ (수동태)

8 Gyeongbokgung Palace is loved by many tourists.
➡ _____ (의문문)

9 The bill was not paid by Yuri.
➡ _____ (능동태)

10 Jake was hurt by his brother in the park yesterday.
➡ _____ (의문문)

PSS 4 수동태의 시제

태 시제	능동태	수동태
현재	Minho **plants** trees. 민호는 나무를 심는다.	Trees **are planted** by Minho. 나무들이 민호에 의해 심어진다.
과거	Minho **planted** trees. 민호는 나무를 심었다.	Trees **were planted** by Minho. 나무들이 민호에 의해 심어졌다.
미래	Minho **will plant** trees. 민호는 나무를 심을 것이다.	Trees **will be planted** by Minho. 나무들이 민호에 의해 심어질 것이다.
현재완료	Minho **has planted** trees. 민호는 나무를 심어왔다.	Trees **have been planted** by Minho. 나무들이 민호에 의해 심어져 왔다.

cf. 행위의 주체가 일반인이거나 말하지 않아도 알 수 있는 경우, 또는 나타낼 필요가 없을 때는 「by+목적격」을 생략할 수 있다.
Someone stole my purse. ➡ My purse was stolen **(by someone)**.
누군가가 내 지갑을 훔쳤다.　　　내 지갑이 (누군가에 의해) 도난당했다.

PRACTICE 4

다음 능동태 문장을 수동태 문장으로 바꾸어 쓰세요. (경우에 따라, 「by+목적격」의 생략이 가능합니다.)

1 Some people saw the thief.
➡ The thief was seen by some people.

2 The man will deliver the magazine.
➡ _____

3 Somebody will clean the room later.
➡ _____

4 Reagan has built a new restaurant.
➡ _____

5 People will cut down more trees in the future.
➡ _____

6 Everyone has believed his lies.
➡ _____

7 Directors make movies or TV programs.
➡ _____

8 We have painted the chair.
➡ _____

9 The people have built this building for three years.
➡ _____

10 He will use the money to buy a new game character.
➡ _____

PRACTICE 5

그림을 보고, 괄호 안의 동사를 알맞은 형태로 바꾸어 수동태 문장을 완성하세요.

1 The light bulb _____ by Thomas Edison in 1879. (invent)

2 The chair _____ yesterday. (move)

3 My work _____ by next Friday. (do)

4 This picture _____ by Marie last week. (paint)

5 The river _____ since 2000. (pollute)

조동사가 있는 수동태

조동사가 있는 수동태는 다음과 같은 어순으로 쓴다.

주어 + 조동사 + be동사 원형 + 과거분사 + by + 목적격.

You **can** easily **find** the restaurant. 너는 그 식당을 쉽게 찾을 수 있다.
➡ The restaurant **can be** easily **found**. 그 식당은 쉽게 찾아질 수 있다.

You **must fix** the car right now. 너는 그 차를 지금 당장 수리해야 한다.
➡ The car **must be fixed** right now. 그 차는 지금 당장 수리되어야 한다.

PRACTICE 6

정답 p.22

다음 능동태 문장을 수동태 문장으로 바꾸어 쓰세요.

1 Kelly can finish the work.
➡ The work can be finished by Kelly.

2 Tony may do it tomorrow.
➡ _____

3 He must solve the problem.
➡ _____

4 They should obey the rules for this game.
➡ _____

5 We might change the plans for the summer.
➡ _____

6 I couldn't prepare dinner last night.
➡ _____

7 Suji must use a computer for this task.
➡ _____

8 We should not put them here.
➡ _____

9 Tom may not keep the promise.
➡ _____

10 The people could see the view very well.
➡ _____

PRACTICE 7

그림을 보고, 괄호 안의 단어를 알맞은 형태로 바꾸어 수동태 문장을 완성하세요.

1 　2　3 　4 　5

1 Your clothes _____ soon. (should, wash)
2 A lot of resources _____ . (can, save)
3 They _____ by Paul. (will, cook)
4 This house _____ by tomorrow. (must, paint)
5 My dog _____ forever. (will, love)

 주의해야 할 수동태

1. 4형식의 수동태

4형식은 간접목적어와 직접목적어 둘 다를 수동태의 주어로 할 수 있지만, 주로 사람을 나타내는 간접목적어를 주어로 하는 경우가 많다. 직접목적어가 수동태의 주어가 되는 경우에는 간접목적어 앞에 to, for, of와 같은 전치사가 온다.

Mom gave me some old pictures. 엄마가 내게 오래된 사진 몇 장을 주셨다.
➡ **I** was given some old pictures by Mom. 나는 엄마에 의해 오래된 사진 몇 장을 받았다.
➡ **Some old pictures** were given **to me** by Mom.
　오래된 사진 몇 장이 엄마에 의해 내게 주어졌다.

She asked the students their names. 그녀는 학생들에게 그들의 이름을 물었다.
➡ **The students** were asked their names by her.
　학생들은 그녀에 의해 그들의 이름을 질문 받았다.
➡ **Their names** were asked **of the students** by her.
　그들의 이름이 그녀에 의해 학생들에게 물어졌다.

cf. 직접목적어만을 수동태의 주어로 하는 동사 – buy, write, cook, make
　I bought my brother an interesting book. 나는 내 남동생에게 재미있는 책을 사 주었다.
　　➡ **An interesting book** was bought **for my brother** by me.
　　　재미있는 책이 나에 의해 내 남동생에게 사 주어졌다.

2. 5형식의 수동태

5형식 문장을 수동태 문장으로 전환할 때, 목적격 보어가 명사나 형용사인 경우에는 「be동사＋과거분사」 뒤에 목적격 보어를 이어서 쓴다.

They call her Liz. 그들은 그녀를 Liz라고 부른다.
➡ She is called **Liz** by them. 그녀는 그들에 의해 Liz라고 불린다.

The news made me happy. 그 소식은 나를 행복하게 만들었다.
➡ I was made **happy** by the news. 나는 그 소식에 의해 행복해졌다.

PRACTICE 8

정답 p.22

〈보기〉와 같이 능동태 문장을 수동태 문장으로 바꾸어 쓰세요.

> 보기
> Sora gave me a book. ➡ I was given a book by Sora.
> ➡ A book was given to me by Sora.
> His music makes me sad. ➡ I am made sad by his music.

1 Mr. Kim bought the boy a new bag.
➡ _____

2 I made my brother angry.
➡ _____

3 They elected him the president.
➡ _____

4 They showed Bob their pictures.
➡ _____
➡ _____

5 Nick gave me lovely flowers.
➡ _____
➡ _____

6 Jenny kept the place clean.
➡ _____

7 My daughter named the fish "Wish".
➡ _____

8 People call the restaurant George's.
➡ _____

9 My mom cooked me spaghetti yesterday.
➡ _____

10 Minho lent me 5,000 won yesterday.
➡ _____
➡ _____

 수동태의 관용 표현

---

1. **be made of** '~로 만들어지다'(재료의 성질이 변하지 않는 경우)
   be made from '~로 만들어지다'(일련의 과정을 거쳐 재료의 성질이 변하는 경우)
   This notebook **is made of** used paper. 이 공책은 쓰고 난 종이로 만들어진다.
   Wine **is made from** grapes. 와인은 포도로 만들어진다.

2. **be filled with** '~로 가득 차 있다'
   Her eyes **were filled with** tears. 그녀의 눈은 눈물로 가득 차 있었다.

3. **be interested in** '~에 흥미가 있다'
   I**'m interested in** English. 나는 영어에 흥미가 있다.

4. **be covered with** '~로 덮여 있다'
   The mountain **is covered with** snow. 그 산은 눈으로 덮여 있다.

5. **be surprised at** '~에 놀라다'
   I **was surprised at** the news. 나는 그 소식에 놀랐다.

6. **be known to** '~에게 알려져 있다'
   be known for '~로[때문에] 알려져 있다(유명하다)'
   be known as '~로서 알려져 있다'
   The Mona Lisa **is known to** many people around the world.
   모나리자(그림)는 전 세계의 많은 사람들에게 알려져 있다.
   He **is known for** the poem. 그는 그 시로 알려져 있다.
   He wants to **be known as** an actor rather than a singer.
   그는 가수보다는 배우로서 알려지기를 원한다.

7. **be pleased with[about]** '~에 기뻐하다, 좋아하다'
   My dad **was pleased with[about]** the shirt. 우리 아빠는 그 셔츠를 좋아하셨다.

8. **be satisfied with** '~에 만족하다'
   I **am satisfied with** the result. 나는 그 결과에 만족한다.

9. **be excited about** '~에 흥분해 있다'
   He **was excited about** the trip. 그는 그 여행에 흥분해 있었다.

10. **be worried about** '~에 대해 걱정하다'
    I **am worried about** your health. 나는 너의 건강에 대해 걱정한다.

PRACTICE 9

정답 p.23

다음 문장의 빈칸에 알맞은 전치사를 쓰세요.

1 He was satisfied _____ my answer.
2 Are you interested _____ our project?
3 They were really excited _____ the party.
4 Mr. White is known _____ everyone in the town.
5 I am very pleased _____ your present.
6 My mom was worried _____ my brother's exam.
7 Plastic is made _____ oil and natural gas.
8 His heart is filled _____ joy.
9 Weren't you surprised _____ his words?
10 The land is covered _____ grass.
11 Paper is made _____ wood.
12 This area is known _____ heavy snow in winter.

PRACTICE 10

정답 p.23

다음 능동태 문장을 수동태 문장으로 바꾸어 쓰세요.

1 The crowd welcomed the president.
   ➡ _____

2 I could finish the work easily.
   ➡ _____

3 Mr. Song will teach science.
   ➡ _____

4 Yumi didn't do the dishes.
➡ _____

5 My kids clean the living room and the bathroom.
➡ _____

6 Susan has postponed the party.
➡ _____

7 John gave us some information.
➡ _____
➡ _____

8 My brother made my parents a family photo album.
➡ _____

9 Alex calls me Jen.
➡ _____

10 My son asked me some difficult questions.
➡ _____
➡ _____

11 Mike can fix the photocopier.
➡ _____

12 Cathy didn't paint this wall.
➡ _____

13 You must invite Bill to the show.
➡ _____

14 His story made us bored.
➡ _____

15 Seho paid me 30,000 won.
➡ _____
➡ _____

16 You can grow many herbs at home.
➡ _____

17 He named his cat Garfield.
➡ _____

18 He made me sandwiches.
➡ _____

Chapter Review Test

CHAPTER 4
수동태

1 다음 중 어법상 어색한 문장은?

① Japanese is spoken in Japan.
② The window was broken by Sam.
③ The red car is had by our grandmother.
④ The principal was respected by all of the students.
⑤ Our dog has been taken care of by my father.

2 다음 주어진 문장이 수동태가 되도록 빈칸에 알맞은 말을 쓰세요.

- Mrs. Smith helps many poor kids.
  ➡ Many poor kids _____ _____ by Mrs. Smith.

3 다음 중 어법상 어색한 문장을 모두 고르세요.

① Computers are used by many people.
② The boy will be teached by her.
③ This fish should not be overcooked.
④ The red dress was worn by Kate.
⑤ The book was wrote by an old woman.

4 다음 대화의 빈칸에 들어갈 알맞은 단어는?

A: Are you _____ in music?
B: Yes, I am. I like it very much.

① to interest   ② interesting   ③ interest
④ interested   ⑤ interestingly

5 다음 대화에서 밑줄 친 부분 중 어법상 자연스러운 것은?

A: What is this article about?
B: It says that a thief ① was catch by the police.
A: You mean the one who ② was stolen jewelry a week ago? I heard the store owner ③ was very shocked because of the incident.
B: Yes. Fortunately, the police ④ was seen him at the mall. The thief ⑤ was arrest by the police.

6 다음 중 밑줄 친 부분이 어법상 올바른 것은?

① The report must be released tomorrow morning.
② Dinner should prepared by five.
③ These shoes made from rubber tires.
④ This novel were written by Tolstoy.
⑤ They has been taught math by Ms. Pierce.

Chapter Review Test

7 주어진 문장을 수동태 문장으로 바꿔 쓰세요.

> • He cooked his friends rice noodles.
> ➡ _____

8 다음 수동태로의 문장 전환 중 어색한 것은?

① Tom cooked this food.
　➡ This food was cooked by Tom.
② Dad made the pencil case.
　➡ The pencil case was made by Dad.
③ My friend read a poem to me.
　➡ A poem is read to me by my friend.
④ The company built a new building.
　➡ A new building was built by the company.
⑤ People speak English in Canada.
　➡ English is spoken in Canada.

9 다음 문장을 수동태 문장으로 바꿔 쓰세요.

> • People called me Alex.
> ➡ _____

10 다음 중 어법상 어색한 문장은?

① It was made by me.
② My dog is loved by everyone.
③ Was this one found by your brother?
④ He wrote the letter to them.
⑤ My hair cut last Wednesday.

11 다음을 수동태 문장으로 바꿀 때, 빈칸에 알맞은 전치사를 쓰세요.

> • I asked him many questions about Mr. Stevenson.
> ➡ Many questions about Mr. Stevenson were asked _____ him by me.

12 주어진 문장을 능동태로 바르게 바꾼 것은?

> The ring was kept in the box by Jiho.

① Jiho keeps the ring in the box.
② Jiho kept the ring in the box.
③ Jiho has kept the ring in the box.
④ Jiho had kept the ring in the box.
⑤ Jiho is keeping the ring in the box.

13 괄호 안의 단어를 이용하여 문장을 완성하세요.

- English _____ _____ in Australia. (speak)
- The World Cup _____ _____ every four years. (hold)

14 다음 중 어법상 어색한 문장만 짝지은 것은?

ⓐ The city was ruined by the war.
ⓑ All the puppies have being washed.
ⓒ She is loved by her neighbors.
ⓓ It is surrounded by beautiful mountains.
ⓔ Many of them were chose by Mary.

① ⓐ, ⓑ ② ⓐ, ⓔ ③ ⓑ, ⓒ
④ ⓑ, ⓔ ⑤ ⓒ, ⓓ

15 괄호 안의 단어를 이용하여 문장을 완성하세요.

Hangeul _____ _____ by King Sejong in 1443. (invent)

16 다음 중 빈칸에 들어갈 단어가 나머지 넷과 다른 것은?

① She is interested _____ watching movies.
② This book was written _____ my friend, Minji.
③ These stamps were collected _____ Mr. Kim.
④ The white horse was sold to James _____ the old couple.
⑤ The vase was broken _____ the baby.

17 다음 중 수동태로 만들 수 있는 문장을 모두 고르세요.

① My brother resembles my grandfather.
② Jake found the subject very interesting.
③ They disappeared without a word last year.
④ Joseph gave his wife a bunch of roses.
⑤ The clothes suited me very well.

18 다음 중 어법상 어색한 문장은?

① They will be surprised at the news.
② The museum was built not in 2011.
③ My uncle's store was robbed yesterday.
④ Was the article read by many people?
⑤ I have been loved by my grandmother since I was born.

19 다음 문장을 수동태 문장으로 바꿔 쓰세요.

(1) I will give you a lot of time.
   ➡ _____

(2) Someone has stolen my car.
   ➡ _____

(3) They can explain the mystery.
   ➡ _____

20 다음 중 어법상 어색한 문장은?

① The letter was written to me by Paul last week.
② Rosa was given a pencil by her brother.
③ A cake was baked for me by my mother.
④ He was made spaghetti with cream sauce by his wife.
⑤ The teacher was asked a lot of personal questions by her students.

21 다음 글의 ①~⑤ 중 어법상 어색한 것은?

There are many interesting things in my room. Look at this photo. It ① was taken last week. The girl in the photo is my best friend, Jimin. She is very good at ② painting. Do you see those paintings on the wall? They ③ were painted by her. You should also ④ check out the table over there. It was made by my father. Don't you think that my room is clean? It is ⑤ cleaning every morning.

22 다음 중 어법상 옳은 대화를 모두 고르면?

① A: When was this house built?
   B: It built in 1960.
② A: Was the poem written by Mr. Black?
   B: No, it wasn't. It was written by his son.
③ A: What do you call this game in Korean?
   B: It calls *Yunnori* in Korean.
④ A: Who caught the bird?
   B: It is caught by my cousin.
⑤ A: Did you go to the party yesterday?
   B: No, I wasn't invited.

23 다음 중 우리말과 의미가 통하도록 영작한 것 중 문법적으로 옳은 것은?

① 그 고기는 피자를 만들기 위해서 얇은 조각들로 잘려진다.
   → The meat is cutted into thin slices to make a pizza.
② 모차르트는 그의 음악적 지능 때문에 천재로 여겨졌다.
   → Mozart is considered a genius because of his musical intelligence.
③ 칼슘은 우유에서 가장 풍부하게 발견된다.
   → Calcium is founded most abundantly in milk.
④ 그 목걸이는 그 신부를 위해 특별히 만들어졌다.
   → The necklace was specially made to the bride.
⑤ 장난감 자동차 한 대가 내 아들을 위해 나의 가장 친한 친구에 의해 구입되었다.
   → A toy car was bought for my son by my best friend.

24 밑줄 친 (A), (B)를 각각 알맞은 형태로 바꾸어 쓰세요.

- The ring (A) steal yesterday.
- Thanks to the firefighters, more than 20 people's lives (B) save yesterday.

(A) _____   (B) _____

25 주어진 단어를 활용하여 〈보기〉와 같이 문장을 만들 때 어법상 잘못된 것은?

보기
the land / discover / Mr. William
➡ The land was discovered by Mr. William.

① the watch / break / James
   ➡ The watch was broken by James.
② the cookies / bake / I
   ➡ The cookies was baked by me.
③ the pencil / find / she
   ➡ The pencil was found by her.
④ the book / read / my brother
   ➡ The book was read by my brother.
⑤ this garbage / throw out / that boy
   ➡ This garbage was thrown out by that boy.

26 우리말과 같은 뜻이 되도록 빈칸에 알맞은 단어를 쓰세요.

- 이 의자는 나무로 만들어진다.
  = This chair is _____ _____ wood.

27 다음 중 어법상 어색한 문장은?

① Football is played in many countries.
② Many fish have been caught by me.
③ The letter will be written by Sue.
④ They were made be happy by the news.
⑤ The news was reported last week.

28 밑줄 친 부분을 어법에 맞게 고친 것 중 틀린 것을 고르세요.

① This boat is belonged to my grandfather.
   → belongs to
② I was given to an interesting book by Mark.
   → an interesting book
③ Chinese dishes were cooked to me by my sister.
   → for me
④ This beautiful house is made by bricks.
   → made of
⑤ A doll was bought her by her father.
   → to her

29 다음 중 수동태로의 전환이 어색한 것은?

① My friend made a wooden box.
   ➡ A wooden box was made by my friend.
② Her boyfriend sent a postcard to her.
   ➡ A postcard is sent her by her boyfriend.
③ Josh calls me Ben.
   ➡ I am called Ben by Josh.
④ The students will clean the playground.
   ➡ The playground will be cleaned by the students.
⑤ People speak Chinese in Hong Kong.
   ➡ Chinese is spoken in Hong Kong.

30 다음 우리말과 같도록 <보기>의 단어를 배열할 때, 네 번째에 오는 단어는?

• 그 준비는 다음 주 금요일까지 완료되어야 한다.

보기
should, next, preparation, be, the, Friday, completed, by

① should   ② be   ③ the
④ Friday   ⑤ preparation

31 다음 문장을 수동태 문장으로 바꿔 쓰세요.

• We have watered all the plants.
→ _____

32 우리말과 같은 뜻이 되도록 괄호 안에 주어진 단어를 반드시 포함하여 6단어로 영작하세요. (단, 필요시 형태 변화 가능.)

• 이 컵은 물로 가득 차 있다. (fill)

→ _____

33 다음 중 밑줄 친 부분을 생략해도 의미 변화가 없는 것은?

① The question was asked at the conference by James.
② Apple Inc. was founded by Steve Jobs in 1974.
③ Canned food was invented by Appert.
④ German is spoken by people in Germany and Austria.
⑤ The island was discovered by an English explorer, James Cook.

34 다음 빈칸 ⓐ, ⓑ, ⓒ에 들어갈 말로 바르게 짝지어진 것을 고르세요.

• The bag ____ⓐ____ lots of gold coins by the merchant.
• The building ____ⓑ____ since last year.
• Nothing ____ⓒ____ my dad — he was always complaining.

	ⓐ	ⓑ	ⓒ
①	was filled of	was built	satisfied
②	was filled with	has been built	was satisfied
③	was filled with	was built	was satisfied
④	was filled of	has been built	was satisfied
⑤	was filled with	has been built	satisfied

35 주어진 문장을 <보기>와 같이 바꿔 쓰세요.

보기
• Einstein discovered the theory of relativity.
→ The theory of relativity was discovered by Einstein.   *theory of relativity: 상대성 이론

• Ernest Hemingway wrote *The Old Man and the Sea*.
→ _____
_____

36 다음 중 밑줄 친 부분이 어법상 바르지 <u>않은</u> 것은?

① We were surprised <u>at</u> the noise.
② The singer is known <u>to</u> everybody.
③ I was pleased <u>with</u> the gift.
④ He was satisfied <u>to</u> the result.
⑤ I am worried <u>about</u> his health.

37 우리말과 같은 뜻이 되도록 괄호 안의 말을 바르게 배열하여 문장을 완성하세요. (단, 필요시 어형을 변화시킬 것)

- 점심 식사 후 짧은 낮잠은 스페인 사람들에 의해 시에스타라고 불린다.
  = A short nap after lunch _____
  _____.
  (the Spanish, call, by, a siesta, be)

38 다음 중 어법상 <u>어색한</u> 문장은?

① I was given some hard work by my boss.
② The room was kept quiet by the old lady.
③ Lots of letters were sent to him by her.
④ She was elected mayor in 2020.
⑤ Look at our house. It needs to be painting.

39 다음을 읽고, 괄호 안의 동사를 이용하여 빈칸에 알맞은 말을 쓰세요.

In 1950, the Korean War broke out. The Korean War took the lives of 5 million men and women. Most of them were not soldiers but children, women, and old people. The war ended in 1953 but many things were ruined.

➡ Many people _____ _____ during the Korean War. (kill)

40 다음 글을 읽고, 괄호 ⓐ와 ⓑ에 주어진 단어를 알맞은 형태로 바꾸세요.

Steve Jobs ⓐ (bear) in 1955. He was interested in a lot of things, especially machines in his childhood. In his twenties, he founded a company. He wanted to make something that could change the world, and now he ⓑ (know) for his creativity.

ⓐ _____ ⓑ _____

41 다음 빈칸에 알맞은 단어를 순서대로 쓰세요.

(1) The whole hill is covered _____ tall trees.
(2) The house was made _____ glass, wood, and stone.
(3) I'm excited _____ my holiday trip.

42 다음 조건에 맞게 괄호 안의 단어를 활용하여 문장을 완성하세요.

<u>조건</u>
- 수동태 문장으로 만들 것.
- 시제는 미래형으로 할 것.

➡ Over four million lives _____
_____.
(save, this medicine)

CHAPTER 5
명사와 관사

성취도 자기 평가 활용법

구분	평가 기준
ⒺxcelIent	문법 내용을 모두 이해하고, 문제를 모두 맞힘.
Ⓥery good	문법 내용은 충분히 이해했으나 실수로 1~2문제 틀림.
Ⓖood	문법 내용이 조금 어려워 3~4문제 틀림.
needs Ⓡeview	문법 내용 이해가 어렵고, 5문제 이상 틀림, 복습 필요.

PSS 1 명사의 복수형	페이지	학습날짜	성취도 자기평가 Ⓔ Ⓥ Ⓖ Ⓡ	학습체크
PSS 1-1 명사의 복수형 Ⅰ	116	/		☐
PSS 1-2 명사의 복수형 Ⅱ	117	/		☐
PSS 1-3 명사의 복수형 Ⅲ	118	/		☐
PSS 2 명사의 쓰임	페이지	학습날짜	성취도 자기평가 Ⓔ Ⓥ Ⓖ Ⓡ	학습체크
PSS 2-1 명사의 종류	119	/		☐
PSS 2-2 셀 수 있는 명사	120	/		☐
PSS 2-3 셀 수 없는 명사	122	/		☐
PSS 2-4 물질명사의 쓰임	124	/		☐
PSS 2-5 주의해야 할 명사의 수	126	/		☐
PSS 2-6 명사의 소유격	127	/		☐
PSS 2-7 동격	128	/		☐
PSS 3 부정관사 a, an	페이지	학습날짜	성취도 자기평가 Ⓔ Ⓥ Ⓖ Ⓡ	학습체크
PSS 3-1 a, an의 쓰임	130	/		☐
PSS 3-2 a, an의 의미	131	/		☐
PSS 4 정관사 the	페이지	학습날짜	성취도 자기평가 Ⓔ Ⓥ Ⓖ Ⓡ	학습체크
PSS 4-1 the의 쓰임 Ⅰ	133	/		☐
PSS 4-2 the의 쓰임 Ⅱ	134	/		☐
PSS 4-3 the의 쓰임 Ⅲ	136	/		☐
PSS 5 관사를 쓰지 않는 경우	137	/		☐
Chapter Review Test	140	/		☐

명사의 복수형

PSS 1-1 명사의 복수형 I

일반적인 경우	명사+s	shoe – shoes month – months custom – customs student – students animal – animals neighbor – neighbors	friend – friends book – books egg – eggs bicycle – bicycles place – places classmate – classmates
-s, -x, -ch, -sh 로 끝나는 경우	명사+es	bus – buses fox – foxes watch – watches brush – brushes	class – classes box – boxes match – matches dish – dishes

정답 p.25

PRACTICE 1

다음 명사의 복수형을 쓰세요.

1. egg ➡ _____
2. watch ➡ _____
3. horse ➡ _____
4. pen ➡ _____
5. shoe ➡ _____
6. glass ➡ _____
7. book ➡ _____
8. dish ➡ _____
9. church ➡ _____
10. classmate ➡ _____
11. bottle ➡ _____
12. class ➡ _____
13. girl ➡ _____
14. camera ➡ _____
15. bus ➡ _____
16. month ➡ _____
17. beach ➡ _____
18. box ➡ _____
19. neighbor ➡ _____
20. brush ➡ _____
21. house ➡ _____
22. place ➡ _____
23. custom ➡ _____
24. friend ➡ _____
25. fox ➡ _____
26. match ➡ _____

27 sandwich ➡ _____
28 wish ➡ _____
29 bicycle ➡ _____
30 animal ➡ _____

PSS 1-2 명사의 복수형 II

자음+y로 끝나는 경우	자음+i+es	country – countries factory – factories city – cities party – parties hobby – hobbies	penny – pennies diary – diaries baby – babies family – families activity – activities
모음+y로 끝나는 경우	명사+s	day – days boy – boys monkey – monkeys	donkey – donkeys way – ways key – keys

정답 p.25

PRACTICE 2

다음 명사의 복수형을 쓰세요.

1 lady ➡ _____
2 story ➡ _____
3 key ➡ _____
4 party ➡ _____
5 diary ➡ _____
6 song ➡ _____
7 couch ➡ _____
8 monkey ➡ _____
9 baby ➡ _____
10 activity ➡ _____
11 city ➡ _____
12 donkey ➡ _____
13 student ➡ _____
14 culture ➡ _____
15 day ➡ _____
16 family ➡ _____
17 boy ➡ _____
18 habit ➡ _____
19 way ➡ _____
20 factory ➡ _____
21 hobby ➡ _____
22 ferry ➡ _____
23 candy ➡ _____
24 computer ➡ _____
25 bench ➡ _____
26 country ➡ _____

27 memory ➡ _____   **28** doctor ➡ _____
29 penny ➡ _____   **30** community ➡ _____

PSS 1-3 명사의 복수형 Ⅲ

-o로 끝나는 경우	명사+es	potato – potato**es** hero – hero**es**	tomato – tomato**es** mosquito – mosquito**(e)s**
	명사+s	kangaroo – kangaroo**s** radio – radio**s**	zoo – zoo**s** piano – piano**s**
-f, -fe로 끝나는 경우	f, fe → v+es	yourself – yoursel**ves** life – li**ves** knife – kni**ves**	leaf – lea**ves** wolf – wol**ves** calf – cal**ves**
	명사+s	roof – roof**s** belief – belief**s**	safe – safe**s** chief – chief**s**
불규칙 변화		goose – **geese** tooth – **teeth** woman – **women** sheep – **sheep** mouse – **mice** Chinese – **Chinese**	foot – **feet** man – **men** fish – **fish/fishes** deer – **deer** child – **children** ox – **oxen**

정답 p.26

PRACTICE 3

다음 명사의 복수형을 쓰세요.

1 video ➡ _____   **2** child ➡ _____
3 wolf ➡ _____   **4** belief ➡ _____
5 life ➡ _____   **6** ox ➡ _____
7 potato ➡ _____   **8** mouse ➡ _____
9 sheep ➡ _____   **10** man ➡ _____
11 photo ➡ _____   **12** goose ➡ _____
13 roof ➡ _____   **14** tooth ➡ _____
15 tomato ➡ _____   **16** fish ➡ _____

17 knife ➡ _____	18 clock ➡ _____
19 calf ➡ _____	20 yourself ➡ _____
21 mosquito ➡ _____	22 radio ➡ _____
23 wife ➡ _____	24 memo ➡ _____
25 leaf ➡ _____	26 deer ➡ _____
27 hero ➡ _____	28 loaf ➡ _____
29 blouse ➡ _____	30 safe ➡ _____
31 shelf ➡ _____	32 foot ➡ _____
33 kangaroo ➡ _____	34 thief ➡ _____
35 studio ➡ _____	36 chief ➡ _____
37 woman ➡ _____	38 zoo ➡ _____
39 piano ➡ _____	40 emergency ➡ _____

PSS 2 명사의 쓰임

PSS 2-1 명사의 종류

셀 수 있는 명사	\multicolumn{2}{l	}{a(n)을 붙이거나 복수형으로 쓸 수 있고, many, (a) few, some, any, no처럼 수를 나타내는 형용사와 함께 쓸 수 있다.}
	보통명사	bag student book pencil computer tree dish animal
	집합명사	class family team audience
셀 수 없는 명사	\multicolumn{2}{l	}{a(n)을 붙이거나 복수형으로 쓸 수 없고, 물질명사와 추상명사는 much, (a) little, some, any, no처럼 양을 나타내는 형용사와 함께 쓸 수 있다.}
	고유명사	David Insuk Korea Chicago Monday Christmas
	물질명사	water salt money juice air milk ice bread paper gold sugar flour
	추상명사	love peace knowledge beauty health honesty information news happiness hope kindness advice

PRACTICE 4

밑줄 친 단어 앞에 a나 an을 붙여야 하는 것을 골라 ○표 하세요.

1 I went to restaurant for dinner yesterday. _____
2 Would you like to drink juice? _____
3 There is church across the street. _____
4 Lady came to see you while you were out. _____
5 We can't live without air. _____
6 Excuse me. I'm looking for supermarket. _____
7 A bird was singing on tree. _____
8 Most artists try to find and express beauty. _____
9 Have you ever raised animal? _____
10 She always eats apple in the morning. _____
11 I go swimming on Monday. _____
12 They decided to write letter to Mr. Lee. _____
13 I met student whose name was Inho. _____
14 Do you have knowledge about this subject? _____
15 It is very tiring to take exam. _____

PSS 2-2 셀 수 있는 명사

1. **보통명사** – 사람이나 동물, 사물을 나타내는 명사로, 단·복수형이 모두 가능하다.

   I bought a **computer** last Friday. 나는 지난 금요일에 컴퓨터를 샀다.
   Jenny didn't bring an **umbrella**. Jenny는 우산을 가져오지 않았다.
   The **students** were playing soccer in the **playground**.
   학생들은 운동장에서 축구를 하고 있었다.

2. **집합명사** – 사람이나 사물의 집합체를 나타내는 명사로, 집합체를 하나의 단위로 보아 단수 취급하거나 개별 구성원에 중점을 두어 복수 취급할 수도 있다.

   My **class** consists of 28 boys and girls. 우리 반은 28명의 남녀로 이루어져 있다.
   There are only two **classes** in this school. 이 학교에는 단지 두 개의 반이 있다.

   My **family** lives in Incheon. 우리 가족은 인천에 산다.
   My **family are** all healthy. 우리 가족은 모두 건강하다. (개별 구성원에 중점을 두어 family를 복수 취급함.)

> Seven **families** live in this town. 일곱 가구가 이 도시에 산다.
>
> The **team** consists of nine people. 팀은 아홉 명으로 구성되어 있다.
>
> Mr. Lee supports three baseball **teams**. Lee 씨는 세 개의 야구팀을 후원한다.

정답 p.26

PRACTICE 5

괄호 안에 들어갈 단어로 알맞은 것을 고르세요. (복수 정답 가능)

1 Lisa bought two (book, books) for me.
2 The (scientist, scientists) was happy to solve the problem.
3 I think your (dog, dogs) are all very cute.
4 There is a (hospital, hospitals) around the corner.
5 Five (team, teams) will take part in the contest.
6 They invited more than a hundred (person, people) to their wedding.
7 I got a (letter, letters) from my friend, John.
8 My family (was, were) very glad to meet Mr. Park.
9 I met three (friend, friends) of Minsu's yesterday.
10 There (is, are) seven classes in 4th grade at the elementary school.
11 The brave (girl, girls) never cries in front of others.
12 The (class, classes) is going to go on a trip.
13 Many (family, families) in America have pets.
14 My team (is, are) ready to start the game.
15 We found a new (building, buildings) in our town.

정답 p.26

PRACTICE 6

다음 문장에서 밑줄 친 부분을 바르게 고쳐 쓰세요.

1 About ten <u>family</u> joined the tour.　　　　　　　　　　_families_
2 My class <u>are</u> usually very cheerful.　　　　　　　　　_____
3 I have been to many <u>country</u>.　　　　　　　　　　　_____
4 Mary is saving money to buy <u>car</u>. She has always wanted to have one.　_____

5   My family live in Chicago. _____

6   Leaf fall down to the ground every autumn. _____

7   Our teeth is very useful and important. _____

8   My boyfriend gave me bag for my birthday present. I like it so much. _____

9   My sister works in restaurant downtown. It offers 24-hour service seven days a week.

 _____

10   The book written by my teacher were published last month. _____

PSS 2-3 셀 수 없는 명사

1. **고유명사** – 사람, 장소, 요일 등의 고유한 이름을 나타내는 명사로, 첫 글자는 대문자로 쓴다.

    My niece **Becky** is a talented swimmer. 내 여자 조카 Becky는 재능있는 수영 선수이다.
    Paris is a beautiful city. 파리는 아름다운 도시이다.
    I'm leaving this city next **Saturday**. 나는 다음 토요일에 이 도시를 떠날 것이다.
    cf. 요일의 경우 '매주 토요일'의 의미로 쓸 때에는 on Saturdays 또는 every Saturday로 쓰인다.

2. **물질명사** – 일정한 형태가 없는 물질을 나타내는 명사로 much, (a) little, some, any, no, all과 같은 양을 나타내는 형용사와 함께 쓸 수 있다.

    We can't live without **water**. 우리는 물 없이 살 수 없다.
    I have **little money** in my purse. 내 지갑에는 돈이 거의 없다.
    Can I have **some juice**? 주스 좀 마실 수 있을까요?

3. **추상명사** – 눈에 보이지 않는 개념을 나타내는 명사로 much, (a) little, some, any, no와 같은 양을 나타내는 형용사와 함께 쓸 수 있다.

    Bill doesn't have **much knowledge** about science.
    Bill은 과학에 대한 많은 지식을 가지고 있지 않다.
    Too much coffee is not good for your **health**. 너무 많은 커피는 너의 건강에 좋지 않다.
    Honesty is the best **policy**. 정직은 최선의 방책이다.

정답 p.26

PRACTICE 7

괄호 안에 주어진 말 중 알맞은 것을 고르세요.

1   I want to drink (a water, water).

2   (A Saturday, Saturday) is my favorite day of a week.

3   I need (a computer, computer) to work from home.

4   Some people think (a beauty, beauty) inside is important.

5   One of the biggest cities in the world is (a New York, New York).

6   Most people want (happiness, happinesses) in their lives.

7   Both plants and animals need (an air, air).

8   My friend Bill has three cute (dog, dogs).

9   (A death, Death) is the end of life.

10 (A family, Family) moved into our town last week.

11 My friend Robert likes (September, Septembers) the best.

12 Mrs. Jones uses a lot of (salt, salts) when she cooks.

13 I'm looking forward to (a Christmas, Christmas).

14 We need some (paper, papers) to write on.

15 Thank you for your great (advice, advices).

PRACTICE 8

〈보기〉에서 알맞은 단어를 골라 빈칸에 어법에 맞게 쓰세요.

보 기	Jane	Seoul	class	apple	question
	time	family	information	juice	happiness

1   The Internet gives us lots of _____.

2   There is little _____ in the bottle.

3   I really enjoy living in _____, the largest city in Korea.

4   You can find _____ in small things.

5   Let me introduce my best friend, _____.

6   It takes a lot of _____ to finish this work.

7   We had dinner with those _____ yesterday.

8   Each _____ has 30 students in my school.

9   The teacher had to answer a lot of _____.

10 Can you buy two _____ on your way home? I need them now.

PSS 2-4 물질명사의 쓰임

물질명사의 수량은 단위명사를 이용하여 「수사＋단위명사＋of＋물질명사」의 어순으로 표현한다.

1. **piece**
   - a piece of **paper** 종이 한 장
   - three pieces of **cheese** 치즈 세 조각
   - seven pieces of **bread** 빵 일곱 조각
   - five pieces of **advice** 충고 다섯 마디
   - six pieces of **cloth** 천 여섯 조각
   - four pieces of **cake** 케이크 네 조각
   - two pieces of **furniture** 가구 두 점

   cf. 물질명사는 아니지만 advice(추상명사), furniture(의미상으로는 집합명사)도 수량 표현 시 piece를 사용한다.

2. **slice**
   - a slice of **cheese** 치즈 한 장
   - two slices of **bread** 빵 두 조각

3. **glass**
   - a glass of **milk** 우유 한 잔
   - three glasses of **juice** 주스 세 잔
   - two glasses of **water** 물 두 잔
   - four glasses of **wine** 와인 네 잔

4. **bar**
   - a bar of **soap** 비누 한 개
   - two bars of **chocolate** 초콜릿 두 개

5. **bottle**
   - a bottle of **juice** 주스 한 병
   - two bottles of **beer** 맥주 두 병

6. **cup**
   - a cup of **tea** 차 한 잔
   - two cups of **coffee** 커피 두 잔

7. **sheet**
   - a sheet of **paper** 종이 한 장

8. **spoonful[teaspoonful]**
   - a spoonful of **sugar** 설탕 한 스푼
   - two teaspoonfuls of **salt** 소금 두 티스푼

9. **loaf**
   - a loaf of **bread** 빵 한 덩어리
   - two loaves of **bread** 빵 두 덩어리

10. **pound**
    - a pound of **meat** 고기 1파운드
    - two pounds of **beef** 소고기 2파운드

11. **bowl**
    - a bowl of **rice** 밥 한 공기
    - two bowls of **soup** 수프 두 그릇

PRACTICE 9

그림을 보고, <보기>와 같이 빈칸에 알맞은 말을 쓰세요.

보 기
　two cups of coffee

1 　2 　3 　4 　5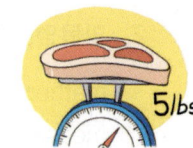

*lb: (무게 단위) 파운드의 약어
(라틴어 libra에서 옴.
약 453그램)

6 　7 　8 　9 　10

1 _____ paper
2 _____ bread
3 _____ juice
4 _____ sugar
5 _____ beef
6 _____ cake
7 _____ tea
8 _____ beer
9 _____ soap
10 _____ cheese

PRACTICE 10

단위명사를 이용하여 괄호 안에 주어진 단어를 빈칸에 알맞게 쓰세요.

1　I had a ___bowl of soup___ for breakfast. (soup)
2　Mom baked a _____ and cut it into ten pieces. (bread)
3　I'd like to give you a _____. (advice)
4　I brought them three _____. (water)
5　We need to buy two more _____. (furniture)
6　Pass me two _____, please. (bread)
7　Can you make a _____ for me? (tea)
8　Susie put three _____ in the soup. (salt)
9　Mrs. Ford bought four _____ for dinner. (meat)
10　Mark drank a _____ at my party. (wine)

PSS 2-5 주의해야 할 명사의 수

1. 한 쌍을 이루어야 하나의 물건으로 제 기능을 하는 명사는 복수형으로 쓰고 복수 취급한다.

   pants   scissors   socks   gloves   glasses   shoes

   cf. 이와 같은 명사의 수를 셀 때는 a pair of, two pairs of … 를 쓴다.
   a pair of pants 바지 한 벌   **two pairs of shoes** 신발 두 켤레

2. 과목명, 국가명, 병명 등의 일부 명사들은 형태상 복수형 같지만 단수 취급한다.

   mathematics 수학   economics 경제학   politics 정치학   the Philippines 필리핀
   measles 홍역   news 뉴스, 소식   customs 세관

3. 「수사+명사」가 뒤에 이어지는 명사를 수식하는 형용사처럼 쓰일 때는 수사 다음의 명사를 복수형으로 쓰지 않는다.

   a six-years-old girl (×) ➡ a **six-year-old** girl (○) 여섯 살짜리 소녀
   a two-months vacation (×) ➡ a **two-month** vacation (○) 두 달간의 휴가
   two five-dollars bills (×) ➡ two **five-dollar** bills (○) 5달러짜리 지폐 2장

PRACTICE 11

정답 p.27

괄호 안에 주어진 말 중 알맞은 것을 고르세요.

1 The news about the earthquake (was, were) very shocking.

2 Customs (is, are) the place where people pay taxes on goods from foreign countries.

3 My mom bought me a pair of (sock, socks).

4 Politics (is, are) the study about countries and governments.

5 Did you see my (glass, glasses)? I can't read without (it, them).

6 I live on the second floor of a (five-story, five-stories) building.

7 Economics (is, are) my favorite subject.

8 Be careful with (that scissor, those scissors).

9 Have you heard about that (two-hour, two-hours) movie?

10 David wants to buy two (pair, pairs) of (shoe, shoes).

11 Mr. Smith loved my (three-month-old, three-months-old) baby.

12 Nayoung got very nice (pant, pants) on her birthday.

13 I need five (ten-dollar, ten-dollars) bills now.

14 Mathematics (make, makes) me really bored.

15 James bought the handmade (glove, gloves) from Italy.

PSS 2-6 명사의 소유격

1. 사람이나 동물을 나타내는 명사는 '(s)를 이용하여 소유격을 만든다.

① 단수 명사+'s
- **Jenny's** book — Jenny의 책
- **the boy's** umbrella — 그 소년의 우산
- **Dr. Kim's** office — 김 박사의 사무실
- **the cat's** eyes — 고양이의 눈
- **Youngsu's** desk — 영수의 책상
- **my mother's** hand — 나의 어머니의 손

② 복수 명사+'
- **kids'** toys — 아이들의 장난감
- a **girls'** high school — 여자 고등학교
- **ladies'** shirts — 여성용 셔츠
- **parents'** day — 어버이날
- **farmers'** festival — 농부들의 축제
- **teachers'** room — 교무실

cf. 명사의 복수형이 -s로 끝나지 않으면 명사 뒤에 's를 붙인다.
- **children's** wear — 아동복
- **women's** magazines — 여성 잡지

③ 명사의 반복을 피하기 위해서나 가리키는 대상이 명백할 때는 소유격 뒤의 명사를 생략할 수도 있다.

This is my room and that is **my brother's**. 여기는 내 방이고, 저기는 내 남동생의 방이다.
　　　　　　　　　　　　　　(= my brother's room)

Where are you going to stay? 너는 어디에서 머무를 거니?
– I'm going to stay at **my uncle's**. 나는 삼촌 댁에서 머무를 거야.
　　　　　　　　　　　(= my uncle's house)

2. 무생물의 소유격은 주로 of를 이용한다.

- the title **of the movie** — 영화의 제목
- the top **of the mountain** — 산꼭대기

cf. 시간, 가격, 거리, 무게를 나타내는 명사는 '(s)를 이용하여 소유격을 만든다.
- **yesterday's** newspaper — 어제 신문
- **two dollars'** worth of salt — 2 달러어치의 소금
- **one hour's** walk — 한 시간의 산책

PRACTICE 12

그림을 보고, 빈칸에 알맞은 말을 쓰세요.

1 Mira (student)
2 Peter (friend)
3 Ms. Song (wife)
4 Minho (son)
5 Sujin (niece)
Mr. Kim

1 Mira is ___Mr. Kim's student___.
2 Peter is _____.
3 Ms. Song is _____.
4 Minho is _____.
5 Sujin is _____.

PRACTICE 13

다음에 주어진 단어나 구를 '(s) 또는 of를 이용하여 하나로 연결하세요.

1 Dave, black cap ➡ ___Dave's black cap___
2 my dog, tail ➡ _____
3 the exit, the building ➡ _____
4 the owner, this car ➡ _____
5 today, TV programs ➡ _____
6 the bottom, the bottle ➡ _____
7 my students, report cards ➡ _____
8 Mr. Brown, blanket ➡ _____
9 the result, the test ➡ _____
10 my sisters, clothes ➡ _____

PSS 2-7 동격

명사나 대명사를 보충 설명하거나 강조하기 위해 그 뒤에 다른 명사(구, 절)를 쓸 수 있는데 이런 관계를 동격이라 한다.

1. 콤마(,)를 이용한 동격
   I like **Mina, the tallest girl in this picture**.
   나는 이 사진에서 가장 키가 큰 소녀인 Mina를 좋아한다.
   This is **my friend, Mariah**.
   이 사람은 내 친구인 Mariah이다.

2. that을 이용한 동격
   I know **the fact that he likes you**.
   나는 그가 너를 좋아한다는 사실을 알고 있다.
   It is important to follow **the advice that you should exercise**.
   네가 운동을 해야 한다는 충고를 따르는 것은 중요하다.

3. of를 이용한 동격
   The news of his leaving us is very sad.
   그가 우리를 떠난다는 소식이 너무 슬프다.
   I was surprised at **the result of our winning the contest**.
   나는 우리가 그 대회에서 이겼다는 결과에 놀랐다.

PRACTICE 14

〈보기〉에서 알맞은 것을 골라 빈칸에 넣으세요.

보기	of / , / that

1 We know the fact _____ the Earth moves around the Sun.
2 Tom _____ the man in a blue shirt, is our English teacher.
3 Jimmy has a dream _____ he wants to be a famous actor.
4 BTS _____ my favorite boy group, is very famous.
5 The news _____ her coming to Seoul made him excited.
6 She has the idea _____ moving to Chicago.
7 He agreed to our opinion _____ he should attend the meeting.
8 There is no hope _____ winning the game.
9 The rumor _____ she stole the money was true.
10 Ms. Scott _____ the ballet teacher, recommended her ballet classes to Jane.

PRACTICE 15

밑줄 친 부분이 동격으로 쓰였으면 ○표, 아닌 경우에는 ×표를 하세요.

1 He likes the song that is easy to sing. [ ]
2 He saw the picture of my little dog. [ ]
3 I heard surprising news that we would go to an amusement park. [ ]
4 I can't believe the fact of his not coming to the class. [ ]
5 This is a book that I borrowed from my friend. [ ]
6 David, my boss, is a diligent man. [ ]
7 The advice that I should drink more water is very important. [ ]
8 Mary, Kate and Tom are good friends. [ ]
9 I'm sure that he will finish the work. [ ]
10 You are the one that I love most. [ ]

부정관사 a, an

PSS 3-1   a, an의 쓰임

1. a는 첫소리가 자음으로 발음되는 명사의 단수형 앞에, an은 모음으로 발음되는 명사의 단수형 앞에 쓰인다.

a dog	**a** man	**a** bus	**a** cat
a house	**a** nurse	**a** pen	**an** animal
an egg	**an** idea	**an** office	**an** umbrella

2. 명사 앞의 형용사의 첫소리가 자음으로 발음되면 a, 모음으로 발음되면 an을 쓴다.

a large apartment   **a** sweet orange   **an** easy question   **an** old lady

3. 철자는 모음으로 시작하지만 첫소리가 자음으로 발음되는 명사 앞에는 a, 철자는 자음으로 시작하지만 모음으로 발음되는 명사 앞에는 an을 쓴다. 명사 앞에 형용사가 있을 경우에는 그 형용사의 첫 소리 발음에 따라 a와 an을 구별하여 쓴다.

a university   **an** hour   **an** honest man   **a** uniform   **a** unique experience

PRACTICE 16

다음 문장의 빈칸에 a나 an 중 알맞은 것을 쓰세요.

1 I used to live in _____ apartment.
2 That is _____ good idea!
3 *Mission Impossible* is _____ interesting movie.
4 He is looking for _____ university student to study with.
5 _____ honest boy brought my lost wallet.
6 We have _____ important meeting tomorrow morning.
7 I have to wear _____ uniform in the workplace.
8 They saw _____ baby crying in the restaurant.
9 The company needs _____ larger office for the new workers.
10 There is _____ old house on the hill.
11 Did you bring _____ umbrella with you?
12 My little brother drew a picture of _____ cute animal.
13 It will take about _____ hour to wash my car.
14 Jina took _____ bus to go to Incheon.
15 The customer is looking for _____ unique design for his clothes.

PSS 3-2 a, an의 의미

one 하나의	Susan gave me **an** apple this morning. Susan은 오늘 아침에 내게 사과 한 개를 주었다.
a certain 어떤	Jenny visited **a** Korean family yesterday. Jenny는 어제 어떤 한국 가정을 방문했다.
some 약간의, 어느 정도	I'll tell him the truth in **a** moment. 나는 잠시 후에 그에게 사실을 말할 것이다.
the same 같은, 동일한	Ingyu and Sumi are of **an** age. 인규와 수미는 동갑이다.

per ~당, ~마다	Mr. Brown goes jogging twice **a** week. Brown 씨는 일주일에 두 번 조깅을 하러 간다.
대표 단수	**A** dog is a very cute animal. 개는 매우 귀여운 동물이다.

정답 p.28

PRACTICE 17

그림을 보고, 〈보기〉에서 알맞은 단어를 골라 a(n)을 이용하여 빈칸에 알맞은 말을 쓰세요.

보 기	glass tree elephant house egg monitor baby police officer

1  2  3  4

5 6  7  8

1 I'll have _____ for breakfast.

2 They are building _____ .

3 There is _____ on the street.

4 Mr. and Mrs. Kim have _____ girl.

5 There is _____ on the table.

6 _____ is controlling traffic.

7 There is _____ in the zoo.

8 Minsu bought _____ for his computer.

PRACTICE 18

밑줄 친 a(n)의 올바른 의미를 <보기>에서 찾아 괄호 안에 번호를 쓰세요.

| 보기 | ① one ② a certain ③ some ④ the same ⑤ per ⑥ 대표 단수 |

1 He came back after a while. (   )
2 Dad had a sandwich for lunch. (   )
3 Birds of a feather flock together. (   )
4 A child needs parents. (   )
5 This book is about an artist. (   )
6 I have an older sister. (   )
7 I visit my grandparents once a month. (   )
8 How many glasses of water do you drink a day? (   )
9 A girl came to see you yesterday. (   )
10 A whale is one of the heaviest animals. (   )
11 We are of an age. (   )
12 Mark and Sena sat at a distance from each other. (   )

정관사 the

PSS 4-1 the의 쓰임 I

1. 앞에 나온 명사가 반복될 때

   There is a book on the desk. **The book** is about science.
   책상 위에 책 한 권이 있다. 그 책은 과학에 관한 것이다.

2. 듣는 사람이 무엇을 가리키는지 알 수 있을 때

   Could you pass me **the sugar**, please? 설탕 좀 건네주시겠어요?

3. 유일한 것을 나타낼 때

   The Sun sets in the west. 해는 서쪽으로 진다.

> **4. 명사 뒤에 명사를 수식하는 구나 절이 있을 때**
>
> Seoul is **the** capital of Korea. 서울은 한국의 수도이다.

PRACTICE 19

정답 p.28

괄호 안에 주어진 단어 중 알맞은 것을 고르세요.

1. People once believed (an, the) Earth was flat.
2. Will you hold (a, the) door for me?
3. It's getting cold. I need to buy (a, the) jacket.
4. I have seen John and Mary's baby. (A, The) baby is so lovely.
5. Today people can go to (a, the) Moon on a spaceship.
6. Jina called you (a, the) while ago.
7. Look at (a, the) bird! It's so beautiful.
8. Insu gave me a pen. (A, The) pen is blue.
9. I had two apples and (a, the) glass of water.
10. We have two long vacations (a, the) year.
11. Did you go to (a, the) concert that you told me about?
12. (A, The) book on my desk is about psychology.
13. I bought a skirt at a flea market. I'm going to wear (a, the) skirt tomorrow.
14. There is (a, the) restaurant near my house. (A, The) restaurant is really good.
15. Who are they? – (A, The) boy is my brother and (a, the) girl is my sister.

PSS 4-2 the의 쓰임 Ⅱ

> **1. 서수, 최상급, only, very, same 앞**
>
> She was **the first** woman to win the award. 그녀는 그 상을 수상한 첫 번째 여성이었다.
> This is **the best** way to solve the problem. 이것이 그 문제를 푸는 가장 좋은 방법이다.
> It's **the only** money I have. 그것이 내가 가지고 있는 유일한 돈이다.
> These are **the very** pants I wanted. 이것이 내가 원했던 바로 그 바지이다.
> Your pen is **the same** as mine. 네 펜은 내 것과 같다.

2. 대표 단수 앞

　　The cat is a smart animal. 고양이는 영리한 동물이다.

3. 악기의 이름 앞

　　Mark can play **the violin** very well. Mark는 바이올린을 매우 잘 연주할 수 있다.

PRACTICE 20

다음 대화의 빈칸에 a(n)나 the 중 알맞은 것을 쓰세요.

1　A: Can I borrow your pencil?
　　B: I'm sorry, but this is _____ only pencil I have.

2　A: Where should I sit?
　　B: At _____ second seat in _____ first row.

3　A: I'm going shopping. Is there anything you want?
　　B: Well, I need _____ notebook.

4　A: Who is Mr. Park?
　　B: He is _____ very person who built the house.

5　A: What color do you want?
　　B: _____ same color as yours.

6　A: Don't you have _____ older brother?
　　B: No. I don't have any.

7　A: Did you like _____ movie?
　　B: Yes. It was the most exciting movie I've ever seen.

8　A: What is Linda doing?
　　B: She is playing _____ piano.

9　A: I met _____ really handsome boy the other day.
　　B: Great! How did you meet him?

10　A: Do you know Mike?
　　B: Yes. He is _____ most popular guy in my school.

11　A: What happened last night?
　　B: _____ thief broke into my neighbor's house.

PSS 4-3 the의 쓰임 Ⅲ

1. **특정 고유명사 앞**

   the Pacific 태평양　　**the** Alps 알프스 산맥　　**the** Philippines 필리핀
   the Netherlands 네덜란드　　**the** Thames 템즈 강　　**the** New York Times 뉴욕타임즈지

2. **the＋형용사/분사 '～한 사람들'**

   You should respect **the** old. 당신은 노인들을 공경해야 한다.

3. **어떤 동작을 가하는 신체의 일부를 나타내는 단어 앞**

   He looked me in **the** eye. 그는 내 눈을 똑바로 쳐다보았다.

정답 p.29

PRACTICE 21

밑줄 친 부분이 올바르면 ○, 틀리면 바르게 고쳐 쓰세요.

1　They tried to help <u>a poor</u>.　　　　　　　　　_____

2　Ben was hit in <u>a face</u> by a stranger.　　　　_____

3　The sailors crossed <u>Pacific</u>.　　　　　　　　_____

4　I see Jenny once <u>the week</u>.　　　　　　　　_____

5　I have been to <u>Netherlands</u>.　　　　　　　　_____

6　<u>A rich</u> tend to spend money carelessly.　　_____

7　Peter took me by <u>the hand</u>.　　　　　　　　_____

8　Excuse me. Is there <u>the post office</u> around here?　_____

9　<u>The young</u> like to be with friends.　　　　_____

10　We should be quiet for <u>a while</u>.　　　　　_____

11　Emily's house is near <u>a Thames</u>.　　　　　_____

12　Do you read <u>a New York Times</u>?　　　　　_____

13　This morning I bought <u>a newspaper</u> on the street.　_____

14　Someone pushed me on <u>a back</u>.　　　　　_____

15　<u>The Alps</u> are always covered with snow.　_____

PRACTICE 22

다음 글을 읽고, 괄호 안에 주어진 단어 중 알맞은 것을 고르세요.

(A, An, The) old want to live a comfortable life. (A, An, The) *Korean Times* reported that these days many of them move to Southeast Asian countries after they retire. (A, An, The) Philippines is one of (a, an, the) most popular countries for them to live in. It is on (a, an, the) Pacific Ocean. It has beautiful scenery and warm weather. My family visits the country about once (a, an, the) year because my grandparents live there, too.

관사를 쓰지 않는 경우

1. **식사를 나타내는 명사 앞**

   I didn't have **breakfast** this morning. 나는 오늘 아침에 아침을 먹지 않았다.

2. **운동 경기를 나타내는 명사 앞**

   John usually plays **basketball** on weekends. John은 대개 주말마다 농구를 한다.

3. **by + 교통수단**

   My sister and I went to Busan **by train**. 내 여동생과 나는 기차를 타고 부산에 갔다.

4. **장소, 기구를 나타내는 명사가 본래의 목적으로 쓰일 때**

   Jack doesn't go to **school** on Saturday. Jack은 토요일에 학교에 가지 않는다.
   I go to **church** every Sunday. 나는 매주 일요일마다 교회에 간다.
   Sumi went to **bed** late last night. 수미는 지난 밤 늦게 잠자리에 들었다.

5. **가족을 나타내는 명사 앞**

   : Mother, Mom, Father, Dad, Uncle, Aunt와 같은 명사 앞에는 관사를 쓰지 않는다.
   (단, brother, sister는 무관사로 쓰지 않는다.)
   I bought **Dad** a muffler for his birthday gift. 나는 아빠의 생신 선물로 머플러를 사드렸다.

6. **관직, 신분을 나타내는 명사 앞**

   Professor Kim is going to leave for Australia. 김 교수님은 호주로 떠날 것이다.

7. 과목을 나타내는 명사 앞

   My favorite subject is **science**. 내가 가장 좋아하는 과목은 과학이다.

8. 그 외의 경우 – listen to music과 watch TV는 관용적으로 관사 없이 쓴다.

   Mark likes **listening to music**. Mark는 음악을 듣는 것을 좋아한다.
   I usually **watch TV** until late at night. 나는 대개 밤 늦게까지 TV를 본다.

PRACTICE 23

〈보기〉에서 알맞은 단어를 골라 빈칸에 쓰세요.

보 기	bus mom Professor TV lunch home math school tennis bed

1 My family went to the East Sea by _____.
2 She plays _____ very well after the lesson.
3 I help my _____ wash the dishes on weekends.
4 What do you want to have for _____?
5 _____ is the most difficult subject for me.
6 I am so tired. I will go to _____ earlier tonight.
7 Giho was watching _____ when I called him.
8 What time did Liz leave _____?
9 Most students really liked _____ Choi's class.
10 Yumi didn't go to _____ today because she was sick.

PRACTICE 24

다음 문장의 빈칸에 a(n)나 the 중 알맞은 것을 쓰고, 필요 없는 곳에는 ×표 하세요.

1 Where did you have _____ lunch?
2 Jenny used to play _____ piano when she was young.
3 He was _____ only boy in the group.
4 Would you like to play _____ baseball together?
5 She looked me in _____ face.

6   I watched _____ interesting movie with Nancy yesterday.

7   I think it's _____ very place that I have lost my book.

8   I usually listen to _____ music on my way to work.

9   We go to the library twice _____ month.

10 Koreans tend to respect _____ old.

11 Junho used to go to _____ church when he was little.

12 This is not _____ first time that Julie and I met.

13 She didn't say anything for _____ while.

14 Ask _____ Dad what time he comes home.

15 _____ friend of mine loves swimming.

16 I usually have _____ breakfast at 7:30.

17 Generally speaking, _____ dog is friendlier than _____ cat.

18 Lory plays _____ cello very well.

19 Every evening I take _____ walk with my dog.

20 _____ moon looks really bright tonight.

21 Here is _____ pencil I borrowed.

22 She works six hours _____ day, five days _____ week.

23 Did you come here by _____ bus or by _____ subway?

24 The police caught the thief, and now he is in _____ prison.

25 Have you met _____ Dr. Choi before?

26 I like _____ math more than any other subject.

27 My brother watches _____ TV from morning to night.

28 _____ children in the room are all of _____ age.

29 _____ young have the future in their hands.

30 We are going to play _____ badminton in the playground.

31 There is a special fish in _____ East Sea of Korea.

32 Junha is _____ only man on our team.

33 He didn't go to _____ bed last night.

34 _____ hotel we stayed at wasn't very good.

Chapter Review Test

정답 p.30

CHAPTER 5
명사와 관사

1 다음 중 단어의 단수 – 복수의 연결이 올바른 것은?

① piano – pianoes
② wife – wives
③ wolf – wolfes
④ tooth – tooths
⑤ beauty – beautys

2 다음 중 어법상 올바른 문장은?

① I bought five furniture.
② He wants two cheese.
③ I had three coffee yesterday.
④ She needs a piece of paper.
⑤ Nora had two cereal for lunch.

3 다음 중 어법상 올바른 문장을 <u>모두</u> 고르면?

① He toasted two piece of breads.
② I'd like a bar of chocolate, please.
③ Can I offer a piece of advice?
④ Mom put two salt in the soup.
⑤ She bought five meat for dinner.

4 우리말과 같은 뜻이 되도록 빈칸에 알맞은 단어를 쓰세요.

- 나는 커피 한 잔과 케이크 네 조각을 먹었다.
  = I had _____ _____ _____ _____ and _____ _____ _____ .

5 다음 문장의 빈칸에 들어갈 말로 알맞은 것은?

There are _____ in the park.

① three donkeys
② two mouses
③ several benchs
④ some birdes
⑤ five foxs

6 다음 밑줄 친 <u>these</u>와 바꿔 쓸 수 없는 것은?

I need to buy <u>these</u> at the supermarket.

① two bars of soap
② five pounds of pork
③ some juices
④ five apples
⑤ three loaves of bread

7 다음 중 어법상 <u>틀린</u> 것의 개수를 고르시오.

ⓐ Do you know the best way to master English?
ⓑ He was first man to set foot on the Moon.
ⓒ David is the only person I trust.
ⓓ The copier and the computer were bought at same year.
ⓔ I heard Rose playing piano yesterday.

① 0개　② 1개　③ 2개　④ 3개　⑤ 4개

Chapter Review Test

8 우리말과 같은 뜻이 되도록 빈칸에 알맞은 단어를 쓰세요.

- James는 그녀의 딸을 위해 신발 한 켤레를 샀다.
  = James bought _____ _____ _____ _____ for his daughter.

9 다음 두 문장의 빈칸에 공통으로 알맞은 것은?

- I need a glass _____ water.
- He has a plan _____ studying for the test.

① at   ② to   ③ of   ④ by   ⑤ in

10 다음 중 어법상 올바른 문장만 짝지은 것은?

ⓐ Would you like some apple?
ⓑ Moon goes round Earth every 27 days.
ⓒ What is the longest river in the world?
ⓓ She works seven hours a day.
ⓔ Seoul is capital of Korea.

① ⓐ, ⓒ   ② ⓐ, ⓔ   ③ ⓑ, ⓓ
④ ⓒ, ⓓ   ⑤ ⓓ, ⓔ

11 다음 중 밑줄 친 부분을 어법상 옳게 고친 것은?

① Suji drinks milks (→ milkes) every day.
② Gidong had meats (→ meates) for dinner yesterday.
③ There are two cup (→ cups) of coffee on the table.
④ Could you pass me the sugar (→ sugars), Linda?
⑤ I want to have a bottle of juice (→ juices).

12 다음 대화의 ①~⑤ 중 어법상 어색한 것은?

A: ① How many ② childrens do you ③ have?
B: I have ④ three sons and ⑤ two daughters.

13 다음 중 어법상 올바른 문장은?

① Are you student?
② Jiho is a newspaper reporter.
③ Today is a second day of school.
④ Sam's uncle is math teacher.
⑤ She looks a very honest.

14 다음 글의 밑줄 친 부분 중 어법상 어색한 것은?

When the teacher came into ① the classroom, he got very upset. The students were making a lot of ② noisy. Some were playing the radio ③ loudly and some were playing ④ games. The teacher tried to stop ⑤ them, but he failed.

15 다음 중 어법상 바른 문장을 <u>모두</u> 고르세요.

① I didn't have the lunch because I was very busy.
② I used to play the violin in my room on weekends.
③ She doesn't go to the school tomorrow.
④ Mary likes the economics.
⑤ I'm the only child in my family.

16 각 문장의 빈칸에 들어갈 알맞은 단어를 <보기>에서 골라 올바른 형태로 바꿔 쓰세요.

보 기
glass   piece   bowl   bottle   pair   slice

(1) I'm so hungry. I want a _____ of rice right now. (밥 한 그릇)
(2) Bring me two _____ of water, please. (물 두 병)
(3) Last Christmas, my father bought me three _____ of shoes. (신발 세 켤레)
(4) I'd like to drink a _____ of orange juice. (오렌지 주스 한 잔)

17 다음 중 어법상 바르지 <u>않은</u> 문장은?

① This is bag of Jenny's.
② I went to a girls' middle school.
③ Hana stayed at her grandparents'.
④ Do you know the owner of this building?
⑤ What's the title of the book?

18 다음 글의 ①~⑤ 중 어법상 <u>어색한</u> 것은?

According to the news, this winter ① <u>is predicted</u> to be colder than usual. So, it is necessary ② <u>to buy</u> warm pairs of pants to withstand the cold. Also, it would be nice to have ③ <u>several pairs of gloves</u>. I am not good with ④ <u>the cold</u>, so I hope the news report was wrong. If the news is right this ⑤ <u>three-months-long winter</u> is going to feel very long to me.

19 다음 조리법의 ①~⑤ 중 어법상 <u>어색한</u> 것은?

How to Make Cucumber Yogurt Dip

What You Need
① <u>two cup of plain yogurt</u>
② <u>1 cup of sour cream</u>
③ <u>1 spoonful of lemon juice</u>
④ <u>salt and black pepper</u>
⑤ <u>two cucumbers</u>

1. Cut the cucumbers in half, grind them and put them into a bowl.
2. Add yogurt, sour cream, and lemon juice.
3. Stir everything.
4. Season with salt and pepper.
5. Refrigerate for at least 1 hour.

20 다음 빈칸에 들어갈 알맞은 말은?

You can see many _____ here.

① leaf　　② baby　　③ sheep
④ man　　⑤ child

21 다음 우리말과 같은 뜻이 되도록 괄호 안에 주어진 단어를 알맞게 배열하세요.

• 나는 그가 마라톤에서 우승했다는 소식을 들었다.
= I heard the news _____.
　(a marathon, he, that, won)

22 다음의 밑줄 친 a와 그 쓰임이 같은 것은?

Dr. Calvin said, "If you want to be taller, you should drink at least three glasses of milk <u>a</u> day."

① <u>A</u> dog is a very faithful animal.
② We have <u>a</u> difficult problem to solve.
③ I wanted to get paid once <u>a</u> month.
④ Birds of <u>a</u> feather flock together.
⑤ There is <u>a</u> Mr. Johnson on the phone.

23 다음 중 빈칸에 The[the]가 들어가야 할 것은?

① Did you have _____ lunch, Mike?
② I went to Daegu by _____ bus.
③ His favorite subject is _____ Korean.
④ I like to listen to _____ music at night.
⑤ _____ Sun rises in the East.

24 밑줄 친 부분을 바르게 고친 것 중 잘못된 것은?

① The Thames is <u>in the London</u>.
　　　　　　　　→ in London
② The rich <u>tends</u> to ignore the poor.
　　　　→ tend
③ Have you ever been to <u>Netherlands</u>?
　　　　　　　　→ the Netherlands
④ Then, he began hitting me <u>on arm</u>.
　　　　　　　　　→ on the arm
⑤ Would you look her <u>in an eye</u>?
　　　　　　　　→ in eye

25 다음 글의 ①~⑤ 중 어법상 어색한 것은?

Tom is going to have ①<u>a party</u> tonight with ②<u>his friends</u>. There will be ③<u>five men and four women</u>. Tom went to the market to buy some ④<u>food</u> for the party. When he came back home, he found out that he forgot to buy ⑤<u>a bread</u>.

26 다음 빈칸에 들어갈 수 없는 것은?

> How many _____ do you want?

① dogs ② pencils ③ informations
④ boxes ⑤ children

27 다음 밑줄 친 that과 용법이 같은 것은?

> Tom told me the news that he would have a birthday party on Sunday.

① I think that is a wonderful dress.
② Look at that dog over there.
③ Everybody knows the fact that he is innocent.
④ I know that he is kind.
⑤ Jim has a car that is red.

28 다음 중 어법상 어색한 문장은?

① They liked to help a poor.
② Could you do me a favor?
③ I enjoy surfing the Internet on Fridays.
④ They will have a lot of fun.
⑤ He went to the airport by bus.

29 다음 밑줄 친 부분 중 어법상 틀린 것을 두 개 찾아 고치세요.

> (A) He skipped a breakfast this morning.
> (B) Lisa went on a two-week-long vacation.
> (C) That day, she was listening to music on the way home.
> (D) I recently bought two pair of shoes.
> (E) Jude led the old man by the hand.

(1) _____ ➡ _____
(2) _____ ➡ _____

30 다음 그림의 내용과 일치하도록 빈칸에 알맞은 말을 <보기>에서 골라 올바른 형태로 바꿔 쓰세요. (단, 필요시 같은 단어를 한 번 이상 쓸 수 있음.)

| 보 기 | bar bottle loaf slice piece |

> There are three ⓐ _____ of cheese, two ⓑ _____ of chocolate, three ⓒ _____ of bread and a ⓓ _____ of juice on the table. There are four ⓔ _____ of paper and three ⓕ _____ of soap under the table.

CHAPTER 6
대명사

성취도 자기 평가 활용법

구분	평가 기준
Excellent	문법 내용을 모두 이해하고, 문제를 모두 맞힘.
Very good	문법 내용은 충분히 이해했으나 실수로 1~2문제 틀림.
Good	문법 내용이 조금 어려워 3~4문제 틀림.
needs **R**eview	문법 내용 이해가 어렵고, 5문제 이상 틀림. 복습 필요.

	페이지	학습날짜	성취도 자기평가 E V G R	학습체크
PSS 1 인칭대명사				
PSS 1-1 주격, 목적격	146	/		☐
PSS 1-2 소유격, 소유대명사	147	/		☐
PSS 1-3 재귀대명사	149	/		☐
PSS 2 it의 쓰임	페이지	학습날짜	성취도 자기평가 E V G R	학습체크
PSS 2-1 비인칭주어 it	150	/		☐
PSS 2-2 it의 특별 용법	151	/		☐
PSS 2-3 가주어 it / 가목적어 it	152	/		☐
PSS 3 지시대명사	페이지	학습날짜	성취도 자기평가 E V G R	학습체크
PSS 3-1 this, that	153	/		☐
PSS 3-2 that/those의 특별 용법	155	/		☐
PSS 4 부정대명사	페이지	학습날짜	성취도 자기평가 E V G R	학습체크
PSS 4-1 one	156	/		☐
PSS 4-2 other, another	157	/		☐
PSS 4-3 관용 표현	159	/		☐
PSS 4-4 each, every	160	/		☐
PSS 4-5 all, both, rest	162	/		☐
PSS 4-6 some-, any-	164	/		☐
PSS 5 의문대명사	페이지	학습날짜	성취도 자기평가 E V G R	학습체크
PSS 5-1 who	166	/		☐
PSS 5-2 which, what	167	/		☐
Chapter Review Test	169	/		☐

인칭대명사

격 인칭	단수					복수				
	주격	소유격	목적격	소유대명사	재귀대명사	주격	소유격	목적격	소유대명사	재귀대명사
1	I	my	me	mine	myself	we	our	us	ours	ourselves
2	you	your	you	yours	yourself	you	your	you	yours	yourselves
3	he	his	him	his	himself	they	their	them	theirs	themselves
	she	her	her	hers	herself					
	it	its	it	-	itself					

PSS 1-1 주격, 목적격

1. 주격 – '~은(는), ~이, ~가'로 해석되고, 문장의 주어 자리에 온다.

   I know Mr. Jones. **He** is a lawyer. 나는 Jones 씨를 안다. 그는 변호사이다.

   I ate an apple. **It** was so sweet. 나는 사과를 먹었다. 그것은 매우 달았다.

2. 목적격 – '~을(를), ~에게'로 해석되고, 동사나 전치사의 목적어 자리에 온다.

   Jane and Paul are kind. People **like them**. Jane과 Paul은 친절하다. 사람들은 그들을 좋아한다.

   Susan and I are going shopping. Would you like to come **with us**?
   Susan과 나는 쇼핑을 갈 거야. 너도 우리와 함께 갈래?

정답 p.32

PRACTICE 1

괄호 안에 주어진 단어 중 알맞은 것을 고르세요.

1 Mr. Kim is one of the most popular people in the office. I like (he, him).

2 John and I went to the movies. (We, Us) had fun.

3 Thank you for helping me. (You, Your) are very kind.

4 A boy looked at (I, me) through the window.

5　Did (they, them) visit you last week?

6　Mrs. Park wanted to see my family, so she invited (we, us) to dinner.

7　Susie is my brother's friend. I don't know (she, her) very well.

8　This book is very interesting. I've read (it, them) twice already.

9　My wife bought a new pair of shoes and gave (they, them) to me.

10　Yoonji likes playing musical instruments. (She, Her) likes singing, too.

PSS 1-2 소유격, 소유대명사

1. **소유격** – '~의'로 해석되고, 명사가 뒤따른다.

   I am wearing a hat. **My hat** is blue. 나는 모자를 쓰고 있다. 나의 모자는 파란색이다.
   Is this **his bag** or **your bag**? 이것은 그의 가방이니, 아니면 너의 가방이니?

   cf. its와 it's의 구분: its는 소유격으로 '그것의'라는 뜻을 가지며 it's는 'it is' 혹은 'it has'의 줄임말이다.

   My dog was wagging **its** tail. 나의 개는 꼬리를 흔들고 있었다.
   It's(= It is) not mine. 그것은 나의 것이 아니다.

2. **소유대명사** – '~의 것'으로 해석되고, 명사가 뒤따르지 않는다.

   I have her pencil. This is **hers**. 나는 그녀의 연필을 가지고 있다. 이것은 그녀의 것이다.
   　　　　　　(= her pencil)
   Are these pants **yours**? 이 바지는 너의 것이니?
   　　　　　　(= your pants)

   cf. 대명사 it은 소유대명사의 형태를 가지지 않는다.

정답 p.32

PRACTICE 2

다음 문장의 빈칸에 알맞은 대명사를 쓰세요.

1　　Sora has a bicycle.
　　This is ___her___ bicycle.
　　This is ___hers___.

2　　Tom has a cap.
　　This is _____ cap.
　　This is _____.

3  Mr. and Mrs. Choi have a house.
This is _____ house.
This is _____ .

4  I have a dog.
It is _____ dog.
It is _____ .

5 Your name is on the cover.
It's _____ book.
It's _____ .

6  We study in this classroom.
This is _____ classroom.
This is _____ .

정답 p.32

PRACTICE 3

괄호 안에 주어진 대명사 중 알맞은 것을 고르세요.

1 I met Jinho yesterday. (He, His) is leaving for London tomorrow.

2 Yumi is (my, mine) friend. I like (she, her) a lot.

3 Have you met Tina and Bob? (They, Them) are my cousins.

4 They brought (our, us) some sandwiches.

5 I've eaten Miyoung's cake. I didn't know it was (her, hers).

6 Do you know the gentleman over there? What is (his, him) name?

7 Did you see the dogs in the picture? Those are (our, ours).

8 Jenny will tell (he, him) the truth.

9 I hope (your, yours) dream will come true in the future.

10 I heard the news but I didn't realize (it's, its) importance.

PSS 1-3 재귀대명사

1. **재귀 용법** – 문장의 주어와 목적어의 대상이 같을 때는 인칭대명사의 목적격 대신 재귀대명사를 쓴다. 재귀 용법으로 쓰인 재귀대명사는 생략할 수 없다.

   I saw **myself** in the mirror. 나는 거울 속에 있는 나 자신을 보았다.
   cf. I saw **me** in the mirror. (×)

   Jina is very proud of **herself**. 지나는 자신을 매우 자랑스러워한다.
   cf. Jina is very proud of **her**. (×)
   　　　　　　　　　　　　　Jina 자신일 때

2. **강조 용법** – 주어, 목적어, 보어를 강조하기 위해 쓰이는 재귀대명사는 강조하고자 하는 (대)명사 바로 뒤에 오거나 문장의 끝에 올 수 있고, 생략할 수 있다. 강조 용법의 재귀대명사를 생략하면 강조의 의미도 사라진다.

   I (myself) fixed the computer. 내가 (직접) 컴퓨터를 고쳤다.
   = **I** fixed the computer **(myself)**.
   I've seen **the singer (himself)**. 나는 그 가수를 (직접) 본 적이 있다.
   It was **Tom (himself)**. 그것은 Tom (그 자신)이었다.

3. **전치사 + 재귀대명사**

   ① by oneself '혼자, 다른 사람 없이'
   　I couldn't go there **by myself**. 나는 혼자서 그곳에 갈 수 없었다.

   ② for oneself '혼자 힘으로, 스스로'
   　Peter did his homework **for himself**. Peter는 혼자 힘으로 숙제를 했다.

PRACTICE 4

다음 문장의 빈칸에 알맞은 재귀대명사를 쓰고, 어떤 용법으로 쓰였는지 고르세요.

1　James could fix the car _____.　　　[재귀 / 강조]
2　Sujin wants to stay here by _____.　　[재귀 / 강조]
3　I _____ promised to come back soon.　[재귀 / 강조]
4　Take good care of _____, will you?　　[재귀 / 강조]
5　History repeats _____.　　　　　　　[재귀 / 강조]
6　We had to solve the problem for _____.[재귀 / 강조]
7　He is proud of _____ for not giving up.[재귀 / 강조]
8　The guests made _____ at home there.　[재귀 / 강조]

PRACTICE 5

괄호 안에 주어진 단어 중 알맞은 것을 고르세요.

1. Tony lent (me, myself) the book yesterday.
2. Frank prepared the meeting by (him, himself).
3. He introduced (them, themselves) to his wife.
4. They gave (us, ourselves) something to drink.
5. She cannot live by (her, herself).
6. I have something to tell (you, yourself).
7. A robot cannot think by (it, itself).
8. I looked at (me, myself) in the mirror.
9. I will be proud of (me, myself).
10. Peter asked (her, herself) to marry him.

 **it의 쓰임**

PSS 2-1 비인칭주어 it

문장의 주어로 쓰이지만 특별한 의미를 가지지 않기 때문에 '그것은, 그것이'로 굳이 해석하지 않는다.

날씨	It will be rainy and windy tomorrow.	내일은 비가 오고 바람이 불 것이다.
거리	It is two kilometers to the office.	그 사무실까지는 2km이다.
시간	It is five o'clock now.	지금은 5시이다.
요일	It is Monday today.	오늘은 월요일이다.
날짜	It is April 6.	4월 6일이다.
온도	It is 17 degrees Celsius in this room.	이 방은 섭씨 17도이다.
계절	It is winter in Korea now.	지금 한국은 겨울이다.

PRACTICE 6

다음 문장의 밑줄 친 부분이 대명사이면 '대', 비인칭주어이면 '비'를 쓰세요.

1. It was dark in the room. [　　]
2. Let's go inside. It is freezing out here. [　　]
3. Look at the cat. It is so cute. [　　]
4. It is hot and humid in summer. [　　]
5. I love autumn. It is a beautiful season. [　　]
6. How far is it to the station? [　　]
7. It is already eight o'clock. We should hurry. [　　]
8. Don't blame yourself. It was not your fault. [　　]

PSS 2-2 it의 특별 용법

1. It seems that ~ '~ 인 것 같다'

   It seems that you are a little tired. 너 약간 피곤한 것 같다. = You **seem to** be a little tired.
   It seemed that she had a cold. 그녀는 감기에 걸린 것 같았다. = She **seemed to** have a cold.

2. 「It is[was] ~ that ....」 강조구문 – 강조하고자 하는 말을 It is[was]와 that 사이에 쓴다. 단, 동사와 형용사는 It is[was]와 that 사이에 쓸 수 없다.

   It is a new laptop **that** we need to buy. 우리가 사야 할 것은 새 노트북 컴퓨터이다.
   It was under the bed **that** I found my socks. 내가 내 양말을 찾은 곳은 침대 밑이었다.

정답 p.32

PRACTICE 7

다음 문장을 It을 주어로 하는 문장으로 바꿔 쓰세요.

1 You seem to be upset about what happened.
   ➡ _____

2 My sister seems to have a plan to stay at Sumi's for a while.
   ➡ _____

3 You seemed to be very confident when you made a speech.
   ➡ _____

4 They always seem to live in a fantasy world.
   ➡ _____

5 She seems to walk like a professional model.
   ➡ _____

6 You seemed to be satisfied with your decision.
   ➡ _____

7 He seems to know what he is doing now.
   ➡ _____

8 They seemed to sit very close to each other.
   ➡ _____

PRACTICE 8

다음 문장을 It ~that 강조구문으로 바꿔 쓰세요.

1 I saw Minji's brother at the theater yesterday. (Minji's brother 강조)
➡ _____

2 I met Sumin at the amusement park a week ago. (a week ago 강조)
➡ _____

3 My uncle was seriously injured in the car accident. (my uncle 강조)
➡ _____

4 I'm going to meet the children at the bus stop this Sunday. (at the bus stop 강조)
➡ _____

5 We were supposed to meet in front of the statue at five. (at five 강조)
➡ _____

PSS 2-3 가주어 it / 가목적어 it

1. **가주어 it** – 문장에서 주어로 쓰인 부정사(구), 동명사(구), 명사절의 길이가 길 때는, 이들을 뒤로 보내고 원래의 주어 자리에는 가주어 it을 쓴다. 이때 원래의 주어인 부정사(구), 동명사(구), 명사절은 진주어라고 한다.

   It is very important **to have breakfast**. 아침식사를 하는 것은 매우 중요하다.
   가주어   진주어

   It is interesting **teaching kids**. 아이들을 가르치는 것은 재미있다.
   가주어   진주어

   It is surprising **that Mina left Korea**. 미나가 한국을 떠났다는 것은 놀랍다.
   가주어   진주어

2. **가목적어 it** – 문장에서 목적어로 쓰인 부정사(구), 동명사(구), 명사절의 길이가 길 때는, 이들을 뒤로 보내고 원래의 목적어 자리에는 가목적어 it을 쓴다. 이때 원래의 목적어는 진목적어라고 한다.

   I found **it** exciting **to ride a roller coaster**. 나는 롤러코스터를 타는 것이 신난다는 것을 알았다.
   가목적어   진목적어

PRACTICE 9

우리말과 일치하도록 주어진 단어를 바르게 배열하세요.

1 병을 재활용하는 것은 중요하다. (the bottles, it, to, recycle, important, is)
➡ _____

2 공상 과학 소설을 읽는 것은 매우 흥미롭다. (very, science fiction, it, exciting, reading, is)
→ _____

3 나는 네가 그렇게 말하는 것이 이상하다고 생각했다. (that, so, I, it, strange, you, thought, said)
→ _____

4 네가 또 거짓말을 했다는 것은 실망스럽다. (you, again, is, that, disappointing, it, lied)
→ _____

5 나는 매일 새로운 단어를 외우는 것이 어렵다는 것을 알았다.
(it, memorize, every day, I, difficult, found, new words, to)
→ _____

6 우리 팀이 경기에서 이겼다는 것은 나를 행복하게 했다.
(won, that, made, it, happy, me, the game, our team)
→ _____

7 팀을 위해 경기하는 것이 중요하다. (to, the team, important, it, for, is, play)
→ _____

8 그가 위기 상황에서도 평정을 유지하다니 놀랍다. (a crisis, he, keep, amazing, it, cool, that, in, can, is)
→ _____

지시대명사

PSS 3-1 this, that

this/these	that/those
가까이에 있는 사람이나 사물을 나타낸다.	멀리 떨어져 있는 사람이나 사물을 나타낸다.
This is my friend, Paul. 이 사람은 내 친구인 Paul이야. **These** are my friends, Paul and Jane. 이 사람들은 내 친구들인 Paul과 Jane이야.	**That** is my friend, Paul. 저 사람은 내 친구인 Paul이야. **Those** are my friends, Paul and Jane. 저 사람들은 내 친구들인 Paul과 Jane이야.
cf. 지시형용사로서 명사를 수식할 수도 있다. **This book** is my brother's. 이 책은 내 형의 것이다. **These pants** are my brother's. 이 바지는 내 형의 것이다.	*cf.* 지시형용사로서 명사를 수식할 수도 있다. **That book** is my brother's. 저 책은 내 형의 것이다. **Those pants** are my brother's. 저 바지는 내 형의 것이다.

this	that
전화상에서 전화를 건 사람과 받는 사람을 가리킨다. Hello, **this** is Minsu. 여보세요, 저는 민수예요. Is **this** Sujin? 수진이니?	전화상에서 전화를 받는 사람을 가리킨다. Is **that** Mr. Jones? Jones 씨이십니까?

PRACTICE 10

정답 p.33

그림을 보고, this나 these, that이나 those를 이용하여 빈칸에 알맞은 말을 쓰세요.

1 _____ _____ your pen, Inho?

2 _____ _____ is very expensive.

3 _____ _____ are Paul's sisters.

4 Hello, _____ is Mary.

5 How high are _____ _____?

6 _____ is Ms. Kim.

7
_____ are mine.

8
_____ are Tony's cats.

PSS 3-2 that/those의 특별 용법

1. 앞에 나오는 명사의 반복을 피하기 위해 쓴다. 앞에 나오는 명사가 단수면 that, 복수면 those를 쓴다.

   The temperature of Jejudo is higher than **that** of Incheon.
   제주도의 기온은 인천의 그것보다 더 높다.   (= the temperature)
   Chinese **customs** are very different from **those** of Australia.
   중국의 관습은 호주의 그것과 매우 다르다.   (= customs)

2. those는 who와 함께 쓰여 '~하는 사람들'의 의미를 갖는다.

   Heaven helps **those who** help themselves. 하늘은 스스로를 돕는 자를 돕는다.
   Those who want to meet Dr. Park should usually wait for 30 minutes.
   박 박사님을 만나기를 원하는 사람들은 보통 30분을 기다려야 한다.

정답 p.33

PRACTICE 11

다음 문장의 빈칸에 that이나 those 중 알맞은 것을 쓰세요.

1 The population of Japan is larger than _____ of Korea.
2 I love _____ who love me, and _____ who seek me diligently will find me.
3 Giho's shoes are bigger than _____ of Minsu.
4 My living room is smaller than _____ of Yumi.
5 The buildings of this city are older than _____ of Seoul.
6 _____ who work hard often succeed in life.
7 The price of your jacket is twice as high as _____ of my jacket.

8 The employees of this year work better than _____ of last year.

9 My brother is one of _____ who love peace.

10 My vacation is shorter than _____ of my sister.

 부정대명사

PSS 4-1 one

1. 앞에 나온 명사와 종류는 같지만 대상이 다른 경우에 명사의 반복을 피하기 위해 one을 쓴다.

   cf. it은 특정한 것을 가리킬 때 쓴다.

   A: Would you like to have a hamburger?
   　햄버거 먹을래?
   B: No, thanks. I already had **one**.
   　고맙지만, 괜찮아. 난 이미 먹었어.
   햄버거를 의미하지만, 앞에서 A가 권한 햄버거를 가리키는 것은 아니므로 one을 쓴다.

   A: Where did you find the ring?
   　너는 그 반지를 어디서 찾았니?
   B: I found **it** under the bed.
   　나는 그것을 침대 밑에서 찾았어.
   앞에서 A가 언급한 그 반지(the ring)를 가리키므로 one이 아닌 it을 쓴다.

2. 명사가 복수형일 때는 ones를 쓴다.

   Are these your shoes? – No, the brown **ones** are mine.
   이것들은 네 신발이니?　　아니, 갈색 신발이 내 거야.

   cf. 명사가 복수형이고 앞에서 언급한 명사와 동일한 대상을 지칭할 때는 they[them]를 쓴다.
   Did you get my letters? – Yes, **they** arrived yesterday.
   내 편지들을 받았니?　　응, 그것들은 어제 도착했어.

3. 일반적인 사람들을 나타낸다.

   One should follow the traffic rules. 사람들은 교통 규칙을 따라야 한다.

PRACTICE 12

〈보기〉에서 알맞은 단어를 골라 빈칸에 쓰세요.

보 기	one　ones　it　them

1   Did you see my cell phone? – No, I didn't see _____.

2   They have only yellow flowers. I need pink _____.

3   Katie gave me a small balloon, but I wanted a big _____.

4   I made three resolutions. Would you like to hear _____?

5   _____ usually finds that friendship is very important.

6   I need an eraser. Do you have _____?

7   Alice bought a book and gave _____ to me.

8   Jane really likes those blue jeans. She will buy _____.

9   Ted has a nice bicycle. I have _____, too.

10 Are these pens yours? – No, mine are the _____ on the desk.

11 We have a dog and a cat. I wash _____ twice a week.

12 _____ should save energy for the future.

13 Robert took the papers and threw _____ away.

14 Here is your cap. – Where did you find _____?

15 Who are Denny's children? – The smiling _____ in the front row.

16 Those sneakers don't look very nice. – How about buying these white _____ instead?

17 We stayed at a famous hotel on Jeju Island, but _____ wasn't worth the money.

PSS 4-2　other, another

1. **others** '(불특정한) 다른 사람[것]들'

    Ann always tries to help **others**. Ann은 항상 다른 사람들을 도와주려고 한다.

2. **the other** '(둘 중) 다른 하나'

    I gave my son this one, but he wanted **the other**.
    나는 나의 아들에게 (둘 중) 이것을 주었지만, 그는 (남은) 다른 것을 원했다.

3. **the others** '(나머지) 다른 사람[것]들'

   I don't like these. Can I have **the others**?
   저는 이것들이 마음에 들지 않아요. (남은) 다른 것들을 가져도 될까요?

4. **another** '또 하나'

   This apple tastes good. Can I have **another**? 이 사과는 맛이 좋군요. 하나 더 먹어도 될까요?

   cf. other는 「other+복수 명사」의 형태로 쓰이며, 이 때의 other는 '다른, 그 밖의'라는 뜻이다. 반면 another는 「another+단수 명사」의 형태로 쓰이며, 이 때의 another는 '또 하나의, 또 다른'이라는 뜻이다.
   Can I ask you **other** questions? 다른 질문들을 해도 될까요?
   Can I ask you **another** question? 또 다른 질문을 해도 될까요?

PRACTICE 13

정답 p.33

괄호 안에 주어진 말 중 알맞은 것을 고르세요.

1 Please, show me (another, other).

2 One of the twins is my friend. (The other, Others) is a friend of my brother's.

3 They gave me (other, another) chance.

4 Do you have any (other, another) books?

5 We should be kind to (another, others).

6 Here are two cats. One is mine and (the other, another) is his.

7 I saw only Alex and Becky. Where are (the other, the others)?

8 I bought four bottles. Two of them are red. (The others, Others) are yellow.

9 Don't care too much about what (others, the other) say about it.

10 Sally entered the room, and (other, another) girls followed her.

11 Some (other, the other) people already took good seats.

12 I've still got a headache. I need (other, another) aspirin.

13 You should keep quiet in the library for (others, another).

14 The bakery is on (another, the other) side of the street.

15 This is my favorite kind of cookie. Can I have (other, another)?

16 You shouldn't talk like that to (the other, others).

PSS 4-3 관용 표현

one ~ the other …
(둘 중에) 하나는 ~, 다른 하나는 …

There are **two men** here. **One** is from Korea, and **the other** is from Canada.

여기에 두 명의 남자들이 있다. 한 명은 한국 출신이고, 다른 한 명은 캐나다 출신이다.

one ~ another … the other −
(셋 중에) 하나는 ~, 다른 하나는 …, 나머지 하나는 −

There are **three men** here. **One** is from Korea, **another** is from Canada and **the other** is from Japan.

여기에 세 명의 남자들이 있다. 한 명은 한국 출신이고, 다른 한 명은 캐나다 출신이고, 나머지 한 명은 일본 출신이다.

some ~ others …
(불특정한 수의 사람[것]들 중에서)
몇몇은 ~, 다른 사람[것]들은 …

There are **a lot of students** in this room. **Some** are wearing glasses, and **others** aren't.

이 방에는 많은 학생들이 있다. 몇몇은 안경을 쓰고 있고, 다른 학생들은 쓰고 있지 않다.

some ~ the others …
(특정한 수의 사람[것]들 중에서)
몇몇은 ~, 나머지는 …

There are **ten students** in this room. **Some** are wearing glasses, and **the others** aren't.

이 방에는 10명의 학생들이 있다. 몇몇은 안경을 쓰고 있고, 나머지는 쓰고 있지 않다.

cf. the가 붙으면 '나머지, 전부'의 의미가 더해진다.

PRACTICE 14

〈보기〉에서 알맞은 말을 골라 빈칸에 쓰세요.

보기	one some the other others the others another

1 Mary has two cups. One is big, and _____ is small.

2 Some like pets, but _____ don't like them.

3 I invited ten people to my birthday party. Some came, but _____ didn't.

4 There are three tables. One is white, another is brown, and _____ is black.

5 Look at the two birds. _____ is small, and _____ is big.

6 John has five sons. _____ like baseball, and _____ like soccer.

7 Do you see the three men there? One is tall. _____ is short. _____ is thin.

8 Some believe in God while _____ don't believe at all.

9 I have two sweaters. _____ is blue, and _____ is red.

10 Some people go jogging in the morning, and _____ go jogging at night.

11 Mr. Hong has three children. _____ is Gildong, another is Sumi, and _____ is Bora.

12 There are a lot of people in the airport. _____ are Koreans, and _____ are Americans.

13 Three people applied for the job. _____ majored in History, _____ majored in Philosophy, and the other majored in English Literature.

14 Helen has two brothers. _____ is 23 years old, and _____ is 20 years old.

15 There are a dozen pens. _____ are black, and _____ are red.

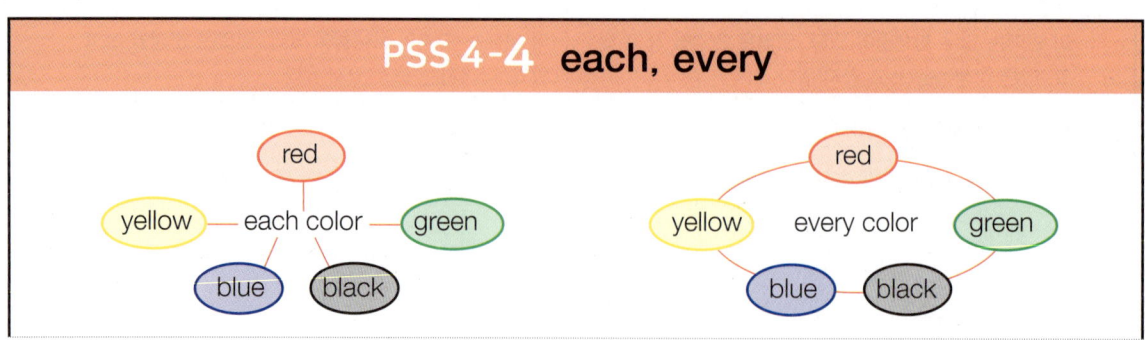

PSS 4-4 each, every

1. each – '각자, 각기, 각각의' 의 뜻으로 명사를 수식하고 단수 취급한다.

   ① each+단수 명사+단수 동사
      Each participant has to tell one story. 각각의 참가자는 한 가지의 이야기를 말해야 한다.

   ② each of+복수 명사+단수 동사 – each 뒤에 of가 올 때는 명사 앞에 관사나 소유격 등의 수식어가 붙는다.
      Each of the girls is from a different country. 그 소녀들 각각은 다른 나라 출신이다.

2. every – '모든' 의 뜻으로 명사를 수식하고 단수 취급한다.

   ① every+단수 명사+단수 동사
      Every kid was excited to see the dolphin show. 모든 어린이들은 돌고래 쇼를 보고 흥분했다.

   ② '~마다, 매 ~'
      My brother and I go to the beach **every summer**. 나의 형과 나는 여름마다 그 해변에 간다.

   cf. every는 not과 같은 부정어와 함께 쓰이면 일부를 부정하는 부분 부정이 된다.
      Not every man likes playing soccer. 모든 남자들이 축구를 좋아하는 것은 아니다.

PRACTICE 15

우리말과 일치하도록 괄호 안에 주어진 단어를 바르게 배열하세요.

1 그 꽃들 각각은 다른 색을 가지고 있다.
   (each, a, different color, of the flowers, has)
   ➡ _____

2 김 선생님은 지난 밤 모든 학생들에게 전화를 했다.
   (every student, Mr. Kim, called, last night)
   ➡ _____

3 각각의 테이블은 녹색 천으로 덮여 있다.
   (each table, covered, is, green cloth, with)
   ➡ _____

4 나는 매주 일요일마다 할머니 댁에 가곤 했다.
   (every Sunday, I, go to my grandmother's house, used to)
   ➡ _____

5 각각의 선수들은 빨간색 바지를 입고 있다.
   (each player, is, red pants, wearing)
   ➡ _____

6 이 방에 있는 모든 책들이 다 정치학에 관한 것은 아니다.
   (every book, is, about politics, in this room, not)
   ➡ _____

PSS 4-5 all, both, rest

1. **all** – '모든, ~ 모두'의 뜻으로, all 뒤에 of가 올 때는 명사 앞에 관사나 소유격 등의 수식어가 붙는다.

   ① all+셀 수 있는 명사의 복수형+복수 동사
      All passengers are sleeping in the bus. 모든 승객들이 버스에서 잠을 자고 있다.

   ② all (of)+셀 수 있는 명사의 복수형+복수 동사
      All (of) the passengers are sleeping in the bus. 승객들 모두가 버스에서 잠을 자고 있다.

   ③ all (of)+셀 수 없는 명사+단수 동사
      All (of) her money is stolen. 그녀의 돈 전부가 도난 당했다.

2. **both** – '양쪽, ~ 둘 다'의 뜻으로 both 뒤에 of가 올 때는 명사 앞에 관사나 소유격 등의 수식어가 붙는다.

   ① both+셀 수 있는 명사의 복수형+복수 동사
      Both dictionaries are very old. 양쪽 사전 다 매우 낡았다.

   ② both (of)+셀 수 있는 명사의 복수형+복수 동사
      Both (of) the dictionaries are very old. 그 사전들 둘 다 매우 낡았다.

   cf. all과 both는 not과 같은 부정어와 함께 쓰이면 일부를 부정하는 부분 부정이 된다.
      Not all the information is useful. 모든 정보가 유용한 것은 아니다.
      I **don't** know **both** of them. 나는 두 사람 다 아는 것은 아니다.

3. **rest** – '나머지'의 뜻으로 정관사 the와 함께 쓰이며, 뒤에 of가 올 때는 명사 앞에 관사나 소유격 등의 수식어가 붙는다.

   ① the rest of +셀 수 있는 명사의 복수형+복수 동사
      The rest of the actors are working through the whole night.
      나머지 배우들이 밤새 작업을 하고 있다.

   ② the rest of+셀 수 없는 명사+단수 동사
      The rest of my life is going to be much brighter than it was before.
      내 남은 인생은 이전보다 훨씬 더 희망적일 것이다.

   cf. the rest 단독으로 '나머지 것들, 나머지 사람들'의 복수의 의미로 쓰인다.
      The first two questions were difficult, but **the rest were** pretty easy.
      처음 두 문제는 어려웠지만 나머지는 꽤 쉬웠다.

PRACTICE 16

우리말과 일치하도록 괄호 안에 주어진 단어를 바르게 배열하세요.

1. 너는 이 방에 있는 책 모두를 읽어야 한다.
   (all the books, in this room, you, should, read)
   ➡ _____

2. Ford 부인이 내 생일 선물로 그 접시들 모두를 내게 주었다.
   (all of those dishes, Ms. Ford, for my birthday present, gave, me)
   ➡ _____

3. 그녀는 네게 모든 정보를 말해줄 것이다.
   (all of the information, she, you, is going to, tell)
   ➡ _____

4. 나는 두 친구 모두를 내 공연에 초대할 거야.
   (both friends, will, I, to my performance, invite)
   ➡ _____

5. 그 시험 둘 다 내게 매우 어려웠다.
   (both of the tests, for me, were, very difficult)
   ➡ _____

6. 그는 그 규칙들을 둘 다 지키지는 않았다.
   (both of the rules, didn't, he, follow)
   ➡ _____

7. 그녀는 식탁 위에 있던 나머지 케이크를 먹었다.
   (ate, on the table, she, the cake, the rest of)
   ➡ _____

8. 너희들 나머지는 지금 집에 가도 좋다.
   (may, home, the rest, go, you, of, now)
   ➡ _____

9. 나머지 승무원들이 불타는 배에서 구조되었다.
   (rescued, from, the crew, the rest of, were, the burning ship)
   ➡ _____

10. 모든 참가자들은 종이 울렸을 때 피곤해 보였다.
    (looked, rang, when, the participants, tired, all of, the bell)
    ➡ _____

11. 모든 사람들이 그 변화에 만족하는 것은 아니다.
    (the changes, are, not, all people, happy with)
    ➡ _____

CHAPTER 6 _ 대명사

PRACTICE 17

괄호 안에 주어진 말 중 알맞은 것을 고르세요.

1. Each (worker, workers) has his own desk.
2. All of (the taxis, taxis) were taken.
3. Both (parent, parents) were cooking in the kitchen.
4. Jack studies for a master's degree every (night, nights).
5. (Do, Does) each girl know the truth?
6. All of my cheese (was, were) gone all of a sudden.
7. I drink a cup of milk every (morning, mornings).
8. Both of (the restaurants, restaurants) are very nice.
9. You should say each of (the word, those words) correctly.
10. Mr. Lee talked to every (parent, parents) in the room.
11. All the guests (is, are) waiting for you.
12. Each of them (has, have) a different answer.
13. The rest of the employees (have to, has to) work in their office.
14. Here (is, are) the rest of your change.
15. (The rest of, Both of) your money was used to buy eggs at the grocery.
16. Both of us (is, are) quite shy.
17. You should always look both (way, ways) before crossing.
18. All of the furniture there (was, were) made in China.
19. Every (minute, minutes) feels like an hour.
20. Only two of the hats are my brother's, and the rest (is, are) mine.

PSS 4-6 some-, any-

somebody, someone, something

1. 긍정문에 쓰인다.

   I want to ask **somebody** about it. 나는 그것에 대해 누군가에게 물어보고 싶다.

2. 권유나 요구를 나타내는 의문문에 쓰인다.

   Can you do **something** for me? 날 위해 무언가를 해줄 수 있니?

3. 긍정의 대답을 예상하는 의문문에 쓰인다.

   Did **someone** call my name? 누군가 내 이름 불렀니?

---

anybody, anyone, anything

1. 부정문에 쓰인다.

   Jenny didn't eat **anything**. Jenny는 아무것도 먹지 않았다.

2. 의문문에 쓰인다.

   Does **anybody** have a dictionary? 누구 사전 가지고 있는 사람 있니?

3. '어떠한 ~라도'의 뜻일 때는 긍정문에도 쓸 수 있다.

   I can do **anything** for you. 난 널 위해 어떠한 것이라도 할 수 있어.

4. 조건을 나타내는 if절에 쓸 수 있다.

   If you know **anyone** to help them, please let me know.
   만약 당신이 그들을 도와줄 누군가를 안다면, 제게 알려주세요.

PRACTICE 18

정답 p.35

주어진 우리말에 유의하여 밑줄 친 부분을 올바르게 고치세요. (단, 틀린 부분이 없다면 ○표를 쓸 것)

1 당신이 나가 있던 동안에 누군가 전화했어요.
   <u>Anyone</u> called while you were out. ➡ _____

2 저를 도와줄 누군가가 필요해요.
   I need <u>anyone</u> to help me. ➡ _____

3 어떤 것이라도 말할 것이 있다면, 어서 하세요.
   If you have <u>anything</u> to say, go ahead. ➡ _____

4 그녀는 그 밖의 다른 것을 사길 원한다.
   She wants to buy <u>anything</u> else. ➡ _____

5 Is <u>anyone</u> interested in my suggestion?
   제 제안에 관심 있으신 분이 계신가요? ➡ _____

6 경찰은 그녀에게서 아무런 혐의점도 찾을 수 없었다.
The police couldn't find something suspicious about her. ➡ _____

7 어떤 사람이라도 우리 파티에 와서 참여할 수 있다.
Someone can come and join our party. ➡ _____

8 뭔가 마실 것을 원하세요?
Would you like something to drink? ➡ _____

9 Eddie는 돈이 거의 없었기 때문에 아무것도 살 수 없었다.
Eddie couldn't buy something because he had little money. ➡ _____

10 어젯밤 무슨 일이 발생했고, 당신은 그것에 대해 알아야 한다.
Anything happened last night and you should know about it. ➡ _____

11 오늘 아침에 누군가 당신을 만나러 왔어요.
Anybody came to see you this morning. ➡ _____

12 당신은 시장에서 뭔가를 구입했나요?
Did you buy anything at the market? ➡ _____

PSS 5 의문대명사

PSS 5-1 who

who는 사람을 가리킬 때 쓴다.

who	주격	**Who** broke the window? – Minho did. 누가 창문을 깨뜨렸니? 민호가 그랬어.
whose	소유격	**Whose** bag is this? – It's Ann's. 이것은 누구의 가방이니? Ann의 것이야. = **Whose** is this bag? 이 가방은 누구의 것이니?
who(m)	목적격	**Who(m)** did you write to? 누구에게 편지를 썼니? = **To whom** did you write? *cf.* 전치사를 의문대명사 앞으로 보낼 경우에는 who를 쓸 수 없다.

PRACTICE 19

괄호 안에 주어진 단어 중 알맞은 것을 고르세요.

1 (Who, Whom) will come with me?
2 (Who, Whose) pens are these?
3 To (whose, whom) are you talking?
4 (Who, Whom) dropped by your house last night?
5 For (who, whom) does he work?
6 (Whose, Whom) name did you forget?
7 (Who, Whom) does not agree with this decision?
8 (Who, Whose) is that car over there?
9 (Whose, Whom) bag did you carry?
10 With (whom, who) are you going there?

PSS 5-2 which, what

which	사람이나 동물, 사물을 가리킬 때 쓴다. 주로 A or B와 같이 구체적인 선택의 범위가 주어진다. **Which** is bigger, Busan **or** Seoul? 부산과 서울 중 어디가 더 크니? **Which** do you like better, coffee **or** tea? 너는 커피와 차 중 어떤 것을 더 좋아하니? *cf.* 명사를 수식하는 의문형용사로도 쓰인다. 　　**Which bag** is yours? 어느 가방이 너의 것이니?
what	동물이나 사물, 그리고 사람의 직업이나 신분을 나타낼 때 쓴다. **What** will you buy? – I'll buy a pair of jeans. 너는 무엇을 살 거니?　나는 청바지 한 벌을 살 거야. **What** is his name? – His name is Dan. 그의 이름은 무엇이니?　그의 이름은 Dan이야. *cf.* 명사를 수식하는 의문형용사로도 쓰인다. 　　**What color** do you like best? 너는 어떤 색깔을 가장 좋아하니?

PRACTICE 20

괄호 안에 주어진 단어 중 알맞은 것을 고르세요.

1. (What, Which) does your father do?
2. (What, Which) book of these two did you borrow?
3. (What, Whom) did the director try to talk to?
4. (Which, What) kind of movies are popular in Korea?
5. (What, Which) is special about January 26th?
6. (What, Which) is your brother among these boys?
7. (Whose, Which) is this jacket? I found it under the table.
8. (What, Which) are cheaper, the apples or the oranges?
9. (What, Which) part do you mean, Part 1 or Part 2?
10. (What, Which) did the man say to you?

PRACTICE 21

우리말과 일치하도록 괄호 안에 주어진 단어를 바르게 배열하세요.

1. 너는 어느 좌석을 원하니?
   (seat, you, which, want, do)?
   ➡ _____

2. 너는 내일 어떤 계획이 있니?
   (do, what, you, plans, have, tomorrow)?
   ➡ _____

3. Cathy는 어느 음식을 좋아하니?
   (food, Cathy, does, which, like)?
   ➡ _____

4. 그는 어떤 나라를 방문하길 원하니?
   (to visit, does, want, what, countries, he)?
   ➡ _____

5. 네 방에 어느 벽지가 좋을까?
   (is, your room, for, wallpaper, which, good)?
   ➡ _____

Chapter Review Test

CHAPTER 6 대명사

정답 p.35

1 다음 글의 (A) ~ (C)에 알맞은 말끼리 바르게 연결된 것은?

> Carl Edward Sagan (A) was / were an American astronomer and author. He is known for (B) he's / his popular science book, *Cosmos*. (C) It / They was published in 1980.
> *astronomer: 천문학자

	(A)	(B)	(C)
①	was	he's	It
②	were	his	They
③	was	his	It
④	were	he's	They
⑤	was	he's	They

2 다음 밑줄 친 himself와 용법이 같은 것은?

> He introduced himself in English.

① Why don't we try it ourselves?
② She painted the wall herself.
③ My father himself designed this house.
④ I looked at myself for a long time.
⑤ The members of this club made the logo themselves.

3 다음 밑줄 친 It과 쓰임이 같은 것은?

> It is still cold out there.

① It is in the closet.
② It is summer now.
③ She wanted to buy it.
④ It was full of treasures.
⑤ I'll check it for you.

4 다음 빈칸에 들어갈 말로 알맞은 것은?

> • 또 다른 예를 들어보시겠어요?
> = Can you give me _____ example?

① other   ② others   ③ the others
④ some   ⑤ another

5 다음 중 밑줄 친 부분을 생략할 수 있는 것은?

① You have to do that yourself.
② She always thinks of herself.
③ He said to himself, "Shall I try?"
④ I prepared breakfast by myself.
⑤ I solved the problem for myself.

6 다음 빈칸에 들어갈 말로 알맞은 것은?

> They did _____ best to save the people in the building.

① their   ② them   ③ theirs
④ they   ⑤ those

9 어법상 잘못 쓰인 부분을 <u>2개</u> 찾아 바르게 고쳐 쓰세요.

> Laura and I has umbrellas. This yellow one is mine and that red one is her. However, I like the red one better than the yellow one.

(1) _____ ➡ _____
(2) _____ ➡ _____

7 다음 중 어법상 잘못된 문장은?

① It's not for sale.
② We arrived in Busan around 3 p.m.
③ I am going to go to France.
④ Each of the girls have her own desk.
⑤ All the seats are taken.

10 다음 대화의 밑줄 친 우리말을 영어로 쓰세요.

> A: Do you have any special plans for summer vacation?
> B: Yes, I visit my grandfather in Paris <u>여름마다</u>.
> A: Wow, sounds nice.

➡ _____

8 다음 밑줄 친 alone과 바꿔 쓸 수 있는 것은?

> A: Can I help you?
> B: No, thanks. I prefer to do everything <u>alone</u>.

① by myself   ② of itself
③ in itself   ④ beside myself
⑤ to myself

11 다음 빈칸에 알맞은 말끼리 짝지어진 것은?

> Look at _____ pictures over there. _____ are my drawings.

① those – That
② this – That
③ that – This
④ those – Those
⑤ this – Those

12 다음 중 밑줄 친 It[it]의 용법이 나머지와 다른 하나는?

① Is it really spicy?
② It is Friday.
③ Is it snowing now?
④ What time is it in Seoul?
⑤ It takes five minutes by bus.

13 다음 빈칸에 알맞은 말끼리 바르게 짝지어진 것은?

> She has two cats. _____ is white and _____ is brown.

① One – two
② One – the other
③ One – others
④ Other – the other
⑤ Other – others

14 다음 대화의 빈칸에 들어갈 알맞은 의문사는?

> A: With _____ should I talk about this?
> B: I think you should talk with Dr. Kim.

① who ② whom ③ what
④ which ⑤ whose

15 다음 중 밑줄 친 부분이 바르게 쓰인 것은?

① He came back to his' house.
② How do astronauts wash himself in space?
③ Three days later, her got a bill from the dentist.
④ All the neighbors liked herself a lot.
⑤ Please take good care of yourself.

16 다음 대화의 빈칸에 들어갈 말로 알맞은 것은?

> A: We're going shopping now. Do you want to join us?
> B: Sorry, but I have _____ else to do now. I'll go with you next time.

① something ② anything
③ everything ④ thing
⑤ things

17 다음 빈칸에 알맞은 말끼리 짝지어진 것은?

> There are three flowers. One of them is a rose. _____ is a lily and _____ is a sunflower.

① Other – the other
② Other – another
③ The other – the third
④ Another – the other
⑤ Another – the others

18 다음 중 대화의 흐름이 어색한 것은?

① A: Did you get the postcard he sent from Paris?
   B: Yes! It was so pretty and unique.
② A: Who made these beautiful dishes?
   B: My mom made them herself.
③ A: Anyone came to see you this afternoon.
   B: Really? Who was it?
④ A: How far is it to your school?
   B: It's about half a kilometer from here.
⑤ A: Is this bottle yours?
   B: No, the black one on the table is mine.

19 다음 빈칸에 알맞은 말끼리 짝지어진 것은?

- _____ food do you like better, Korean or Chinese?
  – I like Chinese food better.
- _____ do you think of Mr. Lee?
  – I think he's very nice.

① Which – When   ② What – Why
③ Which – What   ④ What – What
⑤ Which – Why

20 다음 밑줄 친 It과 쓰임이 같은 것은?

It is interesting to learn about new cultures.

① It is going to rain tonight.
② It is very hot today.
③ It is on the table in the kitchen.
④ It is one kilometer to the office.
⑤ It is not easy to speak English fluently.

21 다음 글의 빈칸에 들어갈 말로 알맞은 것은?

I dropped my phone the other day. The screen was totally broken. So, I decided to buy a new phone. I have two options. One is an Android phone, and _____ is an iOS phone.

① one   ② some   ③ others
④ the other   ⑤ the others

22 다음 중 밑줄 친 부분의 쓰임이 다른 하나는?

① Who's calling, please?
② He asked me who bought the book.
③ Do you know who the woman is?
④ There were many people who were sleeping.
⑤ Who will be the winner of this race?

23 밑줄 친 부분을 바르게 고친 것 중 잘못된 것을 고르시오.

① I lost my bag but I found one (→ it) yesterday.
② These who (→ Those who) are sitting there are waiting for the bus.
③ The climate of the U.S. is milder than this of (→ these of) Canada.
④ There are three girls. One is Susan, other (→ another) is Margaret and the other is Kate.
⑤ We have a lot of pollution in the city those days (→ these days).

24 다음 빈칸 (A)~(C)에 들어갈 말로 알맞은 것은?

Do you like exercising? ___(A)___ of you may, but ___(B)___ may not. People's opinions about exercising are very different. However, the fact that daily exercise helps improve your strength is clear. So, ___(C)___ who work out daily will be stronger than those who do not work out daily.

	(A)	(B)	(C)
①	One	other	they
②	Some	other	they
③	One	others	those
④	Some	others	those
⑤	Some	other	those

25 다음 빈칸에 공통으로 들어갈 한 단어를 쓰세요.

My family doesn't spend much time talking to each _____. In the evening, my children usually do their homework or play computer games. On the _____ hand, my husband and I read the newspaper or watch TV.

26 다음 밑줄 친 It[it]에 대한 설명으로 옳은 것은?

① It is June 19th. (인칭대명사)
② What a beautiful rock it is! (비인칭 주어)
③ It is difficult to make a website. (가주어)
④ How far is it from here to the station? (강조구문)
⑤ It is a new camera that I need to buy. (인칭대명사)

27 다음 밑줄 친 It과 쓰임이 같지 않은 것을 모두 고르세요.

It's very important to exercise every day.

① A: Where did you put the notebook?
   B: I put it on my desk.
② A: Hey, it's rude to stare at people.
   B: Oh, sorry.
③ A: Is it true that the boy is smart?
   B: No, it isn't.
④ A: How's the weather today?
   B: It's sunny. Let's go on a picnic.
⑤ A: What time is it?
   B: It's three o'clock.

28 다음 빈칸에 들어갈 수 없는 말은?

_____ doctors are worried about the spread of the disease.

① All the   ② Every   ③ Both of the
④ Some   ⑤ The rest of the

29 다음 밑줄 친 one의 쓰임이 나머지 넷과 다른 것은?

① I'd like an apple. Are you having one, too?
② My car broke down, so I got a new one.
③ She was wearing her new dress, the purple one.
④ He asked me where a pencil was. I told him there wasn't one.
⑤ He is the one person I can really trust.

30 다음 중 밑줄 친 부분의 쓰임이 어색한 것은?

① He bought a big car and I bought a small one.
② There were ten people in the gym. But now I can see only two. Where are others?
③ I saw a lot of entertainers. Some were kind. Others were not.
④ He has three shirts. One is red, another is blue, and the other is green.
⑤ I don't want this one. Show me another, please.

31 다음 빈칸에 들어갈 말끼리 바르게 짝지어진 것은?

> _____ think keeping a pet teaches us many things, but _____ think having a pet gives us a lot of hard work.

① Some – other
② Some – others
③ Some – the other
④ Other – others
⑤ Other – the other

32 다음 글에서 밑줄 친 that이 가리키는 두 단어를 찾아 쓰세요.

> Yesterday, we had the lowest temperature of this year. Many people say that they are afraid of going out these days, and they are worried about having an accident. The winter of this year is colder than that of last year.

➡ _____

33 다음 중 어법상 틀린 문장은?

① Not all of them are enjoying the party.
② Both of us were very tired after work.
③ I want to be with you for the rest of my life.
④ Both my sisters lived in Paris ten years ago.
⑤ All of my money were stolen last night.

34 다음 빈칸에 공통으로 들어갈 단어는?

> • The cookies are pretty big, not tiny _____.
> • Fix the blinds or buy new _____.
> • I want some gloves, some warm _____.

① them
② it
③ ones
④ others
⑤ the others

35 〈보기〉의 단어를 한 번씩 써서 빈칸을 채우세요.

보기	this that these those

(1) All the buildings built in _____ days were destroyed.

(2) We have mid-term exams _____ Friday.

(3) _____ are not mine. Those are mine.

(4) The population of China is much larger than _____ of Korea.

36 다음 빈칸에 들어갈 수 없는 단어를 고르세요.

- He burned _____.
  (그는 화상을 입었다.)
- My little daughter can't look after _____.
  (내 딸은 자기 자신을 돌볼 수 없다.)
- They set up their tents by _____.
  (그들은 스스로 텐트를 설치했다.)
- You should be proud of _____.
  (너는 너 자신을 자랑스럽게 생각해야 한다.)

① himself ② yourself ③ themselves
④ herself ⑤ itself

37 다음 밑줄 친 부분을 주어로 하여 문장을 다시 쓰세요.

It seems that <u>everyone</u> is thinking the same thing now.

➡ _____

38 다음 빈칸에 공통으로 들어갈 단어를 쓰세요.

- I don't live with my parents. I live by _____.
- I picked up a boiling teapot and burned _____.
- I was invited to the dinner party and I enjoyed _____.

39 밑줄 친 우리말과 같은 의미가 되도록 괄호 안에 주어진 단어들을 배열하세요.

A: Have you ever read *Snow White*?
B: Yes. <u>여왕이 거울로 자기 자신을 보곤 했잖아.</u>
A: She also asked the mirror who the most beautiful person in the world was.
B: Right. I remember it.

➡ _____
_____

(herself, in the mirror, the queen, look at, used to)

40 다음 괄호 안에 들어갈 말로 바르게 짝지어진 것은?

(A) There are two girls in the room. One is from Korea and (　　) is from Taiwan.
(B) I bought some books but I lost (　　).
(C) This is (　　) reason why I study very hard.

	(A)	(B)	(C)
①	the other	them	another
②	the other	them	other
③	the other	it	other
④	another	it	other
⑤	another	them	another

41 다음 대화의 빈칸에 들어갈 알맞은 단어는?

> A: _____ violin is this?
> B: It used to be mine, but it's my sister's now.

① Who   ② How   ③ Why
④ Whose   ⑤ Whom

42 다음 우리말 문장을 영어로 바르게 옮긴 것은?

> Ted는 혼자서 자기 프로젝트를 마칠 수가 없었다.

① Ted couldn't finished his project by him.
② Ted was able to finish his project by him.
③ Ted wasn't able to finish his project by himself.
④ Ted cannot able to finish his project by himself.
⑤ Ted could finished his project by himself.

43 다음 우리말과 뜻이 같도록 괄호 안에 주어진 말을 바르게 배열하세요.

> • 내가 어떤 동호회에 가입해야 할지를 결정하는 것은 쉽지 않다.

➡ _____
_____
(which club, to decide, easy, it, should, join, not, is, I)

[44 - 45] 다음 글을 읽고 물음에 답하세요.

> Most of the employees will be moved to the other parts of the company. More than half of the employees are satisfied with their new parts. However, the ⓐ <u>rest</u> of them didn't want to move their parts. I was one of ⓑ <u>those who</u> wanted not to move my part but I had to move my department.

44 윗글의 ⓐ와 같은 뜻으로 쓰인 것은?

① The doctor told me to <u>rest</u>.
② We wanted to stop for a <u>rest</u>.
③ <u>Rest</u> your head on my shoulder.
④ How would you like to spend the <u>rest</u> of the day?
⑤ The matter cannot <u>rest</u> there.

45 윗 글의 ⓑ를 바르게 해석한 것은?

① 저 사람들   ② ~한 사람들
③ 저것들   ④ ~한 것들
⑤ 해석할 필요 없음

46 〈보기〉에서 알맞은 단어를 골라 빈칸에 한 번씩 쓰세요.

보기	whose what which

(1) _____ jacket is cheaper?
(2) _____ happened to Paul?
(3) I like the story. _____ idea is it?

> ***cf.*** Suji **didn't** promise **to send** an email to John.
> 수지는 John에게 이메일을 보낼 것을 약속하지 않았다.

정답 p.38

PRACTICE 3

괄호 안의 단어를 알맞은 형태로 바꾸어 빈칸에 쓰세요.

1 I wish ____to lose____ weight. (lose)
2 I'd love _____ the artist now. (meet)
3 Yumi is planning _____ a diary in English. (keep)
4 He wants _____ the exam. (not, fail)
5 I hope _____ nature. (protect)
6 You need _____ something. (eat)
7 They decided _____ a garage sale. (not, have)
8 I learned _____ two years ago. (swim)
9 Mom expected _____ Ms. Smith at the party. (see)
10 I agree _____ about it again. (not, talk)
11 I'd like _____ a shower. (take)
12 He promised _____ my birthday. (not, forget)
13 Insu refused _____ Jina in the hospital. (visit)
14 We decided _____ a new bridge. (build)
15 I hope _____ my vacation at home. (not, spend)

PSS 1-3 목적격 보어로 쓰이는 to부정사

다음은 「동사＋목적어＋to부정사」의 형태로 자주 쓰이는 동사들이다.

> want   ask   tell   allow   would like   expect   order
> warn   advise   cause   enable   get

They **want me to become** a doctor. 그들은 내가 의사가 되기를 원한다.

4 To visit foreign countries is a lot of fun.
➡ _____

5 To watch English TV programs is helpful.
➡ _____

6 To spend so much time playing computer games is not good.
➡ _____

정답 p.37

PRACTICE 2

〈보기〉에서 알맞은 표현을 골라 to부정사의 형태로 바꾸어 빈칸에 쓰세요.

| 보 기 | jog every day | go to Europe | be a famous singer |
| | take care of patients | watch movies | see things clearly |

1 I love singing. My dream is _____ .

2 Mike has bad eyesight. His wish is _____ .

3 Jiyeon is a nurse. Her job is _____ .

4 Jenny likes movies. Her hobby is _____ .

5 Minho travels a lot. His plan for the next vacation is _____ .

6 I know a lot of good ways to exercise. One of the best ways is _____ .

PSS 1-2 목적어로 쓰이는 to부정사

1. 다음 동사들 뒤에 다른 동사가 목적어로 올 때, 목적어는 「to+동사원형」의 형태로 쓴다.

| want   wish   decide   promise   would like   would love |
| plan   expect   refuse   hope   need   learn   agree |
| afford   choose   offer   fail |

We **decided to take** a picture of him. 우리는 그의 사진을 찍기로 결정했다.
I**'d like to be** a musician. 나는 음악가가 되기를 원한다.
I'm **planning to go** to the party. 나는 그 파티에 갈 계획이다.

2. to부정사의 부정형은 「not to+동사원형」의 어순으로 쓴다.

Suji promised **not to send** an email to John.
수지는 John에게 이메일을 보내지 않을 것을 약속했다.

PSS 1　명사적 용법

PSS 1-1　주어와 주격 보어로 쓰이는 to부정사

1. 「to+동사원형」의 형태로 문장에서 명사, 형용사, 부사의 역할을 하는 것을 to부정사라고 한다.

   A: It's very difficult **to get** a good grade in major course.
   전공과목에서 좋은 성적을 받는 것은 매우 어려워.
   B: I know. My goal is **to get** an A.
   알아. 내 목표는 A를 받는 거야.

   cf. to부정사가 명사로 쓰일 때는 주어(~하는 것은), 목적어(~하는 것을), 보어(~하는 것이다)의 역할을 할 수 있다.

2. to부정사가 문장의 맨 앞에서 주어의 역할을 할 때는 it을 주어의 자리에 두고, to부정사는 문장의 뒤로 보낸 형태를 주로 쓴다. 이때의 it을 가주어, to부정사가 이끄는 구를 진주어라고 한다.

   To study foreign languages is not easy. 외국어를 공부하는 것은 쉽지 않다.
   = **It** is not easy **to study** foreign languages.
   　가주어　　　　　　　　　진주어

3. to부정사는 주어에 대한 설명을 보충하는 보어의 역할로도 쓰인다.

   The easiest way is **to take** the subway. 가장 쉬운 방법은 지하철을 타는 것이다.
   My dream is **to be** a lawyer. 내 꿈은 변호사가 되는 것이다.

PRACTICE 1

주어진 문장을 가주어 It으로 시작하는 문장으로 바꾸어 쓰세요.

1. To read a lot of books is important.
   ➡ _____

2. To go to a concert is exciting.
   ➡ _____

3. To make my dream come true was not easy.
   ➡ _____

CHAPTER 7
부정사

성취도 자기 평가 활용법

구분	평가 기준
Excellent	문법 내용을 모두 이해하고, 문제를 모두 맞힘.
Very good	문법 내용은 충분히 이해했으나 실수로 1~2문제 틀림.
Good	문법 내용이 조금 어려워 3~4문제 틀림.
needs **R**eview	문법 내용 이해가 어렵고, 5문제 이상 틀림. 복습 필요.

PSS 1 명사적 용법	페이지	학습날짜	성취도 자기평가 E V G R	학습체크
PSS 1-1 주어와 주격 보어로 쓰이는 to부정사	178	/		☐
PSS 1-2 목적어로 쓰이는 to부정사	179	/		☐
PSS 1-3 목적격 보어로 쓰이는 to부정사	180	/		☐
PSS 1-4 의문사+to부정사	182	/		☐
PSS 2 형용사적 용법	183	/		☐

PSS 3 부사적 용법	페이지	학습날짜	성취도 자기평가 E V G R	학습체크
PSS 3-1 목적을 나타내는 to부정사	184	/		☐
PSS 3-2 형용사 수식, 결과를 나타내는 to부정사	187	/		☐
PSS 4 to부정사의 의미상의 주어	188	/		☐
PSS 5 too ~ to, enough to	189	/		☐
PSS 6 원형부정사	191	/		☐
Chapter Review Test	193	/		☐

The doctor **told** me **to drink** lots of warm water.
의사는 나에게 따뜻한 물을 많이 마시라고 말했다.
I'd like you **to meet** my friend, Judy. 나는 네가 내 친구 Judy를 만났으면 해.

PRACTICE 4

정답 p.38

Tony와 Becky의 대화를 참고하여 문장을 완성하세요.

	Tony	Becky
1	I have a bad cold now.	Why don't you go and see a doctor?
2	Could you open the door?	Sure.
3	Do you have time to meet my parents?	No. I'm very busy.
4	Can you come to my place?	Sure. I'll be right there.
5	Could you clean the room?	No problem.
6	Did you call me yesterday?	Yes. Can you repair my car?
7	I finished my paper.	Good. You can go out to play.
8	Shut the door.	OK, I will.
9	Don't touch anything.	All right.
10	What should I do?	You'd better say sorry to your brother first.

1 Becky told _Tony to go and see a doctor_____.

2 Tony asked _____.

3 Tony would like _____.

4 Tony expects _____.

5 Tony wants _____.

6 Becky asks _____.

7 Becky allowed _____.

8 Tony ordered _____.

9 Tony warned _____.

10 Becky advised _____.

PSS 1-4 의문사+to부정사

다음 동사들 뒤에는 「의문사(how, what, where, when)+to부정사」의 형태가 올 수 있다.

> know   show   tell   talk about   learn   teach   explain

1. **how to**+동사원형 '어떻게 ~할지'

    I **learned how to make** a cake. 나는 케이크를 어떻게 만드는지를 배웠다.

2. **what to**+동사원형 '무엇을 ~할지'

    I don't **know what to do** for him. 나는 그를 위해 무엇을 해야 할지 모른다.

3. **where to**+동사원형 '어디서 ~할지'

    Bill didn't **tell** us **where to stay**. Bill은 우리에게 어디에서 머물지 말하지 않았다.

4. **when to**+동사원형 '언제 ~할지'

    The teacher **explained when to begin** the test. 선생님은 언제 그 시험을 시작할지 설명하셨다.
    cf. 「의문사+to부정사」는 「의문사+주어+should[can]+동사원형」으로 바꾸어 쓸 수 있다.
    She **showed** me **how to grow** vegetables.
    그녀는 내게 어떻게 채소를 재배하는지 보여주었다.
    = She **showed** me **how I should[can] grow** vegetables.

PRACTICE 5

정답 p.38

〈보기〉에서 알맞은 단어를 골라 빈칸에 「how/what+to부정사」 구문을 쓰세요.

보 기	help grow say read wear use solve buy

1 I learned _____how to read_____ French.

2 We talked about _____ the problem.

3 I explained _____ the elderly.

4 Did you choose _____ for the party?

5 She showed me _____ the machine.

6 I don't know _____ to her. She looks so sad.

7 He taught the students _____ crops.

8 I can't decide _____ for my mother's birthday present.

형용사적 용법

1. to부정사는 '~할'의 뜻으로 명사 또는 대명사를 뒤에서 꾸며주는 형용사의 역할을 한다.

   I have so many **friends to help** me. 나에게는 나를 도와줄 아주 많은 친구들이 있다.

2. something, anything, everything, nothing과 같은 대명사 뒤에 이들을 수식하는 형용사가 나오면 to부정사는 형용사 뒤에 위치한다.

   Do you have **something interesting to read**? 너에게는 흥미로운 읽을 것이 있니?

3. 「It's (about) time ~」은 '~할 시간이다'의 뜻으로 time 뒤에 동사가 올 때는 to부정사의 형태로 쓴다.

   It's time **to go** to bed. 잠자리에 들 시간이다.

정답 p.38

PRACTICE 6

우리말과 일치하도록 괄호 안에 주어진 단어를 바르게 배열하세요.

1 Bob에게는 그를 이해해줄 사람이 아무도 없다. (understand, no, one, to, him)
   ➡ Bob has _____.

2 너는 먹을 것을 원하니? (eat, to, something)
   ➡ Do you want _____?

3 나는 그에게 줄 돈이 하나도 없다. (give, money, no, to, him)
   ➡ I have _____.

4 당신은 저를 도와줄 충분한 시간이 있나요? (help, enough, to, time, me)
   ➡ Do you have _____?

5 Kevin은 차가운 마실 것을 원한다. (something, drink, to, cold)
   ➡ Kevin wants _____.

6 나는 사랑할 누군가가 필요해. (love, someone, to)
   ➡ I need _____.

7 살 것들이 많이 있다. (a lot of, buy, to, things)
   ➡ There are _____.

8 그녀는 생각할 충분한 시간을 가지고 있지 않다. (time, to, enough, think)
   ➡ She doesn't have _____.

9 이것이 그곳에 도착할 최선의 방법이다. (there, the, way, to, best, get)

➡ This is _____.

10 그녀는 세 가지 할 일이 있다. (three things, do, to)

➡ She has _____.

정답 p.38

PRACTICE 7

다음은 Bill의 하루 일과입니다. 각각의 시간에 해야 할 일이 무엇인지 쓰세요.

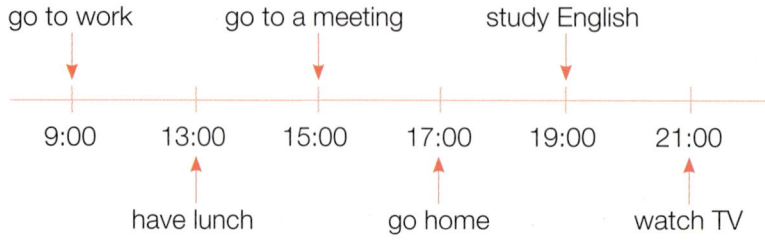

1 9 A.M. – It's time to go to work. _____

2 1 P.M. – _____

3 3 P.M. – _____

4 5 P.M. – _____

5 7 P.M. – _____

6 9 P.M. – _____

부사적 용법

PSS 3-1 목적을 나타내는 to부정사

1. to부정사가 '~하기 위해서'의 뜻으로 목적이나 의도를 나타낼 때는 in order to나 so as to로 바꾸어 쓸 수 있다.

   She went to Tokyo **to visit** her grandparents.
   그녀는 그녀의 조부모님을 방문하기 위해 도쿄에 갔다.
   = She went to Tokyo **in order to visit** her grandparents.
   = She went to Tokyo **so as to visit** her grandparents.

I got up early **to get** ready for the game. 나는 그 경기 준비를 하기 위해 일찍 일어났다.
= I got up early **in order to get** ready for the game.
= I got up early **so as to get** ready for the game.
cf. 「in order to(so as to)+동사원형」이 「to+동사원형」보다 좀 더 격식을 차린 표현이다.

2. '~하지 않기 위해서'는 「(in order/so as) not to+동사원형」으로 표현한다.

They always spoke quietly **(in order/so as) not to be** overheard by anyone.
그들은 아무도 엿듣지 못하도록 항상 조용히 말했다.
Watch your step **(in order/so as) not to slip**. 미끄러지지 않게 조심히 걸어라.

3. to부정사 대신 「for+명사」를 써서 목적과 의도를 나타낼 수 있다.

You can spend money **to help** poor people. 너는 가난한 사람들을 돕기 위해 돈을 쓸 수 있다.
= You can spend money **for** poor people.
I'm going to study much harder **to get** better grades.
나는 더 좋은 점수를 얻기 위해 훨씬 더 열심히 공부할 것이다.
= I'm going to study much harder **for** better grades.

정답 p.38

PRACTICE 8

〈보기〉에서 알맞은 표현을 골라 to부정사의 형태로 바꾸어 빈칸에 쓰세요.

보 기	buy a present for his mom	take care of the sick	check her email
	ask about the test	pass the exam	protect your eyes
	say hello to me	stay healthy and slim	

1 He put his hand on his hat _____.
2 Becky turned on the computer _____.
3 You'd better wear sunglasses _____.
4 Dr. Park went to Africa _____.
5 Mike went downtown _____.
6 Ann visited the professor's office _____.
7 He studied harder _____.
8 She exercises regularly _____.

PRACTICE 9

〈보기〉와 같이 주어진 문장과 같은 뜻이 되도록 괄호 안의 표현을 이용하여 빈칸을 채우세요.

> 보 기   I met Peter to give him the information. (in order to)
> = I met Peter <u>in order to give him the information</u>.

1 Hana went to the library to study for the final exam. (in order to)
   = Hana went to the library _____.

2 I called Minho to ask if he could go shopping with me. (so as to)
   = I called Minho _____.

3 Mom stopped the car to pick up Kelly. (so as to)
   = Mom stopped the car _____.

4 Tony opened the door to watch the birds in the tree. (in order to)
   = Tony opened the door _____.

5 I turned on the computer to surf the Internet. (in order to)
   = I turned on the computer _____.

6 Jenny bought some vegetables to make salad. (so as to)
   = Jenny bought some vegetables _____.

PRACTICE 10

빈칸에 to나 for 중 알맞은 것을 쓰세요.

1 I'm calling to thank you _____ your nice card.
2 We should keep some money _____ a rainy day.
3 He does his best _____ solve the problem.
4 A kind old man came _____ help them.
5 I went to the store _____ some cookies.
6 He studied hard _____ become a doctor.
7 I got out of the car _____ clean the windshield.
8 Let's go out _____ lunch next Friday.
9 People nod their heads _____ mean 'yes'.
10 I have to buy some books _____ my homework.

PSS 3-2 형용사 수식, 결과를 나타내는 to부정사

1. to부정사가 형용사를 뒤에서 수식할 때는 '~하기에(형용사 수식)', '~하다니(판단의 근거)'의 의미를 가진다.

   Hangeul is not **easy to learn**. 한글은 배우기에 쉽지 않다.
   I'm so **lucky to have** such great friends. 그런 멋진 친구들이 있다니 나는 매우 운이 좋다.

2. to부정사가 다음과 같은 감정을 나타내는 형용사를 수식할 때는 '~해서, ~하게 되어'의 뜻으로 감정의 원인을 나타낸다.

   | sorry | happy | pleased | surprised |
   | glad | disappointed | sad | excited |

   Everybody was **surprised to see** him. 모든 사람들이 그를 보고 놀랐다.
   I'm **sorry to hear** the bad news. 안 좋은 소식을 듣게 되어 유감이다.

3. to부정사는 '~해서 (결국) …되다'의 뜻으로 결과를 나타내기도 한다.

   Jenny **grew up to be** a pianist. Jenny는 자라서 피아니스트가 되었다.
   My grandmother **lived to be** eighty. 나의 할머니는 80세까지 사셨다.
   He studied hard for the exam **only to fail**. 그는 시험을 위해 열심히 공부했지만 결국 시험에 떨어졌다.

정답 p.39

PRACTICE 11

〈보기〉와 같이 to부정사를 이용하여 두 문장을 한 문장으로 연결하세요.

보 기	I met Mr. Park. I was happy.
	➡ I was happy to meet Mr. Park.

1 I went back to my hometown. I was really excited.
   ➡ _____

2 I saw Nancy on the street. I was surprised.
   ➡ _____

3 I got a new computer. I was so happy.
   ➡ _____

4 Jason was stupid. He believed such an obvious lie.
   ➡ _____

5 I introduced my family to you. I was glad.
   ➡ _____

6 Sora was lucky. She passed such a difficult test.
   ➡ _____

PRACTICE 12

다음 문장의 밑줄 친 to부정사의 용법이 무엇인지 〈보기〉에서 골라 각각에 해당하는 번호를 쓰세요.

| 보 기 | ① 명사적 용법　② 형용사적 용법　③ 부사적 용법 |

1 Sumi decided <u>to visit</u> China this winter. (　　)

2 Sora was glad <u>to see</u> Sujin again. (　　)

3 It's about time <u>to go</u> for a walk. (　　)

4 I was so happy <u>to receive</u> the letter. (　　)

5 I don't know anyone <u>to ask</u> for help. (　　)

6 It is essential for you and me <u>to trust</u> each other. (　　)

 **4 to부정사의 의미상의 주어**

1. to부정사의 의미상의 주어는 to부정사가 나타내는 동작의 주체를 의미하고, to부정사 앞에 「for+목적격」으로 쓴다.

   It was too important **for us to forget**. 그것은 우리가 잊기에는 너무 중요했다.
   Was it difficult **for you to find** a job? 네가 직업을 찾는 것은 어려웠니?

2. to부정사가 사람의 성격을 묘사하는 형용사를 꾸며줄 때는 의미상의 주어를 「of+목적격」으로 나타낸다.

   | kind　nice　foolish　wise　silly　stupid　generous |

   It is very **kind of you to say** so. 네가 그렇게 말하는 것을 보니 참 친절하구나.
   It was **foolish of him to make** the same mistake again.
   그가 또 다시 똑같은 실수를 저지르다니 어리석었다.

PRACTICE 13

괄호 안에 주어진 단어 중 알맞은 것을 고르세요.

1 It's important (to, for, of) me to exercise regularly.

2 This skirt is too small (to, for, of) me to wear.

3 It is very good (to, for, of) see you again.

4 It was very nice (to, for, of) you to help the old man.

5 It's hard (to, for, of) me to wake up early.

6 It's so stupid (to, for, of) him to talk like that.

7 I'm too tired (to, for, of) go hiking with you.

8 It's very kind (to, for, of) you to take me home.

9 His questions were too confusing (to, for, of) me to answer.

10 It is very wise (to, for, of) her to act like that.

11 It was generous (to, for, of) him to donate a million dollars.

12 This soup is too hot (to, for, of) me to eat.

too ~ to, enough to

1. 「too+형용사/부사+to부정사」는 '~하기에는 너무 …한'의 의미를 가지고, 「so+형용사/부사+that+주어+can't」로 바꾸어 쓸 수 있다.

    I'm **too nervous to sleep**. 나는 잠을 자기에는 너무 불안하다.
    = I'm **so nervous that I can't** sleep. 나는 매우 불안해서 잠을 잘 수 없다.

    cf. 「too+형용사/부사+to부정사」를 「so+형용사/부사+that+주어+can't」로 바꿀 때에는 시제에 유의한다.
    She was **too busy to give** it much thought. 그녀는 많은 생각을 하기에는 너무 바빴다.
    = She was **so busy that she couldn't** give it much thought.
    그녀는 너무 바빠서 많은 생각을 할 수 없었다.

2. 「형용사/부사+enough+to부정사」는 '~할 정도로 충분히 …한'의 의미를 가지고, 「so+형용사/부사+that+주어+can」으로 바꾸어 쓸 수 있다.

    This room is **large enough to have** ten people in.
    이 방은 10명의 사람들이 있기에 충분히 넓다.
    = This room is **so large that it can** have ten people in it.
    이 방은 매우 넓어서 10명의 사람들이 있을 수 있다.

    cf. 「so that+주어+can」은 '~하기 위해서'의 뜻으로 (in order/so as) to와 바꾸어 쓸 수 있다.
    I save money every month **so that I can** buy a car.
    나는 차를 사기 위해서 매달 돈을 저축한다.
    = I save money every month **(in order/so as) to** buy a car.

> 3. so ~ that 표현을 too ~ to / enough to 구문으로 전환할 때 to부정사의 목적어가 주어와 일치하는 경우 to부정사 뒤에는 목적어를 쓰지 않음에 유의해야 한다.
>
> The problem is **so easy that** she **can** solve it. 그 문제는 너무 쉬워서 그녀는 그것을 풀 수 있다.
> = The problem is **easy enough for her to solve**. (O) 그 문제는 그녀가 풀기에 충분히 쉽다.
> = The problem is **easy enough for her to solve** it. (X)
>
> The problem is **so difficult that** she **can't solve** it.
> 그 문제는 너무 어려워서 그녀는 그것을 풀 수 없다.
> = The problem is **too difficult for her to solve**. (O)
> = The problem is **too difficult for her to solve** it. (X)

정답 p.39

PRACTICE 14

주어진 문장과 의미가 같도록 빈칸에 알맞은 문장을 쓰세요. (단, 밑줄 친 부분에 절이 포함되어 있으면 구로, 구가 포함되어 있으면 절로 바꾸어 쓸 것)

1 The box is so heavy that I can't lift it.
   = The box is too heavy for me to lift.

2 The book was interesting enough for me to read twice.
   = _____

3 I studied very hard so that I could pass the bar exam.
   = _____

4 The curry was too spicy for me to eat.
   = _____

5 The dress was too expensive for her to buy.
   = _____

6 Mina went to Canada so that she could study English.
   = _____

7 The movie was too scary for children to watch.
   = _____

8 The blue shirt is so big that I can't wear it.
   = _____

9 The stadium was big enough for ten thousand people to fit into.
   = _____

10 The box is so light that I can carry it.
   = _____

원형부정사

> 원형부정사는 to부정사와는 달리 사역동사나 지각동사의 목적격 보어 역할만을 할 수 있으며, 그 형태는 to 없이 동사원형으로만 이루어져 있다.
>
> 1. **사역동사(let, make, have)의 목적격 보어**
>
>   Mary **made** her son **go** to the university. Mary는 그녀의 아들이 그 대학에 가게 했다.
>   I **helped** her **(to) do** her homework. 나는 그녀가 그녀의 숙제를 하는 것을 도왔다.
>   *cf.* help는 준사역동사로 목적격 보어 자리에 원형부정사 대신 to부정사를 쓰기도 한다.
>
> 2. **지각동사(see, watch, hear, feel)의 목적격 보어**
>
>   We **saw** the dog **run** after him. 우리는 그 개가 그를 쫓아 달리는 것을 보았다.
>   She **heard** James **play** the violin. 그녀는 James가 바이올린을 켜는 것을 들었다.
>
>   *cf.* 지각동사의 목적어의 동작이 진행 중임을 강조할 때는 원형부정사 대신 현재분사를 쓰기도 한다.
>   She **heard** James **playing** the violin. 그녀는 James가 바이올린을 켜고 있는 것을 들었다.

정답 p.39

PRACTICE 15

괄호 안에 주어진 단어를 이용하여 문장을 완성하세요.

1 My sister doesn't let me _____ her jacket. (wear)
2 I felt the house _____ heavily. (shake)
3 I helped my son _____ his desk upstairs. (carry)
4 Peter heard Susan _____ the bell. (ring)
5 The teacher had his students _____ their homework. (do)
6 The songs made me _____ comfortable. (feel)
7 I saw the policeman _____ the building. (enter)
8 The old lady helped the boy _____ his parents. (find)
9 I watched my daughter _____ the flowers. (plant)
10 The piano teacher made me _____ the new song every day. (practice)

PRACTICE 16

각각의 대화를 보고, 빈칸에 알맞은 말을 써서 문장을 완성하세요.

1

3

2

4

1   Liz saw Tom play[playing] tennis   .
2   She made her son _____ .
3   Brian heard Jane _____ .
4   Kate won't let Bill _____ .
5   Jack had his daughter _____ .
6   Shelly feels _____ .

Chapter Review Test

정답 p.40　CHAPTER 7 부정사

1 주어진 문장의 밑줄 친 부분과 용법이 같은 것은?

> I study English to talk with foreigners.

① I want to be a teacher.
② Jihye is going to the library to study.
③ Minho likes to take care of sick people.
④ I need something to eat.
⑤ It is exciting to play tennis.

2 다음 문장을 읽고 질문에 알맞은 답을 두 단어로 쓰세요.

> Lisa is going to New York. She'll attend a meeting there.

Q: Why is Lisa going to New York?
A: She is going to New York _____ _____ a meeting.

3 주어진 단어들을 우리말과 같은 뜻이 되도록 배열할 때 다섯 번째에 오는 단어는?

- 나는 버스를 타고 학교에 가는 데 한 시간이 걸린다.
  = _____
  _____
  (go, by, to, hour, school, it, me, bus, to, takes, an)

① go　　② me　　③ to
④ school　⑤ hour

4 우리말과 같은 의미가 되도록 빈칸에 알맞은 말을 넣을 때 ⓑ에 들어갈 말은?

- 제가 물리를 공부하는 것이 필요한가요?
  = Is it ⓐ_____ ⓑ_____ ⓒ_____ ⓓ_____ ⓔ_____ physics?

① necessary　② me　③ for
④ study　　　⑤ to

5 〈보기〉에서 적절한 의문사를 골라 빈칸에 쓰세요.

> 보기 | what　where　when　how

(1) I don't know _____ to go. Should I go now, or in two hours?
(2) Can you tell me _____ to get to the post office? Can I go there on foot?

6 주어진 문장의 밑줄 친 부분과 용법이 같은 것은?

> There is an easy way to protect the river.

① My hobby is to read comic books.
② A clerk came to clean the floor.
③ He was surprised to hear the news.
④ She decided to study hard.
⑤ I have a pet to play with.

7 두 문장이 같은 뜻이 되도록 빈칸을 채우세요.

- Mina wanted to buy some snacks, so she went to the market.
= Mina went to the market _____ _____ some snacks.

8 다음 빈칸에 들어갈 단어로 알맞은 것은?

A: I don't know _____ to do now.
B: You have to finish your homework.

① that   ② why   ③ what
④ when   ⑤ where

9 우리말과 같은 뜻이 되도록 괄호 안의 단어를 알맞게 배열하여 문장을 완성하세요.

- 그 상자는 내가 들기에 너무 무거웠다.
= The box was _____ _____. (too, heavy, me, lift, for, to)

10 다음 중 밑줄 친 to부정사의 용법이 나머지 넷과 다른 것은?

① It is necessary to read a lot of books.
② To stare at someone is very rude.
③ Her dream was to be a famous actress.
④ His grandfather lived to be eighty.
⑤ They expected to be invited to Gerald's birthday party.

11 다음 빈칸에 들어갈 말로 알맞은 것은?

The red shirt made her _____ better.

① looks   ② look   ③ looked
④ looking   ⑤ to look

12 다음 ⓐ~ⓕ 중 어법상 틀린 문장의 개수로 알맞은 것은?

ⓐ I enjoy talking with my grandmother.
ⓑ Do you mind if I borrow your pen?
ⓒ When will you decide meeting him?
ⓓ He has many books to read for two days.
ⓔ My dad made me to take out the trash.
ⓕ I want you bring me my car key.

① 1개   ② 2개   ③ 3개
④ 4개   ⑤ 5개

13 다음 중 빈칸에 들어갈 단어가 나머지 넷과 다른 것은?

① It's important _____ me to do my best.
② It's very nice _____ you to take care of the baby.
③ It's too heavy _____ me to carry.
④ It's hard _____ her to tell him the truth.
⑤ It's not easy _____ him to live by himself.

14 다음 밑줄 친 우리말을 영어로 바르게 옮긴 것은?

> I was very happy 나의 고등학교 동창들을 다시 봐서.

① see my high school classmates again
② seeing my high school classmates again
③ to be seen my high school classmates again
④ to see my high school classmates again
⑤ have seen my high school classmates again

15 다음 중 밑줄 친 부분의 용법이 같은 것끼리 바르게 짝지어진 것은?

> ⓐ It is difficult to explain exactly why.
> ⓑ Jiyoung went to America to study English.
> ⓒ Why did you agree to do this project?
> ⓓ The fastest way to get there is by bus.
> ⓔ He studied hard to pass the exam.

① ⓐ, ⓑ   ② ⓐ, ⓔ   ③ ⓑ, ⓒ
④ ⓑ, ⓔ   ⑤ ⓒ, ⓓ

16 다음 중 밑줄 친 부분을 어법상 옳게 고친 것은?

① Would you bring something warm to wear?
   (→ warm something)
② I hope to see you soon and heard your travel stories. (→ hearing)
③ Dad told my sister coming home before it gets too late. (→ come)
④ She stopped to buy lunch, as she was very hungry. (→ buying)
⑤ To working twelve hours a day is very tiring.
   (→ work)

17 다음 빈칸에 들어갈 말로 알맞은 것은?

> They are ready _____ the train.

① take   ② took   ③ taken
④ to take   ⑤ taking

18 다음 문장의 밑줄 친 부분과 용법이 같은 것은?

> I have some books to buy.

① I wish to travel around the world.
② Give him something to eat.
③ I went to the cafe to meet him.
④ I'd love to see you at the party.
⑤ It's fun to teach the students.

19 다음 중 어법상 어색한 문장을 모두 고르세요.

① Dad wanted me to clean his car.
② There are a lot of places visit in Korea.
③ I'm planning to take a business course.
④ Would you like to have dinner with us?
⑤ What should I do sing well?

20 다음 중 밑줄 친 부분이 어색한 것은?

① I want to learn how to fly a kite.
② They had trouble deciding which to buy.
③ Let me know where to turn right or left in advance.
④ My friend and I talked about when to meet tomorrow.
⑤ I taught my grandmother what to use the computer.

21 다음 대화의 (A)~(E) 중 빈칸에 들어갈 말이 나머지 넷과 다른 것은?

> Kevin: I don't know ___(A)___ to edit the video I filmed today. Giho, please help me with my video editing.
> Giho: Sure. I can help you.
> Kevin: Wow, I don't know ___(B)___ to thank you.
> Giho: What are friends for?
> Kevin: Then can you come to my house tomorrow?
> Giho: I'm sorry, but I can't. I'm busy. I'm learning ___(C)___ to bake cookies tomorrow. ___(D)___ are you going to do this Saturday?
> Kevin: My cousin is going to teach me ___(E)___ to swim. Is Sunday OK for you, then?
> Giho: Yes, it is. Let's meet on Sunday.

① (A) ② (B) ③ (C)
④ (D) ⑤ (E)

22 우리말과 같은 뜻이 되도록 주어진 단어를 올바른 순서로 배열하세요.

> • 나는 하늘을 날고 싶다.
> = _____.
> (would, I, in, fly, to, the, like, sky)

23 주어진 문장의 밑줄 친 It과 쓰임이 같은 것은?

> It is good to get up early in the morning.

① It's raining now.
② What is it?
③ I saw it yesterday.
④ It's March 18th.
⑤ It's fun to play table tennis.

24 주어진 말을 활용하여 〈보기〉와 같이 문장을 완성하세요.

> 보기 | (dangerous, swim, in the deep sea)
> ➡ It is dangerous to swim in the deep sea.

(useful, learn, a second language)
➡ _____
_____

25 다음 중 어법상 어색한 문장은?

① She is very polite to me.
② It isn't easy to follow that rule.
③ Let's order something to eat cold.
④ I often go hiking with my father.
⑤ How about going shopping on Saturday?

26 다음 조건에 맞게 주어진 우리말과 일치하도록 문장을 완성하세요.

조 건
• 동사 say를 활용할 것. • to부정사를 진주어로 포함할 것. • how many를 사용할 것.

• 얼마나 많은 사람들이 그것을 사용하는지를 말하는 것은 어렵다. = It is difficult _____ _____ .

27 다음 중 어법상 어색한 문장은?

① You're in the wrong seat.
② She is planning to going to Europe.
③ How shall I start my new business?
④ I've been helpful to the students.
⑤ I'm looking forward to seeing you.

28 다음 빈칸에 들어갈 단어가 나머지 넷과 다른 하나는?

① It was necessary _____ him to get the answer.
② It is very kind _____ you to say so.
③ It is not difficult _____ her to win the prize.
④ It is helpful _____ me to wear a mask.
⑤ It was exciting _____ them to reach the top of the mountain.

29 어법상 틀린 것을 바르게 고친 것 중 잘못된 것은?

① I told him take a break and get some sleep.
　　　　　　→ to take
② He made his son to keep a promise.
　　　　　　　　→ keep
③ Mom didn't allow me going to the movies.
　　　　　　　　　→ go
④ I helped him moved the desk.
　　　　　　　→ to move
⑤ Jenny saw them to hide in the closet.
　　　　　　　　→ hiding

30 다음 대화의 밑줄 친 부분과 바꾸어 쓸 수 있는 것은?

A: Are you going to the concert this Friday? B: Of course. I'm dying to see it.

① I don't like music.
② I don't know.
③ I really hate to see it.
④ I can't go there.
⑤ I really want to see it.

31 다음 글의 밑줄 친 부분과 쓰임이 같은 것은?

> Dear Emma,
> How have you been? I wanted to call you, but I forgot to ask for your new number. Writing this letter is the only way to reach you. A lot of things happened after you moved to Seoul. I have many interesting stories to tell you. I hope you will read this letter soon.
> Your friend,
> Sena

① His goal is to win the contest.
② It is not difficult to solve the problem.
③ Jenny refused to take my advice.
④ I am only doing it to earn some money.
⑤ They need something fresh to eat.

32 두 문장이 같은 뜻이 되도록 빈칸에 알맞은 말을 쓰세요.

> • He doesn't know what he should do.
> = He doesn't know _____ _____ _____.

33 다음 밑줄 친 부분을 동명사로 바꾸어 쓸 수 있는 것을 모두 고르세요.

① I advise you to be kind to others.
② Dad helped me fix the radio yesterday.
③ To keep a diary in English every day is not easy.
④ I'm sorry to hear that you are sick.
⑤ Jenny started to practice an hour ago.

34 주어진 문장의 밑줄 친 부분과 용법이 같은 것은?

> Mrs. Lee has a special way to cook rice.

① I know someone to finish the work.
② Do you promise to return the book?
③ I have to study hard to get a good grade.
④ You should exercise to stay healthy.
⑤ We went to the pool to swim.

35 다음 두 문장이 같은 뜻이 되도록 빈칸에 들어갈 알맞은 말은?

> • Adam was too proud to apologize.
>   = Adam was _____ proud that he couldn't apologize.

① such ② so as ③ to
④ enough ⑤ so

36 다음 중 어법상 어색한 문장은?

① It's time for dinner.
② It's time for have a meeting.
③ It's time for the yoga class to start.
④ It is about time to go out.
⑤ It is about time to play basketball.

37 다음 중 〈보기〉의 문장을 바르게 영작한 것을 고르세요.

> 보기 | 나를 용서해 주다니 그녀는 정말 관대하지 않니?

① Is it very generous of her to forgiving me?
② Is it very generous of her to forgive me?
③ Isn't it very generous for her forgiving me?
④ Isn't it very generous for her to forgive me?
⑤ Isn't it very generous of her to forgive me?

38 다음 중 밑줄 친 부분의 쓰임이 같은 것끼리 짝지어진 것을 모두 고르세요.

(A) My grandmother agreed to visit her hometown with me.
(B) I bought a digital camera to take pictures on our trip.
(C) He studied very hard to become a doctor.
(D) Amanda would be the last person to tell a lie.
(E) Why did she decide to end it all?

① (A), (E) ② (A), (C) ③ (B), (C)
④ (C), (E) ⑤ (C), (D)

39 다음 중 밑줄 친 부분이 바르게 쓰인 것은?

① What is she do there?
② Mihye studies with us last night.
③ The 30-years-old woman is my sister.
④ We need to helps him at school.
⑤ I would love to give him a hand.

40 우리말과 같은 뜻이 되도록 주어진 단어를 알맞게 배열하세요.

• 그 물은 너무 더러워서 난 그것을 마실 수 없었다.
= _____
  _____
(I, water, the, it, could, so, was, dirty, not, drink, that)

41 다음은 Minji네 가족이 어제 주고 받은 메시지 내용입니다. ask를 활용하여 Mom이 Minji에게 요청한 것을 영어로 완성하세요. (단, 8단어로 쓸 것.)

➡ Mom _____
_____.

42 다음 중 어법상 어색한 문장은?

① The orange smells good.
② My bag is as heavy as Denny's.
③ He refused taking my advice.
④ Tom will try to read a book every day.
⑤ She looks beautiful.

43 다음 두 문장이 같은 뜻이 되도록 괄호 안의 말을 이용하여 문장을 완성하세요.

- I ran so fast that I could catch him in a minute.
  = I _____ in a minute. (enough, to)

44 주어진 우리말과 같은 뜻이 되도록 괄호 안의 말을 바르게 배열하세요.

- 네 친구의 생일을 기억하는 것은 중요하다.
  ➡ _____
     _____
  (important, your friend's, birthday, is, to, it, remember)

45 다음 중 어법상 <u>어색한</u> 문장은?

① It's hard for him to get a driver's license.
② It's important for me to practice English.
③ It's generous of you to visit him every week.
④ It's easy for her to pass the exam.
⑤ It's impossible of me to find my lost backpack.

46 주어진 단어들을 알맞게 배열하여 문장을 완성하세요.

Do you want _____?
(to, how, a cake, learn, to, make)

47 다음 빈칸에 들어갈 말로 알맞은 것은?

He promised _____ a diary in English.

① keep   ② kept   ③ keeps
④ keeping ⑤ to keep

48 다음 글의 빈칸 (A)~(C)에 들어갈 표현이 바르게 연결된 것은?

How do you usually celebrate the new year? I ____(A)____ to the east coast to watch the sunrise and make wishes for the coming year. Many people come for a similar purpose. Some people might plan ____(B)____ better people, and some might wish to become filthy rich. Last year, I wished for my family's good health. And I am happy ____(C)____ that my wish came true.

	(A)	(B)	(C)
①	always have gone	to become	seeing
②	have always gone	becoming	seeing
③	have always gone	to become	seeing
④	always have gone	becoming	to see
⑤	have always gone	to become	to see

49 다음 빈칸에 들어갈 단어로 알맞은 것은?

- When I see the stars in the sky, I feel happy.
  ➡ The stars in the sky _____ me feel happy.

① want   ② ask   ③ tell
④ make   ⑤ allow

50 주어진 문장의 밑줄 친 부분과 쓰임이 다른 것은?

You need a key <u>to get</u> out of here.

① John went to the library <u>to borrow</u> books.
② He flew to America <u>to visit</u> his grandmother.
③ I called her <u>to ask</u> about the meeting.
④ She came to me <u>to pick</u> up her umbrella.
⑤ I am so happy <u>to hear</u> that.

51 다음 대화의 밑줄 친 우리말을 바르게 영작한 문장을 고르세요.

M: Honey, let's make a shopping list of home appliances.
W: OK. I think <u>우리는 우리의 삶을 더 편하게 만들기 위해서 식기 세척기를 사야한다</u>.
M: Yes. We can disinfect our dishes by using the machine.
W: And how about buying a clothes dryer?
M: Sure. That would mean we wouldn't need to hang our washing to dry.

① we should buy a dishwasher that makes it our life easier
② we should buy a dishwasher in order that make our life easier
③ we should buy a dishwasher so as to make our life easier
④ we should buy a dishwasher to be made our life easier
⑤ we should buy a dishwasher so order to make our life easier

52 다음 글의 ⓐ~ⓔ를 바꾸어 쓸 때, 어법상 어색한 것은?

Hola! My name is Diego. I'm from Spain and ⓐ<u>my job is cutting hams</u>! In Spain, people love hams and every famous restaurant has professional ham cutters. While I was working in a restaurant, I learned ⓑ<u>how to slice hams thinly</u>. Last year, I practiced ⓒ<u>so hard that I could win</u> the ham cutting contest and I won first prize. I was ⓓ<u>happy to win the contest</u>. My next goal is traveling the world and ⓔ<u>helping people enjoy</u> the Spanish ham.

① ⓐ: my job is to cut hams
② ⓑ: how I should slice hams thinly
③ ⓒ: too hard to win
④ ⓓ: happy because I won the contest
⑤ ⓔ: helping people to enjoy

53 다음 밑줄 친 부분의 의미로 알맞은 것은?

A: What would you like to have?
B: A hamburger, please.
A: For here or to go?
B: <u>To go</u>.

① I'll cancel my order.
② I'll take it out.
③ I'll stay at the restaurant.
④ I'll pay for it.
⑤ I'll go back home.

54 다음 그림을 보고 〈보기〉에 주어진 표현을 골라 각 상황에 알맞은 문장을 완성하세요.

보 기
what   how   to wear   to play the cello

(1) I don't know _____.

(2) I can't decide _____.

55 다음 그림과 조건을 참고하여 문장을 완성하세요.

조 건
1. 주어진 가주어 문장을 완성할 것. 2. help, go up, the를 사용할 것.

➡ It's very kind _____ them _____ _____ the old lady _____ _____ _____ _____.

56 주어진 그림을 묘사하는 대화를 만들 때 빈칸 ⓐ, ⓑ에 들어갈 말로 가장 알맞은 것은?

Mom : I want you ___ⓐ___ food to sick grandma. Also, I order you ___ⓑ___ to strangers!
Red Riding Hood: Okay, Mom. I'll keep it in mind.

　　　　ⓐ　　　　　ⓑ
① to deliver　　to not talk
② delivering　　to not talk
③ to deliver　　not talk
④ delivering　　not to talk
⑤ to deliver　　not to talk

57 다음 우리말 문장을 괄호 안의 단어를 이용하여 조건에 맞게 영어로 쓰세요.

• 그는 너무 졸려서 늦게까지 깨어있을 수 없었다.
 (sleepy, stay up, late)

(1) _____
 _____
 (too, to를 이용할 것)

(2) _____
 _____
 (so, that을 이용할 것)

CHAPTER 8
동명사

성취도 자기 평가 활용법

구분	평가 기준
Excellent	문법 내용을 모두 이해하고, 문제를 모두 맞힘.
Very good	문법 내용은 충분히 이해했으나 실수로 1~2문제 틀림.
Good	문법 내용이 조금 어려워 3~4문제 틀림.
needs **R**eview	문법 내용 이해가 어렵고, 5문제 이상 틀림, 복습 필요.

Problem Solving Skill	페이지	학습날짜	성취도 자기평가 E V G R	학습체크
PSS 1 주어와 보어로 쓰이는 동명사	204	/		☐
PSS 2 동사의 목적어로 쓰이는 동명사	페이지	학습날짜	성취도 자기평가 E V G R	학습체크
PSS 2-1 동사+동명사	205	/		☐
PSS 2-2 동사+동명사/to부정사 Ⅰ	206	/		☐
PSS 2-3 동사+동명사/to부정사 Ⅱ	207	/		☐
PSS 3 전치사의 목적어로 쓰이는 동명사	209	/		☐
PSS 4 동명사의 관용 표현	211	/		☐
Chapter Review Test	213	/		☐

주어와 보어로 쓰이는 동명사

「동사원형+-ing」의 형태로 문장에서 주어, 보어, 목적어의 역할을 하는 것을 동명사라고 한다.

1. **주어로 쓰이는 동명사**

    Listening to music is a lot of fun. 음악을 듣는 것은 아주 재미있다.
    = **It**'s a lot of fun **listening** to music. = **It**'s a lot of fun **to listen** to music.
    　가주어　　　　　　　진주어　　　　　　　가주어　　　　　　진주어

2. **보어로 쓰이는 동명사**

    My plan for this weekend is **going** fishing. 이번 주말 동안의 내 계획은 낚시하러 가는 것이다.
    = My plan for this weekend is **to go** fishing.

정답 p.43

PRACTICE 1

우리말과 일치하도록 우리말 주어에 유의하여 괄호 안에 주어진 단어를 바르게 배열하세요.

1 일주일에 7일을 일하는 것은 힘들다. (is, seven days, a week, working, challenging)
➡ _____

2 그녀의 직업은 신발을 디자인하는 것이다. (her job, shoes, is, designing)
➡ _____

3 샤워를 하는 것은 당신에게 상쾌한 기분이 들도록 한다. (you, taking, refreshed, a shower, feel, makes)
➡ _____

4 영어를 배우는 것은 많은 시간과 노력이 든다. (English, takes, time and effort, learning, a lot of)
➡ _____

5 내 취미는 야외에서 사진을 찍는 것이다. (my hobby, taking, is, photos, outside)
➡ _____

6 너의 실수는 너무 빠르게 말한 것이었다. (speaking, too fast, your mistake, was)
➡ _____

정답 p.43

PRACTICE 2

두 문장의 의미가 같도록 동명사를 이용하여 빈칸에 알맞은 말을 쓰세요.

1 It is not easy to practice the violin. = _____ is not easy.

2 It is sometimes necessary to be honest. = _____ is sometimes necessary.

3 My wish is to travel around the world. = My wish is _____.

4 It would be nice to make new friends. = _____ would be nice.

5 My job is to teach English to kids. = My job is _____.

6 It is interesting to live in the countryside. = _____ is interesting.

동사의 목적어로 쓰이는 동명사

PSS 2-1 동사 + 동명사

1. 다음 동사들 뒤에 다른 동사가 목적어로 올 때, 목적어는 동명사의 형태로 쓴다.

   > enjoy   mind   finish   stop   give up   practice
   > put off   deny   imagine   quit   suggest   dislike   avoid

   Susan **enjoys talking** with her grandmother. Susan은 그녀의 할머니와 이야기하는 것을 즐긴다.
   When did you **finish reading** that book? 너는 언제 그 책을 읽는 것을 끝냈니?
   Do you **mind turning** down the volume? 볼륨을 줄여도 괜찮겠니?

2. 동명사의 부정형은 동명사 앞에 not을 붙여 만든다.

   I imagined **not moving** to Suwon. 나는 수원으로 이사가지 않는 것을 상상했다.
   cf. I **didn't** imagine **moving** to Suwon. 나는 수원으로 이사가는 것을 상상하지 않았다.

PRACTICE 3

괄호 안의 동사를 알맞은 형태로 바꾸어 빈칸에 쓰세요.

1 I'll call you when I finish _____. (work)

2 I decided _____ the fireworks show. (watch)

3 She stopped _____ to me for a week. (talk)

4 Mr. Han put off _____ a meeting. (have)

5 They promised _____ him there. (send)

6 Jane enjoys _____ for her family. (cook)

7 My grandmother finally quit _____ at age 73. (work)

8 We didn't plan _____ there tonight. (go)

9 I'll keep _____ this paper until I finish it. (write)

10 Sujin hopes _____ us again soon. (see)

PRACTICE 4

정답 p.44

Becky

Tony와 Becky의 대화를 보고, 괄호 안의 단어를 알맞은 형태로 바꾸어 빈칸에 쓰세요.

	Becky	Tony
1	Do I have to open the door?	No, you don't have to. I'm fine.
2	I don't want to have lunch. I'm still full.	Me, too. Let's skip it.
3	You didn't go to the library, did you?	Yes, I did!
4	Eat dinner. You don't have to lose weight.	I know. I can't do this anymore.
5	You have to stay late at school this Friday.	I hate it.

Tony

1 Becky doesn't mind __*not opening*__ the door. (open)

2 Becky suggested _____ lunch. (have)

3 Becky denied _____ to the library. (go)

4 Becky stopped _____ dinner. (eat)

5 Becky doesn't enjoy _____ late at school this Friday. (stay)

PSS 2-2 동사 + 동명사/to부정사 I

다음은 동명사와 to부정사를 모두 목적어로 취하고, 그 중 어느 것을 목적어로 취하든지 뜻이 달라지지 않는 동사들이다.

> like   love   prefer   hate   begin   start   continue   intend

Do you **like playing** baseball? = Do you **like to play** baseball?
너는 야구 하는 것을 좋아하니?

It **began raining**. = It **began to rain**. 비가 내리기 시작했다.

When did you **start exercising**? = When did you **start to exercise**?
넌 언제 운동하는 것을 시작했니?

PRACTICE 5

괄호 안에 주어진 말 중 알맞은 것을 <u>모두</u> 고르세요.

1   I don't like (to eat, eating) late at night.

2   I should quit (to waste, wasting) my time.

3   John finished (to read, reading) the book.

4   We decided (to move, moving) to Busan.

5   Tony loves (to paint, painting) in the park.

6   It began (to snow, snowing) this morning.

7   Bill refused (to be, being) the chairman of the club.

8   I intended (to go, going) on a picnic, but I couldn't.

9   I'd like (to drink, drinking) some wine.

10 Did you practice (to play, playing) the cello?

11 Mom dislikes (to make, making) the same mistakes.

12 Sujin hates (to spend, spending) much money buying clothes.

13 They continued (to throw, throwing) away their trash on the street.

14 I wish (to get, getting) the perfect score on the test.

15 Peter started (to run, running) an hour ago.

PSS 2-3 동사 + 동명사/to부정사 Ⅱ

다음은 동명사와 to부정사를 모두 목적어로 취하고, 그 중 어느 것을 목적어로 취하느냐에 따라 뜻이 달라지는 동사들이다.

> try   regret   remember   forget

1. try+동명사 '(시험 삼아) ~ 해보다' / try+to부정사 '~하려고 노력하다, 애쓰다'

   I **tried calling** Bob yesterday. 나는 어제 Bob에게 전화를 해봤다.
   I **tried to call** Bob yesterday. 나는 어제 Bob에게 전화하려고 노력했다.

2. regret+동명사 '~한 것을 후회하다' / regret+to부정사 '~하게 되어 유감이다'

   I **regret telling** her that you failed the exam. 네가 시험에 떨어졌다고 그녀에게 말한 것을 후회한다.
   I **regret to tell** her that you failed the exam. 네가 시험에 떨어졌다고 그녀에게 말하게 되어 유감이다.

3. **remember + 동명사** '~한 것을 기억하다' / **remember + to부정사** '~할[하는] 것을 기억하다'

You should **remember telling** this to Sam. 넌 Sam에게 이걸 말했다는 것을 기억해야 해.
You should **remember to tell** this to Sam. 넌 Sam에게 이걸 말할 것을 기억해야 해.

4. **forget + 동명사** '~한 것을 잊다' / **forget + to부정사** '~할[하는] 것을 잊다'

Did you **forget calling** me this morning? 넌 오늘 아침에 내게 전화한 것을 잊었니?
Did you **forget to call** me this morning? 넌 오늘 아침에 내게 전화하는 것을 잊었니?

cf. stop 뒤에는 동명사와 to부정사가 모두 올 수 있지만, 이때 to부정사는 목적어가 아닌 부사구이다.
stop + 동명사 '~하는 것을 멈추다' / stop + to부정사 '~하기 위해 멈추다'
The man **stopped talking** to the woman. 남자는 여자에게 말하는 것을 멈추었다.
The man **stopped to talk** to the woman. 남자는 여자에게 말하기 위해 멈추었다.

정답 p.44

PRACTICE 6

괄호 안의 단어를 알맞은 형태로 바꾸어 빈칸에 쓰세요.

1. Ann tried _____ the answer, but she couldn't get it. (find)
2. Everyone stopped _____ and left the room. (talk)
3. I regret _____ my smartphone because it was too expensive for me. (buy)
4. The old lady kept _____ to her husband. (not, talk)
5. Jason forgot _____ the alarm, so he got up late this morning. (set)
6. Do you mind _____ the window for a while? (open)
7. When you make potato chips, try _____ salt to your potatoes. (add)
8. I stopped _____ up the gas tank, but the gas station was closed. (fill)
9. Linda dislikes _____ lies to people. (tell)
10. I won't forget _____ the famous movie star last night. (see)
11. I decided _____ the summer vacation on Jejudo. (not, spend)
12. Do you remember _____ Hana at the beach last Saturday? (meet)
13. I promised _____ late for work again. (not, be)
14. The boy didn't finish _____ his room. (clean)
15. Nari didn't come in the end. She must have forgotten _____ my office. (visit)

전치사의 목적어로 쓰이는 동명사

전치사의 목적어로 동사가 올 때는 동명사의 형태로 써야 한다.

1. thank A for -ing '~에 대해 A에게 감사하다'
   Thank you **for listening** to my speech. 저의 연설을 들어주셔서 감사합니다.

2. be interested in -ing '~에 관심 있다'
   Are you **interested in dancing** with people? 사람들과 춤추는 것에 관심이 있어요?

3. be good at -ing '~을 잘하다'
   Sangmin **is good at playing** the violin. 상민은 바이올린 연주를 잘한다.

4. be responsible for -ing '~에 책임이 있다'
   You **are responsible for caring** for the baby. 너는 그 아기를 돌보는 데 책임이 있다.

5. be worried about -ing '~에 대해 걱정하다'
   She **is worried about taking** an exam tomorrow. 그녀는 내일 시험을 치를 것에 대해 걱정한다.

6. dream of[about] -ing '~을 꿈꾸다'
   Jeff always **dreams of[about] buying** a nice car. Jeff는 항상 멋진 차를 사는 것을 꿈꾼다.

7. think of[about] -ing '~하는 것에 대해 생각하다'
   He **thought of[about] having** a meeting with them.
   그는 그들과 회의를 하는 것에 대해 생각했다.

8. talk about -ing '~에 대해 말하다'
   We **talked about moving** to a smaller city. 우리는 더 작은 도시로 이사가는 것에 대해 말했다.

9. be excited about -ing '~에 대해 흥분되다'
   Are you **excited about meeting** Mr. Smith? 너는 Smith 씨를 만나는 것에 대해 흥분되니?

10. be tired of -ing '~을 지겨워하다'
    I**'m tired of taking** care of the kids. 나는 아이들을 돌보는 것이 지겹다.

11. look forward to -ing '~을 고대하다'
    I'm **looking forward to visiting** there some day.
    나는 언젠가 그곳을 방문하기를 고대하고 있다.

12. feel like -ing '~하고 싶다'

Jason doesn't **feel like talking** about her. Jason은 그녀에 대해서 말하고 싶지 않다.

13. on -ing '~하자마자'

On arriving home, I went to sleep. 집에 도착하자마자 나는 잠을 잤다.

14. be used to -ing '~에 익숙하다'

Mr. Smith **is used to getting** up early in the morning.
Smith 씨는 아침에 일찍 일어나는 것에 익숙하다.

15. prevent A from -ing 'A가 ~하는 것을 못하게 하다'

The rain **prevented** them **from playing** the game.
그 비는 그들이 그 경기를 치르는 것을 못하게 했다.

정답 p.44

PRACTICE 7

괄호 안의 단어를 알맞은 형태로 바꿔서 빈칸을 완성하세요.

1. Jinho is very interested _____ _____ computer games. (play)
2. Mr. Kim thought _____ _____ to Busan. (move)
3. I feel _____ _____ noodles today. (have)
4. Sujin is worried _____ _____ the test next week. (take)
5. I dream _____ _____ back to my hometown. (go)
6. I'm tired _____ _____ TV these days. (watch)
7. She's responsible _____ _____ the house. (clean)
8. Jenny was good _____ _____ when she was a kid. (sing)
9. David and I were talking _____ _____ our old car. (fix)
10. You are excited _____ _____ Europe, aren't you? (visit)
11. Thank you _____ _____ so kind to me. (be)
12. I'm looking forward _____ _____ wonderful food at the Christmas party. (have)
13. Her illness prevented her _____ _____ here. (come)
14. On _____ the news, she began to cry. (hear)
15. Bill is used _____ _____ in the city. (live)

동명사의 관용 표현

1. How[What] about+-ing? = What do you say to+-ing? '~하는 게 어때?'

   How[What] about going on a picnic tomorrow? 내일 소풍을 가는 게 어때?
   = **What do you say to going** on a picnic tomorrow?

2. be busy+-ing '~하느라 바쁘다'

   Mom **was busy cleaning** the house. 엄마는 집을 청소하느라 바빴다.

3. go+-ing '~하러 가다'

   Let's **go fishing** this afternoon. 오늘 오후에 낚시하러 가자.
   I **went swimming** with Mark. 나는 Mark와 함께 수영하러 갔다.
   I'm planning to **go camping** with my parents. 나는 부모님과 함께 캠핑을 갈 계획이다.
   My brother doesn't like **going shopping**. 내 남동생은 쇼핑 가는 것을 좋아하지 않는다.
   Did you **go skating** last winter? 너 지난 겨울에 스케이트 타러 갔니?

4. spend+시간[돈]+-ing '~하느라 시간[돈]을 쓰다'

   I **spend** too much **time sleeping**. 나는 잠을 자느라 너무 많은 시간을 쓴다.

5. need+-ing '~되어야 할 필요가 있다'

   My house **needs painting**. 나의 집은 페인트 칠해질 필요가 있다.
   = My house **needs to be painted**.

6. It's no use+-ing '~해봐야 소용없다'

   It's no use crying over spilt milk. 엎질러진 우유 때문에 울어봐야 소용없다.

7. cannot help+-ing '~하지 않을 수 없다'

   I **couldn't help giving** money to him. 나는 그에게 돈을 주지 않을 수 없었다.

8. have trouble[difficulty, a hard time]+-ing '~하는 데 어려움을 겪다'

   Jane **had trouble choosing** her major. Jane은 전공을 선택하는 데 어려움을 겪었다.

9. There is no+-ing = It is impossible+to부정사 '~할 수 없다'

   There is no denying the fact that he told a lie to us.
   그가 우리에게 거짓말을 했다는 그 사실을 부인할 수가 없다.
   = **It is impossible to deny** the fact that he told a lie to us.

PRACTICE 8

우리말과 일치하도록 괄호 안의 단어를 이용하여 빈칸에 알맞은 말을 쓰세요.

1 나는 겨울에 종종 언니와 함께 스케이트를 타러 간다.
 ➡ I often _____ with my sister in winter. (skate)

2 나는 새 옷을 사느라 돈을 너무 많이 소비했다.
 ➡ I _____ too much money _____ new clothes. (buy)

3 네 컴퓨터는 고칠 필요가 있다.
 ➡ Your computer needs _____. (fix)

4 잠시 산책하는 게 어때?
 ➡ _____ a walk for a while? (take)
 ➡ _____ a walk for a while?

5 Shelly는 시험 공부를 하느라 바빴다.
 ➡ Shelly has been _____ for the exam. (study)

6 그를 말리려 해봐야 소용없다.
 ➡ It's _____ to stop him. (try)

7 나는 그 순간 웃지 않을 수 없었다.
 ➡ I _____ at that moment. (laugh)

8 Bill은 새 직장을 구하는 데 어려움을 겪고 있다.
 ➡ Bill is _____ a new job. (get)

9 우리는 새 정책에 대해 생각하느라 한 시간을 소비했다.
 ➡ We _____ an hour _____ about the new policy. (think)

10 내 딸은 다음 주말에 스키를 타러 갈 것이다.
 ➡ My daughter is going to _____ next weekend. (ski)

11 논쟁에서는 무식한 사람을 이길 수가 없다.
 ➡ _____ an ignorant man in an argument. (defeat)

12 Sam은 대부분의 시간을 책을 읽으며 보낸다.
 ➡ Sam _____ most of his time _____ books. (read)

13 나는 지난 주말에 캠핑을 갔고, 좋은 시간을 보냈다.
 ➡ I _____ last weekend and had a good time. (camp)

14 우리는 그의 언어를 이해하는 데 어려움을 겪었다.
 ➡ We _____ his language. (understand)

Chapter Review Test

정답 p.45

CHAPTER 8
동명사

1 다음 빈칸에 들어갈 단어로 알맞은 것은?

> A: Would you _____ turning off the TV?
> B: Of course not.

① hope　② mind　③ want
④ like　⑤ wish

2 다음 우리말 해석과 일치하도록 빈칸에 알맞은 영어 표현을 쓰세요.

> • He's good at (ⓐ) and (ⓑ).
>   그는 노래하고 춤추는 것을 잘합니다.
> • I'm used to (ⓒ) early.
>   나는 일찍 일어나는데 익숙합니다.
> • I forgot (ⓓ) him the news.
>   나는 그에게 그 소식을 말해주는 것을 깜빡했습니다.

ⓐ _____
ⓑ _____
ⓒ _____
ⓓ _____

3 다음 중 밑줄 친 부분의 쓰임이 나머지와 다른 하나는?

① My battery is running out.
② His goal is finishing the given tasks.
③ Her recent hope is traveling across Europe.
④ His bad habit is biting his nails.
⑤ The key point is keeping your word.

4 다음 중 우리말 해석이 잘못된 것은?

① I tried moving the piano by myself.
   → 난 혼자서 그 피아노를 옮겨봤다.
② Daniel stopped to talk to his friend.
   → Daniel은 친구랑 이야기하려고 멈추셨다.
③ Do you remember sending a letter to Mr. Watson today?
   → 너 오늘 Watson 씨에게 편지 보내야 하는 것을 기억하니?
④ She forgot to visit her grandparents.
   → 그녀는 조부모님 찾아 뵙는 것을 잊어버렸다.
⑤ My father stopped drinking.
   → 우리 아버지는 술 마시는 걸 끊으셨다.

5 다음 대화의 빈칸에 들어갈 말로 어색한 것은?

> Mike : What do you usually do on weekends?
> Jenny : _____

① I like watching YouTube videos.
② I enjoy watching YouTube videos.
③ I have fun watching YouTube videos.
④ I am tired of watching YouTube videos.
⑤ I spend time watching YouTube videos.

6 다음 두 문장에서 **틀린** 부분을 고쳐 문장을 다시 쓰세요.

(1) I really dislike be interrupted by people.

　➡ _____
　_____

(2) Don't forget feeding our dog after school tomorrow.

　➡ _____
　_____

7 다음 (A)~(E) 중 어법상 올바른 문장의 개수는?

(A) He is running a business.
(B) My elder brother advise me to take Japanese, Chinese and art this semester.
(C) Do you mind taking a picture with me?
(D) She grew up to be a famous scientist.
(E) I am used to be alone.

① 0개　② 2개　③ 3개
④ 4개　⑤ 5개

8 다음 대화의 빈칸에 들어갈 말로 알맞은 것은?

Tom : Hi, Diana.
Diana : Oh, Tom! I was looking forward _____ you.

① see　② seeing　③ saw
④ to see　⑤ to seeing

9 다음 글을 읽고 〈보기〉에 주어진 단어를 이용하여 빈칸에 알맞은 말을 쓰세요. (단, 필요시 어형을 변화시킬 것)

| 보기 | misjudge　deny |
| | communicate　understand |

Cultural awareness means being aware of different cultures. It helps people (A)_____ and embrace cultural differences from different countries and backgrounds. As globalization advances, there is no (B)_____ the fact that trying to understand different values, beliefs, and customs has become more and more important. It helps us to avoid (C)_____ people from various cultural backgrounds. By (D)_____ effectively with people of different cultures, we can break down cultural barriers and be integrated into one community.

10 다음 (A)~(C)에 들어갈 말들이 알맞게 연결된 것은?

- Miranda was very busy ____(A)____ Oliver's birthday party.
- They kept ____(B)____ together at the park.
- We wished ____(C)____ each other to make a happy home.

	(A)	(B)	(C)
①	prepare	jogging	to understand
②	preparing	to jog	understand
③	preparing	jogging	to understand
④	to prepare	jog	understanding
⑤	to prepare	to jog	understanding

11 다음 중 어법상 알맞은 문장은?

① I don't feel like to talk to you.
② I decided taking a bus to school.
③ He denied stealing my money.
④ Would you mind to turn on the radio?
⑤ I agreed changing the schedule.

12 다음 중 어법상 어색한 문장은?

① I couldn't help falling in love with Jessie because she was very lovely.
② This computer needs upgrading now.
③ Let's go shopping to buy your jacket after lunch.
④ What do you say to go for a walk?
⑤ It's no use telling him that because he won't listen.

13 우리말과 같은 뜻이 되도록 빈칸에 알맞은 말을 쓰세요.

- 그는 우표를 수집하는 것과 신문을 읽는 것을 좋아한다.
  = He likes _____ stamps and _____ newspapers.

14 다음 빈칸에 들어갈 말로 알맞은 것은?

When I see weak people, I always try _____ them.

① help   ② to help   ③ to helping
④ helped   ⑤ being help

15 다음 문장에서 틀린 곳을 한 군데 찾아 고치세요.

Exercise every day is good for your health.

_____ ➡ _____

16 다음은 효과적으로 시험을 대비하는 방법을 열거한 글이다. 빈칸 ⓐ, ⓑ, ⓒ에 들어갈 알맞은 말끼리 바르게 연결된 것은?

Are you worried ___ⓐ___ an exam?
There are many ways to study for an exam.

1. Use charts and diagrams ___ⓑ___ your notes.
2. Try to explain your answers ___ⓒ___ your friends.
3. Do not stay up all night to study, and have a good sleep!

	ⓐ	ⓑ	ⓒ
①	about taking	organize	to
②	for taking	organizing	from
③	about taking	to organize	to
④	for taking	organizing	about
⑤	about taking	to organize	from

17 다음 중 밑줄 친 부분의 쓰임이 나머지와 다른 하나는?

① I imagined flying in the sky.
② She quit working for the company.
③ Ben is watching TV now.
④ Minhee likes taking pictures.
⑤ My hobby is playing soccer.

18 다음 대화의 빈칸에 들어갈 알맞은 말은?

> Susan: I'm leaving for France for my summer vacation next Wednesday.
> Ted: Wow, _____.
> Susan: Don't worry. I won't forget.

① don't forget sending me a postcard
② remember to send me a postcard
③ forget to send me a postcard
④ remember sending me a postcard
⑤ don't remember to send me a postcard

19 다음 중 밑줄 친 부분의 쓰임이 잘못된 것은?

① I hope to be a scientist.
② I love writing letters.
③ Jihoon and I practiced to play the guitar.
④ She began to learn how to cook.
⑤ They gave up fixing the computer.

20 우리말과 같은 뜻이 되도록 빈칸에 들어갈 알맞은 말을 세 단어로 쓰세요.

> • 아침에 일찍 일어나는 것은 나에게 때때로 도전이다.
> = _____ in the morning is sometimes a challenge for me.

21 다음 우리말과 뜻이 같도록 괄호 안의 단어를 배열하세요.

> • 그들은 이 문제를 해결하는 데 어려움을 겪고 있다.
> = _____
> _____

(solving, they, difficulty, this, are, having, problem)

22 다음 대화의 빈칸에 공통으로 들어갈 말로 알맞은 것은?

> A: What's your hobby?
> B: I like _____ movies. I'm interested in _____ romantic movies.

① watch   ② to watch   ③ watching
④ watched   ⑤ to be watching

23 다음 중 어법상 틀린 곳을 한군데 찾아 고쳐 쓰세요.

> It was very sunny this morning. I thought of take a walk with my dog.

_____ ➡ _____

분사의 역할

PSS 2-1 명사를 수식하는 분사

1. 분사가 단독으로 쓰일 때는 명사의 앞에서 명사를 수식한다.

   The **crying boy** is my son. 울고 있는 소년이 내 아들이다.

   Look at the **broken window**. 깨진 창문을 보아라.

2. 분사가 구를 이루어 명사를 수식할 때는 명사의 뒤에서 명사를 수식한다.

   The **girl sitting on the chair** is Ann. 의자에 앉아 있는 소녀는 Ann이다.

   Mom swept the **leaves fallen on the ground**. 엄마는 땅에 떨어진 나뭇잎을 쓸었다.

정답 p.48

PRACTICE 2

〈보기〉에서 알맞은 동사를 골라 분사의 형태로 바꾸어 빈칸에 쓰세요.

보기	write	shock	speak	talk	burn
	paint	interest	use	bark	break

1 That word isn't used in ___spoken___ English.

2 I'm afraid of dogs _____ at people.

3 Be careful with the _____ glasses.

4 I like the wall _____ in red.

5 _____ cars are cheaper than new ones.

6 I saw a _____ accident on the road.

7 Have you read a book _____ by James Joyce?

8 That boy _____ with the old lady looks very happy.

9 Andy asked some _____ questions about the movie.

10 A _____ child dreads the fire.

PRACTICE 3

〈보기〉와 같이 분사를 이용하여 두 문장을 한 문장으로 연결하세요.

보 기	The boy is sleeping under the tree. He is my brother. ➡ The boy <u>sleeping under the tree</u> is my brother.

1. I lost my wallet. It was found by my sister.
   ➡ My _____ was found by my sister.

2. The students were dancing. They were happy.
   ➡ The _____ were happy.

3. The leaves have fallen on the ground. Let's pick them up.
   ➡ Let's pick up the leaves _____.

4. The girl is reading a book. She is Kate.
   ➡ The girl _____ is Kate.

5. I ate those cookies. They were burned.
   ➡ I ate those _____.

6. I saw her eyes. They were filled with tears.
   ➡ I saw her eyes _____.

7. The children are exercising in the gym. They are Sena and Minsu.
   ➡ The children _____ are Sena and Minsu.

8. The top of the mountain is covered with snow. It looks great.
   ➡ The top of the mountain _____ looks great.

9. We couldn't look at the sun. It was shining.
   ➡ We couldn't look at the _____.

10. I know the boy. He is singing on the stage.
    ➡ I know the boy _____.

PSS 2-2 보어로 쓰이는 분사

1. 주격 보어 – 주어의 상태나 행위를 설명한다.

   The news sounded **surprising** to us. 그 소식은 우리에게 놀랍게 들렸다.

   주어와 주격 보어가 능동의 관계일 때는 현재분사를 쓴다. 주로 '~하게 하는', '~하면서'로 해석된다.

Dad looked **surprised** to see his brother. 아빠는 그의 형을 보고 놀란 것처럼 보였다.

주어와 주격 보어가 수동의 관계일 때는 과거분사를 쓴다. 주로 '~한, ~된, ~해진'으로 해석된다.

2. 목적격 보어 – 목적어의 상태나 행위를 설명한다.

I heard **the professor calling** my name. 나는 교수님이 내 이름을 부르는 것을 들었다.

목적어와 목적격 보어가 능동의 관계일 때는 현재분사를 쓴다. '(목적어가) ~하는 것을'로 해석된다.

I heard **my name called** in the classroom. 나는 강의실에서 내 이름이 불리는 것을 들었다.

목적어와 목적격 보어가 수동의 관계일 때는 과거분사를 쓴다. '(목적어가) ~ 되는 것을'로 해석된다.

정답 p.48

PRACTICE 4

괄호 안의 동사를 분사의 형태로 바꾸어 빈칸에 쓰고, 문장 안에서 어떤 역할(명사 수식, 주격 보어, 목적격 보어)을 하는지 쓰세요.

1 We were _watching_ TV. (watch) (주격 보어)
2 I watched Mary _____ at the camp. (cook) ( )
3 I want my car _____ by tomorrow. (fix) ( )
4 She felt _____ because of the weather. (depress) ( )
5 He kept me _____ in that room. (wait) ( )
6 I know the boy _____ with the old man. (dance) ( )
7 The people were _____ about watching the game. (excite) ( )
8 Mr. Kim found the students _____ away. (run) ( )
9 Let's pick up the _____ leaves. (fall) ( )
10 Jenny wanted her room _____. (clean) ( )
11 The boy is _____. (smile) ( )
12 John was _____ to music in his room. (listen) ( )
13 What an _____ book this is! (interest) ( )
14 The cookies _____ by Mr. Kim were really good. (bake) ( )
15 I saw your daughter _____ toward the station. (walk) ( )
16 I felt my shoulder _____ and turned around. (touch) ( )

현재분사와 동명사

현재분사와 동명사는 형태는 같지만 현재분사는 형용사, 동명사는 명사의 역할을 한다.

	현재분사	동명사
명사 앞	'~하는, ~인' (명사의 동작, 상태) Look at the **crying** baby. 울고 있는 아기를 보아라.	'~을 하기 위한, ~로 쓰는' (용도) I bought a **sleeping** bag. 나는 침낭을 샀다.
Be동사 뒤	'~중인' (진행시제) I'm **baking** a cheese cake. 나는 치즈 케이크를 굽고 있어.	'~하는 것' (주격 보어 역할의 명사) My dream is **studying** in Germany. 내 꿈은 독일에서 공부하는 것이다.
타동사, 전치사 뒤	명사를 꾸며주는 형용사 역할로, 앞에 정관사나 소유격이 올 수 있다. I like the **dancing** girl. 난 저 춤추는 소녀가 좋아.	타동사, 전치사의 목적어로 명사 역할 I enjoy **listening** to the radio. 난 라디오 듣는 걸 즐겨.

정답 p.49

PRACTICE 5

다음 문장의 밑줄 친 부분의 용법이 〈보기〉의 A와 같으면 A, B와 같으면 B를 쓰세요.

| 보 기 | A. They are playing soccer. | B. She gave me a pair of running shoes. |

1 She is holding a car key. ( )
2 I need to buy a frying pan. ( )
3 My job is driving a taxi. ( )
4 He was reading a paper on the sofa. ( )
5 Let's buy some drinking water. ( )
6 The boring class made us sleepy. ( )
7 Their decision was leaving the country. ( )
8 The boy liked her smiling face. ( )
9 It's exciting to live in the big city. ( )
10 There's a TV in the living room. ( )

PSS 4 감정을 나타내는 분사

This game is very **exciting**.
이 게임은 매우 흥미진진하다.
I am very **excited** about this game.
나는 이 게임에 대해 매우 흥분된다.

-ing (~한 감정을 느끼게 하는) / -ed (~한 감정을 느끼는)

The lecture is **boring**.
그 강의는 지루하다.
I'm **bored** with the lecture.
나는 그 강의에 지루함을 느낀다.

Walking to work is **tiring**.
직장에 걸어가는 것은 피곤하다.
Walking to work makes me **tired**.
직장에 걸어가는 것은 나를 피곤하게 만든다.

Your question is **confusing**.
네 질문은 혼란스럽다.
I'm **confused** by your question.
나는 네 질문에 혼란스러움을 느낀다.

Today's weather is very **depressing**.
오늘의 날씨는 매우 우울하다.
Today's weather makes me **depressed**.
오늘의 날씨는 나를 우울하게 만든다.

The news was **disappointing**.
그 소식은 실망스러웠다.
I was **disappointed** with the news.
나는 그 소식에 실망했다.

Playing baseball is **exciting**.
야구를 하는 것은 흥미진진하다.
I'm **excited** about playing baseball.
나는 야구를 하는 것에 흥분된다.

The service was **satisfying**.
서비스는 만족스러웠다.
The customer was **satisfied** with the service.
그 고객은 서비스에 만족했다.

That novel is **interesting**.
그 소설은 흥미롭다.
I am **interested** in that novel.
나는 그 소설에 흥미를 느낀다.

The story was very **surprising**.
그 이야기는 매우 놀라웠다.
I was very **surprised** at the story.
나는 그 이야기에 매우 놀랐다.

His speech was very **embarrassing**.
그의 연설은 매우 당황스러웠다.
I was very **embarrassed** by his speech.
나는 그의 연설에 매우 당황했다.

The movie was **moving**.
그 영화는 감동적이었다.
I was **moved** by the movie.
나는 그 영화에 감동 받았다.

The accident was **shocking**.
그 사고는 충격적이었다.
I was **shocked** by the accident.
나는 그 사고에 충격을 받았다.

The performance was **amazing**.
그 공연은 놀라웠다.
I was **amazed** at the performance.
나는 그 공연을 보고 놀랐다.

The weather is very **pleasing**.
날씨가 아주 만족스럽다.
I am very **pleased** with the weather.
나는 날씨에 매우 만족한다.

All of the questions were **puzzling**.
그 질문들 모두가 곤혹스러웠다.
I was **puzzled** by all of the questions.
나는 그 모든 질문들에 곤혹함을 느꼈다.

PRACTICE 6

〈보기〉와 같이 분사를 이용하여 빈칸을 채우세요.

> 보 기 Your story interested me.
> ➡ Your story was <u>interesting</u>. / I was <u>interested</u> in your story.

1 This book bores me.
   ➡ This book is _____. / I am _____ with this book.

2 The weather depressed him.
   ➡ He was _____ by the weather. / The weather was _____.

3 Her letter confused me.
   ➡ I was _____ by her letter. / Her letter was _____.

4 Ben's grades disappointed himself.
   ➡ Ben's grades were _____. / Ben was _____ with his grades.

5 The play moved all the audiences.
   ➡ All the audiences were _____ by the play. / The play was _____.

6 The book interests the kids.
   ➡ The book is _____. / The kids are _____ in the book.

7 The news surprised my family.
   ➡ My family felt _____ at the news. / The news was _____ to my family.

8 My idea satisfied them.
   ➡ They were _____ with my idea. / My idea was _____.

9 Too much exercise tires me.
   ➡ Too much exercise is _____. / Too much exercise makes me _____.

10 Ann's essay puzzles me.
   ➡ Ann's essay is _____. / I am _____ by Ann's essay.

11 The party excited everyone.
   ➡ Everyone was _____ about the party. / Everyone found the party _____.

12 The picture shocked the public.
   ➡ The public was _____ by the picture. / The picture was _____.

13 The food festival amazed people.
   ➡ The food festival was _____. / People were _____ at the food festival.

14 The pop music pleased Mina.
   ➡ Mina was _____ with the pop music. / The pop music was _____.

15 His questions embarrassed the teacher.
➡ His questions were _____. / The teacher was _____ by his questions.

정답 p.49

PRACTICE 7

다음은 민지의 일기입니다. 괄호 안의 동사를 알맞은 형태로 바꾸어 빈칸에 쓰세요.

I'm on summer vacation. I was so happy at first, but after a while, I started to feel _____ (bore). I wanted to go somewhere or do something _____ (interest). Yesterday, my friend Yumi called and suggested going to a concert. She said, "They are great singers. You won't be _____ (disappoint)." We went to the art center for the concert today. It was a little _____ (tire) to go there by bus, but the concert was very _____ (excite). Both of us had a lot of fun and were _____ (satisfy).

분사구문

PSS 5-1 분사구문 만드는 법

분사를 이용하여 부사절을 부사구로 바꾼 형태를 분사구문이라고 한다.

After she arrived home, she went to bed. 그녀는 집에 도착한 후, 잠자리에 들었다.
　　　부사절　　　　　주절

① After she arrived home, she went to bed.
　부사절의 접속사(After)를 뺀다.
② she arrived home, she went to bed.
　주절의 주어(she)와 같으면 부사절의 주어(she)를 뺀다.
③ arrived home, she went to bed.
　부사절의 동사(arrived)를 -ing 형태로 바꾼다.
　➡ **Arriving** home, she went to bed.

1. 시간

　When I saw him at the station, I felt very happy.
　그를 역에서 봤을 때, 나는 매우 행복하다고 느꼈다.
　➡ **Seeing** him at the station, I felt very happy.

CHAPTER 9 _ 분사 | 229

2. 원인, 이유

   Because she is young, she can't go there.

   그녀는 어리기 때문에 그곳에 갈 수 없다.

   ➡ **Being young**, she can't go there.

3. 동시동작

   While Andy passed my house, he called me. Andy는 우리 집을 지나가면서 나를 불렀다.

   ➡ **Passing my house**, Andy called me.

4. 연속동작

   Sena turned off the light, **and listened to the music.**

   세나는 불을 끄고 그 음악을 들었다.

   ➡ Sena turned off the light, **listening to the music.**

5. 양보

   Although I know nothing about you, I want to meet you.

   너에 대해 아무것도 모르지만 난 너를 만나고 싶다.

   ➡ **Knowing nothing about you**, I want to meet you.

PRACTICE 8

정답 p.49

짝지어진 두 문장의 의미가 같도록 분사구문을 이용하여 빈칸을 채우세요.

1 I entered my room, and turned on the TV.
   = I entered my room, _turning on the TV_____.

2 As he studied hard, he passed the exam.
   = _____, he passed the exam.

3 As Kelly cooked in the kitchen, she sang some pop songs.
   = _____, Kelly sang some pop songs.

4 After I met Hana at the bookstore, I went back home.
   = _____, I went back home.

5 While they took a walk, they talked about Bob's birthday.
   = _____, they talked about Bob's birthday.

6 This train leaves Daejeon at 9:00, and arrives in Busan at 11:10.
   = This train leaves Daejeon at 9:00, _____.

7 While Tom listened to the radio, he looked at the pictures.
= _____, Tom looked at the pictures.

8 After I pushed a boy by mistake, I said, "I'm sorry."
= _____, I said, "I'm sorry."

9 Because they planned to stay at home, they didn't go out.
= _____, they didn't go out.

10 Because I knew him well, I couldn't believe his story.
= _____, I couldn't believe his story.

PSS 5-2 with + 명사 + 분사

「with + 명사 + 분사」는 '~이(가) …한 채로'의 뜻으로 동시동작을 나타내고, 명사와 분사의 관계가 능동이면 현재분사를, 수동이면 과거분사를 쓴다.

I was having dinner while my dog was sitting beside me.
나의 개가 내 옆에 앉아 있는 동안 나는 저녁을 먹고 있었다.
➡ I was having dinner, **with my dog sitting** beside me.
　　　　　　　　　　　　　　　　└─능동─┘
　나는 나의 개가 내 옆에 앉아 있게 한 채로 저녁을 먹고 있었다.

Nick was listening to music, and his eyes were closed.
Nick은 음악을 듣고 있었고, 그의 눈은 감겨 있었다.
　　　　　　　　　　　　　　　　　　　　┌─수동─┐
➡ Nick was listening to music, **with his eyes closed**. Nick은 눈이 감긴 채로 음악을 듣고 있었다.

PRACTICE 9

〈보기〉와 같이 짝지어진 두 문장의 의미가 같도록 빈칸을 채우세요.

| 보 기 | Mr. Kim was sitting on the sofa and he was crossing his legs.
= Mr. Kim was sitting on the sofa, <u>with his legs crossed</u>. |

1
My son was walking, and my daughter was following him.
= My son was walking, _____.

2
Ted is reading the book, and his lamp is turned on.
= Ted is reading the book, _____.

3
They left the place and the trash was cleaned up.
= They left the place, _____.

4
We ran together and our legs were tied.
= We ran together, _____.

5
He is singing a song while his friends are dancing.
= He is singing a song, _____.

6
I kept sleeping while my alarm clock was ringing.
= I kept sleeping, _____.

Chapter Review Test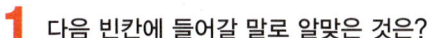

CHAPTER 9 분사

정답 p.50

1 다음 빈칸에 들어갈 말로 알맞은 것은?

> He listened to Hannah's story very carefully. She told him everything, from beginning to end. "That's a very _____ story," he said and smiled.

① boring
② excited
③ confused
④ interesting
⑤ moved

2 〈보기〉의 문장에서 밑줄 친 부분이 틀린 것을 두 개 찾아 그 기호를 쓰고 바르게 고쳐 쓰세요.

> 보기
> ⓐ Gidong is quite depressed.
> ⓑ Those pictures were taking by my mom.
> ⓒ They might get burned if they play with fire.
> ⓓ I saw her eyes filling with tears.

( ) _____ ➡ _____
( ) _____ ➡ _____

3 주어진 문장의 밑줄 친 부분과 쓰임이 같은 것은?

> He was planting some flowers.

① Reading a newspaper every day is important.
② How about going to the beach?
③ I stopped thinking about Jane.
④ She is making some cookies for her parents.
⑤ His hobby is watching movies.

4 다음 중 밑줄 친 부분이 어법상 틀린 것은?

① The audience was bored with the new movie.
② The students are interested in English.
③ The manager was satisfying with Jane's report.
④ The speech was so moving that I shed tears.
⑤ All the people in the hall were surprised at the news.

5 다음 빈칸에 들어갈 말로 알맞은 것은?

> Jane heard her name _____ outside.

① calling
② to call
③ called
④ to calling
⑤ have called

6 다음 문장의 밑줄 친 부분과 쓰임이 다른 것을 2개 고르세요.

> I'm interested in learning German.

① I like the girl dancing on the stage.
② She is drawing pictures in the field.
③ He gave up talking to his Canadian friend in English.
④ I was waiting for my mother in the waiting room.
⑤ Keeping your body warm in winter is important.

7 다음 대화의 빈칸 (A)~(C)에 들어갈 말이 바르게 연결된 것은?

> A: What are you reading?
> B: *A Walk to Remember* written by Nicholas Sparks. It's very ___(A)___ .
> A: Uh, romantic novels make me ___(B)___ .
> B: They are never boring. Then, what kind of books are you ___(C)___ in?
> A: I like science fiction.

	(A)	(B)	(C)
①	moving	bored	interesting
②	moved	bored	interesting
③	moving	bored	interested
④	moved	boring	interesting
⑤	moved	boring	interested

8 다음 밑줄 친 부분과 바꾸어 쓸 수 있는 것은?

> Bill talked to Cathy on the phone <u>while he cleaned</u> the room.

① he cleaning ② cleaning
③ clean ④ cleaned
⑤ to clean

9 다음 중 밑줄 친 부분을 어법상 옳게 고친 것은?

① Ben's grades were disappointing (→ disappointed).
② Too much exercise makes me tiring (→ tired).
③ I was shocked (→ shocking) by the accident.
④ This movie was very touching (→ touched).
⑤ Jenny wanted her room cleaned (→ cleaning).

10 다음 빈칸 (A)~(C)에 들어갈 말이 바르게 연결된 것은?

> **How to Make ___(A)___ Peanuts**
> 1. Put peanuts with water into a pot.
> 2. Boil them at high heat.
> 3. Reduce heat to medium-low.
> 4. ___(B)___ once in a while, boil the peanuts until they get ___(C)___ .
> 5. Cool them before serving.

	(A)	(B)	(C)
①	Boiled	Stirring	tenderly
②	Boiled	Stirred	tender
③	Boiling	Stir	tenderness
④	Boiling	Stir	tenderly
⑤	Boiled	Stirring	tender

11 다음 빈칸에 들어갈 단어로 알맞은 것은?

> Jason went to the park with his 5-year-old daughter. But he couldn't find her after he came back from the restroom. He was very _____.

① worries ② to worry ③ worried
④ worry   ⑤ worrying

12 다음 중 밑줄 친 부분의 쓰임이 나머지 넷과 다른 것은?

① Nari couldn't help crying.
② I heard some surprising news.
③ I enjoy spending time with my parents.
④ My hobby is playing baseball.
⑤ Ted likes going hiking on weekends.

13 다음의 두 문장을 하나의 문장으로 연결할 때 빈칸에 들어갈 말로 적절한 것은?

> • Jane was lying on the grass. I saw her.
> = I saw Jane _____ on the grass.

① lied   ② lay   ③ lying
④ to lie ⑤ to have lay

14 밑줄 친 ⓐ~ⓓ 중 어법상 틀린 것을 있는 대로 고른 것은?

> A: The movie was ⓐ fantastic.
> B: I don't think so. The actors were ⓑ terrible.
> A: But the story was really ⓒ move.
> B: No, It was very boring. I almost fell ⓓ sleeping.

① ⓐ, ⓑ   ② ⓑ, ⓒ   ③ ⓒ, ⓓ
④ ⓐ, ⓑ, ⓒ   ⑤ ⓑ, ⓒ, ⓓ

15 쓰임이 어색한 것을 있는 대로 고른 것은?

> The Moon is a barren, rocky satellite that ⓐ orbit around the Earth. It is Earth's only natural satellite and its distance from Earth is about 385,000 km. The Moon gets its light from the Sun ⓑ since it cannot produce light on its own. The Moon's cratered and ⓒ pitting surface is a result of comet and asteroid impacts. Earth's Moon is the only place beyond Earth ⓓ where humans have set foot. And the Moon's presence helps ⓔ stabilizing our planet's wobble and moderate our climate.

① ⓐ   ② ⓑ, ⓔ   ③ ⓐ, ⓒ
④ ⓐ, ⓒ, ⓔ   ⑤ ⓑ, ⓓ, ⓔ

16 다음 중 밑줄 친 부분이 어법상 어색한 것을 모두 고르세요.

① All the people were excited.
② You should recycle using paper.
③ This book was written by Thomas Hardy.
④ I think the book is so confused.
⑤ The flowers in my garden have been watered.

17 다음 빈칸에 들어갈 말이 알맞게 짝지어진 것은?

> A: Were you _____ at the news?
> B: Yes, the news was very _____.

① surprised – surprising
② surprised – surprised
③ surprising – surprised
④ surprising – surprising
⑤ surprise – surprised

18 다음 중 밑줄 친 부분의 쓰임이 옳지 않은 것은?

① Her speech was shocked to me.
② I was excited when I played the game.
③ My brother is an amazing person.
④ I was tired when I arrived home.
⑤ Drinking a lot of water is good for your health.

19 다음 밑줄 친 부분을 분사구문으로 바꿀 때 빈칸에 알맞은 말을 쓰세요.

> • I am waiting for her and I am listening to music.
> ➡ I am waiting for her _____.

20 다음 글의 (A)~(E) 중 어법상 어색한 것끼리 바르게 짝지은 것은?

> I was at a pet store when I was a puppy. (A) There were a lot of animals waited for their new owners. One day, a cute girl came into the store with her mother. She took me home. (B) At first, she took good care of me. However, after a few months, (C) she seemed busy and even forgot feeding me. (D) Her schedule was filled with her homework. I was sent to this house after all. Fortunately, my new owner takes good care of me. When I was in the park yesterday, some kids came near me. (E) I thought of the little girl. I hope she's doing well.

① (A), (E) ② (B), (C) ③ (B), (D)
④ (A), (C) ⑤ (A), (D)

21 밑줄 친 단어가 문맥에 맞게 쓰인 것은?

① A: Are you going to the gym?
　B: No, too much exercise is tired.
② A: The chocolate cake was amazing!
　B: I know! I want to have it again.
③ A: Did you hear what happened to Tom?
　B: Yes, we were shocking to hear that.
④ A: That movie was so interested.
　B: Do you mean *Spider Man*?
⑤ A: Did you show your mom your grades?
　B: Yes. She was disappointing with my grades.

22 우리말과 같은 뜻이 되도록 밑줄 친 부분을 부사절로 바꿔 쓰세요.

- 우리는 일을 마친 후에 저녁을 먹으러 나갔다.
  ➡ We went out for dinner <u>finishing the work</u>.

= We went out for dinner _____ _____.

23 다음 두 문장을 분사를 이용하여 한 문장으로 쓰세요.

- The woman is my mother.
- The woman is waving to my father.

➡ _____
_____

24 다음 대화의 빈칸에 알맞지 <u>않은</u> 말은?

A: What did you do last holiday?
B: I went to the amusement park with my family.
A: How was it?
B: It was _____.

① exciting ② great ③ awesome
④ surprised ⑤ disappointing

25 우리말과 같은 뜻이 되도록 빈칸에 알맞은 단어를 쓰세요.

- 그는 그의 눈을 감은 채 소파에 누워 있었다.
  = He was lying on the sofa _____ _____ _____ _____.

26 다음 글의 밑줄 친 (A)~(D) 중 어법상 어색한 것을 <u>2개</u> 골라 그 기호와 오류 부분을 쓰고, 바르게 고치세요.

Igloo
(A) <u>An igloo is a type of house building of snow, originally by the Inuit.</u> (B) <u>The name is from the Inuit word</u>, *iglu*. (C) <u>Igloo means snowhouse in English</u>. Have you ever imagined living in an igloo? (D) <u>It would be very excited.</u>

(1) • 기호: _____
 • 오류 부분: _____
 • 오류 수정: _____
(2) • 기호: _____
 • 오류 부분: _____
 • 오류 수정: _____

27 밑줄 친 ⓐ~ⓔ에 각각 들어갈 단어로 어색한 것은?

- Jay usually ___ⓐ___ basketball after lunch.
- With her arms ___ⓑ___, my mom was deep in thought.
- My son reads only ___ⓒ___ books a year.
- She was ___ⓓ___ to see her favorite singer.
- Yesterday I fell down and ___ⓔ___ my arm.

① ⓐ: plays ② ⓑ: folded ③ ⓒ: a few
④ ⓓ: excited ⑤ ⓔ: broken

28 다음 대화의 빈칸에 가장 알맞은 말은?

Sora : Look! There are some dolls over there. Which one do you like?
Jenny: Well, I like the one ___ a hat.

① wearing ② wear ③ to wear
④ wears ⑤ wore

29 주어진 우리말과 같은 뜻이 되도록 괄호 안의 단어를 바르게 바꾸어 쓰세요.

- 우리는 그 꽃병이 깨진 것을 발견하고 모두 놀랐다.
  = We were all surprised to find the vase _____. (break)

30 다음 중 밑줄 친 부분의 쓰임이 나머지와 다른 하나는?

① Going to the beach is exciting.
② The man kept looking at me.
③ I watched Linda crossing the street.
④ I just finished washing the dishes.
⑤ I love eating cookies.

31 다음 중 어법상 옳은 문장의 개수는?

ⓐ Looked after his sister, the boy was getting tired.
ⓑ With her legs crossing, Sara was sitting in front of them.
ⓒ The man wearing a red necktie is my boss, Mr. Lim.
ⓓ She found the guys talking behind her back.
ⓔ The door painting white looks bright and pretty.
ⓕ When Son finally scored a goal, the crowd got so excited.

① 0개 ② 1개 ③ 2개 ④ 3개 ⑤ 4개

32 다음 우리말을 영어로 바르게 옮긴 문장을 모두 고르세요.

Sally는 청구서를 보면서 앉아 있었다.

① Sally was sitting looked at the bill.
② Sally was sitting while look at the bill.
③ Sally was sitting while she looks at the bill.
④ Sally was sitting looking at the bill.
⑤ Sally was sitting while she was looking at the bill.

Chapter Review Test

33 다음 빈칸에 들어갈 말끼리 바르게 짝지어진 것은?

> M: What did you think of the movie?
> W: It was very ___(A)___ . I was really looking forward to this movie's release because the original novel was really good. But it didn't meet my expectations at all.
> M: I agree that the plot was changed a little. But, I didn't think it was that bad.
> W: Come on! Sophie was not supposed to be that active.
> M: But that made the movie more lively. It wasn't that ___(B)___ .

      (A)   (B)
① annoyed – confusing
② disappointed – confused
③ disappointing – disturbing
④ pleasing – disturbed
⑤ annoying – confused

34 다음 대화의 빈칸에 들어갈 말끼리 바르게 짝지어진 것은?

> Tom : What are you going to do this Saturday?
> Mary: I'm going to the Science Fair.
> Tom : Oh, that will be _____ .
> Mary: Are you _____ in science?
> Tom : Of course. Can I join you?
> Mary: Sure.

① interesting – interested
② interested – interesting
③ interesting – interesting
④ interested – interested
⑤ interest – interests

35 다음 주어진 문장을 분사구문으로 바꿀 때, 빈칸에 알맞은 말을 쓰세요.

> • When I dropped by his house, I found him sleeping.
> ➡ _____, I found him sleeping.

36 다음 대화의 밑줄 친 (A)~(E) 중 어법상 올바른 표현으로만 짝지어진 것은?

> Sam : Kate, where are you going?
> Kate: (A) <u>I'm going to a concert held in Seoul.</u>
> Sam : (B) <u>Whom concert is it?</u>
> Kate: Jay Zhang. He's a singer from China.
> Sam : (C) <u>I'm surprising that you are a fan of a Chinese singer.</u> Will there be an interpreter at the concert?
> Kate: No, but (D) <u>I used to live in China for several years,</u> (E) <u>so it's not difficult for me understand Chinese.</u>
> Sam : Wow, I didn't know that. Then can you teach me some Chinese later?
> Kate: Sure! I'd be happy to.

① (A), (C)   ② (B), (D)   ③ (A), (D)
④ (C), (E)   ⑤ (C), (D)

37 우리말과 같은 뜻이 되도록 밑줄 친 부분을 부사절로 바꿔 쓰세요.

- 버스를 놓쳐서 나는 직장에 늦었다.
  ➡ <u>Missing the bus</u>, I was late for work.

= _____, I was late for work.

38 다음 대화의 ⓐ~ⓔ 중에서 그 쓰임이 같은 것끼리 짝지어진 것은?

Mina: Jake, what are you doing?
Jake: I am ⓐ <u>drawing</u> cartoons. My hobby is ⓑ <u>drawing</u> cartoons.
Mina: Well, what are you ⓒ <u>drawing</u>?
Jake: I am ⓓ <u>drawing</u> Mickey Mouse.
Mina: Wow. It's very cute. ⓔ <u>Drawing</u> cartoons is really hard, isn't it?
Jake: No, it isn't.

① ⓐ,ⓒ,ⓔ   ② ⓑ,ⓒ,ⓓ   ③ ⓐ,ⓑ,ⓒ
④ ⓒ,ⓔ   ⑤ ⓑ,ⓔ

39 다음 우리말을 영어로 바르게 옮긴 것은?

Michael은 눈을 감은 채 거기 서 있었다.

① Michael was standing there with his eyes closed.
② Michael was standing there his closed eyes.
③ Michael stood there with his eyes closing.
④ Michael was standing there with his eyes closing.
⑤ Michael was standing there with his eye closed.

40 〈보기〉에서 어법상 틀린 것을 있는 대로 고른 것은?

보기
ⓐ She stood at the door <u>read</u> a newspaper.
ⓑ I can express my emotions by <u>writing</u> them down.
ⓒ I know the man <u>picking</u> up the garbage.
ⓓ We were standing by the bed <u>watched</u> the baby sleeping.
ⓔ James looked at me <u>sang</u> a song.

① ⓐ, ⓑ   ② ⓑ, ⓔ   ③ ⓐ, ⓑ, ⓒ
④ ⓐ, ⓓ, ⓔ   ⑤ ⓑ, ⓒ, ⓓ, ⓔ

41 다음 두 문장의 뜻이 같도록 빈칸에 들어갈 알맞은 말은?

- Though I go to university in this foreign country now, I have lots of friends in my home country.
  = _____ in this foreign country now, I have lots of friends in my home country.

① Go to university
② Going to university
③ Been gone to university
④ Being gone to university
⑤ Gone to university

42 두 문장의 빈칸에 공통으로 들어갈 단어로 가장 적절한 것은?

- I _____ to the countryside last month because of my work.
- He was _____ by her speech about loving one another.

① found   ② moved   ③ made
④ touched ⑤ ran

CHAPTER 10
형용사

성취도 자기 평가 활용법

구분	평가 기준
Excellent	문법 내용을 모두 이해하고, 문제를 모두 맞힘.
Very good	문법 내용은 충분히 이해했으나 실수로 1~2문제 틀림.
Good	문법 내용이 조금 어려워 3~4문제 틀림.
needs **R**eview	문법 내용 이해가 어렵고, 5문제 이상 틀림, 복습 필요.

Problem Solving Skill	페이지	학습날짜	성취도 자기평가 E V G R	학습체크
PSS 1 형용사의 쓰임	242	/		☐
PSS 2 -thing, -one, -body+형용사	244	/		☐
PSS 3 주의해야 할 형용사의 용법	244	/		☐
PSS 4 형용사의 어순	247	/		☐
PSS 5 수나 양을 나타내는 형용사	페이지	학습날짜	성취도 자기평가 E V G R	학습체크
PSS 5-1 many, much	248	/		☐
PSS 5-2 few, little	250	/		☐
PSS 5-3 a few, a little	251	/		☐
PSS 5-4 some, any	253	/		☐
PSS 6 수사	페이지	학습날짜	성취도 자기평가 E V G R	학습체크
PSS 6-1 분수와 소수	255	/		☐
PSS 6-2 연도와 날짜	256	/		☐
PSS 6-3 배수사	257	/		☐
Chapter Review Test	258	/		☐

형용사의 쓰임

한정적 용법	명사의 앞에서 명사를 수식한다. Mr. Kim is a **great** teacher. 김 선생님은 훌륭한 선생님이다. I went to a **fancy** restaurant yesterday. 나는 어제 근사한 음식점에 갔다.
서술적 용법	주격 보어나 목적격 보어로 쓰여 주어나 목적어에 대한 설명을 한다. **The boy** over there is very **tall**. 저기 있는 소년은 키가 매우 크다. 　　　　　　　　　　　　주격 보어 We think **the garden beautiful**. 우리는 그 정원이 아름답다고 생각한다. 　　　　　　　　　목적격 보어 *cf.* afraid, alike, alive, alone, ashamed, asleep, glad, sorry와 같은 형용사는 서술적 용법에만 사용된다. 　　This ant is **alive**. (○) 이 개미는 살아있다. 　　This is an **alive** ant. (×) 　　My sister is **asleep**. (○) 내 여동생은 잠들었다. 　　The **asleep** girl is my sister. (×)

PRACTICE 1

괄호 안에 주어진 형용사를 알맞은 곳에 넣어 문장을 다시 쓰세요.

1　Becky has a car. (old)
　➡ Becky has an old car.

2　Ms. Song is a doctor. (famous)
　➡ _____

3　Mary is wearing a necklace. (beautiful)
　➡ _____

4　I'd like to have coffee. (hot)
　➡ _____

5　Paul watched a movie yesterday. (exciting)
　➡ _____

6　Look at the bird over there. (small)
　➡ _____

7 Inho used to live in an apartment. (large)
➡ _____

8 Could you pass me the ball? (blue)
➡ _____

9 Put them on the table. (plastic)
➡ _____

10 I drank tea last night. (Irish)
➡ _____

정답 p.53

PRACTICE 2

〈보기〉와 같이 주어진 문장을 바꾸어 쓰세요.

보 기	This is a long story.
	➡ This <u>story is long</u>.

1 She is an intelligent woman.
➡ The _____ .

2 It was an impressive movie.
➡ The _____ .

3 This is an empty house.
➡ This _____ .

4 That is a broken computer.
➡ That _____ .

5 She is a diligent student.
➡ That _____ .

6 These are famous artists.
➡ These _____ .

정답 p.53

PRACTICE 3

괄호 안에 주어진 단어 중 알맞은 것을 고르세요.

1 The kids are (sleep, asleep) on the sofa.

2 The (sleeping, asleep) boy is my son.

3 What's she (like, alike)?

4 Did you see the (live, alive) starfish?

5 The boys look (like, alike).

6 The bird is still (live, alive).

7 I'm (glad, gladly) to hear the news.

8 Look at that (glad, cheerful) girl.

9 That (scared, afraid) boy is Minho.

10 I'm (scaring, afraid) of birds.

 **-thing, -one, -body + 형용사**

> -thing, -one, -body로 끝나는 대명사는 형용사가 뒤에서 수식한다.
>
> Don't you have **anything special**? 너는 특별한 무언가를 가지고 있지 않니?
> Jenny met **someone handsome** yesterday. Jenny는 어제 잘생긴 누군가를 만났다.
> Do you know **anybody funny**? 너는 재미있는 누군가를 아니?
> There was **nothing important** to see. 볼 만한 중요한 것이 없었다.
>
> **cf.** 한 단어인 명사 thing은 형용사가 앞에서 수식한다.
> I don't want to eat **sweet things**. 나는 달콤한 것들을 먹고 싶지 않다.

PRACTICE 4

정답 p.53

괄호 안에 주어진 단어를 바르게 배열하여 빈칸에 쓰세요.

1. I'd like to _____. (something, eat, spicy)
2. Was there _____? (familiar, you, anybody, to)
3. I'm looking for _____. (for, the, diligent, someone, job)
4. Don't you _____? (else, need, anything)
5. Would you like _____? (something, drink, to, hot)
6. Have you _____ in the police office? (friendly, met, anyone)
7. She _____ when she needs help. (somebody, to, close, her, calls)
8. I couldn't _____. (expensive, yesterday, buy, anything)
9. I _____ to tell you. (nothing, have, new)
10. I have _____ near my home. (famous, seen, nobody)

 **주의해야 할 형용사의 용법**

> 1. 「the+형용사」는 '~한 사람들'의 뜻으로, 복수 명사처럼 쓰인다.
>
>   He has helped **the poor** for three years. 그는 3년 동안 불쌍한 사람들을 도왔다.
>   　　　　　　(= poor people)

This seat is for **the old**. 이 자리는 노인들을 위한 것이다.
(= old people)

The young are interested in foreign languages. 젊은 사람들은 외국어에 흥미가 있다.
(= Young people)

2. 국가와 관련된 형용사는 주로 국가명에 -n, -sh, -ch, -s, -ese를 붙여 만든다. 이 형태는 형용사뿐 아니라 해당 국가의 언어, 그 국가의 사람을 나타내는 명사로도 쓰인다.

England 영국(명사)
English 영국(인)의, 영어의(형용사), 영국인, 영어(명사)
They don't enjoy **English** breakfast. 그들은 영국식 아침식사를 즐기지 않는다.

주요 국가명과 형용사형

국가명	형용사형	국가명	형용사형
Korea 한국	Korean 한국의	Spain 스페인	Spanish 스페인의
America 미국	American 미국의	China 중국	Chinese 중국의
Canada 캐나다	Canadian 캐나다의	Japan 일본	Japanese 일본의
Poland 폴란드	Polish 폴란드의	France 프랑스	French 프랑스의
Denmark 덴마크	Danish 덴마크의	Germany 독일	German 독일의
Switzerland 스위스	Swiss 스위스의	the Netherlands 네덜란드	Dutch 네덜란드의

cf. 「the+국가명의 형용사」는 '국민 전체'를 의미한다.
the Chinese 중국인 전체   **the French** 프랑스인 전체

단, 형용사 형태가 -sh, -ch, -s, -ese로 끝나지 않는 경우는 -s를 붙인 복수 형태로 국민 전체를 나타낸다.
the Koreans 한국인들   **the Americans** 미국인들

PRACTICE 5

〈보기〉와 같이 주어진 문장을 바꾸어 쓰세요.

| 보 기 | You should respect old people.
➡ You should respect the old. |

1 Rich people have their own problems.
   ➡ _____

2 He did a lot of good things for poor people.
   ➡ _____

3 These days blind people keep dogs to help themselves.
➡ _____

4 There are some special schools for deaf people.
➡ _____

5 Mr. Park encourages young people to be brave.
➡ _____

6 I took care of sick people in the hospital yesterday.
➡ _____

PRACTICE 6

정답 p.54

다음 문장의 밑줄 친 부분을 바르게 고쳐 쓰세요.

1 The old has to exercise regularly. _____

2 Does the sick take a lot of medicine? _____

3 Is the rich getting richer? _____

4 The blind learns a special way of reading. _____

5 The hospital for the elderly were built last year. _____

6 The young tends to learn more easily. _____

PRACTICE 7

정답 p.54

다음 밑줄 친 단어가 문장에서 어떤 의미로 쓰였는지 빈칸에 쓰세요.

1 Mike has always wanted to learn Korean. _____

2 Sarah is an American but she doesn't like traditional American food. _____ , _____

3 The Polish feel proud of their country. _____

4 French women don't gain weight. _____

5 My sister has studied German for five years. _____

6 Danish dairy products are world-famous. _____

7 Have you ever eaten Japanese food? _____

8 Chinese is hard to learn because of four intonations. _____

9 She found Korean culture similar to Canadian culture. _____

10 Spanish is the language spoken by the Argentine people. _____

 **형용사의 어순**

1. 2개 이상의 형용사가 함께 쓰일 때는 주로 다음과 같은 어순을 원칙으로 한다.

서수	기수	성질	크기	신구	색깔	국적	재료
first	two	nice	big	new	blue	Korean	wooden
third	four	pretty	small	old	green	English	plastic
tenth	seven	delicious	large	young	red	French	metal

2. 다음은 형용사 앞에 다른 수식어가 올 때의 어순이다.

all   both
double   half
+

정관사	the
지시형용사	this that these those
소유격	my your his her its our their

PRACTICE 8

괄호 안에 주어진 단어를 바르게 배열하여 빈칸에 쓰세요.

1 _____ dogs (big, white)
2 _____ girls (four, all, Korean)
3 _____ gardens (green, large)
4 _____ vases (metal, small, seven)
5 _____ shirts (nice, blue, those)
6 _____ roses (red, the, beautiful)
7 _____ friend (French, young, my)
8 _____ sentences (first, the, two)
9 _____ chairs (wooden, comfortable)
10 _____ people (million, a, half)
11 _____ buildings (beautiful, both, these)
12 _____ matches (her, three, all)

PRACTICE 9

다음 문장의 밑줄 친 부분을 바르게 고쳐 쓰세요.

1 I met tall a Japanese woman yesterday.　　　　　a tall Japanese
2 He knows the both pretty girls.
3 She loved her new nice friends.
4 Would you like small this piece of cake?
5 Look at high three those buildings!
6 I like the American exciting movies.
7 They threw black ugly the plastic boxes away.
8 Dain bought these all lovely dolls.
9 My older wise brother told me what to do.
10 Put the book on that white big table.
11 The restaurant is famous for Chinese its nice food.
12 Samuel is the English fifth happy traveler that we've met.
13 I have seen her all three pink sweaters.
14 We were watching young healthy four lions.
15 Abby had red two fresh apples for breakfast.

PSS 5 수나 양을 나타내는 형용사
Problem Solving Skill

PSS 5-1 many, much

many+셀 수 있는 명사의 복수형　　much+셀 수 없는 명사

many – '많은'의 뜻으로 셀 수 있는 명사의 수를 나타낸다.	much – '많은'의 뜻으로 셀 수 없는 명사의 양을 나타낸다.
many trees 많은 나무들 = **a lot[number] of** trees = **lots of** trees = **plenty of** trees **Many people** use computers. 많은 사람들이 컴퓨터를 사용한다. How **many students** are there? 얼마나 많은 학생들이 있니?	**much** money 많은 돈 = **a lot of** money = **lots of** money = **plenty of** money I have so **much work** to do. 나는 아주 많은 할 일이 있다. How **much food** did you buy? 얼마나 많은 음식을 샀니?

PRACTICE 10

다음 문장의 빈칸에 many나 much 중 알맞은 것을 쓰세요.

1. Were there _____ kids in the park?
2. There isn't _____ time to waste.
3. There were _____ cars on the road.
4. How _____ water do you drink a day?
5. Kitty has _____ kinds of toys in her room.
6. Did he make _____ money through the business?
7. _____ old people live alone in this town.
8. He made so _____ mistakes.
9. How _____ children does he have?
10. Make sure you don't drink too _____ coffee at night.

PRACTICE 11

밑줄 친 부분을 many나 much로 바꾸어 문장을 다시 쓰세요.

1. Does Minho have a lot of friends?
   → _____

2. Does it take lots of time to get there on foot?
   → _____

3 Are there plenty of flowers in the vase?
➡ _____

4 Lots of drivers drive very fast.
➡ _____

5 Should I give the plants a lot of water?
➡ _____

6 Plenty of students stayed in the classroom after school.
➡ _____

7 There isn't a lot of furniture in my room.
➡ _____

8 Did they spend plenty of money on this house?
➡ _____

9 We didn't have lots of fun.
➡ _____

10 Did you borrow a lot of books from the library?
➡ _____

PSS 5-2 few, little

| few + 셀 수 있는 명사의 복수형 | little + 셀 수 없는 명사 |

few – '거의 ~없는'의 뜻으로 셀 수 있는 명사의 수를 나타낸다.

There are **few people** on the street.
거리에 사람들이 거의 없다.
Peter has **few friends**.
Peter는 친구들이 거의 없다.

little – '거의 ~없는'의 뜻으로 셀 수 없는 명사의 양을 나타낸다.

There is **little water** in the bottle.
병에 물이 거의 없다.
I had **little time** to prepare dinner.
나는 저녁을 준비할 시간이 거의 없었다.

PRACTICE 12

다음 문장의 빈칸에 few나 little 중 알맞은 것을 쓰세요.

1 I'm not busy today. I have _____ things to do.
2 She couldn't buy the clothes because she had _____ money then.
3 We have _____ milk in the refrigerator. Let's buy some.
4 I like to go jogging, but there are _____ parks in this city.
5 Nami did the job very well. She made _____ mistakes.
6 It's hotter today because there is _____ wind.
7 I met _____ foreigners in this small village.
8 There is _____ space left in the car.
9 Help yourself to these cookies. I put _____ sugar in them.
10 There were _____ people in the gallery.

PSS 5-3 a few, a little

a few + 셀 수 있는 명사의 복수형

a little + 셀 수 없는 명사

a few – '조금의, 몇 개의'의 뜻으로 셀 수 있는 명사의 수를 나타낸다.

There are **a few pens** on the desk.
책상에 몇 개의 펜들이 있다.
I borrowed **a few books** yesterday.
나는 어제 몇 권의 책을 빌렸다.

a little – '약간의'의 뜻으로 셀 수 없는 명사의 양을 나타낸다.

There is **a little sugar** left.
약간의 설탕이 남아 있다.
Andy had **a little bread** for lunch.
Andy는 점심으로 약간의 빵을 먹었다.

PRACTICE 13

다음 문장의 빈칸에 a few나 a little 중 알맞은 것을 쓰세요.

1 I bought this bag _____ days ago.
2 You need _____ water to take this medicine.
3 _____ girls were talking about the movie.
4 Tom has _____ trouble paying the rent.
5 It will take _____ time to solve the problem.
6 My neighbor has _____ dogs and cats.
7 I melted _____ butter on the pan.
8 Sangmin knows _____ Spanish words.
9 Do you have _____ knowledge about computers?
10 She came home _____ hours later.

PRACTICE 14

다음 밑줄 친 부분을 바르게 고쳐 쓰세요. (단, 문장에서 원래 의도한 의미를 그대로 살리세요.)

1 I don't have many hope for that. _____
2 He has been reading this book for a little days. _____
3 I have a few money. Shall I buy you an ice cream? _____
4 Alex used to exercise for much hours. _____
5 My brother has little bad teeth. _____
6 There is few ice in the refrigerator. _____
7 Insu has been there a little times. _____
8 There was few light in the dark street. _____
9 There aren't much restaurants in this town. _____
10 They bought a few meat for dinner. _____
11 There's not many traffic now. _____
12 Little members voted for him. _____

PSS 5-4 some, any

A: Would you like **some** sandwiches?
B: No, thanks. I don't have **any** time. I have to go out now.

some과 any는 '얼마간의, 약간의'의 뜻으로 셀 수 있는 명사나 셀 수 없는 명사 모두와 함께 쓸 수 있다.

some	any
1. 일반적으로 긍정문에 쓰인다. Junho gave me **some** eggs. 준호는 내게 약간의 달걀을 주었다. 2. 권유, 요구를 나타내는 의문문에 쓰인다. Would you like **some** salad? 샐러드 좀 드실래요? Can I have **some** water? 물 좀 마실 수 있을까요? 3. 긍정의 대답을 예상하는 의문문에 쓰인다. Were there **some** phone calls for me? 내게 온 전화가 좀 있었나요? 4. some이 불특정한 일부를 나타낼 때는 부정문에 쓸 수 있다. **Some** students don't obey the school's policy. 몇몇 학생들은 학교의 방침을 준수하지 않는다.	1. 일반적으로 부정문과 의문문에 쓰인다. 부정문에서는 '조금도 ~ (아니다)'로 해석한다. I don't have **any** classes this Saturday. 나는 이번 토요일에 수업이 하나도 없다. Do you have **any** ideas about how to help her? 넌 그녀를 어떻게 도울지에 대한 생각이 좀 있니? 2. '어떠한 ~라도'의 뜻으로 긍정문에 쓰인다. You can take **any** bus here. 넌 여기에서 어떠한 버스라도 탈 수 있다. 3. 조건을 나타내는 if절에 쓰인다. If you have **any** questions, call me anytime. 질문이 있으면, 내게 언제든 전화해요.

PRACTICE 15

우리말에 맞게 다음 문장의 빈칸에 some이나 any 중 알맞은 것을 쓰세요.

1 그녀는 아침에 약간의 과일을 먹었다.
   ➡ She had _____ fruit in the morning.

2 그는 필기할 펜이 하나도 없었다.
   ➡ He didn't have _____ pens to write with.

3 도서관에서 약간의 책을 빌릴 수 있나요?
   ➡ Can I borrow _____ books from the library?

4 이 챕터에 대해 어떠한 질문이라도 있나요?
   ➡ Are there _____ questions about this chapter?

5 어떤 기차라도 당신을 그곳에 데려다 줄 거예요.
   ➡ _____ train will take you there.

6 밥을 좀 더 (드시길) 원하세요?
   ➡ Do you want _____ more rice?

7 Mary는 그들로부터 어떠한 충고도 얻지 못했다.
   ➡ Mary didn't get _____ advice from them.

8 Jina와 나는 오늘밤 약간의 계획이 있다.
   ➡ Jina and I have _____ plans for tonight.

9 만약 내게 어떤 문제라도 생긴다면, 당신에게 편지를 쓸게요.
   ➡ If I have _____ trouble, I'll write to you.

10 저는 당신으로부터 어떠한 도움도 필요하지 않아요.
    ➡ I don't need _____ help from you.

PRACTICE 16

〈보기〉에서 알맞은 단어를 골라 some이나 any를 이용하여 문장을 완성하세요.

| 보 기 | people   medicine   friends   money   problems   flowers |
| | time   cake   homework   place   food |

1 Mr. Kim gave the students __*some homework*__ for today.

2 I'm very hungry, but I don't have _____ to eat.

3 The news said _____ died in the accident last night.

4 If you have _____, let me know. I can help you.

5 I bought _____ from the drugstore.

6 We can go to _____ except that unpleasant restaurant.

7 Giho gave me _____ for my new vase.

8 Do you have _____ living around here?

9 I don't have _____ to take care of it. I have to go out.

10 Would you like _____ and juice for dessert?

11 Would you mind lending me _____? I'll pay you back soon.

PSS 6 수사

PSS 6-1 분수와 소수

1. 분수 – 분자는 기수로, 분모는 서수로 읽고, 분자가 2 이상이면 분모에 '-s'를 붙여 읽는다.

   1/5 ➡ a fifth 또는 one-fifth   3/8 ➡ three-eighths
   5 3/4 ➡ five and three-fourths[three-quarters]
   cf. 1/2 ➡ a half 또는 one-half   1/4 ➡ a quarter 또는 one-quarter

2. 소수 – 소수점까지는 기수로, 소수점은 point, 소수점 이하는 한 자리씩 읽는다.

   4.25 ➡ four point two five   13.87 ➡ thirteen point eight seven

정답 p.56

PRACTICE 17

다음 분수와 소수를 영어로 읽을 때의 표기법을 쓰세요.

1 1/3 ➡ _____   **2** 2/5 ➡ _____

3 2 7/11 ➡ _____   **4** 5/6 ➡ _____

5 1/2 ➡ _____   **6** 9/13 ➡ _____

7 1/4 ➡ _____   **8** 4 3/7 ➡ _____

9 3.14 ➡ _____   **10** 5.56 ➡ _____

11 16.29 ➡ _____   **12** 50.15 ➡ _____

13 127.93 ➡ _____

14 612.49 ➡ _____

15 2,105.89 ➡ _____

PSS 6-2 연도와 날짜

1. 연도 – 두 자리씩 끊어 읽는다.

   1785년 ➡ seventeen eighty-five   1998년 ➡ nineteen ninety-eight
   cf. 2002년 ➡ two thousand (and) two   2019년 ➡ two thousand (and) nineteen
                                                     twenty nineteen

2. 날짜 – 서수를 이용한다.

   9월 22일 ➡ September (the) twenty-second 또는 the twenty-second of September

정답 p.56

PRACTICE 18

다음 연도와 날짜를 영어로 읽을 때의 표기법을 쓰세요.

1 1826년 ➡ _____

2 1983년 ➡ _____

3 2004년 ➡ _____

4 2020년 ➡ _____

5 5월 1일 ➡ _____

6 7월 12일 ➡ _____

7 2월 18일 ➡ _____

8 11월 24일 ➡ _____

9 4월 23일 ➡ _____

10 12월 9일 ➡ _____

PSS 1-4 형용사 형태의 부사에 '-ly'를 붙이면 다른 뜻이 되는 부사

close	가까이	She came **close** to me. 그녀는 나에게 가까이 다가왔다.
closely	주의 깊게, 면밀히	You should look at it **closely**. 너는 주의 깊게 그것을 봐야 한다.
hard	열심히	I worked very **hard** in a restaurant. 나는 식당에서 매우 열심히 일했다.
hardly	거의 ~않는	Mike could **hardly** read the letters. Mike는 글자를 거의 읽을 수 없었다.
high	높이	The kite was flying **high**. 연이 높이 날고 있었다.
highly	크게, 매우(=very)	He is a **highly** creative artist. 그는 매우 창의적인 예술가이다.
late	늦게	We had dinner **late**. 우리는 늦게 저녁을 먹었다.
lately	최근에	Have you seen Becky **lately**? 너는 최근에 Becky를 본 적이 있니?
near	가까이	Insu lives **near** the park. 인수는 그 공원 가까이에 산다.
nearly	거의	**Nearly** 1,000 people died from the earthquake. 거의 1,000명의 사람들이 그 지진으로 죽었다.

정답 p.60

PRACTICE 5

괄호 안에 주어진 단어 중 알맞은 것을 고르세요.

1. I haven't seen any movies (late, lately).
2. This apple tastes (sweet, sweetly).
3. Christmas is coming (near, nearly).
4. I read the paper (close, closely).
5. The temperature goes up (high, highly) in summer.
6. Ann (hard, hardly) watches television.
7. Mrs. Smith talked to me (gentle, gently).
8. She runs a (high, highly) successful business in our town.
9. Dad came home (late, lately) all this week.
10. I like sweets very much, but I (rare, rarely) eat them.

6 I usually catch a cold in early spring. _____
7 Alex tried hard to lose weight. _____
8 Don't be late next time. _____
9 Sudong came out of the room last. _____
10 She walked fast to be on time. _____
11 It was the last train for Seoul. _____
12 There aren't enough chairs for everyone. _____
13 I hit my head on the hard floor. _____
14 Is the water warm enough for you? _____

정답 p.59

PRACTICE 4

다음 문장의 밑줄 친 부분이 맞으면 O표, 틀리면 바르게 고쳐 쓰세요.

1 Jason arrived home lately. _____
2 You have to think about it careful. _____
3 I didn't stay there long. _____
4 Who arrived lastly at the party? _____
5 He is a fast speaker. _____
6 You should talk polite to the elderly. _____
7 I have breakfast early in the morning. _____
8 You don't need to run so fastly. _____
9 They practiced hardly for the contest. _____
10 I finally finished reading this book. _____
11 We couldn't solve the problem easy. _____
12 He smiled sad and shook his head. _____
13 Ben visited me sudden yesterday. _____
14 They were waiting for the doctor anxiously. _____
15 She is certain honest. _____
16 He got on the plane last. _____
17 Giraffes are main found in East Africa. _____
18 Cathy told them the story quiet. _____

PSS 1-3 형용사와 형태가 같은 부사

fast	빠른	Shelly is a **fast** runner. Shelly는 빠른 주자이다.
	빨리	Time flies very **fast**. 시간은 아주 빨리 흘러간다.
late	늦은	Dan is sometimes **late** for work. Dan은 가끔 직장에 지각한다.
	늦게	Inho came home **late** at night. 인호는 밤늦게 집에 왔다.
hard	열심인, 단단한	My dad is a **hard** worker. 나의 아빠는 열심히 일하는 사람이다.
	열심히, 단단히	I studied **hard** to pass the exam. 나는 그 시험에 합격하기 위해 열심히 공부했다.
last	마지막인	Today is the **last** day of December. 오늘은 12월의 마지막 날이다.
	마지막으로	When did you see him **last**? 너는 언제 마지막으로 그를 보았니?
long	오래된	They are proud of their **long** history. 그들은 그들의 오랜 역사를 자랑스러워한다.
	오래	My grandmother lived **long**. 나의 할머니는 오래 사셨다.
early	이른	Six o'clock is too **early** to get up. 6시는 일어나기에 너무 이르다.
	일찍	Why did you go home so **early**? 왜 너는 집에 그렇게 일찍 갔니?
enough	충분한	I don't have **enough** money. 나는 충분한 돈을 가지고 있지 않다.
	충분히	The room is large **enough** for me. 그 방은 나에게 충분히 크다. *cf.* enough가 부사로서 형용사 또는 부사를 수식할 때에는 뒤에서 수식한다.

정답 p.59

PRACTICE 3

밑줄 친 부분의 역할이 〈보기〉의 (A)와 같으면 A, (B)와 같으면 B라고 쓰세요.

보 기	My (A)<u>good</u> friend, John, speaks Korean (B)<u>well</u>.

1 We walked for a <u>long</u> time. _____

2 I have to go to work quite <u>early</u> tomorrow. _____

3 The cold weather will last <u>long</u>. _____

4 My mom doesn't like <u>fast</u> food. _____

5 I'm sorry to call you so <u>late</u>. _____

PSS 1-2 형용사를 부사로 만드는 법 II

-le로 끝나는 경우	-le → -ly	gentle – gent**ly** 온화한 온화하게 terrible – terrib**ly** 무서운 무섭게 visible – visib**ly** 눈에 보이는 눈에 보이게	simple – simp**ly** 간단한 간단히 reasonable – reasonab**ly** 합리적인 합리적으로 comfortable – comfortab**ly** 편안한 편안하게
-ue로 끝나는 경우	-ue → -uly	true – tru**ly** 진실의 진실로	
-ll로 끝나는 경우	-ll → -lly	full – ful**ly** 충분한 충분히	dull – dul**ly** 우둔한 우둔하게

정답 p.59

PRACTICE 2

다음 형용사의 부사형을 쓰세요.

1 visible ➡ _____
2 simple ➡ _____
3 dull ➡ _____
4 true ➡ _____
5 loud ➡ _____
6 gentle ➡ _____
7 nice ➡ _____
8 serious ➡ _____
9 heavy ➡ _____
10 clear ➡ _____
11 safe ➡ _____
12 full ➡ _____
13 pretty ➡ _____
14 anxious ➡ _____
15 main ➡ _____
16 foolish ➡ _____
17 terrible ➡ _____
18 reasonable ➡ _____
19 comfortable ➡ _____
20 rude ➡ _____
21 personal ➡ _____
22 possible ➡ _____
23 probable ➡ _____
24 casual ➡ _____
25 rare ➡ _____
26 responsible ➡ _____
27 proper ➡ _____
28 sensitive ➡ _____

부사의 형태

PSS 1-1 형용사를 부사로 만드는 법 I

일반적인 경우	형용사+ly	polite – polite**ly** 예의 바른 예의 바르게 real – real**ly** 진짜의 정말로 final – final**ly** 마지막의 마지막으로 sincere – sincere**ly** 진실의 진정으로	sudden – sudden**ly** 갑작스러운 갑자기 certain – certain**ly** 확실한 확실히 quick – quick**ly** 빠른 빨리 slight – slight**ly** 약간의 약간
자음+y로 끝나는 경우	자음+i+ly	lucky – luck**ily** 운 좋은 운 좋게도 angry – angr**ily** 화난 노하여 busy – bus**ily** 바쁜 바쁘게	happy – happ**ily** 행복한 행복하게 easy – eas**ily** 쉬운 쉽게 heavy – heav**ily** 무거운 무겁게

정답 p.59

PRACTICE 1

다음 형용사의 부사형을 쓰세요.

1 wide   ➡ _____
2 sincere ➡ _____
3 happy   ➡ _____
4 polite ➡ _____
5 slow   ➡ _____
6 slight ➡ _____
7 final   ➡ _____
8 easy   ➡ _____
9 lucky   ➡ _____
10 quiet   ➡ _____
11 careful ➡ _____
12 certain ➡ _____
13 sudden ➡ _____
14 sad   ➡ _____
15 busy   ➡ _____
16 beautiful ➡ _____
17 real   ➡ _____
18 angry   ➡ _____
19 quick   ➡ _____
20 soft   ➡ _____

CHAPTER 11
부사

성취도 자기 평가 활용법

구분	평가 기준
Excellent	문법 내용을 모두 이해하고, 문제를 모두 맞힘.
Very good	문법 내용은 충분히 이해했으나 실수로 1~2문제 틀림.
Good	문법 내용이 조금 어려워 3~4문제 틀림.
needs **R**eview	문법 내용 이해가 어렵고, 5문제 이상 틀림. 복습 필요.

PSS 1 부사의 형태	페이지	학습날짜	성취도 자기평가 E V G R	학습체크
PSS 1-1 형용사를 부사로 만드는 법 Ⅰ	266	/		☐
PSS 1-2 형용사를 부사로 만드는 법 Ⅱ	267	/		☐
PSS 1-3 형용사와 형태가 같은 부사	268	/		☐
PSS 1-4 형용사 형태의 부사에 '-ly'를 붙이면 다른 뜻이 되는 부사	270	/		☐
PSS 2 여러 가지 부사의 용법	페이지	학습날짜	성취도 자기평가 E V G R	학습체크
PSS 2-1 빈도부사의 위치	272	/		☐
PSS 2-2 already, yet, still	274	/		☐
PSS 2-3 too, either	276	/		☐
PSS 2-4 very, much	277	/		☐
PSS 2-5 else, even	278	/		☐
PSS 2-6 「타동사+부사」의 어순	280	/		☐
PSS 2-7 의문부사	282	/		☐
Chapter Review Test	284	/		☐

33 다음 밑줄 친 말과 바꾸어 쓸 수 있는 것은?

> There are a number of monkeys in this zoo.

① much ② many ③ a lot
④ huge ⑤ few

34 우리말과 같은 뜻이 되도록 빈칸에 알맞은 단어를 쓰세요.

> • 나는 Tim이 가진 것보다 세 배 많은 책을 가지고 있다.
> = I have _____ _____ as many books as Tim has.

35 다음 밑줄 친 부분을 옳게 고친 것은?

① I want to eat hot something (→ something hot).
② You look happy (→ happily).
③ I saw an interesting photo (→ a photo interesting) yesterday.
④ The 25-year-old (→ 25-years-old) woman is my sister.
⑤ She bought much (→ many) butter to make a cake.

36 다음 중 12월 13일을 영어로 바르게 표기한 것은?

① December thirteen
② Thirteen of December
③ Thirteen in December
④ The thirteenth of December
⑤ December of the thirteenth

37 다음 중 어법상 올바르지 않은 문장은?

① Giho went on a picnic.
② I made some money last vacation.
③ Do good something for your mother.
④ Finish your work by 7 o'clock.
⑤ There once lived a famous singer in the town.

38 다음 빈칸에 공통으로 들어갈 말로 알맞은 것은?

> • I didn't eat _____ meat today.
> • She isn't feeling _____ better.

① some ② any ③ many
④ few   ⑤ little

Chapter Review Test

27 다음 두 문장이 같은 뜻이 되도록 빈칸에 알맞은 단어를 쓰세요.

- People who are old have a lot of experiences.
 = The _____ _____ a lot of experiences.

28 괄호 안의 단어들을 알맞게 배열하여 대화를 완성하세요.

Danny: What's the problem? Why are you so depressed?
Sunny: There is nothing I can do for your concert.
Danny: It's OK. Cheer up! Look at this. Here's _____.
(you, special, for, something)

29 ⓐ~ⓔ 중 어법상 올바른 것끼리 묶인 것은?

ⓐ Her song makes me sadly.
ⓑ The injured need to be moved to the hospital quickly.
ⓒ Could you give me warm something to drink?
ⓓ My mother planted some white big flowers in the garden.
ⓔ A little bread is left on the table.

① ⓑ, ⓓ   ② ⓑ, ⓔ   ③ ⓐ, ⓓ, ⓔ
④ ⓐ, ⓑ, ⓓ   ⑤ ⓑ, ⓓ, ⓔ

30 다음 중 어법상 어색한 문장은?

① If you have any questions, feel free to ask me.
② Any child could sing better than those people.
③ Would you like some dessert?
④ I don't have some money.
⑤ Some people don't like the idea.

31 다음 중 밑줄 친 부분의 뜻이 틀린 것은?

① <u>Koreans</u> want to master foreign languages in a short time. (한국인들)
② It's difficult to learn <u>French</u>. (프랑스어)
③ He fell in love with a <u>German</u>. (독일인)
④ <u>The Chinese</u> drink tea at any time of day. (중국인 한 명)
⑤ <u>American</u> restaurants often serve iced water with meals. (미국의)

32 다음 대화에서 틀린 부분을 2개 찾아 바르게 고치세요.

Tutor: I won't give you some homework today.
Student: Wow, thank you. I have few time to do homework today.
Tutor: Why?
Student: I have to take care of my three little brothers this evening.

(1) _____ ➡ _____
(2) _____ ➡ _____

22 다음 대화의 밑줄 친 (A)~(E) 중 어법상 어색한 것은?

> Insu : Would you like (A) some chocolate?
> Yunji: No, thank you. I've gained too (B) much weight, so I'm on a diet.
> Insu : Really? My sister gets stressed when she is on a diet.
> Yunji: Why?
> Insu : She likes eating (C) something sweet such as chocolate.
> Yunji: Actually, I'm under (D) a number of stress, too.
> Insu : Well, do you exercise to lose weight?
> Yunji: No, I dislike (E) exercising.

① (A)　② (B)　③ (C)　④ (D)　⑤ (E)

23 다음 중 밑줄 친 부분의 뜻이 틀린 것을 모두 고르세요.

① My sister has a few friends to help her.
　　　　　　　(거의 없는)
② We didn't have much rain last summer.
　　　　　　　　(많은)
③ I bought some oranges.
　　　　(약간의)
④ Plenty of people were laughing at me.
　(몇몇의)
⑤ There are many students in the playground.
　　　　(많은)

24 다음을 영어로 바르게 읽은 것을 모두 고르세요.

① 3/5: three-fifth
② 2013년: two thousand (and) thirteen
③ 5월 15일: the fifteen of May
④ 25.43: twenty-five point four three
⑤ 1974년: one thousand nine hundred and seventy four

25 다음 중 밑줄 친 부분의 쓰임이 올바른 것은?

① I have a white small cat.
② My all neighbors are very kind.
③ Her big brown eyes are beautiful.
④ These both sweaters are mine.
⑤ I need a wooden new box.

26 다음 중 어법상 올바른 문장은?

① The asleep baby is my nephew.
② That is an alive bird.
③ He was a very afraid boy.
④ She is an alone girl.
⑤ Mina and you look alike.

18 다음 글의 밑줄 친 (A)~(E) 중 어법상 어색한 것 2개를 골라 그 기호를 쓰고 바르게 고치세요.

(A) Have you ever seen this painting?
(B) Its title is *Portrait of Doctor Gachet* and it is one of the most famous paintings by Vincent van Gogh. The subject of the painting is Paul Gachet, a doctor (C) who took care of Van Gogh during the last months of his life. In May 1990, the portrait was sold at auction for $82.5 million to a (D) Japan paper manufacturer, Ryoei Saito. This surprised (E) much people at the auction, since no one expected that the painting would sell for so much. It continues to be one of the highest prices ever paid for a painting at auction.

➡ _____ , _____

19 다음 빈칸 (A), (B)에 들어갈 말이 바르게 짝지어진 것은?

- You look ___(A)___ .
- I can't see ___(B)___ with the final report.

	(A)	(B)
①	sad	anything wrong
②	sadly	anything wrong
③	sad	wrong anything
④	sadly	wrong anything
⑤	sadly	something wrong

20 다음 대화 중 흐름상 어색한 것은?

① A: How much money do you have now?
   B: About 5 dollars.
② A: How old is your grandmother?
   B: She is 89 years old.
③ A: How long does it take to get to the airport?
   B: It takes about 30 minutes.
④ A: How often do you take a shower?
   B: I took a shower yesterday.
⑤ A: How many eggs do you have?
   B: I don't have any.

21 다음 밑줄 친 (A)~(E) 중 어법상 어색한 것을 모두 고르세요.

People can change (A) well-known proverbs for a big laugh. You've learned that proverbs teach you lessons. However, twisted proverbs can make you (B) to see life in a different way and help you enjoy it more. Now you know (C) a little secrets about (D) how to tell a good joke. Do you think you can tell a joke (E) on your own? It's not that difficult to do. You can use the secrets you've learned.

① (A)   ② (B)   ③ (C)
④ (D)   ⑤ (E)

12 우리말 뜻과 일치하도록 괄호 안의 단어들을 바르게 배열하여 문장을 완성하세요.

> • 셰익스피어는 보통 사람의 3배만큼 많은 어휘를 알았다.
> = Shakespeare knew _____
> _____.
> (average, three times, as, person, words, an, many, as)

13 그림을 보고 주어진 단어를 사용하여 다음 대화를 완성하세요.

> A: How much food is left in the refrigerator?
> B: _____
> _____ (there, little, food)

14 다음 대화의 밑줄 친 부분 중 어법상 어색한 것은?

> Ted : ① This Friday is Minji's birthday.
> Jiyeon: I know. ② What should we get her?
> Ted : Well, ③ how about a really interesting book?
> Jiyeon: That sounds good. ④ Did you hear that she's going to invite her all friends?
> Ted : No, I didn't know that. ⑤ It'll be very fun.

15 다음 중 밑줄 친 부분이 어법상 어색한 것은?

① Would you like some coffee?
② He put some food in his bag.
③ He doesn't have any friends.
④ Do you have any special plans?
⑤ I bought any oranges at the market.

16 다음 각 대화의 빈칸에 들어갈 말이 바르게 짝지어진 것은?

> A: ___(A)___ books a month does your daughter read?
> B: She usually reads four books a month.
>
> A: ___(B)___ do you go to the gym?
> B: I try to go there at least four times a week.

	(A)	(B)
①	How often	How much
②	How much	How often
③	How many	How often
④	How many	How many
⑤	How often	How many

17 다음 문장의 밑줄 친 부분과 동일한 의미의 다른 표현 2개를 영어로 쓰세요.

> Is there a lot of paper on the desk?

➡ _____
_____

6 다음 빈칸에 들어갈 말로 알맞은 것은?

_____ minutes later, a stranger came up to me and asked me for some money.

① Much ② A few ③ Little
④ A little ⑤ Any

7 그림을 보고, 밑줄 친 우리말에 맞도록 괄호 안의 단어를 바르게 배열하세요.

A: Are you hungry?
B: Yes. 뭐 먹을 만한 맛있는 것 좀 있니?
➡ _____
_____ (something, to eat, you, do, have, delicious)

8 다음 밑줄 친 부분과 바꿔 쓸 수 있는 표현은?

There are lots of people in the fitness center.

① many ② much ③ few
④ a few ⑤ little

9 다음 중 올바른 표현은 몇 개인가?

ⓐ A few years ago, Jina gave piano lessons.
ⓑ I'd like to have a few more soup.
ⓒ The chef added a little hot sauce to the dish.
ⓓ Very few students understood her speech.
ⓔ He's on a diet and eats little sugar.

① 1개 ② 2개 ③ 3개 ④ 4개 ⑤ 5개

10 다음 빈칸에 들어갈 말이 바르게 연결된 것은?

• I borrowed _____ books from the library.
• Does she have _____ friends?
• Do you drink _____ water?
• There is _____ money left.

① a few – much – a few – a little
② a few – many – much – a little
③ a few – many – a little – few
④ much – a little – many – a few
⑤ much – few – a few – a little

11 수미가 테니스를 치는 날을 색칠해둔 달력을 보고 질문에 대한 답을 완성하세요.

Sun	Mon	Tue	Wed	Thu	Fri	Sat
			1	2	3	4	5
6	7	8	9	10	11	12
13	14	15	16	17	18	19
20	21	22	23	24	25	26
27	28	29	30			

Q: How often a week does Sumi play tennis?
A: She plays tennis _____ _____ _____.

Chapter Review Test

정답 p.56   **CHAPTER 10** 형용사

1 다음 글의 빈칸 (A)~(C)에 들어갈 말이 바르게 나열된 것은?

> People in the world greet each other in different ways. When ___(A)___ meet their neighbors or friends, they say *Annyeonghaseyo*. Indian people say *Namaste* when they meet somebody. It means "I respect you." They usually put their hands together at their chest and bow a little when saying this. In ___(B)___, the weather changes quickly. For example, the sun shines strongly in the morning, but later it rains. Then the rain suddenly stops. So, ___(C)___ people are happy when the weather is fine. They always wish for good weather when they say hello.

	(A)	(B)	(C)
①	Korea	English	English
②	Korean	England	England
③	Koreans	England	English
④	Korea	England	English
⑤	Koreans	English	England

2 다음 중 어법상 잘못된 것은?

① There's nothing wrong with the machine.
② Is there anyone left in the bus?
③ Two thirds of the audience at the theater was women.
④ Amanda's suitcase is twice as heavy as her brother's.
⑤ She said that she didn't enjoy things sweet.

3 밑줄 친 우리말과 같은 뜻이 되도록 괄호 안에 주어진 단어를 배열하여 문장을 만들 때, 네 번째로 오는 단어는?

> W: What are you up to tonight?
> M: I'm going to stay home and watch TV.
> W: You don't usually watch TV. <u>TV에서 뭐 재미있는 것이라도 하니?</u>
> (on, anything, TV, interesting, is, there)
> M: Yes! The World Cup final will be broadcast on TV starting at 9 p.m. tonight.

① there   ② interesting   ③ on
④ anything   ⑤ TV

4 다음 중 어법상 올바른 문장은?

① He wore a long black jacket and a red nice tie.
② He wore a black long jacket and a nice red tie.
③ He wore a black long jacket and a red nice tie.
④ He wore a long black jacket and a nice red tie.
⑤ He weared a black long jacket and a nice red tie.

5 다음 문장에서 틀린 부분을 찾아 바르게 고치세요.

> Some people think it is more important to be health than to have a lot of money.

_____ ➡ _____

PSS 6-3 배수사

배수사는 once(1배), twice[two times](2배), 그 이후부터는 「기수＋times」(~배)로 나타낸다.

My bag is **three times** as heavy as yours. 내 가방은 네 것보다 3배 무겁다.
= My bag is **three times** heavier than yours.
Insu has **four times** as many clothes as I have.
인수는 내가 가지고 있는 것보다 4배 많은 옷을 가지고 있다.

cf. 배수사를 이용하여 횟수를 나타낼 수 있으며, 횟수를 물어볼 때는 How often ~?을 쓴다.
once a week 일주일에 한 번   **twice** a month 한 달에 두 번
I have been to Europe **once**. 나는 유럽에 한 번 가본 적이 있다.

정답 p.56

PRACTICE 19

우리말과 같은 뜻이 되도록 빈칸에 알맞은 말을 쓰세요.

1 나는 그녀를 딱 한 번 만났다.
   ➡ I have met her only _____.

2 글루텐 프리 빵은 일반 빵보다 거의 3배만큼 비싸다.
   ➡ Gluten-free bread is nearly _____ as expensive as regular bread.

3 나는 일주일에 6번 수영하러 가곤 했다.
   ➡ I used to go swimming _____ a week.

4 이 연필은 저 연필보다 4배 길다.
   ➡ This pencil is _____ as long as that one.

5 저 나무들은 이 나무들보다 5배 크다.
   ➡ Those trees are _____ taller than these ones.

6 그들은 부산에 두 번 가본 적이 있다.
   ➡ They have been to Busan _____.

7 노란 상자는 빨간 상자보다 10배 무겁다.
   ➡ The yellow box is _____ as heavy as the red box.

8 우리 부모님은 한 달에 한 번 등산을 하신다.
   ➡ My parents go hiking _____ a month.

9 그녀의 개는 너의 개보다 세 배 크다.
   ➡ Her dog is _____ bigger than yours.

10 나는 1년에 8번 제주도에 간다.
   ➡ I go to Jejudo _____ a year.

11 She sang (beautiful, beautifully) in the concert hall.

12 Jane lives (close, closely) to my house.

13 Did you study (hard, hardly) for the exam?

14 (Near, Nearly) 150 countries joined the Olympics.

15 You look (happy, happily) today.

PRACTICE 6

정답 p.60

〈보기〉와 같이 주어진 단어를 이용하여 빈칸을 채우세요.

보 기	polite ① Yumi is a very <u>polite</u> girl. ② Yumi speaks very <u>politely</u>.

1 easy
① That was an _____ question.
② I solved the question very _____.

2 clear
① Could you speak _____?
② The sky is very _____.

3 late
① I had lunch _____, so I'm not hungry.
② Bill was _____ for the meeting.

4 careful
① You should be more _____ of cars.
② Peter drives a car _____.

5 last
① This is the _____ chance to get the key.
② Jinho finished the test _____.

6 early
① Mom woke up _____ this morning.
② They visited me at an _____ hour.

7 lucky
① You are such a _____ guy.
② _____, she was safe.

8 certain
① She eats only _____ kinds of food.
② She'll _____ win first prize.

9 hard
① I've never seen him working so _____.
② I could _____ breathe at the top of the mountain.

10 close
① The cat came _____ to the box.
② Look at these questions _____.

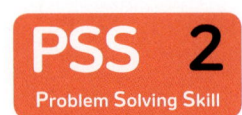

PSS 2 여러 가지 부사의 용법

Problem Solving Skill

PSS 2-1 빈도부사의 위치

always – usually – often – sometimes – seldom – rarely – never

항상 / 보통, 대개 / 종종 / 때때로 / 드물게 / 좀처럼 ~ 않는 / 결코 ~ 않는

100% ⟷ 0%

1. 일반동사 앞

Mary	often	**goes**	to the beach in summer.
I	never	**eat**	fast food.
Minho	seldom	**reads**	the newspaper.
주어	+ 빈도부사	+ 일반동사 ~	

Mary는 여름에 종종 해변에 간다. | 나는 결코 패스트푸드를 먹지 않는다. | 민호는 드물게 신문을 읽는다.

2. be동사나 조동사 뒤

They	**are**	usually	at home on weekends.
My room	**is**	always	very cold.
Andy	**will**	sometimes	write to you.
I	**can**	rarely	see Jack nowadays.
주어	+ be/조동사	+ 빈도부사 ~	

그들은 주말에 대개 집에 있다. | 내 방은 항상 매우 춥다. | Andy가 때때로 네게 편지를 쓸 것이다.
나는 요즘 좀처럼 Jack을 보지 못한다.

cf. sometimes / often / usually와 같은 빈도부사는 문장의 맨 앞이나 뒤에도 올 수 있지만, 많은 경우 일반동사 앞 또는 be동사나 조동사 뒤에 쓴다.

정답 p.60

PRACTICE 7

괄호 안에 주어진 부사를 알맞은 곳에 넣어 문장을 다시 쓰세요. (단, 빈도부사를 문장 맨 앞, 뒤에는 오게 하지 말 것.)

1 I go to Incheon to visit my grandparents. (sometimes)
➡ ______________________________

2 Susie is late for work. (never)
➡ ______________________________

3 Sangmin could come to our club meetings. (rarely)
➡ _____

4 They are ready to go on a trip. (always)
➡ _____

5 We will go to the movies together. (sometimes)
➡ _____

6 They shake hands to greet each other. (usually)
➡ _____

7 I should help my mom with the housework. (often)
➡ _____

8 He is excited about the trip. (seldom)
➡ _____

9 He keeps his room dirty. (never)
➡ _____

10 You don't clean your room, do you? (often)
➡ _____

정답 p.61

PRACTICE 8

다음 괄호 안에 주어진 단어를 바르게 배열하세요. (단, 빈도부사를 문장 맨 앞, 뒤에는 오게 하지 말 것.)

1 (I, go jogging, in the morning, usually)
➡ _____

2 (they, listen to, sometimes, must, others)
➡ _____

3 (often, swimming, we, practice, will)
➡ _____

4 (Hana, brightly, smiles, always)
➡ _____

5 (can, understand, seldom, Nick, Korean)
➡ _____

6 (dangerous, sometimes, is, climbing mountains)
➡ _____

7 (Giho, watches, comic dramas, never)
➡ _____

8 (take care of, younger, I, my, sisters, usually)
➡ _____

9 (buys, she, expensive clothes, rarely)
➡ _____

10 (depressed, often, by, I, bad weather, am)
➡ _____

PSS 2-2 already, yet, still

already	이미, 벌써	already는 긍정문과 놀람을 나타내는 의문문에 쓰인다. Have you **already** forgotten what happened yesterday? 어제 무슨 일이 있었는지 벌써 잊은 거니? I've **already** read the book twice. 나는 벌써 그 책을 두 번 읽었다.
yet	이미, 벌써, 이제, 아직	yet은 의문문과 부정문에 쓰이는데, 의문문에서는 '이미, 벌써, 이제'의 뜻으로, 부정문에서는 '아직'의 뜻으로 해석되고 주로 문장의 끝에 위치한다. Have you seen the movie **yet**? 너는 벌써 그 영화를 봤니? I haven't finished it **yet**. 나는 아직 그것을 끝내지 못했다.
still	여전히, 아직도	still은 긍정문과 의문문에 쓰이고, 계속되는 행위를 강조하고자 할 때는 부정문에도 쓰인다. Sujin **still** enjoys hiking on weekends. 수진은 여전히 주말마다 하이킹을 즐긴다. Do you **still** have the picture? 너는 아직도 그 그림을 가지고 있니? I **still** haven't called my teacher. 나는 아직도 선생님께 전화하지 않았다. ***cf.*** still이 부정문에 쓰일 때는 부정어보다 앞에 온다. ***cf.*** 형용사 still은 '가만히 있는, 고요한'의 뜻을 지닌다. 　　My little son finds it difficult to sit **still** for very long. 　　나의 어린 아들은 오랫동안 가만히 앉아 있는 것을 어렵게 여긴다.

정답 p.61

PRACTICE 9

〈보기〉와 같이 빈칸에 already, yet, still 중 알맞은 것을 쓰세요.

보 기	① I've <u>already</u> quit working there. ② I'm <u>still</u> working there. ③ I haven't quit working there <u>yet</u>.

1 ① I've _____ talked to David.
   ② I haven't talked to David _____.
   ③ I'm _____ talking to David.

2 ① Are you _____ reading the newspaper?
   ② Have you _____ read the newspaper?
   ③ Have you read the newspaper _____? – No, I haven't.

3 ① Junho hasn't written that letter _____.
   ② Junho is _____ writing that letter.
   ③ Junho has _____ written that letter.

4 ① They are _____ having dinner.
   ② They haven't finished having dinner _____.
   ③ They have _____ finished having dinner.

5 ① Has she cleaned the room _____? If not, I'll do it now.
   ② Has she _____ cleaned the room?
   ③ She is _____ cleaning the room.

PRACTICE 10

괄호 안에 주어진 단어 중 알맞은 것을 고르세요.

1 I haven't finished the ironing (yet, still).
2 I've (already, still) had my lunch.
3 Jenny is (yet, still) doing the dishes.
4 Have you met Mr. Smith (yet, still)?
5 Do you (yet, still) go jogging every morning?
6 Kevin has (yet, already) graduated from high school.
7 They haven't sent the email (yet, already).
8 Is he (already, still) nineteen years old? Time flies!
9 Mina (yet, still) wants to go to Europe.
10 Are you (yet, still) working on that report?
11 Have you (still, already) cleaned the room?
12 There is (already, still) no news about the accident.
13 She has (already, still) gone somewhere.
14 We haven't decided what to buy (yet, already).
15 Are my clothes dry (already, still)? I washed them just an hour ago.

PSS 2-3 too, either

too	~ 또한	too는 긍정문에 쓰인다. Jiyeon can play the piano. I can play the piano, **too**. (= Me, too.) 지연이는 피아노를 칠 수 있다. 나도 역시 피아노를 칠 수 있다.
either		either는 부정문에 쓰인다. She doesn't like baseball. I don't like baseball, **either**. (= Me, neither.) 그녀는 야구를 좋아하지 않는다. 나도 역시 야구를 좋아하지 않는다.

PRACTICE 11

Tony / Becky

빈칸에 too, either, neither 중 알맞은 것을 넣어 대화를 완성하세요.

	Tony	Becky
1	I miss Mr. Smith.	I miss Mr. Smith, _____.
2	I'm not going out now.	Me, _____.
3	She likes movies.	Me, _____.
4	I don't live here.	I don't live here, _____.
5	Seho will buy some books.	I will buy some books, _____.
6	I can't speak French.	Me, _____.
7	They won't study tonight.	I won't study tonight, _____.
8	Tom can cook well.	Me, _____.
9	I don't like those noisy dogs.	I don't like those noisy dogs, _____.
10	Nami doesn't get up early.	Me, _____.
11	I am not watching TV.	Me, _____.
12	I can't attend the meeting.	I can't attend the meeting, _____.
13	He wants to see the movie.	I want to see the movie, _____.
14	Semin is not tall.	I'm not tall, _____.
15	I didn't break this glass.	Me, _____.

PSS 2-4 very, much

very	매우	1. 형용사의 원급을 수식한다. Your question is **very** difficult. 너의 질문은 매우 어렵다. 2. 부사의 원급을 수식한다. David speaks Korean **very** well. David는 한국어를 매우 잘 말한다.
much	훨씬	1. 형용사의 비교급을 수식한다. Bill is **much** taller than Alex. Bill은 Alex보다 훨씬 더 키가 크다. 2. 부사의 비교급을 수식한다. Kelly runs **much** faster than Hana. Kelly는 하나보다 훨씬 더 빨리 달린다.

PRACTICE 12

정답 p.61

〈보기〉와 같이 빈칸에 very나 much 중 알맞은 것을 쓰세요.

> 보 기
> ① Jane studies <u>very</u> hard.
> ② Jane studies <u>much</u> harder than anyone else.

1. ① The KTX is _____ fast.
   ② The KTX is _____ faster than the Saemaul train.

2. ① My mom gets up _____ earlier than anyone of us.
   ② My mom gets up _____ early in the morning.

3. ① Jina has a _____ nice voice.
   ② Jina has a _____ nicer voice than Mary.

4. ① The airplane was flying _____ high.
   ② The airplane was flying _____ higher than we had thought.

5. ① Today is _____ cold.
   ② Today is _____ colder than yesterday.

6. ① I found the house _____ smaller than I had imagined.
   ② I found the house _____ small.

7 ① Lydia plays the piano _____ well.
　　② Lydia plays the piano _____ better than I do.

8 ① He arrived here _____ later than the other people.
　　② He arrived here _____ late.

9 ① Those cookies are _____ more delicious than the other cookies.
　　② Those cookies are _____ delicious.

10 ① Namsik finished the work _____ quickly.
　　　② Namsik finished the work _____ more quickly than I had expected.

정답 p.62

PRACTICE 13

괄호 안에 주어진 단어 중 알맞은 것을 고르세요.

1 The traffic was (very, much) heavy.

2 The gentleman was (very, much) older than he looked.

3 You have to listen to them (very, much) carefully.

4 After the rain, the weather became (very, much) cooler.

5 The task took me (very, much) longer than I had thought.

6 The book was (very, much) useful.

7 Things are (very, much) cheaper to buy here.

8 That is a (very, much) good idea.

9 She speaks English (very, much) better than Namsu.

10 I tried (very, much) hard to keep the promise.

11 This game is (very, much) more exciting than that game.

12 The blue whale is a (very, much) large mammal.

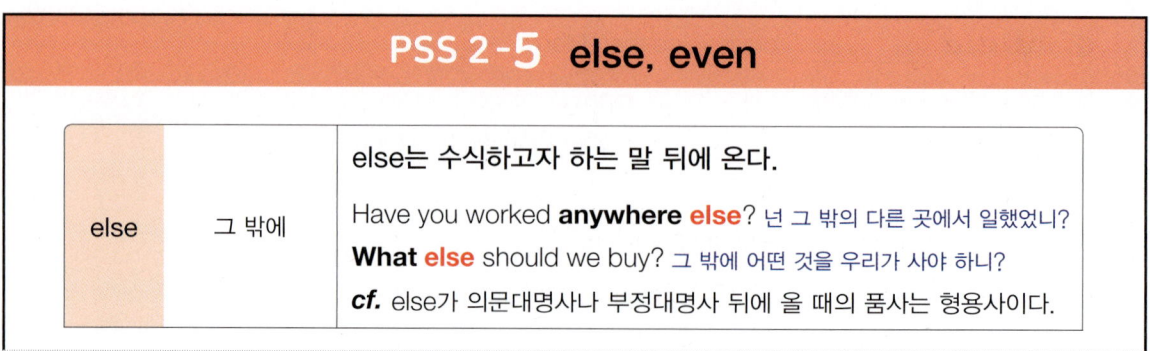

PSS 2-5 else, even

else	그 밖에	else는 수식하고자 하는 말 뒤에 온다. Have you worked **anywhere else**? 넌 그 밖의 다른 곳에서 일했었니? **What else** should we buy? 그 밖에 어떤 것을 우리가 사야 하니? *cf.* else가 의문대명사나 부정대명사 뒤에 올 때의 품사는 형용사이다.

even	~조차	even은 수식하고자 하는 말 앞에 온다. I didn't **even know** it was his birthday. 나는 그의 생일이었다는 것조차 알지 못했다. I believe in the sun, **even when it rains**. 심지어 비가 올 때조차도 나는 햇빛이 있을 거라고 믿는다. Inho is **even mean** to his sister. 인호는 그의 누나에게조차 짓궂다. You are not quiet **even in the library**. 너는 도서관에서조차 조용하지 않구나. **Even children** can do it. 어린이들조차도 그것을 할 수 있다.

정답 p.62

PRACTICE 14

괄호 안에 주어진 단어가 밑줄 친 부분을 수식하도록 문장을 다시 쓰세요.

1. <u>What</u> can I do for you? (else)
 ➡ _____

2. I didn't <u>imagine</u> it was possible. (even)
 ➡ _____

3. It was <u>sad</u> to say goodbye to everyone. (even)
 ➡ _____

4. <u>Where</u> did you visit in London? (else)
 ➡ _____

5. He <u>took</u> some medicine to fall asleep. (even)
 ➡ _____

6. They kept practicing soccer <u>when it rained heavily</u>. (even)
 ➡ _____

7. The child brings his toy <u>to the bathroom</u>. (even)
 ➡ _____

8. A <u>small pet</u> can give you a lot of trouble. (even)
 ➡ _____

9. Jessica <u>gets angry</u> if I don't call her often. (even)
 ➡ _____

10. David can run faster than <u>anyone</u> in his class. (else)
 ➡ _____

11 Dad sometimes works on Sunday. (even)
➡ _____

12 You can order a pizza on the Internet. (even)
➡ _____

13 Babies need to be watched while they are sleeping. (even)
➡ _____

14 You'd better write these rules somewhere. (else)
➡ _____

15 He speaks English, Chinese, French, and Spanish. (even)
➡ _____

정답 p.62

PRACTICE 15

괄호 안에 주어진 단어 중 알맞은 것을 고르세요.

1 You should not (else, even) look at him like that.

2 I like this place more than anywhere (else, even).

3 The little child couldn't (else, even) hold a spoon.

4 Did you meet anyone (else, even) on your way home?

5 I (else, even) had to dance to make her laugh.

6 What (else, even) do I need to remember?

7 Why should we study (else, even) during the vacation?

8 My friend Susan (else, even) knows where my grandparents are now.

9 This store is too crowded. Let's go somewhere (else, even).

10 Where (else, even) can I get information about the city?

PSS 2-6 「타동사+부사」의 어순

1. 목적어가 명사일 때, 목적어는 부사의 뒤에 오거나 동사와 부사의 사이에 온다. 즉, 「동사+부사+목적어」나 「동사+목적어+부사」의 어순 둘 다 가능하다.

   Insu **took off his coat** in the room. 인수는 방에서 그의 코트를 벗었다.
   = Insu **took his coat off** in the room.

2. 목적어가 대명사일 때, 목적어는 반드시 동사와 부사의 사이에 온다. 즉, 「동사+목적어+부사」의 어순만 가능하다.

   Insu **took it off** in the room. 인수는 방에서 그것을 벗었다.
   Insu took off it in the room. (×)

   cf. 자동사 뒤에 전치사가 올 때, 전치사의 목적어는 반드시 전치사 뒤에 온다. 즉, 「동사+전치사+목적어」의 어순만 가능하다.
   I'm **looking for Jack and Cathy**. (○) 나는 Jack과 Cathy를 찾고 있다.
   I'm looking Jack and Cathy for. (×)
   I'm **looking for them**. (○) 나는 그들을 찾고 있다.
   I'm looking them for. (×)

정답 p.62

PRACTICE 16

괄호 안에 주어진 말 중 알맞은 것을 고르세요.

1 I'd like to try (them on, on them).
2 She doesn't care (money about, about money).
3 Could you turn (on the radio, on it)?
4 Never give (up it, it up). Try hard.
5 Look (at the picture, the picture at) on the wall.
6 Did she hand (in the homework, in it) to the teacher?
7 I listened (the radio to, to the radio) last night.
8 Would you mind turning (off it, it off)?
9 The manager called (the show off, off it).
10 The cat was sitting (the chair on, on the chair).
11 I don't know the answer. Did you find (out it, it out)?
12 You should not throw (away it, it away) here.
13 Will you pick (up the paper, up it) for me?
14 I checked (them out, out them) at the Central Library.
15 I have your key. Were you looking (it for, for it)?
16 Let's talk (it about, about it) this evening.

PRACTICE 17

〈보기〉에서 알맞은 부사를 골라 빈칸에 쓰세요.

보기	on off in out up away

1 We have to find _____ who the thief is by tomorrow.
2 Did you throw _____ the paper on the floor?
3 Do you mind if I turn the TV _____? I need to watch the 9 o'clock news.
4 Would you like to try the blue shirt _____?
5 Sora picked _____ the coins and gave them to the boy.
6 You need to hand _____ the paper by this Friday.
7 Will you turn the light _____? I have to sleep now.
8 Could you check _____ the books about Korea for me?
9 My dad called _____ our plan, so I was very disappointed.
10 It rained heavily. We had to give _____ the soccer game.

PSS 2-7 의문부사

when	언제	**When** did you visit Jeff? 넌 언제 Jeff를 방문했니? – I visited him **last Friday**. 난 지난 금요일에 그를 방문했어.
where	어디에	**Where** did you buy those pants? 넌 어디에서 그 바지를 샀니? – I bought them **at a department store**. 난 백화점에서 그것들을 샀어.
how	어떻게	**How** do you go to school? 넌 학교에 어떻게 가니? – I go to school **by bus**. 난 버스로 학교에 가.
	얼마나 ~한	**How long** does it take to get there? 그곳에 도착하는 데 얼마나 걸리니? – It takes **5 minutes**. 5분 걸려. **How many** pencils do you have? 넌 얼마나 많은 연필을 가지고 있니? – I have **five pencils**. 난 5자루의 연필을 가지고 있어. **How old** is your mother? 너의 어머니는 연세가 어떻게 되시니? – She's **55 years old**. 그녀는 55세이셔.

how	얼마나 ~한	**How far** is it from here to the police office? 여기서 경찰서까지 얼마나 머니? – It's **about three kilometers**. 약 3km 정도야. **How much** is this candy? 이 사탕은 얼마야? – It's **five hundred won**. 500원이야. **How often** do you go to the library? 너는 얼마나 자주 도서관에 가니? – I go there about **twice a week**. 나는 약 일주일에 두 번 정도 그곳에 가.
why	왜	**Why** didn't you buy it? 넌 왜 그것을 사지 않았니? – **Because it was too expensive**. 그것은 너무 비쌌기 때문이야.

PRACTICE 18

정답 p.63

Becky의 대답을 보고, Tony의 질문을 완성하세요.

1	_____ are you from?	I'm from Toronto, Canada.
2	_____ can we get there?	We can take the 502 bus.
3	_____ were you late?	Because I got up late this morning.
4	_____ dogs do you have?	I have three dogs.
5	_____ does it take to finish lunch?	It takes almost 30 minutes.
6	_____ is your birthday?	It's April 30th.
7	_____ are you?	I'm twenty-seven.
8	_____ is the admission?	It's 5,000 won.
9	_____ is your home from here?	It's about a ten-minute walk from here.
10	_____ is my notebook?	It's on the desk.
11	_____ did you see him last?	Last Wednesday.
12	_____ do you know Jinho?	He is my old colleague.
13	_____ didn't you call me yesterday?	Because I forgot your number.
14	_____ did the delivery cost?	It cost 3,500 won.
15	_____ do you ride a bike?	About 3 times a month.

Tony

Chapter Review Test

CHAPTER 11 부사

정답 p.63

1 다음 중 두 단어의 관계가 나머지 넷과 <u>다른</u> 것은?

① anxious – anxiously
② foolish – foolishly
③ careful – carefully
④ luck – luckily
⑤ terrible – terribly

2 다음 대화의 빈칸에 들어갈 단어로 알맞은 것은?

A: Have you ever read the book, *Little Women*?
B: No, I haven't read it _____.

① either   ② already   ③ too
④ neither ⑤ yet

3 다음의 우리말을 영어로 바르게 옮긴 것은?

그 또한 형제가 없었다.

① He didn't have few brothers, too.
② He didn't have few brothers, either.
③ He didn't have any brothers, too.
④ He didn't have any brothers, either.
⑤ He didn't have some brothers, either.

4 〈보기〉의 문장 중 어법상 옳은 것의 개수는?

보 기
ⓐ He took them out and looked them at.
ⓑ Inho came home lately at night.
ⓒ The airplane was flying highly.
ⓓ I don't have money enough.
ⓔ I usually catch a cold in early spring.

① 1개   ② 2개   ③ 3개   ④ 4개   ⑤ 5개

5 다음 빈칸에 공통으로 들어갈 단어를 쓰세요.

Sam: Jane, did you see the movie that I recommended?
Jane: Yes. I saw it last Saturday.
Sam: _____ was it?
Jane: I was deeply impressed.
Sam: Were you?
Jane: Yes. _____ could you find such a great movie?

6 다음 중 어법상 <u>어색한</u> 문장을 <u>모두</u> 고르세요.

① Do your best at studying.
② I haven't seen him lately.
③ You should cross the street careful.
④ Kate is always diligent.
⑤ I studied hardly for the exam.

284 마더텅 영문법 3800제 2 – INTERMEDIATE

7 다음 대화의 빈칸에 들어갈 단어로 알맞은 것은?

> A: How was your weekend?
> B: It was not good. I was very sad.
> A: _____ were you so sad?
> B: One of my best friends left for Canada.

① Why   ② How   ③ What
④ Which   ⑤ Where

8 다음 ⓐ~ⓔ 중 어법상 틀린 것을 있는 대로 고른 것은?

> ⓐ They haven't finished it already.
> ⓑ I couldn't visit her, too.
> ⓒ It's more important than anything else.
> ⓓ Please make her stopping crying.
> ⓔ This is very more expensive than that.

① ⓐ, ⓑ   ② ⓑ, ⓒ   ③ ⓑ, ⓒ, ⓓ
④ ⓐ, ⓓ, ⓔ   ⑤ ⓐ, ⓑ, ⓓ, ⓔ

9 다음 대화의 (A)~(E) 중 어법상 어색한 것은?

> Andy : (A)Why are you still reading the book?
> Brenda: Well, I don't know (B)what the author's intention is.
> Andy : (C)Actually, me, too.
> Brenda: By the way, (D)why are you still here?
> Andy : (E)I'm waiting for my friend to pick me up.
> Brenda: I see.

① (A)   ② (B)   ③ (C)   ④ (D)   ⑤ (E)

10 다음 빈칸에 알맞은 단어를 넣어 대화를 완성하세요.

> Mom: Who broke the vase?
> Mina : I didn't break it.
> Jinho: I didn't break it, _____.

11 다음 중 어법상 어색한 문장은?

① Suji always is kind.
② I never drink milk.
③ Nami is often late for work.
④ Ted sometimes goes swimming.
⑤ He usually eats his lunch at home.

12 다음 문장의 빈칸에 알맞은 단어끼리 바르게 나열된 것은?

> • Don't come too ___(A)___!
> • Have you seen Helen ___(B)___?
> • I've worked here for ___(C)___ two years.

	(A)	(B)	(C)
①	closely	lately	near
②	close	lately	nearly
③	close	late	near
④	closely	late	nearly
⑤	close	lately	near

13 다음 중 어법상 어색한 문장은?

① I got a bad grade, too.
② He's very better now.
③ Eating regularly is good for your health.
④ I always meet my friends on Saturday night.
⑤ Sudong sometimes goes to the park near his house.

14 다음 문장에서 어법상 틀린 곳을 찾아 바르게 고치세요.

Sora finished the job interview successful yesterday.

_____ ➡ _____

15 다음 중 <보기>의 답들에 대한 질문이 될 수 없는 것은?

보 기
(A) Once a week.
(B) It takes about two hours to get there.
(C) It's three hundred dollars.
(D) It's 8 miles from here.

① How far is it from here?
② How long does it take to get to Daegu?
③ How often do you play the piano?
④ How come you measured the distance?
⑤ How much is it?

16 다음 문장의 밑줄 친 much와 의미가 다른 것은?

Lisa is much kinder than Jeff.

① Inho is much taller than Giho.
② She is much healthier than before.
③ I enjoyed the movie very much.
④ Sally can run much faster than her sister.
⑤ I feel much better today.

17 다음 밑줄 친 부분 중 어법상 어색한 것은?

① It was not ② hard ③ to find the station. We could ④ easy find ⑤ it.

18 다음 대화 중 가장 어색한 것을 고르세요.

① A: How often do you exercise?
   B: I swim at least twice a week.
② A: What made you hurt so much?
   B: I slipped and fell hardly on the floor.
③ A: How long does it take to take a shower?
   B: In my case, it takes about 40 minutes.
④ A: It is quite difficult for me to enjoy Sudoku.
   B: As you know, Sudoku is a highly intellectual game.
⑤ A: Why didn't he tell you about the due date?
   B: Because he thought I already knew it.

19 다음 빈칸에 들어갈 말로 알맞은 것은?

A: Do you speak Chinese?
B: No, I don't. How about you?
A: _____ But I'm going to take a Chinese class this vacation.

① I do, too.   ② Me, too.
③ Me, neither.   ④ I do, either.
⑤ I don't, neither.

20 밑줄 친 ⓐ~ⓔ 중 어법상 틀린 것을 있는 대로 고른 것은?

In Korea, people take off their shoes when they enter a house, but ⓐ Americans don't take off them. ⓑ So they used to make mistakes. However, these days most of them know that ⓒ they should take their shoes off before entering a house in Korea. ⓓ Some of them even think that ⓔ taking off shoes are good for their feet.

① ⓐ, ⓑ ② ⓐ, ⓔ ③ ⓒ, ⓓ
④ ⓑ, ⓓ, ⓔ ⑤ ⓑ, ⓒ, ⓔ

21 다음 밑줄 친 부분 중 어법상 어색한 것은?

Sumi ① must feel very ② hungry. She ③ only drank ④ a cup of water and had ⑤ else nothing today.

22 다음 글에서 어법상 올바른 것을 모두 고르세요.

Hi, I'm Gina and I live in Los Angeles, often known as L.A. I want to tell you about it. (A) Los Angeles means "the angels" in Spanish. In the central region, there is Hollywood, (B) which visited by many movie fans. Every year, (C) near 3.5 million tourists come to see the famous Hollywood sign. Oh, (D) when the weather gets hot in summer, people go to the Santa Monica Beach to enjoy swimming and water sports. (E) I want you come to L.A. someday.

① (A) ② (B) ③ (C) ④ (D) ⑤ (E)

23 다음 글에서 빈칸 ⓐ~ⓒ에 들어갈 말로 가장 알맞은 것은?

Welcome back to Daily Reminders. Today we will talk about public transportation etiquette. First, and most _____ⓐ_____, we need to be respectful of fellow passengers. Second, avoid using the phone as much as possible. If you need to talk on the phone, try to keep the conversation _____ⓑ_____ and do not speak with a loud voice. Third, offer your seat to _____ⓒ_____ or disabled passengers. Last, do not use multiple seats and be considerate of others. If everyone follows this etiquette, we can make public transportation a more enjoyable experience for everyone. So, let's keep these in mind when you take the bus or subway.

	ⓐ	ⓑ	ⓒ
①	important	short	elder
②	important	shortly	elderly
③	importantly	short	elder
④	importantly	short	elderly
⑤	importantly	shortly	elder

24 다음 빈칸에 들어갈 수 없는 말은?

Jinho : Who is the best player on your team?
Minsu: I think Bill is the best.
Jinho : _____
Minsu: Because he always does his best.

① How come?
② What makes you think so?
③ Why do you say that?
④ What do you think about it?
⑤ What is your reason for saying so?

25 다음 중 밑줄 친 단어의 쓰임이 올바른 것은?

① I sat and watched everyone very close.
② Michelle hard ever calls her parents.
③ His desk was piled high with books.
④ My grandfather hasn't been sleeping well late.
⑤ A bomb exploded somewhere nearly here.

26 다음 빈칸에 알맞도록 괄호 안의 단어를 바르게 배열한 것은?

Nari _____ to work on time. (not, come, does, always)

① does not always come
② does not come always
③ always come does not
④ come always does not
⑤ does always not come

27 다음 두 문장의 빈칸에 공통으로 들어갈 단어로 알맞은 것은?

• _____ I heard the news, I was very surprised. • _____ is your birthday?

① For   ② That   ③ How
④ Since   ⑤ When

28 다음 빈칸 (A)~(C)에 알맞은 말이 바르게 나열된 것은?

A: _____(A)_____ is the river? B: It's 25 kilometers long. A: _____(B)_____ is your dad? B: He is 57 years old. A: _____(C)_____ are there in your class? B: About 25.

	(A)	(B)	(C)
①	How long	How old	How much student
②	How long	How old	How many students
③	How length	How old	How many students
④	How long	How older	How many student
⑤	How length	How older	How much students

29 다음 중 밑줄 친 부분을 어법상 옳게 고친 것은?

① Today is much (→ very) colder than yesterday.
② I can't attend the meeting, either (→ too).
③ Kevin yet (→ already) graduated from college.
④ Do you still (→ yet) have the picture?
⑤ We will often (→ often will) practice swimming.

30 다음 중 밑줄 친 부분이 어법상 어색한 것은?

① John had a seat on the bus, but he offered to give it up to an elderly lady.
② As soon as Jack saw me watching TV, I turned it off.
③ He stays in the playground alone until his mom picks up him.
④ I heard you sent me a picture, but I don't have time to look at it.
⑤ She usually listens to pop songs every night, but she won't listen to them tonight.

31 괄호 안에 주어진 우리말과 일치하도록 빈칸에 알맞은 단어를 쓰세요. (단, 한 단어로 쓸 것.)

> A: Wow, your skin looks ___(A)___ better than before.
> (와, 네 피부가 전보다 훨씬 더 좋아 보여.)
> B: I started putting some ___(B)___ good cream on it a few days ago.
> (며칠 전에 아주 좋은 크림을 피부에 바르기 시작했거든.)
> A: ___(C)___ can I get it?
> (그거 어디서 구할 수 있니?)
> B: My mom gave it to me. I'll let you know later.
> (엄마가 내게 그걸 주셨어. 나중에 알려줄게.)

(A) _____ (B) _____
(C) _____

32 다음 중 밑줄 친 단어의 위치가 잘못된 것은?

① My sister never cleans her room.
② He gets often angry at her.
③ My mother and I will rarely go to the market together.
④ Our boss is always kind to us.
⑤ I usually walk to work.

33 다음 밑줄 친 부분 중 어색한 것끼리 바르게 짝 지어진 것은?

> Jessie: Look out the window! Snow is piling up ⓐ so fast.
> Monica: Interesting. It snows ⓑ rarely in this area.
> Jessie: Let's build a snowman. I'll ⓒ put my mittens on the snowman.
> Monica: Sounds good! I want to build a ⓓ very taller snowman than my height.
> Jessie: Good. Please ⓔ wait for me to put on my coat.

① ⓐ, ⓓ ② ⓒ, ⓓ ③ ⓑ, ⓒ
④ ⓑ, ⓓ ⑤ ⓓ, ⓔ

34 다음 중 어법상 어색한 문장을 모두 고르세요.

① I feel quite well.
② It is very cold outside.
③ He spends usually a lot of money.
④ She often forget to bring her umbrella.
⑤ I sometimes go to church alone.

35 다음 글의 밑줄 친 ①~⑤ 중 어법상 어색한 문장은?

> ① The garage sale was hard work. There were many things to do. ② First, we collected plenty of old things. ③ Then, we cleaned everything carefully. ④ Next, early on Sunday morning, we brought everything out and set up it. ⑤ A lot of people came to the sale and we sold so many things.

36 다음 (A)의 말에 어울리는 말을 (B)에서 골라 그 기호를 쓰세요.

(A)
① Mark has already packed everything for camping.
② Did you eat lunch?
③ I remember that you lived in Seattle.
④ Will you show me your drawing?

(B)
ⓐ Of course I did. It's already three o'clock.
ⓑ I still live there.
ⓒ He seems to be very excited.
ⓓ I haven't finished it yet.

① - _____ ② - _____ ③ - _____ ④ - _____

37 괄호 안의 우리말과 뜻이 같도록 빈칸에 들어갈 질문을 조건에 맞게 영어로 쓰세요.

조건
• 의문부사 how로 시작할 것.
• 동사 get을 사용할 것.
• 조동사 can을 쓸 것.
• 9 단어로 만들 것.

Molly : _____
_____
(내가 여기서 공항까지 어떻게 갈 수 있어?)
Sophia : You can take a taxi. It will take about 20 minutes.
Molly : Thank you.

38 다음 중 밑줄 친 부분이 어색한 것을 모두 고르세요.

① Nick carried it very carefully.
② Why do you walk so fastly?
③ Have you seen any movies late?
④ You can get there quickly.
⑤ They look so much different.

39 (A)~(C)의 빈칸에 알맞은 말끼리 바르게 짝지어진 것은?

The interview was over. Suddenly, the lights came upon the set, and I could not believe my eyes. My favorite actor was there! He was rehearsing with the other actors. Then the director said, "Ready, action!" My dad and the other camera operators were looking through their cameras ____(A)____. The director asked the actors to do the same scene many times. A lot of people worked ____(B)____ to make the one-hour drama, and my dad was one of them. My dad looked really ____(C)____. I felt proud of him.

	(A)	(B)	(C)
①	careful	hardly	wonderfully
②	careful	hard	wonderful
③	careful	hardly	wonderful
④	carefully	hard	wonderful
⑤	carefully	hard	wonderfully

CHAPTER 12
가정법

성취도 자기 평가 활용법

구분	평가 기준
Excellent	문법 내용을 모두 이해하고, 문제를 모두 맞힘.
Very good	문법 내용은 충분히 이해했으나 실수로 1~2문제 틀림.
Good	문법 내용이 조금 어려워 3~4문제 틀림.
needs **R**eview	문법 내용 이해가 어렵고, 5문제 이상 틀림. 복습 필요.

Problem Solving Skill	페이지	학습날짜	성취도 자기평가 E V G R	학습체크
PSS 1 조건을 나타내는 if	292	/		☐
PSS 2 가정법 과거	페이지	학습날짜	성취도 자기평가 E V G R	학습체크
PSS 2-1 if+가정법 과거	293	/		☐
PSS 2-2 I wish+가정법 과거	295	/		☐
PSS 2-3 동사의 현재형+as if+가정법 과거	296	/		☐
PSS 3 가정법 과거완료	페이지	학습날짜	성취도 자기평가 E V G R	학습체크
PSS 3-1 if+가정법 과거완료	297	/		☐
PSS 3-2 I wish+가정법 과거완료	298	/		☐
PSS 3-3 동사의 현재형+as if+가정법 과거완료	299	/		☐
Chapter Review Test	301	/		☐

조건을 나타내는 if

1. if는 '~한다면, ~라면'의 뜻으로 현재나 미래에 실제로 일어날 수 있는 상황에 대한 조건을 나타낸다.

    If it's 10 a.m. in New York, it's 8 p.m. in Seoul. 뉴욕이 오전 10시이면, 서울은 오후 8시이다.
    If it doesn't rain tomorrow, I will go out. 내일 비가 오지 않으면, 나는 밖에 나갈 거야.
    cf. 미래의 일을 나타낸다고 하더라도 조건을 나타내는 if절의 동사는 항상 현재형으로 쓴다.
    　　　If it **won't rain** tomorrow, I will stay home. (×)
    cf. 「명령문＋and ~」는 If 조건문으로, 「명령문＋or ~」는 If 조건문의 부정형으로 나타낼 수 있다.
    　　　Study hard, **and** you will pass the exam.
    　　　＝ **If you study hard**, you will pass the exam.
    　　　　네가 열심히 공부하면 너는 시험에 합격할 것이다.
    　　　Help him right now, **or** he will be in danger.
    　　　＝ **If you don't help him right now**, he will be in danger.
    　　　　네가 당장 그를 도와주지 않는다면 그는 위험에 처하게 될 것이다.

2. if와 when

    A: Are you going to buy the book? 너는 그 책을 살 거니?
    B: I'm not sure. **If** I buy mine, I will buy yours, too. 확실하지 않아. 내 것을 산다면, 네 것도 살게.
    　　(책을 살 것인지 말 것인지가 확실하지 않은 경우를 나타낸다.)

    A: Are you going to buy the book? 너는 그 책을 살 거니?
    B: Yes, I am. **When** I buy mine, I will buy yours, too. 응, 살 거야. 내 것을 살 때, 네 것도 살게.
    　　(분명히 책을 살 경우를 나타낸다.)

정답 p.65

PRACTICE 1

〈보기〉에 주어진 단어를 알맞은 형태로 바꾸어 빈칸에 쓰세요.

보 기	study　finish　rain　find　be　hurry　leave　change　meet　come

1 If I _____ your notebook, I'll call you.

2 Can I go home early if I _____ my work for the day?

3 If he _____ here within two hours, we can see him.

4 Let's stay home if it _____ tomorrow.

5 I will say hello to Jack for you if I _____ him.

6 If your mom _____ her mind, let me know.

7 If she _____ for the office, call me please.

8 Sumi can pass the exam if she _____ hard.

9 Jina can catch the bus if she _____.

10 If you _____ busy now, I will visit you later.

PSS 2 가정법 과거
Problem Solving Skill

PSS 2-1 if+가정법 과거

If + 주어 + 동사의 과거형 ~, 주어 + would, could, should, might + 동사원형 …

1. 가정법 과거는 '만약 ~한다면 …할 텐데'의 뜻으로 현재 사실에 반대되는 일을 가정할 때 쓴다.

   If we **were** on vacation, we **would be** in Hawaii.
   우리가 휴가 중이라면, 우리는 하와이에 있을 텐데.
   ➡ As we are not on vacation, we are not in Hawaii.
   우리는 휴가 중이 아니므로, 우리는 하와이에 있지 않다.

2. if절의 be동사는 인칭에 상관없이 were를 쓴다.

   My son could take care of me if **he were** here.
   내 아들이 여기에 있다면, 나를 돌봐줄 수 있을 텐데.
   ➡ My son can't take care of me because he is not here.
   내 아들이 여기에 있지 않기 때문에, 그는 나를 돌봐줄 수 없다.

   cf. 구어체에서는 was를 쓰기도 한다.
   If I **was** in New York, I would travel with Linda. 내가 뉴욕에 있다면, Linda와 여행을 할 텐데.

PRACTICE 2

괄호 안의 단어를 알맞은 형태로 바꾸어 빈칸에 쓰세요.

1. If she _____ the answer, she could win a prize. (know)
2. If we _____ enough time, we would discuss the rule. (have)
3. If I were busy, I _____ so much. (not, travel)
4. If it _____ a little cheaper, I could buy it. (be)
5. If he were richer, he _____ a nice car. (get)
6. If she liked the boy, she _____ him to the party. (invite)
7. If I had an oven, I _____ some pies. (bake)
8. If you _____ hard, you could pass the exam. (study)
9. If it _____ sunny, we couldn't take a walk. (not, be)
10. If I knew her phone number, I _____ to her right now. (talk)

PRACTICE 3

다음 문장을 if를 이용한 가정법 문장으로 바꾸어 쓰세요.

1. As Mary is sick, she can't visit her grandparents' house.
   ➡ *If Mary weren't sick, she could visit her grandparents' house.*

2. As Steve doesn't know the reason, he isn't angry.
   ➡ _____

3. As this movie isn't fun, I am bored.
   ➡ _____

4. As you aren't honest, you don't have many friends.
   ➡ _____

5. As I don't have enough money, I can't buy you a piano.
   ➡ _____

6. As you aren't old enough, you can't understand this better.
   ➡ _____

7. As my brother is not hungry, he won't go out for dinner.
   ➡ _____

8. As I am tired, I can't go swimming now.
   ➡ _____

9 As she doesn't agree with the writer, she doesn't like his book.
➡ _____

10 As I have other plans, I can't go shopping with you.
➡ _____

PSS 2-2 I wish+가정법 과거

「I wish+가정법 과거」는 '~라면 좋을 텐데'의 뜻으로 현재나 미래의 사실과 반대되거나 이룰 수 없는 일을 소망할 때 쓴다.

I wish + 주어 + 동사의 과거형 ~

I wish I **had** a sister. 여동생이 한 명 있으면 좋을 텐데.
➡ I'm sorry that I don't have a sister.
나는 여동생이 없어서 유감이다.

I wish Dave **would come** to see me.
Dave가 날 보러 온다면 좋을 텐데.
➡ I'm sorry that Dave will not come to see me.
Dave가 날 보러 오지 않을 것이라서 유감이다.

정답 p.66

PRACTICE 4

괄호 안의 단어를 알맞은 형태로 바꾸어 빈칸에 써서 가정법 과거 문장을 완성하세요.

1 I wish I _____ taller. (be)

2 I wish I _____ more subscribers on my YouTube channel. (have)

3 I wish it _____ so much. (not, snow)

4 I wish I _____ Chinese. (can, speak)

5 I wish she _____ me more often. (will, call)

6 I wish I _____ him a hand. (can, give)

7 I wish they _____ here with us now. (be)

8 I wish Mark _____ Korea. (will, not, leave)

9 I wish I _____ well. (can, sing)

10 I wish I _____ more time with you. (have)

PRACTICE 5

다음 주어진 문장과 반대되는 일을 소망하는 뜻이 되도록 문장을 바꾸어 쓰세요.

1. I don't live in the country.
   ➡ I wish I lived in the country.

2. It is cold here.
   ➡ _____

3. I am not diligent.
   ➡ _____

4. I don't know how to drive.
   ➡ _____

5. Angela can't join our club.
   ➡ _____

6. There aren't trees around here.
   ➡ _____

7. Windows update won't finish soon.
   ➡ _____

8. I can't play the violin.
   ➡ _____

9. Mark will move to another city.
   ➡ _____

10. I'm not good at sports.
    ➡ _____

PSS 2-3 동사의 현재형＋as if＋가정법 과거

「as if＋가정법 과거」는 '마치 ~인 것처럼'의 뜻으로 현재의 사실과 반대되는 일을 나타낸다.

[동사의 현재형] ＋ [as if] ＋ [주어] ＋ [동사의 과거형] ~

He **talks** to me **as if** I **were** his son. 그는 마치 내가 그의 아들인 것처럼 내게 말한다.
➡ In fact, I'm not his son. 사실, 나는 그의 아들이 아니다.

Ann **acts as if** she **were** a doctor. Ann은 마치 그녀가 의사인 것처럼 행동한다.
➡ In fact, Ann is not a doctor. 사실, Ann은 의사가 아니다.

PRACTICE 6

〈보기〉와 같이 주어진 문장을 as if를 이용한 가정법 문장으로 바꾸어 쓰세요.

> 보기 In fact, Matt is not Italian.
> ➡ Matt talks <u>as if he were Italian</u>.

1. In fact, you are not his friend.
   ➡ You talk about him _____.

2. In fact, she doesn't live here.
   ➡ It seems _____.

3 In fact, Akiko is not Korean.
➡ Akiko appears _____.

4 In fact, he is not a king.
➡ He acts _____.

5 In fact, the play isn't exciting.
➡ It sounds _____.

6 In fact, today is not Saturday.
➡ It feels _____.

7 In fact, David doesn't know everybody in my family.
➡ David speaks _____.

8 In fact, Kelly isn't very smart.
➡ Kelly talks _____.

9 In fact, you are not a child.
➡ You act _____.

10 In fact, they aren't sick.
➡ It seems _____.

가정법 과거완료

PSS 3-1 if+가정법 과거완료

가정법 과거완료는 '만약 ~했다면 …했을 텐데'의 뜻으로 과거 사실에 반대되는 일을 가정할 때 쓴다.

If I **had had** a car, I **could have given** him a ride.
만약 내게 차가 있었다면, 나는 그를 태워줬을 텐데.
➡ As I didn't have a car, I couldn't give him a ride.
나는 차가 없었기 때문에, 그를 태워줄 수 없었다.

If we **had practiced** harder, we **could have won** the match.
만약 우리가 더 열심히 연습했다면, 우리는 그 경기에서 우승할 수 있었을 텐데.

→ Because we didn't practice harder, we couldn't win the match.
우리는 더 열심히 연습하지 않았기 때문에, 그 경기에서 우승할 수 없었다.

PRACTICE 7

정답 p.66

괄호 안의 단어를 알맞은 형태로 바꾸어 빈칸에 쓰세요.

1 If I _____ the book, I would have lent it to him. (finish)
2 If I _____ her then, I could have helped her. (know)
3 If I _____ you, I would listen to his advice. (be)
4 If they had heard the news, they _____ you. (call)
5 If Ben had any free time, he _____ to see the movie. (go)
6 If she _____ about our party, she could have come. (not, forget)
7 If we had taken the subway, we _____ there on time. (arrive)
8 If you _____ the book, I would give it to you. (like)
9 If Jihoon had been more careful, he _____ the accident. (prevent)
10 If she had slept enough, she _____ so tired. (not, feel)

PSS 3-2 I wish + 가정법 과거완료

「I wish + 가정법 과거완료」는 '~했더라면 좋았을 텐데'의 뜻으로, 과거의 사실과 반대되는 일을 소망할 때 쓴다.

I wish + 주어 + had + 과거분사 ~

I wish I **had had** breakfast. 내가 아침을 먹었더라면 좋았을 텐데.
→ I'm sorry that I didn't have breakfast.
나는 아침을 먹지 않아서 유감이다.

I wish she **had not moved** to Jejudo.
그녀가 제주도로 이사를 가지 않았더라면 좋았을 텐데.
→ I'm sorry that she moved to Jejudo.
그녀가 제주도로 이사를 가서 유감이다.

I wish I had studied last night.

PRACTICE 8

다음 문장을 I wish로 시작하는 가정법 문장으로 바꾸어 쓰세요.

1 I didn't do my best. I'm sorry about that.
→ I wish I had done my best.

2 She didn't keep her promise. I'm sorry about that.
→ _____

3 Jinsu didn't come to my house. I miss him.
→ _____

4 I'm not in Europe now, but I'd like to be there.
→ _____

5 They didn't finish cleaning the room. I'm sorry about that.
→ _____

6 Mina didn't attend the meeting. I'm sorry about that.
→ _____

7 My brother doesn't read books, but I want him to.
→ _____

8 My dog died. I miss it.
→ _____

9 We didn't visit him in the hospital. I'm sorry about that.
→ _____

10 I can't go back to my country this month, but I want to.
→ _____

PSS 3-3 동사의 현재형 + as if + 가정법 과거완료

「as if + 가정법 과거완료」는 '마치 ~이었던 것처럼'의 뜻으로 과거의 사실과 반대되는 일을 나타낸다.

[동사의 현재형] + [as if] + [주어] + [had + 과거분사] ~

It **sounds as if** he **had not studied** last night.
마치 그가 지난밤에 공부를 하지 않았다는 것처럼 들린다.
→ In fact, he studied last night. 사실, 그는 지난밤에 공부를 했다.

CHAPTER 12 _ 가정법

They **talk as if** they **had graduated** from high school.
그들은 마치 고등학교를 졸업한 것처럼 말한다.
➡ In fact, they didn't graduate from high school. 사실, 그들은 고등학교를 졸업하지 않았다.

PRACTICE 9

정답 p.67

〈보기〉와 같이 as if를 이용한 가정법 문장으로 바꾸어 쓰세요.

보 기	In fact, it was not his car.
	➡ He talks <u>as if it had been his car</u>.

1 In fact, she slept well last night.
   ➡ She looks _____.

2 In fact, Jennifer is not married.
   ➡ Jennifer looks _____.

3 In fact, I didn't break the glass.
   ➡ He speaks _____.

4 In fact, they weren't rich in their youth.
   ➡ It seems _____.

5 In fact, I didn't lose my watch.
   ➡ I feel _____.

6 In fact, you were not right all the time.
   ➡ You talk _____.

7 In fact, Mr. Park doesn't know those students.
   ➡ Mr. Park acts _____.

8 In fact, Paul isn't popular among his students.
   ➡ Paul talks _____.

9 In fact, they weren't bored by the lecture.
   ➡ They look _____.

10 In fact, it wasn't your idea.
   ➡ You sound _____.

Chapter Review Test

CHAPTER 12 가정법

1 주어진 동사를 이용하여 빈칸에 알맞은 단어를 쓰세요.

> If it _____, we will not be able to play tennis. (rain)

2 다음 두 문장의 뜻이 같아지도록 각각의 빈칸에 알맞은 단어를 쓰세요.

> • Get up early, and you won't miss the bus.
> = _____ you get up early, you _____ miss the bus.

3 다음 중 어법상 어색한 문장은?

① If you work hard, you'll succeed.
② If she passes the test, she'll be so happy.
③ If it will snow tomorrow, I will stay at home.
④ If you come to my party, we'll have a good time.
⑤ If you lose weight, you'll be healthy.

4 다음 빈칸에 들어갈 알맞은 말은?

> If she doesn't take a taxi, she _____ late.

① is   ② was   ③ be
④ does   ⑤ will be

5 다음의 직설법 문장을 가정법으로 알맞게 고친 것은?

> As he doesn't know her telephone number, he won't call her.

① If he knows her telephone number, he will call her.
② If he knew her telephone number, he will call her.
③ If he had known her telephone number, he would have called her.
④ If he knew her telephone number, he would call her.
⑤ If he knew her telephone number, he would called her.

6 다음 밑줄 친 부분 중 어법상 잘못된 것은?

> If she ① went there ② by car, ③ she won't ④ arrive ⑤ on time.

7 다음 중 어법상 어색한 문장은?

① I wish you could spend Christmas with me.
② This book is three times as expensive as that one.
③ If you didn't tell me about the problem, I couldn't have helped.
④ I wish there were no pollution in the world.
⑤ I hope that I can meet many good friends and teachers.

8 다음 중 어법상 어색한 문장은?

① I wish you could come with me.
② You talk as if you are my father.
③ I wish you were here with us.
④ If I were you, I would marry her.
⑤ If I don't get it, I will try it again.

9 다음 중 어법상 올바른 문장을 두 개 고르세요.

① If you eat too many candies, you would have bad teeth.
② If you want to stay healthy, exercise regularly.
③ If you turn the music app on, you can listen to music.
④ If you got up early, you might have caught the first train.
⑤ If you study hard, you may passed the test.

10 주어진 문장을 가정법으로 올바르게 바꾼 것은?

> As I am busy, I can't go to the concert with you.

① If I am busy, I can go to the concert with you.
② If I am not busy, I could go to the concert with you.
③ If I weren't busy, I could go to the concert with you.
④ If I were busy, I could go to the concert with you.
⑤ If I were busy, I can't go to the concert with you.

11 다음 문장에서 어법상 틀린 부분을 한 군데 찾아 바르게 고쳐 쓰세요.

> My sister went to America to study music last month. I always think of her and miss her a lot. If I am a bird, I could fly to her. I wish I could go to America this summer.

_____ ➡ _____

12 다음 ⓐ~ⓔ 중, 어법상 어색한 문장의 개수를 고르시오.

> ⓐ If she were not sick, she could have come to the party.
> ⓑ If she had not been at work, she could have come here.
> ⓒ If I had known the truth, I would have told them.
> ⓓ If we had the key, we could have entered now.
> ⓔ If I had lived there, I would have visited him often.

① 0개 ② 1개 ③ 2개 ④ 3개 ⑤ 4개

13 다음 빈칸에 알맞은 단어를 넣어 문장을 완성하세요.

> • I didn't finish it by myself. I'm sorry about that.
> ➡ I _____ I _____ _____ it by myself.

14 다음 중 앞뒤 문장의 연결이 의미상 어색한 것은?

① I don't have a lot of free time. I wish I had a lot of free time.
② I am not good at running. I wish I were good at running.
③ I can't swim in the sea. I wish I could swim like a fish.
④ I don't know Chinese. I wish I didn't know Chinese.
⑤ I can't sleep well at night. I wish I could sleep well at night.

15 우리말과 같은 뜻이 되도록 주어진 동사를 활용하여 빈칸에 알맞은 말을 쓰세요.

- 내가 작년에 세계 여행을 했더라면 좋았을 텐데.
  = I wish I _____ _____ around the world last year. (travel)

16 다음을 가정법 문장으로 전환할 때 빈칸에 알맞은 말을 쓰세요.

- My grandmother was not there. I miss her.
  ➡ I wish my grandmother _____ _____ there.

17 우리말과 같은 뜻이 되도록 빈칸에 알맞은 단어를 쓰세요.

- 그녀는 마치 자신이 여왕인 것처럼 행동한다.
  = She acts as if she _____ a queen.

18 빈칸에 알맞은 단어를 써서 주어진 문장을 as if 가정법 문장으로 바꾸세요.

- In fact, Mary is not my close friend.
  ➡ Mary speaks as if she _____ _____ _____ _____.

19 다음 주어진 문장과 의미가 같은 것은?

If I had enough money, I could buy all the items I want.

① Because I didn't have enough money, I couldn't buy all the items I wanted.
② Although I don't have enough money, I can buy all the items I want.
③ Because I don't have enough money, I can't buy all the items I want.
④ As I have enough money, I can buy all the items I want.
⑤ Though I have enough money, I can't buy all the items I want.

20 다음을 가정법 문장으로 바꿀 때 빈칸에 알맞은 단어를 쓰세요.

- In fact, he didn't meet Ms. Kim.
  ➡ He talks as if _____ _____ _____ Ms. Kim.

21 주어진 우리말과 같은 뜻이 되도록 다음 각 빈칸에 알맞은 한 단어를 쓰세요.

> A: I wish I _____ music traveling all over the world.
> (내가 전 세계를 여행하며 음악을 연주한다면 좋을 텐데.)
> B: I wish I _____ English as well as you.
> (난 너만큼 영어를 잘 말한다면 좋을텐데.)

22 주어진 문장과 같은 뜻이 되도록 if로 시작하는 가정법 문장을 쓰세요.

> • As I am not invited to her party, I can't go there.

➡ _____

23 다음 우리말과 같은 뜻이 되도록 괄호 안의 말을 바르게 배열하여 문장을 완성하세요.

> • 회의에 참석할 수 없다면, 저희에게 알려주세요.

➡ Please let us know _____.
(can't, you, the meeting, if, attend)

24 다음 우리말을 영어로 바르게 옮긴 것은?

> • 내가 설거지하는 걸 네가 도와주지 않으면, 난 너한테 쿠키를 구워주지 않을 거야.

① If you help me do the dishes, I won't bake you cookies.
② If you don't help me do the dishes, I won't bake you cookies.
③ If you help me do the dishes, I will bake you cookies.
④ If you didn't help me do the dishes, I bake you cookies.
⑤ If you helped me do the dishes, I will bake you cookies.

25 다음 빈칸에 들어갈 말을 〈보기〉에서 골라 순서대로 바르게 나열한 것은?

> • If I were born as the son of a king, _____
> • If I knew all the answers to the test, _____
> • If I won the lottery, _____
> • If I were a movie director, _____
> • If I had a driver's license, _____

보 기
ⓐ I could drive to the country to relax.
ⓑ I could get a good grade.
ⓒ I would be a prince.
ⓓ I could help the poor in our neighborhood.
ⓔ I could make movies with famous actors.

① ⓒ - ⓑ - ⓓ - ⓔ - ⓐ ② ⓒ - ⓐ - ⓓ - ⓔ - ⓑ
③ ⓓ - ⓐ - ⓒ - ⓔ - ⓑ ④ ⓒ - ⓑ - ⓐ - ⓔ - ⓓ
⑤ ⓐ - ⓒ - ⓓ - ⓔ - ⓑ

CHAPTER 13
비교구문

성취도 자기 평가 활용법

구분	평가 기준
Excellent	문법 내용을 모두 이해하고, 문제를 모두 맞힘.
Very good	문법 내용은 충분히 이해했으나 실수로 1~2문제 틀림.
Good	문법 내용이 조금 어려워 3~4문제 틀림.
needs **R**eview	문법 내용 이해가 어렵고, 5문제 이상 틀림, 복습 필요.

	페이지	학습날짜	성취도 자기평가 E V G R	학습체크
PSS 1 비교급과 최상급 만드는 법				
PSS 1-1 규칙 변화 Ⅰ	306	/		☐
PSS 1-2 규칙 변화 Ⅱ	306	/		☐
PSS 1-3 규칙 변화 Ⅲ	307	/		☐
PSS 1-4 불규칙 변화	309	/		☐
PSS 2 원급을 이용한 비교	페이지	학습날짜	성취도 자기평가 E V G R	학습체크
PSS 2-1 as+원급+as	311	/		☐
PSS 2-2 as+원급+as+주어+can[could]	313	/		☐
PSS 3 비교급을 이용한 비교	페이지	학습날짜	성취도 자기평가 E V G R	학습체크
PSS 3-1 비교급+than	315	/		☐
PSS 3-2 비교급 강조	317	/		☐
PSS 3-3 less+원급+than	318	/		☐
PSS 3-4 the+비교급, the+비교급	319	/		☐
PSS 3-5 There is nothing ~ 비교급+than ⋯	320	/		☐
PSS 3-6 비교급+and+비교급	322	/		☐
PSS 4 최상급을 이용한 비교	페이지	학습날짜	성취도 자기평가 E V G R	학습체크
PSS 4-1 the+최상급	322	/		☐
PSS 4-2 one of+the+최상급+복수 명사	324	/		☐
PSS 4-3 최상급의 다른 표현	325	/		☐
Chapter Review Test	327	/		☐

비교급과 최상급 만드는 법

PSS 1-1 규칙 변화 I

일반적인 경우	형용사/부사의 원급+er, est	old – older – oldest tall – taller – tallest kind – kinder – kindest	small – smaller – smallest hard – harder – hardest high – higher – highest
-e로 끝나는 경우	형용사/부사의 원급+r, st	close – closer – closest nice – nicer – nicest	large – larger – largest strange – stranger – strangest

정답 p.69

PRACTICE 1

다음 형용사나 부사의 비교급과 최상급을 쓰세요.

1 cold – _____ – _____
2 young – _____ – _____
3 nice – _____ – _____
4 high – _____ – _____
5 fresh – _____ – _____
6 small – _____ – _____
7 strange – _____ – _____
8 fast – _____ – _____
9 low – _____ – _____
10 new – _____ – _____
11 hard – _____ – _____
12 close – _____ – _____
13 long – _____ – _____
14 slow – _____ – _____
15 tall – _____ – _____
16 old – _____ – _____
17 kind – _____ – _____
18 warm – _____ – _____
19 large – _____ – _____
20 smart – _____ – _____

PSS 1-2 규칙 변화 II

자음+y로 끝나는 경우	자음+ i+er, est	early – earlier – earliest happy – happier – happiest pretty – prettier – prettiest healthy – healthier – healthiest	heavy – heavier – heaviest easy – easier – easiest

단모음+단자음으로 끝나는 경우	원급+마지막 자음+er, est	hot – hot**ter** – hot**test** thin – thin**ner** – thin**nest**	big – big**ger** – big**gest**

정답 p.69

PRACTICE 2

다음 형용사나 부사의 비교급과 최상급을 쓰세요.

1 happy   – _____ – _____
2 healthy – _____ – _____
3 hot   – _____ – _____
4 easy   – _____ – _____
5 heavy   – _____ – _____
6 early   – _____ – _____
7 wise   – _____ – _____
8 thin   – _____ – _____
9 funny   – _____ – _____
10 pretty   – _____ – _____
11 dirty   – _____ – _____
12 lucky   – _____ – _____
13 friendly – _____ – _____
14 tasty   – _____ – _____
15 sweet   – _____ – _____
16 lazy   – _____ – _____
17 noisy   – _____ – _____
18 big   – _____ – _____
19 busy   – _____ – _____
20 dry   – _____ – _____
21 wet   – _____ – _____
22 ugly   – _____ – _____
23 hungry   – _____ – _____
24 strict   – _____ – _____

PSS 1-3 규칙 변화 Ⅲ

-y, -er로 끝나는 형용사를 제외한 대부분의 2음절 이상의 형용사	more+원급, most+원급	helpful – **more** helpful – **most** helpful useless – **more** useless – **most** useless beautiful – **more** beautiful – **most** beautiful expensive – **more** expensive – **most** expensive
분사 형태의 형용사	more+원급, most+원급	tired – **more** tired – **most** tired surprised – **more** surprised – **most** surprised boring – **more** boring – **most** boring shocking – **more** shocking – **most** shocking

CHAPTER 13 _ 비교구문

'형용사+ly' 형태의 부사	more+원급, most+원급,	exactly – **more** exactly – **most** exactly slowly – **more** slowly – **most** slowly easily – **more** easily – **most** easily fluently – **more** fluently – **most** fluently

정답 p.69

PRACTICE 3

다음 형용사나 부사의 비교급과 최상급을 쓰세요.

1. useful – _____ – _____
2. serious – _____ – _____
3. cheap – _____ – _____
4. afraid – _____ – _____
5. excited – _____ – _____
6. hard – _____ – _____
7. tired – _____ – _____
8. scary – _____ – _____
9. curious – _____ – _____
10. popular – _____ – _____
11. handsome – _____ – _____
12. large – _____ – _____
13. slowly – _____ – _____
14. famous – _____ – _____
15. helpful – _____ – _____
16. surprised – _____ – _____
17. expensive – _____ – _____
18. poor – _____ – _____
19. boring – _____ – _____
20. anxious – _____ – _____
21. convenient – _____ – _____
22. wide – _____ – _____

23 lonely – _____ – _____
24 foolish – _____ – _____
25 patient – _____ – _____
26 strong – _____ – _____
27 useless – _____ – _____
28 deep – _____ – _____
29 beautiful – _____ – _____
30 creative – _____ – _____
31 exactly – _____ – _____
32 mild – _____ – _____
33 easily – _____ – _____
34 important – _____ – _____
35 fluently – _____ – _____
36 great – _____ – _____
37 quickly – _____ – _____
38 difficult – _____ – _____
39 interesting – _____ – _____
40 nervous – _____ – _____

PSS 1-4 불규칙 변화

good – better – best	좋은	This car is **better** than that one. 이 차가 저 차보다 더 좋다.
well – better – best	건강한, 잘	Kelly speaks French **better** than Nick. Kelly가 Nick보다 프랑스어를 더 잘 말한다.
bad – worse – worst	나쁜	The movie is **worse** than I thought. 그 영화는 내가 생각했던 것보다 더 나쁘다.
ill – worse – worst	병든, 건강이 나쁜	Jim is **worse** than yesterday. Jim은 어제보다 상태가 더 나쁘다.

old – older – oldest	나이든, 오래된	My purse is **older** than yours. 내 지갑은 네 것보다 더 오래되었다.
old – elder – eldest	연상의, 손위의	Jason is my **elder** brother. Jason은 내 형이다.
late – later – latest	〈시간〉 늦은	Sujin arrived in Korea **later** than I had expected. 수진은 내가 기대했던 것보다 한국에 더 늦게 도착했다.
late – latter – last	〈순서〉 늦은	The **latter** part of this book is very interesting. 이 책의 후반부는 매우 흥미롭다.
far – farther – farthest	〈거리〉 먼	I can't go **farther** because I'm very tired. 나는 매우 피곤하기 때문에 더 멀리 갈 수 없다. **cf.** 시간, 공간상으로 먼 것을 나타낼 때 further, furthest를 쓰는 경우도 있다.
far – further – furthest	〈정도〉 더욱, 한층	We'd better discuss this problem **further**. 우리는 이 문제에 대해 더 논의해 보는 게 좋겠어요.
many – more – most	〈수〉 많은	Susan has **more** friends than Jeff has. Susan은 Jeff보다 더 많은 친구가 있다.
much – more – most	〈양〉 많은	Give me some **more** water. 내게 물을 좀 더 주세요.
few – fewer – fewest	〈수〉 적은	**Fewer** students attended the class today. 더 적은 학생들이 오늘 수업에 참석했다.
little – less – least	〈양〉 적은	You have to eat **less** meat. 너는 고기를 덜 먹어야 한다.

정답 p.70

PRACTICE 4

다음 형용사나 부사의 비교급과 최상급을 쓰세요.

1 good   – _____ – _____
2 late(시간) – _____ – _____
3 old(나이든) – _____ – _____
4 bad   – _____ – _____
5 many   – _____ – _____
6 far(거리)   – _____ – _____
7 well   – _____ – _____
8 few   – _____ – _____
9 old(손위의) – _____ – _____
10 late(순서) – _____ – _____
11 little   – _____ – _____
12 ill   – _____ – _____
13 far(정도)   – _____ – _____
14 much   – _____ – _____

PSS 2 원급을 이용한 비교

PSS 2-1 as+원급+as

1. 「as+원급+as」 '~만큼 …한'

   Sumi is **as tall as** Mira.
   수미는 미라만큼 키가 크다.
   Today is **as cold as** yesterday.
   오늘은 어제만큼 춥다.
   John speaks Korean **as well as** Kelly.
   John은 Kelly만큼 한국어를 잘 말한다.
   I go shopping **as often as** you.
   나는 너만큼 자주 쇼핑하러 간다.

   cf. 「배수+as+원급+as」 '~배 더 …한'
   The train is **three times as fast as** the car. 그 기차는 그 차보다 3배 빠르다.

2. 「not as[so]+원급+as」 '~만큼 …하지 않은'

   The bread **is not as[so] heavy as** the banana.
   빵은 바나나만큼 무겁지 않다.
   = The banana is **heavier than** the bread.
   바나나가 빵보다 더 무겁다.
   I **didn't** get up **as[so] early as** you.
   나는 너만큼 일찍 일어나지 않았다.
   = You got up **earlier than** I did.
   너는 나보다 더 일찍 일어났다.
   = You got up **earlier than** me.

   cf. than 뒤의 「주어+동사」는 목적격으로 바꾸어 쓸 수 있다.

PRACTICE 5

정답 p.70

<보기>와 같이 짝지어진 두 문장의 의미가 같도록 as ~ as 구문을 사용하여 빈칸을 채우세요.

| 보 기 | Insu studies harder than Giho.
= Giho doesn't study as[so] hard as Insu. |

1 Tony is more polite than Jack.
= Jack _____ Tony.

2 Jieun is taller than Minyoung.
 = Minyoung _____ Jieun.

3 My dog is cuter than my cat.
 = My cat _____ my dog.

4 The train to Busan is faster than the bus.
 = The bus to Busan _____ the train.

5 My shirt is whiter than his shirt.
 = His shirt _____ my shirt.

6 We bought more books than they did.
 = They _____ we did.

7 I speak English better than Sumi does.
 = Sumi _____ I do.

8 This sofa is more comfortable than that sofa.
 = That sofa _____ this sofa.

9 I like baseball more than basketball.
 = I _____ baseball.

10 Math is more difficult than science for me.
 = Science _____ math for me.

PRACTICE 6

다음 대화를 읽고, 괄호 안의 단어를 알맞은 형태로 바꾸어 as ~ as 구문을 완성하세요.

	Tony	Becky
1	I'm 25 years old.	I'm 25 years old, too.
2	My bag was 30,000 won.	My bag was 40,000 won.
3	I go to bed at eleven o'clock.	I go to bed at eleven o'clock, too.
4	I have two brothers.	I have two brothers, too.
5	I'm so tired. I can't run any longer. How about you?	I'm OK. I think I can run longer.
6	It took me 2 hours to finish the report.	The report took me 2 hours, too.

Tony

1 Tony is _____ Becky. (old)

2 Tony's bag was _____ Becky's. (expensive)

3 Tony goes to bed _____ Becky. (late)

4 Tony has _____ Becky does. (many)

5 Becky is _____ Tony. (tired)

6 Becky's report took _____ Tony's. (long)

PSS 2-2 as+원급+as+주어+can[could]

「as+원급+as+주어+can[could]」은 '~가 할 수 있는 한 …하게'의 뜻으로 「as+원급+as possible」로 바꾸어 쓸 수 있다.

I'll finish it **as quickly as I can**. 나는 내가 할 수 있는 한 빨리 그것을 끝낼 것이다.
= I'll finish it **as quickly as possible**.

Jim ran **as fast as he could**. Jim은 그가 할 수 있는 한 빨리 달렸다.
= Jim ran **as fast as possible**.

정답 p.70

PRACTICE 7

괄호 안에 주어진 단어를 바르게 배열하세요.

1 Jane always _____. (she, can, studies, hard, as, as)

2 I tried to _____. (possible, clearly, as, as, speak)

3 Frank _____. (early, could, got, up, as, he, as)

4 She threw the ball _____. (as, she, high, could, as)

5 Can you _____? (me, possible, soon, as, as, call)

6 Yuri _____. (as, as, helped, possible, us, much)

7 I _____. (counted, as, I, exactly, could, as, the number)

8 Ben _____. (goes, swimming, as, can, often, as, he)

9 They'll _____. (the questions, as, possible, as, make, easy)

10 Sujin wants to _____. (look, possible, as, young, as)

PRACTICE 8

짝지어진 두 문장의 의미가 같도록 문장을 완성하세요.

1. I spoke to her as slowly as possible.
   = I spoke to her <u>as slowly as I could</u>.

2. Carrie sang as loud as she could.
   = Carrie sang _____.

3. I'll help you as much as possible.
   = I'll help you _____.

4. Ingyu wrote back to me as quickly as he could.
   = Ingyu wrote back to me _____.

5. Let's work as hard as possible.
   = Let's work _____.

6. I usually have breakfast as fast as I can.
   = I usually have breakfast _____.

7. Ann talked to him as kindly as possible.
   = Ann talked to him _____.

8. I'll wait for you as long as I can.
   = I'll wait for you _____.

9. She tries to eat food as little as possible.
   = She tries to eat food _____.

10. They read the report as closely as they could.
    = They read the report _____.

11. Try to experience as many things as possible.
    = Try to experience _____.

12. He walked as quietly as possible not to get caught.
    = He walked _____ not to get caught.

13. We woke up as early as we could to take the first train.
    = We woke up _____ to take the first train.

14. I wanted to see deep sea animals, so I dived as deep as I could.
    = I wanted to see deep sea animals, so I dived _____.

비교급을 이용한 비교

PSS 3-1 비교급+than

「비교급+than」 '~보다 더 …한'

My sister is **smarter than** I am.
나의 언니는 나보다 더 똑똑하다.
= My sister is **smarter than** me.

I can cook **better than** he can.
나는 그보다 요리를 더 잘할 수 있다.
= I can cook **better than** him.

I have **more** books **than** she does.
나는 그녀보다 더 많은 책들을 갖고 있다.
= I have **more** books **than** her.

cf. 비교의 대상이 같은 종류이면 소유대명사로 나타낼 수 있다.
My bag is heavier than **your bag**. 내 가방이 네 가방보다 더 무겁다.
= My bag is heavier than **yours**.

정답 p.71

PRACTICE 9

괄호 안의 단어를 비교급 형태로 바꾸어 빈칸에 쓰세요.

1 Ann made _____ money than I did. (much)
2 This flower is _____ than that one. (beautiful)
3 Tom looks _____ than Brad. (short)
4 I was _____ than he was. (nervous)
5 He arrived at the airport _____ than us. (late)
6 Jenny came to the office _____ than I did. (early)

PRACTICE 10

짝지어진 두 문장의 의미가 같도록 빈칸에 알맞은 말을 쓰세요.

1 I studied harder than him.
   = I studied harder than ___he___ ___did___.

2 Your cake looks larger than my cake.
   = Your cake looks larger than _____.

3 My elder brother is more patient than me.
   = My elder brother is more patient than _____ _____.

4 Lisa was happier than we were.
   = Lisa was happier than _____.

5 He can type more quickly than she can.
   = He can type more quickly than _____.

6 My dog is smarter than your dog.
   = My dog is smarter than _____.

PRACTICE 11

다음 대화를 읽고, 비교급을 사용하여 빈칸에 알맞은 말을 쓰세요.

Becky

	Tony	Becky
1	I'm 28 years old.	I'm 25 years old.
2	I'm 173cm tall.	I'm 160cm tall.
3	I can't play the guitar well.	I can play the guitar well.
4	I'm very diligent.	I'm not very diligent.
5	I weigh 65kg.	I weigh 50kg.
6	I'm very excited about the vacation.	I'm not so excited about the vacation.
7	I'm not so popular.	I'm very popular.
8	I run 7 meters per second.	I run 5 meters per second.
9	I study very hard.	I don't study very hard.
10	I'm not so active.	I'm very active.

Tony

1 Tony is ___older than___ Becky.
2 Tony is _____ Becky.
3 Becky can play the guitar _____ Tony.
4 Tony is _____ Becky.
5 Tony is _____ Becky.
6 Tony is _____ about the vacation _____ Becky.
7 Becky is _____ Tony.
8 Tony runs _____ Becky.
9 Tony studies _____ Becky.
10 Becky is _____ Tony.

PSS 3-2 비교급 강조

much, still, even, far, a lot은 비교급 앞에서 '훨씬'의 뜻으로 비교급을 강조한다.

I feel **much happier** now than before. 나는 전보다 지금 훨씬 더 행복하다고 느낀다.
Nami is **still busier** than Yuri. 나미는 유리보다 훨씬 더 바쁘다.
This bag is **even smaller** than I thought. 이 가방은 내가 생각했던 것보다 훨씬 더 작다.
It's **far colder** here than in Korea. 여기가 한국에서보다 훨씬 더 춥다.
Jinho speaks English **a lot better** than I expected.
진호는 내가 기대했던 것보다 훨씬 더 영어를 잘 말한다.

cf. very는 '매우'의 뜻으로 원급을 강조한다.
Your tie looks **very nice**. 네 넥타이는 매우 멋져 보인다.
Minsu was walking **very slowly**. 민수는 매우 천천히 걷고 있었다.

정답 p.71

PRACTICE 12

다음 중 밑줄 친 부분의 쓰임이 바른 것은 ○표, 바르지 않은 것은 ×표 하세요.

1 Mike is <u>even</u> lazier than Suji. _____
2 Helen is <u>very</u> shorter than my sister. _____
3 This computer is <u>far</u> expensive. _____
4 Minji is <u>much</u> kinder than other students. _____

5   You look very sleepy.   _____

6   Jeff dances very better than anyone else.   _____

7   I can swim still faster than he can.   _____

8   You are very smarter than I am.   _____

9   Peter sang the song very well.   _____

10 This information is a lot important for the test.   _____

정답 p.71

PRACTICE 13

다음 문장의 빈칸에 주어진 철자로 시작하는 비교급 강조어를 쓰세요.

1   His score is s_____ higher than mine.

2   The patient felt a_____ better than a week ago.

3   Steve was e_____ funnier than Daniel.

4   The car is f_____ more expensive than I expected.

5   She made the work m_____ easier for us.

6   They invited e_____ more people than we had wanted.

7   Her idea was f_____ more creative than yours.

8   Miss Ford looks m_____ younger than she is.

9   The cost of digital books is s_____ lower than that of print versions.

10 The movie star has become a_____ more famous since her last movie.

PSS 3-3 less+원급+than

「less+원급+than」은 '~보다 덜 …한'을 의미하고, 「not as[so]+원급+as」로 바꾸어 쓸 수 있다.

Brian watches the news **less often than** Kate. Brian은 Kate보다 뉴스를 덜 자주 본다.
= Brian **doesn't** watch the news **as[so] often as** Kate.

Driving in the country is **less hard than** driving in the city.
시골에서 운전하는 것은 도시에서 운전하는 것보다 덜 힘들다.
= Driving in the country is **not as[so] hard as** driving in the city.

PRACTICE 14

〈보기〉와 같이 짝지어진 두 문장의 의미가 같도록 as ~ as 구문을 사용하여 빈칸을 채우세요.

> 보 기   This bed is less comfortable than that bed.
> = This bed isn't as[so] comfortable as that bed.

1. Fishing is less exciting than hiking.
   = Fishing _____ .

2. This bag is less expensive than that one.
   = This bag _____ .

3. I met Insu less often than you did.
   = I _____ .

4. Money is less important than friendship.
   = Money _____ .

5. Your article is less interesting than mine.
   = Your article _____ .

6. Nami speaks Japanese less fluently than Seho.
   = Nami _____ .

7. The movie version was less boring than the book itself.
   = The movie version _____ .

8. He spends less money than his sister.
   = He _____ .

PSS 3-4   the+비교급, the+비교급

「the+비교급, the+비교급」 '~하면 할수록 더 …하다'

The more you eat, **the more** weight you will gain.
더 많이 먹으면 먹을수록 너는 몸무게가 더 늘 것이다.

The harder you study, **the smarter** you will become.
더 열심히 공부하면 할수록 너는 더 똑똑해질 것이다.

The heavier it is, **the more expensive** it is.
더 무거우면 무거울수록 더 비싸다.

PRACTICE 15

〈보기〉와 같이 「the+비교급, the+비교급」을 이용하여 주어진 문장을 바꾸어 쓰세요.

> **보 기**
> If the weather is worse, I feel more depressed.
> ➡ The worse the weather is, the more depressed I feel.

1 When you give more, you feel happier.
➡ _____

2 As I walked faster, the building became closer.
➡ _____

3 If you want more, you will be more disappointed.
➡ _____

4 If you get to know him more, you will like him more.
➡ _____

5 As I listened to the music longer, I became more cheerful.
➡ _____

6 As he went farther, he looked smaller.
➡ _____

7 If you practice more, you will play better.
➡ _____

8 When it grew darker, we felt more scared.
➡ _____

9 If you stay longer, it will be harder to leave.
➡ _____

10 As it gets colder, people drink more hot chocolate.
➡ _____

PSS 3-5 There is nothing ~ 비교급+than …

「There is nothing ~ 비교급+than …」은 '…보다 더 ~한 것은 없다'의 뜻으로 최상급의 의미를 나타낸다.

1. 「There is nothing + 비교급 + than …」

   There is nothing more interesting than reading books.
   책을 읽는 것보다 더 흥미로운 것은 없다.

= Reading books is **the most interesting**. 책을 읽는 것이 가장 흥미롭다.

There is nothing more boring than waiting for somebody on the street.

길에서 누군가를 기다리는 것보다 더 지루한 것은 없다.

= Waiting for somebody on the street is **the most boring** thing to do.

길에서 누군가를 기다리는 것이 하기에 가장 지루한 일이다.

2. 「There is nothing + 주어 + 동사 + 비교급 + than …」

There is nothing I do **better than** drawing. 그림을 그리는 것보다 내가 더 잘하는 것은 없다.

= I draw **(the) best**. 나는 그림 그리는 것을 가장 잘한다.

There is nothing I enjoy **more than** teaching kids.

아이들을 가르치는 것보다 내가 더 즐기는 것은 없다.

= I enjoy teaching kids **(the) most**. 나는 아이들을 가르치는 것을 가장 즐긴다.

PRACTICE 16

정답 p.72

괄호 안의 단어들을 어법에 맞게 배열하여 문장을 완성하세요.

1 내가 가장 잘하는 것은 요리하는 것이다. (nothing, I, than, there is, do, better)
  → _____ cooking.

2 수학이 나에게 가장 어렵다. (there is, than, more, difficult, nothing)
  → _____ math for me.

3 그가 가장 관심이 있는 것은 축구이다. (there is, he, interested in, nothing, is, than, more)
  → _____ soccer.

4 내 엄마의 쿠키는 가장 맛있다. (there is, more, delicious, nothing, than)
  → _____ my mom's cookies.

5 액션 영화는 가장 흥분된다. (there is, than, exciting, nothing, more)
  → _____ action movies.

6 나는 내 아이들을 가장 걱정한다. (than, I, nothing, more, there is, worry about)
  → _____ my children.

7 John은 영어를 가장 잘 말한다. (than, there is, better, John, nothing, speaks)
  → _____ English.

8 내가 가장 좋아하는 것은 사진을 찍는 것이다. (like, than, is, there, nothing, better, I)
  → _____ taking pictures.

PSS 3-6 비교급＋and＋비교급

「-er＋and＋-er」 또는 「more and more ~」 '점점 더 ~한'

The sky is getting **darker and darker**. 하늘은 점점 더 어두워지고 있다.
Mark is becoming **thinner and thinner**. Mark는 점점 더 야위어가고 있다.
The man ran **more and more slowly**. 그 남자는 점점 더 천천히 달렸다.

정답 p.72

PRACTICE 17

〈보기〉와 같이 괄호 안의 단어와 「비교급＋and＋비교급」 구문을 이용하여 빈칸을 채우세요.

| 보 기 | Her voice was getting <u>louder and louder</u>. (loud) |

1 The weather is getting _____. (cold)
2 Sue will become _____. (pretty)
3 The tree is growing _____. (tall)
4 We are getting _____. (old)
5 The man was getting _____. (well)
6 The child was growing _____. (tired)
7 Jerry is becoming _____. (popular)
8 The bird was flying _____. (high)
9 I started walking _____. (fast)
10 The houses became _____. (expensive)

최상급을 이용한 비교

PSS 4-1 the＋최상급

「the＋최상급」은 '가장 ~한'의 뜻으로, 비교의 대상을 한정할 때는 주로 최상급 뒤에 in, of 가 이끄는 전치사구나 절이 나온다. in 뒤에는 장소나 집단을 나타내는 단수 명사가 오며, of 뒤에는 복수 명사 및 복수의 의미를 나타내는 명사가 온다.

> What's **the longest** river **in the world**? 세계에서 가장 긴 강은 무엇이니?
> Bob is **the tallest** of the students. Bob은 그 학생들 중에서 가장 키가 크다.
> That's **the most boring** book **I've ever read**.
> 그것은 내가 지금껏 읽은 것 중 가장 지루한 책이다.

PRACTICE 18

괄호 안의 단어를 최상급의 형태로 바꾸어 빈칸에 쓰세요.

1 This is _____ restaurant in the city. (cheap)
2 Jim is _____ of my friends. (young)
3 It was _____ thing I've done. (foolish)
4 Angela is _____ friend of mine. (close)
5 That is _____ story I've ever heard. (strange)
6 Seho is _____ swimmer in his school. (good)
7 This is _____ problem I've ever had. (serious)
8 This is _____ car in our company. (new)
9 I had _____ birthday in my life. (bad)
10 The computer is _____ invention I've ever used. (convenient)

PRACTICE 19

그림을 보고, 주어진 단어를 이용하여 빈칸에 비교하는 말을 바르게 쓰세요.

1 (hot)
① July is _____ June.
② August is _____ .

2
(tall)
① The elephant is _____ the lion.
② The giraffe is _____ .

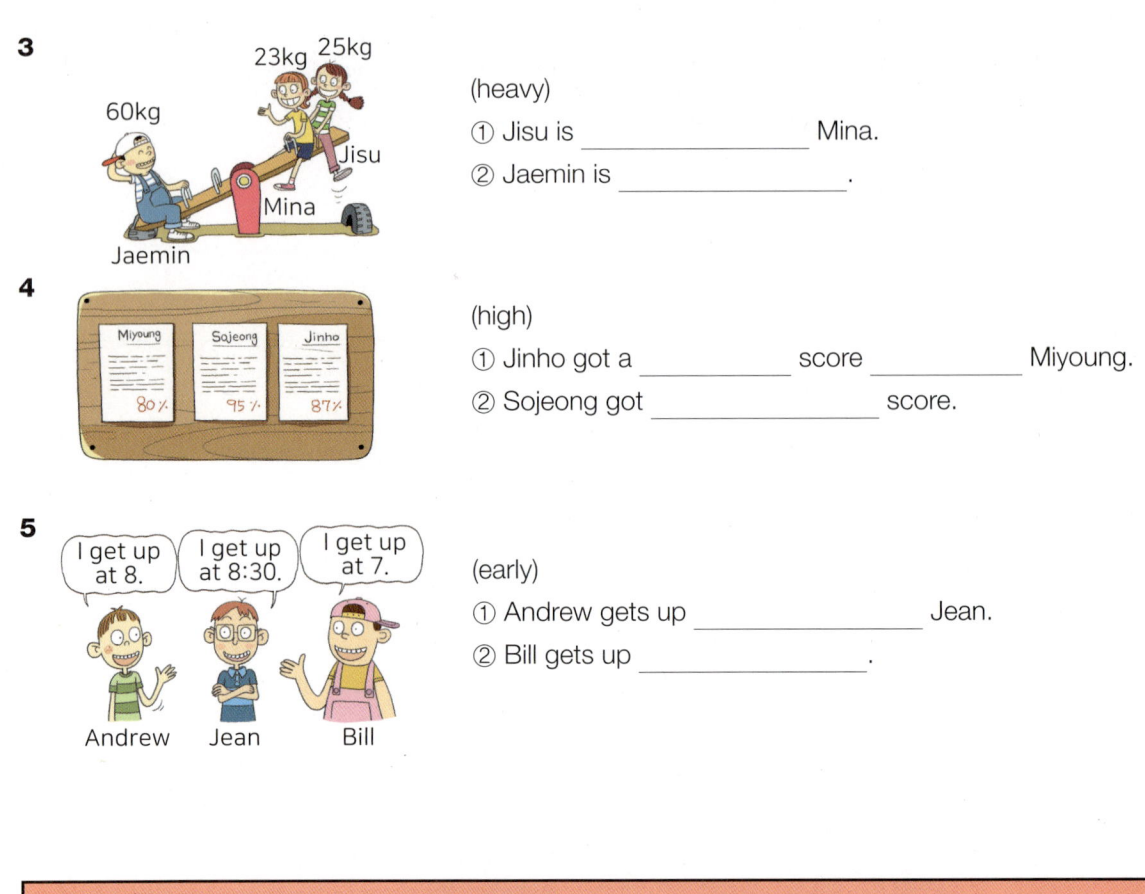

3 (heavy)
① Jisu is _____ Mina.
② Jaemin is _____.

4 (high)
① Jinho got a _____ score _____ Miyoung.
② Sojeong got _____ score.

5 (early)
① Andrew gets up _____ Jean.
② Bill gets up _____.

PSS 4-2 one of+the+최상급+복수 명사

「one of+the+최상급+복수 명사」 '가장 ~한 것 중의 하나'

Shakespeare is **one of the greatest writers**. 셰익스피어는 가장 위대한 작가들 중 한 명이다.
One of the easiest ways is to use public transportation.
가장 쉬운 방법들 중 하나는 대중교통을 이용하는 것이다.
This is **one of the most expensive rings** I have. 이것은 내가 가진 가장 비싼 반지들 중 하나이다.

정답 p.73

PRACTICE 20

〈보기〉와 같이 최상급 표현을 이용하여 빈칸에 알맞은 말을 쓰세요.

| 보 기 | It is a very large city. It is <u>one of the largest cities</u> in the world. |

1 The Han River is a very long river. It is _____ in Korea.
2 Gandhi is a very famous man. He is _____ in the world.
3 Sumi is a very diligent student. She is _____ in her class.
4 Mt. Halla is a very high mountain. It is _____ in Korea.

5 China is a very big country. It is _____ in the world.

6 Ralph is a very happy boy. He is _____ in the town.

7 This is a very boring movie. It is _____ I've ever seen.

8 Mr. Kim is a very kind teacher. He is _____ I've ever met.

9 Mira is a very beautiful girl. She is _____ I know.

10 This is a very popular restaurant. It is _____ in Seoul.

PSS 4-3 최상급의 다른 표현

다음과 같은 표현을 사용하여 최상급의 의미를 나타낼 수 있다.

「No (other) ~ as[so]+원급+as」 ~만큼 …한 것은 없다
= 「No (other) ~ 비교급+than」 ~보다 …한 것은 없다
= 「비교급+than any other+단수 명사」 ~는 다른 어떤 –보다도 더 …하다
= 「비교급+than all the other+복수 명사」 ~는 다른 모든 –보다도 더 …하다

Alex is **the strongest boy** in his class. Alex는 그의 반에서 가장 힘이 센 소년이다.
= **No (other) boy** in his class is **as[so] strong as** Alex.
　그의 반에서 Alex만큼 힘이 센 소년은 없다.
= **No (other) boy** in his class is **stronger than** Alex.
　그의 반에서 Alex보다 힘이 센 소년은 없다.
= Alex is **stronger than any other boy** in his class.
　Alex는 그의 반에서 다른 어떤 소년보다도 더 힘이 세다.
= Alex is **stronger than all the other boys** in his class.
　Alex는 그의 반에서 다른 모든 소년들보다도 더 힘이 세다.

This is **the most interesting** book of all. 이것은 모든 책 중에서 가장 재미있는 책이다.
= **No (other) book** is **as[so] interesting as** this book.
　이 책만큼 재미있는 책은 없다.
= **No (other) book** is **more interesting than** this book.
　이 책보다 더 재미있는 책은 없다.
= This is **more interesting than any other book**.
　이것은 다른 어떤 책보다도 더 재미있다.
= This is **more interesting than all the other books**.
　이것은 다른 모든 책들보다도 더 재미있다.

PRACTICE 21

다음 문장들이 같은 뜻이 되도록 빈칸에 알맞은 말을 쓰세요.

1 This is the most expensive bag in the shop.

= _____ in the shop is _____ this bag.

= _____ in the shop is _____ this bag.

= This is _____ in the shop.

= This is _____ in the shop.

2 Chloe is the kindest employee in our workplace.

= _____ in our workplace is _____ Chloe.

= _____ in our workplace is _____ Chloe.

= Chloe is _____ in our workplace.

= Chloe is _____ in our workplace.

3 He was the most popular singer in the 1990s.

= _____ in the 1990s was _____ him.

= _____ in the 1990s was _____ him.

= He was _____ in the 1990s.

= He was _____ in the 1990s.

4 This is the most difficult question of all.

= _____ is _____ this.

= _____ is _____ this.

= This is _____ .

= This is _____ .

5 Snoopy was the cutest dog in my town.

= _____ in my town was _____ Snoopy.

= _____ in my town was _____ Snoopy.

= Snoopy was _____ in my town.

= Snoopy was _____ in my town.

6 The Red Sea is the saltiest sea in the world.

= _____ in the world is _____ the Red Sea.

= _____ in the world is _____ the Red Sea.

= The Red Sea is _____ in the world.

= The Red Sea is _____ in the world.

Chapter Review Test

CHAPTER 13
비교구문

정답 p.73

1 다음 괄호 안에 주어진 단어의 형태가 바르게 짝지어진 것은?

- I consider time (important) than money.
- Water is the (important) thing in the desert.
- Saving money is as (important) as making money.

① important – important – important
② important – most important – more important
③ most important – important – more important
④ more important – most important – important
⑤ more important – more important – important

2 다음 각 빈칸에 알맞은 말로 바르게 짝지어진 것은?

- This product is _____ better than that one.
- This cake tastes _____ good. I'd like to have another piece.

① much – much
② even – much
③ even – very
④ very – still
⑤ very – very

3 다음 주어진 문장과 의미가 같은 것은?

This room is not so dark as that room.

① That room is not dark at all.
② This room is as dark as that room.
③ This room is darker than that room.
④ That room is darker than this room.
⑤ That room is not so dark as this room.

4 다음 문장의 밑줄 친 much와 쓰임이 같은 것은?

They found out that she had a much better sense of humor than others in the room.

① She did not use much butter.
② How much money do you have now?
③ I don't like classical music that much.
④ You should not spend too much time watching TV.
⑤ It will be much more expensive than you imagined.

[5 - 6] 괄호 안에 주어진 조건대로 다음 우리말을 영작하세요.

5

그가 더 열심히 노력할수록, 그는 춤을 더 잘 출 수 있다. (hard를 활용하여 9단어로)

➡ _____

6

우리가 더 많은 시간을 함께 보낼수록, 우리는 더 가까워진다. (become을 활용하여 10단어로)

➡ _____

7 다음 중 어법상 어색한 문장은?

① I need to get up earlier.
② Sujin is even more beautiful than her sister.
③ His hands are bigger than his brother.
④ My grandfather really wants to look better than now.
⑤ He arrived in Japan later than I had expected.

8 우리말 해석에 맞게 빈칸을 완성하세요.

- _____ we save, _____ we become.
= 더 많이 절약할수록, 우리는 더 부유해진다.

➡ _____, _____

9 다음 글의 밑줄 친 ⓐ~ⓔ를 바르게 고친 것은?

I went to the zoo with my daughter last week. The zoo was ⓐ the large. She was ⓑ much happy to see a lot of animals. She especially liked the elephants, bears, lions, and kangaroos. The elephants were ⓒ very bigger than the kangaroos. The bears were as ⓓ bigger as the lions. My daughter said that the kangaroo was ⓔ much cutest animal.

① ⓐ the → much
② ⓑ much → very
③ ⓒ very → the
④ ⓓ bigger as → bigger than
⑤ ⓔ much cutest → more cutest

10 주어진 단어들을 반드시 사용하여 다음 우리말을 바르게 영작하세요.

- 그녀의 이구아나는 나의 이구아나보다 빠르지 않다.
 (iguana, fast, mine, as)

➡ _____

11 다음 중 주어진 도표와 내용이 다른 것은?

	Lions	Elephants	Bears	Giraffes
Height (m)	1	3.1	1.8	5.3
Weight (kg)	200	1,600	1,000	1,400

① Lions are the shortest of the four animals.
② Giraffes are the tallest among the four animals.
③ Elephants are taller than lions and bears.
④ Lions are as heavy as giraffes.
⑤ Bears are heavier than lions.

12 다음 빈칸에 들어갈 알맞은 표현은?

Junho: Hey, Sunmi. I heard you caught a bad cold.
Sunmi: I did. That's why I couldn't come to school yesterday.
Junho: Are you okay?
Sunmi: Yeah, _____. Thanks for asking.
Junho: That's good to hear.

① I'm feeling much good yesterday than
② I'm feeling much good than yesterday
③ I'm feeling much better than yesterday
④ I'm feeling much better yesterday than
⑤ I'm feeling much well than yesterday

13 다음 밑줄 친 우리말에 맞는 영어 표현을 세 단어로 쓰세요.

Grandma: You are getting 점점 더 키가 커지는 every year.
Chris   : Right. I'm the tallest in my class.

➡ _____ _____ _____

14 괄호 안에 주어진 단어를 알맞게 배열하여 문장을 완성하세요.

> Minsu hit the ball _____.
> (he, as, could, as, hard)

15 다음 중 어법상 잘못된 문장 2개는?

① She is singing as loudly as she can.
② Can cats jump twice so high as dogs?
③ That dress is the most pretty one in this store.
④ The whale is the biggest mammal in the world.
⑤ This stamp is one of the most expensive stamps in the country.

16 다음 중 어법상 어색한 것을 모두 고르세요.

① Suji is as kind as Jiyeon.
② My brother speaks Japanese as better as you.
③ I ran as fastly as I could.
④ Today is as hot as yesterday.
⑤ Paul spoke as slowly as he could.

17 우리말과 같은 뜻이 되도록 빈칸에 알맞은 한 단어를 쓰세요.

> • 너는 가능한 한 집에 빨리 와야 한다.
> = You should get home as quickly as _____.

18 다음의 빈칸에 공통으로 들어갈 단어는?

> • 공부를 적게 할수록 너의 성적은 더 나빠진다.
> = The _____ you study, the worse your grades become.
> • Alex는 Jim보다 덜 먹는다.
> = Alex eats _____ than Jim.

① little ② less ③ few
④ fewer ⑤ more

19 다음 ⓐ~ⓔ 중 어법상 틀린 것을 있는 대로 고른 것은?

> ⓐ I can't run as faster as you.
> ⓑ Turtles live longer than wolves.
> ⓒ Chimpanzees are one of the smartest animal on earth.
> ⓓ The harder the wind blows, the colder we feel.
> ⓔ A cheetah is a very fastest of all land animals.

① ⓐ, ⓑ ② ⓑ, ⓒ ③ ⓐ, ⓒ, ⓔ
④ ⓐ, ⓓ, ⓔ ⑤ ⓑ, ⓒ, ⓓ, ⓔ

20 다음 표의 내용과 일치하지 <u>않는</u> 것은?

Name	Weight	Height
Michelle	48kg	165cm
Tina	53kg	170cm
Ronnie	60kg	155cm
Hannah	45kg	150cm

① Michelle is taller than Hannah.
② Ronnie is lighter than all the other women.
③ Ronnie is shorter than Tina.
④ Tina is the tallest of all the women.
⑤ No other woman is lighter than Hannah.

21 다음 밑줄 친 far를 문맥에 맞게 바르게 고치세요.

> Jason ran far than anyone else.

➡ _____

22 다음 중 어법상 틀린 문장의 개수로 알맞은 것은?

> ⓐ I'm not as smartest as my sister.
> ⓑ I studied for the exam as hard as I could.
> ⓒ If I were an English teacher, I would make my student speak English more fluently.
> ⓓ The well you eat, the healthier you become.
> ⓔ Vostok Station is the coldest area in the world.
> ⓕ There is nothing difficulter than math.
> ⓖ No other country is large than Russia.
> ⓗ I didn't forget to call my grandparents.

① 3개 ② 4개 ③ 5개
④ 6개 ⑤ 8개

23 다음 주어진 문장과 같은 뜻으로 쓰인 것은?

> Jiyeon is not as funny as Inho.

① Jiyeon is as funny as Inho.
② Inho is funnier than Jiyeon.
③ Jiyeon is very funny.
④ Jiyeon is the funniest.
⑤ Inho is not funnier than Jiyeon.

24 다음 그림에 대한 설명 중 옳지 않은 것은?

A B C D

① A is bigger than B.
② B is as big as D.
③ C is smaller than A.
④ C isn't as big as D.
⑤ D is the biggest of all.

25 두 문장이 같은 뜻이 되도록 할 때 빈칸에 들어갈 말이 순서대로 짝지어진 것은?

> • Which do you _____, apples or bananas?
> = Which do you like _____, apples or bananas?

① better – a lot   ② like – prefer
③ better – better   ④ prefer – better
⑤ prefer – prefer

26 다음 문장과 의미가 같도록 조건에 맞게 문장을 완성하세요.

> Others' problems were worse than mine.
>
> 조건
> • as ~ as 비교구문을 사용할 것.
> • 단어의 수는 제시된 빈칸의 수에 일치시킬 것.

➡ My problems were _____ _____ _____ _____ _____.

27 우리말 해석에 맞게 주어진 단어를 활용하여 빈칸을 완성하세요.

> Who's _____ (handsome) _____ in Italy?
> (누가 이탈리아에서 가장 잘생긴 가수인가?)

➡ _____

28 다음 밑줄 친 단어의 올바른 형태끼리 짝지어진 것은?

> • Reading is often <u>easy</u> than writing.
> • The question was the <u>hard</u> of all.

① easy – hard
② easy – harder
③ easier – harder
④ easier – hardest
⑤ easiest – hardest

29 두 문장이 같은 뜻이 되도록 할 때 빈칸에 들어갈 말로 알맞은 것은?

> • I like spaghetti more than any other food.
> = I like _____.

① only spaghetti
② spaghetti most
③ spaghetti more
④ spaghetti very much
⑤ spaghetti better

30 다음 대화에서 틀린 부분을 찾아 바르게 고치세요.

> A: Paris is one of the most famous city in the world.
> B: I know. I'm going there this summer.

_____ ➡ _____

31 다음 빈칸에 알맞은 말끼리 바르게 짝지어진 것은?

> • Money and fame are not as important as health.
> = Money and fame are _____ important _____ health.

① less – than
② more – than
③ so – as
④ either – or
⑤ the – of

32 다음 중 어법상 올바른 문장은?

① I ran as fast as possibly.
② The least we have, the happiest we become.
③ It was getting darkest and darkest.
④ This question is very easier than that one.
⑤ There is nothing greater than the mother's love for her child.

33 다음 표를 보고, 괄호 안의 조건에 맞게 두 사람씩 비교하는 긍정문을 완성하세요.

	Calvin	Jason	Brad
Age	25	24	25
Height	175cm	170cm	165cm
50-meter race record	8.1 sec	7.5 sec	6.9 sec

(1) Calvin is _____ Brad. (Age)
(2) Jason is _____ Calvin. (Height)
(3) Brad is _____ Jason. (50-meter race record)

34 다음 대화의 빈칸에 들어갈 말로 알맞은 것은?

> A: How long have you been living in this city?
> B: It's been 5 years. How about you?
> A: I've been living here for 3 and a half years.
> B: You haven't lived here _____ I have.

① as longer as   ② shorter than
③ as long as   ④ as the long as
⑤ long than

35 다음 빈칸에 들어갈 말이 순서대로 연결된 것은?

> • _____ of the fastest growing sports _____ China is baseball.
> • It's not easy to say who is _____ wisest man _____ all.

① Ones – of – most – in
② One – of – the – in
③ One – in – the – of
④ One – in – very – of
⑤ Ones – in – very – of

36 다음 문장의 밑줄 친 부분 중 어법상 어색한 것은?

> • 그것은 유럽에서 가장 높은 건물 중 하나이다.
> = ① It is ② one of ③ highest ④ buildings ⑤ in Europe.

37 다음 대화의 빈칸에 들어갈 알맞은 말은?

> A: We don't have enough time.
> B: Let's take a taxi. It must be _____ than a bus.

① the fastest   ② faster   ③ fast
④ fastest   ⑤ more fast

38 우리말과 같은 뜻이 되도록 주어진 단어를 바르게 배열하여 문장을 완성하세요.

> • 그녀는 예전보다 더 커 보인다.
> = She _____.
> (than, taller, before, looks)

39 다음 문장의 빈칸에 들어갈 수 없는 것은?

> This truck is _____ better than that one.

① very   ② much   ③ even
④ far   ⑤ a lot

40 괄호 안에 주어진 단어를 알맞게 배열하여 문장을 완성하세요.

> • The Rocky Mountains are _____.
> (than, beautiful, I, more, expected)

41 다음 대화의 빈칸에 들어갈 단어끼리 알맞게 짝지어진 것은?

> A: I like this shirt, but it is too _____ for me. Do you have it in a larger size?
> B: I'm very sorry, but it is the _____ one in our store.

① smallest – largest
② smaller – to large
③ small – to large
④ small – largest
⑤ to small – largest

42 다음 중 그 의미가 나머지 넷과 다른 하나는?

① Sue is the tallest girl in the class.
② Sue is taller than any other girl in the class.
③ No other girl in the class is taller than Sue.
④ No other girl in the class is as tall as Sue.
⑤ Sue is one of the tallest girls in the class.

43 다음 빈칸에 들어갈 단어끼리 알맞게 짝지어진 것은?

> • 많으면 많을수록 더욱 즐겁다.
> = The _____, the _____.

① much – merry
② many – merry
③ much – merrier
④ more – merrier
⑤ more – merry

44 다음 중 어법상 어색한 것은?

① The students were so calmer today.
② The woman is far taller than her brothers.
③ Bob is much heavier than Jenny.
④ This statue is a lot higher than that statue.
⑤ Heesun is even more beautiful than her friends.

45 밑줄 친 (A)~(E) 중 어법에 맞는 문장끼리 짝지어진 것은?

> (A) Insects are one of the most fascinating creature on Earth. More than 800,000 species are known to exist. Despite their somewhat frightening appearance, many insects are beneficial to humans. In fact, (B) some products that we use in our daily life is made by insects.
> First, (C) silk is a valuable product that has been around for over 5,000 years. It is used for all sorts of clothing. Silk is made from cocoons of silkworms. (D) Beeswax is other thing made by insects. It is a natural wax produced by honey bees. This wax is used to make lotions, ointments, and even candles. Lastly, red dyes are produced by insects called cochineals.
> People tend to dislike insects, but (E) they aren't as scary as they seem. Actually, we use products made from them every day without even knowing it.
>
> *cochineal: 코치닐 연지벌레 (멕시코와 같은 중미 지방에서 선인장에 기생하는 벌레로, 그 암컷을 말려 붉은빛 안료나 물감을 만듦.)

① (A), (C)   ② (B), (D)   ③ (B), (E)
④ (C), (D)   ⑤ (C), (E)

46 다음 문장의 틀린 부분을 모두 찾아 문장을 바르게 고쳐 쓰세요. (단, 최상급을 사용하세요.)

It is one of the most simplest way to succeed in your life.

➡ _____

_____

47 그림을 보고 괄호 안의 말을 이용하여 주어진 우리말을 원급 비교 구문의 문장으로 쓰세요.

• 내 여동생의 얼굴은 CD만큼 작다.

➡ _____

_____

(sister, face, small)

48 다음 대화의 (A), (B)에 알맞은 말을 골라 쓰세요.

Mira: What's wrong, Dan? You look (A) [paler/better] than usual.
Dan: I caught a cold, so I haven't been eating well.
Mira: I see. Are you okay now?
Dan: Yes, thank you. By the way, you look (B) [more and more beautiful/beautifuller and beautifuller]. What's your secret?
Mira: I've started eating more fruit and vegetables.

(A) _____ (B) _____

49 다음 표를 보고 괄호 안의 조건에 맞게 두 스마트폰을 비교하는 긍정문을 쓰세요. (단, 비교급 강조 표현을 함께 쓰세요.)

Smartphone	Price	Weight
Optimum 6	$360	200g
Galas	$900	130g

(1) Optimum 6 is _____

_____. (Price)

(2) Galas is _____

_____. (Weight)

50 다음 중 어법상 올바른 것을 모두 고르세요.

① Teresa weighs 60kg. Terry weighs 60kg. Terry is as heavier as Teresa.
② I got two presents from my friends. My sister got three presents. She got more presents than I did.
③ Samuel was happy when he ate two pieces of pizza. He was happier when he ate four pieces of pizza. More he ate, happier he became.
④ Susie runs 1km every day. Simon runs 2km every day. I run 3km every day. No one runs farther than me every day.
⑤ My brother is very diligent. My parents are diligent. I'm not so diligent than they are.

CHAPTER 14
관계사

성취도 자기 평가 활용법

구분	평가 기준
Excellent	문법 내용을 모두 이해하고, 문제를 모두 맞힘.
Very good	문법 내용은 충분히 이해했으나 실수로 1~2문제 틀림.
Good	문법 내용이 조금 어려워 3~4문제 틀림.
needs **R**eview	문법 내용 이해가 어렵고, 5문제 이상 틀림, 복습 필요.

PSS 1 관계대명사	페이지	학습날짜	성취도 자기평가 E V G R	학습체크
PSS 1-1 who	336	/		☐
PSS 1-2 which	338	/		☐
PSS 1-3 that	339	/		☐
PSS 1-4 what	341	/		☐
PSS 1-5 관계대명사의 생략	342	/		☐
PSS 1-6 계속적 용법	343	/		☐
PSS 2 관계부사	페이지	학습날짜	성취도 자기평가 E V G R	학습체크
PSS 2-1 관계부사의 종류	344	/		☐
PSS 2-2 관계부사의 주의해야 할 용법	345	/		☐
Chapter Review Test	347	/		☐

관계대명사

관계대명사는 앞에 오는 선행사를 수식하며, 「접속사+대명사」의 역할을 한다.

선행사 \ 격	주격	소유격	목적격
사람	who	whose	who(m)
사물, 동물	which	whose	which
사물, 동물, 사람	that	–	that
사물 (선행사 포함)	what	–	what

PSS 1-1 who

who는 선행사가 사람일 때 쓴다.

1. **주격 who** – 관계대명사가 이끄는 절 안에서 주어의 역할을 한다.

   She is **my friend**. + **She** helps me a lot.

   → She is **my friend who** helps me a lot.

   그녀는 나를 많이 도와주는 친구이다.

   cf. 주격 관계대명사가 쓰인 관계대명사절의 동사의 수는 관계대명사의 선행사에 따라 결정된다.
   I remember **the boys who were** kind to me.
   나는 나에게 친절했던 그 소년들을 기억한다.

2. **소유격 whose** – 관계대명사가 이끄는 절 안에서 관계대명사 바로 뒤에 나오는 명사를 꾸며주는 역할을 한다.

   I saw a man. **His** hair was red. 나는 한 남자를 보았다. 그의 머리는 빨간색이었다.
   → I saw a man **whose hair** was red. 나는 머리가 빨간색이었던 한 남자를 보았다.

3. **목적격 who(m)** – 관계대명사가 이끄는 절 안에서 목적어의 역할을 한다. 구어체에서는 whom 대신 who를 쓰기도 한다.

   They are the students. Mr. Smith taught **them**. 그들은 학생들이다. Smith 씨는 그들을 가르쳤다.
   → They are the students **who(m)** Mr. Smith taught. 그들은 Smith 씨가 가르쳤던 학생들이다.

PRACTICE 1

다음 문장의 빈칸에 who, whose, whom 중 알맞은 것을 쓰세요.

1 Do you know the people? They live near the school.
  ➡ Do you know the people _____ live near the school?

2 A boy is standing there. His name is Charlie.
  ➡ A boy _____ name is Charlie is standing there.

3 The woman left for India. I wanted to meet her.
  ➡ The woman _____ I wanted to meet left for India.

4 The man looks so sad. His dog is sick.
  ➡ The man _____ dog is sick looks so sad.

5 I met the old lady. She used to walk around the park.
  ➡ I met the old lady _____ used to walk around the park.

6 Do you remember the boy? I met him at church.
  ➡ Do you remember the boy _____ I met at church?

7 There are a few children. They are playing baseball.
  ➡ There are a few children _____ are playing baseball.

8 My grandparents live in Incheon. I visit them once a month.
  ➡ My grandparents _____ I visit once a month live in Incheon.

9 His sister is beautiful. Her nose is sharp.
  ➡ His sister _____ nose is sharp is beautiful.

10 The boy always tells lies. I don't like him.
  ➡ The boy _____ I don't like always tells lies.

PRACTICE 2

괄호 안에 주어진 단어 중 알맞은 것을 고르세요.

1 I had dinner with the boy who (is, are) my student.

2 The girl who (was, were) hurt in the accident is my neighbor.

3 My friend whose eyes (is, are) very big left Korea.

4 I want to talk to the people who (loves, love) cooking.

5 My sister whose dream (is, are) to be a doctor studies hard.

6 The man whose books (is, are) popular is a great writer.

7 I like the singer who (sings, sing) very well.

8 I met the girl whose brothers (is, are) my friends.

9 I have three brothers whose favorite sport (is, are) basketball.

10 The boys who (is, are) best friends are jogging together.

PSS 1-2 which

which는 선행사가 사물이나 동물일 때 쓴다.

1. 주격 which

    This is a book. **It** is about nature. 이것은 책이다. 그것은 자연에 관한 것이다.
    ➡ This is a book **which** is about nature. 이것은 자연에 관한 책이다.

2. 소유격 whose

    This is a book. **Its** cover is red. 이것은 책이다. 그것의 표지는 빨갛다.
    ➡ This is a book **whose** cover is red. 이것은 표지가 빨간 책이다.

3. 목적격 which

    This is a book. Minho bought **it**. 이것은 책이다. 민호가 그것을 샀다.
    ➡ This is a book **which** Minho bought. 이것은 민호가 산 책이다.

정답 p.76

PRACTICE 3

which나 whose를 이용하여 두 문장을 한 문장으로 연결하세요.

1 I took some pictures. Jason liked them.
   ➡ I took some pictures which Jason liked.

2 There is a tree. My family planted it.
   ➡ _____

3 I have a dog. Its name is Happy.
   ➡ _____

4 The dolls are my sister's. They are on the sofa.
   ➡ _____

5 This is the room. Its walls are blue.
   ➡ _____

6 Heejun is reading the book. You gave him the book.
➡ _____

7 The flowers are beautiful. He brought them.
➡ _____

8 He made the movie. It became famous.
➡ _____

9 This is the computer. Its keyboard is broken.
➡ _____

10 You should take the CD. It is on my desk.
➡ _____

정답 p.76

PRACTICE 4

괄호 안에 주어진 단어 중 알맞은 것을 고르세요.

1 The boxes which (is, are) on the table are mine.

2 We are looking for the parents whose children (is, are) here.

3 My mother loves movies which (have, has) happy endings.

4 Jim is wearing the shoes which (is, are) too big for him.

5 The police caught the thieves whose bag (was, were) full of money.

6 I'll buy a table whose legs (doesn't, don't) break easily.

7 She has a lot of work which (takes, take) many hours.

8 They have a small garden which (looks, look) beautiful.

9 Cathy entered the room whose windows (was, were) closed.

10 Give me the book whose cover (is, are) hard.

PSS 1-3 that

1. that은 who와 which의 주격, 목적격을 대신할 수 있다.

I talked to the people **that** live there. 나는 거기에 사는 사람들에게 말했다.
= I talked to the people **who** live there.

Jinsu has some photos **that** I took. 진수는 내가 찍었던 몇 장의 사진을 갖고 있다.
= Jinsu has some photos **which** I took.

2. 선행사에 다음이 포함되어 있을 경우에는 주로 that을 쓴다.

형용사의 최상급	Sora is **the most beautiful** woman **that** I've ever seen. 소라는 지금껏 내가 봤던 가장 아름다운 여자이다.
서수	I'm **the first** player **that** heard the news. 나는 그 소식을 들은 첫 번째 선수이다.
all, much, little, no	These are **all that** I can do for you. 이것들이 내가 널 위해 할 수 있는 전부이다. There isn't **much** information **that** you can get. 네가 얻을 수 있는 정보가 많지 않다.
something, anything	You can eat **anything that** is on the table. 너는 테이블 위에 있는 것은 무엇이든지 먹을 수 있다.

정답 p.76

PRACTICE 5

괄호 안에 주어진 관계대명사 중 알맞은 것을 모두 고르세요.

1 The man (whom, which, that) I talked to was very nice.

2 This is the most interesting book (who, whom, that) I've ever read.

3 There is little food (who, whose, that) I can eat.

4 He wanted to meet the people (who, whom, that) work for this company.

5 This is the first movie (whom, who, that) Mr. Smith has made.

6 Why did you take the book (who, which, that) belongs to Sora?

7 Mt. Halla is the highest mountain (whom, who, that) we've ever been to.

8 Mom didn't like those cats (whom, which, that) I brought home.

9 I saw something (who, whose, that) is very shocking.

10 Let me introduce my friend (who, which, that) is an excellent tennis player.

정답 p.77

PRACTICE 6

다음 문장의 밑줄 친 부분을 바르게 고쳐 쓰세요.

1 Is there anything <u>who</u> you'd like to say? _____

2 Look at the man <u>who he is</u> wearing jeans. _____

3 An employee which spoke English well helped me. _____
4 It is the most surprising news which I've heard. _____
5 These are the glasses whom I wear. _____
6 I called my friend whom likes watching movies. _____
7 This is my new friend whom I met her at the party. _____
8 I said something which made him angry. _____
9 We gave him the toys that they were made in China. _____
10 He was the first man which used the machine. _____
11 Jeff is the tallest boy whom I've ever met. _____
12 This is my sister whom birthday was a week ago. _____
13 I saw a boy whose jeans was too long for him. _____
14 I went to the mountain who was covered with snow. _____
15 She liked the doll which she got it from her mom. _____

PSS 1-4 what

what은 선행사를 자체에 포함하는 관계대명사이므로 선행사가 따로 있지 않고, 그 자체로서 the thing(s) which[that]의 뜻을 나타낸다.

That is **what** James said. 그것이 James가 말했던 것이다.
= That is **the thing which**[that] James said.

What I really want to be is a judge. 내가 정말로 되고 싶은 것은 판사이다.
= **The thing which**[that] I really want to be is a judge.

정답 p.77

PRACTICE 7

괄호 안에 주어진 관계대명사 중 알맞은 것을 고르세요.

1 I can't believe (what, which) Tom said.
2 I gave Nick a watch (what, which) he liked very much.
3 This is (what, which) we were looking for.
4 Today's meeting was (what, which) I've waited for.
5 Here is the fish (what, which) you should take care of.

6   The 9 o'clock news is (what, which) I usually watch.

7   Taking pictures is (what, which) he does in his free time.

8   That's not (what, which) I meant.

9   Mr. Hong suggested an idea (what, which) sounded wonderful.

10 Think about (what, which) you should do first.

11 (What, Which) she said made me laugh.

12 He packed the clothes (what, which) he would need for the winter.

PSS 1-5 관계대명사의 생략

1. 목적격 관계대명사 whom, which, that은 생략 가능하다.

   This is the boy **(whom)** I found at the hotel. 이 아이가 내가 호텔에서 찾은 소년이다.
   This is the building **(which)** I built. 이것이 내가 지은 건물이다.
   Everything **(that)** she told you is true. 그녀가 당신에게 이야기했던 모든 것은 사실이다.

2. 주격 관계대명사 뒤에 be동사가 있고 그 뒤에 분사가 올 때, 「관계대명사+be동사」는 생략할 수 있다.

   The girl **(who is)** standing over there is my sister. 저쪽에 서 있는 소녀가 나의 여동생이다.
   The car **(which is)** parked here is my father's. 여기에 주차된 차는 나의 아버지의 것이다.

PRACTICE 8

다음 문장에서 생략해도 되는 부분이 있으면 그 단어에 괄호 표시하세요.

1   Try this cake which I've just baked.

2   The girl whom I met yesterday was John's sister.

3   My cousin who loves camping will join our trip.

4   Look at those birds which are flying in the sky.

5   I'm worried about the exam which follows the holiday.

6   We spent all the money that Jenny saved for the vacation.

7   I recommend the pants that have pockets.

8   The lady paid for the window which was broken by her kid.

PRACTICE 9

다음 문장의 빈칸에 관계대명사를 활용한 알맞은 말을 쓰세요.

1 The man ___who[that]___ ___is___ planting trees now is my dad.
2 I love the songs _____ _____ played in the 1970s.
3 The shoes _____ _____ washed clean looked like new ones.
4 I called those people _____ _____ waiting there for tickets.
5 The water _____ _____ boiling on the stove is for tea.
6 We like to see the stars _____ _____ shining brightly.
7 The president _____ _____ known as a gentleman before disappointed us.
8 There are lots of people _____ _____ working in the office.
9 The house _____ _____ located on top of the hill is my uncle's.
10 You will find a man _____ _____ making cotton candies for children.

PSS 1-6 계속적 용법

선행사에 대해 부가적인 설명을 덧붙일 때는 관계대명사 앞에 ,(comma)를 쓰며 순차적으로 해석한다.

I made a new friend, **who** is from China.
나는 새 친구를 사귀었는데, 그녀는 중국 출신이다.
= I made a new friend, **and she** is from China.

She is wearing a watch, **which** was a gift from her mother.
그녀는 시계를 차고 있는데, 그것은 그녀의 어머니에게 받은 선물이었다.
= She is wearing a watch, **and it** was a gift from her mother.

cf. 계속적 용법으로 쓰인 관계대명사는 that으로 바꿔 쓸 수 없다.

PRACTICE 10

관계대명사의 계속적 용법을 이용하여 두 개의 문장을 한 개의 문장으로 바꾸어 쓰세요.

1 Kevin has an uncle. He teaches English at a middle school.
→ _____

2 She bought a blouse. It was on sale.
  ➡ _____

3 He was a great scientist. We all respected him.
  ➡ _____

4 Jenny has lost her watch. Her father bought it for her.
  ➡ _____

5 They climbed Mount Everest. It is the highest mountain in the world.
  ➡ _____

관계부사

PSS 2-1 관계부사의 종류

관계부사는 앞에 오는 선행사를 수식하는 절을 이끌어 접속사와 부사의 역할을 동시에 하며, 「전치사＋관계대명사」로 바꾸어 쓸 수 있다.

	선행사	관계부사	전치사＋관계대명사
장소	the place, the house, the town, the city	where	at/in/to which
시간	the time, the day, the month, the year	when	at/in/on which
이유	the reason	why	for which
방법	(the way)	how	in which

This is the city **where** I met Jim. 이곳은 내가 Jim을 만났던 도시이다.
= This is the city **in which** I met Jim.
April 15th is the day **when** I met Jim. 4월 15일은 내가 Jim을 만났던 날이다.
= April 15th is the day **on which** I met Jim.
That's the reason **why** I met Jim. 그것이 내가 Jim을 만났던 이유이다.
= That's the reason **for which** I met Jim.
That's **how** I met Jim. 그것이 내가 Jim을 만났던 방법이다.
= That's the way **in which** I met Jim.
 cf. the way와 how는 함께 쓸 수 없으므로 둘 중 하나를 생략해야 한다.
    That's **the way** I met Jim. (○)
    That's **the way how** I met Jim. (✕)

PRACTICE 11

다음 문장의 빈칸에 알맞은 관계부사를 쓰세요.

1. December 24th is the day. Hana was born then.
   ➡ December 24th is the day _____ Hana was born.

2. Do you know the reason? She left so early for the reason.
   ➡ Do you know the reason _____ she left so early?

3. Seoul is the city. I live there.
   ➡ Seoul is the city _____ I live.

4. 2022 is the year. My brother got his first job that year.
   ➡ 2022 is the year _____ my brother got his first job.

5. This is the way. We use chopsticks in the way.
   ➡ This is _____ we use chopsticks.

6. This is the place. They found the lost purse here.
   ➡ This is the place _____ they found the lost purse.

7. Nicole learned the way. Koreans make *gimchi* in the way.
   ➡ Nicole learned _____ Koreans make *gimchi*.

8. Kevin told me the reason. He didn't come for the reason.
   ➡ Kevin told me the reason _____ he didn't come.

9. He is looking for a nice hotel. He can stay there for a week.
   ➡ He is looking for a nice hotel _____ he can stay for a week.

10. He teaches the way. We wash our hands in the way to fight germs.
    ➡ He teaches _____ we wash our hands to fight germs.

PSS 2-2 관계부사의 주의해야 할 용법

선행사의 생략

주로 구어체에서 굳이 나타내지 않아도 모두가 알 수 있는 일반적인 명사가 관계부사의 선행사로 올 경우 생략할 수 있다.

I'll never forget **(the day) when** we first met.
난 우리가 처음 만난 날을 절대 잊지 않겠어.

This is **(the place) where** I was born.
이곳은 내가 태어난 곳이다.

That's **(the reason) why** we study English.
그것이 우리가 영어를 공부하는 이유이다.

관계부사의 생략	주로 구어체에서 선행사 다음에 오는 관계부사를 생략할 수 있으며, 선행사의 생략과 마찬가지로 일반적인 명사가 선행사로 올 때 생략한다. I remember **the day (when)** I graduated from high school. 나는 내가 고등학교를 졸업한 날을 기억한다. Can you tell me **the reason (why)** he is upset? 그가 언짢은 이유를 내게 말해줄 수 있니? ***cf.*** 관계부사 where은 place, somewhere, anywhere, everywhere, nowhere가 선행사로 올 때만 생략할 수 있으며 특정한 장소가 선행사로 올 경우에는 생략할 수 없다. The shopping mall is **the place (where)** we used to go. (where 생략) 그 쇼핑몰은 우리가 가던 곳이다. California is **the state where** he lives. (where 생략 X) 캘리포니아는 그가 살고 있는 주이다.

PRACTICE 12

정답 p.78

다음 문장들이 같은 뜻이 되도록 빈칸에 알맞은 단어를 쓰세요.

1 Tomorrow is the day when my friends will come.
= Tomorrow is ___the___ ___day___ my friends will come.
= Tomorrow is ___when___ my friends will come.

2 That is the place where I taught kids.
= That is _____ _____ I taught kids.
= That is _____ I taught kids.

3 I don't know the reason why she canceled the meeting.
= I don't know _____ she canceled the meeting.
= I don't know _____ _____ she canceled the meeting.

4 2002 was the year when people were excited about the World Cup.
= 2002 was _____ _____ people were excited about the World Cup.
= 2002 was _____ people were excited about the World Cup.

5 This is the way it happened.
= This is _____ it happened.

6 There should be somewhere where we can have a chat.
= There should be _____ we can have a chat.

Chapter Review Test

CHAPTER 14 관계사

1 다음 중 밑줄 친 단어를 생략할 수 있는 것을 모두 고르면?

① I ate all the cake that Lily made for her friend.
② I can't see that small print even with my glasses on.
③ I think that is the biggest turtle I've ever seen.
④ Jenny is the first female player that received an award.
⑤ My mom thinks that I've gained weight.

2 다음 중 어법상 자연스러운 문장은?

① The dog which has big ears are very cute.
② Can you return the book who you borrowed from me?
③ The man I met was Jimin's father.
④ I like the girl whom is wearing glasses.
⑤ Nobody knows who are they.

3 우리말 해석에 맞게 주어진 단어를 활용하여 빈칸을 완성하세요. (단, 필요시 어형을 변화시킬 것)

I can't understand _____ (say, you) .
(나는 네가 말한 것을 이해할 수 없다.)

➡ _____

4 그림을 보고, 이 사람의 직업을 나타내는 우리말과 뜻이 같도록 관계대명사를 이용하여 알맞은 말을 쓰세요.

• 교사는 학교에서 학생들을 가르치는 사람이다.
= A teacher is a person _____ _____ _____ at school.

5 다음 (1)~(4)의 이야기가 자연스럽도록 〈보기〉에서 알맞은 말을 골라 그 번호를 쓰세요.

보기
① who felt hungry after playing baseball
② which Sarah liked so much
③ who likes cakes and cookies
④ which made it possible to keep the cake cold

(1) Sarah is a girl _____.
(2) One day, her mother baked a strawberry cake _____.
(3) Her mother put the cake in the refrigerator _____.
(4) However, Sarah's youngest brother _____ ate up the cake.
Sarah's mother was surprised that there was no cake left in the refrigerator.

6 다음 밑줄 친 관계대명사 중 문장에서의 쓰임이 다른 하나는?

① I like the dress that Anna is wearing.
② This is the story which my father wrote.
③ This is the table that John made.
④ Here are some of the techniques which they use.
⑤ This is the girl that uses magic.

7 다음 두 문장을 한 문장으로 바르게 바꾼 것은?

> She wrote many fables. They taught me good lessons.

① They taught me good lessons she wrote many fables.
② She wrote many fables who taught me good lessons.
③ She wrote many fables which taught me good lessons.
④ She wrote many fables what taught me good lessons.
⑤ She wrote many fables taught me good lessons.

8 다음 빈칸에 들어갈 관계대명사로 알맞은 것은?

> I like story books _____ have many interesting stories.

① what   ② whose   ③ who
④ whom   ⑤ which

9 다음 중 어법상 어색한 것을 모두 고르세요.

① The girl who has a pony tail is my sister.
② People who exercise regularly are healthy.
③ Look at the police officer, that caught the thief.
④ The shoes which he is wearing are new.
⑤ The book which cover is green was written by him.

10 다음 ⓐ~ⓔ 중, 어법상 틀린 것을 있는 대로 고른 것은?

> ⓐ It's the house which they have lived for a long time.
> ⓑ I didn't know the reason why he left me.
> ⓒ This is the way she cuts the cost of living.
> ⓓ I'm the first man which came to the office today.
> ⓔ She likes the cats, that are living next door.

① ⓐ, ⓑ   ② ⓑ, ⓒ   ③ ⓐ, ⓑ, ⓒ
④ ⓐ, ⓓ, ⓔ   ⑤ ⓐ, ⓒ, ⓓ, ⓔ

11 다음 두 문장의 뜻이 같다고 할 때 빈칸에 알맞은 단어는?

> • They had two daughters, who became famous actresses.
> = They had two daughters, _____ they became famous actresses.

① but   ② or   ③ so
④ and   ⑤ for

12 우리말을 어법상 바르게 영작한 것은?

① 그녀는 내가 어울리고 싶은 학교에서 가장 인기 있는 학생이다.
→ She is the most popular student in school who I would like to hang out.

② 내가 무척 보고 싶어 했던 그 영화는 결말이 뻔하다.
→ The movie that I was eager to watch have an obvious ending.

③ 수지는 그녀의 부모님을 존경하는데, 그들은 매주 고아원으로 자원봉사 하러 가신다.
→ Susie looks up to her parents, who goes to an orphanage to do volunteer work every weekend.

④ 내 아들이 정말로 가고 싶어 하는 놀이공원은 보수 작업을 위해서 문을 닫았다.
→ The amusement park which my son really wants to go to is closed for repair work.

⑤ 그 출판업자가 원래 다음 달로 예정되었던 출시일을 앞당겼다.
→ The publisher moved up the release date which it was originally scheduled for next month.

13 다음 중 어법상 옳은 문장의 개수로 알맞은 것은?

ⓐ I often visit the elderly who lives alone.
ⓑ She painted a picture of peasants who were working.
ⓒ He played two songs that sounded similar.
ⓓ They liked watching the ballerinas who were moving.
ⓔ I know the boys who standing over there.

① 1개　② 2개　③ 3개
④ 4개　⑤ 5개

14 다음 빈칸에 들어갈 말로 알맞게 짝 지어진 것은?

- She painted a man _____ was sitting on the bench.
- Ted has an alarm clock _____ goes off at seven o'clock.

① who – that　② that – who
③ who – what　④ that – what
⑤ which – that

15 다음 중 밑줄 친 부분을 생략할 수 있는 문장은 모두 몇 개인가?

ⓐ Sara is the girl who Mr. Kim is shaking hands with.
ⓑ Mike is my friend that works in New York.
ⓒ He told me that he had something important to discuss.
ⓓ My dog likes any person who gives him a treat.
ⓔ London is one of the places that I've never been to.

① 1개　② 2개　③ 3개
④ 4개　⑤ 5개

16 다음 중 주어진 문장의 밑줄 친 what과 쓰임이 같은 것은?

Soccer is what I like to do.

① They showed you what to do.
② I don't know what to say.
③ What did you do last night?
④ What he said to me was unbelievable.
⑤ I thought about what kind of leader I was.

17 다음 주어진 두 문장을 한 문장으로 바르게 바꾸어 쓴 것은?

> She made spaghetti sauce with the tomatoes. She grew the tomatoes.

① She made spaghetti sauce she grew the tomatoes.
② She made spaghetti sauce with the tomatoes whom she grew.
③ She made spaghetti sauce with the tomatoes she grew.
④ She grew the tomatoes whose she made spaghetti sauce.
⑤ She grew the tomatoes that made spaghetti sauce with the tomatoes.

18 다음 우리말과 같은 뜻이 되도록 괄호 안에 주어진 단어들을 알맞게 배열하세요.

> • 소방대원은 불을 끄고 사람들을 구출해내는 사람이다.
> = _____
> _____ .
> (puts out, is, rescues, a person, a firefighter, people, who, and, fires)

19 다음 중 밑줄 친 부분의 쓰임이 다른 하나는?

① Everything that I told him was true.
② How did Andy know that I was smiling?
③ They show that these people are very rich.
④ The clean sheep knew that the other sheep was dirty.
⑤ I didn't know the fact that he came to Korea.

20 다음 중 두 문장을 올바르게 연결한 것은?

① He is my friend. He is from America.
  ➡ He is my friend who is from America.
② This is Kelly's sister. She is a singer.
  ➡ This is Kelly's sister whose is a singer.
③ This is the camera. I'm looking for it.
  ➡ This is the camera whose I'm looking for.
④ Jack has a girlfriend. Her job is a teacher.
  ➡ Jack has a girlfriend who job is a teacher.
⑤ Mr. Lee is a painter. He drew this picture.
  ➡ Mr. Lee is a painter whom drew this picture.

21 다음 빈칸에 들어갈 알맞은 단어는?

> A: What's the reason _____ we can't buy that car?
> B: Because it is very expensive and we don't have enough money.

① why ② what ③ when
④ how ⑤ which

22 다음 중 밑줄 친 who[Who]의 쓰임이 같은 것끼리 바르게 짝지어진 것은?

> ⓐ He is the teacher who taught us music.
> ⓑ She is the police officer who brought me here.
> ⓒ Do you know who that girl is?
> ⓓ Who borrowed your umbrella?
> ⓔ There are children who can't focus in class.
> ⓕ Tell me who you are, right now!

① ⓐ, ⓒ ② ⓐ, ⓕ ③ ⓑ, ⓔ
④ ⓒ, ⓔ ⑤ ⓔ, ⓕ

23 주어진 문장의 밑줄 친 that과 쓰임이 같은 것은?

> I like books that have beautiful pictures.

① Who is that girl?
② I think that she is Chinese.
③ That is my sister.
④ She is so kind that everyone likes her.
⑤ I know some girls that sing very well.

24 다음 중 밑줄 친 곳의 표현이 바른 것은?

① She likes peaches that are soft.
② He is the one who play the piano.
③ An elephant has a nose that act like a hand.
④ There is an old lady who tell stories to the kids.
⑤ Sam is looking for a shirt which have blue stripes.

25 다음 빈칸 (A)~(C)에 들어갈 말을 순서대로 배열한 것은?

> Yesterday, I saw a documentary ___(A)___ was about a man ___(B)___ tried to live without doing any harm to the environment. After watching it, I decided to start my own project ___(C)___ I named "Project Green." First, I decided to take a shower every other day, instead of every day.

	(A)	(B)	(C)
①	what	who	which
②	that	who	which
③	which	which	that
④	who	which	that
⑤	that	who	who

26 다음 두 문장을 소유격 관계대명사를 사용하여 한 문장으로 쓰세요.

> I saw the house. Its roof was covered with snow.

➡ _____

27 다음 주어진 문장의 밑줄 친 What과 쓰임이 다른 것은?

> What Samantha bought at the market was cheap-looking.

① This is what I want.
② Ron asked me what the problem was.
③ The girl only eats what she likes.
④ He accepted what she offered.
⑤ Thomas listened to what his teacher explained.

28 다음 중 밑줄 친 부분을 생략할 수 있는 것을 모두 고르세요.

① Tell me how you made a lot of money.
② He danced with the woman who wore a blue jacket.
③ The man who is baking an apple pie in the kitchen is my uncle.
④ I know the city that the first Olympic Games were held in.
⑤ He couldn't understand what his sister said.

29 다음 중 어법상 어색한 문장은?

① Jane is the first one that arrived here.
② What I need is some cold water.
③ He is the only person that helped me.
④ Mom bought me a skirt which color is red.
⑤ I met someone who works at the bank.

30 우리말 해석에 맞게 주어진 단어를 활용하여 빈칸을 완성하세요.

> We should respect _____ (live, others) _____.
> (우리는 다른 사람들이 살아가는 방식을 존중해야 한다.)

➡ _____

31 다음 글에서 어법상 틀린 곳을 한 군데 찾아 바르게 고치세요.

> Helen Keller was the first deaf blind person to earn a BA degree, that was born in Alabama on June 27, 1880. At the age of 19 months, an illness left her both deaf and blind. However, she was able to communicate with people and became an author, political activist, and lecturer.

_____ ➡ _____

32 다음 빈칸 (A)~(D)의 어디에도 들어갈 수 없는 말은?

> • Look at the dog ____(A)____ is walking down the street.
> • The Nile, ____(B)____ is the longest river in the world, is in Egypt.
> • Dr. Einstein was a scientist ____(C)____ was awarded the Nobel Prize for physics in 1921.
> • ____(D)____ he wanted was to play basketball after school.

① which   ② who   ③ that
④ how   ⑤ what

33 다음 각 우리말과 같은 뜻이 되도록 조건에 맞게 문장을 완성하세요.

> 조건
> • 반드시 관계대명사를 포함시킬 것.
> • that은 사용할 수 없음.
> • 주어진 칸 수에 맞게 단어를 쓸 것.

(1) 놀이터에서 놀고 있는 그 소년은 매우 잘생겨 보인다.
➡ The boy _____ _____ _____ in the playground looks very handsome.

(2) 이게 내가 어제 Harry한테서 빌린 그 만화책이야.
➡ This is the comic book _____ _____ _____ _____ Harry yesterday.

34 주어진 두 문장을 관계대명사를 사용하여 한 문장으로 연결하세요.

(1) I know a girl. She can speak Spanish very well.
  ➡ _____

(2) The book is easy to read. I bought it last night.
  ➡ _____

(3) Look at the house. Its roof is red.
  ➡ _____

35 다음 조건에 맞게 그림을 묘사하는 문장을 한 개 쓰세요.

조건
- There is ~ 구문을 사용할 것.
- A, B, C에서 각각 한 단어씩 골라 사용할 것.
- 관계대명사 who나 which를 반드시 포함할 것.
- 동사의 현재 진행형을 사용할 것.

A	cat	boy	girl
B	watch	draw	eat
C	TV	fish	a picture

➡ _____

36 다음 중 어법상 어색한 문장은?

① The lady who was sitting on the chair looked ill.
② This is the restaurant where I saw on TV.
③ A planet is a large round object which moves around a star.
④ A bat is an animal which lives in a cave.
⑤ I have a nephew who lives in Busan.

37 다음 밑줄 친 부분을 생략할 수 없는 것은?

① This is the essay which my father wrote.
② I like the glasses that my dad is wearing.
③ The man who is working in the garden is my uncle.
④ She loves the house that her grandfather built.
⑤ Some advertisers use tricks that are performed by magicians.

38 다음 문장의 빈칸에 공통으로 들어갈 단어로 알맞은 것은?

- Send me the money _____ you saved to buy a computer.
- She is the smartest girl _____ I have ever seen.
- Please tell him _____ I am Sam.

① that ② how ③ who
④ what ⑤ which

39 다음의 두 문장을 관계대명사를 이용하여 한 문장으로 쓰세요.

> These are the books. My girlfriend bought them for me.

➡ _____

_____

40 다음 보고서의 밑줄 친 우리말 (A)와 (B)를 괄호 안의 말을 이용하여 조건에 맞게 영어로 쓰세요.

Report on Green Project

| Name: Gina Soros |
| Date: July, 31st |
| Place: Knoxville Park |
| What I did: I cleaned Knoxville Park with my friends. A lot of children came there for a picnic. (A) <u>우리는 그들에게 공원에서 그들이 해서는 안 되는 것을 말했다.</u> For example, no dumping garbage, no walking on the grass. (B) <u>그들은 우리가 말한 것을 주의 깊게 들었다.</u> We thanked them for doing so. We finished cleaning the park at 5 in the afternoon. |
| How I felt: I was very happy to see the clean park. |

조건 | • 두 문장 모두 what을 사용할 것.

(A) _____

_____ (shouldn't do, in the park)

(B) _____

_____ (carefully)

41 다음 중 어법상 <u>어색한</u> 문장은?

① Mary was the only person that received the call.
② It's the most difficult problem what I've ever solved.
③ He bought the book whose title I can't remember.
④ In this cold weather, what I want is to stay inside the house.
⑤ There is someone at the door who wants to see you.

42 다음 문장의 빈칸에 알맞은 말을 쓰세요.

> • This is the city. She was born in the city.
> = This is the city _____ _____ she was born.

43 다음 (A)와 (B)에서 각각 한 문장씩을 택해 관계대명사로 연결하세요.

> (A) • I want to make a machine.
>   • Emily was my friend.
> (B) • She won first prize in the dancing contest.
>   • It can fly me to the moon.

(1) _____

_____

(2) _____

_____

CHAPTER 15
접속사

성취도 자기 평가 활용법

구분	평가 기준
Excellent	문법 내용을 모두 이해하고, 문제를 모두 맞힘.
Very good	문법 내용은 충분히 이해했으나 실수로 1~2문제 틀림.
Good	문법 내용이 조금 어려워 3~4문제 틀림.
needs **R**eview	문법 내용 이해가 어렵고, 5문제 이상 틀림, 복습 필요.

Problem Solving Skill	페이지	학습날짜	성취도 자기평가 E V G R	학습체크
PSS 1 and, but, or	356	/		☐
PSS 2 명령문+and/or	357	/		☐
PSS 3 상관접속사	358	/		☐
PSS 4 because, so	359	/		☐
PSS 5 if	361	/		☐
PSS 6 so that ~, so ~ that …	363	/		☐
PSS 7 명사절을 이끄는 that	364	/		☐
PSS 8 시간을 나타내는 접속사	366	/		☐
PSS 9 even though, although, though	367	/		☐
PSS 10 접속부사	368	/		☐
Chapter Review Test	370	/		☐

and, but, or

and	~와, 그리고, ~하고 나서	앞뒤의 내용이 대등하거나 비슷한 것을 연결한다. Linda **and** Paul went to the movies. Linda와 Paul은 영화를 보러 갔다. *cf.* 접속사의 앞뒤 절의 주어가 같을 때는 접속사 뒤의 주어를 생략할 수 있다. 　I went back home **and** (I) prepared dinner. 　나는 집으로 돌아가서 저녁 식사를 준비했다.
but	하지만, 그러나	앞뒤의 내용이 반대되는 것을 연결한다. I was very sick **but** (I) didn't go to the doctor. 나는 매우 아팠지만 의사에게 가지 않았다. *cf.* not A but B 'A가 아니라 B' 　My garden is **not** large **but** beautiful. 　나의 정원은 크지는 않지만 아름답다.
or	또는, 아니면	둘이나 둘 이상의 대상 중에서 선택을 할 때 쓴다. Have you been to New York **or** Chicago? 뉴욕이나 시카고에 가본 적이 있니? *cf.* 세 개 이상의 단어가 나열될 때는 마지막 단어 앞에 접속사를 쓴다. 　Have you been to New York, Chicago, **or** Los Angeles? 　뉴욕, 시카고 또는 로스앤젤레스에 가본 적이 있니?

정답 p.81

PRACTICE 1

괄호 안에 주어진 접속사 중 알맞은 것을 고르세요.

1　I met Jinsu (and, but, or) Minho on the street yesterday.

2　Where is he going, to gym (and, but, or) home?

3　You made the mistake. It is not I (and, but, or) you who are to blame.

4　Who's your brother, Tim, John, (and, but, or) Ryan?

5　They left Seoul (and, but, or) arrived in Daejeon 2 hours later.

6　Which do you like better, pizza (and, but, or) spaghetti?

7 Eric bought a bottle of milk (and, but, or) a piece of cake.

8 I like music (and, but, or) my brother doesn't.

9 The students entered the classroom (and, but, or) started to clean up.

10 Did you meet Mrs. Park (and, but, or) did you talk to her on the phone?

 명령문＋and/or

명령문＋and	~해라, 그러면	Wake up now, **and** you'll catch the bus. 지금 일어나라. 그러면 너는 그 버스를 탈 거야. = If you wake up now, you'll catch the bus. 만약 네가 지금 일어난다면, 너는 그 버스를 탈 거야.
명령문＋or	~해라, 그렇지 않으면	Wake up now, **or** you'll miss the bus. 지금 일어나라. 그렇지 않으면 너는 그 버스를 놓칠 거야. = If you don't wake up now, you'll miss the bus. 만약 네가 지금 일어나지 않는다면, 너는 그 버스를 놓칠 거야.

정답 p.81

PRACTICE 2

두 문장이 같은 뜻이 되도록 빈칸에 and나 or 중 알맞은 것을 쓰세요.

1 If you exercise regularly, you'll be healthy.
   = Exercise regularly, _____ you'll be healthy.

2 If you don't take the subway, you'll be late.
   = Take the subway, _____ you'll be late.

3 If you hurry up, you won't be late.
   = Hurry up, _____ you won't be late.

4 If you don't study hard, you can't pass the exam.
   = Study hard, _____ you can't pass the exam.

5 If you don't go there, she will be disappointed.
   = Go there, _____ she will be disappointed.

6 If you are kind to others, they'll be nice to you.
   = Be kind to others, _____ they'll be nice to you.

7 If you don't write it down, you'll forget it soon.

= Write it down, _____ you'll forget it soon.

8 If you are honest with her, she'll forgive you.

= Be honest with her, _____ she'll forgive you.

9 If you don't buy a new refrigerator, you will spend more money to fix it.

= Buy a new refrigerator, _____ you will spend more money to fix it.

10 If you get up earlier, you can have breakfast.

= Get up earlier, _____ you can have breakfast.

상관접속사

1. 「both A and B」 'A와 B 둘 다'

    Both Jim **and** Sue like sports. Jim과 Sue는 둘 다 운동을 좋아한다.

    cf. 「both A and B」는 항상 복수 동사를 쓴다.

2. 「not only A but also B」 'A뿐만 아니라 B도' = 「B as well as A」

    Jim is good at **not only** singing **but also** swimming. Jim은 노래뿐만 아니라 수영도 잘한다.
    = Jim is good at swimming **as well as** singing.

    cf. 「not only A but also B」와 「B as well as A」 뒤에 오는 동사는 B의 수에 일치시킨다.

3. 「either A or B」 'A와 B 중 어느 하나'

    Either Jim **or** Sue likes sports.
    Jim과 Sue 중 어느 한 명은 운동을 좋아한다.

    cf. 「either A or B」 뒤에 오는 동사는 동사에 더 가까이 있는 B의 수에 일치시킨다.
    Either she or I **have** to take this bag. 그녀와 나 중 어느 한 명은 이 가방을 가져가야 한다.

4. 「neither A nor B」 'A도 B도 ~ 아닌'

    Neither Jim **nor** Sue likes sports.
    Jim도 Sue도 운동을 좋아하지 않는다.

    cf. 「neither A nor B」 뒤에 오는 동사는 동사에 더 가까이 있는 B의 수에 일치시킨다.
    Neither she nor I **have** to take this bag. 그녀도 나도 이 가방을 가져가야 할 필요가 없다.

PRACTICE 3

다음 문장의 빈칸에 알맞은 접속사를 쓰세요.

1. Jina has gone to China. Minsu has gone to China, too.
   → _____ Jina _____ Minsu have gone to China.

2. Alice is going to major in journalism. Or she is going to major in law.
   → Alice is going to major in _____ journalism _____ law.

3. Paul doesn't play baseball. He doesn't play basketball, either.
   → Paul plays _____ baseball _____ basketball.

4. Henry speaks French. He speaks German, too.
   → Henry speaks _____ French _____ German.

5. The company gave him a car. It gave him a house, too.
   → The company gave him _____ a car _____ a house.

6. She not only wrote a poem but also a novel.
   → She wrote a novel _____ a poem.

7. She must be at home now. Or she must be at the office now.
   → She must be _____ at home _____ at the office now.

8. Making mistakes is necessary. And it is also important.
   → Making mistakes is _____ necessary _____ important.

9. We didn't go into the room. We didn't leave the building, either.
   → We _____ went into the room _____ left the building.

10. He can swim. He can skate, too.
    → He can _____ swim _____ skate.

PSS 4 — because, so

Problem Solving Skill

because	~때문에	because가 이끄는 절은 원인을 나타낸다. Linda often goes to concerts **because** she likes music. Linda는 음악을 좋아하기 때문에 종종 콘서트에 간다. **Because** the food is delicious, the restaurant is popular. 음식이 맛있기 때문에 그 음식점은 인기가 있다.

because	~때문에	**cf.** because of 뒤에는 명사(구)가 온다. The restaurant is popular **because of** the food. 그 음식점은 음식 때문에 인기가 있다.
so	그래서	**so가 이끄는 절은 결과를 나타낸다.** Linda likes music, **so** she often goes to concerts. Linda는 음악을 좋아해서 종종 콘서트에 간다. The food is delicious, **so** the restaurant is popular. 음식이 맛있어서 그 음식점은 인기가 있다.

cf. as나 since도 이유를 나타내는 접속사로 쓰인다.
He couldn't arrive on time **as** he missed the bus.
그는 버스를 놓쳤기 때문에 제시간에 도착할 수 없었다.
Since it is fine tomorrow, we will go on a picnic. 내일 날씨가 좋기 때문에 우리는 소풍을 갈 것이다.

PRACTICE 4

〈보기〉와 같이 because나 so를 이용하여 두 문장을 한 문장으로 연결하세요.

보 기	I was very happy. I got a lot of birthday presents. ➡ I was very happy because I got a lot of birthday presents. ➡ I got a lot of birthday presents, so I was very happy.

1 We are excited. We are going to interview a popular singer.
  ➡ _____
  ➡ _____

2 Martin couldn't call you. He was very busy this week.
  ➡ _____
  ➡ _____

3 Jiyoon has a lot of friends. She is very nice.
  ➡ _____
  ➡ _____

4 I can't study tonight. I'm really sick.
  ➡ _____
  ➡ _____

5 Julie cut her long hair short. She wanted to refresh her look.
  ➡ _____
  ➡ _____

PRACTICE 5

다음 문장의 빈칸에 because나 because of 중 알맞은 것을 쓰세요.

1 I was very tired today _____ I didn't get enough sleep last night.
2 The traffic was terrible _____ the heavy snow.
3 I like John _____ his kindness.
4 Minho had a big lunch _____ he was very hungry.
5 Sena wants to be a teacher _____ she loves children.
6 They bought these flowers _____ the color.

PSS 5 if

if	~ 한다면	**If** you read the book, you can do your homework. 네가 그 책을 읽는다면, 너는 숙제를 할 수 있다. **If** you do **not** read the book, you can't do your homework. 네가 그 책을 읽지 않는다면, 너는 숙제를 할 수 없다. = **Unless** you read the book, you can't do your homework. *cf.* 「if ~ not」은 unless로 바꾸어 쓸 수 있다.
if ~ (or not)	~ 인지 (아닌지)	I don't know **if** she works there **(or not)**. 나는 그녀가 거기에서 일하는지 (아닌지) 알지 못한다. = I don't know **whether** she works there **(or not)**. *cf.* 「if ~ (or not)」는 「whether ~ (or not)」으로 바꾸어 쓸 수 있다.

PRACTICE 6

주어진 문장과 의미가 같도록 unless를 이용하여 다시 쓰세요.

1 I'll do the laundry if it doesn't rain.
   = _____

2 Let's watch a movie together if you aren't busy.
   = _____

3 I can help you if it doesn't take too long.
= ___

4 He will be in trouble if the train doesn't arrive on time.
= ___

5 She can finish the work if she doesn't go home early.
= ___

6 They will forgive you if you don't lie to them.
= ___

7 You'll miss the last bus if you don't hurry.
= ___

8 I'll buy this shirt if I don't change my mind.
= ___

9 We can go swimming if the pool isn't closed.
= ___

10 You can just walk if it's not too far from here.
= ___

PRACTICE 7

정답 p.82

〈보기〉와 같이 빈칸에 알맞은 말을 쓰세요.

> 보 기 Is she married?
> ➡ Do you know **if** she is married (or not)?
> ➡ Do you know **whether** she is married (or not)?

1 Is the news true?
 ➡ Do you know ___ ?
 ➡ Do you know ___ ?

2 Can I go home now?
 ➡ Do you know ___ ?
 ➡ Do you know ___ ?

3 Will he come soon?
 ➡ Do you know ___ ?
 ➡ Do you know ___ ?

4 Is that girl Chinese?
  ➡ Do you know _____?
  ➡ Do you know _____?

5 Does she like Bob?
  ➡ Do you know _____?
  ➡ Do you know _____?

PSS 6 so that ~, so ~ that …

so that ~	~하기 위해서, ~할 수 있도록	목적을 나타낼 때 쓴다. I studied hard **so that** I could enter the university. 나는 그 대학교에 들어가기 위해서 열심히 공부했다. = I studied hard **in order to** enter the university. = I studied hard **so as to** enter the university.
so+형용사/부사 +that …	너무 ~해서 …한	결과를 나타낼 때 쓴다. The book was **so** boring **that** I couldn't finish it. 그 책은 아주 지루해서 나는 그것을 다 읽을 수가 없었다. = The book was **too** boring for me **to** finish.

정답 p.82

PRACTICE 8

〈보기〉와 같이 주어진 문장과 의미가 같도록 빈칸에 알맞은 문장을 쓰세요. (단, 밑줄 친 부분에 절이 포함되어 있으면 구로, 구가 포함되어 있으면 절로 바꾸어 쓸 것)

> 보기 Jiyoung saved her money in order to travel to Europe.
>   ➡ Jiyoung saved her money so that she could travel to Europe.

1 I hurried in the morning so as to catch the train.
  ➡ _____

2 We were too tired to go to the party.
  ➡ _____

3 They practiced hard in order to win the game.
➡ _____

4 The coffee was so hot that she couldn't drink it.
➡ _____

5 I was too busy to answer the phone.
➡ _____

6 I drink a cup of coffee every morning so that I can stay awake.
➡ _____

7 The table was too heavy for me to move.
➡ _____

8 The questions are so difficult that I can't answer them.
➡ _____

9 Animals live in a pack so as to reduce the danger of attack.
➡ _____

10 Mike took a taxi so that he could arrive there in time.
➡ _____

명사절을 이끄는 that

역할	의미	설명
주어	~라는 것은	that절이 주어 역할을 할 때는 주로 문장의 맨 앞에 가주어 it을 쓰고 진주어인 that절은 뒤로 보낸다. **That** she has a twin sister is interesting. 그녀에게 쌍둥이 여동생이 있다는 것은 흥미롭다. = **It**'s interesting **that** she has a twin sister. 　가주어　　　　　　　진주어
목적어	~라는 것을	목적어 역할을 하는 명사절을 이끄는 that은 생략할 수 있다. Some people think **(that)** I'm very polite. 어떤 사람들은 내가 매우 예의바르다고 생각한다.
보어	~라는 것인	The problem is **that** you didn't give it back to me. 문제는 네가 내게 그것을 돌려주지 않았다는 것이다.

PRACTICE 9

〈보기〉와 같이 주어진 문장을 바꾸어 쓰세요.

> 보 기
> I can't see Jenny for a while. It is sad.
> ➡ It is sad that I can't see Jenny for a while.

1 He lied to me. It is disappointing.
➡ _____

2 We are going to Jejudo. It is exciting.
➡ _____

3 They didn't come. It is strange.
➡ _____

4 The story had an unhappy ending. It is a pity.
➡ _____

5 Giho plays the piano well. It is true.
➡ _____

> 보 기
> You are leaving for Canada. (I heard)
> ➡ I heard that you are leaving for Canada.

6 Yumi is Sujin's sister. (I know)
➡ _____

7 She was going to cry. (I thought)
➡ _____

8 Her son is diligent. (I believe)
➡ _____

9 You were having dinner at that restaurant. (I thought)
➡ _____

10 You gave Mike a lot of books. (I knew)
➡ _____

> 보 기
> Sue lost the key. That is the problem.
> ➡ The problem is that Sue lost the key.

11 She doesn't like her new job. That is the fact.
➡ _____

CHAPTER 15 _ 접속사

12 We can't wait any longer. That is the point.
  ➡ _____

13 Minho broke the window. That is the truth.
  ➡ _____

14 Tom and Kate got married. That was the big news.
  ➡ _____

15 He didn't know how to drive. That was the problem.
  ➡ _____

시간을 나타내는 접속사

when	~할 때	**When** I was a child, my family lived in Busan. 내가 어린아이였을 때, 나의 가족은 부산에서 살았다.
as	~하고 있을 때, ~하면서	Ann sometimes listens to music **as** she works. Ann은 일을 하면서 때때로 음악을 듣는다. *cf.* as는 '~대로', '~함에 따라' 또는 '~때문에'라는 뜻의 접속사로도 쓰인다. She did **as** I did. 그녀는 내가 하는 대로 했다. **As** Jack is honest, everybody trusts him. Jack은 정직하기 때문에, 모든 사람이 그를 신뢰한다.
before	~하기 전에	I take off my shoes **before** I enter a room. 나는 방에 들어가기 전에 신발을 벗는다.
after	~한 후에	Let's go for a walk **after** you finish your dinner. 네가 저녁을 다 먹은 후에 산책 가자.
until	~할 때까지	My sister didn't go to bed **until** I got home. 나의 누나는 내가 집에 도착할 때까지 잠자리에 들지 않았다.
while	~하는 동안	**While** I was waiting for the bus, I read a book. 나는 버스를 기다리는 동안 책을 읽었다.
as soon as	~하자마자	He got a job **as soon as** he finished school. 그는 학교를 마치자마자 취업을 했다.

cf. 시간을 나타내는 접속사가 쓰인 부사절에서는 현재시제가 미래시제를 대신한다.
  I'll leave for Busan **as soon as** I **finish** the project.
  나는 그 프로젝트를 끝내자마자 부산으로 떠날 것이다.

PRACTICE 10

괄호 안에 주어진 접속사 중 알맞은 것을 고르세요.

1 Did Cathy go out (as soon as, while) I was washing the dishes?
2 Susan had dinner (after, until) she came home from work.
3 What do you usually do (before, when) you have free time?
4 The food should be ready (before, after) the customers arrive.
5 He met his friend (as, until) he walked down the street.
6 She read a storybook for her child (while, until) he fell asleep.
7 He brushes his teeth (as soon as, until) he gets up.
8 Robert entered the room (while, after) he opened the door.
9 Somebody called me (before, while) I was taking a shower.
10 I'll keep trying (until, as) my dreams come true.

PSS 9 even though, although, though

even though although though	비록 ~일지라도, ~에도 불구하고	It was raining, **but** I went shopping. 비가 내리고 있었지만, 나는 쇼핑하러 갔다. ➡ **Even though** it was raining, I went shopping. ➡ **Although** it was raining, I went shopping. ➡ **Though** it was raining, I went shopping. 비가 내리고 있었음에도 불구하고, 나는 쇼핑하러 갔다.

cf. in spite of와 despite는 '비록 ~일지라도, ~에도 불구하고'라는 의미이지만 전치사이므로, 그 뒤에 절이 아니라 명사 상당어구가 옴에 유의한다.
In spite of the weather, we went on a picnic. 날씨에도 불구하고, 우리는 소풍을 갔다.
Despite her great success, she wasn't satisfied. 그녀의 위대한 성공에도 불구하고, 그녀는 만족하지 않았다.

PRACTICE 11

다음 문장을 even though, although, though로 시작하는 문장으로 바꾸어 쓰세요.

1 My room is very small, but I like it.
   ➡ _____
   ➡ _____
   ➡ _____

2 Betty didn't want to read the book, but she bought it.
→ _____
→ _____
→ _____

3 This computer is very old, but it still works all right.
→ _____
→ _____
→ _____

4 English is difficult, but I like learning it.
→ _____
→ _____
→ _____

5 Andy doesn't eat regularly, but he is quite healthy.
→ _____
→ _____
→ _____

PSS 10 접속부사
Problem Solving Skill

for example	예를 들면	Mina does a lot of things for her family. **For example**, she helps her mom cook. 미나는 그녀의 가족을 위해 많은 것을 한다. 예를 들어, 그녀는 그녀의 엄마가 요리하는 것을 돕는다.
however	그러나	Everyone agreed with Mark. **However**, I had a different idea. 모든 사람들이 Mark의 의견에 찬성했다. 그러나 나는 다른 생각을 가지고 있었다.
therefore	그러므로	He doesn't have enough money. **Therefore**, he cannot afford to buy the new car. 그는 충분한 돈을 갖고 있지 않다. 그러므로 그는 그 새 차를 살 만한 여유가 없다.

in addition, besides	게다가	I like the restaurant. The food is very delicious. **In addition[Besides]**, the service is very good. 나는 그 식당을 좋아한다. 음식이 매우 맛있다. 게다가 서비스도 매우 좋다. ***cf.*** in addition과 in addition to의 쓰임을 헷갈리기 쉬운데, in addition to 다음에는 명사 상당어구가 오며 '~일 뿐 아니라, ~에 더하여'로 해석된다. I can speak Spanish **in addition to** English. 나는 영어뿐만 아니라 스페인어를 말할 수 있다. besides는 접속부사 말고도 전치사로도 쓰이는데 그때는 '~외에'라는 뜻을 갖는다. What other sports do you like **besides** soccer? 너는 축구 외에 무슨 다른 스포츠를 좋아하니?
finally	결국	Sena was interested in law. **Finally**, she became a lawyer. 세나는 법에 관심이 많았다. 결국 그녀는 변호사가 되었다.

정답 p.83

PRACTICE 12

〈보기〉에서 알맞은 말을 골라 빈칸에 쓰세요.

보 기	for example however therefore in addition finally

1 Our team has prepared very hard for this project. We have worked until late at night for two weeks. _____, we have finished it successfully.

2 Junsu's parents didn't want him to be an actor. _____, he became a famous actor.

3 We can send an email through the Internet. _____, we can even talk to each other through it.

4 You can protect the environment in your daily life. _____, you can take a bicycle instead of a car.

5 Rachel was absent yesterday. _____, she didn't hear about the festival.

6 There are several big holidays in Korea. _____, Chuseok and New Year's Day are two big holidays.

7 I was caught in a traffic jam. _____, I could get to work on time.

8 All of the workers will have a vacation for the next two weeks. _____, the office will be empty.

9 I can't go out with you because I have to clean the house. _____, I have to do the laundry.

10 I sent Ms. Lee an e-mail hours ago and I waited for her answer. _____, I got a short reply now.

Chapter Review Test

정답 p.83
CHAPTER 15 접속사

1 다음 중 그 의미가 자연스러운 문장은?

① Take the subway, and you'll get there on time.
② Work hard, and you'll not succeed.
③ Love your friends, or you'll be loved.
④ Start now, or you will catch the bus.
⑤ Don't practice, and you will win the contest.

2 다음 중 두 문장의 의미가 같지 <u>않은</u> 것을 모두 고르세요.

① He didn't go out because of the bad weather.
  = He didn't go out because the weather was bad.
② He runs so fast that I can't catch him.
  = He runs fast in order not to catch him.
③ Get up right now, or you'll be late for work.
  = If you get up right now, you'll be late for work.
④ The meal was not only delicious but also nutritious.
  = The meal was nutritious as well as delicious.
⑤ If you aren't sure, don't use them.
  = Unless you are sure, don't use them.

3 주어진 우리말과 같은 뜻이 되도록 빈칸에 알맞은 표현을 쓰세요.

> 많은 책을 읽어라, 그러면 너는 더 현명해질 것이다.

➡ _____ _____ _____, _____ _____ _____ be wiser.

4 다음 빈칸에 들어갈 말로 알맞은 것을 <u>모두</u> 고르세요.

> He was disappointed _____ he didn't get any Christmas cards.

① because   ② because of   ③ so
④ but   ⑤ as

5 우리말과 같은 뜻이 되도록 주어진 단어를 포함하여 8단어로 영작하세요.

> 지금 출발해라, 그렇지 않으면 너는 회사에 늦을 것이다.

➡ _____
  _____ (leave)

6 밑줄 친 부분을 생략할 수 <u>없는</u> 것은?

① Yuna told me <u>that</u> she would leave for Russia soon.
② Do you know <u>that</u> pretty girl carrying a red bag?
③ He got the concert ticket <u>that</u> he wanted so badly.
④ We all know <u>that</u> Jina is in love with Bill.
⑤ She said <u>that</u> she needed some time to think alone.

7 주어진 표현 중 내용과 가장 어울리는 것을 골라 〈보기〉처럼 because를 사용해 문장을 완성하세요. (필요할 경우 동사의 시제를 바꾸세요.)

보 기
People think that I'm satisfied because I don't complain.

• be too cold	• have a new car
• tell me to do that	• live in London

➡ We didn't stay outside long _____ .

8 〈보기〉에서 문장의 밑줄 친 부분을 바르게 고친 것을 <u>모두</u> 고르면?

보 기
ⓐ Ronald <u>not</u> listens to K-pop but also enjoys Korean dramas.
 ➡ not → only
ⓑ Neither Jackson <u>or</u> Eric is good at driving.
 ➡ or → nor
ⓒ Seulgi as well as I <u>work</u> in the sales department.
 ➡ work → works
ⓓ Not only my sister but also my parents <u>likes</u> the *Harry Potter* series.
 ➡ likes → like
ⓔ Jina's cousins as well as Jina <u>are</u> planning to travel Paris.
 ➡ are → is

① ⓐ, ⓑ　　② ⓑ, ⓒ　　③ ⓐ, ⓒ, ⓔ
④ ⓑ, ⓒ, ⓓ　　⑤ ⓑ, ⓓ, ⓔ

9 다음 우리말과 같은 뜻이 되도록 빈칸에 들어갈 알맞은 한 단어를 쓰세요.

• 비록 그가 시각장애인이긴 했지만, 그는 그의 꿈을 절대 포기하지 않았다.
= _____ he was blind, he never gave up his dream.

10 다음 빈칸에 들어갈 단어로 가장 적절한 것은?

_____ he was riding the roller coaster, we took some pictures.

① And　　② But　　③ While
④ So　　⑤ Finally

11 다음 중 밑줄 친 <u>that</u>의 쓰임이 <u>다른</u> 하나는?

① Sumi gave him the book <u>that</u> he wanted to borrow.
② The problem was <u>that</u> the library was noisy.
③ Are you sure <u>that</u> he wants to go there?
④ We know <u>that</u> fast food is not good for us.
⑤ She feels <u>that</u> she is very lucky.

12 다음의 빈칸에 들어갈 알맞은 말은?

_____ you have an open mind, you'll make a lot of friends.

① That　　② Though　　③ If
④ But　　⑤ Because of

13 다음 중 밑줄 친 If[if]의 뜻이 나머지 넷과 다른 것은?

① Give her this flower if you see her.
② He will tell you the truth if you ask him.
③ I wonder if I should wear a coat or not.
④ If you leave your name, we'll call you as soon as possible.
⑤ If you sit down for a few moments, I'll tell him you're here.

14 다음 빈칸에 알맞은 단어가 바르게 연결된 것은?

- This restaurant is popular _____ the food is very cheap and delicious.
- _____ you go to bed early in the evening, it'll be easy to get up in the morning.

① because – Although ② so – If
③ but – If   ④ because – If
⑤ so – Because

15 주어진 문장과 같은 뜻이 되도록 문장을 바꾸어 쓰세요. (단, as well as 구문을 활용할 것.)

A good sleep is important for not only adults but also kids.
= _____
_____

16 우리말과 같은 뜻이 되도록 빈칸에 알맞은 단어를 쓰세요.

- 그녀의 가족은 런던과 뉴욕 두 곳 모두에서 살았습니다.
= Her family has lived in _____ London _____ New York.

17 다음 빈칸에 들어갈 가장 알맞은 단어는?

- My father read the newspaper. And then he had breakfast.
= _____ my father read the newspaper, he had breakfast.

① As   ② When   ③ Before
④ Because   ⑤ After

18 다음 글에서 밑줄 친 ⓐ와 ⓑ에 공통으로 들어갈 알맞은 말을 고르세요.

M: Good morning. Thank you for calling International Hotel. This is John. How may I help you?
W: Hi, I'd like to reserve a suite for December 24th.
M: Oh, Christmas Eve! Let me see. That day is so popular __ⓐ__ the suites are fully booked.
W: It's my mistake __ⓑ__ I didn't make a reservation in advance. Are there other types of rooms available on that day?
M: There is only one twin room left, and it is $300 per night.
W: I have no choice. I'll reserve that room.

① which   ② when   ③ that
④ since   ⑤ because

19 다음 두 문장이 같은 뜻이 되도록 빈칸에 알맞은 단어를 쓰세요.

- At the age of 7, he learned to ride a bike.
= _____ he was 7, he learned to ride a bike.

20 다음 빈칸에 알맞은 말끼리 바르게 짝지어진 것은?

- Everyone likes her _____ she is kind.
= Everyone likes her _____ her kindness.

① because   – because
② because   – because of
③ because of   – because of
④ because of   – because
⑤ as   – because

21 다음 글의 빈칸에 들어갈 말로 알맞은 것은?

Sumi, Junho and I were talking about the TOEIC. Sumi and Junho said it was very easy compared to the last test. _____, I couldn't agree with them. It was very difficult for me.

① And   ② However   ③ Or
④ For example ⑤ Because

22 다음 문장의 빈칸에 들어갈 알맞은 단어는?

_____ most of his friends like western food, Jack likes Korean food better than any other food.

① So   ② Although   ③ Because
④ Since   ⑤ But

23 〈보기〉의 우리말에 맞도록 괄호 안의 표현에 한 단어를 추가하여 (가)에 들어갈 영어 문장을 쓰세요.

보기

셋째 돼지의 집은 너무 튼튼해서 내가 그것을 부술 수 없어.
(destroy, sturdy, the third pig's house, can't, is, it, I, that)

(가) _____
_____

24 다음 밑줄 친 When[when]의 쓰임이 나머지 넷과 다른 하나는?

① When I was young, I lived in Mexico.
② When I saw my daughter, she smiled at me.
③ Bring your lunch when we go on a picnic.
④ He asked me when I could return the book.
⑤ Call me when you are free.

25 다음 빈칸에 들어갈 가장 알맞은 단어는?

I want to have many chances to watch new movies, _____ I'm going to join the movie club.

① though   ② while   ③ so
④ but   ⑤ however

26 다음 문장에서 that이 들어가야 할 곳은?

An interesting ① fact ② about eating with hands ③ is ④ they use only the right hand ⑤ when they eat.

27 다음 문장의 밑줄 친 As와 같은 의미로 쓰인 것은?

As I was passing by Bill's house, I saw his sister.

① They were used as money.
② Jenny is as tall as Alex.
③ She got prettier as she grew older.
④ As I was talking with Minsu, someone called.
⑤ As he missed the train, he couldn't be there on time.

28 다음 빈칸에 들어갈 말로 알맞은 것은?

I studied very hard _____ I could pass the bar exam.

① but   ② while   ③ besides
④ so that   ⑤ instead of

29 다음 빈칸에 들어갈 말로 알맞은 것은?

Mr. Kim is a very good person. He likes to help people. _____, when he sees the elderly carrying heavy bags, he goes to them and asks if they need any help.

① However   ② Finally
③ If   ④ Even though
⑤ For example

30 다음 중 빈칸 ⓐ와 같은 단어가 들어갈 문장은?

I couldn't go to the concert __ⓐ__ I got a bad cold.

① I am too tired _____ do the laundry.
② I can go to the party, _____ I'm very happy.
③ _____ I was young, I used to listen to the radio.
④ I had a stomachache _____ I ate a lot yesterday.
⑤ Get up early, _____ you'll be late for the train.

31 주어진 문장의 밑줄 친 when의 쓰임과 같은 것은?

> Make sure to close the window when it rains.

① I don't know when the show begins.
② I remember the day when we became best friends.
③ When to leave is very important.
④ When she came back home, she looked tired.
⑤ Can you tell me when we should meet?

32 다음 글의 (A)~(C)에 들어갈 말로 적절한 것은?

> Barry didn't feel well when he got up this morning, ___(A)___ he went to work anyway. He had to attend an important meeting in the morning. Luckily, the meeting was cancelled and he could relax a little. ___(B)___, he still couldn't concentrate on his work. ___(C)___, his boss got angry at him because of some errors in the report written by him.

	(A)	(B)	(C)
①	or	However	In addition
②	but	However	In addition
③	or	However	Besides
④	since	As a result	But
⑤	but	As a result	Therefore

33 다음 밑줄 친 부분과 바꾸어 쓸 수 있는 것은?

> Mark didn't give up and kept running for two hours. In the end, he won second place in the marathon.

① At most
② At least
③ Finally
④ However
⑤ Sometimes

34 다음 중 빈칸에 들어가지 않는 단어는?

> a. _____ I was tired, I went to bed early last night.
> b. Eat breakfast, _____ you can't focus on your study.
> c. Preheat the oven _____ you put the potatoes in it.
> d. I don't know _____ I should go there or not.

① if[If]
② or[Or]
③ but[But]
④ because[Because]
⑤ before[Before]

35 우리말 해석에 맞게 주어진 단어를 활용하여 빈칸을 완성하세요.

> The problem is _____ (throw away, tend, the trash, that) _____ on the street.
> (문제는 사람들이 거리에 쓰레기를 버리는 경향이 있다는 것이다.)

➡ _____

36 다음 문장의 빈칸에 들어갈 단어로 알맞은 것은?

> Robert is very healthy and has a very good memory, _____ his old age.

① although   ② because of   ③ despite
④ after   ⑤ so

37 다음 빈칸에 들어갈 말로 알맞은 것은?

> After I _____ my report, I'll go out to play soccer.

① finished   ② will finish
③ finishes   ④ had finished
⑤ finish

38 다음 중 밑줄 친 단어의 문법적 쓰임이 서로 같은 것끼리 짝지은 것은?

① • <u>Who</u> do you think will win the singing contest?
   • By joining a club, you can meet people <u>who</u> share your interests.
② • <u>As</u> she tasted the tea, she put on a smile.
   • <u>As</u> a famous movie star, he has lots of fans.
③ • To live a happy life, you must learn to love <u>yourself</u>.
   • Did you really make this sweater <u>yourself</u>?
④ • I think <u>that</u> she's a very talented writer.
   • Dad often tells us <u>that</u> he wants to live in a country town.
⑤ • Sara enjoys <u>watching</u> the stars from time to time.
   • <u>Watching</u> her walk away, the boy stood there for a while.

39 다음 두 문장의 뜻이 같도록 빈칸에 들어갈 단어로 알맞은 것은?

> • I went home because it grew darker.
> = It grew darker, _____ I went home.

① but   ② because   ③ for
④ so   ⑤ though

40 다음 글의 빈칸에 들어갈 알맞은 단어는?

> I have a niece whose name is Sora. I love her very much. She studies really hard. She won first prize in the English contest for students in her school. _____, she's very polite and honest.

① Besides   ② However   ③ Although
④ Instead   ⑤ Therefore

41 다음 빈칸에 들어갈 알맞은 말은?

> My friend John has a lot of clothes, _____ _____. He always buys his clothes at garage sales.

① and he spends much money on clothes
② and he doesn't spend much money on clothes
③ but he spends much money on clothes
④ but he doesn't spend much money on clothes
⑤ but he spends many money on clothes

42 다음 밑줄 친 if와 바꿔 쓸 수 있는 것은?

I asked her if she had done it all by herself or if someone had helped her.

① unless ② as ③ because
④ for ⑤ whether

43 다음 중 어법상 옳은 문장을 고르세요.

① Both you and him live in Canada.
② Both my mom and dad was busy harvesting the rice.
③ Guests should choose either to eat or not eat breakfast.
④ Neither he nor I am excited about this SF movie.
⑤ My friend seemed neither surprised or worried.

44 다음 주어진 문장을 괄호 안의 표현을 활용해 같은 의미의 문장으로 바꿔 쓰세요.

- Water is not only the most common substance on Earth but also one of the most unusual things.

➡ _____
_____
(as well as)

45 다음 글에서 밑줄 친 표현과 바꾸어 쓸 수 있는 것은?

Did you know that more than a hundred thousand pets are abandoned each year? These animals are rescued by animal shelters. But the number of homeless pets is so large that the shelters cannot house them all. For this reason, there is a campaign called "Adopt a Friend," which encourages people to adopt a pet from one of the shelters. So instead of buying a pet, why don't you adopt a friend?

① so that the shelters cannot house
② too large for the shelters to house
③ large enough for the shelters to house
④ large for the shelters in order to house
⑤ so large because the shelters cannot house

46 다음 두 문장을 한 문장으로 알맞게 바꾸어 쓴 것은?

I'm hungry. I can eat lunch within ten minutes.

① I'm hungry so that I can't eat lunch within ten minutes.
② I'm so hungry that I can't eat lunch within ten minutes.
③ I'm so hungry that I can eat lunch within ten minutes.
④ I am hungry so that I could eat lunch within ten minutes.
⑤ I'm so hungry that I couldn't eat lunch within ten minutes.

47 다음 빈칸에 알맞은 단어끼리 바르게 짝지어진 것은?

> _____ I was standing on the stage, my legs were shaking. I was very nervous. I started singing. _____ I finished the song, the whole audience gave me a big hand. I said to myself, "I did it."

① While – If
② While – How
③ However – If
④ While – After
⑤ However – After

48 다음 빈칸에 알맞은 단어끼리 바르게 짝지어진 것은?

> • _____ you do your best, you will get the chance.
> • _____ Mina doesn't have many friends, she feels lonely.

① If – After
② Though – If
③ If – Because
④ Although – Because
⑤ Before – Before

49 주어진 문장의 밑줄 친 As와 같은 의미로 쓰인 것을 모두 고르세요.

> As you were out, I left a message.

① As she isn't honest, she won't tell the truth.
② When I was in high school, I started working as a magician's helper.
③ On October 31st, American children dress up as ghosts and monsters.
④ As he got up late, he was late for work.
⑤ My puppy barked as it came into the room.

50 다음 두 문장을 한 문장으로 만들 때 빈칸에 들어갈 단어끼리 알맞게 짝지어진 것은?

> • Semin can't speak Chinese. Juyoung can't speak Chinese, either.
> ➡ _____ Semin _____ Juyoung can speak Chinese.

① Between – and
② Both – and
③ Either – or
④ Neither – or
⑤ Neither – nor

51 다음 빈칸에 들어갈 알맞은 말은?

> My niece ran so fast _____.

① to me I can catch her
② to cannot catch her
③ that I couldn't catch her
④ that I could catch her
⑤ that I can catch her

52 다음은 Cristiano Ronaldo (크리스티아누 호날두)의 인생에서 일어났던 일입니다. 접속사 when을 사용하여 〈보기〉와 같이 영어로 답하세요.

17 years old (2002)	make his professional debut
23 years old (2008)	win his first FIFA World Player of the Year award
31 years old (2016)	help Portugal win the European Championship for the first time

보기

Q: What happened to Ronaldo in 2002?
A: He made his professional debut when he was 17 years old.

(1) Q: What happened to Ronaldo in 2008?
   A: _____

(2) Q: What happened to Ronaldo in 2016?
   A: _____

53 다음 빈칸에 들어갈 말로 알맞은 것은?

_____ has to go to China for a business trip.

① Either she or I
② Both Mary and Ron
③ Neither she nor you
④ Either Jake or Tim
⑤ Both you and I

54 주어진 문장과 의미가 같은 것은?

This English book was so difficult that I couldn't read it.

① This English book was not difficult to read to me.
② This English book was too difficult for me to read it.
③ This English book was so difficult to me read.
④ This English book was too difficult for me to read.
⑤ This English book was too difficult for me to have read.

55 다음 빈칸에 들어갈 알맞은 말은?

_____, it wasn't very warm.

① Because the sun was shining
② Since the sun was shining
③ Although the sun was shining
④ If the sun shines
⑤ As soon as the sun was shining

56 다음 빈칸에 들어갈 표현으로 적절한 것은?

The old lady's name is Kim Younghee. _____ she is 70 years old, she is very healthy.

① But   ② In spite of   ③ Or
④ If   ⑤ Even though

57 그림을 보고 〈보기〉의 말을 사용하여 조건에 맞게 각각의 문장을 완성하세요.

(1)

(2)

조 건
- 「so ~ that …」 구문을 사용할 것.
- 〈보기〉의 말을 중복하여 쓸 수 있음.

보 기 | good   bad   can   couldn't
       the weather   I   go on a picnic

(1) Yesterday, _____ .

(2) Today, _____ .

58 다음 문장에서 틀린 부분을 한 군데 찾아 바르게 고치세요.

Our plans were cancelled because the bad weather.

_____ ➡ _____

59 다음 빈칸에 알맞은 말끼리 순서대로 짝지어진 것은?

Pets can make us happy and keeping pets can teach us many things. Even small pets, _____, need a lot of care. It takes both a huge amount of money and time to keep them. You should think carefully _____ you adopt a pet.

① but   – because
② however   – before
③ because   – before
④ however   – after
⑤ but   – if

60 다음 빈칸에 들어갈 단어로 가장 알맞은 것은?

Helen Keller was born in 1880. She was a healthy little baby _____ she was eighteen months old. Then, she became very sick. When she got better, she couldn't see or hear anything at all.

① but   ② until   ③ after
④ because   ⑤ so

61 다음 빈칸에 들어갈 말로 알맞은 말은?

Seho: When I go to bed, I put my smartphone far away where I can't reach it. I used to stay up very late because of the smartphone. It made me sleepy in the office _____ I work. So, I put it far away from my bed, and now I get to sleep earlier. It's making a difference, and now I can really focus on my work.

① and   ② from   ③ for   ④ when   ⑤ but

CHAPTER 16
전치사

성취도 자기 평가 활용법

구분	평가 기준
Excellent	문법 내용을 모두 이해하고, 문제를 모두 맞힘.
Very good	문법 내용은 충분히 이해했으나 실수로 1~2문제 틀림.
Good	문법 내용이 조금 어려워 3~4문제 틀림.
needs **R**eview	문법 내용 이해가 어렵고, 5문제 이상 틀림, 복습 필요.

PSS 1 시간을 나타내는 전치사	페이지	학습날짜	성취도 자기평가 E V G R	학습체크
PSS 1-1 at, on, in Ⅰ	382	/		☐
PSS 1-2 at, on, in Ⅱ	383	/		☐
PSS 1-3 from, since	385	/		☐
PSS 1-4 by, until	386	/		☐
PSS 1-5 before, after	387	/		☐
PSS 1-6 for, during	389	/		☐

PSS 2 장소, 방향을 나타내는 전치사	페이지	학습날짜	성취도 자기평가 E V G R	학습체크
PSS 2-1 at, in, on Ⅰ	391	/		☐
PSS 2-2 at, in, on Ⅱ	392	/		☐
PSS 2-3 above, below, over, under	394	/		☐
PSS 2-4 up, down, into, out of	395	/		☐
PSS 2-5 across, along, through, around	397	/		☐
PSS 2-6 by, in front of, behind	398	/		☐
PSS 2-7 between, among	400	/		☐
PSS 2-8 to, for	401	/		☐

PSS 3 그 밖의 전치사	페이지	학습날짜	성취도 자기평가 E V G R	학습체크
PSS 3-1 with, about, like	402	/		☐
PSS 3-2 by, as, in	403	/		☐
PSS 3-3 형용사·분사와 함께 쓰이는 전치사	405	/		☐
PSS 3-4 동사와 함께 쓰이는 전치사	406	/		☐
Chapter Review Test	410	/		☐

시간을 나타내는 전치사

PSS 1-1 at, on, in I

at		구체적인 시각 앞에 온다. I usually get up **at** 7 o'clock. 나는 대개 7시에 일어난다. The movie starts **at** 4:50. 그 영화는 4시 50분에 시작한다.
on		날짜나 요일 앞에 온다. My brother was born **on** June 25th, 2007. 내 남동생은 2007년 6월 25일에 태어났다. Mark and Shelly arrived here **on** Monday. Mark와 Shelly는 월요일에 이곳에 도착했다. We visit our grandparents **on** Saturdays. 우리는 토요일마다 조부모님을 방문한다.
in		연도, 월, 계절과 같은 비교적 긴 시간 앞에 온다. My family moved to Tokyo **in** 2007. 우리 가족은 2007년에 도쿄로 이사했다. My parents married **in** March. 나의 부모님은 3월에 결혼하셨다. I like to go skating **in** winter. 나는 겨울에 스케이트 타러 가는 것을 좋아한다.

정답 p.87

PRACTICE 1

괄호 안에 주어진 전치사 중 알맞은 것을 고르세요.

1 Jenny is leaving for Busan (at, on, in) Sunday.

2 I'm going to meet Ted (at, on, in) 2 p.m.

3 My younger sister was born (at, on, in) 1998.

4 Let's go shopping (at, on, in) Friday.

5 I plan to visit England (at, on, in) summer.

6 The class will begin (at, on, in) half past three.

7 We usually have dinner (at, on, in) 6:30.

8 Jack bought a new car (at, on, in) December.

9 They will take the exam (at, on, in) November 8th.

10 The piano lesson starts (at, on, in) noon.

11 I'll go to his concert (at, on, in) the 3rd of February.

12 The first modern Olympic Games were held (at, on, in) 1896.

13 Mom buys the weekly magazine (at, on, in) Wednesdays.

14 This email was sent (at, on, in) 9 in the morning.

15 I traveled in Alaska (at, on, in) June, 2006.

PSS 1-2　at, on, in Ⅱ

다음은 시간을 나타내는 전치사 at, on, in과 함께 쓰이는 명사(구)이다.

> at night　　at lunchtime　　at Christmas　　at present　　at sunset

Jenny doesn't drink even water **at night**. Jenny는 밤에는 물조차 마시지 않는다.
What are you going to do **at Christmas**? 넌 크리스마스에 뭘 할 거니?
Let's play tennis **at lunchtime**. 점심시간에 테니스 치자.

> on Christmas Day　　on New Year's Eve　　on Tuesday evening
> on Sunday night　　on my birthday

My family went to a nice restaurant **on New Year's Eve**.
우리 가족은 새해 전날 밤에 근사한 식당에 갔다.
Did you meet Mr. Park **on Friday night**? 너는 금요일 밤에 박 선생님을 만났니?
What did you get **on your birthday**? 너는 네 생일에 무엇을 받았니?

> in the morning　　in the 21st century　　in the 1990s
> in the past　　in the future

I wash my hair **in the evening**. 나는 저녁에 머리를 감는다.
Can you imagine living **in the 19th century**? 너는 19세기에 사는 것을 상상할 수 있니?
We may work with robots **in the future**. 우리는 미래에 로봇과 일할지도 모른다.

cf. every, this, last, next 등이 붙어 시간을 나타내는 부사구를 이룰 때는 그 앞에 at, on, in을 쓰지 않는다.
Bob goes to the mountains **every Sunday**. Bob은 일요일마다 산에 간다.
Can I visit your office **this evening**? 오늘 저녁에 네 사무실을 방문해도 될까?
I spoke to Mr. Baker on the phone **last night**. 나는 어젯밤에 Baker 씨와 전화 통화를 했다.

PRACTICE 2

괄호 안에 주어진 전치사 중 알맞은 것을 고르세요.

1. We gave presents to each other (at, on, in) Christmas Day.
2. I like watching TV (at, on, in) night.
3. There weren't many cars (at, on, in) the past.
4. Julia sent me a lovely card (at, on, in) my birthday.
5. We had lunch with Mr. Lee (at, on, in) noon.
6. Suji usually reads the newspaper (at, on, in) the morning.
7. I'll call you (at, on, in) lunchtime.
8. Can you come to my house (at, on, in) Monday afternoon?
9. Einstein made many important discoveries (at, on, in) the 20th century.
10. Are you planning to go to church (at, on, in) New Year's Eve?

PRACTICE 3

다음 문장의 빈칸에 at, on, in 중 알맞은 전치사를 쓰세요. 필요하지 않은 곳에는 ×표 하세요.

1. ① Where were you _____ April?
   ② Where were you _____ April 27th?
2. ① I go to the library _____ Thursdays.
   ② I go to the library _____ every Thursday.
3. ① They will meet _____ noon.
   ② They will meet _____ the afternoon.
4. ① Changho writes a diary _____ night.
   ② Changho wrote a diary _____ last night.
5. ① My family gets together _____ Christmas.
   ② My family gets together _____ Christmas Day.
6. ① What do you usually do _____ the evening?
   ② What are you going to do _____ this evening?
7. ① Have you been to the restaurant _____ night?
   ② Have you been to the restaurant _____ Friday night?
8. ① I went to the dentist _____ Tuesday.
   ② I'll go to the dentist _____ next Tuesday.

9 ① Mom was very busy _____ the morning.
   ② Mom was very busy _____ Sunday morning.

10 ① The soccer season begins _____ August 1st.
   ② The soccer season begins _____ August.

PSS 1-3 from, since

from	~부터	동작이나 사건이 시작되는 시점을 나타낸다. I will live in Paris **from** March. 나는 3월부터 파리에 살 것이다. *cf.* 「from ~ to …」 '~부터 …까지' I lived in Paris **from** 2015 **to** 2023. 나는 2015년부터 2023년까지 파리에 살았다.
since	~ 이래로	주로 완료시제와 함께 쓰이며, 과거에 시작된 사건이 현재에도 영향을 끼치고 있음을 나타낸다. I **have lived** in Paris **since** 2015. 나는 2015년 이래로 파리에서 살아왔다.

정답 p.88

PRACTICE 4

다음 문장의 빈칸에 from이나 since 중 알맞은 전치사를 쓰세요.

1 Miyoung has played the piano _____ 2017.

2 I will learn Chinese _____ next year.

3 Jane worked for that company _____ January to September.

4 It has been cold _____ yesterday.

5 This program was on TV _____ 2019 to 2020.

6 My brother has been sick _____ last weekend.

7 We will get up earlier _____ tomorrow.

8 Mike has stayed at my house _____ Monday.

9 Julie and I have been friends _____ last year.

10 They have a meeting _____ one o'clock.

PSS 1-4 by, until

by	~까지	동작이나 상태가 완료되는 시점을 나타낼 때 쓴다. The rain will stop **by** Tuesday. 비가 화요일까지는 그칠 것이다. I will turn off the TV **by** 3 o'clock. 나는 3시까지는 TV를 끌 것이다.
until		동작이나 상태가 한 시점까지 계속되는 것을 나타낼 때 쓴다. The rain won't stop **until** Tuesday. 비는 화요일까지 그치지 않을 것이다. (화요일까지 그치지 않고 계속 내린다는 의미) I will watch TV **until** 3 o'clock. 나는 3시까지 TV를 볼 것이다. (3시까지 TV를 계속해서 볼 것이라는 의미)

정답 p.88

PRACTICE 5

괄호 안에 주어진 전치사 중 알맞은 것을 고르세요.

1. I'm going to stay at the hotel (by, until) next Friday.
2. I have to finish my work (by, until) tomorrow.
3. Heejin kept surfing the Internet (by, until) midnight.
4. Let me know the result (by, until) the weekend.
5. The students have to stay at school (by, until) 3:30.
6. You should return the car (by, until) this Wednesday.
7. Robert will be back (by, until) April.
8. We have to drive (by, until) the night.
9. The dinner should be prepared (by, until) six o'clock.
10. Mr. Jones will leave Korea (by, until) 2014.

정답 p.88

PRACTICE 6

〈보기〉에서 알맞은 전치사를 골라 빈칸에 쓰세요.

보기	at · on in from since by until

1. The news starts _____ eight o'clock.

386 | 마더텅 영문법 3800제 2 - INTERMEDIATE

2 I will exercise harder _____ today!

3 We have to decide it _____ next Monday.

4 Beth sent this letter to me _____ the 3rd of November.

5 I stayed in bed _____ late in the morning.

6 Minsu has kept an English diary _____ last summer.

7 My family moved to Seoul _____ 2003.

8 I usually watch TV _____ Sunday night.

9 She must come back from Japan _____ next month.

10 My cousins will visit us _____ Christmas.

11 I haven't seen Samuel _____ the day he left this town.

12 You should wait for the result _____ next week.

13 Mrs. Song likes to drink coffee _____ the morning.

14 We played baseball _____ two thirty to five.

15 I got those shoes _____ my birthday.

PSS 1-5 before, after

before	~ 전에	She can answer the phone **before** 4 o'clock. 그녀는 4시 이전에 전화를 받을 수 있다. I'm not going to watch TV **before** finishing my report. (= before I finish my report) 나는 과제를 끝내기 전에 TV를 보지 않을 것이다.
after	~ 후에	She can't answer the phone **after** 4 o'clock. 그녀는 4시 이후에 전화를 받을 수 없다. I'm going to watch TV **after** finishing my report. (= after I finish my report) 나는 과제를 끝낸 후에 TV를 볼 것이다.

PRACTICE 7

다음은 유미가 지난 토요일에 한 일입니다. 빈칸에 before나 after 중 알맞은 전치사를 쓰세요.

> **Yumi's schedule**
>
> 09:00 - had breakfast
> 10:00 - did the laundry
> 11:00 - read the history book
> 13:00 - had lunch
> 14:00 - went to the movies
> 16:00 - went to the library
> 18:00 - went to a Chinese restaurant for dinner
> 19:30 - got home

1. Yumi had breakfast _____ 10:00.

2. Yumi did the laundry _____ breakfast.

3. Yumi read the history book _____ lunch.

4. Yumi went to the movies _____ lunch.

5. Yumi went to the library _____ 5:00 p.m.

6. Yumi got home _____ dinner.

PRACTICE 8

〈보기〉와 같이 문장을 바꿔 쓰세요.

> 보 기　　I cleaned my room, and I watched TV shows.
> ➡ After cleaning my room, I watched TV shows.

1　He turned off the light, and he went out.
　➡ Before _____.

2　Jessica and Inho saw a movie, and they had dinner.
　➡ After _____.

3　Mom looked at the oranges carefully, and she bought them.
　➡ Before _____.

4　I decided what to do, and I told him about it.
　➡ After _____.

5　Nick usually prays, and he eats food.
　➡ Before _____.

6　We read the book, and we discussed it together.
　➡ After _____.

PSS 1-6　for, during

for	~ 동안	for 다음에는 시간의 길이를 나타내는 명사(구)가 온다. Alex has to stay in hospital **for two months**. Alex는 두 달 동안 입원해 있어야 한다. It rained **for a while**. 잠시 동안 비가 내렸다.
during		during 다음에는 특정 기간을 나타내는 명사(구)가 온다. Alex has to stay in hospital **during his vacation**. Alex는 그의 휴가 기간 동안 입원해 있어야 한다. It rained **during the night**. 밤새 비가 내렸다.
cf. while		while은 접속사이므로, while 다음에는 '주어+동사'가 옴에 주의한다. Someone knocked the door **while I was** asleep. 내가 잠들어 있는 동안 누군가 문을 두드렸다.

PRACTICE 9

다음 문장의 빈칸에 for나 during 중 알맞은 전치사를 쓰세요.

1. ① I was standing _____ almost two hours.
   ② I was standing _____ the concert.

2. ① Betty felt sleepy _____ the class.
   ② Betty felt sleepy _____ a while.

3. ① Minju will stay in London _____ the summer.
   ② Minju will stay in London _____ two months.

4. ① I turned off my cell phone _____ three hours.
   ② I turned off my cell phone _____ the movie.

5. ① Junho exercised very hard _____ a week.
   ② Junho exercised very hard _____ the week.

6. ① We talked about the meeting _____ about thirty minutes.
   ② We talked about the meeting _____ lunch.

7. ① Many soldiers fought _____ the war.
   ② Many soldiers fought _____ ten months.

8. ① I've been reading the book _____ the afternoon.
   ② I've been reading the book _____ some hours.

9. ① Sally went to the beach _____ two weeks.
   ② Sally went to the beach _____ the holiday.

10. ① My mom cooked and cleaned _____ many hours.
    ② My mom cooked and cleaned _____ the day.

PRACTICE 10

〈보기〉에서 알맞은 전치사를 골라 빈칸에 쓰세요.

보 기	before after for during

1. He got very tired _____ walking around the city.
2. The player moved very fast _____ the game.
3. I have taken tennis lessons _____ two years.
4. Let's clean the house _____ going out.
5. I asked the price _____ paying the money.

6 Charlie was talking to her _____ over an hour.

7 Somebody entered the room _____ knocking on the door loudly.

8 _____ going to bed, I took a shower.

9 My family doesn't talk a lot _____ meals.

10 Andy has taught us English _____ six months.

PSS 2 장소, 방향을 나타내는 전치사

PSS 2-1 at, in, on I

at	~에	특정한 한 지점을 나타내거나 비교적 좁은 장소 앞에 쓰인다. I was sitting **at** the table. 나는 탁자에 앉아 있었다. Jack was waiting for me **at** the bus stop. Jack은 버스 정류장에서 나를 기다리고 있었다.
in	~ (안)에	공간 안에 속해 있는 느낌을 나타내거나 비교적 넓은 장소 앞에 쓰인다. He took off his shoes **in** the room. 그는 방에서 신발을 벗었다. There are two birds **in** the cage. 새장 안에 새가 두 마리 있다.
on	~ (위)에	표면에 접촉해 있는 것을 나타낸다. A book lies **on** the desk. 책이 책상 위에 놓여 있다. I found some coins **on** the floor. 나는 바닥에서 동전 몇 개를 찾았다.

정답 p.89

PRACTICE 11

그림을 보고, 빈칸에 at, in, on 중 알맞은 전치사를 쓰세요.

1

2

3

1   There is a picture _____ the door.

2   Flowers are _____ the vase.

3   I met my friend Steve _____ the bus stop.

4   The books are _____ the desk.

5   My brother is standing _____ the door.

6   I left my bag _____ the classroom.

7   There is a boat _____ the lake.

8   She was sitting _____ the window reading a book.

9   There are books _____ the bag.

PSS 2-2 at, in, on Ⅱ

다음은 장소를 나타내는 전치사 at, in, on과 함께 쓰이는 명사(구)이다.

at home	at school	at work
at an airport	at the bottom	at a meeting
at a garage sale	at a contest	at a party
at a gym	at my grandparents' house	

Where is Junho now? – He's **at work**. 준호는 지금 어디에 있니? – 그는 직장에 있어.
There is the answer **at the bottom of** the paper. 종이 아래쪽에 답이 있다.
I met Yumi **at the party** last Saturday. 나는 지난 토요일 파티에서 유미를 만났다.

in bed	in hospital	in prison	in a mirror
in a car	in a taxi	in the middle	in a picture
in the sky	in a book	in a dictionary	

We went to the museum **in a car**. 우리는 차를 타고 박물관에 갔다.
Shelly had a car accident yesterday. She's **in hospital** now.
Shelly는 어제 교통 사고를 당했다. 그녀는 지금 병원에 있다.
Mark is sitting **in the middle** of the meeting room. Mark는 회의실의 중앙에 앉아 있다.

on a bus	on a subway	on a train	on a plane
on a boat	on a street	on a road	on an island
on a farm	on the first floor	on one's[the] way home	

We went to Japan **on a boat**. 우리는 배를 타고 일본에 갔다.
There are so many cars **on the road**. 도로 위에는 아주 많은 차들이 있다.
The room is **on the second floor**. 그 방은 2층에 있다.
I met my uncle **on my way home**. 나는 집에 가는 길에 나의 삼촌을 만났다.

PRACTICE 12

정답 p.89

다음 빈칸에 at, in, on 중 알맞은 전치사를 쓰세요.

1. Why don't you look up the words _____ the dictionary?
2. Namsik goes to work _____ a bus.
3. Mrs. Lee's idea was welcomed _____ the meeting.
4. I worked _____ the farm during my vacation.
5. Alex has been sick _____ bed since yesterday.
6. How many people were there _____ the rock concert?
7. He got so excited while traveling _____ a plane.
8. Hurry up! You should be _____ the airport in an hour.
9. It's difficult to stop _____ the middle of the street.
10. How did you get to the city, _____ a train or _____ a car?
11. I think I read the story _____ a book.
12. I want to stay _____ home today.
13. My grandparents live _____ an island.
14. I saw my old friend _____ the street yesterday.
15. We are going to watch a soccer match _____ my friend's house.

PSS 2-3 above, below, over, under

above	(~ 보다) 위에	The clock is **above** the TV. 시계는 TV 위에 있다.
below	(~ 보다) 아래에	The TV is **below** the clock. TV는 시계 아래에 있다.
over	~ (뒤덮듯이) 바로 위에	Look at the rainbow **over** the tree. 나무 위에 있는 무지개를 보아라.
under	~ 아래에	There is a dog **under** the tree. 나무 아래에 개 한 마리가 있다.

정답 p.89

PRACTICE 13

그림을 보고, 괄호 안에 주어진 전치사 중 알맞은 것을 고르세요.

1 There is a bridge (over, under) the river.

2 A few birds are flying (above, below) the people.

3 Two people are walking (above, below) the birds.

4 There is a small village (over, under) the mountain.

5 Some white clouds are (above, below) the mountain.

6 The sun is shining (over, under) the mountain.

7 Fish are swimming (above, below) the bridge.

8 We can see some flowers (over, under) the tree.

PSS 2-4 up, down, into, out of

up	~ 위로	Minji and I walked **up** the mountain. 민지와 나는 산 위로 걸어 올라갔다.
down	~ 아래로	Minji and I walked **down** the mountain. 민지와 나는 산 아래로 걸어 내려갔다.
into	~ 안으로	Three students came **into** the classroom. 세 명의 학생들이 교실 안으로 들어갔다.
out of	~ 밖으로	Three students got **out of** the classroom. 세 명의 학생들이 교실 밖으로 나왔다.

정답 p.89

PRACTICE 14

그림을 보고, 〈보기〉에서 알맞은 전치사를 골라 빈칸에 쓰세요.

1    2    3   4

5   6    7    8

보기	up　down　into　out of

1　A man is going _____ the stairs.

2　Sejin is climbing _____ the hill.

3　A few people were coming _____ the building.

4　Mom was cooking when I walked _____ the kitchen.

5　I had to go _____ the ladder to reach the shelf.

6　Bob took a cat _____ the box.

7 She helped her grandmother to get _____ a car.

8 It was easy to row a boat _____ the river.

PRACTICE 15

정답 p.89

그림을 보고, 괄호 안에 주어진 전치사 중 알맞은 것을 고르세요.

1    2   3    4

5    6    7    8

1 The girl is looking (into, out of) the window.
The dog is coming (up, down) the hill.

2 The sofa lies (above, below) the window.
The window is (above, below) the sofa.

3 My brother went (up, down) the tree to get the kite.
I was waiting (over, under) the tree.

4 The player served the ball (over, under) the net.
The ball is now (into, out of) the court.

5 A boy came (into, out of) the room.
He found a picture (above, below) the desk.

6 The rabbit was running (up, down) the mountain.
It has just jumped (over, under) the rock.

7 Sumi went (into, out of) the bed.
Her dog was lying (above, under) the bed.

8 I walked (up, down) the street.
I saw a man standing (above, below) the streetlight.

PSS 2-5 across, along, through, around

across	~을 가로질러	I walked **across** the road. 나는 도로를 가로질러 걸었다.
along	~을 따라	I walked **along** the river. 나는 강을 따라 걸었다.
through	~을 통과하여	I walked **through** the forest. 나는 숲을 통과하여 걸었다.
around	~ 주위에(를)	I walked **around** the building. 나는 그 건물 주위를 걸었다.

정답 p.89

PRACTICE 16

그림을 보고, 〈보기〉에서 알맞은 전치사를 골라 빈칸에 쓰세요.

1
2
3
4

5
6
7
8

| 보 기 | across　along　through　around |

1 Jim walked _____ the street.
2 Many cars are moving _____ the road.
3 We often take walks _____ the park with our little daughter.
4 Dad likes driving _____ the town.
5 A cool wind entered the room _____ the window.
6 I tried to swim _____ the river.
7 The postbox is just _____ the corner.
8 She was walking _____ the street.

PSS 2-6 by, in front of, behind

by	~ 옆에	Peter is sitting **by** Jane. Peter는 Jane 옆에 앉아 있다. = Peter is sitting **beside** Jane. = Peter is sitting **next to** Jane.
in front of	~ 앞에	Nami is sitting **in front of** Peter. 나미는 Peter 앞에 앉아 있다.
behind	~ 뒤에	Sudong is sitting **behind** Jane. 수동은 Jane 뒤에 앉아 있다.

정답 p.89

PRACTICE 17

그림을 보고, 〈보기〉에서 알맞은 전치사를 골라 빈칸에 쓰세요.

1
2
3
4
5
6
7
8
9

보 기	by in front of behind

1 The tree is _____ the rock.

2 Billy is waiting for his friend _____ the school.

3 The police station is _____ the hospital.

4 There are four more people _____ me.

5 The girl _____ Paul is Lisa.

6 I have been to the mountain _____ these houses.

7 I saw some foreigners taking photos _____ the tower.

8 The children are hiding _____ the curtain.

9 I left my glasses _____ the book.

정답 p.89

PRACTICE 18

그림을 보고, 괄호 안에 주어진 전치사 중 알맞은 것을 고르세요.

1  2  3  4

5  6  7  8

1 There is a tree (in front of, behind) the school.
A girl is walking (across, along) the street.

2 A man is running (through, around) the park.
A dog is running (in front of, behind) him.

3 The post office is (behind, by) the bank.
The drug store is (across, around) the corner.

4 Some people walk (across, along) the river.
Other people walk (across, under) the bridge.

5 My family was driving (by, through) the town.
There was a truck (behind, around) our car.

6 Sally is standing (by, behind) me.
Peter and Julie are standing (in front of, behind) Sally and me.

7 My parents and I were sitting (through, around) the table.
Someone knocked on the door (in front of, behind) Mom.

8 I was standing (by, behind) the tree.
Jenny came to me (across, along) the street.

PSS 2-7 between, among

between	(둘) 사이에	The war **between** the two countries has ended. 그 두 국가 사이의 전쟁이 끝났다. Korea is located **between** China **and** Japan. 한국은 중국과 일본 사이에 위치해 있다. ***cf.*** between은 「between A and B」의 형태로도 쓰인다.
among	(셋 이상의) 사이에	Jeremy is a popular singer **among** young people. Jeremy는 젊은 사람들 사이에서 인기 있는 가수다.

정답 p.89

PRACTICE 19

괄호 안에 주어진 전치사 중 알맞은 것을 고르세요.

1 Cathy is the girl sitting (between, among) Mark and Sam.

2 Bill has a good reputation (between, among) his fellows.

3 How many girls do you know (between, among) those five?

4 You have to choose (between, among) the two colors.

5 It was difficult to find Yujin (between, among) thousands of children.

6 There's a soccer game (between, among) Korea and Taiwan today.

7 The time difference (between, among) the two countries is an hour.

8 The TV show is very popular (between, among) my friends.

PSS 2-8 to, for

to	~로, ~에	go, come, return 동사와 함께 도착지를 나타낼 때 쓰인다. I **went to** the hospital to visit my uncle. 나는 나의 삼촌을 방문하기 위해 병원에 갔다. Smith **came to** Korea three months ago. Smith는 3개월 전에 한국에 왔다. She **returned to** China in 2018. 그녀는 2018년에 중국으로 돌아갔다.
for	~로, ~을 향하여	leave, start 동사와 함께 방향을 나타낼 때 쓰인다. Linda **left for** Los Angeles yesterday. Linda는 어제 로스앤젤레스로 떠났다. My family is going to **start for** Busan. 우리 가족은 부산을 향해 출발할 것이다.

cf. to와 for는 4형식 문장을 3형식 문장으로 전환할 때 간접목적어 앞에 놓여 '~에게, ~께'로 해석된다.

My brother gave Mom a bunch of roses. 나의 남동생은 엄마께 장미꽃 한 다발을 드렸다.
➡ My brother gave a bunch of roses **to** Mom.

She bought her father a necktie. 그녀는 그녀의 아버지께 넥타이를 사드렸다.
➡ She bought a necktie **for** her father.

정답 p.89

PRACTICE 20

다음 문장의 빈칸에 to와 for 중 알맞은 전치사를 쓰세요.

1. We're going _____ Madrid next month.
2. Seho started _____ school ten minutes ago.
3. They came _____ my house to see me.
4. Jina will return _____ Seoul in a week.
5. The train is leaving _____ Daegu in a few minutes.
6. I returned _____ the bookstore and bought the book.
7. You'd better start _____ the airport now to be on board in time.
8. She went _____ the gym to meet Chris.
9. Jaehui made bibimbap _____ Sarah yesterday.
10. Eddie wrote a letter _____ his grandmother in Korea.

PSS 3 그 밖의 전치사

PSS 3-1 with, about, like

with	~와 함께	I live **with** my grandparents. 나는 나의 조부모님과 함께 산다.
	~의 몸에 지니고	You'd better take an umbrella **with** you. 넌 우산을 가져가는 것이 좋을 거야.
	~을 가지고 있는	The dog **with** a long tail is Max. 긴 꼬리를 가진 개가 Max야.
	~을 사용하여, ~으로	What did you make **with** snow? 넌 눈으로 무엇을 만들었니?
about	~에 대해 (=on)	We were talking **about** having pets. 우리는 애완 동물을 갖는 것에 대해 이야기하고 있었다.
like	~와 같은 (=such as)	I love Italian food **like** spaghetti and pizza. 나는 스파게티와 피자 같은 이탈리아 음식을 대단히 좋아한다.
	~처럼	Alex and Matthew look **like** brothers. Alex와 Matthew는 형제처럼 보인다.

cf. without '(사람, 물건, 경험 등이) 없이'
Can you see well **without** your glasses? 넌 네 안경 없이 잘 볼 수 있니?

PRACTICE 21

괄호 안에 주어진 전치사 중 알맞은 것을 고르세요.

1. The book is (with, about) Korean history.
2. Tony enjoys sports (about, like) baseball and basketball.
3. I'd like to take a trip (about, with) my friends.
4. Did you hear the news (about, like) the traffic accident last night?
5. Do you know the boy (like, with) glasses over there?
6. What's your opinion (with, about) Sora's birthday present?
7. She made a cake (with, about) sugar, butter, and flour.
8. My sister sings very well (about, like) a singer.
9. We found the place (without, like) difficulty.
10. Yunju and Sunhee look (like, with) twins.

PRACTICE 22

우리말 해석과 일치하도록 〈보기〉에서 알맞은 전치사를 골라 빈칸에 쓰세요.

보 기	between　among　to　for　with　about　like　without

1 Let's go _____ the park after lunch. (점심 식사 후에 공원에 가자.)

2 When do you plan to start _____ Daejeon? (너는 대전으로 언제 출발할 계획이니?)

3 You can't make an omelet _____ eggs. (너는 계란 없이 오믈렛을 만들 수 없다.)

4 I saw a movie _____ World War II on TV.
   (나는 TV에서 2차 세계대전에 대한 영화를 봤다.)

5 A squirrel was making rustling noises _____ the leaves.
   (다람쥐 한 마리가 나뭇잎들 사이에서 바스락 거리는 소리를 내고 있었다.)

6 The patient _____ the disease has to take medicine twice a day.
   (그 병을 가진 환자는 하루에 두 번 약을 복용해야 한다.)

7 People say that I look _____ my father. (사람들은 내가 나의 아빠를 닮았다고 말한다.)

8 I can't decide which to eat _____ pizza and steak.
   (나는 피자와 스테이크 중에 어느 것을 먹을지 정할 수 없다.)

PSS 3-2　by, as, in

by	~를 타고	I went to Chicago **by** plane. 나는 비행기를 타고 시카고에 갔다. ***cf.*** by 뒤에 교통수단이 올 때는 관사를 쓰지 않는다.
	〈방법〉 ~로	Mike and I keep in touch **by** email. Mike와 나는 이메일로 계속 연락한다.
	~에 의해	This novel was written **by** James Joyce. 이 소설은 James Joyce에 의해 쓰여졌다.
	〈정도〉 ~로, ~만큼	My team lost the game **by** 3 to 1. 나의 팀은 3대 1로 경기에 졌다.

by	~함으로써, ~하며	What can you make **by** using the paper? 그 종이를 사용함으로써 너는 무엇을 만들 수 있니?	
as	~로서	I used to use this bowl **as** a cup. 나는 이 사발을 컵으로 이용하곤 했다.	
in	~을 입고 있는	Look at the woman **in** red. 빨간 옷을 입고 있는 여자를 보아라.	
	〈크기〉 ~로	Cut the bread **in** half. 빵을 반으로 잘라라.	
	〈방법〉 ~로	They spoke **in** English during the meeting. 그들은 회의 동안 영어로 말했다.	

PRACTICE 23

정답 p.89

〈보기〉에서 알맞은 전치사를 골라 빈칸에 쓰세요.

| 보 기 | by | as | in |

1 Luke works _____ a manager in the restaurant.
2 This famous play was written _____ Shakespeare.
3 Mom sliced the bread _____ three pieces.
4 She tries to lose weight _____ swimming every morning.
5 My brother is taller than I am _____ three centimeters.
6 We think of her _____ the best volleyball player in Korea.
7 I sketched the picture _____ pencil first.
8 It is pleasant to travel _____ train.
9 Ten men _____ black are standing in front of the building.
10 You can learn how to communicate with other people _____ working together.
11 You have to speak _____ Korean during this class.
12 Could you send it to me _____ fax?
13 The island was discovered _____ an English explorer, James Cook.
14 The couch can also be used _____ an extra bed.

PSS 3-3 형용사 · 분사와 함께 쓰이는 전치사

1. **full of** '~로 가득한' = filled with
   This garden is **full of** beautiful flowers. 이 정원은 아름다운 꽃들로 가득하다.

2. **built of** '~로 지어진'
   This house is **built of** brick. 이 집은 벽돌로 지어졌다.

3. **made of** '~로 만들어진'
   The chair is **made of** wood. 그 의자는 나무로 만들어졌다.
   cf. 화학적 변화를 거쳐 만들어질 때는 made from을 쓴다.

4. **upset about** '~에 대해 화난, 기분이 나쁜'
   I'm **upset about** the poor service. 나는 형편없는 서비스에 대해 기분이 나쁘다.

5. **good at** '~을 잘하는'
   Jina is **good at** playing the flute. 지나는 플룻 연주를 잘한다.

6. **poor at** '~에 서툰'
   I'm **poor at** driving. 나는 운전에 서툴다.

7. **proud of** '~을 자랑스러워 하는'
   Kevin is **proud of** his son. Kevin은 그의 아들을 자랑스러워 한다.

8. **famous for** '~로 유명한'
   Sumi is **famous for** her paintings. 수미는 그녀의 그림들로 유명하다.

9. **interested in** '~에 흥미가 있는, 관심이 있는'
   My father is **interested in** classical music. 나의 아버지는 클래식 음악에 관심이 있으시다.

10. **afraid of** '~을 두려워하는'
    John is **afraid of** birds. John은 새를 두려워한다.

11. **tired of** '~에 싫증난, ~이 지겨운'
    I'm **tired of** eating at the same restaurant every day. 난 매일 똑같은 식당에서 밥 먹는 게 지겨워.

12. **similar to** '~와 비슷한'
    This question is **similar to** that question. 이 문제는 그 문제와 유사하다.

PRACTICE 24

괄호 안에 주어진 전치사 중 알맞은 것을 고르세요.

1 James is very good (at, in) many kinds of sports.
2 I'm proud (of, at) my family and country.
3 Are you interested (at, in) romantic movies?
4 Most books are made (of, in) paper.
5 Your teacher is upset (from, about) your rude manners.
6 Her eyes were full (of, with) tears.
7 Tim is poor (at, in) speaking in public.
8 All of the children were afraid (of, at) ghosts.
9 This building is built (of, in) stones.
10 Mr. Park is famous (of, for) his TV show.
11 I'm tired (from, of) cold weather, heavy coats, and boots.
12 He thought that Korean culture was similar (of, to) Canadian culture.

PSS 3-4 동사와 함께 쓰이는 전치사

1. **belong to** '~에 속하다, ~의 소유물이다'
   The huge house **belongs to** Mr. Simpson. 그 거대한 집은 Simpson 씨 소유이다.

2. **look for** '~을 찾다'
   I'm **looking for** my brown bag. 나는 내 갈색 가방을 찾고 있다.

3. **die of** '~로 죽다'
   My grandfather **died of** cancer. 나의 할아버지는 암으로 돌아가셨다.

4. **consist of** '~로 구성되어 있다'
   The test **consists of** speaking and listening. 그 시험은 말하기와 듣기로 구성되어 있다.

5. **wait for** '~을 기다리다'
   The lady is **waiting for** the bus for 30 minutes. 그 숙녀는 30분 동안 버스를 기다리고 있다.

6. listen to '~을 듣다'
   Giho was **listening to** the radio. 기호는 라디오를 듣고 있었다.

7. thank … for '(…에게) ~을 감사하다'
   Thank you **for** your quick response. 당신의 빠른 답변에 감사드립니다.

8. believe in '~을 믿다'
   I **believe in** God. 나는 하나님을 믿는다.

9. care about '~에 대해 신경 쓰다, 관심을 가지다'
   Doctors **care about** their patients. 의사들은 자신의 환자들에 대해 신경을 쓴다.

10. laugh at '~을 보고 웃다, 비웃다'
    They **laughed at** Tom's stupid question. 그들은 Tom의 어리석은 질문을 비웃었다.

11. run into[across] '~와 우연히 마주치다'
    I **ran into** your brother today. 나는 오늘 너희 오빠와 우연히 마주쳤다.

12. take pride in '~에 자부심을 가지다'
    They **take pride in** their school. 그들은 그들의 학교에 자부심을 가진다.

정답 p.90

PRACTICE 25

다음 문장의 빈칸에 알맞은 전치사를 쓰세요.

1 The team consists _____ doctors and nurses.
2 My sister is looking _____ a new job.
3 Jake enjoys listening _____ rap music.
4 The concert hall was full _____ people.
5 I've always been interested _____ cooking.
6 Does this bag belong _____ you?
7 Mr. White is proud _____ his school.
8 We were waiting _____ the guest speaker in the lecture hall.
9 Everybody is afraid _____ death.
10 Brazil and Columbia are famous _____ their coffee.

11 My grandmother died _____ old age.

12 People laughed _____ the clown's walking.

13 Thank you all _____ coming tonight.

14 A few people believe _____ UFOs.

15 She doesn't care _____ the prize. It's not important to her.

16 She ran _____ an old friend at the party.

17 The Korean team took pride _____ winning the game against the Brazilian team.

정답 p.90

PRACTICE 26

괄호 안에 주어진 전치사 중 알맞은 것을 고르세요.

1 I stayed at Jinho's house (for, during) five days.

2 Thank you (to, for) inviting me to dinner.

3 I like the pretty table cloth (on, above) that table.

4 I wrote my name (down, below) my father's.

5 I'm going to a concert (at, in) Christmas.

6 Mike is poor (in, at) looking after babies.

7 There is a carpet (on, in) the floor.

8 Are you good (at, of) singing?

9 Jinyoung is not interested (in, at) making things.

10 There's a mirror (as, above) the TV.

11 People feel more tired (in, on) Mondays.

12 I'll return (to, for) my house at about 8:30.

13 Jack is proud (of, with) his height.

14 She was beautiful (in, of) white.

15 I usually go swimming (from, since) 7 to 8.

16 Mr. Smith came to Korea (at, in) 1998.

17 I've waited (for, on) his reply since last year.

18 We need to think (with, about) moving to another city.

19 My family consists (of, with) Dad, Mom, my brother, and me.

20 Mom and I planted pretty flowers (around, above) our garden.
21 I read the newspaper (at, in) the evening.
22 I haven't seen Helen (for, during) 3 months.
23 I don't know how to say this (by, in) English.
24 Do you know what happened (between, among) Nancy and Carrie?
25 This baby looks (like, with) an angel.
26 Ann put some books (down, under) the desk.
27 Go and wash your hands first (before, after) eating lunch.
28 These jeans belong (to, for) my sister.
29 We visited our grandparents (in, during) the holiday.
30 We climbed (up, down) the hill to go higher.
31 He should have finished writing it (by, until) now.
32 They ran (down, under) the stairs to get the door.
33 Many children are dying (in, of) hunger in Africa.
34 What are you going to do (by, with) the money?
35 My cats are sleeping (in, at) the living room.
36 (Under, After) getting dressed, I went out in a hurry.
37 Birds are flying high (in, at) the sky.
38 The students were standing (through, along) the white line.
39 Wine is made (in, from) grapes.
40 I can stay in Tokyo (by, until) next week.
41 They went to Australia (on, by) a plane.
42 We can save some time if we go there (in, on) a taxi.
43 Yumi has wanted to learn Chinese (from, since) last year.
44 This river flows (out of, through) the city.
45 I saw Sangho going (in, into) the building.
46 The Korean team won the game (by, in) 2 to 1.
47 My heart became full (of, with) joy.
48 Let's get (into, out of) the classroom and have some fresh air.
49 I wanted to see the actor's face (behind, in front of) the mask.
50 When do you leave (for, to) New York?

Chapter Review Test

CHAPTER 16 전치사

정답 p.91

1 다음 빈칸에 들어갈 단어로 알맞은 것은?

> My father was born in Seoul _____ September 17th, 1965.

① to ② of ③ on
④ in ⑤ at

2 다음 빈칸에 들어갈 단어로 알맞은 것은?

> Write your address and stick a stamp _____ the envelope.

① on ② in ③ by
④ at ⑤ into

3 다음 우리말을 영어로 옮길 때 빈칸에 알맞은 세 단어를 쓰세요.

> • 그녀의 생각은 내 생각과 꽤 비슷하다.
> = Her idea is quite _____ _____ _____.

4 주어진 우리말과 같은 뜻이 되도록 빈칸에 알맞은 단어를 쓰세요.

> • 집에 가는 길에, 그는 부모님을 위해 과일을 샀다.
> = _____ _____ _____ _____, he bought some fruit for his parents.

5 다음 빈칸에 공통으로 들어갈 알맞은 단어는?

> • Put some water _____ the bowl.
> • My family is going to move _____ a new house next month.

① of ② about ③ on
④ for ⑤ into

6 주어진 우리말과 같은 뜻이 되도록 빈칸에 알맞은 단어를 쓰세요.

> • 그녀는 은행에 가는 길에 그녀의 이웃과 우연히 마주쳤다.
> = She ran _____ her neighbor on her way to the bank.

7 다음 대화의 빈칸에 들어갈 단어끼리 알맞게 짝지어진 것은?

> A: Do you know _____ we can't meet Mr. Kim anymore?
> B: That's because he died _____ cancer last month.

① what – at ② what – of
③ why – of ④ why – by
⑤ by – in

8 ⓐ~ⓒ에 들어갈 단어끼리 알맞게 짝지어진 것은?

> Two years ago, I visited Mexico with my family. ⓐ (With / At) that time, people were celebrating the Day of the Dead, a Mexican holiday. ⓑ (In / On) this holiday, Mexicans remember and honor their deceased loved ones. It's not a gloomy occasion, but rather it is a colorful holiday. People usually visit cemeteries and decorate the graves. Also, they make *ofrendas*, elaborately decorated altars, ⓒ (with / in) their homes to welcome the spirits.
>
> *deceased: 사망한 **elaborately: 정교하게 ***altar: 제단

	ⓐ	ⓑ	ⓒ
①	With	- In	- with
②	At	- On	- in
③	At	- In	- with
④	With	- On	- with
⑤	At	- In	- in

9 다음 ⓐ~ⓔ의 밑줄 친 부분 중 어법상 틀린 것을 있는 대로 고른 것은?

> ⓐ She speaks English <u>in</u> her first language.
> ⓑ We should protect wild animals <u>as</u> tigers and bears.
> ⓒ I'm going to travel <u>around</u> the countryside.
> ⓓ We are looking <u>for</u> a used car.
> ⓔ The contest was held <u>on</u> April 7th.

① ⓐ, ⓑ   ② ⓑ, ⓒ   ③ ⓐ, ⓑ, ⓒ
④ ⓐ, ⓓ, ⓔ   ⑤ ⓑ, ⓒ, ⓓ, ⓔ

10 다음 우리말과 일치하도록 빈칸에 알맞은 표현을 쓰세요.

> • 내 목걸이는 파란 유리구슬로 만들어져 있다.
> = My necklace _____ _____ _____ blue glass beads.

11 다음 빈칸에 알맞은 단어끼리 바르게 짝지어진 것은?

> • He's good _____ playing tennis.
> • The picture didn't fit _____ the frame.

① for – to   ② for – in
③ at – at   ④ at – to
⑤ at – in

12 다음 빈칸에 공통으로 들어갈 알맞은 단어를 쓰세요.

> • I'll let you know _____ email.
> • The other team was losing _____ one run.
> • The great film was directed _____ Woody Allen.

13 각 문장의 빈칸에 들어갈 알맞은 전치사를 쓰세요.

> • Sora is going to leave Seoul _____ Jejudo.
> • She has gone _____ Jejudo.

14 Albert Einstein에 관한 다음 글의 빈칸에 알맞은 말을 〈보기〉에서 골라 쓰세요.

> After Albert Einstein graduated from the Swiss Federal Polytechnic, he couldn't find a job with his physics degree. However, ___(A)___ working at the patent office, he continued studying physics. Finally, he received the Nobel Prize in physics in 1921. After his emigration to the U.S., he wrote a letter ___(B)___ President Franklin D. Roosevelt to say that the U.S. should not allow Hitler to make atomic bombs first. As a result, he participated in the Manhattan Project ___(C)___ was aimed at making atomic bombs.
> *Swiss Federal Polytechnic: 스위스 연방 공과대학

보기	while　for　who　if　to　which

(A) _____　(B) _____　(C) _____

15 다음 빈칸에 알맞은 단어끼리 바르게 짝지어진 것은?

> • I prefer milk _____ coffee.
> • I am sure she's _____ the airport now.

① than – to
② to　 – with
③ in　 – to
④ to　 – at
⑤ by　 – at

16 다음 빈칸에 들어갈 알맞은 단어를 〈보기〉에서 찾아 한 번씩 쓰세요.

보기	during　for　while

(1) We stayed at Jack's home _____ two weeks.
(2) He hurt his arm _____ he was playing basketball.
(3) I told my friends what I did _____ my trip to New York.

17 다음 빈칸에 알맞은 단어끼리 바르게 짝지어진 것은?

> • He took me _____ a nice restaurant.
> • The interviewer asked me _____ my school days.

① to　 – about
② to – of
③ about – to
④ on – about
⑤ in　 – to

18 주어진 우리말과 같은 뜻이 되도록 빈칸에 알맞은 단어를 쓰세요.

> • 그는 그의 아버지처럼 훌륭한 과학자가 될 것이다.
> = He'll be a good scientist _____ his father.

19 다음 빈칸에 공통으로 들어갈 단어는?

- We went there _____ a car.
- He helped me keep a diary _____ English.

① for   ② in   ③ by
④ on   ⑤ to

20 다음 중 밑줄 친 부분의 쓰임이 어색한 것은?

① Many people go to the beach <u>in</u> summer.
② I talked to Mr. Lee <u>of</u> the phone for an hour.
③ I didn't see your name <u>on</u> the list.
④ Why don't we take a taxi instead <u>of</u> a bus?
⑤ She had intended to take a holiday <u>in</u> Thailand.

21 주어진 문장의 밑줄 친 since와 의미가 같은 것을 모두 고르세요.

We've lived here <u>since</u> 1996.

① We thought that we'd stop by and see him <u>since</u> we were in the area.
② You don't have to go to see her <u>since</u> she's OK.
③ Irene has been working in a bank <u>since</u> leaving school.
④ I haven't eaten anything <u>since</u> breakfast.
⑤ I'm not worried anymore <u>since</u> you're here for me.

22 다음 대화의 빈칸에 들어갈 단어로 알맞은 것은?

A: Have you ever read the book, *Pride and Prejudice*?
B: No, I haven't. What is the book _____?

① of   ② by   ③ from
④ in   ⑤ about

23 다음 빈칸에 공통으로 들어갈 단어는?

- Do you have this shirt _____ size five?
- Cut this cake _____ half.

① from   ② in   ③ out
④ of   ⑤ into

24 다음 글에서 틀린 문장을 2개 찾아 그 기호를 쓰고 완전한 문장으로 다시 쓰세요.

How to Get Along with Coworkers

ⓐ Don't wait until they will speak to you.
ⓑ Speak to them first.
ⓒ Help them ahead before they ask for help.
ⓓ Listen at what they say.
ⓔ If they need your advice, try to give it to them.

(1) _____
(2) _____

25 다음 빈칸에 공통으로 들어갈 단어는?

- The telephone was invented _____ Alexander Graham Bell.
- Is it possible to deliver this package _____ tomorrow?
- He greeted us _____ shaking hands.

① by   ② from   ③ for
④ at   ⑤ to

26 주어진 우리말과 같은 뜻이 되도록 빈칸에 알맞은 단어를 쓰세요.

- 만약 네가 네 자신을 믿는다면, 넌 그것을 해낼 수 있을 것이다.
= If you _____ _____ _____, you'll be able to make it.

27 다음 빈칸에 들어갈 알맞은 단어는?

I am tired _____ eating vegetables.

① as   ② in   ③ of
④ off   ⑤ on

28 각 빈칸에 들어갈 알맞은 전치사를 〈보기〉에서 골라 한 번씩 쓰세요.

| 보기 | on   in   after   with |

(1) I left the books _____ the table.
(2) I'll go to the dentist _____ work.
(3) Is anything wrong _____ your computer?
(4) My brother helped me write a letter _____ English.

29 다음 빈칸에 공통으로 들어갈 말은?

Andrew: What are you reading now?
Carroll: I'm reading *Animal Farm* written by George Orwell.
Andrew: *Animal Farm*? I also _____ reading anti-utopian novels.
Carroll: What does anti-utopian mean?
Andrew: It is the opposite of the word utopian which means "of a perfect or ideal existence." Books _____ *1984* and *Animal Farm* are anti-utopian novels.

*anti-utopian novel: 반이상향 소설

① up   ② like   ③ into
④ around   ⑤ without

30 다음 중 어법상 올바른 문장은?

① I like this restaurant because its delicious food and good service.
② Let's make it on 6 o'clock in front of the department store.
③ My friend James lives at Canada.
④ Why don't we go to the stadium on Saturday afternoon?
⑤ We enjoyed to dance with them.

31 다음 빈칸에 공통으로 들어갈 단어는?

- The woman _____ curly hair is my aunt.
- My daughter walked to school _____ her friend, Jina.

① in ② by ③ on
④ out ⑤ with

32 다음 빈칸 (A)~(E)에 들어갈 수 <u>없는</u> 전치사는?

- It is similar __(A)__ the Korean holiday Chuseok.
- Nobody will laugh __(B)__ you for trying.
- Take pride __(C)__ your health and your figure.
- This book consists __(D)__ 12 chapters.
- I'm good __(E)__ speaking in public.

① for ② to ③ in
④ of ⑤ at

33 다음 빈칸에 들어갈 단어끼리 알맞게 짝지어진 것은?

- Junho usually spends _____ thirty minutes to forty minutes surfing the Internet.
- The box is full _____ letters from my husband.

① from – of
② from – in
③ from – with
④ in – of
⑤ in – on

34 각 빈칸에 들어갈 알맞은 말을 〈보기〉에서 골라 한 번씩 쓰세요.

| 보기 | in with about out of to |

(1) It takes twenty minutes to get from school _____ my house.
(2) I saw smoke coming _____ the house.
(3) Does Yumi live _____ Busan or Ulsan?
(4) Cut the paper _____ your knife carefully.
(5) We need to talk _____ Kevin's strange behavior.

35 다음 빈칸에 알맞은 전치사를 순서대로 바르게 나열한 것은?

- _____ first he was afraid of water, but now he is a good swimmer.
- When Junho arrived at his house, his parents were waiting _____ him anxiously.
- _____ my surprise, I won first prize in the English speech contest.

① For – at – To
② At – to – For
③ To – for – At
④ For – to – At
⑤ At – for – To

36 다음 빈칸에 알맞은 단어끼리 바르게 짝지어진 것은?

- The airplane started _____ Japan.
- Thank you _____ helping me solve the problem.

① to – to
② for – for
③ to – into
④ for – into
⑤ to – for

37 다음 빈칸에 들어갈 알맞은 단어는?

My family was in Canada _____ the summer.

① of
② on
③ at
④ to
⑤ during

38 다음 빈칸에 알맞은 단어끼리 바르게 짝지어진 것은?

- The gates of most _____ the houses were locked.
- When he was young, he was interested _____ invention.

① in – of
② at – in
③ of – in
④ of – to
⑤ in – from

39 다음 우리말과 같은 뜻이 되도록 빈칸에 들어갈 알맞은 단어는?

- 1번부터 시작할까?
  = Shall we start _____ number 1?

① to
② in
③ of
④ for
⑤ with

40 다음 빈칸에 들어갈 알맞은 단어는?

She just kept eating and eating _____ saying a word.

① into
② without
③ from
④ but
⑤ or

41 다음 지도에서 건물 위치를 설명한 문장으로 알맞은 것은?

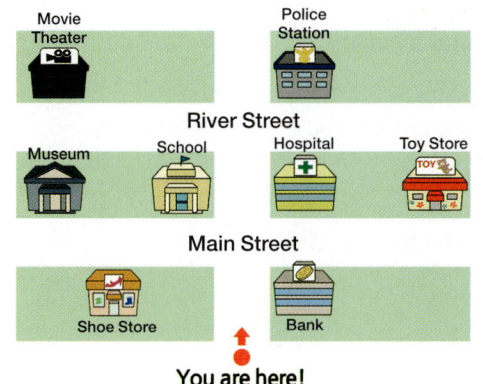

① The museum is next to the bank.
② The police station is across from the shoe store.
③ You have to go straight two blocks and turn right to find the movie theater.
④ Go straight one block and turn left. You will see the school on your right.
⑤ Go straight one block and turn right, then you can see the hospital on your right.

42 〈보기〉의 밑줄 친 like와 쓰임이 같은 것의 개수는?

> 보기
> The box is filled with old things like toys and coins.

ⓐ They like to collect comic books.
ⓑ I grew vegetables like potatoes and tomatoes.
ⓒ My sister sings very well like a singer.
ⓓ Do you also like drawing cartoons?
ⓔ She seems to like watching movies.

① 1개 ② 2개 ③ 3개 ④ 4개 ⑤ 5개

43 다음 빈칸에 공통으로 들어갈 알맞은 단어는?

> • From now _____, I'm going to ride my bike for an hour every day.
> • My family went out for dinner _____ Sunday evening.

① on   ② to   ③ in
④ of   ⑤ with

44 우리말과 같은 뜻이 되도록 할 때 빈칸에 들어갈 단어로 알맞은 것은?

> • 그는 항상 일요일마다 정오까지 잠을 잔다.
>   = He always sleeps _____ noon on Sundays.

① until   ② on   ③ to
④ from   ⑤ at

45 다음 빈칸에 알맞은 전치사를 순서대로 바르게 나열한 것은?

> • The man _____ the brown bag is my dad.
> • The thieves came into the room _____ the window.
> • The house doesn't belong _____ me anymore.

① with – into   – about
② with – through – to
③ with – through – for
④ as   – into   – of
⑤ as   – through – to

46 괄호 안의 단어들을 알맞게 배열하여 문장을 완성할 때, <u>일곱 번째</u>에 오는 단어를 쓰세요.

- Teresa는 1시간 동안 그녀의 친구를 기다렸기 때문에 화가 났다.
  = Teresa got angry (for / friend / she / her / because / for / waited / an hour).

➡ _____

47 다음 빈칸에 공통으로 들어갈 알맞은 단어는?

- You must come back home _____ 6:00.
- I want to build a house _____ the river.

① for ② on ③ at
④ until ⑤ by

48 주어진 문장의 밑줄 친 <u>for</u>와 의미가 같은 것은?

She was standing beside the window <u>for</u> a while.

① My uncle bought a new bike <u>for</u> me.
② This shirt is a little big <u>for</u> you.
③ Many people brought many things <u>for</u> the garage sale.
④ I went there <u>for</u> my swimming lesson.
⑤ She swam in the pool <u>for</u> three hours.

49 다음 빈칸에 알맞은 단어끼리 바르게 짝지어진 것은?

James arrived _____ London at night. He was very tired, so he decided to get some rest _____ a hotel first.

① on – at   ② in – on   ③ in – at
④ on – to   ⑤ in – to

50 다음 빈칸에 공통으로 들어갈 알맞은 단어는?

- He has to hurry up to get to work _____ time.
- He always goes to work _____ foot.

① as   ② on   ③ with
④ in   ⑤ by

51 다음 빈칸에 알맞은 전치사끼리 바르게 짝지어진 것은?

I teach math _____ a girls' middle school in Gwangju. Yesterday was my birthday. When I went _____ the classroom, all the students sang a song for me.

① on – at   ② on – into
③ at – for   ④ at – into
⑤ by – at

52 우리말과 같은 뜻이 되도록 빈칸에 알맞은 단어를 쓰세요.

> • 그는 호주머니에서 그 돈을 꺼냈다.
> = He took the money _____ _____ his pocket.

53 다음 빈칸에 알맞은 단어끼리 바르게 짝지어진 것은?

> *Laura*: Ted, have you seen my passport?
> *Ted* : No. Didn't you put it _____ your bag?
> *Laura*: I can't find it there.
> *Ted* : Have you checked _____ the bed?
> *Laura*: No. Oh, there it is!

① at – on
② in – under
③ on – at
④ in – of
⑤ at – down

54 다음 중 어법상 틀린 문장의 개수를 고르세요.

> I went shopping with my mom at Sunday. We went there by car. There were a lot of goods on sale in the market. My mom bought a cute bag for me. It is made by cotton. My mom also bought a bag which is similar to mine.

① 1개 ② 2개 ③ 3개 ④ 4개 ⑤ 5개

55 다음의 밑줄 친 in과 같은 뜻으로 쓰인 것은?

> In the picture, my cousin David was smiling in his new blue shirt.

① There are cookies in his bag.
② You look very nice in your new skirt.
③ My brother gets up early in the morning.
④ In winter, I go snowboarding with my family.
⑤ Is there a computer in your room?

56 다음 중 짝지어진 두 문장의 의미가 다른 것을 모두 고르세요.

① The box was too heavy for me to carry.
  = The box was heavy enough for me to carry.
② At the age of 10, I could run faster than now.
  = When I was 10, I was able to run faster than now.
③ There used to be a department store here.
  = There was a department store here in the past, but there isn't now.
④ The jar was filled with apple jam.
  = There was a little apple jam left in the jar.
⑤ I'm proud of constructing the building all by myself.
  = I take pride in constructing the building all by myself.

57 다음 빈칸에 공통으로 알맞은 단어를 쓰세요.

- You should bring the book _____ you.
- I like playing _____ my dogs.

58 다음 대화의 우리말 (A)를 조건에 맞게 영작하세요.

W: Will, do you know any good cooking channel on YouTube?
M: Yeah, plenty of them. Why?
W: Well, (A)나는 요리를 매우 못해. So, I'm trying to learn how to cook.
M: Good idea. Let me show you a video for beginners on Chef Baek's cooking class.

조건
- 5단어, 현재시제로 쓸 것
- very, poor를 쓸 것

➡ _____

59 그림을 보고, 각 문장의 밑줄 친 부분을 바르게 고쳐 문장을 다시 쓰세요.

(1) The bear is over the ball.
  ➡ _____

(2) The elephant is in front of the box.
  ➡ _____

(3) The tiger is next to the chair.
  ➡ _____

60 다음 빈칸에 공통으로 들어갈 알맞은 단어는?

The bicycle was invented _____ a toy for the rich. Then, it became a means of transportation. Next, it became a toy again. Now, the bicycle is popular all over the world _____ a means of transportation once more.

① so ② to ③ as
④ of ⑤ by

61 다음 빈칸에 들어갈 알맞은 단어는?

Friends should be there for each other not only in good times but also in bad times. When one friend is _____ trouble, the other friends should be ready to help him or her.

① in ② on ③ for
④ with ⑤ over

62 다음 두 문장의 뜻이 같도록 빈칸에 들어갈 알맞은 단어는?

- Koreans are proud of their traditional clothing, Hanbok.
 = Koreans take pride _____ their traditional clothing, Hanbok.

① at ② on ③ of
④ with ⑤ in

63 다음 빈칸에 알맞은 단어끼리 바르게 짝지어진 것은?

> Wayne: Minsu, look! I got a postcard _____ my older sister.
> Minsu: Oh, that's sweet of her. I love receiving postcards. Where is she?
> Wayne: She's in Hong Kong. She's _____ a trip.

① for – on
② from – to
③ from – on
④ to – in
⑤ for – with

64 다음 글의 빈칸 (A)~(C)에 들어갈 알맞은 말은?

> Hi, my name is Mohamed Rahman. I live in Bangladesh. Last year, I could not go to school for weeks because of the flood. I was very sad. ___(A)___, things are different this year. Today was my first day on a school boat. ___(B)___ going to school, the school came to me! My little sister and I went outside and waited with our friends. When the boat came, we all got excited. I love my school boat. I'm very happy to go ___(C)___ school and study now. I want to teach children like me on a school boat in the future.

	(A)	(B)	(C)
①	And	Instead	to
②	However	Instead of	by
③	However	Instead of	to
④	However	Instead	to
⑤	And	Instead	by

65 다음 대화의 밑줄 친 부분과 바꿔 쓸 수 있는 것은?

> Kim: Hey, what's wrong? You look depressed.
> Tony: I'm worried about my essay.
> Kim: When is your essay due?
> Tony: Next Friday, but I haven't started writing it yet.
> Kim: Don't worry. I think I can help you.
> Tony: Really? How can I ever thank you?

① By when should your essay be handed in?
② By when should you start your essay?
③ When can I write your essay?
④ By when should I help you write your essay?
⑤ Why don't I write the essay for you?

66 다음 그림에 맞게 괄호 안의 단어를 바르게 배열하세요.

➡ _____

_____

(two, glasses, wearing, sat, between, on the subway, a woman, men)

67 다음 대화 중 밑줄 친 부분의 쓰임이 어색한 것은?

① A: How did you come into the house?
　B: Through the window.
② A: Why did you run out of the room so suddenly?
　B: I felt the house shaking.
③ A: Did you find your father?
　B: There were a lot of people in the park. It was impossible to find him between them.
④ A: What are you going to do during your summer vacation?
　B: I'll go camping with my family for two weeks.
⑤ A: I have played the piano since I was five years old.
　B: Wow, you have played the piano for 10 years!

68 다음 중 빈칸에 들어갈 말이 빈칸 ⓐ에 알맞은 말과 다른 것은?

> Ms. Kim : Good morning, Dahye. Are you going to school?
> Dahye　: Yes, I am.
> Ms. Kim : How do you go to school?
> Dahye　: I usually go there ⓐ _____ bus.

① I will turn off the TV _____ 6 o'clock.
② This poem was written _____ my father.
③ I sent you the memo _____ e-mail.
④ He goes to the cinema _____ foot.
⑤ They can learn responsibility _____ doing their homework.

69 다음 중 빈칸에 들어갈 말이 나머지 넷과 다른 하나는?

① I didn't know that his brother was _____ prison at that time.
② I met her _____ a big party last week and we became friends.
③ Her necklace looks so expensive that I can't believe she bought it _____ a garage sale.
④ Do you think you can meet me _____ the airport tomorrow before you take your flight?
⑤ My passport will expire _____ the end of this year.

70 다음 중 짝지어진 두 문장의 뜻이 서로 같지 않은 것은?

① My mother uses this bottle as a vase.
　= This bottle is used as a vase by my mother.
② I think she went to Daegu by plane.
　= I think she took a plane when she went to Daegu.
③ He seems to be in love with that girl in a blue skirt.
　= It seems like he's in love with that girl whose skirt is blue.
④ Jerry's basketball team lost the game by 45:30 score.
　= Jerry's basketball team didn't win the game and the score was 45 to 30.
⑤ It's amazing to see Chloe make such a beautiful candle by using only one hand.
　= It's amazing to see Chloe make such a beautiful candle as one hand.

CHAPTER 17
일치·도치·화법 & 속담

성취도 자기 평가 활용법

구분	평가 기준
Excellent	문법 내용을 모두 이해하고, 문제를 모두 맞힘.
Very good	문법 내용은 충분히 이해했으나 실수로 1~2문제 틀림.
Good	문법 내용이 조금 어려워 3~4문제 틀림.
needs **R**eview	문법 내용 이해가 어렵고, 5문제 이상 틀림. 복습 필요.

PSS 1 시제의 일치	페이지	학습날짜	성취도 자기평가 E V G R	학습체크
PSS 1-1 시제 일치의 원칙	424	/		☐
PSS 1-2 시제 일치의 예외	425	/		☐
PSS 2 도치	426	/		☐
PSS 3 평서문의 화법 전환	428	/		☐
PSS 4 의문문의 화법 전환	430	/		☐
PSS 5 명령문의 화법 전환	432	/		☐
PSS 6 속담	433	/		☐
Chapter Review Test	436	/		☐

PSS 1 시제의 일치

PSS 1-1 시제 일치의 원칙

1. 주절의 동사가 현재시제인 경우 종속절의 동사는 의미에 따라 어떠한 시제든지 쓸 수 있다.

    They **believe** that she **does** her best to overcome her fear.
    그들은 그녀가 그녀의 두려움을 극복하는 데 최선을 다한다고 믿는다.
    They **believe** that she **did** her best to overcome her fear.
    그들은 그녀가 그녀의 두려움을 극복하는 데 최선을 다했다고 믿는다.
    They **believe** that she **will do** her best to overcome her fear.
    그들은 그녀가 그녀의 두려움을 극복하는 데 최선을 다할 것이라고 믿는다.

2. 주절의 동사가 과거시제인 경우 종속절의 동사는 의미에 따라 과거나 과거완료를 써야 한다.

    He **knew** that I **made** a big mistake.
    그는 내가 큰 실수를 한 것을 알았다.
    He **knew** that I **would make** a big mistake.
    그는 내가 큰 실수를 할 것이라는 것을 알았다.
    He **knew** that I **had made** a big mistake.
    그는 내가 큰 실수를 했었다는 것을 알았다.
    cf. 과거완료 시제는 과거의 어느 시점에서 일어난 일보다 더 이전에 있었던 일을 나타낸다.

정답 p.94

PRACTICE 1

다음 문장의 시제를 바꿀 때 빈칸에 알맞은 말을 써서 문장을 완성하세요.

1 I wonder why the subway is extremely crowded.
   ➡ I wondered why _____.

2 The doctor told him that he would get better.
   ➡ The doctor tells him that _____.

3 The taxi driver tells us that there are many fancy restaurants on this street.
   ➡ The taxi driver told us that _____.

4 Everyone said that the Korean team would win the game.
   ➡ _____ that the Korean team will win the game.

5 We are afraid that my son may be late for school on the first day.
   ➡ We were afraid that _____.

PSS 1-2 시제 일치의 예외

1. **현재의 습관, 사실, 격언, 진리는 항상 현재시제로 쓴다.**

   Sally said that she always **starts** her day with a cup of coffee.
   Sally는 그녀가 항상 커피 한 잔으로 그녀의 하루를 시작한다고 말했다.
   I learned that oil **is** lighter than water.
   나는 기름이 물보다 가볍다는 것을 배웠다.
   He taught us that the sun **rises** in the east and **sets** in the west.
   그는 해가 동쪽에서 뜨고 서쪽에서 진다는 것을 우리에게 가르쳤다.
   Mom used to tell me that practice **makes** perfect.
   엄마는 연습이 완벽을 만든다고 나에게 말씀하시곤 하셨다.

2. **역사적 사실은 항상 과거시제로 쓴다.**

   Dad told me that the Korean War **began** in 1950 and **ended** in 1953.
   아빠는 내게 한국 전쟁이 1950년에 일어났고 1953년에 끝났다고 말씀하셨다.

PRACTICE 2

다음 문장의 시제를 바꿀 때 빈칸에 알맞은 말을 써서 문장을 완성하세요.

1 Our history teacher teaches us that Columbus discovered America in 1492.
   ➡ Our history teacher taught us that _____.

2 My best friend, Jack, says that he always goes to school on foot.
   ➡ My best friend, Jack, said that _____.

3 My mom tells my father that the trains leave every 20 minutes.
   ➡ My mom told my father that _____.

4 You learn that water boils at 100℃ and freezes at 0℃.
   ➡ You learned that _____.

5 We hear that nothing is impossible to a willing heart.
   ➡ We heard that _____.

6 My little brother knows that one and one makes two.
   ➡ My little brother knew that _____.

PSS 2 도치

주어와 (조)동사의 어순이 서로 바뀌는 현상을 도치라고 한다. 강조하려는 어구를 문장의 맨 앞으로 가져올 때 도치가 일어난다.

1. 의문문에서의 도치

    의문문에서는 해당 문장이 평서문이 아님을 나타내기 위해 주어와 (조)동사가 도치된다.
    Jina is in her room. ➡ **Is Jina** in her room? Jina는 그녀의 방에 있니?
    You can drive a car. ➡ **Can you** drive a car? 너는 운전을 할 수 있니?
    한편, 의문사가 있는 의문문에서는 의문사가 강조되기 때문에 문장 맨 앞으로 나오고, 주어와 (조)동사가 도치된다.
    What did you do last night? 너는 어젯밤에 무엇을 했니?
    Why is Tim so busy today? Tim은 오늘 왜 그렇게 바쁘니?

    cf. 「How come+주어+동사 ~ ?」
    How come은 Why와 같이 '왜?'라는 의미로 의문문에서 사용된다. 하지만 의문문임에도 How come 뒤에서 주어와 동사의 순서가 바뀌지 않고 평서문과 같이 「주어+동사」의 어순을 유지함을 주의해야 한다.
    How come **you missed** the train? (O) 왜 너는 기차를 놓쳤니?
    How come **did you miss** the train? (X)

2. 「There/Here+동사+주어」

    There **is a bank** across the street.   Here **comes the train**.
    길 건너에 은행이 있다.   (여기에) 기차가 온다.

    cf. 주어가 대명사일 경우에는 주어와 동사의 순서가 바뀌지 않는다.
    Here **they come**.   (여기에) 그들이 온다.

3. 장소나 방향을 나타내는 부사(구)의 도치 – 「부사구+동사+주어」

    A man stood in front of the door.
    ➡ In front of the door **stood a man**. 문 앞에 한 남자가 서 있었다.

    cf. 주어가 대명사일 경우에는 주어와 동사의 순서가 바뀌지 않는다.
    She sat on the bench.
    ➡ On the bench, **she sat**. 벤치에 그녀가 앉았다.

4. 부정어(구)의 도치 – 「부정어+조동사+주어+동사」

    I never saw such a pretty cat.
    ➡ **Never did I see** such a pretty cat. 나는 그렇게 예쁜 고양이는 보지 못했다.

PRACTICE 3

괄호 안의 단어를 바르게 배열하여 문장을 완성하세요.

1. _____ you ordered, sir.
   (are, the pepperoni pizzas, here)

2. _____ that is bound for Busan.
   (the last train, there, goes)

3. _____ standing in a long line, waiting for the tram to arrive.
   (they, here, are)

4. _____ and I didn't?
   (you, got invited, how come)

5. _____ in the past few years.
   (been, there, several, snowstorms, have)

6. If she spent five years in China, _____ so bad?
   (her Chinese, how come, is)

7. _____ to New York, Chicago or Los Angeles?
   (been, you, have)

8. _____ in front of the hospital an hour ago?
   (see, did, who, you)

PRACTICE 4

주어진 문장을 밑줄 친 부분을 강조하는 도치구문으로 바꿔 쓰세요.

1. The sun is still shining <u>behind the clouds</u>.
   ➡ _____

2. He <u>never</u> attended the meeting.
   ➡ _____

3. Charlie understood <u>little</u> about the situation.
   ➡ _____

4. A beautiful tree was <u>on the hill</u>.
   ➡ _____

5. I have <u>never</u> seen such a disaster.
   ➡ _____

평서문의 화법 전환

화법이란 다른 사람의 말을 전달하는 방법이다.

직접 화법: 누군가의 말을 큰 따옴표(" ")를 사용해 직접적으로 전달하는 방법
간접 화법: 누군가의 말을 전달하는 사람의 입장으로 바꿔서 간접적으로 전달하는 방법

직접 화법 He **said**, "**I can't** believe the truth **now**."
그는 "나는 지금 그 사실을 믿을 수 없어."라고 말했다.

⬇

간접 화법 He ① **said** ② (that) ③ **he** ④ **couldn't** believe the truth ⑤ **then**.
그는 그때 그 사실을 믿을 수 없다고 말했다.

① say는 say로, say to는 tell로 전달 동사를 바꾼다.
② 콤마(,)와 큰 따옴표(" ")를 빼고 두 절을 that을 이용하여 연결시킨다. 이때 that은 생략 가능하다.
③ that절의 인칭 대명사는 전달하는 사람의 입장으로 바꾼다.
④ that절의 시제는 전달 동사의 시제에 따라 일치시킨다.
　전달 동사가 현재시제일 때는 종속절의 시제에 변화가 없지만, 과거일 때는 시제 일치의 원칙에 따라 시제를 바꾼다.
⑤ 지시 대명사나 부사(구)는 전달하는 사람의 입장으로 바꾼다.

this[these] ➡ that[those]	here ➡ there	now ➡ then
ago ➡ before	today ➡ that day	
yesterday ➡ the previous day[the day before]		
tomorrow ➡ the next day[the following day]		
last night ➡ the previous night[the night before]		

Tom **said**, "**I'll** go to Jeju Island **tomorrow**."
Tom은 "나는 내일 제주도에 갈 거야."라고 말했다.
➡ Tom **said** (that) **he would** go to Jeju Island **the next day**.
Tom은 다음날 제주도에 갈 거라고 말했다.

Mike **said to** me, "**I am** really interested in music."
Mike는 나에게 "나는 정말 음악에 흥미가 있어."라고 말했다.
➡ Mike **told** me (that) **he was** really interested in music.
Mike는 나에게 자신이 정말 음악에 흥미가 있다고 말했다.

PRACTICE 5

〈보기〉와 같이 주어진 문장을 간접 화법으로 바꿀 때, 빈칸에 알맞은 말을 쓰세요.

> 보 기
> He said to me, "I'm very grateful for your help."
> ➡ He told me that he was very grateful for my help.

1 My brother said, "I know how to play this game."
  ➡ My brother said that _____ how to play _____ game.

2 Jenny said, "My mom may not be at home now."
  ➡ Jenny said that _____ mom _____ at home _____.

3 My friend said to me, "I'm going to learn Taekwondo."
  ➡ My friend _____ me that he _____ Taekwondo.

4 Mom said to us, "It is too cold for you to play baseball outside today."
  ➡ Mom _____ us that it _____ too cold for us to play baseball outside _____.

5 Tom said, "I will meet her tomorrow."
  ➡ Tom said that _____ meet her _____.

PRACTICE 6

〈보기〉와 같이 간접 화법은 직접 화법으로, 직접 화법은 간접 화법으로 바꾸세요.

> 보 기
> He said, "I will go to America."
> ➡ He said that he would go to America.
> Sarah told me that she played golf every weekend.
> ➡ Sarah said to me, "I play golf every weekend."

1 My younger brother said that the computer game was too difficult for him to play.
  ➡ _____

2 The man said to her, "It will take about two hours from now."
  ➡ _____

3 The boy said, "I don't want to eat these carrots."
  ➡ _____

4 The chairman told the members that the money was raised by donations.
  ➡ _____

5 Father said, "It will be nice to visit here again next summer."
  ➡ _____

# 의문문의 화법 전환

1. **의문사가 있는 의문문의 화법 전환**

    He **said to** me, "What is your favorite sport?"
    그는 나에게 "네가 좋아하는 스포츠가 뭐니?"라고 말했다.

    ⬇

    He ① **asked** me ② **what** ③ **my favorite sport was**.
    그는 나에게 내가 좋아하는 스포츠가 무엇인지 물었다.

    ① say나 say to를 ask로 바꾼다.
    ② 콤마(,)와 큰 따옴표(" "), 물음표(?)를 빼고 의문사로 두 절을 연결한다.
    ③ 인칭 대명사와 시제를 적절하게 바꾸고, 어순을 「주어+동사」로 변경한다. 단, 의문사가 주어인 경우에는 「의문사+동사」의 어순을 그대로 유지한다.

    He said to me, "What do you mean?"
    그는 나에게 "무슨 뜻이야?"라고 말했다.
    ➡ He **asked** me **what I meant**.
     그는 나에게 무슨 뜻이냐고 물었다.

    Mina said, "Who can make me a dress?"
    미나는 "누가 나에게 드레스를 만들어 줄 수 있을까?"라고 말했다.
    ➡ Mina **asked who could make her** a dress.
     미나는 누가 그녀에게 드레스를 만들어 줄 수 있는지 물었다.

2. **의문사가 없는 의문문의 화법 전환**

    He **said**, "Are you ready to order?"
    그는 "주문할 준비가 되셨나요?"라고 말했다.

    ⬇

    He ① **asked** ② **if[whether]** ③ **I was** ready to order.
    그는 내가 주문할 준비가 됐는지 물었다.

    ① say나 say to를 ask로 바꾼다.
    ② 콤마(,)와 큰 따옴표(" "), 물음표(?)를 빼고 if나 whether로 두 절을 연결한다.
    ③ 인칭 대명사와 시제를 적절하게 바꾸고, 어순을 「주어+동사」로 변경한다.

    She said, "Is he good at playing baseball?"
    그녀는 "그는 야구를 잘하니?"라고 말했다.
    ➡ She **asked if[whether] he was** good at playing baseball.
     그녀는 그가 야구를 잘하는지 물었다.

The man said to me, "Have you ever been to Hong Kong?"
그 남자는 나에게 "홍콩에 가본 적 있어요?"라고 말했다.
➡ The man **asked** me **if[whether] I had ever been** to Hong Kong.
그 남자는 나에게 홍콩에 가본 적이 있는지 물었다.

PRACTICE 7

정답 p.94

〈보기〉와 같이 주어진 문장을 간접 화법으로 바꾸세요.

> 보 기
> He said to me, "How often do you visit my blog?"
> ➡ He asked me how often I visited his blog.
>
> The man said to me, "Do you enjoy working out?"
> ➡ The man asked me if[whether] I enjoyed working out.

1 Kevin said to her, "May I use your dictionary?"
➡ _____

2 Mom said, "Who's calling?"
➡ _____

3 The coach said to us, "What are your hopes for this year?"
➡ _____

4 He said to Jane, "When do you usually watch TV?"
➡ _____

5 He said to me, "Are you for or against dieting?"
➡ _____

6 Andy said to me, "Do you know how to make a movie clip on your phone?"
➡ _____

7 The man said to her, "Can you say that again?"
➡ _____

8 The gentleman said to the boy, "What makes you think so?"
➡ _____

9 I said to James, "Can you lend me your bike?"
➡ _____

10 Bob said, "Where can I get the ticket?"
➡ _____

 # 명령문의 화법 전환

She **said to** her son, "Stay home."
그녀는 그녀의 아들에게 "집에 있어라."라고 말했다.

⬇

She ① **told** her son ② **to stay** home.
그녀는 그녀의 아들에게 집에 있으라고 말했다.

① 전달 동사는 명령문의 어조에 따라 tell, ask, advise, order 등으로 바꾼다.

명령	tell, order, command
충고	advise
부탁 (주로 please가 있는 문장)	ask, beg

② 명령문의 동사원형을 to부정사로 바꾼다. (부정 명령문의 경우 Don't나 Never를 없애고, 동사원형을 not to부정사로 바꾼다.)

The doctor said to me, "Stop eating spicy foods."
의사가 나에게 "매운 음식을 그만 드세요."라고 말했다.
➡ The doctor **told** me **to stop** eating spicy foods.
의사가 나에게 매운 음식을 그만 먹으라고 말했다.

He said to me, "Don't stand in the middle."
그는 나에게 "중간에 서지 말아라."고 말했다.
➡ He **ordered** me **not to stand** in the middle. 그는 나에게 중간에 서지 말라고 명령했다.

정답 p.95

PRACTICE 8

〈보기〉와 같이 주어진 문장을 괄호 안의 단어를 이용하여 간접 화법으로 바꾸세요.

> 보 기
> He said to me, "Watch out while you are swimming." (advise)
> ➡ He advised me to watch out while I was swimming.
>
> The father said to his son, "Don't go near the fire." (tell)
> ➡ The father told his son not to go near the fire.

1 She said to her neighbor, "Look on the bright side." (advise)
➡

2 Tom said to me, "Bring me a chair." (tell)
➡ _____

3 Jim said to me, "Tell me when her birthday is." (tell)
➡ _____

4 The police officer said to him, "Don't move." (order)
➡ _____

5 Mom said to me, "Pass me the salt, please." (ask)
➡ _____

6 The doctor said to me, "Don't eat too much junk food." (advise)
➡ _____

7 Patrick said to his son, "Wear a helmet on the bike." (order)
➡ _____

8 Mr. Anderson said to us, "Don't be late." (tell)
➡ _____

속담

1. **Time is money.**
   시간이 돈이다.

2. **Haste makes waste.**
   서두름이 낭비를 만든다. (급히 서두르면 일을 망친다.)

3. **Like father, like son.**
   그 아버지에 그 아들. (부전자전)

4. **Better late than never.**
   늦는 것이 안 하는 것보다 낫다.

5. **A watched pot never boils.**
   지켜보는 냄비는 끓지 않는다.

6. **After a storm comes a calm.**
   폭풍 후에 평온함이 온다. (비 온 뒤에 땅이 굳어진다.)

7. **Blood is thicker than water.**
   피는 물보다 진하다.

Time is money.

A watched pot never boils.

8. Strike while the iron is hot.
   쇠가 달았을 때 두드려라. (쇠뿔도 단김에 빼라.)

9. He laughs best who laughs last.
   최후에 웃는 사람이 승자다.

10. The foot of the candle is dark.
    등잔 밑이 어둡다.

11. A rolling stone gathers no moss.
    구르는 돌에는 이끼가 끼지 않는다. (① 자주 옮겨 다니는 사람은 모으는 것이 없다. ② 부지런한 사람은 침체되지 않는다.)

12. Actions speak louder than words.
    말보다 행동이다. (말보다 행동이 더 설득력 있다.)

13. Every cloud has a silver lining.
    모든 구름의 뒤편은 은빛으로 빛난다. (괴로움 뒤에는 기쁨이 있다.)

14. A friend in need is a friend indeed.
    어려울 때 돕는 친구가 참된 친구다.

15. The pen is mightier than the sword.
    펜은 칼보다 더 강하다.

16. Out of the frying pan into the fire.
    튀김 팬에서 불 속으로. (갈수록 태산이다.)

17. Where there is a will, there is a way.
    뜻이 있는 곳에 길이 있다.

18. A bird in the hand is worth two in the bush.
    제 손 안의 한 마리 새는 숲 속의 두 마리보다 낫다.

19. Don't count your chickens before they are hatched.
    부화하기도 전에 병아리 수를 세지 마라. (김칫국부터 마시지 마라.)

PRACTICE 9

다음 우리말에 맞게 빈칸에 알맞은 말을 쓰세요.

1 펜은 칼보다 더 강하다.
→ The pen is _____ the sword.

2 비 온 뒤에 땅이 굳어진다.
→ After a storm _____.

3 쇠뿔도 단김에 빼라.
→ _____ while the iron is _____.

4 튀김 팬에서 불 속으로. (갈수록 태산이다.)
→ _____ the frying pan _____ the fire.

5 어려울 때 돕는 친구가 참된 친구다.
→ A friend _____ is a friend _____.

6 피는 물보다 진하다.
→ Blood is _____ water.

7 말보다 행동이다.
→ Actions _____ than words.

8 지켜보는 냄비는 끓지 않는다.
→ _____ never boils.

9 뜻이 있는 곳에 길이 있다.
→ Where there is _____, there is _____.

10 구르는 돌에는 이끼가 끼지 않는다.
→ A rolling stone _____.

11 제 손 안의 한 마리 새는 숲 속의 두 마리보다 낫다.
→ A bird in the hand _____ two in the bush.

12 늦는 것이 안 하는 것보다 낫다.
→ _____ than _____.

13 서두름이 낭비를 만든다. (급히 서두르면 일을 망친다.)
→ _____ makes _____.

14 최후에 웃는 사람이 승자다.
→ He laughs best _____.

15 부화하기도 전에 병아리 수를 세지 마라. (김칫국부터 마시지 마라.)
→ Don't count your chickens _____.

Chapter Review Test

정답 p.95

CHAPTER 17
일치 · 도치 · 화법 & 속담

1 다음을 간접 화법으로 바꿀 때 어법상 어색한 것은?

She said, "I don't have to finish the report today."
➡ She said that she doesn't have to finish
  ①   ②   ③   ④
  the report that day.
             ⑤

2 다음 문장을 간접 화법으로 바꿀 때 빈칸에 들어갈 말로 알맞은 것은?

My friend said to me, "What do you want to do this weekend?"
➡ My friend asked me _____ to do that weekend.

① what you want   ② whether I wanted
③ what I do want   ④ what I wanted
⑤ whether I want

3 다음 문장의 화법을 올바르게 전환한 것은?

Jack said, "I will keep my mouth closed."

① Jack said that I will keep my mouth closed.
② Jack said that he will keep his mouth closed.
③ Jack told he would keep his mouth closed.
④ Jack told that he kept his mouth closed.
⑤ Jack said that he would keep his mouth closed.

4 다음 문장 중 어법상 어색한 것을 두 개 고르시오.

① How come did you visit his house?
② On the desk lay today's newspaper.
③ Hardly I met a kind person like him.
④ Under the table he is with his son.
⑤ Never has she seen such a gentle boy.

5 다음 빈칸에 알맞은 말끼리 바르게 짝지은 것은?

The general said to his soldiers, "Charge!"
➡ The general _____ his soldiers _____ charge.

① said to   – to   ② said   – to
③ told   – not to ④ advised   – to
⑤ ordered   – to

6 다음을 간접 화법으로 바꿀 때, 빈칸에 알맞은 말끼리 바르게 짝지은 것은?

Mom said, "I'm writing invitation cards to my guests."
➡ Mom said that she _____ invitation cards to _____.

① writing – her guests
② wrote – her guests
③ was writing – my guests
④ wrote – my guests
⑤ was writing – her guests

7 다음 대화의 빈칸에 알맞은 속담은?

A: What are you doing now?
B: I'm collecting data for my report.
A: Do you need my help? I think it will take a long time.
B: No thanks. I don't want to take up your time.
A: _____
You can save time with my help. Let's do it together.

① Many hands make light work.
② After a storm comes a calm.
③ Every cloud has a silver lining.
④ Blood is thicker than water.
⑤ The foot of the candle is dark.

8 다음 글의 내용과 어울리는 속담은?

There once was a goose that always wanted to fly. So he practiced hard, always thinking he could fly someday. His friends thought he was a fool. But he didn't mind and kept trying to fly every day. One day, the goose stood on the roof. He jumped from the roof and began to fly high in the sky. His friends just looked at him with envious eyes.

① Time flies like an arrow.
② Like father, like son.
③ Where there is a will, there is a way.
④ The foot of the candle is dark.
⑤ The pen is mightier than the sword.

9 다음을 간접 화법으로 바꿀 때 빈칸에 들어갈 알맞은 말을 쓰세요.

He said to me, "How do you know the guy?"
➡ He asked me how _____.

10 다음 〈보기〉를 참고하여, 다음 문장을 완성하세요.

| 보기 |
He seldom realizes that he is happy.
➡ Seldom does he realize that he is happy.

(1) I never saw a boring movie like this.
　➡ Never _____.

(2) A pretty girl stood in front of the door.
　➡ In front of the door _____.

(3) He could hardly ride his bike.
　➡ Hardly _____.

11 다음 화법 전환 중 틀린 부분을 한 군데 찾아 바르게 고치세요.

Mr. Kim said to me, "Why do you think she is bad?"
➡ Mr. Kim asked me why I think she was bad.

_____ ➡ _____

12 다음 문장을 간접 화법으로 올바르게 전환한 것은?

> I said to the woman, "May I visit here with my family?"

① I said the woman if may I visit here with my family.
② I told the woman if may I visit there with my family.
③ I asked the woman whether I might visit there with my family.
④ I asked the woman whether I may visit there with my family.
⑤ I asked the woman if I might visit here with my family.

13 다음 글의 내용과 어울리는 속담은?

> A college student named Emily thought riding a bicycle on a busy road was very dangerous. Sometimes cars came close to hitting her when she was riding her bike on the road. She really wanted to ride her bike safely. So, she made a device that produced a laser image in front of her bicycle. Its purpose was to alert drivers that a passing bicycle was nearby. She hoped that the device would reduce bicycle accidents on the road.

① Step by step one goes a long way.
② Necessity is the mother of invention.
③ Out of the frying pan into the fire.
④ A friend in need is a friend indeed.
⑤ A bird in the hand is worth two in the bush.

14 다음을 간접 화법으로 바꿀 때 빈칸에 알맞은 말을 쓰세요.

> Mr. Kim said to me, "Don't forget to pay your utility bill."

➡ Mr. Kim told me _____ _____ forget to pay _____ utility bill.

15 다음 중 어법상 올바른 문장을 모두 고른 것은?

> (a) Rarely does Wendy offer to help.
> (b) In the parking lot were various cars.
> (c) There is a lot of people in the train.
> (d) Under the bridge does the stream flow.
> (e) Here is the most exciting part of the book.

① (a), (b), (c) ② (a), (b), (e) ③ (a), (c), (d)
④ (b), (c), (d) ⑤ (c), (d), (e)

16 대화 (A)를 읽고, 대화 (B)를 완성하세요.

(A) **At school**
Thomas: What are you going to do during summer vacation?
Esther : I will go fishing with my father. How about you?
Thomas: I will go to Canada where my uncle lives.

(B) **At Esther's home**
Esther : Mom, Thomas asked me _____(1)_____ to do during summer vacation.
Mom : What did you say?
Esther : I said I would go fishing with my father. He said that _____(2)_____ where his uncle lives.
Mom : That sounds nice.

(1) ____ ____ ____ ____
(2) ____ ____ ____ ____ ____

17 〈보기〉와 같이 문장을 전환하세요.

보기
Father said to me, "Get out of my car."
➡ Father ordered me to get out of his car.

Deborah said to Davis, "Please buy this necklace for me."
➡ _____
_____

18 다음 글의 밑줄 친 우리말을 영어로 바르게 옮긴 것은?

We have to hand in our homework by tomorrow. Yesterday, I finished my homework and was about to go shopping with my mother. Just then, my friend Michael called me. He said that he couldn't do his homework because he had to take care of his younger brothers. <u>그는 내게 자기 숙제 하는 걸 도와달라고 부탁했다.</u> I decided to help him instead of going shopping.

① He asked me help him do his homework.
② He asks me to help him do his homework.
③ He asked me to help him do his homework.
④ He would ask me help him do his homework.
⑤ He asks me help him do his homework.

19 다음 빈칸에 들어갈 알맞은 말은?

I can't believe ten years have passed since I saw Tim at the meeting. Like they say, _____.
It was as if we had just seen each other yesterday. For ten years, I have always tried to love and respect him.

① a friend in need is a friend indeed
② time flies like an arrow
③ strike while the iron is hot
④ a rolling stone gathers no moss
⑤ every cloud has a silver lining

20 다음 대화의 밑줄 친 부분 중 어법상 어색한 것을 모두 고르세요.

> Father: You're still playing that computer game! Didn't you hear ① what I said to you?
> Son : I did. I know you told me ② to not spend too much time on it.
> Father: Then stop playing it and let's go outside ③ to play basketball together.
> Son : No, the reporter on the news said ④ that it would rain.
> Father: I thought he said it ⑤ will be only cloudy. I'll check it out.

21 다음 문장을 직접 화법으로 바꿀 때 빈칸에 알맞은 말을 쓰세요.

(1) He told me to cheer up.
→ He _____ _____ me, "Cheer up."

(2) Sally told me not to read her diary.
→ Sally _____ _____ me, "_____ read my diary."

(3) Mr. Pacino asked me if I had ever seen his movie.
→ Mr. Pacino _____ _____ me, "_____ you ever seen my movie?"

22 다음 우리말 해석을 괄호 안의 말을 이용하여 영어로 쓰세요.

> Jane은 그에게 그가 충분한 돈을 가지고 있는지 물어보았다.

→ _____
   _____ (ask)

23 다음 영어 속담의 우리말 의미가 잘못된 것은?

① Haste makes waste. (급히 서두르면 일을 망친다.)
② Strike while the iron is hot. (쇠뿔도 단김에 빼라.)
③ A friend in need is a friend indeed. (어려울 때 돕는 친구가 참된 친구다.)
④ Every cloud has a silver lining. (모든 사물은 이면을 가지고 있다.)
⑤ Don't count your chickens before they are hatched. (김칫국부터 마시지 마라.)

24 주어진 문장을 밑줄 친 부분을 강조하는 도치 구문으로 바꿔 쓰세요.

> He has never had any training on the cello.

→ _____

25 주어진 문장을 도치 구문으로 바꿔 쓴 것 중 어법상 어색한 것을 고르세요.

① She seldom drinks coffee at night.
  → Seldom does she drink coffee at night.
② The man stood in front of the mirror.
  → In front of the mirror stood the man.
③ I little imagined he would say such a thing.
  → Little I did imagine he would say such a thing.
④ We lived in the town called Kendal.
  → In the town called Kendal we lived.
⑤ They have never seen such a beautiful picture.
  → Never have they seen such a beautiful picture.

영어의 8품사

		예문
명사	**사람, 사물, 동물의 이름**을 나타내는 말 → 주어, 목적어, 보어 예) Jane, Mr. Brown, desk, chair, computer, bag, dog, bird	This **computer** looks new. 이 컴퓨터는 새것처럼 보인다. I have a **dog**. 나는 개가 한 마리 있다.
대명사	명사를 **대신**하는 말 → 주어, 목적어, 보어 예) I, my, you, he, she, it, them, we, myself, yourself, ourselves	Look at the dog! **It** is cute. 개 좀 봐! 그것은 귀여워. I'm proud of **myself**. 나는 내 자신이 자랑스럽다.
동사	**행위, 동작, 상태를 묘사**하며 '~다'로 해석되는 말 → 서술어 - 일반동사: 주로 움직임을 나타내며 '~하다'라고 해석 예) walk, run, eat, study, play, make, buy, love, like - be동사: 상태나 위치를 주로 묘사하며 '~이다'라고 해석 예) am, are, is, was, were	We **eat** dinner at 7. 우리는 7시에 저녁을 먹는다. She **loves** her daughter. 그녀는 그녀의 딸을 사랑한다. I **am** an artist. 나는 예술가이다.
형용사	**명사**를 꾸미거나 보충 설명하는 말 → 수식어, 보어 **생김새, 색깔, 크기, 성격, 특징**을 묘사하는 말 예) pretty, beautiful, red, tall, big, small, nice, kind, easy, difficult	She has **big** eyes. 그녀는 큰 눈을 가지고 있다. He is a **kind** boy. 그는 친절한 소년이다. The book is **easy**. 그 책은 쉽다.
부사	**형용사, 동사, 다른 부사, 문장 전체**를 자세히 설명하여 문장의 의미를 더욱 풍부하게 하는 말 → 수식어 **시간, 장소, 정도, 빈도**를 묘사하는 말 예) now, here, very, well, always, early, really, happily, sadly	What are you doing **now**? 지금 뭐 하고 있어? Your sister is **very** pretty. 네 언니는 무척 예쁘다. We **really** enjoyed the party. 우리는 정말 그 파티를 즐겼다.
접속사	**단어와 단어, 구와 구, 절과 절**을 이어주는 말 - 등위접속사: **같은 종류**의 말을 연결 예) and, but, or, so - 종속접속사: **명사절, 부사절, 형용사절**을 **주절**에 연결 예) because, when, as, if	She is old **and** wise. 그녀는 나이가 있고 지혜롭다. I slept early, **because** I was tired. 나는 피곤했기 때문에 일찍 잤다.
전치사	명사 앞에서 **시간, 장소, 방향, 위치**를 나타내는 말 예) at, on, in, before, after, under, from, to, for, with, between, in front of	I sleep **at** 11 p.m. 나는 밤 11시에 잔다. Your pen is **under** the chair. 네 펜은 의자 밑에 있다. Let's meet **in front of** the building. 건물 앞에서 만나자.
감탄사	**감정**을 표현하는 말 예) Oh, Wow, Well	**Wow**, you got a new phone! 와, 너 새로운 전화기를 샀구나!

필수문법용어 : 문장의 구성 단위와 성분

		예문
단어	의미를 지니는 **말의 최소 단위** 명사, 대명사, 동사, 형용사, 부사, 전치사, 접속사, 감탄사로 나눌 수 있음	He lied to all of us. 그는 우리 모두에게 거짓말을 했다.
구	완결된 의미를 가지고 있는 두 단어 이상의 모음으로 **주어와 동사를 포함하지 않음** - 명사구 → 주어, 목적어, 보어 - 형용사구 → 명사 수식 - 부사구 → 동사, 형용사, 다른 부사, 문장 전체 수식	There is a pencil on the desk. 책상 위에 연필이 있다. Thank you for helping me. 나를 도와주어서 고마워.
절	완결된 의미를 가지고 있는 두 단어 이상의 모음으로 **주어와 동사를 반드시 포함** - 대등절: 등위접속사로 연결된 대등한 절 - 종속절: 주절에 종속접속사로 연결되어 명사, 형용사, 부사의 역할을 함	She got very angry, but she tried not to show it. 그녀는 매우 화가 났지만, 그것을 보이려고 하지 않았다. Please let me know if he is kind. 그가 친절한지 아닌지 내게 알려 줘.
주어	동작이나 상태의 **주체**를 가리키는 말	She arrived at her office. 그녀는 그녀의 사무실에 도착했다.
동사	주어의 **동작이나 상태**를 나타내는 말	He is a nurse. 그는 간호사이다. They call her an angel. 그들은 그녀를 천사라 부른다.
목적어	동작이나 상태의 **대상**을 가리키는 말	I put this rabbit in the hat. 나는 모자에 이 토끼를 넣는다.
보어	주어나 목적어를 **보충 설명**해 주는 말	I want to become a teacher. 나는 선생님이 되고 싶다. He forced me to hurry. 그는 내가 서두르도록 강요했다.
수식어	문장의 주요 성분을 **부연 설명**하는 역할 생략해도 문법적인 오류를 일으키지 않음	You look pretty tired. 너 꽤 피곤해 보여.

탄탄한 영어 실력을 위한 영문법의 시작

마더텅
영문법 3800제
정답과 해설

토익·토플
TEPS
공무원영어
대비

INTERMEDIATE 2

영문법 기초 개념 정리

문장의 성분

영어 문장은 네 가지 주요 성분(주어, 동사, 목적어, 보어)과 수식어로 이루어진다.

Ruth *started* laughing when he saw the picture.   Ruth는 그가 그 그림을 보았을 때 웃기 시작했다.
주어 / 동사 / 목적어 / 수식어

She *made* him clean up the plate every day.   그녀는 그가 매일 접시를 씻도록 만들었다.
주어 / 동사 / 목적어 / 목적격 보어 / 수식어

1. 주어: 동작이나 상태의 주체를 가리키는 말이다.
   They left for Paris last night.   그들은 지난밤에 파리로 떠났다.

2. 동사: 주어의 동작이나 상태를 나타내는 말이다.
   She **kicked** the ball as hard as she could.   그녀는 최대한 공을 세게 찼다.

3. 목적어: 동작이나 상태의 대상을 가리키는 말이다.
   The factory makes **washing machines**.   그 공장은 세탁기를 만든다.

4. 보어: 주어나 목적어를 보충 설명해 주는 말이다.
   He wants to become **a teacher**.   그는 선생님이 되고 싶어 한다.
   My parents encouraged me **to try new things**.   나의 부모님은 내가 새로운 일을 시도하도록 격려하셨다.

5. 수식어: 문장의 주요 성분을 부연 설명하는 역할을 하며 생략해도 문법적인 오류를 일으키지 않는다.
   The girls (chatting in the classroom) are twins.   교실에서 수다를 떨고 있는 소녀들은 쌍둥이다.
   주어 / 수식어 / 동사 주격 보어

문장의 5형식

영어 문장은 다음과 같이 5가지 형태로 나뉜다.

1형식	주어(S)+동사(V)	The baby cried. 아기가 울었다. S V
2형식	주어(S)+동사(V)+주격 보어(S.C)	He looks happy. 그는 행복해 보인다. S V S.C
3형식	주어(S)+동사(V)+목적어(O)	Amy likes her teacher. Amy는 그녀의 선생님을 좋아한다. S V O
4형식	주어(S)+동사(V) +간접목적어(I.O)+직접목적어(D.O)	We sent him a postcard. 우리는 그에게 엽서를 한 장 보냈다. S V I.O D.O
5형식	주어(S)+동사(V) +목적어(O)+목적격 보어(O.C)	She heard the birds sing. 그녀는 새들이 노래하는 것을 들었다. S V O O.C

정답 및 해설
Problem Solving Skill

Chapter 1	문장의 기초 Introduction to Sentences	p.2
Chapter 2	시제 Tense	p.8
Chapter 3	조동사 Modals	p.16
Chapter 4	수동태 Passive Voice	p.21
Chapter 5	명사와 관사 Nouns and Articles	p.25
Chapter 6	대명사 Pronouns	p.32
Chapter 7	부정사 Infinitives	p.37
Chapter 8	동명사 Gerunds	p.43
Chapter 9	분사 Participles	p.48
Chapter 10	형용사 Adjectives	p.53
Chapter 11	부사 Adverbs	p.59
Chapter 12	가정법 Conditionals	p.65
Chapter 13	비교구문 Comparisons	p.69
Chapter 14	관계사 Relatives	p.76
Chapter 15	접속사 Conjunctions	p.81
Chapter 16	전치사 Prepositions	p.87
Chapter 17	일치·도치·화법 & 속담 Agreement·Inversion·Narration & Proverbs	p.94

마더텅

CHAPTER 1 문장의 기초
Introduction to Sentences

본문 _ p.6

PRACTICE 1

1 Can she get there on time?
2 Aren't those gloves yours?
3 Doesn't he go to church on Sundays?
4 Is your mom angry at you?
5 Was David drawing a picture?
6 Can this be true?
7 Do many people make plans for the New Year?
8 Didn't your brother win the race?

> 1, 6 조동사 can이 포함된 문장을 의문문으로 바꿀 때 조동사를 문장 맨 앞으로 옮겨서 「조동사+주어+동사원형~?」의 형태로 만든다.
> 2, 4, 5 be동사가 있는 문장을 의문문으로 바꿀 때 be동사(와 부정어)를 문장 맨 앞으로 옮겨서 「Be동사(+부정어)+주어~?」의 형태로 만든다.
> 3, 8 부정어를 포함한 일반동사가 있는 문장을 의문문으로 바꿀 때 「do[does, did]+부정어」를 문장 맨 앞으로 옮겨서 「Do[Does, Did]+부정어+주어+동사원형~?」의 형태로 만든다.
> 7 일반동사의 긍정형인 make가 사용된 문장을 의문문으로 바꿀 때 do를 복수 주어(Many people)의 인칭과 동사의 시제에 맞게 사용하여 「Do+주어+동사원형~?」의 형태로 만든다.

PRACTICE 2

1 Yes, he does.
2 No, they don't.
3 Yes, I did.
4 No, he wasn't.
5 Yes, I was.
6 Yes, they can.
7 Yes, he does.
8 No, she isn't.

> 2, 3, 5, 7, 8 부정어가 포함된 동사로 시작하는 의문문에 대한 대답은 질문과 상관없이 대답의 내용이 긍정적이면 yes, 부정적이면 no로 표현한다. 그러나 yes/no에 대한 우리말 해석은 반대로 됨에 유의해야 한다.
> 2 B: 네, 그들은 가지고 있지 않습니다.
> 3 B: 아니오, 저는 (바깥이 춥다고) 느꼈습니다.
> 5 B: 아니오, 저는 배가 고팠습니다.
> 7 B: 아니오, 그는 열심히 공부합니다.
> 8 B: 네, 그녀는 (스포츠를) 잘 하지 못합니다.

PRACTICE 3

1 Who did you meet at the restaurant?
2 Why is Kelly so busy today?
3 What did he say to you?
4 Where did you find the key?
5 When will he return from the trip?
6 How do I use this machine?
7 How is everything with you?

PRACTICE 4

2 When is
3 How was
4 Where did
5 Why were[What made]
6 Who is
7 What did
8 Where do
9 When did
10 Why did[What made]

PRACTICE 5

1 are you
2 isn't it
3 did she
4 doesn't it
5 couldn't he
6 wasn't it
7 do they
8 weren't they
9 are they
10 will she
11 doesn't she
12 didn't he

> 1, 3, 7, 9, 10 부정문의 부가 의문문은 조동사, be동사, do동사의 긍정형으로 만든다. 7, 9번의 경우 주어에 those, these가 포함되어 있으므로 인칭대명사는 they가 적절하다.
> 2, 5, 6, 8 긍정문의 부가 의문문은 조동사, be동사, do동사의 부정형으로 만든다. 8번의 주어 the children은 복수형이므로 인칭대명사는 they가 적절하다.
> 4, 11, 12 일반동사의 긍정형이 사용된 문장의 부가 의문문은 do를 주어의 인칭과 동사의 시제에 맞게 사용하여 「doesn't/didn't+인칭대명사?」의 형태로 만든다.

PRACTICE 6

1 will you
2 don't I
3 isn't it
4 shall we
5 didn't he
6 were they
7 shall we
8 am I not[aren't I]
9 will you[won't you]
10 can they

> 1 부정명령문의 부가 의문문은 'will you?'만 사용한다. 명령문은 주어 you가 생략된 것으로 간주하기 때문에 부가 의문문의 주어는 항상 you이다.
> 4, 7 'Let's~'로 시작하는 문장의 부가 의문문은 'shall we?'를 사용한다.
> 9 긍정명령문의 부가 의문문은 어조에 따라서 명령조일 때는 'will you?', 정중하게 말할 때는 'won't you?'를 쓴다.
> 오늘 밤 내게 전화해 줘, 알겠니? - 명령
> 오늘 밤 내게 전화해 줘, 그렇게 해 주지 않을래? - 권유

PRACTICE 7

1 Steak
2 soccer
3 a skirt
4 noodles
5 My mother
6 by train

CHAPTER 1

PRACTICE 8

1. what that means
2. if[whether] it is important
3. how I can get to the subway station
4. who broke the window
5. if[whether] you passed the exam
6. if[whether] you love Mike
7. if[whether] she can swim
8. if[whether] Kate was seeing him
9. where she lives
10. if[whether] Max bought a new car
11. how much this book costs

> 1, 3, 9, 11 의문사가 있는 의문문을 간접 의문문으로 바꿀 때는 「의문사+주어+동사~」순이 된다. 의문문 구조를 만드는 데 사용되었던 do동사를 없애면서 시제와 수를 일반동사에 적용하면 된다. 11번의 경우 how와 much를 하나의 묶음으로 간주한다.
> 2, 5, 6, 7, 8, 10 의문사가 없는 의문문을 간접 의문문으로 바꿀 때, 의문문의 내용은 if나 whether이 이끄는 명사절의 일부가 되면서 「if[whether]+주어+동사」 구조로 쓰인다. 5번과 10번의 경우 문장의 시제가 과거임을 주의한다.
> 4 의문사 who가 간접 의문문의 주어로 쓰였기 때문에 직접 의문문의 어순을 그대로 사용한다.

PRACTICE 9

1. What do you think he is making?
2. Do you know when he arrived?
3. Who do you believe is right?
4. Why do you think we should learn English?
5. I don't know if[whether] Susan has feelings for me.
6. When do you believe he will come?
7. What do you guess will happen next?
8. Can you tell me if[whether] there are bookstores near here?
9. How do you think we can solve this problem?
10. I wonder how old your brother is.
11. Where do you believe you lost it?
12. Why do you suppose he is so upset?

> 1, 3, 4, 6, 7, 9, 11, 12 간접 의문문이 포함된 문장에서 think, believe, suppose, guess와 같이 생각이나 추측을 나타내는 동사가 주절에 있을 때는 간접 의문문의 의문사가 문장 맨 앞에 위치한다.
> 2, 10 의문사가 있는 의문문을 간접 의문문으로 바꿀 때 「의문사+주어+동사」 구조로 쓴다. 10번의 경우 how와 old를 하나의 묶음으로 간주한다. how your brother is old로 쓰지 않도록 주의한다.

> 5, 8 의문사가 없는 의문문을 간접 의문문으로 바꿀 때 「if[whether]+주어+동사」 구조로 쓴다.

PRACTICE 10

1. How patient you are!
2. How hot and humid it is!
3. What a well-known writer she is!
4. What an excellent painting that is!
5. How angry they were!
6. How exciting this journey is!
7. What terrible players they were!
8. What a friendly teacher she is!
9. How polite he was!
10. What beautiful songs these are!

> 7, 10 What 감탄문의 복수형도 사용 가능하다.
> 「What+형용사+복수명사+복수대명사+복수동사」

PRACTICE 11

1	①, ②, ③, ⑧	2	①, ②, ⑧, ⑧
3	①, ②, ④, ⑤	4	①, ②, ⑥, ⑧
5	①, ②, ③, ⑦	6	①, ②, ⑧
7	①, ②, ⑥	8	①, ②, ④, ⑤
9	①, ②, ③, ⑧	10	①, ②, ③, ⑦
11	①, ②, ⑥, ⑧	12	①, ②, ⑧
13	①, ②, ③, ⑦	14	①, ②, ④, ⑤
15	①, ②, ③, ⑧	16	①, ②, ⑧, ⑧
17	①, ②, ④, ⑤	18	①, ②, ⑥, ⑧

> 보기의 ①~⑦에 해당하는 주어, 동사, 목적어(간접목적어, 직접 목적어), 보어(주격 보어, 목적격 보어)는 문장을 구성하는 필수 구성 요소이다. 문장의 형식은 위와 같은 문장 성분을 통해 구별할 수 있다.
> ⑧부사는 필수 문장성분이 아니며 동사, 형용사, 부사, 문장 전체를 수식하는 역할을 한다. 부사구는 2단어 이상의 묶음이 부사 역할을 하는 것을 가리킨다.
> 1형식: 주어+동사 → 2, 6, 12, 16번 문제
> 2형식: 주어+동사+주격 보어 → 4, 7, 11, 18번 문제
> 3형식: 주어+동사+목적어 → 1, 9, 15번 문제
> 4형식: 주어+동사+간접목적어+직접 목적어
> → 3, 8, 14, 17번 문제
> 5형식: 주어+동사+목적어+목적격 보어 → 5, 10, 13번 문제

PRACTICE 12

1	late	2	healthy	3	cold
4	popular	5	bored	6	quiet
7	tired	8	black		

CHAPTER 1

> 1 be late for: ~에 늦다
> 2 stay healthy: 건강을 유지하다
> 3 turn cold: (날씨가) 추워지다
> 4 become popular: 인기를 얻게 되다
> 5 feel bored: 지루함을 느끼다
> 6 keep quiet: 조용히 하다
> 7 get tired: 피곤하다
> 8 grow black: 어두워지다

PRACTICE 13

1	happy	2	terrible
3	nicely	4	look like
5	well	6	salty
7	good	8	sad
9	easily	10	sweet
11	strange	12	sounds like
13	feels	14	beautifully

> 1, 8, 11 '~해 보이다'라는 의미의 동사 look, appear, seem이 사용되어 보어 자리에 형용사가 온다.
> 2, 6, 7, 10, 13 감각동사(feel, taste, sound, smell)가 사용되어 보어 자리에 형용사가 온다.
> 3 동사 treat이 '대하다, 다루다'라는 의미로 쓰일 때 어떤 태도로 대하는지 부사를 이용하여 설명할 수 있다. (treat nicely: 잘 대접하다)
> 4, 12 동사 다음에 명사가 와야 하기 때문에 형용사만을 보어로 가지는 look과 sounds는 정답이 될 수 없다.
> look like+명사: (명사)처럼 보이다
> sound like+명사: (명사)하게 들리다
> 5, 9, 14 이미 완벽한 문장이므로 동사가 어떻게 수행되는지 꾸며주는 부사가 들어가는 것이 적절하다.

PRACTICE 14

1 My uncle lent me the bike.
2 Mark will buy me a pretty doll.
  [Will Mark buy me a pretty doll?]
3 She told me a surprising story.
4 I'll give you a birthday gift.
5 They got us some food.
6 She made us some cheesecake.
7 I asked him the price of the house.
8 Why don't you show me the picture?
9 Mother cooked them a nice dinner.
10 We send our grandmother a postcard every year.

PRACTICE 15

1 I cooked some soup for my son.
2 The interviewer asked a difficult question of me.
3 Jinho bought a present for her.
4 She sent some pictures of her son to me.
5 I wrote a letter to my cousin.
6 They showed their car to me.
7 He made a cup of hot chocolate for her.
8 Mr. Smith teaches English to us.
9 Can you get a Coke for me?
10 I didn't lend my bicycle to her.

> 1, 3, 7, 9 cook, buy, make, get은 4형식에서 3형식으로 전환 시 전치사 for를 사용한다.
> 2 ask는 4형식에서 3형식으로 전환 시 전치사 of를 사용한다.
> 4, 5, 6, 8, 10 send, write, show, teach, lend는 4형식에서 3형식으로 전환 시 전치사 to를 사용한다.

PRACTICE 16

1	angry	2	sour
3	to come	4	to leave
5	to clean	6	heavy
7	to rest	8	quiet
9	to come	10	more attractive
11	to use		

> 1, 2, 6, 8, 10 make, turn, find, keep은 목적격 보어 자리에 명사나 형용사가 온다. 10번의 경우 부사가 아닌 형용사의 비교급이 오는 것이 적절하다.
> 3, 4, 5, 7, 9, 11 ask, want, tell, advise, get, allow는 목적격 보어로 to부정사가 온다.

PRACTICE 17

1	baking	2	go	3	sing
4	stay	5	to consider	6	laugh
7	shouting	8	remember	9	to marry
10	come	11	to pose	12	to watch
13	touching	14	to study	15	plant
16	carrying	17	to tell		

> 1, 7, 13, 16 지각동사의 목적격 보어로 현재분사가 사용되어 진행중인 상황이나 행동을 강조할 수 있다.
> 2, 4, 6, 10 사역동사 make, have, let의 목적격 보어 자리에는 동사원형이 온다.
> 3, 15 지각동사의 목적격 보어로 동사원형이 온다.
> 5, 9, 11, 12, 14, 17 tell, want, get, allow, advise, ask는 사역동사나 지각동사가 아니고 to부정사를 목적격 보어로 가지는 동사들이다.
> 8 준사역동사 help의 목적격 보어 자리에는 동사원형 또는 to부정사가 올 수 있다.

Chapter Review Test 정답
본문 _ p.24

1 ④ **2** ④ **3** ② **4** ③ **5** ① **6** ⑤ **7** ①
8 ④,⑤ **9** ① **10** What do you think will happen next? **11** ④ **12** ④ **13** ④ **14** ④
15 The movie[film] made her laugh and cry.
16 ③ **17** ③ **18** I wonder if[whether] she was practicing English. **19** The police officer made me stop my car. **20** ③ **21** ④ **22** ④
23 ③ **24** ⑤ **25** ② **26** ③ **27** ③ **28** ④
29 ③,⑤ **30** ④ **31** will[won't] you **32** (1) What do you think our problem is (2) Who do you suppose wrote the letter **33** ① **34** ④
35 ④ **36** ④ **37** ⑤ **38** ④ **39** ④ **40** ⑤
41 (1) Why did he choose to come back? (2) What did she say? **42** ④ **43** ⑤ **44** ②
45 ② **46** ① **47** ①,⑤ **48** How nice her new house is! **49** ③ **50** ② **51** ② **52** ③
53 how many letters Hangeul has **54** ③
55 ④ **56** had **57** ③ **58** (1) healthy (2) cute
59 send a specific address to her **60** make someone feel good **61** ① **62** ③ **63** Amy sent me a book. / Amy sent a book to me.
64 ④ **65** what your hobby is **66** ⓑ cheerful, ⓓ for

Chapter Review Test 해설

1
- '누가'라는 주어의 역할을 하므로 who가 의문사로 온다.
- 의문사가 없는 간접의문문은 의문사 자리에 대신 if[whether](~인지)를 쓴다.

2 B가 No, I haven't라고 대답했고, A는 이야기에 감명 받았다고(I was impressed by its story.) 했으므로 빈칸에 들어갈 말은 Have로 시작하는 의문문이면서 책에 대한 질문인 ④번이다.

3 ② 일반동사가 긍정형인 문장의 부가의문문은 「do 동사의 부정 축약형＋인칭대명사」의 형태로 쓴다. 이때, 동사가 lost이므로 과거시제이기 때문에 doesn't가 아닌 didn't를 써야 한다.
① be동사가 긍정형인 문장의 부가의문문은 「be동사의 부정 축약형＋인칭대명사」의 형태로 쓴다.
③ 일반동사가 부정형인 문장의 부가의문문은 「do동사의 긍정형＋인칭대명사」의 형태로 쓴다.
④ 명령문의 부가의문문은 '명령문, will you?'의 형태로 쓴다. 어조에 따라 '명령문, won't you?'로 쓰는 것도 가능하다.
⑤ 조동사가 부정형인 문장의 부가의문문은 「조동사의 긍정형＋인칭대명사」의 형태로 쓴다.

4 ⓐ feel happy: make＋목적어＋동사원형(목적격 보어)
ⓑ friendly and nice: 형용사가 보어 역할
ⓓ uncomfortable: make＋목적어＋형용사(목적격 보어)

5 「make＋목적어＋동사원형」

6 「What＋a/an＋형용사＋명사＋(주어＋동사)!」

7 ①은 '~하는 것'이라는 뜻의 관계대명사로 쓰였고, ②③④⑤는 간접의문문에서 '무엇'이라는 뜻의 의문사로 쓰였다.
① 나는 네가 원하는 것을 가지고 있다.
② 그녀의 이름이 무엇인지 말해줘.
③ 나는 정답이 무엇일까 궁금하다.
④ 그녀는 나에게 James에게 무슨 일이 생겼냐고 물었다.
⑤ 그는 그녀가 미국에서 무엇을 공부했는지 모른다.

8 ① 주어인 a spider가 3인칭 단수이므로 do가 아니라 3인칭 단수 형태인 does를 써야 한다.
② 주어인 your favorite singer가 3인칭 단수이므로 be동사도 3인칭 단수인 is를 써야 한다.
③ 의문사가 있는 일반동사의 의문문의 경우 「의문사＋do＋주어＋동사원형」의 어순으로 만든다. 이때, 과거시제라면 do를 did로 쓰고, 주어 뒤에 나오는 일반동사는 원형으로 써야한다. 따라서 came은 come으로 고쳐 써야 한다.

9 감탄문은 'What＋(a/an)＋형용사＋명사＋(주어＋동사)!'의 어순으로 만든다. 주어인 그들이 복수이므로 (a, an)은 쓰지 않으며, 친절한 사람들이라는 뜻의 nice people을 What 뒤에 써준다. 주어는 그들이므로, 이어서 they are을 써준다. 이때, 감탄하는 대상이 명사인 '친절한 사람들'이므로 How를 쓰지 않는다.

10 Do you think?와 What will happen next?가 합쳐진 간접의문문이다. 생각이나 추측을 나타내는 동사 think가 있으므로 의문사를 문장 맨 앞에 써서 "What do you think ~?"의 어순으로 쓴다.

11 ④ beautiful flowers는 복수 명사이므로 주어 또한 3인칭 복수인 they, 동사는 are를 써야 한다.
(it is → they are)

12 사역동사 let, make는 목적격 보어로 동사원형을 쓴다.
ⓑ let her to eat → let her eat
ⓓ make her to stop → make her stop

13 간접의문문에서 의문사 뒤의 어순은 「의문사 + 주어 + 동사」이다.

14 ④ 동사가 지각동사인 heard이므로 목적격 보어로 동사원형 또는 -ing형이 와야 한다.
(fell → fall 또는 falling)

15 「make + 목적어 + 동사원형」'~이 …하게 만들다'

16 「How + 부사[형용사] + 주어 + 동사!」

17 ③ seem은 2형식에서 쓰이는 동사로 보어의 자리에 형용사가 온다. 만약 명사를 쓰고 싶을 때는 'seem like + 명사'의 형태로 쓰면 된다. 이 경우 형용사가 보어의 자리에 있으므로 'seem + 형용사'로 써준다.

18 의문사가 없는 간접의문문의 어순은 「주절 + if[whether] + 주어 + 동사」이다.

19 사역동사 make의 목적격 보어로 동사가 오는 문장에서 목적어(me)와 목적격 보어(stop)의 관계가 능동이므로 동사원형인 stop을 쓴다. 시제는 과거시제이므로 make의 과거형인 made로 바꾸어 써야 한다.

20 ①②④⑤ 'Let's ~', 'Shall we ~?', 'How about -ing?', 'Why don't we ~?'는 모두 권유나 제안을 하는 청유문에 쓰이는 표현들이다.
③ 공원에 가는 방법을 묻는 의문문이다.

21 동사 tell은 목적격 보어로 to부정사를 쓴다.
Zack은 나에게 1에서 10 사이에서 숫자 하나를 고르라고 말했다.

22 「call + 목적어 + 목적격 보어」

23 부가의문문이 'did you?'이므로 앞 문장은 You didn't ~ 로 시작해야 한다. 뒤따라오는 A의 말로 보아 문맥상 ③이 와야 한다.

24 ① 목적어의 자리이므로 목적격 대명사 him을 쓴다.
(his → him)
②③④ 5형식 문장의 동사가 make이므로 목적격 보어는 형용사를 써야 한다.
② to be sleepy → sleepy
③ angrily → angry
④ warmly → warm

25 ① 현재완료 'have p.p.'는 have가 조동사 역할을 하는 것으로 본다. 조동사가 긍정형인 문장의 부가의문문은 '조동사의 부정 축약형 + 인칭대명사'의 형태로 쓴다. (have you → haven't you)
③ taste는 감각을 나타내는 동사로 보어 자리에 형용사가 온다. (bitterly → bitter)
④ 4형식 문장은 '동사 + 간접목적어 + 직접목적어'의 어순으로 써준다. 이 경우, 간접목적어인 his mom이 직접목적어인 flowers 보다 앞에 나왔으므로 4형식이다. 따라서 전치사 to는 쓰지 않는다. (to 삭제)
⑤ help는 준사역동사로 목적격 보어로 동사원형이나 to부정사가 온다.
(to choosing → choose 또는 to choose)

26 ③ 질문이 현재시제이므로 답변도 현재시제로 해야 한다. 따라서 didn't의 과거시제는 알맞지 않다.

27 A의 마지막 말로 보아 빈칸에는 사실에 대한 확신을 묻는 표현이 와야 한다.
③ Are you all right? 너 괜찮니?

28 ⓓ 동사 make는 목적격 보어로 명사 혹은 형용사를 취할 수 있다. 따라서 부사 joyfully를 형용사 joyful로 바꾸어야 한다.
ⓐ '보기 위해서'라는 의미로 to부정사의 부사적 용법 (목적)으로 쓰였다.
ⓑ 동사 give는 3형식 문장에서 간접목적어 앞에 to를 쓴다.
ⓒ 감탄문 'What + a + 형용사 + 명사!'
ⓔ 감탄문 'How + 형용사 + 주어 + 동사!'

29 「help + 목적어 + 동사원형[to부정사]」

30 ④ 동사 find는 3형식에서 간접목적어 앞에 to가 아닌 for를 쓴다. (to me → for me)
① 동사 keep의 보어 자리에는 형용사 warm을 쓰는 것이 알맞다.
② 긍정 명령문의 부가의문문에서 명령조에는 will you?를, 정중하게 권할 때는 won't you?를 쓸 수 있다.
③ 동사 ask의 목적격 보어로 to부정사가 온다.
⑤ 나의 결정이 어떻게 될지 모르겠다는 의미이므로, 명사절의 주어(my decision) 다음에는 미래시제 조동사 will을 쓰는 것이 알맞다.
(가) 감기에 걸리지 않도록 몸을 따뜻하게 해야 한다.
(나) 내가 이 테이블을 옮기는 것을 도와줘. 그래 줄래?
(다) 진정한 결혼은 우리에게 신뢰와 충성을 보여줄 것을 요구한다.
(라) 나를 위해 호텔을 찾아줄 수 있니?
(마) 현재로서는 내 결정이 어떻게 될지 모르겠다.

31 명령문의 부가의문문은 will you? 또는 won't you?이다.

32 간접의문문이 think, suppose 등의 동사의 목적어로

쓰일 때는 의문사가 문장 맨 앞에 위치한다.
33 「feel + 형용사」 '~한 느낌이 들다'
34 모두 명령문이므로 부가의문은 will you? 또는 won't you? 가 올 수 있다. 선택지에는 will만 있으므로 ④가 정답이다.
35 look은 '~해 보이다'라는 뜻으로 보어 자리에 형용사가 온다.
36 ④ 'What do you want to be?'는 '너는 무엇이 되고 싶니?'라는 뜻으로 장래희망을 묻는 질문이다.
①②③⑤ 모두 직업을 물어보는 표현이다.
37 ⑤ 의문문에 답할 때는 의문문에 쓰인 동사와 같은 동사를 쓴다. ⑤번의 질문에서는 Is로 물었으므로, 대답 또한 is를 써야 한다. 따라서 올바른 대답은 No, he isn't이다. (doesn't → isn't)
38 • 「hear + 목적어 + 현재분사」
   • 「let + 목적어 + 동사원형」
39 「see + 목적어 + 현재분사」
40 ⑤ sound는 감각동사이므로 동사의 보어로 형용사가 온다. nicely는 부사이므로, 형용사 형태인 nice로 고쳐주어야 한다. (nicely → nice)
41 (1) 간접의문문을 직접의문문으로 되돌릴 때는 동사 (chose)의 과거 시제에 유의해 did he choose로 써야 한다.
   (2) 주절의 동사로 guess가 쓰여 의문사가 문장 맨 앞으로 이동한 문장이다. 의문사로 시작하는 의문문으로 되돌릴 때는 동사(said)의 과거 시제에 유의해 did she say로 써야 한다.
42 (가) "예쁘게 보인다"는 look 뒤에 형용사 good을 쓴다.
   (나) "~처럼 보인다"는 look 뒤에 like+(대)명사를 쓴다.
   내 친구 Alexa는 그녀의 SNS에 셀카를 올리는 것을 좋아한다. 그녀가 필터를 사용하면 셀카가 예쁘게 보인다. 하지만 나는 가끔 그녀의 셀카가 그녀처럼 보이지 않는다고 생각한다.
43 질문에 부정어가 포함된 동사가 있을 때, 대답에 not이 포함되면 No, ~.로 대답한다.
44 ② Don't you remember? 기억 안 나?
45 (A) 감각동사 smell은 형용사를 보어로 취한다.
       smell good: 좋은 냄새가 나다
   (B) 동사 want는 to부정사를 목적격 보어로 취한다.
   (C) 일반동사 긍정문의 부가의문문은 조동사 do의 부정 축약형을 쓴다.

46 「want + 목적어 + to부정사」
47 heard는 지각동사이다. 지각동사는 목적격 보어로 동사원형이나 -ing형을 쓴다. 따라서 빈칸에는 crying 혹은 cry가 들어가야 한다.
48 「How + 형용사 + 주어 + 동사!」
49 ① 부정문의 부가의문문은 be동사의 긍정형으로 만든다. (isn't she → is she)
   ② 긍정문의 부가의문문은 조동사의 부정형으로 만든다. 현재완료시제에서는 have/has가 조동사의 역할을 한다. (didn't he → hasn't he)
   ④ 'Let's ~'로 시작하는 문장의 부가의문문은 shall we?를 사용한다. (will you → shall we)
   ⑤ 긍정문의 부가의문문은 조동사의 부정형으로 만든다. (can you → can't you)
50 「make + 직접목적어 + for + 간접목적어」
51 「look + 형용사」 '~해 보이다'
52 Let's ~, shall we?
53 「주절 + 의문사 + 주어 + 동사 ~」
54 ① 'go + 형용사'는 '~하게 되다'라는 뜻이다. (sourly → sour)
   ② 주어가 복수 명사이므로 동사도 복수형태인 grow가 와야 한다. (grows → grow)
   ③ stay + 주격보어(형용사): '~한 상태를 유지하다'
   ④ 작년에 있었던 일로, 시제가 과거이므로 동사도 과거형인 became을 써야 한다. (becomes → became)
   ⑤ 동사 stay는 2형식 문장에서 동사의 보어 자리에 형용사가 온다. 따라서 openness의 형용사 형태인 open이 와야 한다. (openness → open)
55 A: 넌 팝과 재즈 중에서 어느 것을 더 좋아하니?
   B: 난 재즈를 더 좋아해.
56 • have a good time: 좋은 시간을 보내다
   • 사역동사 have+목적어+동사원형: 목적어가 ~하게 하다
   • have a nice dinner: 근사한 저녁 식사를 하다
   첫 번째 문장과 세 번째 문장에서 과거를 나타내는 표현(yesterday / last night)이 쓰였으므로 빈칸에는 have의 과거형 had가 들어가야 한다.
57 ③ came → come/coming
   지각동사의 목적격 보어 자리에는 동사원형 또는 진행 중인 동작을 강조하여 -ing형이 온다.
58 (1) 동사 make는 형용사를 목적격 보어로 취한다.
   (2) 동사 find는 형용사를 목적격 보어로 취한다.

59 우편번호를 포함한 특정 주소 기입을 요청하는 이메일이다. '그녀는 그 고객이 그녀에게 특정 주소를 보내주기를 원한다.'는 뜻이 되어야 한다. want는 목적격 보어로 to부정사를 취하므로 to 다음에는 동사원형 send를 써준다. send 다음에는 구조상 '간접목적어+직접목적어' 또는 '직접목적어+to+간접목적어'가 올 수 있는데 괄호 안의 단어에 to가 있기 때문에 send+직접목적어(a specific address)+to+간접목적어(her)로 써준다.

60 「make+목적어+동사원형」

61 • 「find+직접목적어+for+간접목적어」
• 「ask+직접목적어+of+간접목적어」

62 ③ 4형식 문장을 3형식으로 전환할 때는 '동사+직접목적어+전치사+간접목적어'의 어순으로 써준다. 동사 ask는 4형식을 3형식으로 전환할 때 전치사 of를 사용한다. (to → of)

63 4형식 문장은 '동사+간접목적어+직접목적어'의 어순으로 쓴다. 동사는 '보냈다'라는 뜻의 sent를 써준다. 간접목적어는 '나'라는 뜻의 1인칭 단수 목적격 대명사인 me, 직접목적어는 책 한 권이므로 'a book'을 써준다. 4형식 문장을 3형식으로 전환할 때는 '동사+직접목적어+전치사+간접목적어'의 어순으로 써준다. send는 4형식을 3형식으로 전환할 때, 전치사로 to를 쓴다. 따라서 me 앞에는 to를 붙여준다.

64 (A)와 ④의 makes는 '~을 …하게 만들다'는 뜻이므로 목적격 보어를 필요로 하는 5형식 동사로 쓰였다. ①②③⑤의 makes는 목적어만을 취하는 3형식 동사이다.
① make '~을 만들다'
② make '(계산하면) …이다'
③ make sense '타당하다[말이 되다]'
⑤ make a living '생계를 꾸리다'

65 의문사가 들어간 간접의문문의 어순은 '의문사+주어+동사'이다.

66 ⓑ feel 다음에는 형용사(또는 분사)가 와야 하므로 부사 cheerfully를 형용사 형태로 고쳐야 한다. (cheerfully → cheerful)
ⓓ 동사 cook이 3형식 문장에서 쓰일 때는 간접목적어 앞에 전치사 for를 써야 한다.
ⓐ 동사 dig '(땅을) 파다', sow '(씨를) 뿌리다'에 이어 and로 연결되어 있으므로 ⓐ에는 동사 형태인 water '(화초 등에) 물을 주다'가 쓰였다.
나는 내 정원에서 땅을 파고, 씨앗들을 뿌리고, 그 식물들에 물을 준다.
ⓒ 지각동사 watch의 목적격 보어 자리이므로 동사원형 come이 쓰였다.
ⓔ 주어 The vegetables를 'I grow'가 부연설명하고 있고, 주어 뒤 ⓔ에는 동사가 위치하는 자리이다. 주어가 복수이므로 복수동사 taste가 쓰였다.

CHAPTER 2 시제 Tense

본문 _ p.36

PRACTICE 1

1	departs	2	rewards
3	bites	4	answers
5	uses	6	sings
7	breathes	8	opens
9	destroys	10	closes
11	changes	12	proves
13	makes	14	cries
15	draws	16	reduces
17	tells	18	misses
19	mixes	20	complains
21	leaves	22	raises
23	shoots	24	lifts
25	likes	26	bears
27	takes	28	elects
29	recycles	30	recommends
31	stops	32	wants
33	exchanges	34	interviews
35	allows	36	keeps

CHAPTER 2

37	marries	38	prays		
39	acts	40	enjoys		
41	rescues	42	starts		
43	vows	44	mentions		
45	imagines	46	brings		
47	does	48	leads		
49	finds	50	fights		
51	wraps	52	flows		
53	argues	54	travels		
55	produces	56	seems		
57	serves	58	gives		
59	follows	60	finishes		
61	adds	62	borrows		
63	copies	64	discovers		
65	admires	66	sinks		
67	understands	68	worries		
69	remembers	70	quits		
71	stretches	72	knocks		
73	hopes	74	wakes		
75	reports	76	introduces		
77	appears	78	saves		
79	supposes	80	agrees		
81	beats	82	hatches		
83	becomes	84	describes		
85	wonders	86	tries		

PRACTICE 2

1	s	2	z	3	z	4	z
5	z	6	s	7	s	8	z
9	iz	10	z	11	s	12	z
13	z	14	iz	15	z	16	z
17	s	18	z	19	iz	20	s
21	z	22	iz	23	z	24	iz
25	s	26	z	27	s	28	s
29	iz	30	z	31	iz	32	s
33	iz	34	s	35	z	36	s
37	z	38	iz	39	s	40	iz
41	s	42	iz	43	s	44	z
45	s						

PRACTICE 3

2	plays	3	sleep	4	is
5	moves	6	go		

> 1, 4 현재의 사실이나 상태를 나타낼 때 현재시제를 쓴다.
> 2, 3, 6 현재의 습관이나 반복적인 동작을 나타낼 때 현재시제를 쓴다.
> 5 불변의 진리나 격언, 과학적 사실을 나타낼 때 현재시제를 쓴다.

PRACTICE 4

2	arrives	3	have	4	leaves
5	comes	6	blames	7	hears
8	visits	9	studies	10	gets
11	reaches	12	completes	13	arrive

> 1, 5 눈앞에서 진행되고 있는 일을 나타낼 때 현재시제를 쓴다.
> 2, 4, 11 왕래발착동사가 미래를 나타내는 부사구와 함께 쓰일 때 현재시제로 미래를 나타낼 수 있다.
> 3, 7, 10, 12, 13 시간과 조건의 부사절에서는 현재시제로 미래를 나타낸다.
> 6 격언이나 속담을 나타낼 때 현재시제를 쓴다.
> *A bad workman always blames his tools.: 서투른 일꾼이 연장 탓한다. (속담)
> 8, 9 현재의 습관이나 반복적인 동작을 나타낼 때 현재시제를 쓴다.

PRACTICE 5

2	was	3	are	4	were
5	are	6	is	7	is
8	were	9	was	10	was

PRACTICE 6

1	were, was	2	Was, wasn't
3	Is, is	4	was, was
5	is, is		

> 1 질문의 시제가 과거이므로 기준 시점에 해당하는 when 뒤의 빈칸과 답변 모두 과거시제가 되어야 알맞다.
> 2 답변 뒤에 덧붙인 문장이 과거시제이므로 질문과 답변 모두 과거시제가 되어야 알맞다.
> 3, 5 답변 뒤에 덧붙인 문장이 현재시제이므로 질문과 답변 모두 현재시제가 되어야 알맞다.
> 4 과거 시점을 나타내는 부사구 last week가 있으므로 과거시제로 질문하고 답변해야 알맞다.

PRACTICE 7

1	stayed	2	ripped
3	smelled	4	caused
5	worried	6	destroyed
7	died	8	bowed
9	preferred	10	applied

11 judged	12 wasted	11 heard – heard	12 sat – sat
13 controlled	14 played	13 bore – borne/born	14 taught – taught
15 watched	16 delayed	15 sang – sung	16 cost – cost
17 invited	18 hurried	17 thought – thought	18 flew – flown
19 copied	20 hoped	19 wore – worn	20 hurt – hurt
21 shopped	22 expected	21 read – read	22 told – told
23 disappeared	24 observed	23 made – made	24 fought – fought
25 studied	26 fixed	25 saw – seen	26 went – gone
27 chatted	28 carried	27 brought – brought	28 paid – paid
29 smiled	30 jogged	29 drew – drawn	30 found – found
31 popped	32 noticed	31 hit – hit	32 bought – bought
33 danced	34 tried	33 spoke – spoken	34 began – begun
35 stopped	36 rushed	35 understood – understood	
37 enjoyed	38 married	36 lay – lain	37 stole – stolen
39 planned	40 waited	38 put – put	39 held – held
41 replied	42 practiced	40 sank – sunk	41 woke – woken
43 picked	44 dropped	42 wrote – written	
45 agreed	46 decided	43 overcame – overcome	
47 fried	48 grabbed	44 led – led	45 knew – known
49 clapped	50 cleaned	46 left – left	47 set – set
51 saved	52 cried	48 rose – risen	49 swept – swept
53 wrapped	54 dried	50 smelled/smelt – smelled/smelt	
		51 ate – eaten	52 forgot – forgotten
		53 had – had	54 became – become
		55 slept – slept	56 let – let
		57 spread – spread	
		58 dreamed/dreamt – dreamed/dreamt	
		59 sent – sent	60 beat – beaten
		61 stood – stood	62 drank – drunk
		63 came – come	64 said – said
		65 felt – felt	66 meant – meant
		67 grew – grown	68 built – built
		69 cut – cut	70 swam – swum
		71 threw – thrown	72 was, were – been
		73 lost – lost	74 blew – blown
		75 drove – driven	76 did – done
		77 hid – hidden	78 got – got(ten)
		79 won – won	80 rode – ridden
		81 sold – sold	82 shut – shut

PRACTICE 8

1	d	2	d	3	id	4	t
5	d	6	d	7	id	8	d
9	t	10	t	11	id	12	t
13	d	14	d	15	t	16	id
17	d	18	t	19	d	20	id
21	t	22	id	23	id	24	d
25	t	26	d	27	id	28	d
29	t	30	id	31	t	32	d
33	d	34	d	35	id	36	t
37	d	38	t	39	id	40	d
41	t	42	id	43	t	44	d
45	id						

PRACTICE 9

1 chose – chosen		2 laid – laid	
3 met – met		4 fell – fallen	
5 rang – rung		6 ran – run	
7 spent – spent		8 took – taken	
9 gave – given		10 kept – kept	

PRACTICE 10

1	sent	2	was	3	spend
4	didn't eat	5	woke	6	didn't hear

7	broke	8	hit	9	fell	23	dying	24 returning
10	didn't play	11	closes	12	lay	25	planning	26 operating
13	read	14	brought	15	saw	27	serving	28 joining
16	ate	17	drew	18	came	29	carrying	30 climbing
19	didn't come	20	leaves	21	drove	31	going	32 setting
22	shut	23	sang			33	studying	34 cleaning

> 1, 2, 6, 14, 15, 16, 17, 18, 19 last week, in 2005, last night, yesterday, last month, three years ago, in 2001 같은 과거를 나타내는 부사구가 있으므로 과거시제가 알맞다.
> 3 현재를 나타내는 부사구 these days가 있으므로 현재시제가 알맞다.
> 4, 5, 7, 8, 9, 12, 21, 22 등위접속사로 연결된 문장의 시제가 과거이므로 주절의 동사 역시 과거시제가 알맞다.
> 10, 13 시간부사절(when ~/after ~)로 제시된 기준 시점이 과거이므로 주절의 시제 역시 과거가 알맞다.
> 11 on weekdays(평일에)로 보아 반복적인 동작을 나타내고 있으므로 현재시제가 알맞다.
> 20 왕래발착동사 leave와 미래를 나타내는 부사구 tomorrow morning이 함께 왔으므로 현재시제로 미래를 나타낼 수 있다.
> 23 과거의 특정 상황에서 일어난 일을 설명하고 있으므로 과거 시제가 알맞다.

PRACTICE 11

1	will	2	Are	3	go
4	are	5	going	6	will join
7	going	8	will	9	am
10	will				

PRACTICE 12

2	Are, going to buy	3	is going to give
4	are going to study	5	is going to rain
6	is going to paint		

PRACTICE 13

1	planting	2	taking
3	getting	4	playing
5	smiling	6	bowing
7	becoming	8	seeing
9	losing	10	breathing
11	standing	12	opening
13	arguing	14	tumbling
15	worrying	16	biting
17	teaching	18	wrapping
19	swimming	20	copying
21	singing	22	baking

35	dating	36	encouraging
37	pulling	38	burning
39	using	40	staying
41	coming	42	acting
43	winning	44	producing
45	celebrating	46	writing
47	denying	48	repeating
49	entering	50	eating
51	making	52	hitting
53	running	54	marrying
55	shining	56	beating
57	enjoying	58	causing
59	moving	60	solving
61	facing	62	destroying
63	fighting	64	rolling
65	washing	66	saying
67	stopping	68	shaking
69	introducing	70	happening
71	flying	72	holding
73	saving	74	sharing
75	visiting	76	putting
77	lying	78	talking
79	riding	80	collecting
81	dreaming	82	controlling
83	trying	84	driving
85	hurting	86	filling
87	paying	88	wearing
89	agreeing	90	cheating
91	cutting	92	selling
93	forming	94	fixing
95	removing	96	turning
97	mentioning	98	increasing
99	waiting	100	picking

PRACTICE 14

2	was having[eating]	3	was reading
4	was cleaning	5	was watching

6 was reading

PRACTICE 15

2	is baking	3	were arguing
4	was riding	5	is sleeping
6	is removing	7	are, leaving
8	is cooking	9	were, doing
10	are going	11	am not working
12	was standing	13	was having
14	is not using	15	am making

> 2, 5, 6, 8, 15 be+-ing가 현재진행시제를 나타낸다.
> 1, 3, 4, 9, 12, 13 be동사의 과거형+-ing는 과거진행시제로, 과거의 한 시점에 진행되고 있던 동작을 나타낸다.
> 7, 10, 11, 14 이미 계획된 일에 대한 가까운 미래를 표현할 때는 현재진행시제가 미래를 대신할 수 있다.

PRACTICE 16

2 have passed
3 Have, thought, haven't
4 haven't touched
5 have hatched
6 has lost
7 Have, visited, have
8 have got(ten)
9 have set
10 have bought
11 has been
12 haven't learned
13 Have, been, haven't
14 has become
15 has changed
16 haven't eaten
17 Have, seen, have
18 has practiced
19 has read
20 haven't seen

> 1 hear of: ~에 대해 듣다
> 2 pass away: 사망하다, 돌아가시다
> 3 think about: ~에 대해 생각하다
> 5 hatch: 부화하다, 부화되다
> 6 lose one's job: 실직하다
> 7 visit+장소 명사: ~를 방문하다
> 9 set up: 준비하다, 설치하다
> 10 buy+사람+A: ~에게 A를 사주다
> 13 have been to+장소: ~에 가본 적이 있다
> 18 practice+-ing: ~하는 것을 연습하다

PRACTICE 17

2 My father has gone, 결과
3 I have already done, 완료
4 She has stayed in Korea, 계속
5 He has been to India, 경험

6 They have just finished, 완료

> 2 has gone은 '가버려서 지금 여기 없다'는 의미로 현재완료의 용법 중 '결과'에 해당한다.
> 3, 6 already(이미)와 just(방금)는 현재완료의 '완료' 용법에서 자주 쓰이는 부사이다.
> 4 for two years(2년 동안)로 지속 기간을 나타내고 있으므로 현재완료의 용법 중 '계속'에 해당한다.
> 5 'have been to+장소'는 ~에 가본 적이 있다'는 말로 현재완료의 '경험' 용법이다.

PRACTICE 18

1	for	2	for	3	since
4	for	5	since	6	for
7	since	8	since	9	for
10	since				

> 1, 2, 4, 6, 9 빈칸 뒤에 기간 표현이 왔으므로 '~ 동안'이라는 뜻으로 어떤 일이 지속된 시간의 길이를 나타내는 for가 알맞다.
> 3, 5, 7, 8, 10 빈칸 뒤에 특정 시점 표현이 왔으므로 '~ 이후로'의 뜻으로 사건이 시작된 시점을 나타내는 since가 알맞다.

PRACTICE 19

1 Jack has been here for four days.
2 I have taught students for fifteen years.
3 Liz has studied Japanese for two years.
4 My mom has had the house since last year.
5 Kate has dated Dave since last April.
6 Mark has played tennis since 2015.

> 1, 2, 3 현재완료시제(주어+have+과거분사) 뒤에 'for+기간'을 쓰면 어떤 일이 일어나 지속된 시간을 나타내어 '~ 동안 …해왔다'라는 의미가 된다.
> 4, 5, 6 현재완료시제(주어+have+과거분사) 뒤에 'since+시점'을 쓰면 어떤 일이 시작된 시점을 나타내어 '~ 이후로 …해왔다'라는 의미가 된다.

PRACTICE 20

1	saw	2	have never read
3	haven't talked	4	got
5	snowed	6	have never driven
7	have just finished	8	cleaned
9	haven't eaten	10	walked

> 1, 5, 8 과거의 특정한 때를 나타내는 부사(구)(last night, this morning, yesterday)가 있으므로 과거시제가 알맞다.
> 2, 6 과거에서부터 지금까지의 경험을 말할 때 현재완료시제를 써서 '~한 적이 있다'라고 표현할 수 있다. never를 넣으면 '~한 적이

없다'라는 뜻이 되며, before(전에, 예전에)는 현재완료의 경험 용법에서 자주 쓰이는 부사이다.
3 '최근에 언니와 얘기하지 않았다'는 것은 과거에 시작되어 현재까지 계속되는 상태를 묘사하고 있으므로 현재완료시제가 알맞다.
4, 10 과거에 종료된 동작이나 상태를 나타내고 있으므로 과거시제가 알맞다.
7 '막 ~했다'라고 표현할 때는 현재완료시제를 사용한다. 완료 용법에 해당하며 just, now, already 같은 부사가 자주 함께 쓰인다.
9 과거의 특정 시점 이후로(since this morning) 계속 지속된 동작이나 상태를 나타내므로 현재완료시제가 알맞다.

PRACTICE 21

1	had	2	잘못된 곳 없음
3	rained	4	잘못된 곳 없음
5	was	6	bought
7	잘못된 곳 없음	8	finished
9	잘못된 곳 없음	10	got

1, 3, 6, 8, 10 과거의 특정한 때를 나타내는 부사(구)(yesterday, last night, in 2013, two hours ago, last month)가 있으므로 현재완료가 아닌 단순 과거시제가 되어야 한다.
5 유미가 광주에서 태어난 것은 과거에 종료된 일이므로 과거시제가 되어야 한다.
*be born in: ~에서 태어나다

PRACTICE 22

2 Mike has played soccer for three hours.
3 Have they worked here since 2010?
4 The train arrived at the station five minutes ago.
5 How did you earn so much last year?
6 Eva hasn't[has not] seen her sister for a long time.

2, 6 지속 기간을 나타내는 표현(for three hours, for a long time)이 있으므로 '~ 동안 계속되다'라는 의미가 되도록 현재완료시제가 되어야 한다.
3 since를 써서 어떤 일이 시작된 시점을 나타내고 있으므로 '~ 이후로 계속되다'라는 의미가 되도록 현재완료시제가 되어야 한다.
4, 5 과거의 특정한 때를 나타내는 표현(five minutes ago, last year)에 어울리는 과거시제가 알맞다.

PRACTICE 23

1	have been studying	2	have been playing
3	has, been sleeping	4	has been working
5	Have, been reading	6	has been repairing
7	have been waiting	8	has been talking
9	Has, been baking	10	has been watching

4 work for: ~을 위해[~에서] 일하다
7 wait for: ~을 기다리다
8 talk to: ~에게 이야기하다

PRACTICE 24

2 Seyeon has been using her laptop for two hours.
3 Two people have been playing tennis since 4 o'clock.
4 Mike has been making lunch since noon.
5 Jisu and Minji have been building a sand castle for an hour.
6 It has been raining since this morning.

2, 5 시간의 길이를 나타내는 표현(two hours, an hour)이 명시되어 있으므로, '~동안 계속되다'라는 의미를 가진 for를 사용하는 것이 적절하다.
3, 4, 6 시점을 나타내는 표현(4 o'clock, noon, this morning)이 주어졌으므로, '~이후로 계속되다'라는 의미의 since를 사용하는 것이 적절하다.

Chapter Review Test 정답 본문 _ p.63

1 ② 2 ② 3 ③ 4 ③ 5 are going to 6 ①
7 have lived in 8 I've[I have] never eaten it.
9 They have served free meals for two years.
10 ④ 11 ② 12 ④ 13 ④ 14 ①
15 ⓐ Did you finish packing your bag yesterday?
16 ② 17 ② 18 ② 19 is washing the[a] car
20 finished, went 21 ④,⑤ 22 ④ 23 ⑤
24 ②,⑤ 25 ③ 26 ⑤ 27 ④ 28 ①,③
29 have been reading, since 30 ④ 31 ④
32 ⑤ 33 ② 34 ⓓ I have not[haven't] been there for two months. 35 ④ 36 ② 37 ①
38 ② 39 ② 40 has been snowing 41 I have [I've] had a great time since I started to work at the library. 42 ③ 43 (1) have visited Brazil once (2) have not [haven't] won a prize in the piano competition (3) has read *Anna Karenina*, has not [hasn't] read *Anna Karenina*[it] 44 ①
45 am, have been, will, will, will

Chapter Review Test 해설

1 ② will take → take

CHAPTER 2

시간이나 조건의 부사절에서는 미래 시제 대신 현재 시제가 쓰인다.

2 ⓐ 「There is ~」는 '~가 있다'라는 뜻으로 동사의 수를 뒤에 나오는 명사에 일치시킨다. 단수 명사 a dog이 쓰였으므로, 동사 또한 단수 동사인 is를 쓴다. There's는 There is의 축약형이다.
ⓑ 지난달부터 현재까지 계속 지속된 사건에 대해 말할 때는 현재완료를 사용한다. 현재완료는 'have/has + 과거분사'로 나타낸다. (had → have)
ⓒ 의문문에 대한 답을 할 때는 의문문에 쓰인 동사에 맞춰 답을 한다. 질문에서 Doesn't로 물었으므로, 긍정의 답변은 does로 한다. (is → does)
ⓓ 현재의 습관이나 반복적인 동작을 나타낼 때는 현재시제를 쓴다. 주어 he는 3인칭 단수이므로, 동사 또한 3인칭 단수 현재형으로 만들기 위해 '-s'를 붙인다.
ⓔ 현재진행시제는 말하고 있는 시점에 진행되고 있는 동작을 나타낼 때 쓰인다. 3인칭 단수 명사 the dog이 주어이므로 'is + -ing'의 형태로 쓴다.

3 ③ 경험 ① 결과 ② 완료 ④⑤ 계속
4 ③ 사건이 시작된 시점은 since와 함께 쓴다.
   (for → since)
5 will = be going to
6 ① 왕래발착동사 현재형이 미래시제를 뜻할 수 있으므로 올바르다.
   ② 과거를 나타내는 부사 yesterday가 쓰였으므로 과거시제를 사용한다. (studies → studied)
   ③ 미래를 나타내는 부사구 next Sunday가 쓰였으므로 미래시제를 사용한다.
   (was playing → will[am going to] play)
   ④ 주어 your parents가 복수이므로 be동사도 수를 일치시킨다. (Was → Were)
   ⑤ 주어 You는 2인칭이므로 부정문을 만들 때 don't을 사용한다. (doesn't → don't)
7 과거에 발생한 동작이나 상태가 현재까지 이어질 때는 「have/has + 과거분사」의 현재완료로 표현한다.
8 「have + never + 과거분사」 '~해본 적이 없다.'
9 2년 전부터 무료 식사를 제공하기 시작해 현재까지 계속 제공하고 있으므로 현재완료 시제와 for(~동안)가 쓰인다.
10 ④ 현재완료 의문문의 Have가 필요하다.
   ①②③ 일반동사 의문문이고 대답을 보아 과거시제를 써야 하므로 Did가 필요하다.
   ⑤ 의문사 의문문의 동사 자리에 do의 과거형 did가 필요하다.

11 ⓐ 현재완료는 「have + 과거분사」로 쓴다.
   (trying → tried)
   ⓒ 과거의 특정한 때를 나타내는 부사구 last year이 쓰였으므로 과거시제로 쓴다.
   (have tried → tried)
   ⓓ ever since로 과거에 시작되어 현재까지 계속되는 상태임을 알 수 있다. 따라서 현재완료시제를 사용한다. (was → has been)
12 각각 경험, 완료를 나타내는 현재완료가 필요하다.
13 과거의 특정한 때를 나타내는 부사구가 쓰였으므로 과거시제로 쓴다.
   ⓐ have met → met   ⓒ swum → swam
14 ① 계속 ②④⑤ 경험 ③ 결과
15 A의 질문에 B가 'Yes, I did.'로 답했고, yesterday는 과거의 특정한 때이므로 과거시제를 써야 한다.
16 주절(he will take care of it)의 내용으로 보아 시간이나 조건의 부사절에 현재시제가 와야 하고, something은 단수 취급한다.
17 주어진 문장은 '너는 이 마을의 노란 새에 대해 들어본 적 있니?'라는 뜻으로, 현재완료의 경험 용법이 사용되었다. ever는 주로 의문문에서 '지금까지, 여태껏'이라는 의미로 사용되는 부사이고 have와 과거분사 사이에 위치한다.
   ① 밑줄 친 부분은 '살아 왔다'라는 의미로 해석할 수 있다. for은 사건이 일어나 지속된 시간의 길이를 나타내는 전치사로, 현재완료의 계속 용법과 함께 쓰인다.
   ② have never seen은 '한 번도 본 적이 없다'는 의미로, '절대/한 번도 …않다'라는 뜻의 부사 never와 현재완료가 함께 쓰여 경험을 나타낸다.
   ③ just는 완료 용법과 함께 쓰여, 주로 have와 과거분사 사이에 위치한다. has just broken은 '방금 깨뜨렸다'라는 의미로, 이미 완료된 일을 나타냄을 알 수 있다.
   ④ has gone은 '가버렸다'라는 뜻으로, 이미 이 곳을 떠났다는 결과를 나타낸다.
   ⑤ have stayed는 '머물러 왔다'라는 의미로, '~이후로'의 뜻을 나타내는 since와 함께 쓰여 머무르는 행동이 계속됨을 나타낸다.
18 ② lie(누워 있다) - lay - lain
19 현재에 진행 중인 동작을 물었으므로 현재진행형으로 대답한다.
20 • 완료를 나타내는 현재완료시제

• 과거의 특정한 때를 나타내는 과거시제
21 「on+요일s」, 「every+요일」 '~요일마다'
22 ⓓ 현재완료의 형태는 'have+과거분사'이다.
(drop → dropped)
ⓐ,ⓑ 과거형 동사
ⓒ '너의 것'을 의미하는 대명사
ⓔ '~에 감동하여'라는 수동의 의미로 쓰인 과거분사
+by
lumberjack 벌목꾼 axe (자루가 긴) 도끼
23 Have you ever been to~? '~에 가본 적 있니?'
24 ① the kitchen → a room
③ was taking a shower → was making spaghetti
④ (Alex 기준) was writing a letter to her dad →
was playing the cello 또는
(Samantha 기준) was listening to the radio
→ was playing a computer game
25 have been (to) '~에 갔었다'
26 미래를 나타내는 부사구(next Monday)가 있으므로
is going to 또는 will이 들어간다.
27 ④ 전체적인 시제가 과거이고 과거의 사건에 대해 말
하므로 과거시제로 쓴다.
(grow and grow → grew and grew)
28 '절대 잃어버린 적이 없다'는 현재완료의 경험을 나타
내는 용법이다. never은 현재완료의 경험 용법에서
해 본 적이 없었다는 의미를 나타낸다.
① '전에 읽은 적이 있다'는 의미로, 현재완료의 경험
용법이다. before는 경험 용법에서 자주 쓰이는 단
어이다.
② '벌써 흰머리가 되었다'라는 의미로, 현재완료의 완
료 용법이다. already는 '이미, 벌써'라는 뜻으로 완
료 용법에서 자주 쓰인다.
③ '두 번 만난 적이 있다'는 경험을 나타내는 용법이
다. twice와 같은 배수사는 경험 용법에서 쓰여, 경
험의 횟수를 나타낸다.
④ '닦았다'라는 뜻으로, 이미 차를 닦았다는 완료된 사
건에 대해 이야기하므로, 현재완료의 완료 용법이
다. just는 현재완료의 완료 용법에서 자주 쓰인다.
⑤ '살아왔다'는 의미로, 계속되고 있는 사건에 대해 이
야기하므로, 현재완료의 계속 용법이다. for은 현
재완료의 계속 용법에서 사건이 일어나 지속된 시
간의 길이를 나타낸다.
29 「have/has+been+-ing+since+사건 시작 시점」
B가 오늘 아침에 만화책을 읽고 있었고 현재까지 계속
읽고 있으므로 현재완료 진행시제가 쓰인다.

30 ④ 현재완료는 「have+과거분사」로 쓴다.
(stole → stolen)
31 ⓐ ever은 '지금까지, 여태껏'이라는 의미로, 현재완료
의 경험 용법과 자주 쓰인다.
ⓑ last year은 과거의 특정한 때를 나타내는 부사구
로, 과거시제와 함께 쓰여야 한다.
(has visited → visited)
ⓒ yesterday는 과거의 특정한 때를 나타내는 부사
이므로, 과거시제와 함께 쓰여야 한다.
ⓓ in 2018은 과거의 특정한 때를 나타낸다. 따라서
과거시제와 함께 쓰여야 한다.
(has lived → lived)
ⓔ six months ago는 과거의 특정한 때를 나타낸다.
따라서 과거시제와 함께 쓰이는 것이 적절하다.
32 • fall - fell - fallen • is - was - been
33 ⓐ 능동의 의미를 지닌 현재완료(has struggled)나
현재완료진행(has been struggling)이 적절하다.
ⓒ The number에 수일치 시켜서 has로 고친다.
ⓔ already는 긍정문과 놀람을 나타내는 의문문에 쓴
다.
ⓕ 과거를 나타내는 부사구 four days ago가 있으므
로 과거시제 met이 적절하다.
34 현재완료 부정문은 「have/has not+과거분사」이
다. 두 달 동안 그곳에 가본 적이 없다는 뜻이므로
since(~이후로)가 아닌 for(~동안)가 와야 한다.
35 과거의 특정한 때를 나타내는 부사구가 있으면 과거
시제로 쓴다.
① have gone → went
② have you taught → did you teach
③ has met → met
⑤ have been → were
36 ② 「be going to+장소」 '~로 가고 있다'
37 for(~동안)는 사건이 일어나 지속된 시간의 길이를 나
타낸다.
38 (A) 과거에 진행되던 동작이므로 과거진행형을 쓴다.
(B) 명백한 과거를 나타내는 부사구(last week)는 과
거시제와 함께 쓰인다.
(C) '나는 태어난 이후로 이와 같은 경험을 해본 적이
없다'는 의미로 '~이후로'의 since가 적합하다.
39 ② Has he ~?에 대한 답은 Yes, he has. 또는 No,
he hasn't.가 되어야 한다.
40 오후 세 시부터 눈이 내리기 시작해 현재까지 계속 내
리는 중이므로 현재완료 진행시제로 표현한다.
41 '~이래로'를 나타내는 since와 현재완료 시제를 함께

써서 즐거운 시간을 보낸 것이 계속됐음(have had a great time)을 나타낸다.
42 (A) 앞에 현재완료 동사(has made)가 술어로 나오고, 뒤에 과거시제 동사(was)가 나와 '어린 시절 이후로 엄마가 계속 타르트를 만들어주셨다'는 의미를 이루므로 since가 적절하다.
(B) 앞에 현재완료의 have('ve)가 나오므로, (B)에는 과거분사인 eaten이 적절하다.

43 현재완료의 문장은 「have/has + 과거분사」로 쓴다. 주어가 복수형이면 have, 단수형이면 has를 사용하며, 부정문은 「have/has not + 과거분사」로 쓴다.
44 빈칸 앞에 No가 있으므로 빈칸에는 해운대에 가본 적이 없다는 내용이 와야 한다.
45 예정된 계획을 나타내는 be going to, 과거에 시작된 동작이 현재까지 계속되는 현재완료진행 have been + -ing, 미래에 대한 의지를 나타내는 will이 필요하다.

CHAPTER 3 조동사 Modals

본문 _ p.72

PRACTICE 1

1	①	2	②	3	①	4	②
5	②	6	①	7	③	8	③
9	①	10	②	11	③	12	②
13	③	14	②	15	②		

1, 2, 3, 5, 6, 7, 8, 10, 11, 12, 13 조동사 뒤에는 동사원형이 와야 한다.
4, 15 주어가 3인칭 단수면 동사도 3인칭 단수 동사가 온다.
9 two weeks ago라는 명백한 과거를 나타내는 시간부사구가 있으므로 과거 시제를 써야 한다.
14 강조의 does 뒤에는 동사원형을 써야 한다.

PRACTICE 2

2 I cannot[can't] wait to meet them.
3 You may not play the computer game now.
4 You must not[mustn't] break your promise.
5 You had better not['d better not] go on a diet.
6 It might not[mightn't] be safe to do so.
7 I could not[couldn't] get to the office early.
8 You had better not['d better not] bring your kids.
9 I will not[won't] bring it to you.
10 You should not[shouldn't] hang it on the wall.
11 I did not use to[didn't use to/used not to] play the guitar.
12 She could not[couldn't] finish the work on time.
13 Denny will not[won't] be fourteen years old soon.
14 We should not[shouldn't] listen to the teacher.
15 You must not[mustn't] cross the street now.

5, 8 had better의 부정형은 had better 뒤에 not을 붙인다.
11 used to의 부정형은 didn't use to 또는 used not to라고 쓴다. 후자는 격식체에서 주로 사용한다.

PRACTICE 3

2 Will Dave play basketball?
3 Should Jihye take the first train?
4 Can he drive a car?
5 Should I give him my notebook?
6 Will he teach English at a middle school?
7 Can Mike speak five languages?
8 Will she take art classes in Italy?
9 Can I order some food?
10 Can they make Chinese dishes?

1~10 조동사로 시작하는 의문문은 「조동사+주어+동사원형 ~?」의 어순으로 쓴다.

PRACTICE 4

1	have	2	must	3	must
4	have	5	have	6	must
7	have	8	must	9	had
10	has				

CHAPTER 3 조동사

1 'to+동사원형'과 함께 '~해야 한다'는 의무를 나타내는 have가 알맞다. Did로 시작되는 의문문이므로 과거동사 had는 올 수 없다.
2, 3, 6, 8 바로 뒤의 동사원형과 함께 '~해야 한다'라는 의무를 나타내야 하므로 조동사 must가 알맞다.
4 'to+동사원형'과 함께 '~해야 한다'는 의무를 나타내야 하고, 현재를 나타내는 부사(now)가 있으므로 have to가 알맞다.
5, 7 조동사 will과 must가 나란히 올 수 없다. 'to+동사원형'과 함께 사용되면서 must처럼 의무를 나타내는 have가 알맞다.
9 과거를 나타내는 부사구 last night이 있으므로 '~해야 했다'라는 의미로 과거의 의무를 나타내는 had to의 had가 알맞다.
10 'to+동사원형'과 함께 '~해야 한다'는 의무를 나타내야 하고, 주어가 3인칭 단수이므로 has가 알맞다.

PRACTICE 5

1	have to[will have to]	2	had to
3	have to[will have to]	4	have to
5	has to[will have to]	6	had to
7	has to[will have to]	8	has to[will have to]
9	had to	10	have to[will have to]

1, 3, 10 의미상 현재 또는 미래의 의무를 나타내는 표현이 적합하므로 have to 또는 will have to가 알맞다.
2, 6, 9 기준 시점이 과거인 경우(when she was young)이거나 과거를 나타내는 부사구(Last Friday, yesterday)가 있으므로 '~해야 했다'라는 의미로 과거의 의무를 나타내는 had to가 알맞다.
4 현재를 나타내는 부사 now가 있으므로 현재의 의무를 나타내는 have to가 알맞다.
5, 7, 8 의미상 현재 또는 미래의 의무를 나타내는 표현이 적합한데, 주어가 3인칭 단수이므로 has to 또는 will have to가 알맞다.

PRACTICE 6

1	must	2	can't	3	must	4	must
5	can't	6	can't	7	must	8	can't
9	must	10	can't				

1, 3, 4, 7, 9 '~임에 틀림없다'라는 뜻으로 강한 추측을 나타내는 must가 알맞다.
2, 5, 10 '~일 리가 없다'라는 의미가 되어야 앞 문장과 자연스럽게 이어진다. '~일 리가 없다'는 「can't+동사원형」으로 나타낼 수 있다.
6, 8 '~할 수 없다'라는 의미가 되어야 하므로 불가능을 나타내는 can't가 알맞다.

PRACTICE 7

1	must not	2	don't have to
3	doesn't have to	4	must not
5	don't have to	6	must not

1, 4, 6 '~해서는 안 된다'는 금지의 의미가 되어야 하므로 must not이 알맞다.
2, 3, 5 '~할 필요가 없다'는 불필요를 나타내는 표현이 적합하므로 don't have to가 알맞다.

PRACTICE 8

2	were able to	3	am able to
4	wasn't able to	5	Aren't, able to
6	won't be able to[isn't able to]		
7	was able to	8	weren't able to
9	will be able to[are able to]		
10	is able to		

1, 5 can't를 be not able to로 바꾸어 쓸 수 있다. 복수주어(The players) 또는 you와 함께 쓰였기 때문에 aren't able to라고 쓴다.
2, 7 can의 과거형 could는 were[was] able to로 바꾸어 쓸 수 있다.
3, 10 can을 be able to로 바꾸어 쓸 수 있다. 주어가 1인칭인 경우 am able to, 3인칭 단수인 경우 is able to라고 쓴다.
4, 8 can't의 과거형 couldn't는 wasn't[weren't] able to로 바꾸어 쓸 수 있다.
6 '(미래에) ~할 수 없다'를 나타낼 때, will과 can't를 함께 쓸 수 없으므로 이를 대신하여 won't[will not] be able to를 쓴다. 또는 be able to의 현재형을 사용하여 미래시제를 나타낼 수 있다. 이때 주어가 3인칭 단수이므로 isn't able to 라고 쓴다.
9 미래에 대한 일을 나타낼 때에는 앞에 will을 붙여 will be able to 라고 쓰거나 be able to의 현재형을 사용한다. 이때 주어가 We이므로 are able to라고 쓴다.

PRACTICE 9

2	추측	3	능력	4	능력
5	추측	6	요청	7	능력
8	요청	9	허가	10	능력

1, 6, 8 'Could you ~?'가 '~해주시겠어요?'라는 요청의 의미로 사용되고 있다.
2, 5 can't/couldn't로 '~일 리가 없다'라는 추측의 의미를 전달하고 있다.
3, 4, 7, 10 '~할 수 있다/없다'라는 가능/불가능의 의미로 can/could를 사용하고 있다.
9 Could I ~?는 '~해도 될까요?'라는 의미로 상대에게 허락을 구하는 표현이다.

PRACTICE 10

1	Do	2	does	3	does	4	did
5	does	6	Do	7	does	8	do
9	don't	10	did				

1, 6 2인칭 주어나 복수 주어를 가진 일반동사의 의문문은 문장 맨 앞에 do가 와서「Do+주어+동사원형 ~?」어순이 된다.
2, 4, 8, 10 동사를 강조할 때 do를 쓴다. 주어의 수나 문장의 시제에 맞춰 do/does/did 중 알맞은 형태를 골라 써야 하며, 원래의 동사는 원형이 되어야 한다.
3, 5, 9 동사구의 반복을 피하기 위해 대동사 do를 쓴다.
7 일반동사의 부정문은 do를 써서 「do/does/did not+동사원형」 형태로 만든다.

PRACTICE 11

1. must be
2. doesn't have to[need not] give
3. will have to take
4. does like
5. can't[cannot] fail

> 1 조동사 must는 '~해야 한다'는 뜻 외에도 '~임에 틀림없다'는 강한 추측의 의미로도 쓰인다.
> 2 doesn't have to는 '~할 필요가 없다'는 의미로, need not과 바꾸어 쓸 수 있다.
> 3 '~해야 할 것이다'라는 미래의 의무를 나타낼 때는 will have to를 쓴다.
> 4 동사를 강조할 때는 3인칭 단수 주어이므로 「does+동사원형」으로 쓴다.
> 5 「can't[cannot]+동사원형」을 써서 '~할 리가 없다'라는 뜻으로 강한 의심을 나타낼 수 있다.

PRACTICE 12

1. You should not talk to your parents like that.
2. Should I go there again?
3. You should stop using your smartphone before bedtime.
4. Jenny should not forget the truth.
5. I should apologize to her.

> 1, 4 should not+동사원형: ~해서는 안 된다
> 2 Should I+동사원형 ~?: 제가 ~해야 하나요?
> 3, 5 should+동사원형: ~해야 한다

PRACTICE 13

2. He'd better get
3. We'd better take
4. You'd better study
5. You'd better not drive

> 1~5 조동사 had better는 일상 대화에서 보통 축약형 「'd better」로 사용된다. 부정형은 「'd better not」으로 '~하지 않는 편이 낫다'는 뜻이다

PRACTICE 14

1	Would	2	Will	3	Would
4	Can	5	Would	6	Can
7	Will	8	Would	9	Could
10	Do	11	Would	12	Could
13	Will	14	Would	15	Will

> 1, 11, 14 상대에게 음식 등을 권할 때 「Would you like+명사?」로 표현할 수 있다.
> 2, 7, 13, 15 Will/Would you ~?는 '~해주시겠습니까?'라는 뜻으로, 상대에게 요청/부탁을 할 때 쓰는 표현이다.
> 3, 5, 8 Would you like to+동사원형 ~?는 '~하시겠습니까?'라는 뜻으로, 상대에게 무언가를 제안할 때 쓰는 표현이다.
> 4, 6, 12 Can/Could I ~?는 '제가 ~해도 되겠습니까?'라는 뜻으로, 상대에게 허락을 구할 때 쓰는 표현이다.
> 9 Could you ~?는 '~해주시겠습니까?'라는 뜻으로, 상대에게 요청/부탁을 할 때 쓰는 표현이다.
> 10 '당신의 새 차가 마음에 드나요?'라고 묻는 일반동사의 의문문이므로 Do가 알맞다.

PRACTICE 15

2	may feel	3	may not know
4	may come	5	may not want
6	may work		

> 1, 2, 4, 6 조동사 may는 '~일지도 모른다, 아마 ~일 것이다'라는 뜻으로 약한 추측을 나타낼 때 쓴다.
> 3 민수가 나의 이름을 부르지 않는 이유로는 '네 이름을 알지 못할 수도 있다.'가 적절하므로 부정형(may not know)으로 쓴다.
> 5 Tom이 전화를 받지 않는 이유로 '누구와도 대화를 원하지 않을 수도 있어.'가 적절하므로 부정형(may not want)으로 쓴다.

PRACTICE 16

1	May	2	might	3	Will
4	did	5	must not	6	Can
7	have to	8	Would	9	be able to
10	May	11	Would		

> 1, 10 상대방에게 허락을 구하는 상황이므로 '~해도 될까요?'라는 뜻의 May I ~? 구문이 알맞다.
> 2 'Jane이 아플지도 모른다'라는 뜻이 되도록 약한 추측을 나타낼 때 쓰는 조동사 might가 알맞다.
> 3 상대방에게 부탁하는 상황이므로 '~해주시겠어요?'라는 의미로 쓰는 Will you ~? 구문이 알맞다.
> 4 동사를 강조하기 위해 do를 쓸 수 있는데, 여기서는 주어가 He이므로 did가 알맞다. 이때 원래의 동사는 원형으로 써야 한다.
> 5 허락을 구하는 말에 거절하는 상황이므로 '~하면 안 된다'는 뜻의 must not이 알맞다.
> 6 상대에게 부탁하는 상황이므로 '~해주시겠습니까?'라는 뜻으로 쓰이는 Can you ~? 구문이 알맞다.
> 7 비 오는 날에는 운전을 조심해야 한다는 내용이므로 '~해야 한다'는 의미로 의무를 나타낼 때 쓰는 have to가 알맞다.
> 8, 11 '~하시겠어요?'라고 상대방에게 무언가를 제안하거나 권하는 상황이므로 Would you like (to) ~? 구문이 알맞다.
> 9 '~할 수 있을 것이다'라는 미래의 능력을 나타낼 때는 will과 can을 함께 사용할 수 없으므로 can을 대신하여 will be able to를 쓴다.

PRACTICE 17

2 used to have
3 used to raise
4 used to[would] play
5 used to[would] ride
6 used to live

> 1, 2, 3, 6 과거의 상태에 대해 '과거에는 ~한 상태였지만 지금은 아니다'라고 할 때는 used to를 쓴다. 이 경우에는 과거의 행위에 대한 것이 아니므로 would를 쓰지 않는다.
> 4, 5 과거에 반복적으로 일어났으나 지금은 더 이상 이뤄지지 않는 행위를 나타내고 있으므로 '~하곤 했다'의 의미의 used to나 would를 쓴다.

PRACTICE 18

1 am used to doing yoga
2 were used to plant
3 used to go to bed
4 were used to carry
5 is not used to driving
6 are used to volunteering
7 is used to make chocolate
8 used to be chubby
9 is used to waking up
10 used to be afraid of

> 1, 5, 6, 9 '~하는 데 익숙하다'는 「be used to + -ing」로 나타낸다.
> 2, 4, 7 '~하는 데 사용되다'는 「be used to + 동사원형」으로 나타낸다.
> 3, 8, 10 '~하곤 했다'는 「used to + 동사원형」으로 나타낸다.

Chapter Review Test 정답 본문_p.89

1 ④   2 ②   3 ③   4 ⑤   5 ④   6 ①   7 ①,⑤
8 ④   9 ①   10 ②   11 ⑤   12 ④   13 There must be another way to solve this problem.
14 ⑤   15 ④   16 ②   17 I used to work at a restaurant near my house.   18 ③   19 ⑤
20 ⑤   21 ④   22 (1) You had better[You'd better] take some medicine. (2) You had better[You'd better] go to bed earlier. (3) She had better[She'd better] check the Lost and Found.   23 ⑤   24 You had better not go out tonight.   25 ④   26 ②   27 ②,③   28 ⑤
29 ①   30 ③   31 ④,⑤   32 ③   33 (1) was not able to (2) were able to   34 will be able to
35 should not turn right

Chapter Review Test 해설

1 ①② could/can과 may는 허가의 의미를 가지며 의문문으로 써서 허락을 구하는 질문(~해도 될까요?)을 만들 수 있다. 이때 대답은 긍정(해도 된다)과 부정(하면 안 된다)의 두 가지가 나올 수 있다.
④ 'Shouldn't you~?'는 '너 ~해야 하지 않아?'라는 의미의 질문이므로 대답은 you가 아닌 I로 해야 한다. 여기서 should는 의무를 나타낸다.
⑤ can은 '~해 주시겠어요?'라는 요청의 의미를 지니며 Can you give me a hand?는 '도와주시겠어요?'라는 의미이다.

2 '~해 주시겠어요?'라는 표현은 Would[Will] you~?로 쓴다. lend는 '(~을) 빌려주다'라는 뜻이고, borrow는 '(~을) 빌리다'라는 뜻이다.

3 ③ '~임에 틀림없다'   ①②④⑤ '~해야 한다'

4 ① 「Here is/are ~」은 뒤에 나오는 명사에 수를 일치시킨다. Donna's plan이 단수 명사구이므로, 동사 또한 단수 동사 is로 써야 한다. (are → is)
② 등위 접속사 and로 인해, 밑줄 친 부분은 vacuum과 병렬구조를 이루고 있다. vacuum은 조동사 다음에 와서 동사원형 형태이므로, wipe도 동사원형이 되어야 한다. (wipes → wipe)
③ want는 목적격 보어로 to부정사를 쓰는 동사이다. (spending → to spend)
④ if처럼 조건을 나타내는 접속사가 쓰인 조건의 부사절에서는 현재시제로 미래를 나타낸다. (will be → is)
⑤ 미래에 일어날 동작을 예측하는 것이므로, 미래시제를 쓰는 것이 알맞다.

5 ⓐ used to는 '~하곤 했다'는 의미의 조동사로, 뒤에 동사원형을 쓴다. (living → live)
ⓑ actress를 설명해주는 관계대명사절에서, 주격 관계대명사는 생략할 수 없다. 선행사가 사람이기 때문에, 주격 관계대명사인 who를 써야 한다. (was → who was)
ⓒ 의문사가 없는 간접의문문은 「if + 주어 + 동사」의 어순으로 쓴다.
ⓓ 조동사는 현재시제의 3인칭 단수형으로 쓰지 않는다. (musts → must)
ⓔ 현재의 사실이나 상태를 나타내므로, 현재시제로 써주어야 하고, 주어 Penny가 3인칭 단수이므로 동사에 -s를 붙여야 한다.
ⓕ stop은 동명사를 목적어로 쓰는 동사이다.

⑨ want는 to부정사를 목적격 보어로 쓰는 동사이다. (attend → to attend)

6 문맥상 can의 과거형 could가 알맞다.

7 ② '주말마다 축구를 하곤 했다'는 뜻이므로 「used to + 동사원형」으로 나타낸다. (playing →play)
③ '고기를 먹곤 했다'는 뜻이므로 「used to + 동사원형」으로 나타낸다. (is used to → used to)
④ '그리는(칠하는) 데 사용되다'라는 뜻이므로 「be used to + 동사원형」으로 나타낸다. (painting → paint)

8 「used to+동사원형」 '(과거에) ~하곤 했다'

9 ① must의 부정형은 must not으로 쓴다. (doesn't must → must not)

10 ② 일반동사 do
①③④⑤ 동사를 강조하는 역할의 do

11 ⑤ knows → know

12 종속절(because ~)의 내용으로 보아 should not이 적절하다.

13 '~가 있다'라는 의미를 가진 「There is/are ~」를 활용한다. '~임에 틀림없다'는 강한 추측은 조동사 must를 활용해 나타낸다. '해결할 다른 방법'이라는 부분은 to부정사의 형용사적 용법을 사용해 명사(another way)를 뒤에서 수식해준다.

14 must의 과거는 had to이므로 의문문에서는 'Did … have to ~?'의 형태가 된다.

15 제주도에 가본 적이 있는 A가 거기서 할 수 있는 활동을 추천하고 이에 긍정적으로 대답하므로 shouldn't(~하지 않는 게 좋다)가 아닌 should(~하는 게 좋다)를 사용하여 추천, 제안을 나타내는 것이 적절하다.

16 ② 동사를 강조하는 do
①⑤ 일반동사 do
③ 동사의 반복을 피하는 대동사 do
④ 의문문에 쓰이는 do

17 현재는 더 이상 하지 않는 과거의 동작이나 상태는 used to로 나타낸다.

18 ① don't have to는 불필요의 의미를 나타내며 need not으로 바꿔 쓸 수 있다.
② 과거의 습관적인 행위(~하곤 했다)를 나타내는 used to는 would로 바꿔 쓸 수 있다.
③ had better는 '~하는 게 낫다'라는 의미의 조동사이고, would like to는 '~하고 싶다'라는 뜻이므로 서로 바꿔 쓸 수 없다.
④ 능력/가능을 의미하는 can은 be able to로 바꿔 쓸 수 있다.

⑤ 'Would you~?'가 '~해 주시겠습니까?'라는 요청의 의미로 쓰였을 때 'Could you~?'로 바꿔 쓸 수 있다.

19 대화의 내용에 따르면 해당 좌석은 몸이 불편한 분들을 위한 것이므로 빈칸에는 '우리는 여기에 앉으면 안 된다.'는 금지의 내용이 들어가야 한다. ⑤ don't have to는 불필요를 의미하므로 빈칸에 들어가기에 적절하지 않다.

20 ⓐⓑⓒⓓ 규칙에 대하여 설명하므로 '~해야 한다'라는 의무나 당위를 나타내는 조동사 must나 should가 들어가야 한다.
ⓔ 규칙을 어기면 일어날 일에 대해서 설명하므로 미래의 일에 대한 가능성이나 추측을 나타내는 조동사 can[could], may[might], will[would]이 들어가야 한다.

21 앞에 나온 cries의 반복을 피하기 위한 대동사로 do의 3인칭 단수형인 does가 적절하다.

22 「had better+동사원형」 '~하는 게 낫다'

23 ① like는 to부정사 또는 동명사를 목적어로 취한다. (read → to read[reading])
② would like to + 동사원형: ~하고 싶다 (having → have)
③ 조동사 might 뒤에는 동사원형이 와야 한다. (looks → look)
④ 등위접속사 and가 where절에 있는 두 개의 동사, talk와 watch를 연결하고 있다. talk 앞에 조동사 can이 있으므로 watch 앞에도 조동사 can이 생략된 것으로 보는 것이 적절하다. 따라서 watching을 watch로 고쳐야 한다. (watching → watch)
⑤ why don't you + 동사원형?: ~ 하는 게 어때? will be able to + 동사원형: ~ 할 수 있을 것이다.

24 had better의 부정문은 「had better not+동사원형」의 어순으로 쓴다.

25 ④ Can을 이용하여 허가(~해도 될까요?)에 대한 질문을 했으므로 불필요(don't have to: ~할 필요 없다)를 나타내는 대답은 적절하지 못하다.

26 동사구의 반복을 피하는 대동사 did

27 긍정이면 Yes, you may.로, 부정이면 No, you may not[must not, can't].로 대답한다.

28 would like to = want to
'~하고 싶어하다, ~하기를 원하다'

29 should not '~하지 말아야 한다'

30 because가 이끄는 절의 주어인 I 뒤에 am이 있으므

로 be able to의 형태가 되어야 한다.
31 '항공권 예약을 도와주시겠어요?'라고 물었으므로 ④ '혼자서 여행하지 그래?' 와 ⑤ '너는 소중한 시간을 낭비해서는 안 돼.'는 대답으로 적절하지 않다.
32 had better은 뒤에 동사원형이 온다. 부정형은 had better not으로 쓴다.
ⓐ I'd not better → I'd better not
ⓒ to answer → answer
ⓓ to bring → bring
33 be able to는 '~할 수 있다'라는 뜻이며, 이때 be는 주어의 인칭과 수, 시제에 따라 변한다. 부정문은 be동사 뒤에 not을 써서 표현한다.
34 '능력'을 뜻하는 조동사 can의 미래형은 will be able to로 쓴다.
35 우회전을 하지 말라는 표지판이므로, should not으로 금지를 나타낸다.

CHAPTER 4 수동태
Passive Voice

본문 _ p.96

PRACTICE 1

2	read	3	stolen	4	sung
5	made	6	broken	7	caught
8	taught	9	written	10	spoken
11	grown	12	fed	13	taken
14	kept				

PRACTICE 2

2 I am loved by my friends.
3 *The Mona Lisa* was painted by Leonardo da Vinci.
4 Plastic bottles are recycled by them.
5 Those black pants were bought by me.
6 Those cookies were made by my mom.
7 A lot of books are read by him.
8 All the classmates were invited to the party by Jason.
9 Thieves are caught by the police.
10 The news was reported by Harry.
11 Stamps and coins are collected by Mrs. Lopez.
12 Two black bears were killed by the hunter.
13 The bus was stopped by the police officer.
14 The meeting was held by Mr. Kim.
15 The rules of the meeting were changed by the president.

> **2~15** 능동태 문장의 목적어를 수동태 문장의 주어로 하고, 능동태 문장의 동사를 「be동사+과거분사」의 형태로 바꾼 다음, 능동태 문장의 주어를 「by+목적격」으로 바꾼다.

PRACTICE 3

2 The cake wasn't made by my mother.
3 English isn't spoken by some people in Japan.
4 Was he invited to Jane's birthday party?
5 Was that book written by him?
6 Shakespeare didn't write that play.
7 Bibimbap isn't sold by[at] Lily's restaurant.
8 Is Gyeongbokgung Palace loved by many tourists?
9 Yuri didn't pay the bill.
10 Was Jake hurt by his brother in the park yesterday?

> **2, 3, 7** 수동태의 부정문은 「주어+be동사+not+과거분사+by+목적격」의 어순으로 쓴다.
> **4, 5, 8, 10** 수동태의 의문문은 「be동사+주어+과거분사+by+목적격?」의 어순으로 쓴다.
> **6, 9** 수동태 부정문을 능동태로 전환하면 「be동사+not+과거분사」 부분이 「don't/doesn't/didn't+동사원형」이 된다.
> *pay the bill: 요금을 지불하다, 대금을 치르다

PRACTICE 4

2 The magazine will be delivered by the man.
3 The room will be cleaned later (by somebody).
4 A new restaurant has been built by Reagan.
5 More trees will be cut down in the future (by people).
6 His lies have been believed (by everyone).
7 Movies or TV programs are made by directors.
8 The chair has been painted by us.

9 This building has been built for three years by the people.
10 The money will be used to buy a new game character by him.

> 2, 3, 5, 10 미래시제의 수동태에서는 동사가 「will be+과거분사」의 형태이다.
> 4, 6, 8, 9 현재완료시제의 수동태에서는 동사가 「have/has been+과거분사」의 형태이다.
> 7 현재시제의 수동태에서는 동사가 「am/are/is+과거분사」의 형태이다.

PRACTICE 5

1 was invented **2** was moved
3 will be done **4** was painted
5 has been polluted

> **1** 과거의 특정 연도(1879)가 있으므로 과거시제 수동태가 알맞다.
> **2, 4** 과거를 나타내는 부사(구) yesterday, last week가 있으므로 과거시제 수동태가 알맞다.
> **3** 미래를 나타내는 부사구 next Friday가 있으므로 미래시제 수동태가 알맞다.
> **5** '~ 이후로'라는 의미의 「since+시점」 표현이 있으므로 현재완료시제 수동태가 알맞다.

PRACTICE 6

2 It may be done tomorrow by Tony.
3 The problem must be solved by him.
4 The rules for this game should be obeyed by them.
5 The plans for the summer might be changed by us.
6 Dinner couldn't be prepared last night by me.
7 A computer must be used for this task by Suji.
8 They should not[shouldn't] be put here by us.
9 The promise may not be kept by Tom.
10 The view could be seen very well by the people.

> **2~10** 조동사가 있는 문장을 수동태로 바꿀 때는 「주어+조동사+be동사 원형+과거분사+by+목적격」 순으로 쓴다.

PRACTICE 7

1 should be washed **2** can be saved
3 will be cooked   **4** must be painted
5 will be loved

> 각 문장을 능동태로 표현하면 다음과 같다.
> **1** You should wash your clothes soon.
> **2** You can save a lot of resources.
> **3** Paul will cook them.
> **4** You must paint this house by tomorrow.
> **5** I will love my dog forever.

PRACTICE 8

1 A new bag was bought for the boy by Mr. Kim.
2 My brother was made angry by me.
3 He was elected the president by them.
4 Bob was shown their pictures by them.
Their pictures were shown to Bob by them.
5 I was given lovely flowers by Nick.
Lovely flowers were given to me by Nick.
6 The place was kept clean by Jenny.
7 The fish was named "Wish" by my daughter.
8 The restaurant is called George's (by people).
9 Spaghetti was cooked for me yesterday by my mom.
10 I was lent 5,000 won yesterday by Minho.
5,000 won was lent to me yesterday by Minho.

> **1, 9** buy, cook은 직접목적어만을 수동태로 하는 동사들이다. 직접목적어가 수동태의 주어가 될 때는 간접목적어 앞에 전치사 for이 온다.
> **4, 5, 10** 4형식 문장이므로 간접목적어와 직접목적어 둘 다 수동태의 주어가 될 수 있지만, 직접목적어가 수동태의 주어가 될 때는 간접목적어 앞에 to, for, of와 같은 전치사가 온다.
> **2, 3, 6, 7, 8** 5형식 문장을 수동태 문장으로 바꿀 때, 목적격 보어가 명사나 형용사인 경우에는 「be동사+과거분사」 뒤에 목적격 보어를 이어서 쓴다.
>
> **1** buy A B: A에게 B를 사주다 (4형식)
> = B be bought for A
> **2** make A B: A를 B하게 만들다 (5형식)
> = A be made B
> **3** elect A B: A를 B로 선출하다 (5형식)
> = A be elected B
> **4** show A B: A에게 B를 보여주다 (4형식)
> = A be shown B
> = B be shown to A
> **5** give A B: A에게 B를 주다 (4형식)
> = A be given B
> = B be given to A
> **6** keep A B: A를 B한 상태로 유지하다 (5형식)
> = A be kept B
> **7** name A B: A를 B라고 이름을 짓다 (5형식)
> = A be named B
> **8** call A B: A를 B로 부르다 (5형식)
> = A be called B
> **9** cook A B: A에게 B를 요리해주다 (4형식)
> = B be cooked for A

10 lend A B: A에게 B를 빌려주다 (4형식)
= A be lent B
= B be lent to A

7, 10, 15 4형식 문장의 수동태는 능동태의 간접목적어나 직접목적어가 주어가 되는데, 직접목적어가 주어가 될 때는 간접목적어 앞에 to, for, of 같은 전치사가 온다.
8, 18 make는 목적어가 2개인 4형식 문장을 만드는 동사지만, 사람(간접목적어)이 주어인 수동태 문장은 의미상 어색하기 때문에 쓰지 않는다. 따라서 수동태의 주어로 직접목적어만 허용된다.
9, 14, 17 목적격 보어가 명사나 형용사인 5형식 문장의 수동태는 「be동사+과거분사」 뒤에 목적격 보어를 이어서 쓴다.

PRACTICE 9

1	with	2	in	3	about
4	to	5	with[about]	6	about
7	from	8	with	9	at
10	with	11	from	12	for

PRACTICE 10

1 The president was welcomed by the crowd.
2 The work could be finished easily by me.
3 Science will be taught by Mr. Song.
4 The dishes weren't done by Yumi.
5 The living room and the bathroom are cleaned by my kids.
6 The party has been postponed by Susan.
7 We were given some information by John.
   Some information was given to us by John.
8 A family photo album was made for my parents by my brother.
9 I am called Jen by Alex.
10 I was asked some difficult questions by my son.
   Some difficult questions were asked of me by my son.
11 The photocopier can be fixed by Mike.
12 This wall wasn't painted by Cathy.
13 Bill must be invited to the show by you.
14 We were made bored by his story.
15 I was paid 30,000 won by Seho.
   30,000 won was paid to me by Seho.
16 Many herbs can be grown at home by you.
17 His cat was named Garfield by him.
18 Sandwiches were made for me by him.

1 과거시제의 수동태는 「주어+was/were+과거분사+by+목적격」 순으로 쓴다.
2, 3, 11, 13, 16 조동사가 있는 수동태는 「주어+조동사+be동사 원형+과거분사+by+목적격」 순으로 쓴다.
4, 12 과거시제 수동태의 부정문은 「주어+was/were+not+과거분사+by+목적격」 순으로 쓴다.
5 현재시제의 수동태는 「주어+am/are/is+과거분사+by+목적격」 순으로 쓴다. 주어의 the living room과 the bathroom이 접속사 and로 연결되어 복수 취급한다.
6 현재완료시제의 수동태는 「주어+have/has been+과거분사+by+목적격」 순으로 쓴다.

Chapter Review Test 정답 본문 _ p.108

1 ③ 2 are helped 3 ②,⑤ 4 ④
5 ③ 6 ① 7 Rice noodles were cooked for his friends by him. 8 ③ 9 I was called Alex (by people). 10 ⑤ 11 of 12 ②
13 is spoken, is held 14 ④ 15 was invented
16 ① 17 ②,④ 18 ② 19 (1) A lot of time will be given to you by me.[You will be given a lot of time by me.] (2) My car has been stolen (by someone). (3) The mystery can be explained by them. 20 ④ 21 ⑤ 22 ②,⑤
23 ⑤ 24 (A) was stolen (B) were saved
25 ② 26 made of 27 ④ 28 ⑤ 29 ②
30 ② 31 All the plants have been watered by us. 32 This cup is filled with water. 33 ④
34 ⑤ 35 *The Old Man and the Sea* was written by Ernest Hemingway. 36 ④ 37 is called a siesta by the Spanish 38 ⑤ 39 were killed 40 ⓐ was born ⓑ is known
41 (1) with (2) of (3) about 42 will be saved by this medicine

Chapter Review Test 해설

1 ③ → Our grandmother has the red car. '가지다, 소유하다'라는 뜻의 have는 수동태 문장으로 만들 수 없다.
2 능동태의 시제가 현재이면 수동태는 「is[are]+과거분사」가 된다. 주어가 복수형이므로 are를 쓴다.
3 수동태는 「be동사+과거분사」로 쓴다.
  ② teached → taught   ⑤ wrote → written
4 be interested in '~에 흥미가 있다'
5 ① 수동태는 「be동사+과거분사」의 형태이다.
   (was catch → was caught)

② 도둑이 훔친 것이므로 능동태를 쓴다.
(was stolen → stole)
④ 경찰이 본 것이므로 능동태를 쓴다.
(was seen → saw)
⑤ 수동태는 「be동사+과거분사」의 형태이다.
(was arrest → was arrested)

6 ② 조동사가 포함된 수동태는 「조동사+be동사+과거분사」로 쓴다. (prepared → be prepared)
③ 수동태는 「be동사+과거분사」로 쓴다.
(made → are[were] made)
④ 주어 This novel이 단수이므로 be동사는 was로 쓴다. (were written → was written)
⑤ 주어 They가 복수이므로 have를 사용한다.
(has been taught → have been taught)

7 4형식 동사 cook은 직접목적어만을 주어로 삼아 수동태로 만들며 「직접목적어+be cooked+for+간접목적어」의 형태로 쓴다.

8 ③ 주어가 3인칭 단수(My friend)인데 동사 read에 -s가 없으므로 read가 과거시제로 쓰였음을 알 수 있다. 따라서 수동태로 전환한 문장 또한 과거시제여야 한다. (is read → was read)

9 목적격 보어가 명사인 5형식 문장을 수동태로 바꿀 때, 목적격 보어는 과거분사 뒤에 이어서 쓴다. 능동태의 시제가 과거이므로 수동태는 「was[were]+과거분사」이며, 수동태의 주어(I)가 단수이므로 was를 쓴다.

10 ⑤ 머리카락이 잘린 것이므로 수동태로 써야 한다. 과거를 나타내는 last Wednesday가 쓰였으므로 과거시제이다. (cut → was cut)

11 4형식 문장의 직접목적어가 수동태의 주어가 될 때는 간접목적어 앞에 전치사를 쓴다. 동사 ask의 간접목적어 앞에는 전치사 of가 온다.

12 수동태의 시제가 과거이므로 능동태도 과거시제가 되어야 한다.

13 수동태 문장은 「be동사+과거분사」의 형태를 사용하여 만든다.
• speak - spoke - spoken   • hold - held - held

14 ⓑ 현재완료시제의 수동태는 「have+been+과거분사」로 쓴다.
(have being washed → have been washed)
ⓔ 수동태는 「be동사+과거분사」로 쓴다. choose의 과거분사는 chosen이다. (chose → chosen)

15 과거의 역사적 사실을 나타내므로 수동태의 시제도 과거가 되어야 한다.

16 be interested in은 '~에 흥미가 있다'는 뜻의 관용표현이다.
① in ②③④⑤ by

17 ①③⑤ 동사 resemble, 자동사 disappear, 동사 suit 등은 수동태 문장으로 만들 수 없다.

18 수동태의 부정문은 「주어+be동사+not+과거분사」의 어순이므로 ②는 The museum was not built in 2011.이 되어야 한다.

19 (1), (3) 「조동사+(not)+be+과거분사」
(2) 「have[has]+been+과거분사」
행위 주체가 someone, anyone 등일 때 'by+목적격'은 생략이 가능하다.

20 ④ → Spaghetti with cream sauce was made for him by his wife.
4형식 동사 make는 직접목적어만을 수동태의 주어로 취한다.

21 ⑤ 방이 매일 아침 청소가 되어지는 것이므로 수동태를 사용해야 한다. (cleaning → cleaned)

22 ① 집이 지어진 것이므로 수동태를 사용해야 한다.
(built → was built)
③ 수동태는 「be동사+과거분사」로 쓴다.
(calls → is called)
④ 과거 시제를 써서 질문했으므로 대답도 과거 시제로 해야 한다. (is caught → was caught)

23 ⑤ 동사 buy는 직접목적어만을 수동태의 주어로 쓸 수 있고, 3형식 문장에서 간접목적어 앞에 전치사 for를 써야 한다. 따라서 주어로 직접목적어인 A toy car가 쓰였고 간접목적어 앞에 전치사 for가 있으므로 적절하다.
① 불규칙 동사 cut은 원형, 과거형, 과거분사형이 같다. (cutted → cut)
② 5형식의 수동태 문장으로 시제가 과거이므로 is가 아닌 was가 적절하다. (is → was)
③ '발견하다'의 의미를 지닌 동사 find의 과거분사는 found이다. '설립하다'의 의미를 지닌 found의 과거분사가 founded이다. (founded → found)
④ 4형식 문장의 직접목적어가 주어로 온 수동태 문장이다. 동사 make는 간접목적어 앞에 전치사 for를 쓴다. (to → for)

24 (A) steal-stole-stolen   (B) save-saved-saved

25 ② 주어 The cookies가 복수이므로 be동사는 were을 사용한다. (was baked → were baked)

26 be made of '~로 만들어지다'(물리적 변화)

27 ④ 5형식 문장을 수동태로 전환할 때 형용사 목적격

보어는 「be동사+과거분사」 뒤에 그대로 쓴다.
(be happy → happy)

28 ⑤ 4형식 문장을 3형식으로 고칠 때, buy는 전치사 for을 수반하는 동사이다. (to her → for her)

29 ② 능동태의 시제가 과거이므로 수동태도 과거로 쓰고 간접목적어 앞에 전치사를 넣는다.
(is sent her → was sent to her)

30 바르게 배열하면 The preparation should be completed by next Friday.가 된다.

31 주어가 3인칭 복수인 현재완료시제의 수동태이므로 「have+been+과거분사」의 형태가 되어야 한다.

32 be filled with '~로 가득 차 있다'

33 행위의 주체가 일반인이거나 굳이 말하지 않아도 알 수 있는 경우에는 「by+목적격」을 생략할 수 있다.

34 ⓐ '가방이 금화로 가득 차 있다'는 의미이므로 빈칸에는 '~로 가득 찬'을 의미하는 'be filled with'가 들어가야 한다. (be filled with = be full of)
ⓑ '~이래로'를 의미하는 since는 현재완료시제와 주로 쓰여 특정 시점 이후로 계속되었음을 나타내므로 has been built가 적절하다.
ⓒ 주어(Nothing)가 사람이 아니기 때문에 '만족감을 느꼈다'는 의미의 'was satisfied'는 적절하지 않

다. '아무것도 내 아버지를 만족시키지 못했다.'는 뜻이므로 satisfied가 들어가야 한다.

35 능동태를 수동태로 바꿀 때에는 능동태의 목적어를 주어 자리로 옮기고, 동사는 「be동사+과거분사」의 형태로, 주어는 「by+목적격」으로 바꾸고 시제는 능동태와 일치시킨다.

36 ④ be satisfied with '~에 만족하다' (to → with)

37 5형식 문장을 수동태로 전환할 때, 동사가 call, 목적격 보어가 명사(a siesta)인 경우에 해당하므로 「be동사+과거분사」 뒤에 목적격 보어를 이어서 쓰고, 그 뒤에 by+목적격을 쓴다.

38 ⑤ 집이 칠해지는 것이므로 수동태를 사용해야 한다.
(painting → painted)

39 주어가 3인칭 복수이고 과거의 역사적 사실을 나타내는 과거시제의 수동태이므로 「were+과거분사」의 형태가 되어야 한다.

40 ⓐ be born '태어나다'
ⓑ be known for '~로(~때문에) 알려지다'

41 (1) be covered with '~로 덮여 있다'
(2) be made of '~로 만들어지다' (물리적 변화)
(3) be excited about '~에 흥분해 있다'

42 수동태의 미래형은 「will be+과거분사」로 쓴다.

CHAPTER 5 명사와 관사
Nouns and Articles

본문 _ p.116

PRACTICE 1

1 eggs		**2** watches	
3 horses		**4** pens	
5 shoes		**6** glasses	
7 books		**8** dishes	
9 churches		**10** classmates	
11 bottles		**12** classes	
13 girls		**14** cameras	
15 buses		**16** months	
17 beaches		**18** boxes	
19 neighbors		**20** brushes	
21 houses		**22** places	
23 customs		**24** friends	
25 foxes		**26** matches	
27 sandwiches		**28** wishes	
29 bicycles		**30** animals	

PRACTICE 2

1 ladies		**2** stories	
3 keys		**4** parties	
5 diaries		**6** songs	
7 couches		**8** monkeys	
9 babies		**10** activities	
11 cities		**12** donkeys	
13 students		**14** cultures	
15 days		**16** families	
17 boys		**18** habits	
19 ways		**20** factories	

21	hobbies	22	ferries
23	candies	24	computers
25	benches	26	countries
27	memories	28	doctors
29	pennies	30	communities

10	are	11	girl	12	class
13	families	14	is, are	15	building

※ 8번의 family, 14번의 team은 집합체를 하나의 단위로 보아 단수 취급하거나 개별 구성원에 중점을 두어 복수 취급할 수 있음.

(밑줄: 정답의 근거)
1 Lisa bought <u>two</u> **books** for me.
2 The **scientist** <u>was</u> happy to solve the problem.
3 I think your **dogs** <u>are</u> all very cute.
4 There <u>is a</u> **hospital** around the corner.
5 <u>Five</u> **teams** will take part in the contest.
6 They invited more than <u>a hundred</u> **people** to their wedding.
7 I got <u>a</u> **letter** from my friend, John.
8 My <u>family</u> **was/were** very glad to meet Mr. Park.
9 I met <u>three</u> **friends** of Minsu's yesterday.
10 There **are** seven <u>classes</u> in 4th grade at the elementary school.
11 The brave **girl** never <u>cries</u> in front of others.
12 The **class** <u>is</u> going to go on a trip.
13 <u>Many</u> **families** in America <u>have</u> pets.
14 My **team** **is/are** ready to start the game.
15 We found <u>a</u> new **building** in our town.

PRACTICE 3

1	videos	2	children
3	wolves	4	beliefs
5	lives	6	oxen
7	potatoes	8	mice
9	sheep	10	men
11	photos	12	geese
13	roofs	14	teeth
15	tomatoes	16	fish/fishes
17	knives	18	clocks
19	calves	20	yourselves
21	mosquito(e)s	22	radios
23	wives	24	memos
25	leaves	26	deer
27	heroes	28	loaves
29	blouses	30	safes
31	shelves	32	feet
33	kangaroos	34	thieves
35	studios	36	chiefs
37	women	38	zoos
39	pianos	40	emergencies

PRACTICE 4

1	○	2	앞에 a나 an을 쓰지 않음.
3	○	4	○
5	앞에 a나 an을 쓰지 않음.	6	○
7	○	8	앞에 a나 an을 쓰지 않음.
9	○	10	○
11	앞에 a나 an을 쓰지 않음.	12	○
13	○	14	앞에 a나 an을 쓰지 않음.
15	○		

PRACTICE 5

1	books	2	scientist	3	dogs
4	hospital	5	teams	6	people
7	letter	8	was, were	9	friends

PRACTICE 6

2	is	3	countries
4	a car	5	lives
6	Leaves[The leaves]	7	are
8	a[the] bag	9	a[the] restaurant
10	was		

2, 5 집합명사는 집합체를 하나의 단위로 보아 단수 취급하거나 개별 구성원에 중점을 두어 복수 취급하기도 하는데, 여기서 my class(우리 반)와 my family(우리 가족)는 하나의 단위로 보아야 하므로 단수 취급한다.
3 country는 셀 수 있는 명사이므로 many의 수식을 받으려면 복수형이 되어야 한다.
4, 8, 9 car, bag, restaurant은 셀 수 있는 명사이므로 단수형으로 쓰려면 앞에 관사가 와야 한다.
6 leaf는 셀 수 있는 명사이므로 단수형 또는 복수형으로 모두 쓸 수 있는데, fall이 복수 동사이므로 복수 명사 Leaves[The leaves]로 써야 한다.
7 teeth는 tooth의 복수형이므로 동사가 복수형 are가 되어야 한다.
10 주어가 단수 명사인 the book이므로 단수 동사 was가 알맞다.

PRACTICE 7

1	water	2	Saturday
3	a computer	4	beauty
5	New York	6	happiness
7	air	8	dogs

CHAPTER 5

9	Death	10	A family
11	September	12	salt
13	Christmas	14	paper
15	advice		

> **1, 7, 12, 14** 일정한 형태가 없는 물질을 나타내는 물질명사는 a/an의 수식을 받을 수 없으며 복수형으로 쓰지 않는다.
> **2, 5, 11, 13** 사람, 장소, 요일 등을 나타내는 고유명사는 a/an의 수식을 받을 수 없으며 복수형으로 쓰지 않는다.
> **3, 8** 셀 수 있는 명사는 관사와 함께 단수형으로 쓰거나 관사가 없을 때는 반드시 복수형으로 써야 한다.
> **4, 6, 9, 15** 눈에 보이지 않는 개념을 나타내는 추상명사는 a/an의 수식을 받을 수 없으며 복수형으로 쓰지 않는다.
> **10** 집합명사 family는 셀 수 있는 명사이므로 단수 형태로 쓰려면 앞에 관사가 있어야 한다.

PRACTICE 8

1	information	2	juice
3	Seoul	4	happiness
5	Jane	6	time
7	families	8	class
9	questions	10	apples

> **1, 2, 4, 6** 추상명사(information, happiness, time)와 물질명사(juice)는 셀 수 없는 명사로, 양을 나타낼 때는 much, (a) little, some, any, no, all, lots of, a lot of 같은 형용사와 함께 쓰인다.
> *lots of information: 많은 정보
> *there is little juice: 주스가 거의 없다
> *take a lot of time: 시간이 많이 걸리다
> **3, 5** 고유명사는 관사 없이 쓰며, 첫 글자는 항상 대문자다.
> **7** 집합명사 family는 셀 수 있는 명사이므로 복수 형태로 those의 수식을 받을 수 있다.
> **8** each는 셀 수 있는 명사 class의 단수형 앞에 와서 '각 학급'이라는 뜻으로 쓰인다.
> **9, 10** 셀 수 있는 명사의 복수형은 수사, many, a lot of, lots of, (a) few 등의 다양한 수량 형용사와 함께 쓸 수 있다.

PRACTICE 9

1	a piece[sheet] of	2	three slices of
3	four glasses of		
4	ten spoonfuls[teaspoonfuls] of		
5	five pounds of	6	a piece of
7	three cups of	8	a bottle of
9	six bars of	10	two slices of

PRACTICE 10

2	loaf of bread
3	piece of advice
4	glasses[cups/bottles] of water
5	pieces of furniture
6	pieces[slices/loaves] of bread
7	cup of tea
8	spoonfuls[teaspoonfuls] of salt
9	pounds of meat
10	glass[bottle] of wine

PRACTICE 11

1	was	2	is
3	socks	4	is
5	glasses, them	6	five-story
7	is	8	those scissors
9	two-hour	10	pairs, shoes
11	three-month-old	12	pants
13	ten-dollar	14	makes
15	gloves		

> **1, 2, 4, 7, 14** the news(뉴스, 소식), customs(세관), politics(정치학), economics(경제학), mathematics(수학)와 같은 명사들은 형태는 복수형으로 보이지만 단수 취급한다.
> **3, 5, 8, 10, 12, 15** 한 쌍을 이루어 사용되는 명사는 복수형으로 쓰고 복수 취급한다.
> **6, 9, 11, 13** 「수사+명사」가 뒤에 이어지는 명사를 수식하는 형용사처럼 쓰일 때는 수사 다음의 명사를 복수형으로 쓰지 않는다.

PRACTICE 12

2	Mr. Kim's friend	3	Mr. Kim's wife
4	Mr. Kim's son	5	Mr. Kim's niece

PRACTICE 13

2	my dog's tail
3	the exit of the building
4	the owner of this car
5	today's TV programs
6	the bottom of the bottle
7	my students' report cards
8	Mr. Brown's blanket
9	the result of the test
10	my sisters' clothes

> **2, 7, 8, 10** 사람이나 동물을 나타내는 명사는 '(s)를 이용하여 소유격을 만든다.
> **3, 4, 6, 9** 무생물의 소유격은 주로 of를 이용한다.
> **5** 시간을 나타내는 명사는 '(s)를 이용하여 소유격을 만든다.

PRACTICE 14

1	that	2	,	3	that	4	,
5	of	6	of	7	that	8	of
9	that	10	,				

> **1, 3, 7, 9** 명사구와 문장이 동격을 이루고 있으므로 동격의 접속사 that을 이용한다.
> the fact = The Earth moves around the Sun. 지구가 태양 주위를 돈다는 사실
> a dream = He wants to be a famous actor. 그가 유명한 배우가 되기를 원한다는 꿈
> our opinion = He should attend the meeting. 그가 회의에 참석해야 한다는 우리의 의견
> the rumor = She stole the money. 그녀가 돈을 훔쳤다는 소문
> **2, 4, 10** 두 명사(구)가 같은 대상을 가리킬 때는 콤마(,)를 이용해 동격을 나타낸다.
> Tom = the man in a blue shirt
> 푸른색 셔츠를 입은 남자 Tom
> BTS = my favorite boy group
> 내가 가장 좋아하는 보이그룹 BTS
> Ms. Scott = the ballet teacher 발레 선생님 Scott 씨
> **5, 6, 8** 명사와 동명사구가 서로 동격일 때는 of를 이용한다.
> The news = her coming to Seoul 그녀가 서울에 온다는 소식
> the idea = moving to Chicago 시카고로 이사한다는 생각
> hope = winning the game 경기에서 이긴다는 가능성

PRACTICE 15

1	×	2	×	3	○	4	○
5	×	6	○	7	○	8	×
9	×	10	×				

> **1, 5, 10** that이 관계대명사로 쓰였다.
> the song that is easy to sing: 부르기 쉬운 노래 (주격 관계대명사)
> a book that I borrowed from my friend: 친구에게 빌린 책 (목적격 관계대명사)
> the one that I love most: 내가 가장 사랑하는 사람 (목적격 관계대명사)
> **2** of가 소유격(~의)을 나타내는 전치사로 쓰였다.
> the picture of my little dog: 내 작은 강아지의 사진
> **3, 7** that이 동격의 접속사로 쓰였다.
> news = we would go to an amusement park: 우리가 놀이공원에 갈 거라는 소식
> the advice = I should drink more water: 내가 물을 더 많이 마셔야 한다는 충고
> **4** of가 동격을 나타내는 전치사로 쓰였다.
> the fact = his not coming to the class: 그가 수업에 오지 않는다는 사실
> **6** 콤마(,)를 이용해 두 명사(구)가 동격임을 나타내고 있다. (David = my boss)
> **8** 콤마(,)가 A, B and C 구조로 세 개의 명사(Mary, Kate, Tom)를 나열하는 데 쓰였다.
> **9** that이 명사절(목적어 역할)을 이끄는 접속사로 쓰였다.

PRACTICE 16

1	an	2	a	3	an	4	a
5	An	6	an	7	a	8	a
9	a	10	an	11	an	12	a
13	an	14	a	15	a		

> **1, 11, 13** 첫소리가 모음으로 발음되는 명사의 단수형 앞에는 an을 쓴다.
> **2, 9, 12, 15** 명사 앞의 형용사의 첫소리가 자음으로 발음되면 a를 쓴다.
> **3, 5, 6, 10** 명사 앞의 형용사의 첫소리가 모음으로 발음되면 an을 쓴다.
> **4, 7, 8, 14** 첫소리가 자음으로 발음되는 명사의 단수형 앞에는 a를 쓴다.

PRACTICE 17

1	an egg	2	a house
3	a tree	4	a baby
5	a glass	6	A police officer
7	an elephant	8	a monitor

PRACTICE 18

1	③	2	①	3	④	4	⑥
5	②	6	①	7	⑤	8	⑤
9	②	10	⑥	11	④	12	③

PRACTICE 19

1	the	2	the	3	a	4	The
5	the	6	a	7	the	8	The
9	a	10	a	11	the	12	The
13	the	14	a, The	15	The, the		

> **1, 5** 유일한 것을 나타낼 때 the를 쓴다.
> the Earth, the Moon
> **2, 7, 15** 듣는 사람이 무엇을 가리키는지 알 수 있을 때 the를 쓴다.
> **3, 9** one(하나의)의 의미일 때 a/an을 쓴다.
> a jacket: 재킷 하나
> a glass of water: 물 한 잔
> **4, 8, 13** 앞에 나온 명사가 반복될 때 the를 쓴다.
> John and Mary's baby → the baby
> a pen → the pen
> a skirt → the skirt
> **6** some(약간의, 어느 정도)의 의미일 때 a/an을 쓴다.
> a while ago: 조금 전에
> **10** per(~당, ~마다)의 의미일 때 a/an을 쓴다.
> two long vacations a year: 1년마다 두 번의 긴 휴가
> **11, 12** 명사 뒤에 명사를 수식하는 구나 절이 있을 때 the를 쓴다.
> the concert that you told me about:

네가 나에게 말했던 그 콘서트
the book on my desk: 책상 위에 있는 그 책
14 앞의 restaurant는 '어떤 식당(a certain restaurant)'을 의미하고, 뒤의 restaurant는 앞에서 언급한 '그 식당'을 의미하므로 각각 a restaurant와 the restaurant가 되어야 알맞다.

PRACTICE 20

1	the	2	the, the	3	a	4	the
5	The	6	an	7	the	8	the
9	a	10	the	11	A		

1, 2, 4, 5, 10 서수, 최상급, only, very, same 앞에는 the를 쓴다.
3, 6 one(하나의)의 의미일 때는 a/an을 쓴다.
7 듣는 사람이 무엇을 가리키는지 알 수 있을 때 the를 쓴다.
8 악기 이름 앞에는 the를 쓴다.
9, 11 a certain(어떤)의 의미일 때는 a/an을 쓴다.

PRACTICE 21

1	the poor	2	the face
3	the Pacific	4	a week
5	the Netherlands	6	The rich
7	○	8	a post office
9	○	10	○
11	the Thames	12	the New York Times
13	○	14	the back
15	○		

1, 6, 9 「the+형용사」를 써서 '~한 사람들'이라고 표현한다.
the poor: 가난한 사람들
the rich: 부유한 사람들
the young: 젊은 사람들
2, 7, 14 어떤 동작을 가하는 신체의 일부를 나타내는 단어 앞에는 the를 쓴다.
hit in the face: 얼굴을 때리다
by the hand: 손을 잡고
push+사람+on the back: ~의 등을 밀다
3, 5, 11, 12, 15 특정 고유명사 앞에는 the를 쓴다.
the Pacific, the Netherlands, the Thames, the New York Times, the Alps
4 per(~당, ~마다)의 의미일 때 a/an을 쓴다.
once a week: 일주일에 한 번
8 맥락상 처음 언급된 정해지지 않은 단수명사에 대해 묻고 있으므로 a/an을 쓴다.
10 some(약간의, 어느 정도의)의 의미일 때 a/an을 쓴다.
for a while: 잠시 후에
13 one(하나의)의 의미일 때 a/an을 쓴다.
a newspaper: 신문 한 부

PRACTICE 22

The, The, The, the, the, a

The old want to live a comfortable life.
→ the+형용사(~한 사람들)
The Korean Times reported ~.
→ the+특정 고유명사
The Philippines is one of the most popular countries for them to live in.
→ the+특정 고유명사 / the+최상급
It is on the Pacific Ocean.
→ the+특정 고유명사
My family visits the country about once a year ~.
→ per(~당, ~마다)를 의미하는 a/an

PRACTICE 23

1	bus	2	tennis	3	mom
4	lunch	5	Math	6	bed
7	TV	8	home	9	Professor
10	school				

1 「by+교통수단」일 때는 교통수단에 해당하는 명사 앞에 관사를 쓰지 않는다.
2 운동 경기를 나타내는 명사 앞에는 관사를 쓰지 않는다.
3 가족 구성원을 나타내는 명사 앞에는 관사를 쓰지 않는다.
4 식사를 나타내는 명사 앞에는 관사를 쓰지 않는다.
5 과목을 나타내는 명사 앞에는 관사를 쓰지 않는다.
6, 10 장소, 기구를 나타내는 명사가 본래의 목적으로 쓰일 때는 앞에 관사를 쓰지 않는다.
7 listen to music과 watch TV는 관용적으로 관사 없이 쓴다.
8 home이 '자기 집, 고향'의 뜻으로 쓰이면 보통 관사 없이 쓴다.
9 관직, 신분을 나타내는 명사 앞에는 관사를 쓰지 않는다.

PRACTICE 24

1	×	2	the	3	the
4	×	5	the	6	an
7	the	8	×	9	a
10	the	11	×	12	the
13	a	14	×	15	A
16	×	17	the[a], the[a]		
18	the	19	a	20	The
21	the	22	a, a	23	×, ×
24	×	25	×	26	×
27	×	28	The, an	29	The
30	×	31	the	32	the
33	×	34	The		

1, 16 식사를 나타내는 명사 앞에는 관사를 쓰지 않는다.
2, 18 악기 이름 앞에는 the를 쓴다.
3, 7, 12, 32 서수, only, very 앞에는 the를 쓴다.
4, 30 운동 경기를 나타내는 명사 앞에는 관사를 쓰지 않는다.
5 어떤 동작을 가하는 신체의 일부를 나타내는 단어 앞에는 the를 쓴다.
6 one(하나의)의 의미일 때 a/an을 쓴다.
8, 27 listen to music과 watch TV는 관용적으로 관사 없이 쓴다.
9, 22 per(~당, ~마다)의 의미일 때 a/an을 쓴다.
10, 29 「the+형용사/분사」를 써서 '~한 사람들'이라고 표현한다.
11, 24, 33 장소, 기구를 나타내는 명사가 본래의 목적으로 쓰일 때는 앞에 관사를 쓰지 않는다.
13, 19 some(약간의, 어느 정도)의 의미일 때 a/an을 쓴다.
14 가족 구성원을 나타내는 명사 앞에는 관사를 쓰지 않는다.
15 a certain(어떤)의 의미일 때는 a/an을 쓴다.
17 어떤 종류의 전체를 나타내는 보통 명사를 대표 단수로 표현할 때 a/an이나 the를 쓴다.
20 유일한 것을 나타낼 때 the를 쓴다.
21, 34 명사 뒤에 명사를 수식하는 구나 절이 있을 때 the를 쓴다.
23 「by+교통수단」일 때는 교통수단에 해당하는 명사 앞에 관사를 쓰지 않는다.
25 관직, 신분을 나타내는 명사 앞에는 관사를 쓰지 않는다.
26 과목을 나타내는 명사 앞에는 관사를 쓰지 않는다.
28 명사 뒤에 명사를 수식하는 구나 절이 있을 때 the를 쓰므로 the children이 알맞고, a/an에 the same(같은, 동일한)의 의미가 있으므로 of an age는 '나이가 같은'이라는 뜻으로 쓰인다.
31 특정 고유명사 앞에는 the를 쓴다.

Chapter Review Test 정답   본문 _ p.140

1 ②   2 ④   3 ②, ③   4 a cup of coffee, four slices[pieces] of cake   5 ①   6 ③   7 ④
8 a pair of shoes   9 ③   10 ④   11 ③   12 ②
13 ②   14 ②   15 ②, ⑤   16 (1) bowl (2) bottles (3) pairs (4) glass   17 ①   18 ⑤
19 ①   20 ③   21 that he won a marathon
22 ③   23 ⑤   24 ⑤   25 ⑤   26 ⑤   27 ⑤
28 ①   29 (1) a breakfast → breakfast   (2) pair → pairs   30 ⓐ slices   ⓑ bars   ⓒ loaves   ⓓ bottle   ⓔ pieces   ⓕ bars

Chapter Review Test 해설

1 ① piano - pianos   ③ wolf - wolves
   ④ tooth - teeth   ⑤ beauty - beauties
2 furniture(집합적 물질명사: 유사한 사물들의 집합체이지만 양으로 나타내는 물질 명사의 성격을 갖는 명사)와 cheese, coffee, cereal(물질명사)은 셀 수 없는 명사로, 수를 나타내는 경우 단위 명사를 이용한다.
   ① five pieces of furniture
   ② two slices of cheese
   ③ three cups of coffee
   ⑤ two bowls of cereal
3 물질명사는 셀 수 없으며 수를 나타내야 할 때는 단위 명사를 사용한다.
   ① piece → pieces, breads → bread
   ④ two salt → two (tea)spoonfuls of salt
   ⑤ five meat → five pounds[pieces] of meat
4 a cup of '한 잔의 ~'
   four slices[pieces] of '네 조각의 ~'
5 ② mouse의 복수형 - mice
   ③ bench의 복수형 - benches
   ④ bird의 복수형 - birds
   ⑤ fox의 복수형 - foxes
6 ③ some juices → some juice
   물질명사인 juice는 복수형으로 쓰일 수 없다.
7 서수, same, 악기의 이름 앞에는 정관사 the를 쓴다.
   ⓑ first → the first   ⓓ same → the same
   ⓔ piano → the piano
8 한 쌍을 이루어 기능하는 명사의 수는 '수사+pair(s) +of+복수형' 어순으로 표현한다.
9 • a glass of '한 잔의 ~'
   • 명사 a plan과 동명사구 studying for the test를 동격으로 연결하는 of
10 ⓐ some은 '몇몇의, 약간의'라는 뜻으로 뒤에 셀 수 있는 명사가 올 경우 복수형으로 써야 한다.
   (apple → apples)
   ⓑ 유일한 것을 나타낼 때는 정관사 the를 쓴다.
   (Moon → The Moon, Earth → the Earth)
   ⓔ 명사 뒤에 명사를 수식하는 구가 있을 때 정관사 the를 쓴다. (capital → the capital)
11 milk와 meat는 물질명사로 셀 수 없는 명사이다.
   ① milks → milk   ② meats → meat
   ④, ⑤는 고치지 않은 형태가 어법상 옳다.
12 ② child의 복수형은 childrens가 아니라 children이다. (childrens → children)
13 ① student가 셀 수 있는 명사이고, 단수형이므로 부정관사 a나 정관사 the를 써야 한다.
   (student → a[the] student)
   ③ second와 같은 서수의 앞에는 정관사 the를 써야 한다. (a second → the second)

④ math teacher는 셀 수 있는 명사이고, 단수형이므로 부정관사 a나 정관사 the를 써야 한다. (math teacher → a[the] math teacher)
⑤ '~해 보이다'는 뜻의 look은 주격 보어로 형용사를 쓴다. 부정관사 a는 명사의 앞에만 쓰이므로 삭제해야 한다. (a very → very)

14 ① 정황상 무엇을 가리키는지 알 수 있으므로 정관사 the를 쓴다.
② a lot of는 '많은'이라는 뜻으로 명사 앞에 온다. 따라서 밑줄 친 부분에는 명사가 들어가야 한다. noisy는 '시끄러운'이라는 형용사이며, '소리, 소음'이라는 뜻의 명사 noise를 쓴다. 참고로 'make a lot of noise'는 '시끄럽게 하다'라는 뜻이다. (noisy → noise)
③ 동사 were playing을 꾸며주고 있으므로 부사인 loudly의 쓰임은 적절하다.
④ games는 셀 수 있는 명사이고, '게임들'이라는 뜻이므로 '-s'를 붙여 복수형으로 만든다.
⑤ 앞에서 언급한 the students를 의미하므로, 대명사 them의 쓰임은 적절하다.

15 식사를 나타내는 명사 앞, 장소를 나타내는 명사가 본래의 목적으로 쓰일 때, 과목을 나타내는 명사 앞에는 관사를 쓰지 않는다.
① the lunch → lunch
③ to the school → to school
④ the economics → economics

16 (1) a bowl of '한 그릇의 ~'
(2) two bottles of '두 병의~'
(3) three pairs of '세 켤레의~'
(4) a glass of '한 잔의 ~'

17 ① 사람을 나타내는 명사는 's를 사용하여 소유격을 만든다. (bag of Jenny's → Jenny's bag)

18 ⑤「수사+명사」가 뒤에 이어지는 명사를 수식하는 형용사처럼 쓰일 때는 수사 다음의 명사를 복수형으로 쓰지 않는다. (three-months-long winter → three-month-long winter)

① 「주어+be동사+과거분사」 형태의 수동태 문장이다.
② it이 가주어, to buy 이하가 진주어이고 to buy는 to부정사의 명사적 용법으로 쓰였다.
③ gloves는 한 쌍을 이루어야 하나의 물건으로 제 기능을 하는 명사로서 단위명사와 함께 쓴다.
④ the cold '추위'

19 ① 컵은 셀 수 있는 명사이므로 여러 개 있을 때는 복수형으로 쓴다. (two cup → two cups)

20 many 뒤에는 명사의 복수형이 와야 하므로, 단·복수의 형태가 같은 sheep이 가능하다.

21 the news와 he won a marathon은 that으로 연결되는 동격 관계이다.

22 ③ per(~당, ~마다)
① 대표 단수   ② one(하나)
④ the same(같은)   ⑤ a certain(어떤)

23 ⑤ 유일한 것을 나타내는 명사 앞에는 the를 쓴다.

24 ⑤ 어떤 동작을 가하는 신체의 일부를 나타내는 단어 앞에 the를 쓴다. (in an eye → in the eye)

25 ⑤ a bread → a loaf of bread
물질명사는 단위명사를 이용하여 수를 나타낸다.

26 셀 수 없는 명사는 many와 함께 쓸 수 없다.

27 ③ 동격
① 지시대명사   ② 지시형용사
④ 명사절을 이끄는 접속사   ⑤ 관계대명사

28 ①「the+형용사」는 '~한 사람들'이라는 뜻을 나타낸다. (a → the)

29 (1) 식사명 앞에는 관사를 쓰지 않는다.
(2) 앞에 복수인 two가 나오므로 pair는 pairs로 고쳐야 한다.

30 ⓐ three slices '세 장'
ⓑ two bars '두 개'
ⓒ three loaves '세 덩어리'
ⓓ a bottle '한 병'
ⓔ four pieces '네 장'
ⓕ three bars '세 개'

CHAPTER 6 대명사
Pronouns

본문 _ p.146

PRACTICE 1

1. him
2. We
3. You
4. me
5. they
6. us
7. her
8. it
9. them
10. She

> 1, 6, 7, 8, 9 동사의 목적어 자리이므로 목적격이 알맞다.
> 2, 3, 10 문장의 주어 자리이므로 주격이 알맞다.
> 4 전치사 다음에는 대명사의 목적격이 들어가는 것이 적절하다.
> 5 의문문에서는 주어-(조)동사 도치가 일어나기 때문에 조동사 Did 다음에 주격인 they가 나오는 것이 적절하다.

PRACTICE 2

2. his, his
3. their, theirs
4. my, mine
5. your, yours
6. our, ours

PRACTICE 3

1. He
2. my, her
3. They
4. us
5. hers
6. his
7. ours
8. him
9. your
10. its

> 1, 3 문장의 주어 자리이므로 주격 대명사가 들어가는 것이 알맞다.
> 2 명사 friend를 앞에서 수식할 수 있는 소유격이 적절하다. / like의 목적어 자리이므로 her이 알맞다.
> 4, 8 수여동사 bring과 tell의 간접목적어 자리이므로 목적격 대명사가 들어가야 한다.
> 5, 7 소유격인 her과 our은 꾸며줄 명사 없이 혼자 쓰일 수 없으므로 소유대명사를 사용하는 것이 적절하다.
> 6, 9, 10 명사의 앞에서 명사를 꾸며줄 수 있는 소유격이 들어가야 한다.

PRACTICE 4

1. himself, 강조
2. herself, 재귀
3. myself, 강조
4. yourself, 재귀
5. itself, 재귀
6. ourselves, 재귀
7. himself, 재귀
8. themselves, 재귀

> 2 by oneself: 혼자
> 5 'repeat itself'는 '같은 방식으로 계속 반복되다'는 의미의 관용적 표현이다. repeat은 타동사로 쓰였기 때문에 itself는 생략할 수 없다.
> 6 for oneself: 혼자 힘으로
> 8 make oneself at home: 느긋하게 쉬다, 자기 집에 있는 것처럼 편하게 지내다

PRACTICE 5

1. me
2. himself
3. them
4. us
5. herself
6. you
7. itself
8. myself
9. myself
10. her

> 1, 3, 4, 6, 10 행동의 주체와 대상이 같지 않으므로 재귀대명사를 사용할 수 없다.
> 8, 9 행동의 주체와 대상이 같으므로 재귀대명사를 사용할 수 있다.
> 2, 5, 7 by oneself: 혼자서, 스스로

PRACTICE 6

1. 비
2. 비
3. 대
4. 비
5. 대
6. 비
7. 비
8. 대

> 1 명암을 가리키는 비인칭주어다.
> 2, 4 날씨를 가리키는 비인칭주어다.
> 3 앞선 문장의 the cat을 가리키는 대명사다.
> 5 앞선 문장의 autumn을 가리키는 대명사다.
> 6 거리를 가리키는 비인칭주어다.
> 7 시간을 가리키는 비인칭주어다.
> 8 문장 내에 언급되지는 않았지만 it이 가리키는 특정 사안이 있음을 알 수 있다. 따라서 it은 대명사로 쓰였다.

PRACTICE 7

1. It seems that you are upset about what happened.
2. It seems that my sister has a plan to stay at Sumi's for a while.
3. It seemed that you were very confident when you made a speech.
4. It seems that they always live in a fantasy world.
5. It seems that she walks like a professional model.
6. It seemed that you were satisfied with your decision.
7. It seems that he knows what he is doing now.
8. It seemed that they sat very close to each other.

PRACTICE 8

1 It was Minji's brother that I saw at the theater yesterday.
2 It was a week ago that I met Sumin at the amusement park.
3 It was my uncle that was seriously injured in the car accident.
4 It is at the bus stop that I'm going to meet the children this Sunday.
5 It was at five that we were supposed to meet in front of the statue.

PRACTICE 9

1 It is important to recycle the bottles.
2 It is very exciting reading science fiction.
3 I thought it strange that you said so.
4 It is disappointing that you lied again.
5 I found it difficult to memorize new words every day.
6 It made me happy that our team won the game.
7 It is important to play for the team.
8 It is amazing that he can keep cool in a crisis.

> 1, 7 to부정사 주어가 길 때는 문장의 맨 뒤로 보내고 이를 대신하여 주어 자리에 가주어 it이 온다.
> 2 동명사구 주어가 길 때는 문장의 맨 뒤로 보내고 대신해서 가주어 it이 온다.
> 3 'that you said so'가 진목적어인 문장이다. 목적어로 쓰인 명사절이 길 때는 그 자리에 it을 쓰고 명사절을 문장의 맨 뒤로 보낸다.
> 4, 6, 8 that이 이끄는 명사절이 진주어인 문장이다. 주어로 쓰인 명사절이 길 때는 그 자리에 it을 쓰고 that절을 문장의 맨 뒤로 보낸다.
> 5 진목적어인 to부정사구의 길이가 길 경우, 목적어 자리에 it을 쓰고 to부정사구를 문장의 맨 뒤로 보낸다.

PRACTICE 10

1	Is this	2	That car
3	These girls	4	this
5	those buildings	6	That
7	These books	8	Those

PRACTICE 11

1	that	2	those, those
3	those	4	that
5	those	6	Those
7	that	8	those
9	those	10	that

> 1 population의 반복을 피하기 위해서 that을 사용한다.
> 2, 6, 9 '~한 사람들'이라는 의미를 가진 those가 적절하다.
> 3 복수명사 shoes를 대신하기 위해 those를 사용한다.
> 4 living room의 반복을 피하기 위해 that을 사용한다.
> 5 복수명사 buildings를 대신하기 위해 those를 사용한다.
> 7 the price의 반복을 피하기 위해 that을 사용한다.
> 8 복수명사 the employees의 반복을 피하기 위해 those를 사용한다.
> 10 vacation의 반복을 피하기 위해 that을 사용한다.

PRACTICE 12

1	it	2	ones	3	one
4	them	5	One	6	one
7	it	8	them	9	one
10	ones	11	them	12	One
13	them	14	it	15	ones
16	ones	17	it		

> 1, 7, 14, 17 앞서 언급한 바로 그 명사를 지칭해야 하기 때문에 대명사 it이 적절하다.
> 2, 16 같은 종류이지만, 다른 속성(색상)을 가진 대상들을 가리키기 위해 ones를 사용한다.
> 3 앞서 언급한 a small balloon과 같은 종류이지만, 다른 속성(big)을 가진 대상을 가리키기 위해 one을 사용한다.
> 4, 8, 11, 13 앞서 언급한 바로 그 명사를 지칭한다. 복수형 명사이므로 대명사 them이 적절하다.
> 5, 12 일반적인 사람들을 가리킬 때는 one을 사용한다.
> 6 an eraser라고 했으므로 명확한 대상이 정해지지 않은 지우개를 언급하였고, 대상이 다르면서 종류는 같은 명사에 대해 반복을 피하기 위해 one을 사용한다.
> 9 앞서 언급한 a nice bicycle과 같은 종류이지만 다른 대상을 가리키기 위해 one을 사용한다.
> 10 특정한 대상을 짚어 질문하였지만 대답에서 그것과 같은 종류의 다른 개체를 지칭하고 있기 때문에 ones가 적절하다.
> 15 앞에 언급한 특정하지 않은 명사를 대신할 때 ones를 쓴다.

PRACTICE 13

1	another	2	The other
3	another	4	other
5	others	6	the other
7	the others	8	The others
9	others	10	other
11	other	12	another
13	others	14	the other
15	another	16	others

> **1, 15** other은 명사 앞에서 꾸며주는 식으로만 사용 가능하기 때문에 '또 다른 하나'를 가리키는 another이 적절하다.
> **2, 6** 전체 범위가 두 가지로 명시된 경우, 무작위로 고른 첫 번째 것은 one, 남은 하나는 the other이라고 쓴다.
> **3, 12** 뒤에 따라오는 단수 명사를 수식할 수 있는 another가 적절하다.
> **4, 10, 11** 뒤에 따라오는 복수 명사를 수식할 수 있는 other이 적절하다.
> **5, 9, 13, 16** 앞서 전체 범위가 몇 명인지 언급되지 않았고, 문맥상 불특정 다수(다른 사람들)을 가리키므로 others가 적절하다.
> **7** 복수형 동사 are와 수를 일치시키려면 the others가 적절하다.
> **8** 앞서 병의 전체 개수가 4개라고 언급되었으므로 색상이 붉은 색인 두 개의 병의 제외한 나머지가 특정되었다. 따라서 '나머지 것들'을 가리키는 the others가 적절하다.
> **14** 길의 반대편을 말할 때 'the other side'를 사용하는 것이 적절하다.

PRACTICE 14

1 the other
2 others
3 the others
4 the other
5 One, the other
6 Some, the others
7 Another, The other
8 others
9 One, the other
10 others
11 One, the other
12 Some, others
13 One, another
14 One, the other
15 Some, the others

> **1, 5, 9, 14** 전체 범위가 두 개로 명시된 경우, 두 개 중 무작위로 먼저 고른 하나는 one, 나머지 하나를 the other이라고 한다.
> **2, 8, 10, 12** 전체 개수가 불특정한 경우, 그 중 일부를 가리킬 때 some, 다른 일부를 언급할 때 others라고 한다.
> **3, 6, 15** 전체 개수가 명시된 경우, 그 중 무작위의 일부를 가리킬 때 some, 그 외 나머지를 언급할 때 the others라고 한다.
> **4, 7, 11, 13** 전체 개수가 3개일 때 처음 고른 하나는 one, 남은 두 개 중 하나를 another, 나머지 하나를 the other이라고 한다.

PRACTICE 15

1 Each of the flowers has a different color.
2 Mr. Kim called every student last night.
3 Each table is covered with green cloth.
4 I used to go to my grandmother's house every Sunday.
5 Each player is wearing red pants.
6 Not every book in this room is about politics.

> **1** each of+관사/소유격+복수명사는 단수 취급하여 단수 동사와 함께 쓰인다.
> **2** every 뒤에는 단수 명사가 온다.
> **3, 5** each+단수명사는 단수 취급한다.
> **4** every Sunday: 매 일요일마다 (=on Sundays)
> **6** every가 not과 함께 쓰여 '모든 책들이 다 ~한 것은 아니다'라는 부분 부정을 나타낸다.

PRACTICE 16

1 You should read all the books in this room.
2 Ms. Ford gave me all of those dishes for my birthday present.
3 She is going to tell you all of the information.
4 I will invite both friends to my performance.
5 Both of the tests were very difficult for me.
6 He didn't follow both of the rules.
7 She ate the rest of the cake on the table.
8 The rest of you may go home now.
9 The rest of the crew were rescued from the burning ship.
10 All of the participants looked tired when the bell rang.
11 Not all people are happy with the changes.

PRACTICE 17

1 worker
2 the taxis
3 parents
4 night
5 Does
6 was
7 morning
8 the restaurants
9 those words
10 parent
11 are
12 has
13 have to
14 is
15 The rest of
16 are
17 ways
18 was
19 minute
20 are

> **1, 4, 7, 10, 19** every/each는 단수 명사만을 꾸밀 수 있다.
> **2** all of the+복수 명사는 복수형 동사와 함께 쓰인다.
> **3, 16, 17** both와 both of는 복수 명사 및 복수 동사와 사용된다.
> **5** each+단수 명사(girl)는 단수형 동사와 함께 쓰인다.
> **6, 18** all of와 셀 수 없는 명사가 함께 쓰일 경우 동사는 단수형으로 사용한다.
> **8** both 뒤에 of가 올 때는 명사 앞에 관사나 소유격 등의 수식어가 붙는다.
> **9, 12** each of는 복수 명사와 함께 쓰이며, 동사는 단수형으로 사용한다.
> **11** all the+복수 명사(guests)는 복수 취급하므로 are과 함께 쓰는 것이 적절하다.
> **13** the rest of와 복수 명사가 함께 쓰일 경우 동사는 복수형으로 사용한다.
> **14, 15** the rest of와 셀 수 없는 명사가 함께 쓰일 경우 동사는 단수형으로 사용한다.
> **20** the rest가 단독으로 쓰일 경우 '나머지 것들(모자)'라는 의미를 나타낸다. 복수형 동사와 함께 사용한다.

PRACTICE 18

1 Someone [Somebody]
2 someone [somebody]
3 ○
4 something
5 ○
6 anything
7 Anyone [Anybody]
8 ○
9 anything
10 Something
11 Someone [Somebody]
12 ○

> 1, 2, 11 anyone[anybody]은 보통 부정문이나 의문문에 쓰이고, 긍정문에 쓰인 경우는 '어떠한 ~라도'의 뜻으로 쓰인다. '누군가'라는 뜻으로 긍정문에서 쓰인 경우, someone[somebody]가 적절하다.
> 3 anything은 긍정문에서 '어떠한 ~라도'라는 의미로 쓰이므로 적절하다.
> 4 anything이 긍정문에 쓰일 경우는 '어떠한 ~라도'의 뜻이다. 긍정문에서 '(어떤) 것'이라는 의미는 something이 적절하다.
> 5 anyone은 의문문에서 '누군가'라는 의미로 쓰이므로 적절하다.
> 6, 9 something은 부정문에 쓰이지 않는다. 이 문장에서는 '아무 것'이라는 의미로 쓰여야 하므로 anything이 적절하다.
> 7 Someone은 긍정문에서 '누군가'라는 의미로 쓰인다. 긍정문에서 '어떤 사람이라도'라는 의미로 쓰여야 하므로 Anyone[Anybody]이 적절하다.
> 8 something은 긍정의 대답을 예상하는 의문문에 쓰이므로 적절하다.
> 10 Anything이 긍정문에 쓰일 경우는 '어떠한 ~라도'의 뜻이다. 이 문장에서는 '무슨 일'이라는 의미의 단어가 쓰여야 하므로 Something이 적절하다.
> 12 anything은 의문문에서 '무언가'라는 의미로 쓰이므로 적절하다.

PRACTICE 19

1 Who
2 Whose
3 whom
4 Who
5 whom
6 Whose
7 Who
8 Whose
9 Whose
10 whom

> 1, 4, 7 문장의 주어가 없기 때문에 주격 의문대명사가 오는 것이 적절하다.
> 2, 6, 9 명사를 앞에서 꾸며줄 수 있어야 하기 때문에 소유격 의문형용사가 오는 것이 적절하다.
> 3, 5, 10 전치사 (to, for, with)의 목적어 역할을 하는 목적격 의문대명사를 사용하는 것이 적절하다.
> 8 사물에 대해 물어보고 있으므로 who는 적절하지 않고, 뒤에 따라오는 명사가 없으므로 whose가 소유격 의문대명사(누구의 것)로 사용되었다.

PRACTICE 20

1 What
2 Which
3 Whom
4 What
5 What
6 Which
7 Whose
8 Which
9 Which
10 What

> 1 사람의 직업을 물어볼 때 what을 사용한다.
> 2 선택지가 주어진 상황에서 질문하므로 which를 사용한다.
> 3 구동사 talk to의 목적어가 없으므로 목적격 의문대명사 whom으로 질문하는 것이 적절하다.
> 4 선택의 범위가 주어지지 않은 상황에서 사물에 대해 질문하므로 what을 사용한다. 여기서 what은 kind를 꾸며주는 의문형용사로 쓰여 '어떤 종류'라는 의미를 나타낸다.
> 5, 10 선택의 범위가 주어지지 않은 상황에서 사람이 아닌 것에 대해 질문하므로 what을 사용한다.
> 6 선택의 범위가 주어진 상황에서 질문하고 있기 때문에 which가 적절하다. Which는 사람을 가리킬 때도 사용 가능하다.
> 7 선택의 범위가 주어지지 않았기 때문에 which로 질문할 수 없다. '누구의 것'을 의미하는 의문대명사 whose를 사용하는 것이 적절하다.
> 8 사과와 오렌지 중 어느 것이 더 저렴한지 묻고 있기 때문에 선택의 범위가 정해져 있다. 따라서 which로 질문하는 것이 적절하다.
> 9 선택의 범위가 part1, 2로 정해져 있으므로 which를 사용한다. 여기서 which는 part를 앞에서 수식하는 의문형용사로 쓰였으며 '어느 파트'라는 의미를 나타낸다.

PRACTICE 21

1 Which seat do you want?
2 What plans do you have tomorrow?
3 Which food does Cathy like?
4 What countries does he want to visit?
5 Which wallpaper is good for your room?

Chapter Review Test 정답 본문_p.169

1 ③ 2 ④ 3 ② 4 ⑤ 5 ① 6 ① 7 ④
8 ① 9 (1) has → have (2) her → hers
10 every[each] summer 11 ④ 12 ① 13 ②
14 ② 15 ⑤ 16 ① 17 ④ 18 ③ 19 ③
20 ⑤ 21 ④ 22 ④ 23 ③ 24 ④ 25 other
26 ③ 27 ①,④,⑤ 28 ② 29 ⑤ 30 ②
31 ② 32 the winter 33 ⑤ 34 ③
35 (1) those (2) this (3) These (4) that 36 ⑤
37 Everyone seems to be thinking the same thing now. 38 myself 39 The queen used to look at herself in the mirror. 40 ① 41 ④
42 ③ 43 It is not easy to decide which club I should join. 44 ④ 45 ② 46 (1) Which (2) What (3) Whose

Chapter Review Test 해설

1. (A) 주어가 단수이므로 be동사는 was다.
   (B) 대명사 he의 소유격이 필요하므로 his가 맞다.
   (C) 앞에 나온 단수 명사 science book, *Cosmos*를 받으므로 It이 올바르다.

2. ④ 재귀 용법 ①②③⑤ 강조 용법

3. ② 비인칭 주어 it ①③④⑤ 인칭대명사 it

4. 「another + 단수 명사」 '또 다른 ~, 또 하나의 ~'

5. ① 강조 용법의 재귀대명사는 생략이 가능하다.
   ②③④⑤ 전치사의 목적어로 쓰인 재귀대명사는 생략할 수 없다.

6. do one's best '최선을 다하다'
   one's 자리에는 인칭대명사의 소유격을 쓴다.

7. ④ have → has
   each는 단수 취급한다.

8. by oneself '혼자서, 홀로'

9. (1) Laura and I는 복수형 주어이므로 has를 have로 바꾼다.
   (2) 문맥상 '저 빨간 것은 그녀의 것이다'라는 뜻이 되어야 하므로 her를 hers로 바꾼다.

10. every[each] 뒤에 시간 관련 명사가 오면 '매, ~마다'의 의미가 된다.

11. 저기 있는 저 그림들을 봐. 저것들은 내 그림들이야.

12. ① 앞에 언급한 것을 지칭하는 '그것'이라는 뜻의 인칭대명사로 쓰였다. (그것은 정말 맵니?)
    ② 요일을 나타내는 비인칭주어 it이다.
    ③ 날씨를 나타내는 비인칭주어 it이다.
    ④⑤ 시간을 나타내는 비인칭주어 it이다.

13. one ~ the other …
    '(둘 중에) 하나는 ~, 다른 하나는 …'

14. 의문대명사가 전치사 뒤에 오면 목적격으로 쓴다.

15. ⑤ 주어와 목적어의 대상이 you로 같으므로, 목적어의 자리에는 재귀대명사(yourself)를 쓰는 것이 알맞다.
    ① his는 이미 그 자체로 소유격이므로, '(어퍼스트로피)를 이용하여 소유격을 만들어줄 필요가 없다.
    (his' → his)
    ② 문장의 주어와 목적어의 대상이 astronauts로 같으므로 재귀대명사를 쓰는 것이 알맞다. 그러나 astronauts는 복수형이므로, 재귀대명사 또한 3인칭 복수형인 themselves가 되어야 한다.
    (himself → themselves)
    ③ 밑줄 친 부분은 문장의 주어 자리이므로 주격 대명사가 나와야 한다. her의 주격은 she이다.
    (her → she)
    ④ 주어와 목적어의 대상이 각각 neighbors와 her로 다르므로 재귀대명사를 쓰지 않는다. 밑줄 친 부분은 목적어 자리이므로 3인칭 단수 여성의 목적격 대명사인 her로 고쳐야 한다. (herself → her)

16. 지금 '다른 할 일'이 있다는 것을 나타내야 하므로, 긍정문에 쓰이는 something이 들어간다.

17. one ~ another … the other -
    '(셋 중에) 하나는 ~, 다른 하나는 …, 나머지 하나는 -'

18. 긍정문에서 '누군가'라는 뜻을 나타내는 대명사는 someone이다. anyone이 긍정문에 쓰이면 '누구라도, 어떤 사람이라도'라는 뜻인데 여기서는 맥락상 적절하지 않다.

19. • 선택의 범위가 주어질 때는 which를 쓴다.
    • What do you think of ~?
    '~에 대해 어떻게 생각하니?'

20. ⑤ 가주어 it   ①②④ 비인칭 주어 it
    ③ 인칭대명사 it

21. one ~ the other …
    '(둘 중에) 하나는 ~, 다른 하나는 …'

22. ④ 관계대명사   ①②③⑤ 의문대명사

23. ③ this of → that of

24. (A), (B) some ~, others …
    '몇몇은 ~, 다른 사람(것)들은 …'
    (C) those who ~ '~하는 사람들'

25. • each other '서로'
    • on the other hand '반면에'

26. ① 날짜를 나타내는 비인칭 주어 it
    ② 인칭대명사 it
    ④ 거리를 나타내는 비인칭 주어 it
    ⑤ It that 강조구문

27. ②③ 가주어 it
    ① 인칭대명사 it
    ④ 날씨를 나타내는 비인칭 주어 it
    ⑤ 시간을 나타내는 비인칭 주어 it

28. every는 뒤에 단수 명사와 단수 동사를 취한다.

29. ①②③④ 명사의 반복을 피하기 위한 부정대명사 one
    ⑤ '유일한'의 의미를 지닌 형용사 one

30. ② 사람들이 10명이라고 명시되어 있다. 특정한 수의 사람들 중에서 나머지를 얘기할 때는, the others를 쓴다. (others → the others)
    ① 앞에 나온 car와 종류는 같지만, 다른 대상이므로 명사의 반복을 피하기 위해 one을 쓰는 것이 적절

하다.
③ 'a lot of entertainers'로 불특정한 수의 사람들을 말하고 있으므로, 그 중 몇몇은 some, 다른 사람들은 others로 쓴다.
④ 세 개의 대상 중에 제일 처음 언급하는 것은 one, 다른 하나는 another, 나머지 하나는 the other로 쓴다.
⑤ 나는 이것이 맘에 들지 않으니 또 하나의 다른 것을 보여달라는 내용이 되어야 한다. 따라서 another의 쓰임은 적절하다.

31 some ~ others …
'(불특정한 수의 사람들 중에서) 몇몇은 ~ 다른 사람들은 …'

32 that은 앞에 나온 명사의 반복을 피하기 위해 쓰였다.

33 ⑤ were → was
「all of+셀 수 없는 명사+단수 동사」

34 앞에 나온 명사가 복수형일 때, 명사의 종류는 같지만 대상이 다른 경우에 그 반복을 피하기 위해 쓰는 부정대명사는 ones이다.

35 (1) those days '그 당시, 그 때'
(2) this Friday '이번 금요일'
(3) these '이것들'
(4) that은 the population을 대신하여 앞에 나온 명사의 반복을 피하기 위해 쓰였다.

36 • He burned himself.
• My little daughter can't look after herself.
• They set up their tents by themselves.
• You should be proud of yourself.

37 It seems that 주어+동사=주어 seem(s) to 동사원형

38 • by oneself '혼자서'
• burn oneself '불에 데다'
• enjoy oneself '즐거운 시간을 보내다'

39 문장의 주어와 목적어의 대상이 같으므로 재귀대명사를 쓴다.

40 (A) one ~ the other… (둘 중에) 하나는 ~, 나머지 하나는 …
(B) 앞에 나온 books를 대신하는 대명사는 them이다.
(C) another+단수명사 '또 다른 ~'

41 「whose+명사」 '누구의 ~'

42 「be able to+동사원형」 '~할 수 있다'
by oneself '혼자서, 홀로'

43 가주어 it을 문장 앞에 놓고, 진주어인 to부정사구는 문장 뒤로 보낸다.

44 글의 ⓐ rest와 ④는 '나머지'라는 의미이다.
① 쉬다 ② 휴식 ③ 받치다, 기대다 ⑤ 그대로 있다

45 those는 뒤에 who가 와서 '~한 사람들'의 의미로 쓰인다.

46 (1) 어느 재킷이 더 싸니?
(2) Paul에게 무슨 일이 일어났니?
(3) 난 그 얘기가 마음에 들어. 그건 누구의 아이디어야?

CHAPTER 7 부정사
Infinitives

본문 _ p.178

PRACTICE 1

1 It is important to read a lot of books.
2 It is exciting to go to a concert.
3 It was not easy to make my dream come true.
4 It is a lot of fun to visit foreign countries.
5 It is helpful to watch English TV programs.
6 It is not good to spend so much time playing computer games.

1~6 to부정사가 문장의 맨 앞에서 주어의 역할을 할 때는 it을 주어의 자리에 두고 to부정사는 문장의 뒤로 보낸 형태를 주로 쓴다. 이때의 it을 가주어, to부정사가 이끄는 구를 진주어라고 한다.

PRACTICE 2

1 to be a famous singer
2 to see things clearly
3 to take care of patients
4 to watch movies
5 to go to Europe
6 to jog every day

1~6 명사처럼 쓰이는 to부정사가 문장 내에서 주격 보어 역할을 할 때, '~하는 것이다'로 해석한다.

PRACTICE 3

2	to meet	3	to keep
4	not to fail	5	to protect
6	to eat	7	not to have
8	to swim	9	to see
10	not to talk	11	to take
12	not to forget	13	to visit
14	to build	15	not to spend

> 1 lose weight: 체중을 감량하다
> 3 keep a diary: 일기를 쓰다
> 4, 7, 10, 12, 15 to부정사의 부정형은 「not to+동사원형」으로 쓴다.
> *fail the exam: 시험에 떨어지다
> 11 take a shower: 샤워하다
> 13 refuse: 거절하다

PRACTICE 4

2 Becky to open the door
3 Becky to meet his parents
4 Becky to come to his place
5 Becky to clean the room
6 Tony to repair her car
7 Tony to go out to play
8 Becky to shut the door
9 Becky not to touch anything
10 Tony to say sorry to his brother first

> 1~10 tell, ask, would like, expect, want, allow, order, warn, advise와 같은 동사는 목적격 보어로 to부정사를 가진다.

PRACTICE 5

2	how to solve	3	how to help
4	what to wear	5	how to use
6	what to say	7	how to grow
8	what to buy		

> 4, 6, 8 문장 내에 wear, say, buy의 목적어가 없으므로 '무엇을 ~할지'라는 의미를 가진 what+to부정사가 적절하다.

PRACTICE 6

1 no one to understand him
2 something to eat
3 no money to give him
4 enough time to help me
5 something cold to drink
6 someone to love
7 a lot of things to buy
8 enough time to think
9 the best way to get there
10 three things to do

> 5 -thing 형태의 명사는 형용사도 뒤에서 꾸민다. 이때, 형용사처럼 쓰인 to부정사는 형용사보다 뒤에서 수식한다.
> 8 일반적으로 명사는 형용사가 앞에서 꾸며준다. 형용사처럼 쓰인 to부정사는 명사를 뒤에서 수식한다.

PRACTICE 7

2 It's time to have lunch.
3 It's time to go to a meeting.
4 It's time to go home.
5 It's time to study English.
6 It's time to watch TV.

PRACTICE 8

1 to say hello to me
2 to check her email
3 to protect your eyes
4 to take care of the sick
5 to buy a present for his mom
6 to ask about the test
7 to pass the exam
8 to stay healthy and slim

PRACTICE 9

1 in order to study for the final exam
2 so as to ask if he could go shopping with me
3 so as to pick up Kelly
4 in order to watch the birds in the tree
5 in order to surf the Internet
6 so as to make salad

PRACTICE 10

1	for	2	for	3	to	4	to
5	for	6	to	7	to	8	for
9	to	10	for				

CHAPTER 7

> 1 thank+사람+for+명사: ~에 대해 …에게 고마워하다
> 2 keep[save] money for a rainy day: 어려울 때에 대비해 돈을 모아두다
> 3, 4, 6, 7, 9 빈칸 다음에 원형부정사가 나오는데 목적/의도를 설명할 수 있도록 연결하려면 to가 들어가야 한다.
> 5, 8, 10 빈칸 다음에 명사가 나오는데 목적/의도를 설명할 수 있도록 연결하려면 전치사 for가 들어가야 한다.
> for some cookies: 쿠키를 좀 사기 위해서
> for lunch: 점심식사를 하기 위해서
> for my homework: 나의 숙제를 하기 위해서

PRACTICE 11

1 I was really excited to go back to my hometown.
2 I was surprised to see Nancy on the street.
3 I was so happy to get a new computer.
4 Jason was stupid to believe such an obvious lie.
5 I was glad to introduce my family to you.
6 Sora was lucky to pass such a difficult test.

> 1, 2, 3, 5 to부정사가 형용사 중 감정을 나타내는 excited, surprised, happy, glad를 수식하여 감정의 원인을 나타낸다.
> 4, 6 to부정사가 형용사 stupid, lucky를 수식하여 판단의 근거를 나타낸다.

PRACTICE 12

1 ① 2 ③ 3 ② 4 ③
5 ② 6 ①

> 1 decide의 목적어로 쓰인 to부정사의 명사적 용법이다.
> 2, 4 감정을 나타내는 형용사를 수식하여 감정의 원인을 서술하는 to부정사의 부사적 용법이다.
> 3 명사 time을 수식하여 '~할 시간'이라는 뜻을 나타내므로 형용사적 용법이다.
> 5 명사 anyone을 수식하는 형용사적 용법이다. '도움을 요청할 사람'으로 해석할 수 있다.
> 6 문장 내에서 진주어로 쓰인 명사적 용법의 to부정사다.

PRACTICE 13

1 for   2 for   3 to   4 of
5 for   6 of   7 to   8 of
9 for   10 of   11 of 12 for

> 1, 2, 5, 9, 12 to부정사의 행위의 주체가 되는 의미상의 주어 앞에 위치하기에는 for이 적절하다.
> 3 to부정사의 명사적 용법으로 to부정사는 진주어, it은 가주어가 된다.
> 4, 6, 8, 10, 11 사람의 성격을 묘사하는 형용사를 꾸며줄 때 의미상의 주어를 「of+목적격」으로 나타낸다.

> 7 형용사를 수식하여 '~하기에'라는 의미를 나타내는 to부정사의 부사적 용법이 오는 것이 적절하다.

PRACTICE 14

2 The book was so interesting that I could read it twice.
3 I studied very hard (in order/so as) to pass the bar exam.
4 The curry was so spicy that I couldn't eat it.
5 The dress was so expensive that she couldn't buy it.
6 Mina went to Canada (in order/so as) to study English.
7 The movie was so scary that children couldn't watch it.
8 The blue shirt is too big for me to wear.
9 The stadium was so big that ten thousand people could fit into it.
10 The box is light enough for me to carry.

> 1, 4, 5, 7, 8 「so+형용사+that+주어+can't[couldn't]~」는 「too+형용사+for+의미상의 주어+to부정사」로 바꾸어 쓸 수 있다.
> 2, 9, 10 「so+형용사+that+주어+can[could]~」는 「형용사+enough+for+의미상의 주어+to부정사」로 바꾸어 쓸 수 있다.
> 3, 6 「so that+주어+can[could]」는 「(in order/so as) to부정사」로 바꾸어 쓸 수 있다.

PRACTICE 15

1 wear   2 shake[shaking]
3 carry[to carry] 4 ring[ringing]
5 do   6 feel
7 enter[entering] 8 find[to find]
9 plant[planting] 10 practice

> 1, 5, 6, 10 사역동사의 목적격 보어 역할은 원형부정사만 가능하다.
> 2, 4, 7, 9 지각동사의 목적격 보어 자리에는 원형부정사를 사용하고, 동작이 진행 중임을 강조할 때 현재분사도 가능하다.
> 3, 8 준사역동사 help의 목적격 보어 자리에는 원형부정사와 to부정사 모두 사용 가능하다.

PRACTICE 16

2 clean the room first
3 play[playing] the guitar
4 know the truth
5 study English for the test
6 the table move[moving]

Chapter Review Test 정답 본문 _ p.193

1 ② 2 to attend 3 ⑤ 4 ③ 5 (1) when (2) how 6 ⑤ 7 to buy 8 ③ 9 too heavy for me to lift 10 ④ 11 ② 12 ③ 13 ② 14 ④ 15 ④ 16 ⑤ 17 ④ 18 ② 19 ②,⑤ 20 ⑤ 21 ④ 22 I would like to fly in the sky 23 ⑤ 24 It is useful to learn a second language. 25 ③ 26 to say how many people use it 27 ② 28 ② 29 ③ 30 ⑤ 31 ⑤ 32 what to do 33 ③,⑤ 34 ① 35 ⑤ 36 ② 37 ⑤ 38 ①,③ 39 ⑤ 40 The water was so dirty that I could not drink it. 41 asked Minji not to miss her piano lesson 42 ③ 43 ran fast enough to catch him 44 It is important to remember your friend's birthday. 45 ⑤ 46 to learn how to make a cake 47 ⑤ 48 ⑤ 49 ④ 50 ⑤ 51 ⑤ 52 ③ 53 ② 54 (1) how to play the cello (2) what to wear 55 of, to help, go up the stairs 56 ⑤ 57 (1) He was too sleepy to stay up late. (2) He was so sleepy that he couldn't stay up late.

Chapter Review Test 해설

1 보기는 '외국인과 대화하기 위해서'라는 뜻으로, 목적을 나타내는 to부정사의 부사적 용법이다.
② '공부하기 위해서'라는 목적을 나타내는 to부정사의 부사적 용법이다.
①③ to부정사의 명사적 용법으로 문장 내에서 목적어로 쓰이고 있다.
④ 앞에 나오는 명사 something을 수식하는 to부정사의 형용사적 용법이다.
⑤ to부정사의 명사적 용법으로, to부정사가 주어의 역할을 하고 있다. 진주어인 to부정사는 뒤로 보내고, 주어의 자리에 가주어인 it을 쓴 구조이다.

2 '참석하기 위해서'라는 뜻의 to부정사의 부사적 용법이다.

3 It takes 사람+시간+to부정사
= It takes 시간+for 사람+to부정사
It takes me an hour to go to school by bus.

4 빈칸에 들어갈 말은 necessary for me to study이

다. to부정사의 의미상 주어는 「for+목적격」으로 표현한다.

5 (1) 시간을 묻는 의문사 when
(2) 방법을 묻는 의문사 how

6 보기는 명사구 an easy way를 수식하는 to부정사의 형용사적 용법이다.
⑤ 명사 a pet을 수식하는 to부정사의 형용사적 용법이다.
① to부정사의 명사적 용법으로, 문장에서 주격 보어로 쓰였다.
② '바닥을 청소하기 위해서'라는 목적을 나타내는 to부정사의 부사적 용법이다.
③ surprised라는 형용사를 수식하여 감정의 원인을 나타내는 to부정사의 부사적 용법이다.
④ 동사 decide의 목적어로 쓰인 to부정사의 명사적 용법이다.

7 '~하기 위해서'라는 뜻을 가진 to부정사의 부사적 용법이 필요하다.

8 「what to+동사원형」 '무엇을 ~할지'

9 「too+형용사+for+목적격+to부정사」 '~가 …하기에 너무 -한'

10 ④ '그의 할아버지는 80세까지 사셨다'는 결과를 나타내는 to부정사의 부사적 용법이다.
① to부정사의 명사적 용법으로, 문장의 주어 역할을 하고 있다. to부정사구는 문장의 뒤로 보내고, 주어 자리에는 가주어 it을 써주었다.
② to부정사의 명사적 용법으로, to부정사가 문장의 주어로 쓰였다.
③ to부정사의 명사적 용법으로, 주어에 대한 설명을 보충하는 보어 역할로 쓰였다.
⑤ to부정사의 명사적 용법으로, to부정사가 expect의 목적어로 쓰였다.

11 사역동사 make의 목적격 보어로는 원형부정사가 온다.

12 ⓒ 동사 decide는 to부정사를 목적어로 한다.
(meeting → to meet)
ⓔ 사역동사 make는 원형부정사를 목적격 보어로 쓴다. (to take → take)
ⓕ 동사 want는 목적격 보어로 to부정사를 쓴다.
(bring → to bring)

13 to부정사의 의미상의 주어는 'for+목적격'으로 나타낸다. to부정사가 사람의 성격을 묘사하는 형용사를 꾸며줄 때는 'of+목적격'으로 쓴다.
② of ①③④⑤ for

14 감정을 나타내는 형용사 뒤에 오는 to부정사는 그 감정을 느끼는 원인이 된다.

15 ⓐ to부정사의 명사적 용법으로, 문장의 진주어 역할을 하고 있다. to부정사구는 문장의 뒤로 보내고, 주어 자리에는 가주어 it을 써주었다.
ⓑ '영어를 공부하기 위해서'라는 목적을 나타내는 to부정사의 부사적 용법이다.
ⓒ agree의 목적어로 쓰인 to부정사의 명사적 용법이다.
ⓓ 명사 the fastest way를 수식해주는 to부정사의 형용사적 용법이다.
ⓔ '시험을 통과하기 위해서'라는 목적을 나타내는 to부정사의 부사적 용법이다.

16 ⑤ to부정사는 to+동사원형의 형태로 만든다. 이 경우, 문장의 주어로 쓰인 to부정사이므로, to work로 써주는 것이 맞다. (working → work)
① something과 같이 -thing 형태의 대명사는 형용사가 뒤에서 수식한다. 따라서 고치지 않은 형태가 맞다.
② 등위 접속사 and가 있으므로 밑줄 친 자리는 to see 혹은 see와 병렬구조를 이루고 있다. 따라서 to부정사나 동사원형으로 써주는 것이 맞다. (heard → (to) hear)
③ 동사 tell은 목적격 보어로 to부정사를 쓴다. (coming → to come)
④ stop은 동명사만을 목적어로 쓰는 동사이지만, 목적을 나타내는 부사적 용법의 to부정사와 함께 쓰기도 한다. 여기에서는 '점심을 사는 것을 멈추다'가 아니라 '점심을 사기 위해'라는 목적을 나타내는 to부정사로 쓰는 것이 적절하다.

17 「ready+to부정사」 '~할 준비가 된'

18 주어진 문장은 명사 some books를 수식해주는 to부정사의 형용사적 용법이다.
② 명사 something을 수식해주는 to부정사의 형용사적 용법이다.
①④ 동사 wish와 would love의 목적어로 쓰인 to부정사의 명사적 용법이다.
③ '그를 만나기 위해서'라는 목적을 나타내는 to부정사의 부사적 용법이다.
⑤ to부정사의 명사적 용법으로, 문장의 진주어로 쓰였다. to부정사는 문장의 뒤로 보내고 주어의 자리에 가주어 it을 써주었다.

19 ② '방문할 장소들'이라는 뜻으로, places를 수식하기 위해서는 to부정사가 필요하다. (visit → to visit)

⑤ '노래를 잘하기 위해'라는 목적을 나타내주어야 하므로, to부정사의 부사적 용법을 활용해야 한다. (sing → to sing)
① want는 목적격 보어로 to부정사를 쓰는 동사이다.
③④ plan과 would like는 목적어로 to부정사를 쓰는 동사이다.

20 ⑤ 할머니께 컴퓨터를 사용하는 방법을 알려드렸다는 뜻이므로 의문사 how를 사용한다. (what → how)

21 (A), (B), (C), (E) how
(D) What

22 「would like+to부정사」 '~하고 싶다'

23 ⑤ 가주어 it
①④ 비인칭 주어 it
②③ 인칭대명사 it

24 「It(가주어) ~ to부정사(진주어)」 구문

25 ③ something과 같은 -thing 형태의 대명사 뒤에 이를 수식하는 형용사가 나오면 to부정사는 형용사 뒤에 위치한다. (to eat cold → cold to eat)

26 「to+동사원형」이 문장의 뒤에서 구를 이끌어 진주어 역할을 한다.

27 ② going → go

28 to부정사의 의미상의 주어는 'for+목적격'으로 쓴다. to부정사가 사람의 성격을 묘사하는 형용사를 꾸며줄 때는 'of+목적격'으로 쓴다.
② of　　　　　　①③④⑤ for

29 ③ allow는 목적격 보어로 to부정사를 쓴다.
① tell은 목적격 보어로 to부정사를 쓰는 동사이다.
② 사역동사 make는 목적격 보어로 원형부정사를 쓴다.
④ 준사역동사 help는 목적격 보어로 to부정사 또는 원형부정사를 쓴다.
⑤ 지각동사 see는 목적격 보어로 원형부정사나 현재분사를 쓴다.

30 「dying+to부정사」 '몹시 ~하고 싶어하는'

31 ⑤ 형용사적 용법
①②③ 명사적 용법
④ 부사적 용법

32 「what to+동사원형」 '무엇을 ~할지'

33 ③ 주어 역할을 하고 있는 자리이므로 to부정사의 명사적 용법 또는 동명사를 쓸 수 있다.
⑤ start는 목적어로 to부정사나 동명사를 쓴다.
① advise는 목적격 보어로 to부정사를 쓴다.
② 준사역동사 help는 목적격 보어로 to부정사 또는 원형부정사를 쓴다.

⑤ to부정사가 sorry라는 형용사를 수식하여 감정의 원인을 나타내는 부사적 용법으로 쓰였다.

34 주어진 문장의 to부정사구는 명사 a special way를 수식하는 형용사적 용법으로 쓰였다. '요리하는 (특별한 방법)'으로 해석한다.
① 명사 someone을 수식해주는 형용사적 용법이다. '일을 끝낼 (누군가)'로 해석한다.
② 동사 promise의 목적어로 쓰였으며, 명사적 용법이다.
③ '좋은 점수를 받기 위해'라는 목적을 나타내는 to부정사의 부사적 용법이다.
④ '건강하게 유지하기 위해'라는 목적을 나타내는 부사적 용법이다.
⑤ '수영하기 위해'라는 목적을 나타내는 부사적 용법이다.

35 「too+형용사+to부정사」=「so+형용사+that+주어+cannot」 '너무 ~해서 …하지 못하다'

36 ② 'It's time ~'은 '~할 시간이다'의 뜻으로, time 뒤에 동사가 올 때는 to부정사의 형태로 쓴다. (for → to)

37 가주어로 it, 진주어로 to부정사를 쓴다. 사람의 성격을 나타내는 형용사인 generous(관대한)를 썼기 때문에 의미상의 주어는 to부정사 앞에 「of+목적격」형태로 쓴다.

38 (A) agree의 목적어로 쓰인 to부정사의 명사적 용법이다.
(B) '사진을 찍기 위해'라는 목적을 나타내는 to부정사의 부사적 용법이다.
(C) '의사가 되기 위해'라는 목적을 나타내는 to부정사의 부사적 용법이다.
(D) 명사 person을 수식해주는 to부정사의 형용사적 용법이다.
(E) decide의 목적어로 쓰인 to부정사의 명사적 용법이다.

39 ① 그녀가 거기서 무엇을 하고 있냐는 뜻이 적절하므로 진행형으로 써야한다. 진행형은 「be+-ing」의 형태로 쓴다. (do → doing)
② 과거를 나타내는 부사구 last night이 쓰였으므로 과거시제로 써야 한다. (studies → studied)
③ 수사+명사가 형용사처럼 명사를 수식할 때는 명사를 복수형으로 쓰지 않는다. (30-years-old → 30-year-old)
④ need는 to부정사를 목적어로 쓰는 동사이다. to부정사는 to+동사원형으로 쓴다. (to helps → to

help)

40 「so+형용사+that+주어+can't」 '너무 ~해서 …할 수 없다'

41 5형식 동사 ask는 to부정사를 목적격 보어로 취한다. 이때 빈칸에는 '하지 말아야' 하는 내용에 대한 요청을 나타내야 하므로 「not+to부정사」를 이용하여(not to miss) 답안을 작성한다. 대명사 your는 목적어에 맞게 her로 바꾼다.

42 ③ 동사 refuse는 목적어로 to부정사를 쓴다.
①⑤ smell, look과 같은 감각동사는 보어 자리에 형용사가 온다.
② '~만큼 …한'이라는 뜻의 원급 비교는 「as+원급+as」의 어순으로 쓴다.
④ try는 to부정사와 동명사 모두 목적어로 쓸 수 있지만, 여기서는 '책을 읽기 위해 노력하다'라는 의미로 쓰였으므로 to부정사로 써야 한다. try의 목적어로 동명사가 올 경우, '(시험 삼아) ~ 해보다'라는 뜻이 된다.

43 「so+형용사/부사+that+주어+can」
=「형용사/부사+enough+to부정사」 '매우 ~해서 …할 수 있다'='…하기에 충분히 ~하다'

44 to부정사를 진주어로, 본래의 주어 자리에 it을 가주어로 쓴 문장이 필요하다.

45 ⑤ to부정사의 의미상의 주어는 'for+목적격'으로 쓴다. 사람의 성격을 묘사하는 형용사가 쓰였을 때는 'of+목적격'으로 쓴다. impossible은 성격을 묘사하는 형용사가 아니므로 for가 적절하다. (of → for)

46 '의문사+to부정사'인 how to make가 learn의 목적어로 쓰였다.

47 promise 뒤에 동사가 목적어로 올 때는 「to+동사원형」의 형태로 쓴다.

48 (A) '항상 가곤 했다'는 의미로 현재완료의 계속 용법으로 쓰였다. 빈도부사 always는 have와 과거분사 gone 사이에 위치한다.
(B) plan은 to부정사를 목적어로 취하는 동사로, '몇몇 사람들은 더 나은 사람이 되는 것을 계획할지도 모른다'는 의미가 된다. plan 뒤에 동명사를 쓰려면 전치사 on과 함께 써야 한다.
filthy rich '대단히 부유한'
(C) '나의 소원이 이루어지는 것을 보게 되어서 행복하다'는 의미이므로 감정의 원인을 나타내는 to부정사가 와야 한다.

49 ④ 사역동사 make의 목적격 보어는 동사원형으로 쓴

다.
①②③⑤ 목적격 보어로 to부정사의 형태를 갖는 동사들이다.

50 ⑤ 감정의 원인을 나타내는 부사적 용법
①②③④ 목적을 나타내는 부사적 용법

51 '우리의 삶을 더 편하게 만들기 위해서'는 「in order to[so as to]+동사원형」 또는 to부정사(부사적 용법 중 '목적')로 쓸 수 있다.

52 ⓒ '매우 ~해서 …할 수 있(었)다'는 뜻인 「so+형용사/부사+that+주어+can/could」는 '…할 정도로 충분히 ~한'의 뜻을 갖는 「형용사/부사+enough+to부정사」와 바꾸어 쓸 수 있다. 「too+형용사/부사+to부정사」는 '~하기에는 너무 …한'이라는 의미이다. (too hard to win→ hard enough to win)
ⓐ 동명사와 to부정사는 모두 주어에 대한 설명을 보충하는 보어의 역할로 쓰일 수 있다. 이때의 to부정사는 명사적 용법이다.
ⓑ 「의문사+to부정사」는 「의문사+주어+should+동사원형」으로 바꾸어 쓸 수 있다.
ⓓ happy와 같이 감정을 나타내는 형용사를 수식하는 to부정사는 '~해서, ~하게 되어'의 뜻으로 감정의 원인을 나타내기 때문에 이유, 원인을 나타내는 접속사 because절로 바꾸어 쓸 수 있다.
ⓔ 준사역동사 help는 목적격 보어로 원형부정사와 to부정사를 모두 쓸 수 있다.

53 To go. (I'll take it out.) 가져갈 것입니다.
For here. 여기서 먹을 것입니다.

54 (1) 「how+to부정사」 '~하는 법'
(2) 「what+to부정사」 '무엇을 ~할지'

55 to부정사가 사람의 성격을 나타내는 형용사를 꾸며줄 때에는 의미상의 주어를 「of+목적격」으로 나타내고, help의 목적격 보어로는 원형부정사 또는 to부정사를 쓴다. 여기서는 빈칸의 수에 맞추려면 원형부정사가 와야 한다.

56 ⓐ want는 목적격 보어로 to부정사를 쓰는 동사이다.
ⓑ order는 목적격 보어로 to부정사를 쓰는 동사이다. 낯선 사람들에게 말을 걸지 말라고 했으므로, to부정사의 부정형을 써준다. to부정사의 부정형은 「not to+동사원형」의 어순으로 쓴다.

57 「too+형용사+to부정사」=「so+형용사+that+주어+couldn't」 '너무 ~해서 …할 수 없었다'

CHAPTER 8 동명사
Gerunds

본문 _ p.204

PRACTICE 1

1 Working seven days a week is challenging.
2 Her job is designing shoes.
3 Taking a shower makes you feel refreshed.
4 Learning English takes a lot of time and effort.
5 My hobby is taking photos outside.
6 Your mistake was speaking too fast.

> 동명사는 「동사원형+-ing」의 형태로 '~하는 것'이라고 해석하며 문장 내에서 주어, 보어, 목적어의 역할을 할 수 있다.
> 1 일주일에 7일을 일하는 것: Working seven days a week (주어)
> 2 신발을 디자인하는 것: designing shoes (주격 보어)
> 3 샤워를 하는 것: Taking a shower (주어)
> 4 영어를 배우는 것: Learning English (주어)
> 5 야외에서 사진을 찍는 것: taking photos outside (주격 보어)
> 6 너무 빠르게 말한 것: speaking too fast (주격 보어)

PRACTICE 2

1 Practicing the violin
2 Being honest
3 travel(l)ing around the world
4 Making new friends
5 teaching English to kids
6 Living in the countryside

> 1, 2, 4, 6 to부정사 주어가 문장 맨 뒤로 가고 가주어 it이 그 자리를 대신하는 문장이다. 진주어인 to부정사의 to를 뗀 후 -ing를 붙여 동명사로 바꾸고 원래 자리인 맨 앞으로 오게 한다.
> 3, 5 보어로 쓰인 to부정사구를 동명사구로 바꾼다.

PRACTICE 3

1 working　2 to watch　3 talking

4	having	5	to send	6	cooking	
7	working	8	to go	9	writing	
10	to see					

> 1, 3, 4, 6, 7 finish, stop, put off, enjoy, quit은 동명사를 목적어로 가지는 동사이다.
> *stop+동명사 ~하는 것을 멈추다
> stop+to부정사 ~하기 위해 멈추다 (부사적 용법)
> 2, 5, 8, 10 decide, promise, plan, hope는 to부정사를 목적어로 가지는 동사이다.
> 9 keep+-ing: 계속 ~하다

PRACTICE 4

2	not having	3	not going
4	not eating	5	staying

> 1 don't mind: 신경 쓰지 않다, 괜찮다
> 3 Tony: You didn't go to the library, did you?
> 너는 도서관에 가지 않았어. 그렇지?
> Becky: Yes, I did!
> 아니야, 나 갔었어!
> 토니는 베키가 도서관에 가지 않은 것으로 생각하고 질문했지만, 베키는 갔었다고 말하며 토니의 질문에 부인했다. 따라서 베키는 '도서관에 안 갔다는 것(not going)을 부인했다.'가 맞다. 여기서 부정의문문의 대답으로 쓰인 yes는 '아니오'로 해석하고, I did는 긍정으로 해석한다.

PRACTICE 5

1	to eat, eating	2	wasting
3	reading	4	to move
5	to paint, painting	6	to snow, snowing
7	to be	8	to go, going
9	to drink	10	playing
11	making	12	to spend, spending
13	to throw, throwing	14	to get
15	to run, running		

> 1, 5, 6, 8, 12, 13, 15 동사 like, love, begin, intend, hate, continue, start는 동명사와 to부정사를 모두 목적어로 취하고, 그중 어느 것을 목적어로 취하든지 뜻이 달라지지 않는 동사들이다.
> 2, 3, 10, 11 동사 quit, finish, practice, dislike는 동명사만을 목적어로 가지는 동사이다.
> 4, 7, 9, 14 동사 decide, refuse, would like, wish는 to부정사만을 목적어로 가지는 동사이다.

PRACTICE 6

1	to find	2	talking
3	buying	4	not talking
5	to set	6	opening
7	adding	8	to fill

9	telling	10	seeing
11	not to spend	12	meeting
13	not to be	14	cleaning
15	to visit		

> 1 tried to find: 찾으려고 노력했다
> 2 stopped talking: 말하기를 멈췄다
> 3 regret buying: 구매한 것을 후회하다 (일어난 일)
> 4 kept not talking: 말하지 않는 것을 계속했다
> 5 forgot to set: 맞추는 것을 잊었다. (일어나지 않은 일)
> 6 mind opening: 여는 것을 꺼려하다
> 7 try adding: 추가하는 것을 시도해봐라
> 8 stopped to fill up: 채우기 위해서 멈췄다 (목적을 나타내는 부사구로 쓰인 to부정사)
> 9 dislike telling lies: 거짓말하는 것을 싫어하다
> 10 won't forget seeing: 본 것을 잊지 않을 것이다 (일어난 일)
> 11 decided not to spend: (여름휴가를 제주도에서) 보내지 않기로 결정했다
> 12 remember meeting: 만난 것을 기억하다 (일어난 일)
> 13 promised not to be late: 늦지 않기로 약속했다
> 14 didn't finish cleaning: 청소하는 것을 끝내지 않았다
> 15 have forgotten to visit: 방문할 것을 잊었다 (일어나지 않은 일)

PRACTICE 7

1	in playing	2	about[of] moving
3	like having	4	about taking
5	about[of] going	6	of watching
7	for cleaning	8	at singing
9	about fixing	10	about visiting
11	for being	12	to having
13	from coming	14	hearing
15	to living		

PRACTICE 8

1	go skating
2	spent, buying
3	fixing[to be fixed]
4	How[What] about taking, What do you say to taking
5	busy studying
6	no use trying
7	couldn't help laughing
8	having trouble[difficulty/a hard time] getting
9	spent, thinking
10	go skiing
11	There is no defeating[It is impossible to defeat]
12	spends, reading

13 went camping
14 had trouble[difficulty/a hard time] understanding

> 1, 10, 13 go+-ing: ~하러 가다
> 2, 9, 12 spend+시간/돈+-ing: ~하느라 시간/돈을 쓰다
> 3 need+to be p.p./-ing: ~될/할 필요가 있다
> 4 How[What] about -ing?/What do you say to+-ing?: ~하는 것 어때?
> 5 be busy+-ing: ~하느라 바쁘다
> 6 It's no use+-ing: ~해도 소용없다
> 7 can't help+-ing: ~하지 않을 수 없다
> 8, 14 have trouble[difficulty/a hard time]+-ing: ~하는 데에 어려움을 겪다
> 11 There is no+-ing = It is impossible to부정사: ~할 수 없다

Chapter Review Test 정답   본문 _ p.213

1 ② **2** ⓐ singing ⓑ dancing ⓒ getting up[waking up] ⓓ to tell **3** ① **4** ③ **5** ④
6 (1) I really dislike being interrupted by people. (2) Don't forget to feed our dog after school tomorrow. **7** ③ **8** ⑤ **9** (A) [to] understand (B) denying (C) misjudging (D) communicating
10 ③ **11** ③ **12** ④ **13** collecting[to collect], reading[to read] **14** ③ **15** Exercise → Exercising[To exercise] **16** ③ **17** ⑤ **18** ②
19 ③ **20** Getting[Waking] up early **21** They are having difficulty solving this problem. **22** ③
23 take, taking **24** ⑤ **25** ① **26** being
27 Playing basketball **28** ① **29** (1) ⓐ, to give → giving (2) ⓒ, to wash → washing **30** ②
31 ③ **32** On hearing his prayer **33** ④
34 ② **35** ① **36** (1) There is → There are (2) to talk → talking (3) theirs → them **37** ④
38 I regret staying up so late last night.
39 ③,④ **40** ③ **41** ③,④ **42** (1) eight glasses water → eight glasses of water (2) enjoy to do → enjoy doing **43** ⑤

Chapter Review Test 해설

1 mind+-ing '~을 꺼리다'
① hope+to부정사 '~을 바라다'
③ want+to부정사 '~을 원하다'
④ would like+to부정사 '~을 하고 싶다'
⑤ wish+to부정사 '~을 희망하다'

2 ⓐⓑ be good at은 동명사와 함께 써서 '~을 잘하다'라는 뜻을 나타낸다.
ⓒ be used to 다음에 동명사와 함께 쓰면 '~ 하는 것에 익숙하다'라는 뜻이다.
ⓓ forget은 to부정사와 동명사 모두를 목적어로 가질 수 있으며, 그 중 어느 것을 목적어로 쓰는지에 따라 의미가 달라진다. '~하는/할 것을 잊다'라고 표현하려면 to부정사와 함께 써야 한다.

3 ① 진행의 의미를 나타내는 현재분사이다.
②③④⑤ 문장에서 보어의 역할을 하는 동명사이다. 해석은 '~하는 것'으로 한다.

4 ③ 너 오늘 Watson 씨에게 편지를 보낸 것을 기억해?
「remember+동명사」 '과거에 했던 일을 기억하다'
「remember+to부정사」 '미래에 할 일을 기억하다'

5 Mike는 Jenny가 주말에 주로 무엇을 하는지 질문했으므로 대답에는 '~하는 것을 좋아한다.' 또는 '~하면서 시간을 보낸다.'는 답변이 적절하다. ④번은 '유튜브 영상을 보는 것이 지겹다.'는 뜻으로 어울리지 않는 답변이다.
① like+-ing: ~하는 것을 좋아하다
② enjoy+-ing: ~ 하는 것을 즐기다
③ have fun+-ing: ~하며 즐거운 시간을 보내다
④ be tired of+-ing: ~에 지겨움을 느끼다, 지긋지긋하다
⑤ spend time+-ing: ~하면서 시간을 보내다

6 (1) dislike는 동명사만을 목적어로 취하는 동사다.
(2) 「forget+to부정사」 '할 일을 잊다'
    cf. 「forget+동명사」 '했던 일을 잊어버리다'

7 (B) advise → advises
(E) be → being
be used to -ing: ~에 익숙하다

8 look forward to+-ing '~을 고대하다'

9 (A) help는 준사역동사로 목적격 보어 자리에 동사 원형 또는 to부정사가 올 수 있다.
(B) There is no+-ing : ~할 수 없다
세계화가 진행됨에 따라 서로 다른 가치, 신념 및 관습을 이해하려는 노력이 점점 더 중요해졌다는 사실을 부인할 수 없다.
(C) avoid의 목적어로 동사가 올 때는 동명사 형태로 쓴다.
(D) 전치사 by의 목적어는 동명사로 써준다.
by+-ing: ~함으로써

10 (A) 「be busy+-ing」 '~하느라 바쁘다'
   (B) 「keep+-ing」 '~을 계속하다'
   (C) 「wish+to부정사」 '~하기를 원하다, 바라다'
11 ③ deny는 동명사를 목적어로 쓰는 동사이다.
   ① feel like은 '~하고 싶다'는 뜻으로 뒤에 동명사가 온다. (feel like to talk → feel like talking)
   ② decide는 to부정사를 목적어로 쓰는 동사이다. (decided taking → decided to take)
   ④ mind는 동명사를 목적어로 쓰는 동사이다. (mind to turn → mind turning)
   ⑤ agree는 to부정사를 목적어로 쓰는 동사이다. (agree changing → agree to change)
12 ④ to go → to going
   「What do you say to+동명사 ~?」
   '~하는 게 어때?'
13 「like+-ing/to부정사」 '~을 좋아하다'
14 「try+to부정사」 '~하려고 노력하다, 애쓰다'
   cf. try+-ing '(시험삼아) ~해보다'
15 문장의 주어로는 동명사(Exercising)나 to부정사(To exercise)가 온다.
16 ⓐ 「be worried about -ing」 '~에 대해 걱정하다'
   ⓑ to부정사의 부사적 용법(목적)
   ⓒ 「explain A to B」 'A를 B에게 설명하다'
17 ③ 현재분사   ①②④⑤ 동명사
18 문맥상 미래의 행동에 관해 말하는 것이므로 「remember+to부정사」(~할 것을 기억하다)인 ②가 맞다.
19 ③ practice+-ing '~을 연습하다'
   (to play → playing)
20 '일찍 일어나다'라는 표현은 'get[wake] up early'이다. 문장의 주어로는 동명사나 to부정사가 올 수 있는데 세 단어로 써야 하므로 답은 'Getting[Waking] up early'가 된다.
21 「have difficulty+동명사」 '~하는 데 어려움을 겪다'
22 • 「like+-ing/to부정사」 '~을 좋아하다'
   • be interested in+-ing '~에 관심 있다'
23 think of+-ing '~하는 것에 대해 생각하다'
24 ⑤ ⓐ 과거진행시제(he was doing his homework)를 나타내는 현재분사이다. (그가 숙제를 하고 있었다.)
   ⓑ 전치사의 목적어로 쓰인 동명사이다. 'be tired of'는 '~을 지겨워하다'는 뜻의 관용표현이다. (너의 질문들에 대답하는 것이 지겹다.)

① 문장의 주어로 쓰인 동명사이다.
   ⓐ Taking a nap: 낮잠을 자는 것
   ⓑ Eating vegetables: 채소를 먹는 것
② 명사를 수식하는 현재분사이다.
   ⓐ the boring news: 지루한 뉴스
   ⓑ The girl sleeping on the couch: 소파에서 자고 있는 소녀
③ 타동사(enjoy/finish)의 목적어로 쓰인 동명사이다.
   ⓐ enjoys swimming: 수영하는 것을 즐기다
   ⓑ finish writing: 쓰는 것을 끝내다
④ 주격 보어로 쓰인 동명사이다.
   ⓐ teaching English: 영어를 가르치는 것
   ⓑ going to Canada: 캐나다에 가는 것
25 ⓐ 「How about+-ing」는 '~하는 게 어때?'라는 관용어구이며 여기서 -ing는 '~하는 것'을 의미하는 동명사이다.
   ⓑ be동사와 함께 쓰여 진행시제를 나타내는 현재분사이다.
   ⓒ 주격 보어 역할로 쓰인 동명사이다. '~하는 것'으로 해석된다.
   ⓓ hear과 같은 지각동사의 목적격 보어로는 동사원형이나 진행의 의미를 강조하는 현재분사를 쓸 수 있다.
   ⓔ 명사(baby)의 앞에서 명사의 동작이나 상태를 수식해주는 현재분사이다. (The sleeping baby: 자고 있는 아기)
   ⓕ 전치사의 다음에 나왔으므로 명사 역할을 하는 동명사이다.
26 deny+-ing '~을 부인하다' 나는 그 사기에 연루된 것을 부인했다.
27 <보기>에서 문장의 주어로 동명사(Learning)가 왔으므로, 동명사로 시작하는 문장이 되어야 한다.
28 「remember+to부정사」 '~할 것을 기억하다'
   cf. remember+-ing '~한 것을 기억하다'
29 ⓐ mind는 동명사를 목적어로 취한다.
   ⓒ finish는 동명사를 목적어로 취하는 동사다.
30 ② like는 to부정사와 동명사 모두를 목적어로 가질 수 있으며 의미가 달라지지 않는 동사이다. 따라서 (나)에 riding이 들어가는 것은 적절하다.
   ① want는 to부정사만을 목적어로 가지는 동사다. (가)에는 to go가 들어가야 한다.
   ③ would like는 to부정사와 함께 쓰여 '~하고 싶다'

라는 뜻을 나타낸다. (다)에는 to drink가 들어가야 한다.
④ 주어 자리에는 동사원형이 들어갈 수 없다. (라)에는 동명사 Yelling 또는 to부정사 To yell이 적합하다
⑤ be used to는 to 다음에 동사원형이 올 경우 '~하는 데에 사용되다'라는 뜻을 나타내고, 동명사가 와서 'be used to -ing'가 될 경우 '~하는 데에 익숙하다'라는 뜻을 나타낸다. 여기서는 '그는 많은 사람들 앞에서 공연하는 데에 익숙하지 않다.' 라는 의미가 적절하므로 (마)에는 동명사 performing이 들어가야 한다.

31 ③의 decide는 to부정사를 목적어로 취하는 동사이고 나머지 동사는 동명사를 취하는 동사이다.

32 on -ing: ~하자마자
그의 기도를 듣자마자 요정은 그 인형에게 생명을 불어넣었다.

33 전치사의 목적어로는 동명사가 온다.

34 「There is no+동명사」=「It is impossible+to부정사」 '~할 수 없다'

35 (A) would love[like] 뒤에는 to부정사만 가능하다.
would love to '~하기를 좋아하다'
(B) 주어가 사물(That copy machine)이므로 need 뒤에는 '~되어야 할 필요가 있다'는 수동 의미로서 동명사를 쓴다. 「need + -ing」 '~되어야 할 필요가 있다'
(C) ask+목적어+to부정사: ~에게 …하도록 요청하다

36 (1) 첫 번째 줄: 「there is+단수명사」, 「there are+복수명사」 (There is → There are)
(2) 밑에서 네 번째 줄: enjoy는 동명사를 목적어로 취한다. (enjoy to talk → enjoy talking)
(3) 마지막 줄: 전치사 뒤에는 목적격이 온다. (with theirs → with them)

37 (A) 우유는 치즈를 만드는 데 사용된다는 뜻이므로 「be used to+동사원형」을 사용하여 나타낸다. (making → make)

(B) cannot[couldn't] help+-ing는 '~하지 않을 수 없다'는 뜻의 관용표현이다. (to buy → buying)
(D) prevent A from -ing는 'A가 ~하는 것을 못하게 하다'는 뜻의 관용표현이다.
(to cross → from crossing)
(E) be responsible for -ing는 '~에 책임이 있다'는 뜻의 관용표현이다. 전치사의 목적어로 동사가 올 때는 동명사의 형태로 쓴다.
(prepare → preparing)

38 regret +동명사: ~한 것을 후회하다
stay up late '늦게까지 자지 않다'

39 「begin+-ing/to부정사」 '~을 시작하다'

40 ③ imagine은 동명사를 목적어로 쓰는 동사이다.
(to meet → meeting)
① suggest는 동명사를 목적어로 쓰는 동사이다.
② hate는 동명사와 to부정사 모두 목적어로 쓰고, 그 중 어느 것을 목적어로 써도 뜻이 달라지지 않는다.
④ to fix가 '(내 컴퓨터를) 고치기 위해서'라는 목적을 나타내는 to부정사의 부사적 용법으로 쓰였다.
⑤ refuse는 to부정사를 목적어로 쓰는 동사이다.

41 ① doing → to do
「expect+목적어+to부정사」 '목적어가 ~하기를 기대하다'
② support → to support
「decide+to부정사」 '~하기로 결심하다'
⑤ to work → working
「dislike+동명사」 '~하기를 싫어하다'

42 (1) 두 번째 줄: 물질명사의 수를 나타내는 단위명사의 뒤에는 of가 와야 한다. (eight glasses water → eight glasses of water)
(2) 밑에서 두 번째 줄: enjoy는 동명사를 목적어로 취한다. (enjoy to do → enjoy doing)

43 if 조건절에서는 현재 시제가 미래 시제를 대신한다. '~하는데 시간을 쓰다'는 「spend time +~ing」로 나타낸다.

CHAPTER 9 분사
Participles

본문 _ p.222

PRACTICE 1

1. repaired
2. surprising
3. sleeping
4. depressing
5. boiled
6. eating
7. given
8. invited
9. taken
10. amazing
11. used
12. rising

> 1 has just repaired: '막, 방금'이라는 의미의 부사 just와 함께 쓰여 현재완료시제의 완료를 나타낸다.
> 2 some surprising news: 현재분사 surprising이 명사 news를 꾸며서 능동(놀라게 하는)의 의미를 나타낸다.
> 3 the sleeping puppy: 현재분사 sleeping이 명사 puppy를 꾸며서 진행(자고 있는)의 의미를 나타낸다.
> 4 depressing: 현재분사 depressing이 문장 내에서 주격 보어로 사용되어 능동(우울하게 하는)의 의미를 나타낸다.
> 5 boiled eggs: 과거분사 boiled가 명사 eggs를 앞에서 수식하여 수동 및 완료(삶아진)의 의미를 나타낸다.
> 6 were eating: 현재분사 eating이 were과 함께 쓰여 과거진행시제를 나타낸다. 여기서 과거분사가 사용될 경우 수동태(They were eaten: 그들은 먹혔다.)가 되어 의미상 적절하지 않다.
> 7 given name: 과거분사 given이 명사를 앞에서 수식하여 수동(주어진)의 의미를 나타낸다. given name은 first name과 같은 뜻으로, 성을 제외한 이름을 가리킨다.
> 8 was invited: 과거분사 invited가 과거시제 be동사와 함께 쓰여 과거 수동태(초대되었다)를 나타낸다. 내가 아닌 그의 생일파티이기 때문에 초대를 받는 수동의 의미가 적절하다.
> 9 were taken: 과거분사 taken이 과거시제 be동사와 함께 쓰여 과거 수동태(찍혔다)를 나타낸다. 사진이 주어이므로 능동보다는 수동태 사용이 적절하다.
> 10 amazing: 현재분사 amazing이 the story를 보충 설명하는 주격 보어로 쓰여 능동(놀라게 하는)의 의미를 나타낸다.
> 11 a used car: 과거분사 used가 car를 앞에서 수식하여 수동 및 완료(사용된)의 의미를 나타낸다.
> 12 a rising sun: 현재분사 rising이 sun을 앞에서 수식하여 진행(뜨고 있는)의 의미를 나타낸다.

PRACTICE 2

2. barking
3. broken
4. painted
5. Used
6. shocking
7. written
8. talking
9. interesting
10. burned[burnt]

> 2 dogs barking at people: 사람을 향해 짖고 있는 개들(진행)
> 3 the broken glasses: 깨진 안경(수동, 완료)
> 4 the wall painted in red: 빨간색으로 칠해진 벽(수동)
> 5 Used cars: 사용된(중고의) 차(수동, 완료)
> 6 a shocking accident: 충격적인 사고(능동)
> 7 a book written by James Joyce: James Joyce에 의해 쓰여진 책(수동)

> 8 That boy talking with the old lady: 노부인과 대화 중인 저 소년(진행)
> 9 some interesting questions: 몇 가지 흥미로운 질문들(능동)
> 10 A burned[burnt] child: 화상을 입은 아이(수동)

PRACTICE 3

1. lost wallet
2. dancing students
3. fallen on the ground
4. reading a book
5. burned cookies
6. filled with tears
7. exercising in the gym
8. covered with snow
9. shining sun
10. singing on the stage

PRACTICE 4

2. cooking, 목적격 보어
3. fixed, 목적격 보어
4. depressed, 주격 보어
5. waiting, 목적격 보어
6. dancing, 명사 수식
7. excited, 주격 보어
8. running, 목적격 보어
9. fallen, 명사 수식
10. cleaned, 목적격 보어
11. smiling, 주격 보어
12. listening, 주격 보어
13. interesting, 명사 수식
14. baked, 명사 수식
15. walking, 목적격 보어
16. touched, 목적격 보어

> 2, 5, 8, 15 목적격 보어로 현재분사를 사용하여 목적어가 하고 있는 행위를 서술한다. 지각동사의 목적격 보어로 현재분사가 사용될 경우 진행의 의미를 강조할 수 있다.
> 3, 10, 16 목적격 보어로 과거분사를 사용하여 목적어가 당하는 행위나 상태를 서술한다. '(목적어가)~되는 것을'로 해석한다.
> 4, 7 주격 보어로 과거분사를 사용하여 주어가 느끼는 감정을 서술한다.
> *depressed: 우울한
> *excited: 신이 난, 들뜬

6, 14 구를 이루는 분사는 명사 뒤에서 명사를 꾸며줄 수 있다.
9, 13 분사가 단독으로 쓰일 때는 명사 앞에서 명사를 꾸며줄 수 있다.
11, 12 be 동사와 함께 현재분사를 사용하여 주어가 하는 행위가 진행 중임을 나타낸다.

PRACTICE 7

bored, interesting, disappointed, tiring, exciting, satisfied

- I started to feel <u>bored</u>: 주어가 사람이고, 주어의 감정/상태를 나타내므로 과거분사를 사용한다.
- something <u>interesting</u>: something을 수식하여 능동(~하게 하는)의 의미를 나타낸다. -thing 형태의 대명사는 뒤에서만 수식해줄 수 있다.
- You won't be <u>disappointed</u> : 주어가 사람이고, 주어의 감정을 나타내므로 과거분사를 사용한다.
- <u>It</u>(가주어) was a little tiring <u>to go there by bus</u>(진주어): 사람이 아닌 주어의 성질을 나타낼 때 현재분사를 사용하여 '피곤한', '피곤하게 하는' 등의 의미를 나타낼 수 있다.
- the concert was very <u>exciting</u> : 사람이 아닌 주어의 주격 보어로 현재분사를 사용한다.
- Both of us … were <u>satisfied</u>: 사람인 주어의 감정을 나타내기 위해 과거분사를 사용하여 '만족스러운'의 의미를 나타낸다.

PRACTICE 5

1	A	2	B	3	B
4	A	5	B	6	A
7	B	8	A	9	A
10	B				

[보기]
A. are playing soccer: 축구를 하는 중이다. (현재분사)
B. running shoes: 달리기용 신발 (동명사)

1, 4 be 동사와 함께 쓰여 진행 시제를 나타내는 현재분사이다.
2, 5, 10 용도를 나타내는 동명사다. '~을 하기 위한,' '~로 쓰는'이라고 해석할 수 있다.
3, 7 주격 보어로 쓰인 동명사이다. '~하는 것' 으로 해석한다.
6, 8 명사를 꾸며주는 형용사 역할의 현재분사이다. 앞에 정관사나 소유격이 온다.
*the boring class: 지루한 수업
*her smiling face: 그녀의 웃는 얼굴
9 현재분사가 주어의 내용을 보충 설명하는 주격 보어로 쓰였다.

PRACTICE 8

2 Studying hard
3 Cooking in the kitchen
4 Meeting Hana at the bookstore
5 Taking a walk
6 arriving in Busan at 11:10
7 Listening to the radio
8 Pushing a boy by mistake
9 Planning to stay at home
10 Knowing him well

PRACTICE 6

1 boring, bored
2 depressed, depressing
3 confused, confusing
4 disappointing, disappointed
5 moved, moving
6 interesting, interested
7 surprised, surprising
8 satisfied, satisfying
9 tiring, tired
10 puzzling, puzzled
11 excited, exciting
12 shocked, shocking
13 amazing, amazed
14 pleased, pleasing
15 embarrassing, embarrassed

PRACTICE 9

1 with my daughter following him
2 with his lamp turned on
3 with the trash cleaned up
4 with our legs tied
5 with his friends dancing
6 with my alarm clock ringing

[보기]
… and he was crossing his legs. (사람 주어, 능동)
= … with his legs crossed. (with+신체 일부+과거분사)

1, 5 접속사 다음에 나오는 주어가 사람이고, 주어가 직접 행위를 하는 내용이기 때문에「with+명사+현재분사」로 나타낼 수 있다.
2, 3, 4 접속사 and 다음의 주어가 사물/신체 일부이고, 주어가 동사의 행위를 당하는 내용이기 때문에「with+명사+과거분사」로 나타낼 수 있다.
6 접속사 while 다음에 나오는 주어가 사물(my alarm clock)이지만, 동사가 '울리다'라는 능동의 의미를 지니기 때문에「with+명사+현재분사」로 나타낼 수 있다.

1~15 수식을 받거나 서술되는 대상이 사람일 때, 보어로 과거분사를 사용하여 '~된', '~감정을 느끼는'이라는 의미를 나타낸다.
한편, 수식을 받거나 서술되는 대상이 사람이 아닐 때, 보어로 현재분사를 사용하여 사물의 성질을 나타낼 수 있고, '~하게 하는'이라고 해석한다.

Chapter Review Test 정답 본문 _ p.233

1 ④　2 ⓑ taking → taken, ⓓ filling → filled
3 ④　4 ③　5 ③　6 ①,②　7 ③　8 ②　9 ②
10 ⑤　11 ③　12 ②　13 ④　14 ③
15 ④　16 ②,④　17 ①　18 ①　19 listening to music　20 ④　21 ②　22 after we finished the work　23 The woman waving to my father is my mother.　24 ④　25 with his eyes closed
26 (1) (A), building, built (2) (D), excited, exciting
27 ⑤　28 ①　29 broken　30 ③　31 ④
32 ④,⑤　33 ③　34 ①　35 Dropping by his house　36 ③　37 Because[As/Since] I missed the bus　38 ⑤　39 ①　40 ④　41 ②
42 ②

Chapter Review Test 해설

1 interesting '흥미로운'
2 ⓑ taking → taken
　수동태 문장이므로 과거분사를 쓴다.
　ⓓ filling → filled
　목적어와 목적격 보어가 수동관계이므로 과거분사를 쓴다.
3 ④ 현재분사
　①②③⑤ 동명사
4 ③ satisfying → satisfied
5 목적어와 목적격 보어가 수동의 관계이므로 과거분사가 필요하다.
6 밑줄 친 부분은 전치사 다음에 쓰였기 때문에 동명사이다.
　① 명사 'the girl'을 수식하는 현재분사이다. (the girl dancing on the stage: 무대 위에서 춤추고 있는 소녀)
　② be동사와 함께 쓰여 진행시제를 나타내는 현재분사이다.
　③ 「give up -ing」는 '-하는 것을 포기하다'라는 의미이며 여기서 -ing는 '~하는 것'을 나타내는 동명사이다.
　④ waiting room은 대기실이라는 뜻으로, 여기서 waiting이 명사의 용도(대기용)를 나타내므로 동명사다.
　⑤ 문장의 주어로 쓰인 동명사이다. (Keeping your body warm: 네 몸을 따뜻하게 유지하는 것)
7 (A) 책이 감동적인 것이므로 현재분사 moving
　(B) 사람이 지루해하는 것이므로 과거분사 bored
　(C) 사람이 관심을 갖게 되는 것이므로 과거분사 interested
8 접속사(while)와 부사절의 주어(he)를 빼고 부사절의 동사(cleaned)를 -ing형으로 바꾸어 분사구문을 만들 수 있다.
9 ② 'me'가 피곤한 감정을 느끼는 대상이므로 과거분사를 써야 한다.
　① 'Ben's grades'가 실망스러운 감정을 느끼게 하는 것이므로 현재분사를 쓰는 것이 맞다.
　③ 'I'가 충격을 받는 대상이므로 과거분사를 써야 한다.
　④ 영화가 감정을 일으키는 주체이므로 현재분사를 써야 한다.
　⑤ 'her room'은 청소가 되는 대상이므로 과거분사를 써야 한다.
10 (A) Peanuts가 삶아지는 대상이므로 과거분사 Boiled가 맞다.
　(B) 동시동작을 나타내는 분사구문이다.
　Stirring once in a while ~.
　= While you stir once in a while ~.
　(C) 「get+형용사」 '~해지다'
11 worried '걱정스러운'
　-ed '~한 감정을 느끼는'
12 ② 현재분사
　①③④⑤ 동명사
13 목적어(Jane)와 목적격 보어(lying)가 능동의 관계일 때는 현재분사를 쓴다.
14 ⓒ 영화가 감동을 느끼게 하는 것이므로 '감동적인'이라는 뜻의 현재분사 moving을 쓴다. (move → moving)
　ⓓ 자동사 fall '(어떤 상태에) 빠지다' 뒤에는 서술적 용법의 형용사 asleep이 온다. (sleeping → asleep)
15 ⓐ 선행사가 3인칭 단수이므로 동사도 3인칭 단수형으로 수일치한다. (orbit → orbits)
　ⓒ pit는 타동사로 '(움푹 패인) 자국[구멍]을 남기다'라는 뜻이다. 달의 표면에 구멍이 나 있는 것이므로 과거분사가 알맞다. (pitting → pitted)
　ⓔ 준사역동사 help는 목적격 보어로 원형부정사나 to부정사만을 가진다. (stabilizing →

stabilize[to stabilize])

16 ② '이미 사용된 종이를 재활용해야 한다'는 뜻이므로 수동과 완료의 의미를 가진 과거분사를 써야 한다. (using → used)
④ 'the book'이 혼란스러운 감정을 느끼게 하는 것이므로 현재분사를 써야 한다. (confused → confusing)
① 'people'이 흥분을 느끼는 대상이므로 과거분사를 써야 한다.
③ 'this book'은 Thomas Hardy에 의해 쓰여진 것이므로, 수동의 의미를 가진 과거분사를 써야 한다.
⑤ 'The flowers'는 물주기(water)라는 행위의 대상이므로 수동의 의미를 가진 과거분사를 써야 한다.

17 surprised '놀란' - surprising '놀라운'

18 ① 'Her speech'가 충격적인 감정을 느끼게 하는 것이므로 현재분사를 써야 한다. (shocked → shocking)
② 'I'가 흥분을 느끼는 대상이므로 과거분사를 써야 한다.
③ 'person'이 놀라운 감정을 느끼게 하는 것이므로 현재분사를 써야 한다.
④ 'I'가 피곤한 감정을 느끼는 것이므로 과거분사를 써야 한다.
⑤ 'Drinking a lot of water'는 문장에서 주어의 역할을 하는 동명사로 쓰였다.

19 접속사(and)와 주어(I)를 빼고, 동사(am listening)을 현재분사로 바꾸어 분사구문을 만들 수 있다. 이때, listening이 이미 진행의 의미를 담고 있으므로 being은 쓰지 않는다.

20 (A) 'a lot of animals'가 기다리는 행위의 주체이므로 능동의 의미를 나타내는 현재분사를 써야 한다. (waited → waiting)
(C) forget은 to부정사를 목적어로 쓰면 '~할 것을 잊다(일어나지 않은 일)'라는 뜻이고 동명사를 목적어로 쓸 경우 '~한 것을 잊다(이미 일어난 일)'를 의미한다. 여기에서는 '먹이를 주는 것을 잊었다'는 뜻이므로 to부정사를 쓰는 것이 맞다.
(B) 「take (good) care of」 '~를 (잘) 돌보다'
(D) 「be filled with」 '~로 가득 차 있다'
(E) 「think of」 '~을 생각하다, 머리에 떠올리다'

21 ① 운동이 피곤함을 느끼게 하는 것이므로 현재분사 tiring을 쓴다. (tired → tiring)
③ 우리가 충격을 받은 것이므로 과거분사 shocked를 쓴다. (shocking → shocked)
④ 영화가 흥미로웠던 것이므로 현재분사 interesting을 쓴다. (interested → interesting)
⑤ 그녀가 실망을 느끼는 것이므로 과거분사를 써야 한다. (disappointing → disappointed)

22 문맥에 맞는 접속사(after)와 주어(we)를 더하고 분사 형태인 동사를 주절의 동사와 시제가 일치하도록 하여(finished) 부사절로 만들 수 있다.

23 현재분사가 뒤의 다른 어구들과 함께 명사를 수식할 때는 명사 뒤에 놓는다.

24 ④ surprised '놀란' → surprising '놀라운'

25 '~을 …한 채로'라는 뜻의 「with+명사+분사」를 이용하여 쓴다. 이때, 'his eyes'와 'close'가 수동의 관계이므로 과거분사를 사용한다.

26 (1) '눈으로 지어진 집'이라는 수동의 의미이므로 과거분사가 되어야 한다.
(2) '~한 감정을 느끼게 하는' 것이므로 현재분사가 되어야 한다.

27 ⓔ 등위접속사 and로 fell down과 병렬구조를 이루고 있다. fell down이 과거시제 동사이므로 break도 과거시제로 써야 한다. (broken → broke)
ⓐ Jay가 3인칭 단수이므로, 동사도 3인칭 단수 현재형의 'plays'를 쓴다.
ⓑ 「with+명사+분사」는 '~을 …한 채로'라는 뜻으로, 'her arms'와 'fold'가 수동의 관계이므로 과거분사를 쓴다.
ⓒ books는 셀 수 있는 명사이므로, 셀 수 있는 명사를 수식하는 a few를 쓴다.
ⓓ 'She'가 흥분을 느끼는 대상이므로 과거분사의 형태로 쓴다.

28 '~하고 있는'의 뜻일 때는 현재분사를 쓴다.

29 broken '깨진' break - broke - broken

30 ③ 현재분사
①②④⑤ 동명사

31 ⓐ the boy가 돌보는 행위(look after)의 주체이므로 현재분사를 써야 한다. (Looked → Looking)
ⓑ 「with+명사+분사」는 '~을 …한 채로'라는 뜻으로, 'her legs'와 'cross'가 수동의 관계이므로 과거분사를 쓴다. (crossing → crossed)
ⓒ 'The man'이 입고 있는 주체이므로 현재 분사(wearing)를 쓴다. 이때, 분사가 구를 이루어 명사를 수식하므로 명사의 뒤에서 수식한다.
ⓓ 'the guys'가 말을 하고 있는 주체이므로 현재 분

사(talking)를 쓴다.
ⓔ 'The door'가 페인트칠 되는 대상이므로 수동의 의미를 가진 과거분사를 쓴다. (painting → painted)
ⓕ 'the crowd'가 흥분을 느끼는 대상이므로 과거분사(excited)를 쓴다.

32 ⑤ '~하면서'라는 뜻의 동시동작은 접속사 while을 사용하여 나타낼 수 있다. 주어는 Sally이므로 반복을 피하기 위해 대명사 she를 쓴다. 보고 있었던 것이므로 과거진행형을 사용한다.
④ ⑤번의 문장에서 접속사와 부사절의 주어를 지우고, 동사를 현재분사로 바꾸어 동시동작을 나타내는 분사구문을 만들 수 있다. 이때 looking이 이미 진행의 의미를 담고 있으므로 being은 쓰지 않는다.

33 (A) 주어 it은 영화를 가리키는 인칭대명사이며 감정을 불러일으키는 것이므로 현재분사가 알맞다.
(B) 주어 it은 Sophie가 적극적인 모습으로 영화에 나왔다는 것을 나타내며, 그다지 불편한 감정을 느끼게 하지는 않았다는 문장이므로 현재분사가 알맞다.

34 interesting '흥미로운'
be interested in '~에 관심 있다'

35 접속사(When)와 부사절의 주어(I)를 빼고 부사절의 동사(dropped)를 -ing형으로 바꾸어 분사구문을 만들 수 있다.

36 (A) 'a concert'가 열리는 대상이므로 수동의 의미를 가진 과거분사 held를 쓴다.
(B) '누구의 콘서트'인지 묻는 것이므로 소유격 의문형용사 whose를 써야 한다. whom은 목적격 의문대명사이다. (whom → whose)
(C) 'I'가 놀라운 감정을 느끼는 대상이므로 과거분사 surprised를 써야 한다. surprising은 '놀라게 하는'의 의미이다. (surprising → surprised)
(D) 'used to'는 '~하곤 했다'는 뜻의 조동사이므로, 뒤에 동사원형을 쓴다.
(E) 진주어를 뒤로 보내고 가주어 it을 주어의 자리에 쓴 형태이다. 의미상의 주어로 「for+목적격(me)」이 쓰인 것으로 보아서 진주어가 to부정사구가 되는 것이 적절함을 알 수 있다. (understand → to understand)

37 원인을 나타내는 접속사 Because[As/Since]와 주어 I를 넣는다. 동사의 시제는 주절과 동일하게 과거시제(missed)로 쓴다.

38 ⓑⓔ 동명사
ⓐⓒⓓ 현재분사

39 '~을 …한 채로'라는 뜻의 「with+명사+분사」를 이용하여 쓴다. 이때, 'his eyes'와 'close'가 수동의 관계이므로 과거분사를 사용한다.

40 ⓐ 한 문장 내에서 접속사 없이 두 개의 동사가 나올 수 없다. stood와 read의 주체가 모두 She이므로 read를 현재분사 reading으로 바꾸어 동시동작(신문을 읽으면서)을 나타낼 수 있다. (read → reading)
ⓑ by+-ing: ~함으로써
ⓒ 'the man'이 줍고 있는 주체이므로 능동의 의미를 가진 현재분사(picking)로 쓴다.
ⓓ 주어인 we가 보고 있는 주체이므로 현재분사를 쓴다. (watched → watching)
ⓔ 지각동사 look at의 목적격 보어로는 동사원형이나 현재분사를 쓴다. (sang → sing/singing)

41 접속사(Though)와 부사절의 주어(I)를 빼고 부사절의 동사(go)를 -ing형으로 바꾸어 분사구문을 만들 수 있다.

42 move는 '이동하다, 이사하다'와 '감동시키다'라는 뜻의 동사이고, move의 과거분사 moved는 '감동한'이라는 뜻의 형용사처럼 사용되어 문장의 주격 보어 역할을 할 수 있다.

• 난 내 일 때문에 지난달에 시골 지역으로 이사했다.
• 그는 서로를 사랑하는 것에 대한 그녀의 연설에 감동했다.

CHAPTER 10 형용사
Adjectives

본문 _ p.242

PRACTICE 1

2 Ms. Song is a famous doctor.
3 Mary is wearing a beautiful necklace.
4 I'd like to have hot coffee.
5 Paul watched an exciting movie yesterday.
6 Look at the small bird over there.
7 Inho used to live in a large apartment.
8 Could you pass me the blue ball?
9 Put them on the plastic table.
10 I drank Irish tea last night.

> 1~10 형용사는 명사의 앞에서 명사를 수식한다. 첫소리가 모음으로 시작하는 형용사가 셀 수 있는 단수 명사를 수식할 경우, 명사의 발음과는 상관없이 형용사 앞에 관사 an이 온다.
> 1 an old car: 오래된 자동차
> 2 a famous doctor: 유명한 의사
> 3 a beautiful necklace: 아름다운 목걸이
> 4 hot coffee: 뜨거운 커피
> 5 an exciting movie: 흥미진진한 영화
> 6 the small bird: 작은 새
> 7 a large apartment: 넓은 아파트
> 8 the blue ball: 파란색 공
> 9 the plastic table: 플라스틱 탁자
> 10 Irish tea: 아일랜드 차

PRACTICE 2

1 woman is intelligent
2 movie was impressive
3 house is empty
4 computer is broken
5 student is diligent
6 artists are famous

PRACTICE 3

1	asleep	2	sleeping
3	like	4	live
5	alike	6	alive
7	glad	8	cheerful
9	scared	10	afraid

> 1, 5, 6, 7 주격 보어 자리이므로 서술적 용법으로 쓸 수 있는 형용사가 알맞다.
> 2, 4, 8, 9 명사 앞에서 명사를 수식하는 자리이므로 한정적 용법으로 쓰일 수 있는 형용사가 알맞다.
> 3 like는 명사나 대명사 앞에서 '~와 유사한'이라는 의미의 전치사로 쓰였다. What's she like?는 '그녀는 어떤 사람이니?'라는 의미이다.
> 10 be afraid of: ~를 두려워하다 (=be scared of)

PRACTICE 4

1 eat something spicy
2 anybody familiar to you
3 someone diligent for the job
4 need anything else
5 something hot to drink[to drink something hot]
6 met anyone friendly
7 calls somebody close to her
8 buy anything expensive yesterday
9 have nothing new
10 seen nobody famous

> 1~10 -thing, -one, -body로 끝나는 대명사는 형용사가 뒤에서 수식한다.
> 1 something spicy: 매콤한 것
> 2 anybody familiar to you: 너에게 친숙한 누구라도
> * familiar to: ~에게 익숙한
> 3 someone diligent: 부지런한 누군가
> 4 anything else: 그밖에 또 다른 것
> 5 something hot: 뜨거운 것
> 6 anyone friendly: 다정한 누군가
> 7 somebody close to her: 그녀와 가까운 누군가
> *close to: ~와 가까운 (사이인)
> 8 anything expensive: 비싼 것
> 9 nothing new: 새로운 것이 없는
> 10 nobody famous: 유명한 사람이 없는

PRACTICE 5

1 The rich have their own problems.
2 He did a lot of good things for the poor.
3 These days the blind keep dogs to help themselves.

4 There are some special schools for the deaf.
5 Mr. Park encourages the young to be brave.
6 I took care of the sick in the hospital yesterday.

> 1~6 「the+형용사」는 '~한 사람들'의 뜻으로, 복수 명사처럼 쓰인다.
> 1 rich people = the rich: 부유한 사람들
> 2 poor people = the poor: 가난한 사람들
> 3 blind people = the blind: 시각 장애인들
> 4 deaf people = the deaf: 청각 장애인들
> 5 young people = the young: 젊은 사람들
> *encourage+사람+to+동사원형: ~를 …하도록 북돋우다, 격려하다
> 6 sick people = the sick: 아픈 사람들

PRACTICE 6

1 have **2** Do **3** Are
4 learn **5** was **6** tend

> 1, 2, 3, 4, 6 주어 자리의 「the+형용사」는 '~한 사람들'이라는 뜻으로, 복수 명사처럼 쓰이므로 복수 동사가 알맞다. 2번의 경우 일반동사 의문문이므로 복수 주어 the sick에 맞춰 문장 맨 앞의 Does가 Do가 되어야 한다.
> 5 문장의 주어는 the elderly가 아니라 The hospital이므로 단수 동사 was가 알맞다.

PRACTICE 7

1 한국어 **2** 미국인, 미국의
3 폴란드 사람들 **4** 프랑스의
5 독일어 **6** 덴마크의
7 일본의 **8** 중국어
9 캐나다의 **10** 스페인어

> 1 learn Korean: 한국어를 배우다
> 2 Sarah is an American.: Sarah는 미국인이다.
> American food: 미국의 음식
> 3 The Polish: 폴란드 사람들
> * 'the+국가명의 형용사'는 '국민 전체'를 의미한다.
> 4 French women: 프랑스의(프랑스 국적의) 여자
> 5 study German: 독일어를 공부하다
> 6 Danish dairy products: 덴마크의 낙농제품
> 7 Japanese food: 일본의 음식
> 8 Chinese is hard to learn.: 중국어는 배우기 어렵다.
> 9 Canadian culture: 캐나다의 문화
> 10 Spanish is the language~: 스페인어는 ~한 언어다

PRACTICE 8

1 big white
2 all four Korean
3 large green
4 seven small metal
5 those nice blue
6 the beautiful red
7 my young French
8 the first two
9 comfortable wooden
10 half a million[a half million]
11 both these beautiful
12 all her three

> 1~12 2개 이상의 형용사가 함께 쓰일 때는 '서수 → 기수 → 성질 → 크기 → 신구 → 색깔 → 국적 → 재료' 순으로 쓰고, 형용사 앞에 다른 수식어가 올 때는 'all/both/double/half → 정관사/지시형용사/소유격 → 형용사' 순으로 쓴다.

PRACTICE 9

2 both the pretty
3 her nice new
4 this small
5 those three high
6 the exciting American
7 the ugly black plastic
8 all these lovely
9 My wise older
10 that big white
11 its nice Chinese
12 the fifth happy English
13 all her three pink
14 four healthy young
15 two fresh red

PRACTICE 10

1 many **2** much
3 many **4** much
5 many **6** much
7 Many **8** many
9 many **10** much

> 1, 3, 5, 7, 8, 9 셀 수 있는 명사의 복수형 앞이므로 many가 알맞다.
> 2, 4, 6, 10 셀 수 없는 명사 앞이므로 much가 알맞다.

PRACTICE 11

1 Does Minho have many friends?
2 Does it take much time to get there on foot?
3 Are there many flowers in the vase?
4 Many drivers drive very fast.
5 Should I give the plants much water?
6 Many students stayed in the classroom after school.
7 There isn't much furniture in my room.
8 Did they spend much money on this house?
9 We didn't have much fun.
10 Did you borrow many books from the library?

> 1, 3, 4, 6, 10 셀 수 있는 명사의 복수형 앞이므로 many로 바꾸어 쓸 수 있다.
> 2, 5, 7, 8, 9 셀 수 없는 명사 앞이므로 much로 바꾸어 쓸 수 있다.

PRACTICE 12

1	few	2	little
3	little	4	few
5	few	6	little
7	few	8	little
9	little	10	few

> 1, 4, 5, 7, 10 빈칸 뒤에 셀 수 있는 명사의 복수형을 썼으므로 few가 알맞다.
> 2, 3, 6, 8, 9 빈칸 뒤에 셀 수 없는 명사를 썼으므로 little이 알맞다.

PRACTICE 13

1	a few	2	a little
3	A few	4	a little
5	a little	6	a few
7	a little	8	a few
9	a little	10	a few

> 1, 3, 6, 8, 10 빈칸 뒤에 셀 수 있는 명사의 복수형을 썼으므로 a few가 알맞다.
> 2, 4, 5, 7, 9 빈칸 뒤에 셀 수 없는 명사를 썼으므로 a little이 알맞다.

PRACTICE 14

1	much	2	a few
3	a little	4	many
5	few	6	little
7	a few	8	little
9	many	10	a little
11	much	12	Few

> 1, 11 many는 '많은'이라는 의미로 셀 수 있는 명사의 수를 나타내는데, hope와 traffic은 셀 수 없는 명사이므로 much로 고치는 것이 알맞다.
> 2, 7 a little은 '약간의'라는 의미로 셀 수 없는 명사의 양을 나타내는데, days와 times는 셀 수 있는 명사의 복수형이므로 a few로 고치는 것이 알맞다. 7번의 times는 '시간'의 뜻으로 쓰일 때는 셀 수 없는 명사이지만, 여기서처럼 횟수를 나타낼 때는 셀 수 있는 명사로 취급한다.
> 3, 10 a few는 '조금의, 몇 개의'라는 의미로 셀 수 있는 명사의 수를 나타내는데, money와 meat는 셀 수 없는 명사이므로 a little이 알맞다.
> 4, 9 much는 '많은'이라는 의미로 셀 수 없는 명사의 양을 나타내는데, hours와 restaurants는 셀 수 있는 명사의 복수형이므로 many로 고치는 것이 알맞다.
> 5, 12 little은 '거의 없는'이라는 의미로 셀 수 없는 명사의 양을 나타내는데, teeth와 members는 셀 수 있는 명사의 복수형이므로 few로 고치는 것이 알맞다.
> 6, 8 few는 '거의 없는'이라는 의미로 셀 수 있는 명사의 수를 나타내는데, ice와 light는 셀 수 없는 명사이므로 little로 고치는 것이 알맞다.

PRACTICE 15

1	some	2	any
3	some	4	any
5	Any	6	some
7	any	8	some
9	any	10	any

> 1, 8 일반적으로 긍정문에서 '얼마간의, 약간의'라는 뜻으로 쓰이며, 셀 수 있는 명사나 셀 수 없는 명사 모두와 함께 쓸 수 있는 some이 알맞다.
> 2, 7, 10 일반적으로 부정문에서 '조금도 ~ (아니다)'라는 의미로 쓰이는 any가 알맞다.
> 3, 6 '~하시겠어요?' 또는 '~할 수 있을까요?'라는 의미의 권유나 요구를 나타내는 의문문에서 쓰이는 some이 알맞다.
> 4 어떠한 질문이라도 있는지 묻는 것이므로 any를 쓴다.
> 5 긍정문에서 '어떠한 ~라도'의 뜻으로 쓰이는 any가 알맞다.
> 9 조건을 나타내는 if절에서는 any를 쓴다.

PRACTICE 16

2	any food	3	some people
4	any problems	5	some medicine
6	any place	7	some flowers
8	any[some] friends	9	any time
10	some cake	11	some money

1 some homework: 약간의 숙제 → some이 셀 수 없는 명사를 수식할 때
2 I don't have any food: 음식이 전혀 없다 → any가 부정문에서 사용될 때
3 some people: 몇몇 사람들 → some이 셀 수 있는 명사를 수식할 때
4 if you have any problems: 너에게 무슨 문제라도 있으면 → any가 조건을 나타내는 if절에서 사용될 때
5 some medicine: 약간의 약 → some이 셀 수 없는 명사를 수식할 때
6 We can go to any place: 우리는 어떤 장소라도 갈 수 있다 → any가 긍정문에서 사용될 때
7 some flowers: 약간의 꽃 → some이 셀 수 있는 명사를 수식할 때
8 Do you have any[some] friends?: 친구가 좀 있니? → 의문문에서는 any를 쓰는 것이 일반적이지만 긍정의 대답을 예상하고 질문하는 경우에는 some을 쓰기도 한다.
9 I don't have any time: 시간이 전혀 없다 → any가 부정문에서 사용될 때
10 Would you like some cake?: 케이크 좀 드시겠어요? → some이 권유를 나타내는 의문문에서 사용될 때
11 Would you mind lending me some money?: 제게 돈 좀 빌려주시겠어요? → some이 요구를 나타내는 의문문에서 사용될 때
*mind -ing: ~하는 것을 꺼리다

PRACTICE 17

1 a third [one-third]
2 two-fifths
3 two and seven-elevenths
4 five-sixths
5 a half [one-half]
6 nine-thirteenths
7 a quarter [one-quarter]
8 four and three-sevenths
9 three point one four
10 five point five six
11 sixteen point two nine
12 fifty point one five
13 a[one] hundred (and) twenty-seven point nine three
14 six hundred (and) twelve point four nine
15 two thousand one hundred (and) five point eight nine

PRACTICE 18

1 eighteen twenty-six
2 nineteen eighty-three
3 two thousand (and) four
4 two thousand (and) twenty [twenty twenty]
5 May (the) first [the first of May]
6 July (the) twelfth [the twelfth of July]
7 February (the) eighteenth [the eighteenth of February]
8 November (the) twenty-fourth [the twenty-fourth of November]
9 April (the) twenty-third [the twenty-third of April]
10 December (the) ninth [the ninth of December]

PRACTICE 19

1 once
2 three times
3 six times
4 four times
5 five times
6 twice
7 ten times
8 once
9 three times
10 eight times

1 only once: 딱 한 번
2, 4, 7 기수+times+as+형용사+as: ~보다 (몇) 배 …한
3, 10 기수+times+a+day/week/month/year: 하루/한 달/일 주일/일 년에 (몇) 번
5, 9 기수+times+as+형용사 비교급+than: ~보다 (몇) 배 …한
6 twice = two times
8 once a day/week/month/year: 하루/일주일/한 달/일 년에 한 번

Chapter Review Test 정답 본문 _ p.258

1 ③ 2 ⑤ 3 ② 4 ④ 5 health → healthy
6 ② 7 Do you have something delicious to eat? 8 ① 9 ④ 10 ② 11 twice a week
12 three times as many words as an average person 13 There is little food left (in it [in the refrigerator]). 14 ④ 15 ⑤ 16 ③ 17 much, lots of, plenty of (3개 중 2개를 골라 썼으면 정답으로 인정) 18 (D) Japanese, (E) many
19 ① 20 ④ 21 ②,③ 22 ④ 23 ①,④
24 ②,④ 25 ③ 26 ⑤ 27 old have
28 something special for you 29 ② 30 ④
31 ④ 32 (1) some → any (2) few → little
33 ② 34 three times 35 ① 36 ④ 37 ③
38 ②

Chapter Review Test 해설

1. (A) 한국인들 (B) 영국 (C) 영국의
2. ⑤ 한 단어인 명사 thing은 형용사가 앞에서 수식한다. (things sweet → sweet things)
   ① -thing으로 끝나는 대명사는 형용사가 뒤에서 수식한다.
   ② '버스에 남겨진'이란 뜻이므로, 수동과 완료의 의미를 가진 과거분사 left를 사용하여 anyone을 뒤에서 수식한다.
   ③ 분수를 표현할 때는, 분자는 기수로 분모는 서수로 쓰고 분자가 2 이상이면 분모에 '-s'를 붙인다.
   ④ 「배수사+as 원급 as」 '배수사만큼 ~한'
3. anything은 꾸미는 말이 뒤에 나오는 부정대명사이므로, 주어진 문장을 영작하면 'Is there anything interesting on TV?'이다. 따라서 네 번째로 오는 단어는 interesting이다.
4. 형용사는 '성질-크기-신구-색깔-국적-재료'의 순으로 쓴다.
5. 명사 health의 형용사인 healthy가 와야 한다.
6. a few minutes later '몇 분 후에'
7. 대명사 something을 형용사 delicious가 뒤에서 수식한다.
8. 「many+셀 수 있는 명사의 복수형」 '많은'
9. ⓐ years는 셀 수 있는 명사의 복수형이므로, a few를 사용하여 수식한다.
   ⓑ soup는 셀 수 없는 명사이므로, a little을 사용하여 수식한다. (a few → a little)
   ⓒ hot sauce는 셀 수 없는 명사이므로, a little을 사용하여 수식한다.
   ⓓ students는 셀 수 있는 명사의 복수형이므로, few를 사용하여 수식한다.
   ⓔ sugar는 셀 수 없는 명사이므로 little을 사용하여 수식한다.
10. • 「a few+셀 수 있는 명사의 복수형」 '몇 개의'
    • 「many+셀 수 있는 명사의 복수형」 '많은'
    • 「much+셀 수 없는 명사」 '많은'
    • 「a little+셀 수 없는 명사」 '약간의'
11. 배수사로 횟수를 표현한다.
12. 「배수사+as+형용사(+명사)+as+비교대상」 '~보다 몇 배 더 …한'
13. food는 셀 수 없는 명사이므로 '거의 없는'이라는 뜻의 little이 수식한다. 주어가 셀 수 없는 명사이므로 be동사는 3인칭 단수형인 is를 쓴다.
14. ④ 명사 앞에 오는 수식어의 어순은 all+소유격이다. (her all → all her)
15. ⑤ 긍정문에서는 some을 쓴다. 긍정문에서 any가 쓰이면 '어떠한 ~라도'라는 뜻이지만 여기에서는 적절하지 않다. (any → some)
16. (A) 셀 수 있는 명사의 수를 물어볼 때는 「How many +명사의 복수형」을 쓴다.
    (B) 횟수나 빈도를 물어볼 때는 How often ~?을 쓴다.
17. 「much+셀 수 없는 명사」 '많은'
    lots of, plenty of 는 셀 수 없는 명사, 셀 수 있는 명사와 모두 같이 쓸 수 있다.
18. (A) 경험을 묻는 현재완료시제가 쓰였다. 해석은 '본 적 있니?'로 한다.
    (B) '그것의'라는 뜻의 3인칭 단수 소유격으로, 소유격+명사의 형태로 나타낸다.
    (C) a doctor를 선행사로 하는 주격 관계대명사이므로 who를 쓴다.
    (D) '일본의'라는 뜻의 형용사는 Japan에 -ese를 붙여 만든다. (Japan → Japanese)
    (E) people은 셀 수 있는 명사의 복수형이므로 many를 사용하여 수식한다. (much → many)
19. (A) 「look+형용사」 '~하게 보이다'
    (B) anything은 형용사가 뒤에서 수식한다.
20. ④ How often은 횟수나 빈도를 물어보는 의문사이므로 배수사를 활용해 횟수로 대답해야 한다.
21. (A) well-known '잘 알려진'
    (B) 사역동사 make는 목적격 보어로 원형부정사를 쓴다. (to see → see)
    (C) secrets는 셀 수 있는 명사의 복수형이므로 a few를 쓴다. a little은 셀 수 없는 명사의 앞에만 온다. (a little → a few)
    (D) 「how to+동사원형」은 명사절로 전치사 뒤에 올 수 있다.
    (E) on one's own '스스로'
22. (A) some은 권유, 요구를 나타내는 의문문에 쓰인다.
    (B) weight는 셀 수 없는 명사이므로 much가 수식한다.
    (C) something과 같이 -thing으로 끝나는 대명사는 형용사가 뒤에서 수식한다.
    (D) 'a number of'는 '많은'이라는 뜻으로 셀 수 있는 명사의 복수형 앞에 온다. many와도 바꾸어 쓸

수 있다. stress는 셀 수 없는 명사이므로 a lot of 나 much를 사용해야 한다.
(a number of → a lot of[much])
(E) dislike는 동명사를 목적어로 쓰는 동사이다.

23 ① a few '약간의, 조금의'
④ Plenty of '많은'

24 ① 분수를 읽을 때는 분자는 기수로, 분모는 서수로 읽고, 분자가 2 이상이면 분모에 '-s'를 붙여 읽는다. (three-fifth → three-fifths)
③ 날짜는 서수를 이용하여 표현한다. (the fifteen of May → the fifteenth of May [May (the) fifteenth]
⑤ 연도는 두 자리씩 끊어 읽는다. (one thousand nine hundred and seventy four → nineteen seventy-four)

25 명사 앞에 오는 형용사의 어순은 all/both+지시형용사/소유격+성질+크기+색깔+재료 순으로 쓴다.
① white small → small white
② My all → All my
④ These both → Both these
⑤ wooden new → new wooden

26 ① asleep, ② alive, ③ afraid, ④ alone과 같은 형용사는 서술적 용법에만 사용되므로 명사를 수식할 수 없다.

27 '~한 사람들'을 뜻하는 「the+형용사」는 복수 취급한다.

28 something은 형용사가 뒤에서 수식한다.

29 ⓐ 부사는 목적격 보어로 쓸 수 없다. (sadly → sad)
ⓒ something은 형용사가 뒤에서 꾸며주는 대명사다. (warm something → something warm)
ⓓ 명사를 꾸미는 형용사가 2개 이상일 때 크기 다음에 색깔을 나타내는 형용사가 와야 한다. (white big → big white)

30 ④ 부정문에서는 some이 아닌 any가 쓰인다.

31 ④ 「the+나라 이름 형용사」는 '그 나라 국민 전체'를 나타낸다.

32 (1) 부정문에서는 some 대신 any를 써야 한다.
(2) time은 셀 수 없는 명사이므로 few가 아닌 little 이 와야 한다.

33 a number of '많은', 뒤의 명사가 셀 수 있는 명사 (monkeys)이므로 many가 적절하다.

34 「기수+times」를 이용하여 배수사('~배, ~번')를 나타낸다.

35 ① -thing으로 끝나는 대명사는 형용사가 뒤에서 수식한다.
② happily → happy
③ a photo interesting → an interesting photo
④ 25-years-old → 25-year-old
⑤ many → much[a lot of]

36 날짜를 읽을 때는 서수를 사용한다.

37 ③ something은 형용사가 뒤에서 수식한다.
(good something → something good)

38 any는 부정문에서 '조금도 ~(아니다)'로 쓰인다.

CHAPTER 11 부사 (Adverbs)

본문 _ p.266

PRACTICE 1

1 widely	2 sincerely
3 happily	4 politely
5 slowly	6 slightly
7 finally	8 easily
9 luckily	10 quietly
11 carefully	12 certainly
13 suddenly	14 sadly
15 busily	16 beautifully
17 really	18 angrily
19 quickly	20 softly

PRACTICE 2

1 visibly	2 simply
3 dully	4 truly
5 loudly	6 gently
7 nicely	8 seriously
9 heavily	10 clearly
11 safely	12 fully
13 prettily	14 anxiously
15 mainly	16 foolishly
17 terribly	18 reasonably
19 comfortably	20 rudely
21 personally	22 possibly
23 probably	24 casually
25 rarely	26 responsibly
27 properly	28 sensitively

PRACTICE 3

1 A	2 B	3 B
4 A	5 B	6 A
7 B	8 A	9 B
10 B	11 A	12 A
13 A	14 B	

[보기]
My good friend, John, speaks Korean well.
형용사 / 부사

1, 4, 6, 11, 12, 13 밑줄 친 부분이 명사를 수식하는 한정적 용법의 형용사로 쓰였다.
2, 3, 5, 7, 9, 10 밑줄 친 부분이 동사를 수식하는 부사로 쓰였다.
8 밑줄 친 부분이 서술적 용법의 형용사로 쓰였다.

14 밑줄 친 부분이 형용사를 수식하는 부사로 쓰였다.
1 We walked for a long time. (긴 시간)
2 I have to go to work quite early tomorrow. (일찍 가다)
3 The cold weather will last long. (오래 지속되다)
4 My mom doesn't like fast food. (빠른 음식: 패스트푸드)
5 I'm sorry to call you so late. (늦게 전화하다)
6 I usually catch a cold in early spring. (이른 봄)
7 Alex tried hard to lose weight. (열심히 노력하다)
8 Don't be late next time. (늦은)
9 Sudong came out of the room last. (마지막으로 나오다)
10 She walked fast to be on time. (빠르게 걷다)
11 It was the last train for Seoul. (마지막 열차)
12 There aren't enough chairs for everyone. (충분한 의자)
13 I hit my head on the hard floor. (딱딱한 바닥)
14 Is the water warm enough for you? (충분히 따뜻한)

PRACTICE 4

1 late	2 carefully
3 ○	4 last
5 ○	6 politely
7 ○	8 fast
9 hard	10 ○
11 easily	12 sadly
13 suddenly	14 ○
15 certainly	16 ○
17 mainly	18 quietly

1 늦게 도착하다 (arrive lately → arrive late)
*lately: 최근에 / late: 늦게
2 그것에 대해 신중하게 생각하다
(think about it careful → think about it carefully)
3 나는 그곳에 오래 머무르지 않았다.
long(오래, 오랫동안)은 동사 stay를 수식하는 부사로 알맞게 쓰였다.
4 마지막으로 도착하다 (arrive lastly → arrive last)
*lastly: 🖲 (무엇을 열거하면서 마지막 요소 앞에서)끝으로 / last: 🖲 마지막에
5 그는 (말이) 빠른 연설가다. (=그는 빠르게 말하는 사람이다.)
speaker(연설가, 말하는 사람)이라는 명사를 앞에서 수식하고 있으므로 여기서 fast는 형용사로 쓰였다.
6 공손하게 말하다 (talk polite → talk politely)
7 나는 아침 일찍 아침밥을 먹는다.
early(일찍)는 동사 have를 수식하는 부사로 알맞게 쓰였다.
8 너무 빨리 달리다 (run so fastly → run so fast)

fast는 형용사와 부사로 모두 사용될 수 있으며 fastly라는 단어는 없다.
9 열심히 연습했다 (practiced hardly → practiced hard)
*hardly: 거의…않는 / hard: ⓑ 열심히
10 나는 마침내 이 책을 읽는 것을 끝냈다.
finally는 동사 finished를 수식하는 부사로 알맞게 쓰였다.
11 문제를 쉽게 해결하다 (solve the problem easy → solve the problem easily)
12 슬프게 미소 짓다 (smiled sad → smiled sadly)
smile은 완전자동사로 보어나 목적어를 가지지 않는 동사이다. 따라서 sad가 아닌 동사를 꾸며줄 수 있는 부사 sadly가 오는 것이 적절하다.
13 갑자기 나를 방문했다 (visited me sudden → visited me suddenly)
14 그들은 걱정스럽게 의사를 기다리고 있었다.
anxiously(걱정스럽게)는 동사 were waiting을 수식하는 부사로 알맞게 쓰였다.
15 분명히 솔직하다 (is certain honest → is certainly honest)
16 그는 마지막으로 비행기에 탔다. (last ⓑ 마지막으로)
last(마지막으로)는 동사 got on을 수식하는 부사로 알맞게 쓰였다.
17 주로 동아프리카에서 발견된다 (are main found in East Africa → are mainly found in East Africa)
18 조용히 그들에게 이야기를 들려줬다 (told them the story quiet → told them the story quietly)

9 아버지가 집에 늦게 오셨다는 뜻이므로 late가 적절하다.
* late: 늦은 / lately: 최근에
10 그것들을 드물게 먹는다는 뜻이므로 rarely가 적절하다.
* rare: 드문, 희귀한 / rarely: 드물게, 좀처럼 하지 않는
11 그녀가 아름답게 노래를 불렀다는 뜻이므로 동사를 수식할 수 있는 부사 beautifully가 적절하다.
12 Jane이 나의 집에 가까이 산다는 뜻이므로 close가 적절하다.
* close to: ~에 가까이 / closely: 면밀히
13 시험공부를 열심히 했냐는 뜻이므로 hard가 적절하다.
* hard: 열심히 / hardly: 좀처럼 ~않다
14 거의 150개에 달하는 국가들이 올림픽에 참가했다는 뜻이므로 nearly가 적절하다.
* near: 가까이 / nearly: 거의
15 감각동사 look은 형용사를 보어로 취하므로 happy가 적절하다. (look happy: 행복해 보이다)

PRACTICE 6

1	① easy		② easily
2	① clearly		② clear
3	① late		② late
4	① careful		② carefully
5	① last		② last
6	① early		② early
7	① lucky		② Luckily
8	① certain		② certainly
9	① hard		② hardly
10	① close		② closely

1 ① an easy question: 쉬운 문제 → 형용사
② solve a question easily: 쉽게 문제를 풀다 → 부사
2 ① speak clearly: 분명하게 말하다 → 부사
② the sky is clear: 하늘이 맑다 → 형용사
3 ① have lunch late: 점심식사를 늦게 하다 → 부사
② late for the meeting: 회의에 늦은 → 형용사
4 ① careful of cars: 차를 조심하는 → 형용사
② drive a car carefully: 차를 주의해서 운전하다 → 부사
5 ① the last chance: 마지막인 기회 → 형용사
② finish last: 마지막으로 끝내다 → 부사
6 ① wake up early: 일찍 일어나다 → 부사
② an early hour: 이른 시각 → 형용사
7 ① a lucky guy: 운 좋은 녀석 → 형용사
② Luckily, she was safe.: 다행스럽게도, 그녀는 안전했다. → 부사
8 ① certain kinds: 특정한 종류 → 형용사
② certainly win first prize: 틀림없이 우승하다 → 부사
9 ① work so hard: 매우 열심히 일하다 → 부사
② could hardly breathe: 거의 숨을 쉴 수가 없었다 → 부사
10 ① come close to: ~에 가까이 오다 → 부사
② look at ~ closely: ~을 면밀히 보다 → 부사

PRACTICE 5

1	lately	2	sweet
3	near	4	closely
5	high	6	hardly
7	gently	8	highly
9	late	10	rarely
11	beautifully	12	close
13	hard	14	Nearly
15	happy		

1 최근에 아무 영화도 보지 않았다는 뜻이므로 lately가 적절하다.
* late: 늦게 / lately: 최근에
2 감각동사 taste는 형용사를 보어로 취하므로 sweet이 적절하다. (taste sweet: 달콤한 맛이 나다)
3 크리스마스가 가까이 다가오고 있다는 뜻이므로 near이 적절하다
* near: 가까이 / nearly: 거의
4 신문(the paper)을 가까이서 자세히 읽었다는 뜻이므로 closely가 적절하다.
* close: 가까운 / closely: 접근하여, 면밀히
5 여름에는 기온이 높이 상승한다는 뜻이므로 high가 적절하다
* high: 높게 / highly: 크게, 대단히
6 Ann은 TV를 거의 보지 않는다는 뜻이므로 hardly가 적절하다.
* hard: 어려운, 딱딱한 / hardly: 좀처럼 ~않는
7 Smith 부인이 내게 상냥하게 말을 걸었다는 뜻이므로 gently가 적절하다.
* gentle: 온화한 / gently: 다정하게
8 대단히 성공적인 사업이라는 뜻이므로 highly가 적절하다.
* high: 높게 / highly: 대단히, 크게

PRACTICE 7

1 I sometimes go to Incheon to visit my

CHAPTER 11

grandparents.
2 Susie is never late for work.
3 Sangmin could rarely come to our club meetings.
4 They are always ready to go on a trip.
5 We will sometimes go to the movies together.
6 They usually shake hands to greet each other.
7 I should often help my mom with the housework.
8 He is seldom excited about the trip.
9 He never keeps his room dirty.
10 You don't often clean your room, do you?

> 1, 6, 9 빈도부사는 일반동사 앞에 온다.
> 2, 4, 8 빈도부사는 be동사 뒤에 온다.
> 3, 5, 7, 10 빈도부사는 조동사 뒤에 온다.

PRACTICE 8

1 I usually go jogging in the morning.
2 They must sometimes listen to others.
3 We will often practice swimming.
4 Hana always smiles brightly.
5 Nick can seldom understand Korean.
6 Climbing mountains is sometimes dangerous.
7 Giho never watches comic dramas.
8 I usually take care of my younger sisters.
9 She rarely buys expensive clothes.
10 I am often depressed by bad weather.

> 1 I usually **go** jogging in the morning.
> → 보통 조깅을 한다
> 2 They **must** sometimes listen to others.
> → 때때로 들어야 한다
> 3 We **will** often practice swimming.
> → 종종 연습할 것이다
> 4 Hana always smiles brightly.
> → 항상 웃는다
> 5 Nick **can** seldom understand Korean.
> → 좀처럼 이해할 수 없다
> 6 Climbing mountains **is** sometimes dangerous.
> → 때때로 위험하다
> 7 Giho never watches comic dramas.
> → 절대 보지 않는다
> 8 I usually take care of my younger sisters.
> → 보통 돌본다
> 9 She rarely buys expensive clothes.
> → 거의 사지 않는다
> 10 I am often depressed by bad weather.
> → 종종 우울하다

PRACTICE 9

	①	②	③
1	already	yet	still
2	still	already	yet
3	yet	still	already
4	still	yet	already
5	yet	already	still

PRACTICE 10

1	yet	2	already	3	still
4	yet	5	still	6	already
7	yet	8	already	9	still
10	still	11	already	12	still
13	already	14	yet	15	already

> 1, 7, 14 부정문에서 '아직'의 의미로 쓰이고, 주로 문장 끝에 위치하는 yet이 알맞다.
> 2, 6, 13 긍정문에서 '이미, 벌써'의 의미로 쓰이는 already가 알맞다.
> 3, 5, 9, 10 긍정문과 의문문에서 '여전히, 아직도'의 의미로 쓰이는 still이 알맞다.
> 4 의문문에서 '이미, 벌써, 이제'의 뜻으로 쓰이는 yet이 알맞다.
> 8, 11, 15 놀람을 나타내는 의문문에서 '이미, 벌써'의 의미로 쓰이는 already가 알맞다.
> 12 부정문에서 계속되는 행위를 강조할 때 쓰이는 still이 알맞다.

PRACTICE 11

1	too	2	neither	3	too
4	either	5	too	6	neither
7	either	8	too	9	either
10	neither	11	neither	12	either
13	too	14	either	15	neither

PRACTICE 12

	①	②
1	very	much
2	much	very
3	very	much
4	very	much
5	very	much
6	much	very
7	very	much
8	much	very
9	much	very
10	very	much

Ch 11 부사

CHAPTER 11

PRACTICE 13

1	very	2	much	3	very
4	much	5	much	6	very
7	much	8	very	9	much
10	very	11	much	12	very

> 1, 6, 8, 12 형용사의 원급을 수식하는 자리이므로 very가 알맞다.
> very heavy: 매우 심한
> very useful: 매우 유용한
> very good: 매우 좋은
> very large: 매우 큰
> 2, 4, 7, 11 형용사의 비교급을 수식하는 자리이므로 much가 알맞다.
> much older: 훨씬 더 나이가 많은
> much cooler: 훨씬 더 시원한
> much cheaper: 훨씬 더 싼
> much more exciting: 훨씬 더 신나는
> 3, 10 부사의 원급을 수식하는 자리이므로 very가 알맞다.
> listen very carefully: 매우 주의 깊게 듣다
> try very hard: 아주 열심히 노력하다
> 5, 9 부사의 비교급을 수식하는 자리이므로 much가 알맞다.
> take much longer: 훨씬 더 오래 걸리다
> speak much better: 훨씬 더 잘 말하다

PRACTICE 14

1 What else can I do for you?
2 I didn't even imagine it was possible.
3 It was even sad to say goodbye to everyone.
4 Where else did you visit in London?
5 He even took some medicine to fall asleep.
6 They kept practicing soccer even when it rained heavily.
7 The child brings his toy even to the bathroom.
8 Even a small pet can give you a lot of trouble.
9 Jessica even gets angry if I don't call her often.
10 David can run faster than anyone else in his class.
11 Dad sometimes works even on Sunday.
12 You can even order a pizza on the Internet.
13 Babies need to be watched even while they are sleeping.
14 You'd better write these rules somewhere else.
15 He speaks English, Chinese, French, and even Spanish.

> 1, 4, 10, 14 else는 '그 밖에'라는 뜻으로 수식하고자 하는 말 뒤에 온다.
> 2, 3, 5, 6, 7, 8, 9, 11, 12, 13, 15 even은 '~조차(도), ~까지도'라는 뜻으로 수식하고자 하는 말 앞에 온다.

PRACTICE 15

1	even	2	else	3	even
4	else	5	even	6	else
7	even	8	even	9	else
10	else				

> 1 You should not even look: 너는 보지조차 말아야 한다
> 2 anywhere else: 그 밖의 다른 곳
> 3 couldn't even hold a spoon: 숟가락조차 들지 못했다
> 4 anyone else: 그 밖의 다른 사람
> 5 I even had to dance: 나는 춤을 추는 것까지도 해야 했다
> 6 what else: 그 밖의 무엇
> 7 even during the vacation: 휴가 동안조차
> 8 even knows where my grandparents are now: 나의 조부모님이 지금 어디에 계신지조차 안다
> 9 somewhere else: 그 밖의 다른 곳
> 10 where else: 그 밖의 어디

PRACTICE 16

1	them on	2	about money
3	on the radio	4	it up
5	at the picture	6	in the homework
7	to the radio	8	it off
9	the show off	10	on the chair
11	it out	12	it away
13	up the paper	14	them out
15	for it	16	about it

> 1, 4, 8, 11, 12, 14 목적어가 대명사일 때는 「동사+목적어+부사」의 어순만 가능하다.
> try ~ on: ~을 입어[신어]보다
> give ~ up: ~을 포기하다
> turn ~ off: ~을 끄다
> find ~ out: ~을 발견하다, 알아내다
> throw ~ away: ~을 버리다
> check ~ out: ~을 대출하다, 확인하다
> 2, 5, 7, 10, 15, 16 자동사 뒤에 전치사가 올 때, 전치사의 목적어는 반드시 전치사 뒤에 온다.
> care about: ~에 대해 신경 쓰다
> look at: ~을 보다
> listen to: ~을 듣다
> sit on: ~에 앉다
> look for: ~을 찾다
> talk about: ~에 대해 얘기하다
> 3, 6, 9, 13 목적어가 일반 명사일 때는 「동사+부사+목적어」나 「동사+목적어+부사」의 어순 둘 다 가능하다.
> turn on: ~을 켜다
> hand in: ~을 제출하다
> call off: ~을 취소하다
> pick up: ~을 줍다, 찾아오다, (차에) 태우다

PRACTICE 17

1	out	2	away[out]	3	on
4	on	5	up	6	in
7	off	8	out	9	off
10	up				

1 find out who the thief is: 누가 범인인지 알아내다
2 throw away[out] the paper: 서류를 버리다
3 turn the TV on: TV를 켜다
4 try the blue shirt on: 푸른색 셔츠를 입어보다
5 pick up the coins: 동전들을 줍다
6 hand in the paper: 서류를 제출하다
7 turn the light off: 전등을 끄다
8 check out the books: 책들을 대출하다
9 call off our plan: 우리의 계획을 취소하다
10 give up the soccer game: 축구 경기를 포기하다

PRACTICE 18

1	Where	2	How
3	Why	4	How many
5	How long	6	When
7	How old	8	How much
9	How far	10	Where
11	When	12	How
13	Why	14	How much
15	How often		

1, 10 장소/지역을 나타내는 표현으로 답하고 있으므로 Where(어디에) 의문문이 알맞다.
2, 12 어떤 곳에 가는 교통편이나 누군가를 알게 된 경위 등으로 답하고 있으므로 방법을 묻는 How(어떻게) 의문문이 알맞다.
3, 13 이유를 설명할 때 쓰는 접속사인 Because(~ 때문에)로 답하고 있으므로 Why(왜) 의문문이 알맞다.
4 수량으로 답하고 있으므로 How many(얼마나 많은) 의문문이 알맞다.
5 소요 시간으로 답하고 있으므로 How long(얼마나 오래) 의문문이 알맞다.
6, 11 특정 시점으로 답하고 있으므로 때를 묻는 When(언제) 의문문이 알맞다.
7 나이로 답하고 있으므로 How old(몇 살인) 의문문이 알맞다.
8, 14 가격으로 답하고 있으므로 How much(얼마인) 의문문이 알맞다.
9 거리로 답하고 있으므로 How far(얼마나 멀리) 의문문이 알맞다.
15 빈도/횟수로 답하고 있으므로 How often(얼마나 자주) 의문문이 알맞다.

Chapter Review Test 정답 본문 _ p.284

1 ④ 2 ⑤ 3 ④ 4 ① 5 How 6 ③,⑤
7 ① 8 ⑤ 9 ③ 10 either 11 ① 12 ②
13 ② 14 successful → successfully 15 ④
16 ③ 17 ④ 18 ② 19 ③ 20 ② 21 ⑤
22 ①,④ 23 ④ 24 ④ 25 ③ 26 ① 27 ⑤
28 ② 29 ③ 30 ③ 31 (A) much[far/still/even] (B) very (C) Where 32 ② 33 ④
34 ③,④ 35 ④ 36 ⓒ,ⓐ,ⓑ,ⓓ 37 How can I get to the airport from here? 38 ②,③ 39 ④

Chapter Review Test 해설

1 ④ 명사 - 부사
   ①②⑤ 형용사 - 부사

2 yet은 부정문에서 '아직'이란 뜻으로 쓰인다.

3 not ~ any는 no와 같고, either는 '~또한'의 의미로 부정문에 쓰인다.

4 ⓐ took out의 목적어가 대명사 them이므로 them은 took와 out 사이에 위치하고, 동사 looked와 전치사 at의 목적어는 항상 전치사 뒤에 위치하므로 looked at them이 된다.
   ⓑ '최근에'라는 의미의 부사 lately
     '늦게'라는 의미의 부사 late
   ⓒ '높게'라는 의미의 부사 high
     '매우'라는 의미의 부사 highly
   ⓓ enough가 형용사로서 명사를 수식할 때는 명사의 앞에 위치한다.
     (money enough → enough money)

5 How was it? 그건 어땠니?
   How could you find such a great movie?
   그렇게 좋은 영화를 어떻게 찾을 수 있었니?

6 ③ '너는 조심스럽게 길을 건너야한다'는 뜻이므로 동사 cross를 수식하는 부사를 써야 한다.
     (careful → carefully)
   ⑤ '나는 시험을 위해 열심히 공부했다'는 뜻이므로 '열심히'라는 뜻의 부사 hard를 써야 한다. hardly는 '거의 ~않는'이라는 뜻이다. (hardly → hard)

7 Why were you so sad? 넌 왜 그렇게 슬펐니?

8 ⓐ '그들은 아직 그것을 끝내지 못했다'라는 뜻이 되어야 하므로, 부정문에서 '아직'이라는 뜻으로 쓰이는 부사 yet을 써야 한다. (already → yet)

ⓑ either은 부정문에서 '~또한'이라는 뜻을 나타낸다. too는 긍정문에 쓰인다. (too → either)
ⓓ 사역동사 make는 목적격 보어로 동사원형을 쓴다. (stopping → stop)
ⓔ 형용사의 비교급은 much로 수식한다. very는 원급을 수식한다. (very → much)

9 (C) '나도 아니다'라는 뜻은 Me, neither.로 쓸 수 있다. too는 긍정문에 쓰인다. (too → neither)

10 either는 '~또한'의 의미로 부정문에 쓰인다.

11 ① 빈도부사는 be동사의 뒤에 위치한다.
(always is → is always)

12 (A) '가까이'라는 의미의 부사로 쓰인 close
(B) '최근에'라는 의미의 부사 lately
(C) '거의'라는 의미의 부사 nearly

13 ② 비교급을 수식할 때는 much를 사용한다. very는 원급을 수식한다. (very → much)

14 successfully '성공적으로'

15 ④ How come은 '왜'라는 뜻으로 why와 같은 의미이다. 보기에는 이에 적절한 답이 없다.
① How far은 '얼마나 머니?'라는 뜻으로 거리를 묻는 질문이다. 따라서 (D)가 적절한 답이다.
② How long은 '(시간이) 얼마나 걸리니?'라는 뜻으로 시간의 길이를 묻는 질문이다. 따라서 (B)가 적절한 답이다.
③ How often은 '얼마나 자주'라는 뜻으로 빈도를 묻는 질문이다. 따라서 (A)가 적절한 답이다.
⑤ How much는 가격을 묻는 표현이다. 따라서 (C)가 적절한 답이다.

16 ③ '많이' ①②④⑤ '훨씬' (비교급 강조)

17 ④ '쉽게 찾을 수 있었다'는 뜻이 되어야 하므로 동사 find를 수식할 수 있는 부사의 형태로 써야 한다. (easy → easily)

18 ② '바닥에 세게 넘어졌다'는 뜻이 되어야 하므로 '세게'라는 뜻의 부사 hard를 써야 한다. hardly는 '거의 ~않는'이라는 뜻이다. (hardly → hard)

19 ③ Me, neither. = I don't, either.

20 ⓐ 「타동사+부사」의 목적어가 대명사일 때, 목적어는 반드시 동사와 부사의 사이에 쓴다.
(take off them → take them off)
ⓑ used to는 '~하곤 했다'는 뜻의 조동사이므로 뒤에 동사원형을 쓴다.
ⓒ 「타동사+부사」의 목적어가 명사일 때, 목적어는 부사의 뒤나 동사와 부사의 사이에 쓴다.

ⓓ even은 수식하고자 하는 말 앞에 온다. 여기에서는 '생각하기도 한다'는 뜻을 나타내고자 think 앞에 쓴다.
ⓔ taking off shoes는 동명사구로, 동명사구가 주어로 올 때는 단수 취급한다. (are → is)

21 ⑤ else는 수식하고자 하는 말 뒤에 온다.
(else nothing → nothing else)

22 (B) 주어인 Hollywood가 많은 영화 팬들이 방문하는 대상이므로 수동태로 고쳐주어야 한다.
(visited → is visited)
(C) near은 형용사와 부사의 형태가 같은 단어이다. 형용사 형태의 부사에 '-ly'를 붙이면 뜻이 달라지는데 이때 nearly의 뜻은 '거의'이다. 여기서는 '거의 3백 5십만 명의 관광객'이라는 의미이므로 nearly가 맞다.
(E) want는 to부정사를 목적격 보어로 취하므로 come을 to come으로 고쳐야 한다.

23 ⓐ 문장 전체를 수식하는 부사구가 나온 경우로, '처음으로 그리고 가장 중요한 것은'이란 의미를 지니며 문장 전체를 수식한다.
ⓑ 5형식 문장으로 목적격 보어 자리에 the conversation을 설명하는 형용사가 나와야 한다. 목적격 보어 자리에 부사는 나올 수 없다.
ⓒ elder과 elderly 둘 다 형용사로 나이가 더 많다는 뜻이지만 의미 차이가 있다. elder은 상대방보다 나이가 더 많은 경우, 손위의 의미일 때 사용하며 elderly는 나이가 많은 노인들을 가리킨다.

24 민수의 말에 이은 진호의 응답은 '왜 그렇게 생각해?'라는 뜻을 가진 말이어야 한다.

25 ③ '책이 높게 쌓여있다'는 의미이므로 '높게'라는 뜻의 부사 high를 쓰는 것이 맞다.
① '주의 깊게, 면밀히'라는 뜻을 가진 closely로 써야 한다. close는 '가까이'라는 뜻의 부사이다.
(close → closely)
② '거의 ~않는'이라는 의미의 hardly로 써야 한다. hard는 '열심히'라는 뜻의 부사이다.
(hard → hardly)
④ '최근에'라는 뜻의 lately로 써야 한다. late는 '늦게'라는 뜻의 부사이다. (late → lately)
⑤ '가까이'라는 의미의 near로 써야 한다. nearly는 '거의'라는 뜻의 부사이다. (nearly → near)

26 빈도부사는 조동사 뒤, 일반동사 앞에 위치한다.

27 • 접속사 when '~할 때' • 의문부사 when '언제'

28 (A) 길이를 묻는 How long ~?
    (B) 나이를 묻는 How old ~?
    (C) 셀 수 있는 명사의 수를 묻는 How many ~?
29 ③ already(이미, 벌써)는 긍정문과 의문문에서 쓰인다. yet은 의문문(이미, 벌써)과 부정문(아직)에서 쓰인다. 긍정문이므로 yet을 already로 고쳐야 한다.
30 ③「타동사+부사」의 목적어가 대명사일 때 목적어는 항상 타동사와 부사 사이에 온다.
31 (A) 비교급을 수식하는 much[far/still/even]
    (B) 원급을 수식하는 very
    (C) 장소에 대한 정보를 묻는 의문사 where
32 ② often은 빈도부사이므로 일반동사 gets 앞에 와야 한다.
33 ⓑ 빈도부사 rarely는 일반동사(snow) 앞에 쓴다.
    ⓓ very는 형용사나 부사의 원급을 수식하는 부사이므로, 비교급을 수식하는 much[far/a lot/even/still]로 바꿔야 한다.
    ⓐ so(아주)가 부사 fast(빠르게)를 수식하는 표현으로 적절하다.
    ⓒ '나는 눈사람에게 내 벙어리장갑을 끼울게.' put something on ~ : ~에 무엇을 끼우다[입히다]
    ⓔ wait for+사람: ~을 기다리다
34 ③ 빈도부사는 일반동사 앞에 위치한다.
    (spends usually → usually spends)
    ④ 주어가 3인칭 단수인 현재시제이므로 동사에 -s를 붙인다. (forget → forgets)
35 ④ 타동사+부사의 어순에서, 목적어가 대명사이면 타동사와 부사의 사이에 온다.
    (set up it → set it up)
36 ① - ⓒ Mark는 이미 캠핑을 위해 모든 것을 챙겼다. – 그는 매우 흥분한 것 같아.
    ② - ⓐ 점심 먹었니? – 당연히 먹었지. 벌써 세 시야.
    ③ - ⓑ 당신이 시애틀에 살던 것을 기억해요. – 전 아직 거기 살아요.
    ④ - ⓓ 네 그림을 보여주겠니? – 아직 끝내지 않았어요.
37 how는 '방법'을 묻는 의문사이며, 뒤에「조동사+주어+본동사 ~?」의 어순이 온다.
38 ② fast는 부사와 형용사의 형태가 같다.
    (fastly → fast)
    ③ '최근에 영화를 봤었니?'라는 뜻이 되어야 하므로 '최근에'라는 뜻의 부사 lately를 써야 한다. late는 '늦게'라는 뜻이다. (late → lately)
39 (A) 동사를 꾸며주는 부사가 와야 한다.
    (B) 문맥상 '열심히'의 의미이므로 hard가 와야 한다.
    (C)「look+형용사」'~하게 보이다'

CHAPTER 12 가정법
Conditionals

본문 _ p.292

PRACTICE 1

1 find   2 finish   3 comes
4 rains   5 meet   6 changes
7 leaves   8 studies   9 hurries
10 are

1~10 조건을 나타내는 if절의 동사는 현재형으로 써야 한다.
2 finish work: 일을 마치다(주어가 'I'이므로 finish가 적절하다.)
3 come here: 이리로 오다(주어가 'He'이므로 comes가 적절하다.)
4 it rains: 비가 오다
5 say hello to: ~에게 안부를 전하다
6 change one's mind: 생각을 바꾸다, 마음을 고쳐먹다
7 leave for: ~을 향해 떠나다
8 study hard: 열심히 공부하다
9 catch a bus: 버스를 잡아타다

PRACTICE 2

1 knew   2 had
3 couldn't travel   4 were

5 would[could/might] get
6 would[might] invite
7 would[could] bake
8 studied
9 weren't
10 would[could] talk

> 가정법 과거는 '만약 ~한다면 …할 텐데'의 뜻으로 현재 사실에 반대되는 일을 가정할 때 쓰며, 「If+주어+동사의 과거형 ~, 주어+would/could/should/might+동사원형 …」으로 나타낸다.
>
> 1, 2, 4, 8, 9 가정법 과거 구문에서, if절의 동사는 과거형으로 쓴다. 단, be동사일 경우에는 인칭에 상관없이 were를 쓴다.
>
> 3, 5, 6, 7, 10 가정법 과거 구문에서, 주절의 동사는 'would/could/should/might+동사원형'으로 쓴다.

PRACTICE 3

2 If Steve knew the reason, he would be angry.
3 If this movie were fun, I wouldn't be bored.
4 If you were honest, you would have many friends.
5 If I had enough money, I could buy you a piano.
6 If you were old enough, you could understand this better.
7 If my brother were hungry, he would go out for dinner.
8 If I weren't tired, I could go swimming now.
9 If she agreed with the writer, she would like his book.
10 If I didn't have other plans, I could go shopping with you.

PRACTICE 4

1	were	2	had
3	didn't snow	4	could speak
5	would call	6	could give
7	were	8	wouldn't leave
9	could sing	10	had

> 1~10 「I wish+가정법 과거」는 '~라면 좋을 텐데'의 뜻으로, 현재나 미래의 사실과 반대되거나 이룰 수 없는 일을 소망할 때 쓰며, 「I wish+주어+동사의 과거형 ~」으로 나타낸다.

PRACTICE 5

2 I wish it weren't cold here.
3 I wish I were diligent.

4 I wish I knew how to drive.
5 I wish Angela could join our club.
6 I wish there were trees around here.
7 I wish Windows update would finish soon.
8 I wish I could play the violin.
9 I wish Mark wouldn't move to another city.
10 I wish I were good at sports.

PRACTICE 6

1 as if you were his friend
2 as if she lived here
3 as if she were Korean
4 as if he were a king
5 as if the play were exciting
6 as if today were Saturday
7 as if he knew everybody in my family
8 as if she were very smart
9 as if you were a child
10 as if they were sick

> 1~10 「as if+가정법 과거」는 '마치 ~인 것처럼'의 뜻으로 현재의 사실과 반대되는 일을 나타내며, 「동사의 현재형+as if+주어+동사의 과거형 ~」으로 쓴다.

PRACTICE 7

1 had finished
2 had known
3 were
4 would[might] have called
5 would[could] go
6 had not forgotten
7 would[could] have arrived
8 liked
9 could have prevented
10 wouldn't have felt

> 1, 2, 6 주절이 'would/could+have+과거분사' 형태로 되어 있으므로 가정법 과거 완료 문장임을 알 수 있다. 따라서 if절의 동사는 'had+과거분사' 형태로 써야 한다.
>
> 3, 8 주절이 'would+동사원형' 형태로 되어 있으므로 가정법 과거 문장임을 알 수 있다. 따라서 if절의 동사는 '과거형'으로 써야 한다.
>
> 4, 7, 9, 10 If절이 'If+주어+had+과거분사 ~'형태로 되어 있으므로 가정법 과거 완료 문장임을 알 수 있다. 따라서 주절은 'would/might/could/wouldn't+have+과거분사' 형태로 써야 한다.
>
> 5 If절이 'If+주어+동사의 과거형 ~'형태로 되어 있으므로 가정법 과거 문장임을 알 수 있다. 따라서 주절은 'would/could+동사' 형태로 써야 한다.

PRACTICE 8

2 I wish she had kept her promise.
3 I wish Jinsu had come to my house.
4 I wish I were in Europe now.
5 I wish they had finished cleaning the room.
6 I wish Mina had attended the meeting.
7 I wish my brother read books.
8 I wish my dog hadn't died.
9 I wish we had visited him in the hospital.
10 I wish I could go back to my country this month.

> 2, 3, 5, 6, 8, 9 과거의 사실과 반대되는 일을 소망하고 있으므로 「I wish+가정법 과거완료」가 적합하다. 따라서 「I wish+주어+had+과거분사 ~」로 표현하는 것이 알맞다.
> 4, 7, 10 현재의 사실과 반대되거나 이룰 수 없는 일을 소망하고 있으므로 「I wish+가정법 과거」가 적합하다. 따라서 「I wish+주어+동사의 과거형 ~」으로 표현하는 것이 알맞다.

PRACTICE 9

1 as if she had not slept well last night
2 as if she were married
3 as if I had broken the glass
4 as if they had been rich in their youth
5 as if I had lost my watch
6 as if you had been right all the time
7 as if he knew those students
8 as if he were popular among his students
9 as if they had been bored by the lecture
10 as if it had been your idea

> 1, 3, 4, 5, 6, 9, 10 '마치 ~이었던 것처럼'이라는 뜻으로 과거의 사실과 반대되는 일을 나타내고 있으므로 「as if+가정법 과거완료」가 적합하다. 따라서 「동사의 현재형+as if+주어+had+과거분사 ~」로 표현하는 것이 알맞다.
> 2, 7, 8 '마치 ~인 것처럼'이라는 뜻으로 현재의 사실과 반대되는 일을 나타내고 있으므로 「as if+가정법 과거」가 적합하다. 따라서 「동사의 현재형+as if+주어+동사의 과거형 ~」으로 표현하는 것이 알맞다.

Chapter Review Test 정답 _본문 p.301_

1 rains 2 If, won't 3 ③ 4 ⑤ 5 ④ 6 ①
7 ③ 8 ② 9 ②,③ 10 ③ 11 am → were
12 ③ 13 wish, had finished 14 ④ 15 had travel(l)ed 16 had been 17 were 18 were my close friend 19 ③ 20 he had met
21 played, spoke 22 If I were invited to her party, I could go there. 23 if you can't attend the meeting 24 ② 25 ①

Chapter Review Test 해설

1 조건을 나타내는 if절의 문장에서 if절의 동사는 현재형으로 미래를 나타낸다.

2 「명령문, and …」는 '~해라, 그러면 …'으로 해석하고 조건을 나타내는 if절로 바꾸어 쓸 수 있다.

3 ③ 조건을 나타내는 if절이 미래의 일을 나타낸다 하더라도 if절의 동사는 현재형으로 쓴다.
  (will snow → snows)

4 미래의 일을 나타내는 조건절이 쓰였으므로 주절은 미래 시제를 쓴다.

5 현재 사실에 반대되는 일을 가정할 때 쓰는 가정법 과거로 바꾸어 쓸 수 있다.

6 주절의 won't로 보아, 문장의 시제가 미래임을 알 수 있다. 그러나 미래의 일을 나타낸다고 하더라도 조건을 나타내는 if절의 동사는 항상 현재시제가 미래시제를 대신한다. (went → goes)

7 ③ 과거의 사실에 대한 가정이므로 가정법 과거완료로 쓴다. 가정법 과거완료는 「If+주어+had 과거분사, 주어+could+have 과거분사」의 어순으로 나타낸다. (didn't tell → had not told)
  ①④ '~라면 좋을 텐데'라는 뜻의 현재사실의 반대를 나타내는 I wish+가정법 과거는 「I wish+주어+동사의 과거형」의 어순으로 쓴다.
  ② 배수사를 사용한 원급의 비교는 「배수사+as+원급+as」의 어순으로 나타낸다.
  ⑤ 주절의 동사가 현재시제인 경우 종속절의 동사는 의미에 따라 어떠한 시제든지 쓸 수 있다.

8 ② 현재 사실과 반대되는 일을 나타내는 as if+가정법 과거는 「동사의 현재형+as if+주어+동사의 과거형」으로 쓴다. (are → were)

9 ②③ 여기서 if는 현재나 미래에 실제로 일어날 수 있

는 상황에 대한 조건을 나타낸다. 이때, 미래의 일을 나타낸다 하더라도, if절의 동사는 항상 현재형으로 쓴다.
ⓐ 현재의 사실에 반대되는 가정을 나타내는 가정법 과거는 「If + 주어 + 동사의 과거형, 주어 + would + 동사원형」의 어순으로 나타낸다. (eat → ate)
ⓓ 현재의 사실에 반대되는 가정을 나타내는 가정법 과거는 「If + 주어 + 동사의 과거형, 주어 + might + 동사원형」의 어순으로 나타낸다.
(have caught → catch)
ⓔ if가 현재나 미래에 실제로 일어날 수 있는 상황에 대한 조건을 나타낸다. may는 조동사이므로 뒤에 항상 동사원형을 쓴다. (passed → pass)

10 현재의 사실에 반대되는 가정을 나타내는 가정법 과거는 「If + 주어 + 동사의 과거형, 주어 + could + 동사원형」의 어순으로 나타낸다. if절의 be동사는 인칭에 상관없이 were를 쓴다.

11 가정법 과거의 be동사는 인칭에 관계없이 were를 쓴다.

12 ⓐ 가정법 과거 또는 가정법 과거완료로 써야 한다.
(could have come → could come 또는 were not → had not been)
ⓓ now로 보아 현재 사실에 반대되는 일을 가정하는 가정법 과거임을 알 수 있다.
(could have entered → could enter)

13 과거의 사실과 반대되는 일을 소망할 때 쓰는 「I wish + 가정법 과거완료」로 바꾸어 쓸 수 있다.

14 ⓓ 「I wish + 가정법 과거」는 현재 사실과 반대되는 일을 소망할 때 쓴다. 중국어를 현재 모른다고 했으므로 '안다면 좋을 텐데.'라는 뜻을 나타내기 위해 knew로 써야 한다. (didn't know → knew)

15 과거의 사실과 반대되는 일을 소망할 때는 「I wish + 가정법 과거완료」 구문을 쓴다.

16 I wish my grandmother had been there.
우리 할머니께서 거기에 계셨더라면 좋았을 텐데.

17 현재의 사실과 반대되는 일을 나타낼 때는 as if 뒤에 동사의 과거형을 쓴다. 가정법 과거의 be동사는 인칭에 관계없이 were를 쓴다.

18 Mary speaks as if she were my close friend.
Mary는 마치 그녀가 나의 친한 친구인 것처럼 말한다.

19 If I had enough money, I could buy all the items I want. 만약 내가 충분한 돈을 가지고 있다면, 내가 원하는 모든 물품들을 살 수 있을 텐데.
= Because I don't have enough money, I can't buy all the items I want. 나는 충분한 돈이 없기 때문에, 내가 원하는 모든 물품들을 살 수 없다.

20 과거의 사실과 반대되는 일을 나타낼 때는 「동사의 현재형 + as if + 주어 + had + 과거분사」를 쓴다.

21 「I wish + 가정법 과거」에서 동사는 과거형을 쓴다.

22 「If + 주어 + 동사의 과거형 ~, 주어 + would/could/should/might + 동사원형」 '만약 ~한다면 …할 텐데'

23 if는 '~한다면'의 뜻으로 조건을 나타내며, 이때 if절의 동사는 현재형으로 미래를 나타낸다.

24 조건문에서는 현재 시제가 미래 시제를 대신하며, 부정의 조건을 내걸었으므로 ②가 맞다.

25
- If I were born as the son of a king, I would be a prince. 내가 왕의 아들로 태어난다면 난 왕자가 될 텐데.
- If I knew all the answers to the test, I could get a good grade. 내가 그 시험의 답을 다 알고 있다면 난 좋은 성적을 얻을 수 있을 텐데.
- If I won the lottery, I could help the poor in our neighborhood. 내가 복권에 당첨된다면 우리 동네의 가난한 사람들을 도와줄 수 있을 텐데.
- If I were a movie director, I could make movies with famous actors. 내가 영화 감독이라면 유명한 배우들과 영화를 만들 수 있을 텐데.
- If I had a driver's license, I could drive to the country to relax. 내가 운전면허를 갖고 있다면 머리를 식히러 시골로 차를 몰고 갈 수 있을 텐데.

CHAPTER 13 비교구문
Comparisons

본문 _ p.306

PRACTICE 1

1 colder – coldest
2 younger – youngest
3 nicer – nicest
4 higher – highest
5 fresher – freshest
6 smaller – smallest
7 stranger – strangest
8 faster – fastest
9 lower – lowest
10 newer – newest
11 harder – hardest
12 closer – closest
13 longer – longest
14 slower – slowest
15 taller – tallest
16 older – oldest
17 kinder – kindest
18 warmer – warmest
19 larger – largest
20 smarter – smartest

PRACTICE 2

1 happier – happiest
2 healthier – healthiest
3 hotter – hottest
4 easier – easiest
5 heavier – heaviest
6 earlier – earliest
7 wiser – wisest
8 thinner – thinnest
9 funnier – funniest
10 prettier – prettiest
11 dirtier – dirtiest
12 luckier – luckiest
13 friendlier – friendliest
14 tastier – tastiest
15 sweeter – sweetest
16 lazier – laziest
17 noisier – noisiest
18 bigger – biggest
19 busier – busiest
20 drier – driest
21 wetter – wettest
22 uglier – ugliest
23 hungrier – hungriest
24 stricter – strictest

PRACTICE 3

1 more useful – most useful
2 more serious – most serious
3 cheaper – cheapest
4 more afraid – most afraid
5 more excited – most excited
6 harder – hardest
7 more tired – most tired
8 scarier – scariest
9 more curious – most curious
10 more popular – most popular
11 more handsome[handsomer]
   – most handsome[handsomest]
12 larger – largest
13 more slowly – most slowly
14 more famous – most famous
15 more helpful – most helpful
16 more surprised – most surprised
17 more expensive – most expensive
18 poorer – poorest
19 more boring – most boring
20 more anxious – most anxious
21 more convenient – most convenient
22 wider – widest
23 lonelier – loneliest
24 more foolish – most foolish
25 more patient – most patient
26 stronger – strongest
27 more useless – most useless
28 deeper – deepest
29 more beautiful – most beautiful
30 more creative – most creative
31 more exactly – most exactly

32 milder – mildest
33 more easily – most easily
34 more important – most important
35 more fluently – most fluently
36 greater – greatest
37 more quickly – most quickly
38 more difficult – most difficult
39 more interesting – most interesting
40 more nervous – most nervous

PRACTICE 4

1 better – best
2 later – latest
3 older – oldest
4 worse – worst
5 more – most
6 farther[further] – farthest[furthest]
7 better – best
8 fewer – fewest
9 elder – eldest
10 latter – last
11 less – least
12 worse – worst
13 further – furthest
14 more – most

PRACTICE 5

1 isn't as[so] polite as
2 isn't as[so] tall as
3 isn't as[so] cute as
4 isn't as[so] fast as
5 isn't as[so] white as
6 didn't buy as[so] many books as
7 doesn't speak English as[so] well as
8 isn't as[so] comfortable as
9 don't like basketball as[so] much as
10 isn't as[so] difficult as

[보기] Insu studies harder than Giho. (인수는 기호보다 더 열심히 공부한다.)
= Giho doesn't study as[so] hard as Insu.
(기호는 인수만큼 열심히 공부하지 않는다.)
1~10 A 비교급 than B(A가 B보다 더 ~ 하다 = B not as[so] 원급 as A(B가 A만큼 ~ 하지 않다)

PRACTICE 6

1 as old as
2 not as[so] expensive as
3 as late as
4 as many brothers as
5 not as[so] tired as
6 as long as

1 Tony의 나이와 Becky의 나이가 같으므로 as old as(~만큼 나이가 든)로 표현한다.
2 Tony의 가방이 Becky의 가방보다 싸므로 not as[so] expensive as(~만큼 비싸지 않은)로 표현한다.
3 Tony와 Becky가 잠자리에 든 시각이 같으므로 as late as(~만큼 늦게)로 표현한다.
4 Tony와 Becky 모두 남자 형제의 수가 같으므로 as many brothers as(~만큼 많은 형제들)로 표현한다.
5 Becky는 Tony만큼 피곤하지 않은 상태이므로 not as[so] tired as(~만큼 지치지 않은)로 표현한다.
6 Tony와 Becky가 보고서를 끝내는 데 걸린 시간이 같으므로 as long as(~만큼 오래)로 표현한다.

PRACTICE 7

1 studies as hard as she can
2 speak as clearly as possible
3 got up as early as he could
4 as high as she could
5 call me as soon as possible
6 helped us as much as possible
7 counted the number as exactly as I could
8 goes swimming as often as he can
9 make the questions as easy as possible
10 look as young as possible

PRACTICE 8

2 as loud as possible
3 as much as I can
4 as quickly as possible
5 as hard as we can
6 as fast as possible
7 as kindly as she could
8 as long as possible
9 as little as she can
10 as closely as possible
11 as many things as you can
12 as quietly as he could

13 as early as possible
14 as deep as possible

PRACTICE 9

1 more		**2** more beautiful	
3 shorter		**4** more nervous	
5 later		**6** earlier	

> **1** much(많이)의 비교급은 more이다. did는 앞에 쓰인 made를 대신하여 쓰인 대동사이다.
> **2** beautiful(아름다운)의 비교급은 more beautiful이다. 앞에 쓰인 This flower와 종류는 같지만 다른 대상을 가리키므로 부정대명사 one이 쓰였다.
> **3** short(키가 작은)의 비교급은 shorter이다.
> **4** nervous(불안한)의 비교급은 more nervous이다.
> **5** late(늦게)의 비교급은 later이다.
> **6** early(일찍)의 비교급은 earlier이다. did는 앞에 쓰인 came을 대신하여 쓰인 대동사이다.

PRACTICE 10

2 mine	**3** I am	**4** us	
5 her	**6** yours		

> **1** 비교급 than 다음의 목적격 대명사(him)는 '주어+동사' 형태로 바꿔 쓸 수 있다. 앞에 쓰인 동사(studied)를 대신하여 대동사 did를 썼다. 앞의 동사가 과거 시제이므로 대동사(do)의 시제도 과거형(did)으로 썼음에 유의한다.
> **2** 비교 대상이 같은 종류이면 소유대명사로 바꿔 쓸 수 있다. (my cake → mine)
> **3** 비교급 than 다음의 목적격 대명사(me)는 '주어+동사' 형태로 바꿔 쓸 수 있다. 앞에 is(be동사의 3인칭 현재 단수형)가 쓰였으므로 than 뒤에 be 동사의 현재형 형태(am)을 써야 한다.
> **4** than 다음의 '주어+동사'는 목적격 대명사로 바꿔 쓸 수 있다. (we were → us)
> **5** than 다음의 '주어+동사'는 목적격 대명사로 바꿔 쓸 수 있다. (she can → her)
> **6** 비교의 대상이 같은 종류이면 소유대명사로 바꿔 쓸 수 있다. (your dog → yours)

PRACTICE 11

2 taller than		**3** better than	
4 more diligent than		**5** heavier than	
6 more excited, than		**7** more popular than	
8 faster than		**9** harder than	
10 more active than			

> **1** Tony가 Becky보다 나이가 많으므로 older than(~보다 나이가 많은)으로 표현한다.
> **2** Tony가 Becky보다 키가 크므로 taller than(~보다 키가 큰)으로 표현한다.
> **3** Becky가 Tony보다 기타를 더 잘 치므로 better than(~보다 더 잘)으로 표현한다.

4 Tony가 Becky보다 부지런하므로 more diligent than(~보다 더 부지런한)으로 표현한다.
5 Tony가 Becky보다 체중이 더 나가므로 heavier than(~보다 더 무거운)으로 표현한다.
6 Tony가 Becky보다 휴가에 대한 기대감이 더 크므로 more excited than(~보다 더 들뜬)으로 표현한다.
7 Becky가 Tony보다 인기가 더 많으므로 more popular than(~보다 더 인기가 많은)으로 표현한다.
8 Tony가 Becky보다 더 빨리 달리므로 faster than(~보다 더 빠른)으로 표현한다.
9 Tony가 Becky보다 공부를 더 열심히 하므로 harder than(~보다 더 열심인)으로 표현한다.
10 Becky가 Tony보다 더 활동적이므로 more active than(~보다 더 활동적인)으로 표현한다.

PRACTICE 12

1 ○		**2** ×		**3** ×		**4** ○
5 ○		**6** ×		**7** ○		**8** ×
9 ○		**10** ×					

> **2, 6, 8** very는 '매우'의 뜻으로 원급을 강조한다. 따라서 비교급 앞에서 '훨씬'의 뜻으로 비교급을 강조하는 much, still, even, far, a lot 중 하나로 바꿔야 한다.
> **3, 10** far나 a lot은 비교급 앞에서 '훨씬'의 뜻으로 비교급을 강조하므로 원급을 강조하는 very로 바꿔야 한다.

PRACTICE 13

1 (s)till		**2** (a) lot		**3** (e)ven
4 (f)ar		**5** (m)uch		**6** (e)ven
7 (f)ar		**8** (m)uch		**9** (s)till
10 (a) lot					

PRACTICE 14

1 isn't as[so] exciting as hiking
2 isn't as[so] expensive as that one
3 didn't meet Insu as[so] often as you did
4 isn't as[so] important as friendship
5 isn't as[so] interesting as mine
6 doesn't speak Japanese as[so] fluently as Seho
7 wasn't as[so] boring as the book itself
8 doesn't spend as[so] much money as his sister

> [보기] This bed is less comfortable than that bed. (이 침대는 저 침대보다 덜 편안하다.)
> = This bed isn't as[so] comfortable as that bed. (이 침대는 저 침대만큼 편안하지 않다.)
> **1~8** A less 원급 than B(A는 B보다 덜 ~하다)= A not as[so] 원급 as B(A는 B만큼 ~ 하지 않다)

PRACTICE 15

1. The more you give, the happier you feel.
2. The faster I walked, the closer the building became.
3. The more you want, the more disappointed you will be.
4. The more you get to know him, the more you will like him.
5. The longer I listened to the music, the more cheerful I became.
6. The farther he went, the smaller he looked.
7. The more you practice, the better you will play.
8. The darker it grew, the more scared we felt.
9. The longer you stay, the harder it will be to leave.
10. The colder it gets, the more hot chocolate people drink.

PRACTICE 16

1. There is nothing I do better than
2. There is nothing more difficult than
3. There is nothing he is interested in more than [There is nothing he is more interested in than]
4. There is nothing more delicious than
5. There is nothing more exciting than
6. There is nothing I worry about more than
7. There is nothing John speaks better than
8. There is nothing I like better than

PRACTICE 17

1. colder and colder
2. prettier and prettier
3. taller and taller
4. older and older
5. better and better
6. more and more tired
7. more and more popular
8. higher and higher
9. faster and faster
10. more and more expensive

> 2 pretty의 비교급은 prettier이다.
> 5 get well: (병세가) 좋아지다 / 형용사 well(건강한, 몸이 좋은)의 비교급은 better이다.
> 6 tired(지친, 피곤한)의 비교급은 more tired이다.
> 7 popular(인기 있는)의 비교급은 more popular이다.
> 10 expensive(비싼)의 비교급은 more expensive이다.

PRACTICE 18

1	the cheapest	2	the youngest
3	the most foolish	4	the closest
5	the strangest	6	the best
7	the most serious	8	the newest
9	the worst	10	the most convenient

> 최상급 표현은 범위를 한정하거나, 지금까지 해 본 경험을 나타내는 표현과 같이 쓰는 경우가 많다.
> 3 foolish(어리석은)의 최상급은 the most foolish이다.
> 6 good(잘 하는)의 최상급은 the best이다.
> 7 serious(심각한)의 최상급은 the most serious이다.
> 9 bad(불쾌한)의 최상급은 the worst이다.
> 10 convenient(편리한)의 최상급은 the most convenient이다.

PRACTICE 19

1	① hotter than	② the hottest
2	① taller than	② the tallest
3	① heavier than	② the heaviest
4	① higher, than	② the highest
5	① earlier than	② (the) earliest

> 1 ① 7월이 6월보다 온도가 높으므로 hotter than(~보다 더 더운)이 알맞다.
> ② 8월의 온도가 가장 높으므로 the hottest(가장 더운)가 알맞다.
> 2 ① 코끼리가 사자보다 키가 크므로 taller than(~보다 더 키가 큰)이 알맞다.
> ② 기린이 가장 키가 크므로 the tallest(가장 키가 큰)가 알맞다.
> 3 ① 지수가 미나보다 무거우므로 heavier than(~보다 더 무거운)이 알맞다.
> ② 재민이가 가장 무거우므로 the heaviest(가장 무거운)가 알맞다.
> 4 ① 진호가 미영이보다 더 높은 점수를 받았으므로 higher score than(~보다 더 점수가 높은)이 알맞다.
> ② 소정이가 가장 점수가 높으므로 the highest(가장 높은)가 알맞다.
> 5 ① Andrew가 Jean보다 더 일찍 일어나므로 earlier than(~보다 더 일찍)이 알맞다.
> ② Bill이 가장 일찍 일어나므로 (the) earliest(가장 일찍)가 알맞다.

PRACTICE 20

1. one of the longest rivers
2. one of the most famous men
3. one of the most diligent students
4. one of the highest mountains
5. one of the biggest countries
6. one of the happiest boys
7. one of the most boring movies
8. one of the kindest teachers
9. one of the most beautiful girls
10. one of the most popular restaurants

> 「one of+the+최상급」 뒤에는 반드시 복수 명사가 와서 '가장 ~한 것 중의 하나'라는 뜻을 나타낸다.
>
> 1 one of the longest rivers: 가장 긴 강 중의 하나
> 2 one of the most famous men: 가장 유명한 남자들 중의 하나
> 3 one of the most diligent students: 가장 부지런한 학생들 중의 하나
> 4 one of the highest mountains: 가장 높은 산들 중의 하나
> 5 one of the biggest countries: 가장 큰 국가들 중의 하나
> 6 one of the happiest boys: 가장 행복한 소년들 중의 하나
> 7 one of the most boring movies: 가장 지루한 영화들 중의 하나
> 8 one of the kindest teachers: 가장 친절한 교사들 중의 하나
> 9 one of the most beautiful girls: 가장 아름다운 소녀들 중의 하나
> 10 one of the most popular restaurants: 가장 인기 있는 식당들 중의 하나

PRACTICE 21

1. No (other) bag, as[so] expensive as
   No (other) bag, more expensive than
   more expensive than any other bag
   more expensive than all the other bags

2. No (other) employee, as[so] kind as
   No (other) employee, kinder than
   kinder than any other employee
   kinder than all the other employees

3. No (other) singer, as[so] popular as
   No (other) singer, more popular than
   more popular than any other singer
   more popular than all the other singers

4. No (other) question, as[so] difficult as
   No (other) question, more difficult than
   more difficult than any other question
   more difficult than all the other questions

5. No (other) dog, as[so] cute as
   No (other) dog, cuter than
   cuter than any other dog
   cuter than all the other dogs

6. No (other) sea, as[so] salty as
   No (other) sea, saltier than
   saltier than any other sea
   saltier than all the other seas

Chapter Review Test 정답 본문 _ p.327

1 ④ 2 ③ 3 ④ 4 ⑤ 5 The harder he tries, the better he can dance. 6 The more time we spend together, the closer we become. 7 ③ 8 The more, the richer 9 ② 10 Her iguana is not as[so] fast as mine. 11 ④ 12 ③ 13 taller and taller 14 as hard as he could 15 ②,③ 16 ②,③ 17 possible 18 ② 19 ③ 20 ② 21 farther[further] 22 ② 23 ② 24 ② 25 ④ 26 not as bad as others' 27 the most handsome singer[the handsomest singer] 28 ④ 29 ② 30 city → cities 31 ① 32 ⑤ 33 (1) as old as (2) shorter than (3) faster than 34 ③ 35 ③ 36 ③ 37 ② 38 looks taller than before 39 ① 40 more beautiful than I expected 41 ④ 42 ⑤ 43 ④ 44 ① 45 ⑤ 46 It is one of the simplest ways to succeed in your life. 47 My sister's face is as small as a CD. 48 (A) paler (B) more and more beautiful 49 (1) far/still/even/much/a lot cheaper than Galas (2) far/still/even/much/a lot lighter than Optimum 6 50 ②,④

Chapter Review Test 해설

1. 「비교급+than」 '~보다 …한', 「the+최상급」 '가장 ~한', 「as+원급+as」 '~만큼 …한'

2. 비교급의 강조는 비교급 앞에 much, still, far, even, a lot을 쓰고, very는 원급 앞에서 원급의 의미를 강조한다.

3. This room is not so dark as that room.

이 방은 저 방만큼 어둡지 않다.
= That room is darker than this room.
저 방은 이 방보다 더 어둡다.

4 ①②④ 수량형용사 '많은'
③ 부사 '많이'   ⑤ 비교급의 수식 '훨씬'

5 「the+비교급 ~, the+비교급 …」을 활용하여 영작한다. '더 열심히'는 The harder, '더 잘'은 the better로 나타낸다.

6 「the+비교급 ~, the+비교급 …」을 활용하여 영작한다. '더 많은 시간'은 The more time, '더 가까운'은 the closer로 쓴다.

7 ③ 비교의 대상이 그의 손과 그의 형의 손이므로 than 뒤에는 his brother's hands를 써야 한다. 반복을 피하기 위해 hands는 생략 가능하다.
(his brother → his brother's (hands))

8 「the+비교급, the+비교급」 '~하면 할수록 더 …한'

9 ① ⓐ the는 정관사로, 명사의 앞에 쓰인다. 주어진 문장에는 주격 보어로 쓰인 형용사 large만 있으므로 이를 수식할 수 있는 very를 써야 한다. (the → very)
③ ⓒ very는 형용사나 부사의 원급을 수식한다. 비교급을 수식하기 위해서는 much, still, far, even, a lot을 써야 한다.
(very → much/ still/far/even/a lot)
④ ⓓ 원급 비교는 「as+원급+as」로 쓴다.
(bigger as → big as)
⑤ ⓔ -e로 끝나는 형용사의 최상급은 -st를 붙여서 만든다. 최상급의 앞에는 정관사 the를 써야 한다. (much cutest → the cutest)

10 「not+as[so]+원급+as」 '~만큼 …하지 않은'

11 ④ 사자는 기린보다 가볍다.
(as heavy as → lighter than)

12 '(몸 상태가) 어제보다 훨씬 낫다'는 표현이 들어가야 하므로 well(건강한)의 비교급인 better를 사용하고, 비교급 앞에 '훨씬'을 나타내는 much를 써서 비교급을 강조한다. than 다음에 비교 대상(yesterday)을 쓴다.

13 「비교급+and+비교급」 '점점 더 ~한'

14 민수는 가능한 한 세게 공을 쳤다.

15 ② 「배수사+as+원급+as」 '~배 만큼 …한' 표현이 쓰였으며 「so+원급+as~」 표현은 부정문에서 쓴다.
(so → as)
③ pretty의 최상급은 the prettiest로 쓴다.
(the most pretty → the prettiest)

16 ② 원급 비교는 「as+원급+as」로 쓴다.
(better → well)
③ fast는 형용사와 부사의 형태가 같다. 또한 원급 비교이므로 원급으로 써야 한다. (fastly → fast)

17 「as+원급+as possible」 '가능한 한 …하게'

18 • 「the+비교급, the+비교급」
'~하면 할수록 더 …한'
• little - less - least

19 ⓐ 원급을 이용한 비교는 「as+원급+as」의 어순으로 나타낸다. (faster → fast)
ⓑ 비교급을 이용한 비교는 「비교급+than」의 어순으로 나타낸다.
ⓒ '가장 ~한 것 중의 하나'라는 의미는 「one of+the+최상급+복수 명사」의 어순으로 나타낸다. (animal → animals)
ⓓ 「the+비교급, the+비교급」은 '~하면 할수록 더 …하다'라는 뜻으로 쓰인다.
ⓔ '가장 ~한'의 뜻으로 쓸 때는 「the+최상급」으로 나타낸다. (a very fastest → the fastest)

20 ② Ronnie가 제일 몸무게가 많이 나가므로 형용사를 heavier로 고치거나, 주어를 제일 몸무게가 가벼운 Hannah로 써야 한다. (Ronnie → Hannah 또는 lighter → heavier)

21 '다른 누구보다 더 멀리 뛰었다'는 뜻이 되어야 하므로 「비교급+than」을 사용하여 써준다.
far - farther[further] - farthest[furthest]
'<거리> 먼'

22 ⓐ 원급을 이용한 비교는 「as+원급+as」의 어순으로 나타낸다. (smartest → smart)
ⓑ 「as+원급+as+주어+can[could]」는 '~가 할 수 있는 한 …하게'라는 뜻이다.
ⓒ 현재의 사실에 반대되는 가정을 나타내는 가정법 과거는 「If+주어+동사의 과거형, 주어+would+동사원형」의 어순으로 나타낸다. 「형용사+ly」 형태의 부사 fluently(유창하게)의 비교급은 more fluently이다.
ⓓ '~하면 할수록 더 …하다'라는 의미는 「the+비교급, the+비교급」으로 나타낸다.
(The well → The better)
ⓔ '가장 ~한'라는 의미의 「the+최상급」의 뒤에는 주로 in, of가 이끄는 전치사구나 절이 나온다. in 뒤에는 장소나 집단을 나타내는 단수 명사가 온다.
ⓕ 「There is nothing ~ 비교급+than …」은 '…보다 더 ~한 것은 없다'의 뜻으로 최상급의 의미를 나

타낸다. difficult는 2음절 이상의 형용사이므로 more을 사용해 비교급을 쓴다.
(difficulter → more difficult)

ⓖ 「No (other) ~ 비교급+than」를 사용하여 최상급의 의미를 나타낼 수 있다. (large → larger)

ⓗ forget은 목적어로 to부정사와 동명사 중 어느 것을 쓰냐에 따라 뜻이 달라진다. '조부모님께 전화드리는 것을 잊지 않았다'는 의미이므로 to부정사를 쓴다.

23 Jiyeon is not as funny as Inho.
지연이는 인호만큼 재미있지 않다.
= Inho is funnier than Jiyeon.
인호가 지연이보다 더 재미있다.

24 ② B는 D보다 작다. (as big as → smaller than)

25 prefer = like ~ better '~을 더 좋아하다'

26 비교급이 쓰인 문장은 '~만큼 …하지 않은'이라는 뜻의 「not as[so]+원급+as」으로 바꾸어 쓸 수 있다. 이때 마지막 빈칸은 명사(problem)의 반복 사용을 피하기 위해서 소유격 뒤의 명사를 생략하여 others'로 쓴다.

27 「the+최상급」 '가장 ~한'

28 • 「비교급+than」 '~보다 더 …한'
• 「the+최상급」 '가장 ~한'

29 「비교급+than any other+단수 명사」는 최상급의 의미를 나타낸다.

30 「one of+the+최상급+복수 명사」
'가장 ~한 것 중의 하나'

31 「not as[so]+형용사/부사 원급+as」
= 「less+원급+than」

32 ① 「as+원급+as+주어+can[could]」은 '~가 할 수 있는 한 …하게'의 뜻으로 「as+원급+as possible」로 바꾸어 쓸 수 있다.
(possibly → possible)
② '~하면 할수록 더 …하다'라는 의미는 「the+비교급, the+비교급」으로 나타낸다. (The least → The less, the happiest → the happier)
③ '점점 더 ~한'이라는 의미는 「비교급+and+비교급」으로 나타낸다.
(darkest and darkest → darker and darker)
④ 비교급을 강조할 때는 much, still, even, far, a lot을 사용한다. very는 '매우'의 뜻으로 원급을 강조한다.
⑤ 「There is nothing ~ 비교급+than …」은 '…보다 더 ~한 것은 없다'의 뜻으로 최상급의 의미를 나타낸다.

33 (1) Calvin은 Brad와 나이가 같다.
(2) Jason은 Calvin보다 키가 작다.
(3) Brad는 Jason보다 빠르다.

34 A는 이곳에 3년 반째 살고 있는 반면, B는 5년째 살고 있다. 따라서 B가 할 말은 '너는 여기서 나만큼 오래 살지는 않았네.'이다.
not as+원급+as: ~만큼 …하지 않은

35 • 「one of+the+최상급+복수명사」 '가장 ~한 … 중의 하나'
「in+단수 명사」 비교문에서 in은 비교 대상인 '장소, 집단' 앞에 쓰인다.
• 「the+최상급+명사+of+복수 명사」 '~중에서 가장 …한'

36 「one of+the+최상급+복수 명사」
'가장 ~한 것 중의 하나'
(highest → the highest)

37 must '~임에 틀림없다'
「비교급+than」 '~보다 더 …한'

38 「look+형용사」 '~해 보이다'
「비교급+than」 '~보다 더 …한'

39 very는 비교급 앞에 올 수 없다.

40 록키 산맥은 내가 예상했던 것보다 더 아름답다.

41 A: 저는 이 셔츠가 좋은데 제게 너무 작군요. 이걸로 더 큰 사이즈 있나요?
B: 매우 죄송합니다만, 그것이 우리 가게에 있는 가장 큰 사이즈입니다.

42 ⑤ Sue는 반에서 가장 키가 큰 소녀들 중 한명이다.
①②③④ Sue는 반에서 가장 키가 크다.

43 「the+비교급, the+비교급」 '~하면 할수록 더 …한'

44 ① so는 비교급을 수식할 수 없다.

45 (A) '가장 ~한 것 중의 하나'라는 의미는 「one of+the+최상급+복수 명사」의 어순으로 나타낸다.
(creature → creatures)
(B) 주어는 some products로, 복수 명사이다. 따라서 동사도 복수형으로 쓴다. (is → are)
(C) 주격 관계대명사절의 동사는 선행사에 일치시킨다. 선행사가 a valuable product로 단수이므로, 동사 또한 3인칭 단수형인 has로 쓴다.
(D) 단수 명사 앞에는, '또 하나의, 또 다른'이라는 뜻으로 another가 쓰인다. other은 복수 명사의 앞에 쓰인다. (other → another)

(E) '~만큼 …하지 않은'이라는 뜻은 「not as[so]+원급+as」의 어순으로 나타낼 수 있다.

46 '가장 ~한 것 중의 하나'라는 의미는 「one of+the+최상급+복수 명사」의 어순으로 나타낸다. simple의 최상급은 -est를 붙여 만들어준다.
(most simplest → simplest, way → ways)

47 「as+원급+as」 '~만큼 …한'

48 (A) 의미상 '더 창백한'이란 뜻이 어울린다.
(B) 「비교급+and+비교급」 '점점 더 ~한'
2음절 이상의 형용사인 beautiful의 비교급은 more로 나타낸다.

49 (1) Optimum 6는 Galas보다 훨씬 더 싸다.
(2) Galas는 Optimum 6보다 훨씬 더 가볍다.

50 ① 몸무게가 같으므로 '~만큼 …한'의 뜻을 나타내는 원급비교를 사용한다. 원급비교는 「as+원급+as」로 쓴다. (heavier → heavy)
③ 먹을수록 더 행복하다는 뜻이므로 '~하면 할수록 더 …하다'는 뜻의 「the+비교급, the+비교급」을 사용한다.
(More → The more, happier → the happier)
⑤ 나는 형과 부모님만큼 부지런하지 않다는 뜻이므로, '~만큼 …하지 않은'이라는 뜻의 「not so+원급+as」를 사용한다. (than → as)

CHAPTER 14 관계사 Relatives

본문 _ p.336

PRACTICE 1

1	who	2	whose	3	who(m)
4	whose	5	who	6	who(m)
7	who	8	who(m)	9	whose
10	who(m)				

> 1, 5, 7 선행사가 사람이고, 관계대명사절 내에서 관계대명사가 주어 역할을 하기 때문에 주격 관계대명사 who가 적절하다.
> 2, 4, 9 선행사가 사람이고, 관계대명사절 내에서 관계대명사가 명사를 꾸며주는 소유격 역할을 하기 때문에 소유격 관계대명사 whose가 적절하다.
> 3, 6, 8, 10 선행사가 사람이고, 관계대명사절 내에서 관계대명사가 목적어 역할을 하기 때문에 목적격 관계대명사 who(m)이 적절하다.

PRACTICE 2

1	is	2	was	3	are	4	love
5	is	6	are	7	sings	8	are
9	is	10	are				

> 1~10 관계대명사절의 동사는 선행사의 수에 일치시킨다.

PRACTICE 3

2 There is a tree which my family planted.
3 I have a dog whose name is Happy.
4 The dolls which are on the sofa are my sister's.
5 This is the room whose walls are blue.
6 Heejun is reading the book which you gave him.
7 The flowers which he brought are beautiful.
8 He made the movie which became famous.
9 This is the computer whose keyboard is broken.
10 You should take the CD which is on my desk.

> 2, 6, 7 선행사가 사물이고, 관계대명사절 내에서 관계대명사가 목적어를 대신하므로 목적격 관계대명사 which를 사용하여 연결한다.
> 3, 5, 9 선행사가 사물 또는 동물이고, 관계대명사가 명사를 수식하는 소유격 역할을 하므로 소유격 관계대명사 whose를 사용하여 연결한다.
> 4, 8, 10 선행사가 사물이고, 관계대명사절 내에서 관계대명사가 주어 역할을 하므로 주격 관계대명사 which를 사용하여 연결한다.

PRACTICE 4

1	are	2	are	3	have	4	are
5	was	6	don't	7	takes	8	looks
9	were	10	is				

> 1, 3, 4, 7, 8 주격 관계대명사절의 동사는 선행사의 수에 일치시킨다.
> 2, 5, 6, 9, 10 소유격 관계대명사가 쓰였을 경우에는 whose 뒤에 오는 명사의 수에 동사를 일치시킨다.

PRACTICE 5

1	whom, that	2	that
3	that	4	who, that
5	that	6	which, that

CHAPTER 14

7	that	8	which, that
9	that	10	who, that

> 1 선행사가 사람이고, 관계대명사가 목적어 역할을 하기 때문에 목적격 관계대명사 whom과 that을 쓸 수 있다.
> 2, 7 선행사에 형용사의 최상급이 포함되어 있기 때문에 목적격 관계대명사로 that이 적절하다.
> 3 선행사에 little이 포함되어 있기 때문에 목적격 관계대명사로 that이 적절하다.
> 4, 10 선행사가 사람이고, 관계대명사가 주어 역할을 하기 때문에 주격 관계대명사 who와 that을 쓸 수 있다.
> 5 선행사에 서수(the first)가 포함되어 있기 때문에 목적격 관계대명사 that이 적절하다.
> 6 선행사가 사물이고, 관계대명사가 주어 역할을 하기 때문에 주격 관계대명사 which와 that을 쓸 수 있다.
> 8 선행사가 동물이고, 관계대명사가 목적어 역할을 하기 때문에 목적격 관계대명사 which와 that을 쓸 수 있다.
> 9 선행사가 something이기 때문에 주격 관계대명사로 that이 적절하다.

PRACTICE 6

1	that	2	who[that] is
3	who[that]	4	that
5	which[that]	6	who[that]
7	I met at the party	8	that
9	that[which] were	10	that
11	that	12	whose
13	were	14	which[that]
15	she got from her mom		

> 1 선행사가 anything이기 때문에 목적격 관계대명사로 that을 써야 한다.
> 2 주격 관계대명사 who가 쓰였기 때문에 관계대명사절의 주어(he)는 생략해야 한다. 주격 관계대명사 who는 that으로 바꿔 쓸 수 있다.
> 3 선행사(An employee)가 사람이기 때문에 주격 관계대명사로 who 또는 that을 써야 한다.
> 4, 11 선행사에 형용사의 최상급이 포함되어 있으므로 목적격 관계대명사로 that을 써야 한다.
> 5 선행사(the glasses)가 사물이므로 목적격 관계대명사로 which 또는 that을 써야 한다.
> 6 선행사가 사람(my friend)이고 관계대명사가 주어 역할을 하므로 주격 관계대명사 who 또는 that을 써야 한다.
> 7 목적격 관계대명사 whom이 쓰였기 때문에 관계대명사절의 목적어(her)는 생략해야 한다.
> 8 선행사가 something이기 때문에 주격 관계대명사로 that을 써야 한다.
> 9 주격 관계대명사 that이 쓰였기 때문에 관계대명사절의 주어(they)는 생략해야 한다.
> 10 선행사에 서수(the first)가 포함되어 있으므로 주격 관계대명사로 that을 써야 한다.
> 12 관계대명사가 명사를 수식하는 소유격 역할을 해야 하므로 소유격 관계대명사 whose를 써야 한다.
> 13 관계대명사절의 주어가 whose jeans(복수명사)이기 때문에 were이 적절하다.

> 14 선행사(the mountain)가 사물이기 때문에 주격 관계대명사로 which 또는 that을 써야 한다.
> 15 목적격 관계대명사 which가 쓰였기 때문에 관계대명사절의 목적어(it)는 생략해야 한다.

PRACTICE 7

1	what	2	which	3	what
4	what	5	which	6	what
7	what	8	what	9	which
10	what	11	What	12	which

> 1, 3, 4, 6, 7, 8, 10, 11 선행사가 없으므로, 선행사를 자체에 포함하는 관계대명사 what을 써야 한다.
> 2, 12 선행사가 사물이고, 관계대명사가 목적어 역할을 하기 때문에 목적격 관계대명사 which가 적절하다.
> 5 선행사가 동물이고, 관계대명사가 목적어 역할을 하기 때문에 목적격 관계대명사 which가 적절하다.
> 9 선행사가 사물이고, 관계대명사가 주어 역할을 하기 때문에 주격 관계대명사 which가 적절하다.

PRACTICE 8

1	(which)	2	(whom)
3	생략해도 되는 부분 없음.	4	(which are)
5	생략해도 되는 부분 없음.	6	(that)
7	생략해도 되는 부분 없음.	8	(which was)

> 1, 2, 6 목적격 관계대명사 which, whom, that은 생략 가능하다.
> 4, 8 주격 관계대명사 뒤에 be동사가 있고 그 뒤에 분사가 올 때, 관계대명사+be동사는 생략할 수 있다
> 3, 5, 7 who, which, that이 주격 관계대명사로 사용되었기 때문에 생략할 수 없다.

PRACTICE 9

2	which[that] were	3	which[that] were
4	who[that] were	5	which[that] is
6	which[that] are	7	who[that] was
8	who[that] are	9	which[that] is
10	who[that] is		

PRACTICE 10

1 Kevin has an uncle, who teaches English at a middle school.
2 She bought a blouse, which was on sale.
3 He was a great scientist, who(m) we all respected.

Ch 14 관계사

4 Jenny has lost her watch, which her father bought for her.
5 They climbed Mount Everest, which is the highest mountain in the world.

> **1** 선행사가 사람이고, 관계대명사가 주어 역할을 하기 때문에 주격 관계대명사 who를 사용하여 계속적 용법으로 두 문장을 연결할 수 있다.
> **2, 5** 선행사가 사물이고, 관계대명사가 주어 역할을 하기 때문에 주격 관계대명사 which를 사용하여 계속적 용법으로 두 문장을 연결할 수 있다.
> **3** 선행사가 사람이고, 관계대명사가 목적어 역할을 하기 때문에 목적격 관계대명사 who(m)을 사용하여 계속적 용법으로 두 문장을 연결 할 수 있다.
> **4** 선행사가 사물이고, 관계대명사가 목적어 역할을 하기 때문에 목적격 관계대명사 which를 사용하여 계속적 용법으로 두 문장을 연결할 수 있다.

PRACTICE 11

1	when	**2**	why	**3**	where
4	when	**5**	how	**6**	where
7	how	**8**	why	**9**	where
10	how				

PRACTICE 12

2	the place, where	**3**	why, the reason
4	the year, when	**5**	how
6	somewhere		

Chapter Review Test 정답 본문 _ p.347

1 ①,⑤ **2** ③ **3** what you said **4** who[that] teaches students **5** (1) ③ (2) ② (3) ④ (4) ① **6** ⑤ **7** ③ **8** ⑤ **9** ③,⑤ **10** ④ **11** ④ **12** ④ **13** ③ **14** ① **15** ③ **16** ④ **17** ③ **18** A firefighter is a person who puts out fires and rescues people. **19** ① **20** ① **21** ① **22** ③ **23** ⑤ **24** ① **25** ② **26** I saw the house whose roof was covered with snow. **27** ② **28** ③,④ **29** ④ **30** the way others live[how others live] **31** that → who **32** ④ **33** (1) who is playing (2) which I borrowed from **34** (1) I know a girl who[that] can speak Spanish very well. (2) The book which[that] I bought last night is easy to read. (3) Look at the house whose roof is red. **35** There is a boy who is drawing a picture. [There is a girl who is watching TV. / There is a cat which is eating fish.] **36** ② **37** ③ **38** ① **39** These are the books which[that] my girlfriend bought for me. **40** (A) We told them what they shouldn't do in the park. (B) They listened carefully to what we said. **41** ② **42** in which **43** (1) I want to make a machine which[that] can fly me to the moon. (2) Emily was my friend who[that] won first prize in the dancing contest./Emily who[that] won first prize in the dancing contest was my friend.

Chapter Review Test 해설

1 ① 목적격 관계대명사
② 지시형용사 (생략 불가)
③ 지시대명사 (생략 불가)
④ 주격 관계대명사 (생략 불가)
⑤ 목적어 역할을 하는 명사절 접속사

2 ① 주어 The dog이 단수 명사이므로, 동사 또한 단수 동사로 일치시켜야 한다. (are → is)
② 선행사 the book이 사물이므로, 관계대명사 which나 that을 써야 한다. who는 선행사가 사람일 때 쓸 수 있다. (who → which[that])
③ The man을 수식하는 관계대명사절 who(m) I met에서 목적격 관계대명사인 who(m)은 생략 가능하다.
④ 선행사를 주어로 하는 관계대명사절이므로, 주격 관계대명사인 who를 쓴다. whom은 목적격 관계대명사이다. (whom → who)
⑤ 간접의문문의 어순은 「의문사+주어+동사」로 나타낸다. (who are they → who they are)

3 선행사를 포함하는 관계대명사 what을 이용하여 understand의 목적어 역할을 하는 절을 완성한다.

4 선행사가 사람일 때 뒤에 오는 주격 관계대명사는 who[that]이다. 선행사는 3인칭 단수이고, 시제가 현재형이므로 동사도 3인칭 단수 현재형인 teaches로 쓴다.

5 (1) 선행사가 사람이므로 주격 관계대명사 who로 시작하는 문장이 뒤따르며, 내용상 ③이 알맞다.
(2) 선행사가 사물(케이크)이므로 목적격 관계대명사

which로 시작하는 절이 뒤따르며, 내용상 ②가 알맞다.
(3) 선행사가 사물(냉장고)이므로 주격 관계대명사 which로 시작하는 절이 뒤따르며, 내용상 ④가 알맞다.
(4) 선행사가 사람이므로 주격 관계대명사 who로 시작하는 절이 뒤따르며, 내용상 ①이 알맞다.

6 ⑤ 주격 관계대명사 ①②③④ 목적격 관계대명사

7 선행사(many fables)가 사물이므로 which를 이용하여 두 문장을 연결한다.

8 선행사(story books)가 사물이고 관계사절에서 주어 역할을 하므로 which가 온다.

9 ③ 관계대명사 that은 계속적 용법으로 쓸 수 없다. 따라서 선행사가 사람일 때 쓰이는 주격 관계대명사 who로 바꾸어야 한다. (that → who)
⑤ 관계대명사절에서 명사(cover)를 앞에서 수식하는 역할을 해야 하므로 소유격 관계대명사 whose가 알맞다. (which → whose)

10 ⓐ 선행사가 장소이고, 뒤 따라오는 절이 완전하므로 관계부사 where을 쓴다. (which → where)
ⓓ 선행사에 서수가 포함되어 있는 경우 관계대명사 that을 주로 쓴다. (which → that)
ⓔ 관계대명사 that은 계속적 용법으로 쓸 수 없다. (that → which)

11 계속적 용법의 관계대명사는 「접속사+대명사」로 바꿔 쓸 수 있다.

12 ① 관계대명사절(who)이 선행사 student를 수식하고 있는 문장으로 전치사 뒤의 명사가 생략된 절이 되어야 한다.
    hang out with: '~와 어울리다, 시간을 보내다'
② 관계대명사 that절이 선행사 the movie를 수식하고 있으므로 단수동사 has가 적절하다.
③ 관계대명사 계속적 용법으로 선행사가 her parents이므로 복수동사 go를 써야 한다.
⑤ 주격 관계대명사 which가 선행사 the release date를 수식하고 있는데 뒤의 절이 완전하므로 주어 it을 삭제해야 한다.

13 ⓐ 「the+형용사」는 '~한 사람들'의 뜻으로, 복수 명사처럼 쓰인다. 따라서 관계대명사절의 동사 또한 복수로 써야 한다. (lives → live)
ⓔ 주격 관계대명사 뒤에 be동사가 있고 그 뒤에 분사가 올 때, 「관계대명사+be동사」는 생략할 수 있다. 이때의 「관계대명사+be동사」는 반드시 함께 생략해야 한다. (who → who are/생략)

14 • 선행사(a man)가 사람이므로 who[that]가 온다.
• 선행사가 사물(an alarm clock)이므로 which[that]가 온다.

15 ⓐⓔ 목적격 관계대명사 who(m), that은 생략 가능하다.
ⓑⓓ 주격 관계대명사는 생략이 불가능하다. 주격 관계대명사 뒤에 be동사가 있고 그 뒤에 분사가 올 때, 「관계대명사+be동사」는 생략할 수 있다.
ⓒ 목적어 역할을 하는 명사절 접속사 that은 생략이 가능하다.

16 ④ 관계대명사 ①②③ 의문대명사 ⑤ 의문형용사

17 선행사(the tomatoes)가 사물이므로 목적격 관계대명사 which나 that을 사용하여 두 문장을 이어준다. 목적격 관계대명사는 생략할 수 있다.
그녀는 그녀가 기른 토마토로 스파게티 소스를 만들었다.

18 who는 주격 관계대명사로 쓰였다.

19 ① 관계대명사 ②③④⑤ 접속사

20 ① 관계대명사절 안에서 주어의 역할을 하며, 선행사가 사람이므로 주격 관계대명사 who를 사용한다.
② 관계대명사절 안에서 주어의 역할을 하며, 선행사가 사람이므로 주격 관계대명사 who나 that을 사용한다. (whose → who/that)
③ 관계대명사절 안에서 목적어의 역할을 하며, 선행사가 사물이므로 목적격 관계대명사 which나 that을 사용한다. (whose → which/that)
④ 관계대명사절 안에서 관계대명사 바로 뒤에 나오는 명사를 꾸며주어야 하므로, 소유격 관계대명사 whose를 사용한다. (who → whose)
⑤ 관계대명사절 안에서 주어의 역할을 하며, 선행사가 사람이므로 주격 관계대명사 who나 that을 사용한다. (whom → who/that)

21 선행사(the reason)가 이유를 나타내므로 관계부사 why가 온다.

22 ⓐⓑⓔ 주격 관계대명사 ⓒⓓⓕ 의문대명사

23 주어진 that은 관계대명사절 안에서 주어의 역할을 하고 있으므로 주격 관계대명사이다.
① 멀리 떨어진 사물을 나타내는 지시형용사로서 뒤에 나오는 명사 girl을 수식하고 있다. (that girl: 저 소녀)
② 명사절을 이끄는 접속사로 쓰였다.
③ 멀리 떨어진 사람이나 사물을 가리키는 지시대명사로 쓰였다. (that: 저 사람)
④ 「so+형용사+that~」은 '너무 …해서 ~하다'라는 뜻으로, 이때의 that은 접속사로 쓰였다.

⑤ 관계대명사절 안에서 주어의 역할을 하는 주격 관계대명사이다.

24 ① 선행사가 사물일 경우 주격 관계대명사는 that을 쓸 수 있고, 관계사절의 동사는 선행사의 수에 맞추어 복수형을 쓴다.
②③④⑤ 선행사가 단수 명사이므로 주격 관계대명사절의 동사도 단수로 일치시켜야 한다.

25 (A) 선행사가 사물인 주격 관계대명사 that[which]
(B) 선행사가 사람인 주격 관계대명사 who[that]
(C) 선행사가 사물인 목적격 관계대명사 which[that]

26 선행사가 사물인 소유격 관계대명사 whose를 Its의 자리에 써서 두 문장을 이어준다.

27 ② '무엇'의 의미를 지닌 의문사
①③④⑤ 선행사를 포함하고 있는 관계대명사

28 ③ 주격 관계대명사 뒤에 be동사가 있고 그 뒤에 분사가 올 때「관계대명사+be동사」는 생략 가능하다.
④ 목적격 관계대명사 that 뒤에 주어+동사가 오고 전치사가 문장의 뒤에 있으므로 that을 생략할 수 있다.

29 ④ 관계대명사절 안에서 관계대명사 바로 뒤에 나오는 명사를 꾸미고 있으므로, 소유격 관계대명사 whose가 알맞다. (which → whose)

30 선행사 the way와 관계부사 how는 함께 쓸 수 없으므로 관계부사와 선행사 둘 중 하나는 생략해야 한다.

31 관계대명사의 계속적 용법에서는 that을 쓸 수 없다.

32 (A) 선행사가 동물이므로 주격 관계대명사 which 혹은 that을 쓴다.
(B) 선행사가 무생물(The Nile: 나일강)이므로 주격 관계대명사 which를 쓴다. 이때, 계속적 용법으로 쓰였으므로 that은 쓸 수 없다.
(C) 선행사가 사람이므로 주격 관계대명사 who 혹은 that을 쓴다.
(D) 선행사가 따로 없는 관계대명사절이므로, 선행사를 자체에 포함하는 관계대명사 What을 쓴다.

33 (1) 선행사가 사람인 The boy이므로 관계대명사는 who이며, 의미상 시제는 현재진행으로 쓴다.
(2) 선행사가 사물인 the comic book이므로 관계대명사는 which이며, 어제의 일이므로 과거시제를 쓴다.

34 (1) 선행사(a girl)가 사람이므로 주격 관계대명사 who[that]을 사용해 연결한다.
나는 스페인어를 매우 잘 말할 수 있는 한 소녀를 안다.
(2) 선행사(The book)가 사물이므로 목적격 관계대명사 which[that]을 사용해 연결한다.
내가 지난밤에 산 책은 읽기 쉽다.
(3) 선행사(the house)가 사물이고, 소유격을 대신해 바로 뒤에 나오는 명사를 수식하므로 소유격 관계대명사 whose를 사용해 연결한다.
지붕이 빨간 그 집을 봐.

35 선행사가 사람일 때는 주격 관계대명사 who를, 동물이거나 사물이면 which를 쓰며 현재진행형은「be동사의 현재형+-ing」로 나타낸다.

36 ② I saw on TV는 목적어가 없는 불완전한 절이므로, 관계부사가 아닌 목적격 관계대명사가 쓰여야 한다. 또한 선행사가 사물(the restaurant)이므로, 관계대명사 which나 that을 쓴다.
(where → which[that])

37 ③ 주격 관계대명사는 단독으로 생략할 수 없다.

38 • 사물을 선행사로 하는 목적격 관계대명사 which나 that이 들어간다.
• 선행사에 형용사의 최상급이 포함되어 있으므로 목적격 관계대명사 that이 들어간다.
• 목적어 역할을 하는 명사절을 이끄는 접속사 that ('~라는 것을')이 들어간다.

39 선행사 the books가 사물이므로 목적격 관계대명사 which나 that을 이용하여 두 문장을 연결한다.

40 (A) what they shouldn't do '그들이 해서는 안 되는 것'
(B) what we said '우리가 말한 것'

41 ② what 이하는 목적어가 없는 불완전한 절이므로, 목적격 관계대명사가 들어가야 한다. 선행사에 형용사의 최상급이 포함되어 있으므로 that이 들어가야 한다. what은 자체에 선행사를 포함하기 때문에 선행사가 없는 경우에만 쓸 수 있는 관계대명사이다. (what → that)

42 「전치사+관계대명사」인 in which로 관계부사 where를 대신할 수 있다.

43 (1) 선행사(a machine)가 사물이므로 주격 관계대명사 which[that]을 사용해 연결한다.
나는 나를 달로 보내줄 기계를 만들고 싶다.
(2) 선행사(Emily/my friend)가 사람이므로 주격 관계대명사 who[that]을 사용해 연결한다.
춤 대회에서 1등 상을 탄 Emily는 나의 친구였다.

CHAPTER 15 접속사
Conjunctions

본문 _ p.356

PRACTICE 1

1 and
2 or
3 but
4 or
5 and
6 or
7 and
8 but
9 and
10 or

> 1 진수와 민호를 대등하게 연결하고 있으므로 and가 적절하다.
> (해석: 나는 어제 거리에서 진수와 민호를 만났다.)
> 2 헬스장 아니면 집으로 가는지 묻고 있으므로 or이 적절하다.
> (해석: 그는 어디로 가는 거니, 헬스장으로 아니면 집으로?)
> 3 문맥상 not A but B구문이 사용되었음을 알 수 있다. 따라서 but이 적절하다. (해석: 네가 실수했어. 비난받아야 할 사람은 내가 아니라 너야.)
> 4 둘 이상의 대상 중에서 선택하고 있으므로 or이 적절하다.
> (해석: Tim, John, 아니면 Ryan 중 누가 네 형이니?)
> 5 서울을 떠났고 대전에 도착했다는 대등한 내용을 연결하고 있으므로 and가 적절하다.
> (해석: 그들은 서울을 떠났고 2시간 후에 대전에 도착했다.)
> 6 둘 이상의 대상 중에서 어떤 것을 좋아하는지 묻고 있으므로 or이 적절하다. (해석: 피자와 스파게티 중 너는 어느 것을 더 좋아하니?)
> 7 우유 한 병과 케이크 한 조각을 대등하게 연결하고 있으므로 and가 적절하다. (해석: Eric은 우유 한 병과 케이크 한 조각을 샀다.)
> 8 나는 음악을 좋아하고, 나의 형은 그렇지 않다는 반대되는 내용을 연결하고 있으므로 but이 적절하다. doesn't 뒤에는 like music이 생략되어 있다.
> (해석: 나는 음악을 좋아하지만 내 형은 그렇지 않다.)
> 9 학생들이 교실에 들어갔고, 청소하기를 시작했다는 대등한 내용을 연결하고 있으므로 and가 적절하다.
> (해석: 학생들은 교실로 들어갔고 청소하기를 시작했다.)
> 10 박 여사를 만났는지, 아니면 전화로 얘기했는지 둘 중의 하나를 선택하도록 묻고 있으므로 or이 적절하다. (해석: 너는 박 여사를 만났니, 아니면 그녀에게 전화로 얘기했니?)

PRACTICE 2

1 and
2 or
3 and
4 or
5 or
6 and
7 or
8 and
9 or
10 and

PRACTICE 3

1 Both, and
2 either, or
3 neither, nor
4 both[not only], and[but also]
5 both[not only], and[but also]
6 as well as
7 either, or
8 both[not only], and[but also]
9 neither, nor
10 both[not only], and[but also]

> 1 Both A and B: A와 B 둘 다, both A and B를 주어로 쓸 때는 복수형의 동사를 쓴다.
> 2, 7 either A or B: A와 B중 어느 하나
> 3, 9 neither A nor B: A도 B도 ~아닌
> 4, 5, 8, 10 both A and B: A와 B 둘 다(A뿐만 아니라 B도) 문맥상 not only A but also B(A뿐만 아니라 B도)가 들어가는 것도 가능하다.
> 6 not only A but also B=B as well as A: A뿐만 아니라 B도

PRACTICE 4

1 We are excited because we are going to interview a popular singer.
We are going to interview a popular singer, so we are excited.
2 Martin couldn't call you because he was very busy this week.
Martin was very busy this week, so he couldn't call you.
3 Jiyoon has a lot of friends because she is very nice.
Jiyoon is very nice, so she has a lot of friends.
4 I can't study tonight because I'm really sick.
I'm really sick, so I can't study tonight.
5 Julie cut her long hair short because she wanted to refresh her look.
Julie wanted to refresh her look, so she cut her long hair short.

PRACTICE 5

1 because
2 because of
3 because of
4 because
5 because
6 because of

> 1~6 because 뒤에는 절이 오고, because of 뒤에는 명사 상당 어구가 와야 한다.

PRACTICE 6

1 I'll do the laundry unless it rains.
2 Let's watch a movie together unless you are busy.
3 I can help you unless it takes too long.

4 He will be in trouble unless the train arrives on time.
5 She can finish the work unless she goes home early.
6 They will forgive you unless you lie to them.
7 You'll miss the last bus unless you hurry.
8 I'll buy this shirt unless I change my mind.
9 We can go swimming unless the pool is closed.
10 You can just walk unless it's too far from here.

PRACTICE 7

1 if the news is true (or not)
   whether the news is true (or not)
2 if I can go home now (or not)
   whether I can go home now (or not)
3 if he will come soon (or not)
   whether he will come soon (or not)
4 if that girl is Chinese (or not)
   whether that girl is Chinese (or not)
5 if she likes Bob (or not)
   whether she likes Bob (or not)

PRACTICE 8

1 I hurried in the morning so that I could catch the train.
2 We were so tired that we couldn't go to the party.
3 They practiced hard so that they could win the game.
4 The coffee was too hot for her to drink.
5 I was so busy that I couldn't answer the phone.
6 I drink a cup of coffee every morning (in order[so as]) to stay awake.
7 The table was so heavy that I couldn't move it.
8 The questions are too difficult for me to answer.
9 Animals live in a pack so that they can reduce the danger of attack.
10 Mike took a taxi (in order[so as]) to arrive there in time.

> 1, 3, 6, 9, 10 '~하기 위해서, ~할 수 있도록' 목적을 의미하는 「so that~」표현은 「(in order[so as]) to+동사원형」으로 바꿔 쓸 수 있다.
> 2, 4, 5, 7, 8 「so+형용사/부사+that+주어+can[could] not...」표현은 「too+형용사/부사+to+동사원형」으로 바꿔 쓸 수 있다.

PRACTICE 9

1 It is disappointing that he lied to me.
2 It is exciting that we are going to Jejudo.
3 It is strange that they didn't come.
4 It is a pity that the story had an unhappy ending.
5 It is true that Giho plays the piano well.
6 I know that Yumi is Sujin's sister.
7 I thought that she was going to cry.
8 I believe that her son is diligent.
9 I thought that you were having dinner at that restaurant.
10 I knew that you gave Mike a lot of books.
11 The fact is that she doesn't like her new job.
12 The point is that we can't wait any longer.
13 The truth is that Minho broke the window.
14 The big news was that Tom and Kate got married.
15 The problem was that he didn't know how to drive.

> 1~5 문장 앞에 가주어 it을 쓰고 진주어인 that절을 뒤로 보내서 써야 한다.
> 6~10 목적어 역할을 하는 명사절을 이끄는 that절 형태로 써야 한다. 이때의 that은 생략 가능하다.
> 11~15 보어 역할을 하는 that절 형태로 써야 한다.

PRACTICE 10

1 while   2 after   3 when
4 before   5 as   6 until
7 as soon as 8 after 9 while
10 until

> 1 과거 진행형(was washing the dishes) 형태가 쓰여 내가 설거지를 하고 있었던 동안이라는 의미가 되어야 하므로 while(~하는 동안)이 적절하다.
> 2 퇴근 후에 집에 와서 저녁을 먹었다는 의미가 되어야 하므로 after(~한 후에)가 적절하다.
> 3 한가할 때 주로 무엇을 하는지 묻는 의미가 되어야 하므로 when(~할 때)이 적절하다.
> 4 손님이 도착하기 전에 음식이 준비되어 있어야 한다는 의미이므로 before(~전에)가 적절하다.
> 5 거리를 걷고 있었을 때 그의 친구를 만났다는 의미이므로 as (~하고 있을 때)가 적절하다.

6 그가 잠들 때까지 이야기책을 읽었다는 의미이므로 until(~할 때까지)이 적절하다.
7 그는 일어나자마자 양치질을 한다는 의미이므로 as soon as (~하자마자)가 적절하다.
8 문을 연 후에 방에 들어왔다는 의미이므로 after(~한 후에)가 적절하다.
9 내가 샤워를 하고 있었던 동안(I was taking a shower) 누군가 전화를 했다는 의미이므로 while(~하는 동안)이 적절하다.
10 꿈이 이뤄질 때까지 계속 시도하겠다는 의미이므로 until(~할 때까지)이 적절하다.

PRACTICE 11

1   Even though my room is very small, I like it.
    Although my room is very small, I like it.
    Though my room is very small, I like it.
2   Even though Betty didn't want to read the book, she bought it.
    Although Betty didn't want to read the book, she bought it.
    Though Betty didn't want to read the book, she bought it.
3   Even though this computer is very old, it still works all right.
    Although this computer is very old, it still works all right.
    Though this computer is very old, it still works all right.
4   Even though English is difficult, I like learning it.
    Although English is difficult, I like learning it.
    Though English is difficult, I like learning it.
5   Even though Andy doesn't eat regularly, he is quite healthy.
    Although Andy doesn't eat regularly, he is quite healthy.
    Though Andy doesn't eat regularly, he is quite healthy.

PRACTICE 12

1 Finally   2 However
3 In addition   4 For example
5 Therefore   6 For example
7 However   8 Therefore
9 In addition   10 Finally

1 우리 팀이 프로젝트를 매우 열심히 준비해 왔고 결국 성공적으로 그것을 마쳤다는 의미이므로 Finally(결국)가 적절하다.
2 준수의 부모님이 그가 배우가 되기를 원하지 않으셨지만 그는 유명한 배우가 되었다는 반대되는 내용이므로 However(그러나)가 적절하다.
3 우리가 인터넷으로 이메일을 보낼 수 있고, 추가적으로 그것을 통해 이야기를 나눌 수 있다는 부가적 사실을 말하고 있으므로 In addition(게다가)이 적절하다.
4 매일의 생활에서 환경을 보호할 수 있는 사례를 들고 있으므로 For example(예를 들면)이 적절하다.
5 어제 결석을 해서 그 결과 축제에 대한 소식을 듣지 못했다는 의미이므로 Therefore(그러므로)가 적절하다.
6 한국의 중요한 명절로 추석과 설날을 예시로 들고 있으므로 For example(예를 들면)이 적절하다.
7 교통 체증이 있었지만, 시간에 맞춰 직장에 도착할 수 있었다는 의미이므로 However(그러나)가 적절하다.
8 모두 다음 2주간 휴가를 가기 때문에 그 결과 사무실이 비어 있을 것이라는 의미이므로 Therefore(그러므로)가 적절하다.
9 집을 청소해야 하고 추가적으로 빨래도 해야 한다는 내용이므로 In addition(게다가)이 적절하다.
10 몇 시간 전에 이메일을 보냈고, 답신을 기다리다가 마침내 지금 짧은 답신을 받았다는 의미이므로 Finally(결국)가 적절하다.

📝 Chapter Review Test 정답 본문 _ p.370

1 ① 2 ②,③ 3 Read many books and you will 4 ①,⑤ 5 Leave now, or you'll be late for work. 6 ② 7 because it was[we were] too cold 8 ④ 9 Although[Though] 10 ③ 11 ① 12 ③ 13 ③ 14 ④ 15 A good sleep is important for kids as well as adults. 16 both, and 17 ⑤ 18 ③ 19 When 20 ② 21 ② 22 ② 23 The third pig's house is so sturdy that I can't destroy it. 24 ④ 25 ③ 26 ④ 27 ④ 28 ④ 29 ⑤ 30 ④ 31 ④ 32 ② 33 ③ 34 ③ 35 that people tend to throw away the trash 36 ③ 37 ⑤ 38 ④ 39 ④ 40 ① 41 ④ 42 ⑤ 43 ④ 44 Water is one of the most unusual things as well as the most common substance on Earth. 45 ② 46 ③ 47 ④ 48 ③ 49 ①,④ 50 ⑤ 51 ③ 52 (1) He won his first FIFA World Player of the Year award when he was 23 years old. (2) He helped Portugal win the European Championship for the first time when he was 31 years old. 53 ④ 54 ④ 55 ③ 56 ⑤ 57 (1) the weather was so bad that I couldn't go on a picnic (2) the weather is so good that

I can go on a picnic 58 because → because of 59 ② 60 ② 61 ④

Chapter Review Test 해설

1 ① 지하철을 타라, 그러면 시간에 맞춰 거기 도착할 것이다.
   ② 열심히 일해라, 그렇지 않으면 성공하지 못할 것이다. (and → or)
   ③ 친구들을 사랑해라, 그러면 너는 사랑받을 것이다. (or → and)
   ④ 지금 출발해라, 그러면 버스를 탈 것이다. (or → and)
   ⑤ 연습해라, 그러면 대회에서 이길 것이다. (Don't practice → Practice)

2 ② 「so+부사+that+주어+can't」는 「too+부사+for+목적격+to부정사」로 바꾸어 쓸 수 있다. in order to는 '~하기 위해서'라는 뜻으로 목적을 나타낸다.
   = He runs too fast for me to catch him.
   ③ 「명령문+or」은 'If you don't ~'의 뜻을 나타낸다.
   = Unless you get up right now, you'll be late for work.

3 「명령문+and」 '~하라, 그러면 …'

4 크리스마스 카드를 받지 못해 실망했다고 했으므로 원인을 나타내는 접속사가 들어가야 한다.
   ① because '~때문에' ⑤ as '~때문에'

5 「명령문+or」 '~해라, 그렇지 않으면'

6 ② 지시형용사   ①④⑤ 명사절 접속사(목적어)
   ③ 목적격 관계대명사

7 너무 추워서 우리는 밖에 오래 있지 않았다.

8 ⓐ 「not only A but also B」 'A뿐만 아니라 B도'
   (not → not only)
   ⓑ 「neither A nor B」 'A도 B도 ~ 아닌'
   ⓒ 「B as well as A」 뒤에 오는 동사는 B에 수를 일치시켜야 한다. 따라서 3인칭 단수 현재형인 works로 고치는 것이 알맞다.
   ⓓ 「not only A but also B」 뒤에 오는 동사는 B에 수를 일치시켜야 한다. 따라서 복수인 my parents에 맞춰 복수형 동사로 고쳐야 한다.
   ⓔ 「B as well as A」 뒤에 오는 동사는 B의 수에 일치시킨다. 따라서, 복수 명사인 Jina's cousins에 맞춰 복수 동사가 나와야 한다. (are → 고칠 필요 없음)

9 although[though] '비록 ~일지라도'

10 롤러코스터를 타는 동안 사진을 찍었다는 의미이므로 동시동작을 나타내는 접속사 while을 써야 한다.

11 ① 관계대명사   ②③④⑤ 접속사

12 '열린 마음을 가진다면, 친구를 많이 만들 것이다.'라는 뜻이므로 조건을 나타내는 접속사 if를 써야 한다.

13 ③ 명사절 접속사 if '~인지 아닌지'
   ①②④⑤ 조건을 나타내는 if '~라면'
   ① 네가 그녀를 본다면 이 꽃을 그녀에게 줘.
   ② 네가 그에게 묻는다면 그는 너에게 진실을 말해줄 것이다.
   ③ 나는 내가 코트를 입어야 하는지 아닌지 궁금하다.
   ④ 당신의 이름을 남겨 주신다면, 우리는 당신께 최대한 빨리 전화 드리겠습니다.
   ⑤ 네가 잠시 앉아있는다면, 나는 네가 여기 있다고 그에게 말할 것이다.

14 • 음식이 싸고 맛있어서 식당이 인기가 있다는 의미이므로 원인을 나타내는 접속사 because를 써야 한다.
   • 저녁에 일찍 잠자리에 들면 아침에 일어나기 더 쉽다는 의미이므로 조건을 나타내는 접속사 if를 써야 한다.

15 「not only A but also B」 = 「B as well as A」
   'A뿐만 아니라 B도'

16 「both A and B」 'A와 B 둘 다'

17 신문을 보고 난 후, 아침을 먹었다고 했으므로 '~한 후에'의 의미인 after을 써야 한다.

18 ⓐ so 형용사 that … : 너무 ~해서 …한
   그 날은 너무 인기 있어서 스위트 룸은 예약이 꽉 찼습니다.
   ⓑ it이 가주어, that 이하가 진주어인 문장이다.
   제가 미리 예약하지 않은 것이 저의 실수입니다.

19 7살 때라는 특정 시점을 말하므로 '~할 때'라는 의미의 when을 써야 한다.

20 because 뒤에는 절이 오고, because of 뒤에는 명사(구)가 온다.

21 수미와 준호는 이번 시험이 더 쉬웠다고 했지만 나는 동의하지 않는다고 했으므로 대조적인 의미의 However을 써야 한다.

22 대부분의 친구들은 양식을 좋아하지만 Jack은 한식을 제일 좋아한다고 했으므로 '비록 ~일지라도'의 의미인 Although를 써야 한다.

23 '너무 ~해서 …할 수 없다'라는 표현은 괄호 안에 주어진 단어들에 so를 추가하여 「so+형용사+that+주어+can't+동사」 구조로 나타낼 수 있다. 이 표현은 늑대가 결국 벽돌집을 부수지 못했다는 결과를 의미한다.

24 ④ 의문부사 when '언제'
①②③⑤ 접속사 when '~할 때'
① 내가 어렸을 때, 나는 멕시코에 살았다.
② 내가 나의 딸을 보았을 때, 그녀는 내게 미소지었다.
③ 우리가 소풍을 갈 때, 너의 점심을 가져와라.
④ 그는 내게 언제 내가 책을 돌려줄 수 있는지 물었다.
⑤ 시간이 될 때, 내게 연락해라.

25 새로운 영화를 볼 기회를 가지고 싶어서 영화 동아리에 가입할 것이라고 했으므로 결과를 나타내는 접속사 so를 써야 한다.

26 is(be 동사)뒤 보어 자리에 절이 오므로, 명사절을 이끄는 접속사 that이 필요하다.

27 밑줄 친 As는 '~할 때'를 의미하는 접속사이다.
④ '~하고 있을 때' (접속사)
① '~로(서)' (전치사)
② '~만큼' (부사)
③ '~함에 따라' (접속사)
⑤ '~때문에' (접속사)

28 ④ so that ~ '~할 수 있도록'

29 Mr. Kim이 사람들을 돕는 것을 좋아한다고 했고, 그에 대한 예시를 들고 있으므로 '예를 들어'라는 뜻의 For example을 써야 한다.

30 ⓐ 콘서트에 갈 수 없는 원인이 나오므로 '~때문에'라는 의미를 가진 because가 나와야 한다.
① 'too+형용사+to부정사'는 '~하기에는 너무 …한'의 의미이다.
② 파티를 가게 돼서 기쁘다는 결과를 나타내는 절을 이끄므로, '그래서'라는 의미의 so가 나와야 한다.
③ '내가 어렸을 때'라는 시간을 의미하므로, '~할 때'라는 의미의 when이 쓰인다.
④ 배가 아픈 원인을 나타내는 절을 이끄므로, '~때문에'라는 의미를 가진 because가 나와야 한다.
⑤ '일찍 일어나지 않으면 기차 시간에 늦을 것이다'라는 의미의 문장이다. '~해라, 그렇지 않으면'의 의미는 '명령문+or'을 사용해 나타낸다.

31 ④ 접속사(~때) ①⑤ 의문부사(언제)
② 관계부사 ③ 의문사+to부정사(언제 ~할지)
[보기] 비가 내릴 때 꼭 창문을 닫아 두어라.
① 나는 언제 공연이 시작할지 모르겠다.
② 나는 우리가 단짝 친구가 되었던 날을 기억한다.
③ 언제 떠날지가 매우 중요하다.
④ 그녀가 집에 돌아왔을 때, 그녀는 피곤해 보였다.
⑤ 우리가 언제 만나야 하는지 내게 말해 줄래?

32 (A) 아침에 일어났을 때 몸이 좋지 않았지만 일에 갔다고 했으므로, 대조적인 의미의 but을 쓴다.
(B) 회사에서 회의가 취소되어 조금 쉴 수 있었다는 내용 뒤에 일에 집중할 수 없었다는 대조적인 내용이 이어지므로 '그러나'라는 뜻의 However을 쓴다.
(C) 일에 집중할 수 없었다는 내용에 더해 상사가 보고서의 오류 때문에 화가 났다고 했으므로, '게다가'라는 뜻의 In addition을 쓴다. Besides도 같은 뜻이다.

33 in the end = finally '결국, 마침내'

34 a. 피곤했기 때문에 어젯밤 일찍 잠자리에 든 것이므로 인과를 나타내는 접속사 Because를 써야 한다.
b. 아침을 먹지 않으면 공부에 집중할 수 없다는 의미이므로 빈칸에는 접속사 or(그렇지 않으면)가 적절하다. 「명령문+or …」: ~해라 그렇지 않으면 …할 것이다.
c. 감자를 오븐 안에 넣기 전에 오븐을 예열해야 하므로, 빈칸에는 접속사 before가 들어가는 것이 적절하다.
d. 내가 그곳에 가야 하는지 아닌지 모르겠다는 의미이므로 빈칸에는 접속사 if(~인지 아닌지)가 적절하다.

35 that이 이끄는 보어 역할을 하는 명사절이 온다.

36 '~에도 불구하고'의 의미이고, 구를 이끄는 전치사 despite가 들어가야 한다. 접속사 although는 뒤에 절이 온다.

37 시간을 나타내는 접속사가 쓰인 부사절에서는 현재시제가 미래시제를 대신한다.

38 ① • 누구인지를 묻는 의문사로 쓰였다.
• 관계대명사절에서 주어의 역할을 하고 있는 주격 관계대명사로 쓰였다.
② • 그녀는 차를 맛보면서 미소를 띠었다.
'~하고 있을 때, ~하면서'라는 뜻의 접속사로 쓰였다.
• 유명한 영화 배우로서, 그는 많은 팬을 가지고 있다.
'~로서'라는 뜻의 전치사로 쓰였다.
③ • 문장의 주어와 목적어가 같으므로 재귀대명사의

재귀 용법이 쓰였다.
　　• '직접'이라는 뜻을 강조해주기 위한 재귀대명사의 강조 용법으로 쓰였다.
　④ 두 문장에서 모두 목적어로 쓰인 명사절을 이끄는 접속사로 쓰였다
　⑤ • 동사 enjoy의 목적어로 쓰인 동명사이다.
　　• 분사구문으로 쓰인 현재분사이다.

39　어두워졌기 때문에 집에 갔다고 했으므로 결과를 나타내는 절을 이끄는 접속사 so를 쓴다. because는 원인을 나타내는 절을 이끈다.

40　소라는 공부를 열심히 하고 영어 대회에서 1등을 했다는 내용에, 그녀는 예의바르고 정직하다는 내용을 덧붙이고 있다. 따라서 '게다가'라는 뜻의 Besides가 들어가는 것이 알맞다.

41　John은 옷이 많지만 중고 거래로 옷을 사므로, 앞과 반대되는 내용을 나타내는 접속사 but과 함께 옷을 사는 데 돈을 많이 쓰지 않는다는 내용이 와야 한다.

42　'~ 인지 (아닌지)'라는 뜻의 if는 whether로 바꾸어 쓸 수 있다.
　　나는 그녀가 그것을 전부 다 직접 했는지, 아니면 누군가 그녀를 도와주었는지 물었다.

43　① 주어 자리에 'both A and B' 구문이 사용된 것으로 주격으로 써야 한다. (him → he)
　② 'both A and B' 구문이 주어로 사용된 경우 복수동사를 쓴다. (was → were)
　③ 'either A or B' 구문이 사용된 것으로 A와 B의 형태는 같아야 한다. (not eat → not to eat)
　④ 'neither A nor B' 구문이 주어로 온 것으로 수일치는 B에 시켜서 동사는 am이 적절하다.
　⑤ '둘 다 ~아닌'이란 의미를 지닌 상관접속사는 'neither A nor B'로 쓴다. (or → nor)

44　not only A but also B = B as well as A

45　「so+형용사/부사+that+주어+cannot(can't)…」은 '너무 ~해서 …할 수 없는' 이라는 뜻으로, 「too+형용사/부사+to부정사」로 바꾸어 쓸 수 있다.
　① so that은 '~하기 위해서'라는 뜻으로 목적을 나타낼 때 쓴다.
　③ 「형용사/부사+enough+to부정사」는 '~할 정도로 충분히 …한'이라는 의미이고 「so+형용사/부사+that+주어+can」으로 바꾸어 쓸 수 있다.
　④ in order to는 '~하기 위해서'라는 목적의 의미를 나타낼 때 쓴다.
　⑤ because는 원인을 나타내는 접속사이다. 따라서 'Because the number of homeless pets is so large, the shelters cannot house them all.' 이라고 해주어야 본문의 문장과 같은 뜻이 된다.

46　so ~ that … '너무 ~해서 …한'

47　• 무대에 서있는 동안 다리가 떨렸다는 의미가 되어야 하므로 '~하는 동안'을 의미하는 while이 들어가야 한다.
　• 노래를 마치고 난 뒤, 관객들이 큰 박수를 보냈다는 의미가 되어야 하므로 '~한 후에'라는 뜻의 after가 들어가야 한다.

48　• 최선을 다하면 기회를 잡을 수 있을 것이라는 의미가 되어야 하므로, 조건을 뜻하는 if가 알맞다.
　• 친구가 많이 없어서 외롭다는 내용이 되어야 하므로 원인을 나타내는 절을 이끄는 because가 들어가야 한다.

49　주어진 문장의 밑줄 친 As는 '~때문에'를 의미한다.
　네가 외출 중이었기 때문에, 나는 메시지를 남겼다.
　①④ '~ 때문에'　　② '~로(서)'
　③ '~처럼'　　　　⑤ '~하면서'
　① 그녀가 정직하지 않기 때문에, 그녀는 진실을 말하지 않을 것이다.
　② 내가 고등학교에 있었을 때, 나는 마술사의 조수로서 일을 시작했다.
　③ 10월 31일에, 미국 아이들은 유령과 괴물처럼 변장을 한다.
　④ 그가 늦게 일어났기 때문에, 그는 직장에 늦었다.
　⑤ 내 강아지는 방에 들어오면서 짖었다.

50　neither A nor B 'A도 B도 ~ 아닌'

51　「so+형용사/부사+that … 」은 '너무 ~해서 …한'의 뜻으로, 결과를 나타낼 때 쓴다. '나의 여자 조카가 너무 빨리 달려서 잡을 수 없었다.'는 뜻이므로 조동사는 couldn't를 쓴다.

52　과거의 사실을 쓰는 것이므로 시제를 과거로 하는 것에 주의한다.

53　①④ either A or B - B에 수 일치
　③ neither A nor B - B에 수 일치
　②⑤ both A and B - 복수 동사

54　「so+형용사+that+주어+can't[couldn't]」는 「too+형용사+to부정사」로 바꾸어 쓸 수 있다.
　This English book was so difficult that I couldn't read it.
　= This English book was too difficult for me to read.

① 읽기에 어렵지 않았다는 뜻으로 주어진 문장과 의미가 상반된다.
② it=This English book이다. 중복 언급이므로 it을 쓰지 않는다. (to read it → to read)
③ 「too+형용사+to부정사」가 의미상의 주어를 가질 때 for me to read라고 쓴다.
⑤ 주어진 문장 내의 시제가 모두 일치하므로 to부정사의 시제도 주절과 동일하게 맞추어 to read라고 써야한다. (to have read → to read)

55 해가 빛나고 있었음에도 불구하고, 아주 따뜻하지는 않았다.

56 70세임에도 매우 건강하다는 의미가 되어야 하므로 '비록 ~일지라도'의 의미인 Even though가 들어가는 것이 알맞다.

57 (1) 「so~that+주어+couldn't…」 '너무 ~해서 …할 수 없었다'
(2) 「so~that+주어+can…」 '매우 ~해서 …할 수 있다'

58 because 뒤에는 절이 오고, because of 뒤에는 명사(구)가 온다.

59 • 애완동물을 키우는 것의 장점에 대한 내용 뒤에 작은 애완동물이라도 많은 보살핌을 필요로 한다(손이 많이 간다)는 대조적인 내용이 이어지므로 '그러나'라는 뜻의 however가 들어가는 것이 알맞다.
• 애완동물을 입양하기 전에 신중하게 생각해봐야 한다는 내용이 되어야 하므로, '~전에'라는 뜻의 before를 써야 한다.

60 18개월까지는 건강한 아기였다는 내용이 되어야 하므로 '~까지'의 의미를 나타내는 until이 알맞다.

61 빈칸 다음에 주어와 동사가 나오므로 빈칸에는 접속사만 들어갈 수 있다.
④ 빈칸이 포함된 문장은 '사무실에서 일할 때 그것(스마트폰을 사용하느라 매우 늦게까지 깨어 있는 것)은 나를 졸리게 했다.'는 의미이므로 '~할 때'를 나타내는 접속사 when이 적절하다.
①⑤ and(그리고), but(그러나)는 빈칸에 들어가기에 의미상 어색하다.
② from은 전치사이므로 빈칸에 들어갈 수 없다.
③ for이 접속사로 쓰일 때는 '왜냐하면'을 의미한다. 그러나 빈칸에 들어가기에 의미상 어색하다.

CHAPTER 16 전치사
Prepositions

본문 _ p.382

PRACTICE 1

1	on	2	at	3	in
4	on	5	in	6	at
7	at	8	in	9	on
10	at	11	on	12	in
13	on	14	at	15	in

PRACTICE 2

| 1 | on | 2 | at | 3 | in |

4	on	5	at	6	in
7	at	8	on	9	in
10	on				

PRACTICE 3

1	① in ② on	2	① on ② ×
3	① at ② in	4	① at ② ×
5	① at ② on	6	① in ② ×
7	① at ② on	8	① on ② ×
9	① in ② on	10	① on ② in

> 1 ① in+월 ② on+날짜
> 2 ① on+요일 ② ×, 「every+요일」 형태의 부사구 앞에 전치사를 쓰지 않는다.
> 3 ① at+구체적인 시각 ② in the afternoon: 오후에
> *noon: 낮 12시
> 4 ① at night: 밤에 ② ×, last night(어젯밤)와 같은 부사구 앞에 전치사를 쓰지 않는다.
> 5 ① at Christmas: 크리스마스에 ② on Christmas Day: 크리스마스 날에
> 6 ① in the evening: 저녁에 ② ×, this evening(오늘 저녁)과 같은 부사구 앞에 전치사를 쓰지 않는다.
> 7 ① at night: 밤에 ② on+요일, on Friday night: 금요일 밤에
> 8 ① on+요일 ② ×, next Tuesday(다음 주 화요일)와 같은 부사구 앞에 전치사를 쓰지 않는다.
> 9 ① in the morning: 아침에 ② on+요일, on Sunday morning: 일요일 아침에
> 10 ① on+날짜 ② in+월

> 1 at+구체적인 시각
> 2 from: ~부터
> 3, 9 by: ~까지(기한), 동작이나 상태가 완료되는 시점을 강조하고 싶을 때 쓴다.
> 4 on+날짜
> 5, 12 until: ~까지(계속), 동작이나 상태가 한 시점까지 계속되는 것을 나타낼 때 쓴다.
> 6, 11 since: ~이래로, 주로 완료 시제와 함께 쓰인다.
> 7 in+연도
> 8 on+요일
> 10 at Christmas: 크리스마스에
> 13 in the morning: 아침에
> 14 from A to B: A로부터 B까지
> 15 on my birthday: 내 생일에

PRACTICE 4

1	since	2	from	3	from
4	since	5	from	6	since
7	from	8	since	9	since
10	from				

> 1, 4, 6, 8, 9 현재완료 시제가 쓰여 '~ 이래로' 과거에서 시작된 사건이 현재까지 계속 영향을 미치고 있다는 의미이므로 since (~이래로)가 적절하다.
> 2, 7, 10 동작이나 사건의 시작 시점을 나타내고 있으므로 from (~부터)이 적절하다.
> 3, 5 from A to B(A로부터 B까지) 구문이 쓰였다.

PRACTICE 5

1	until	2	by	3	until
4	by	5	until	6	by
7	by	8	until	9	by
10	by				

> 1, 3, 5, 8 until: ~까지(계속), 동작이나 상태가 한 시점까지 계속된다는 의미를 강조하고 싶을 때 쓴다.
> 2, 4, 6, 7, 9, 10 by: ~까지(기한), 동작이나 상태가 완료되는 시점을 강조해서 나타내고 싶을 때 쓴다.

PRACTICE 6

1	at	2	from	3	by
4	on	5	until	6	since
7	in	8	on	9	by
10	at	11	since	12	until
13	in	14	from	15	on

PRACTICE 7

1	before	2	after	3	before
4	after	5	before	6	after

PRACTICE 8

1 going out, he turned off the light
2 seeing a movie, Jessica and Inho had dinner
3 buying the oranges, Mom looked at them carefully
4 deciding what to do, I told him about it
5 eating food, Nick usually prays
6 reading the book, we discussed it together

PRACTICE 9

1	① for	② during
2	① during	② for
3	① during	② for
4	① for	② during
5	① for	② during
6	① for	② during
7	① during	② for
8	① during	② for
9	① for	② during
10	① for	② during

PRACTICE 10

1	after	2	during	3	for
4	before	5	before	6	for
7	after	8	Before	9	during
10	for				

PRACTICE 11

1	on	2	in	3	at
4	on	5	at	6	in
7	on	8	at	9	in

PRACTICE 12

1	in	2	on	3	at
4	on	5	in	6	at
7	on	8	at	9	in
10	on, in	11	in	12	at
13	on	14	on	15	at

PRACTICE 13

1	over	2	above	3	below
4	under	5	above	6	over
7	below	8	under		

PRACTICE 14

1	down	2	up	3	out of
4	into	5	up	6	out of
7	into	8	down		

PRACTICE 15

1	out of, down	2	below, above
3	up, under	4	over, out of
5	into, above	6	up, over
7	into, under	8	down, below

PRACTICE 16

1	across	2	along
3	through	4	around
5	through	6	across
7	around	8	along

PRACTICE 17

1	behind	2	in front of
3	by	4	in front of
5	by	6	behind
7	in front of	8	behind
9	by		

PRACTICE 18

1	in front of, along	2	through, behind
3	by, around	4	along, across
5	through, behind	6	by, in front of
7	around, behind	8	by, across

PRACTICE 19

1	between	2	among
3	among	4	between
5	among	6	between
7	between	8	among

PRACTICE 20

1	to	2	for	3	to
4	to	5	for	6	to
7	for	8	to	9	for
10	to				

PRACTICE 21

1	about	2	like	3	with
4	about	5	with	6	about
7	with	8	like	9	without
10	like				

PRACTICE 22

1	to	2	for	3	without
4	about	5	among	6	with
7	like	8	between		

> 1 to: '~로, ~에'란 뜻으로, go, come과 함께 도착지를 나타낸다.
> 2 for: '~로, ~을 향하여'란 뜻으로, start, leave와 함께 목적지를 나타낸다.
> 3 without: ~없이
> 4 about: ~에 대하여
> 5 among: ~(셋 이상) 사이에
> 6 with: ~을 가진
> 7 like: ~처럼
> 8 between: ~(둘) 사이에

PRACTICE 23

1	as	2	by	3	in
4	by	5	by	6	as
7	in	8	by	9	in

10	by	11	in	12	by
13	by	14	as		

> 1 식당에서 매니저로 일한다는 의미이므로 자격을 나타내는 전치사 as(~로서)가 적절하다.
> 2, 13 수동태 문장에서 행위자를 나타내므로 by(~에 의해)가 적절하다.
> 3 빵을 세 조각으로 잘랐다는 의미이므로 크기를 나타내는 in(~로)가 적절하다. in three pieces(세 조각으로)
> 4, 10 by ~ing: ~함으로써
> 5 키가 3 cm 차이가 난다는 의미이므로 정도를 나타내는 by(~만큼)가 적절하다.
> 6 think of A as B: A를 B라고 생각하다
> 7 연필로 먼저 스케치를 했다는 뜻이므로 방법을 나타내는 in(~로)이 적절하다.
> 8 by+교통수단
> 9 in: ~을 입고 있는
> 11 수업에서 한국어로 말해야 한다는 의미이므로 방법을 나타내는 in(~로)이 적절하다.
> 12 그것을 팩스로 보내줄 수 있는지 묻고 있으므로 방법을 나타내는 by(~로)가 적절하다.
> 14 소파는 또한 여분의 침대로도 쓰일 수 있다는 의미이므로 as(~로서)가 적절하다.

PRACTICE 24

1	at	2	of	3	in
4	of	5	about	6	of
7	at	8	of	9	of
10	for	11	of	12	to

PRACTICE 25

1	of	2	for	3	to
4	of	5	in	6	to
7	of	8	for	9	of
10	for	11	of	12	at
13	for	14	in	15	about
16	into[across]	17	in		

PRACTICE 26

1	for	2	for	3	on
4	below	5	at	6	at
7	on	8	at	9	in
10	above	11	on	12	to
13	of	14	in	15	from
16	in	17	for	18	about
19	of	20	around	21	in
22	for	23	in	24	between
25	like	26	under	27	before
28	to	29	during	30	up

31	by	32	down	33	of
34	with	35	in	36	After
37	in	38	along	39	from
40	until	41	on	42	in
43	since	44	through	45	into
46	by	47	of	48	out of
49	behind	50	for		

> 1, 22 for+시간의 길이를 나타내는 명사구, for five days(5일 동안) for 3 months(3달 동안)
> 2 Thank you for ~ing: ~에 대해 감사하다, invite A to dinner (A를 저녁식사에 초대하다)
> 3, 7 on: (위)에
> 4 below: (~보다) 아래에
> 5 at Christmas: 크리스마스에
> 6 be poor at: ~을 잘 못하다, look after(~를 돌보다)
> 8 be good at: ~에 능숙하다
> 9 be interested in: ~에 관심이 있다
> 10 above: (~보다) 위에
> 11 on+요일
> 12 return to: ~로 돌아가다
> 13 be proud of: ~을 자랑스러워하다
> 14 in: ~을 입고 있는, in white: 흰색 옷을 입고 있는
> 15 from A to B: A부터 B까지
> 16 in+연도
> 17 wait for: ~을 기다리다
> 18 think about ~ing: ~에 대해 생각하다, 고려하다
> 19 consist of: ~로 구성되다
> 20 around: ~ 주위에
> 21 in the evening: 저녁에
> 23 in English: 영어로
> 24 between A and B: A와 B 사이에
> 25 look like: ~처럼 보이다
> 26 under: ~ 아래에
> 27 before: ~ 전에
> 28 belong to: ~에 속하다
> 29 during+특정 기간을 나타내는 명사구, during the holiday (연휴 동안)
> 30 더 높이 올라가기 위해서 언덕 위로 올라갔다는 의미이므로 up이 적절하다, climb up the hill(언덕 위로 올라가다), climb down the hill(언덕 아래로 내려가다)
> 31 by: (늦어도) ~까지는[쯤에는]
> 32 run down the stairs: 계단을 뛰어내려가다
> 33 die of hunger: 굶어 죽다, die의 진행형은 dying임에 유의한다.
> 34 with: ~(으)로, ~을 사용하여
> 35 in+비교적 넓은 장소: ~에
> 36 After: ~ 후에
> 37 in the sky: 하늘을, 하늘에서
> 38 stand along the white line: 흰 선을 따라 줄을 서다
> 39 be made from: ~로 만들어지다. 와인은 포도주로 만들어진다는 의미인데, 재료의 형태를 알아볼 수 없을 때는 전치사 from을 사용한다.
> 40 until: ~까지(동작, 상태가 한 시점까지 계속될 때)
> 41 plane 앞에 부정관사(a)가 있으므로 on을 써야 한다. 교통수단 중 plane, train, bus, boat는 전치사 on과 함께 쓴다.
> 42 taxi 앞에 부정관사(a)가 있으므로 in을 써야 한다. 교통수단 중 taxi, car, truck은 전치사 in과 함께 쓴다.
> 43 since: ~ 이래로(주로 완료시제와 함께 사용)

44 through: ~을 통과하여
45 into: ~ 안으로
46 by <정도>: ~로, ~만큼
47 become full of: ~로 가득 차게 되다
48 out of: ~ 밖으로
49 behind: ~ 뒤에
50 동사 leave와 함께 목적지 앞에는 전치사 for를 쓴다.

📖 Chapter Review Test 정답 본문 _ p.410

1 ③ 2 ① 3 similar to mine 4 On his[the] way home 5 ⑤ 6 across[into] 7 ③ 8 ②
9 ① 10 is made of 11 ⑤ 12 by 13 for, to 14 (A) while (B) to (C) which 15 ④
16 (1) for (2) while (3) during 17 ① 18 like
19 ② 20 ② 21 ③,④ 22 ⑤ 23 ②
24 (1) ⓐ Don't wait until they speak to you.
(2) ⓓ Listen to what they say. 25 ①
26 believe in yourself 27 ③ 28 (1) on
(2) after (3) with (4) in 29 ② 30 ④ 31 ⑤
32 ① 33 ① 34 (1) to (2) out of (3) in
(4) with (5) about 35 ⑤ 36 ② 37 ⑤
38 ③ 39 ⑤ 40 ② 41 ④ 42 ② 43 ①
44 ① 45 ② 46 for 47 ⑤ 48 ⑤ 49 ③
50 ② 51 ④ 52 out of 53 ② 54 ②
55 ② 56 ①,④ 57 with 58 I'm very poor at cooking. 59 (1) The bear is on the ball.
(2) The elephant is in the box. (3) The tiger is under the chair. 60 ③ 61 ① 62 ⑤
63 ③ 64 ③ 65 ① 66 A woman wearing glasses sat between two men on the subway. 67 ③ 68 ④ 69 ① 70 ⑤

Chapter Review Test 해설

1 날짜나 요일 앞에는 on을 쓴다.
2 표면에 접촉해 있는 것을 나타낼 때는 on을 쓴다.
3 be similar to '~와 비슷하다'
4 on one's[the] way (to) ~ '~로 가는 길에'
5 • put ~ into … '~을 …안으로 넣다'
• move into ~ '~로 이사하다'
6 run across[into] '우연히 마주치다'
7 • 이유를 나타내는 의문부사 why가 온다.
• die of '~로 죽다'

8 ⓐ at that time '그 당시에'
ⓑ 날짜나 요일 앞에는 전치사 on이 온다.
ⓒ 집 안에서 일어나는 일이므로 전치사 in이 적절하다.
9 ⓐ '그녀는 그녀의 모국어로서 영어를 말한다'는 의미이므로, '~로서'라는 의미를 가진 전치사 as를 쓰는 것이 적절하다. (in → as)
ⓑ '우리는 호랑이와 곰과 같은 야생 동물을 보호해야 한다'는 의미이므로, '~와 같은'의 의미를 가진 전치사 like를 쓰는 것이 적절하다. (as → like)
10 be made of '~로 만들어지다'
cf. be made from은 화학적 변화를 거쳐 만들어질 때 쓴다.
11 • be good at '~을 잘하다'
• 사진이 액자 안에 끼워지지 않는다는 문장이므로 공간을 나타내는 전치사 in을 쓴다.
12 • by email '이메일로' – 방법을 나타내는 by
• by one run '1점 차로' – 정도를 나타내는 by
• directed by '~에 의해 연출된' – '~에 의해'라는 뜻의 by
13 • for는 leave 동사와 함께 방향을 나타낸다.
• to는 go 동사와 함께 도착지 앞에 쓴다.
14 (A) '~하는 동안, ~하면서'라는 의미의 접속사 while
(B) 4형식 문장을 3형식으로 전환할 때, 동사가 write이면 간접목적어 앞에 to가 쓰인다.
(C) 선행사 the Manhattan Project를 수식하는 관계대명사 which
15 • prefer A to B 'B보다 A를 더 좋아하다'
• at the airport '공항에'
16 (1) 시간의 길이를 나타내는 명사구 앞에는 for를 쓴다.
(2) 빈칸 뒤에 절이 나오므로 접속사 while을 쓴다.
(3) 특정 기간을 나타내는 명사구 앞에는 during을 쓴다.
17 • take A to B 'A를 B에 데려가다'
• about '~에 대해'
18 like '~처럼'
19 방법을 나타내는 전치사 in이 들어가야 한다.
• in a car '차를 타고'   • in English '영어로'
20 ② talk on the phone '전화로 이야기하다'
(of → on)
21 ③④ '~이래로'   ①②⑤ '~때문에'
22 ⑤ about '~에 대한'

23 ② in '<크기> ~로'

24 (1) ⓐ 시간과 조건을 나타내는 부사절에서는 현재시제가 미래시제를 대신한다.
(will speak → speak)
(2) ⓓ listen to '~을 듣다' (at → to)

25 ① by '~에 의해', '<시간> ~까지', '~함으로써'

26 '~을 믿다'라는 의미의 구동사 'believe in'을 사용한다. 또한 주어와 목적어가 같으므로 재귀대명사 yourself를 써야 한다.

27 tired of '~에 싫증난, 지겨운'

28 (1) on '~(위)에'
(2) after work '퇴근 후에'
(3) be wrong with '~이 잘못되다, 이상하다'
(4) in English '영어로'

29 like는 동사로 '~을 좋아하다'라는 뜻, 전치사로는 '~ 같은'이라는 뜻을 가진다.

30 ① 명사구의 앞에 쓰였으므로 전치사 because of를 써준다. because는 접속사이므로 뒤에 절이 와야 한다. (because → because of)
② 6 o'clock은 구체적인 시각이므로, 전치사 at을 쓴다. (on → at)
③ Canada는 비교적 넓은 장소이므로, 전치사 in을 사용한다. (at → in)
④ Saturday와 같은 요일 앞에는 전치사 on이 쓰인다.
⑤ enjoy는 목적어로 동명사를 쓰는 동사이다. (to dance → dancing)

31 • with '~을 가진', '~와 함께'

32 • similar to '~와 비슷한'
• laugh at '~을 비웃다'
• take pride in '~에 자부심을 가지다'
• consist of '~로 구성되다'
• be good at '~을 잘하다'

33 • from A to B 'A부터 B까지'
• be full of '~로 가득차다'

34 (1) from A to B 'A부터 B까지'
(2) out of '~밖으로'
(3) 비교적 넓은 장소 앞에는 in을 쓴다.
(4) with '~을 사용하여'
(5) about '~에 대하여'

35 • at first '처음에는'
• wait for '~를 기다리다'
• to one's surprise '놀랍게도, 뜻밖에도'

36 • start for '~로 출발하다'

• thank A for B 'A에게 B에 대해 감사하다'

37 특정 기간을 나타내는 명사구 앞에는 during(~동안)을 쓴다.

38 • most of '대부분의'
• be interested in '~에 관심이 있다'

39 start with '~부터[로] 시작하다'

40 ② without '~하지 않고, ~없이'

41 ① next to는 '~ 옆에'라는 뜻이다. 박물관은 은행이 아니라 학교 옆에 있다. (bank → school)
② across는 '~을 가로질러'라는 의미로, across from으로 쓰면 '~의 건너편에'라는 의미이다. 경찰서는 신발 가게가 아닌, 병원의 건너편에 있다. (shoe store → hospital)
③ '영화관을 찾으려면 두 블록을 똑바로 걸어가서 오른쪽으로 돌아라.'는 뜻이다. 영화관은 두 블록을 걸어가서 왼쪽으로 돌아야 한다. (turn right → turn left)
④ '한 블록을 똑바로 걸어가서 왼쪽으로 돌아라. 오른편에 학교가 보일 것이다'라는 뜻이다.
⑤ '한 블록을 똑바로 걸어가서 오른쪽으로 돌아라. 그러면 오른편에 병원을 볼 수 있다'라는 뜻이다. 한 블록을 걸어가서 오른쪽으로 돌면, 오른편이 아닌 왼편에 병원이 있다. (on your right → on your left)

42 ⓑⓒ 전치사 '~와 같은', '~처럼'
ⓐⓓⓔ 동사 '좋아하다'

43 • from now on '지금부터'
• on Sunday evening '일요일 저녁에'

44 정오까지 잠을 자는 상태가 계속되므로 '~까지'라는 의미의 until을 써야 한다.

45 • with '~을 가지고 있는'
• through '~을 통해'
• belong to '~의 소유이다'

46 단어를 배열하면 because she waited for her friend for an hour가 된다.

47 by '<시간> ~까지', '~옆에'

48 ⑤ '~동안' ①② '~에게' ③④ '~을 위해, 위한'

49 in은 비교적 넓은 장소 앞에, at은 비교적 좁은 장소 앞에 쓰인다.

50 • on time '제시간에'   • on foot '걸어서'

51 • at – 비교적 좁은 장소를 나타낼 때 쓴다.
• into '~안으로'

52 take A out of B 'B에서 A를 꺼내다'

53 in '~안에' under '~아래에'

54 날짜나 요일 앞에는 전치사 on을 쓰므로, 첫째 줄 Sunday 앞의 전치사 at을 on으로 고쳐야 한다. (at → on)
   made by(~에 의해 만들어진) 뒤에는 만든 주체가 나오고, made of(~로 만들어진) 뒤에는 성분이 나온다. 따라서 밑에서 셋째 줄의 made by는 made of로 고쳐야 한다. (by → of)
55 ② '~을 입고' ①⑤ '~(안)에' ③④ 시간을 나타내는 in
56 ① The box was too heavy for me to carry. = The box was so heavy that I couldn't carry it.
   ② could는 '할 수 있다'는 의미의 'be able to'의 과거형 'was/were able to'와 바꾸어 쓸 수 있다.
   ③ used to는 '(과거에) ~하곤 했다'는 의미를 나타내는 조동사이다. 따라서 과거에는 여기 백화점이 있었지만 지금은 없다'는 의미의 문장은 적절하다.
   ④ The jar was filled with apple jam.= The jar was full of apple jam.
   ⑤ 'be proud of'는 '~을 자랑스러워하다'라는 뜻의 관용표현이다. 'take pride in'은 '~에 자부심을 갖다'라는 뜻의 관용표현이다.
57 • with '~의 몸에 지니고'
   • with '~와 함께'
58 be poor at: ~을 못하다, ~에 서툴다
59 (1) on '~ (표면) 위에'   (2) in '~ 안에'
   (3) under '~ 아래에'
60 ③ as '~로서'
61 be in trouble '곤란한 처지에 있다'
62 be proud of = take pride in '~을 자랑스러워 하다'
63 from '~로부터' on a trip '여행 중인'
64 (A) 작년에는 홍수 때문에 학교에 갈 수 없어 슬펐지만, 올해는 다르다는 대조적인 의미이다. 따라서 '그러나'라는 의미의 접속부사 however을 쓴다.
   (B) 빈칸 뒤에 동명사구 going to school이 뒤따라오므로, 동명사를 목적어로 가지는 전치사 instead of를 쓴다. 해석은 '~대신에'로 한다. instead는 부사이다.
   (C) to는 go, come, return 동사와 함께 도착지를 나타낼 때 쓰인다.
65 네 에세이의 마감일이 언제니? = ① 네 에세이는 언제까지 제출되어야 하니?
   due '(언제) ~하기로 되어 있는(예정된)'
66 안경을 쓴 여자가 지하철에서 두 남자 사이에 앉았다.

between '~ 사이에'
67 ③ between은 '(둘) 사이에'라는 뜻으로, 두 개의 사물 또는 사람을 나타내는 말 앞에서 쓰인다. 여기에서는 많은 사람들이 있었다고 했으므로, 셋 이상의 사물 또는 사람 사이를 나타내는 말인 among을 쓰는 것이 적절하다. (between → among)
68 ④ by는 교통수단을 나타내는 말과 함께 쓰여, '~를 타고'라는 뜻을 나타낸다.
   ① by는 시간을 나타내는 말과 함께 쓰여, '~까지'를 의미하며 동작이나 상태가 완료되는 시점을 나타낸다.
   ② by는 수동태와 함께 쓰여 행위자를 나타내며, '~에 의해'라는 뜻을 나타낸다.
   ③ by는 방법을 나타내는데 쓰이고, 해석은 '~로'로 한다.
   ④ '걸어서'라는 뜻은 전치사 on을 활용해 on foot으로 쓴다.
   ⑤ by는 동명사와 함께 쓰여, '~함으로써, ~하며'라는 의미를 나타낸다.
69 ① prison은 in과 함께 쓰이는 명사이다.
   ② a party는 at과 함께 쓰이는 명사이다.
   ③ a garage sale은 at과 함께 쓰이는 명사구이다.
   ④ an airport는 at과 함께 쓰이는 명사이다.
   ⑤ the end of this year은 at과 함께 쓰이는 명사구이다.
70 ① 수동태 문장으로 만들 때는, 목적어를 수동태 문장의 주어로 하여, 동사는 be동사+과거분사의 형태로 바꾼다. 능동태 문장의 주어는 by+목적격으로 바꾼다.
   ② by는 교통수단을 나타내는 말과 함께 쓰여, '~를 타고'라는 뜻을 나타낸다. 'take+교통수단'은 '~를 타다'라는 뜻이다.
   ③ 'seem+to be ~'와 'It seems like+주어+동사'는 '~처럼 보인다'는 뜻으로 서로 바꾸어 쓸 수 있다. 전치사 in은 '~를 입고 있는'이라는 뜻을 나타낸다.
   ④ 전치사 by는 'lost/win the game by+점수'의 형태로 '~점 차로 경기에 지다/이기다'라는 뜻을 나타낸다.
   ⑤ by+동명사는 '~함으로써(수단)'라는 뜻을 나타낸다. as는 '~로서(자격)'라는 뜻이다. 따라서, '~을 사용하여, ~으로'라는 뜻으로 쓸 수 있는 전치사 with로 바꾸는 것이 적절하다. (as → with)

CHAPTER 17 일치·도치·화법 & 속담
Agreement·Inversion·Narration & Proverbs

본문 _ p.424

PRACTICE 1

1. the subway was extremely crowded
2. he will get better
3. there were many fancy restaurants on this street
4. Everyone says
5. my son might be late for school on the first day

PRACTICE 2

1. Columbus discovered America in 1492
2. he always goes to school on foot
3. the trains leave every 20 minutes
4. water boils at 100℃ and freezes at 0℃
5. nothing is impossible to a willing heart
6. one and one makes two

PRACTICE 3

1. Here are the pepperoni pizzas
2. There goes the last train
3. Here they are
4. How come you got invited
5. There have been several snowstorms
6. how come her Chinese is
7. Have you been
8. Who did you see

PRACTICE 4

1. Behind the clouds is the sun still shining.
2. Never did he attend the meeting.
3. Little did Charlie understand about the situation.
4. On the hill was a beautiful tree.
5. Never have I seen such a disaster.

> 1, 4 장소나 방향을 나타내는 부사구(behind the clouds, on the hill)가 문장 맨 앞에 올 경우, 주어 동사가 도치되어 「부사구+동사+주어」 순으로 써야 한다.
> 2, 3, 5 부정어(never, little)가 문장 맨 앞에 올 경우, 「부정어+조동사+주어+동사」 순서로 써야 한다. 조동사 없이 일반동사가 쓰였을 경우, 조동사 do를 시제에 맞추어 쓴다.
> * little: 거의 ~않는

PRACTICE 5

1. he knew, that
2. her, might not be, then
3. told, was going to learn
4. told, was, that day
5. he would, the next day[the following day]

PRACTICE 6

1. My younger brother said, "The computer game is too difficult for me to play."
2. The man told her (that) it would take about two hours from then.
3. The boy said (that) he didn't want to eat those carrots.
4. The chairman said to the members, "The money is raised by donations."
5. Father said (that) it would be nice to visit there again the next[following] summer.

PRACTICE 7

1. Kevin asked her if[whether] he might use her dictionary.
2. Mom asked who was calling.
3. The coach asked us what our hopes for that year were.[The coach asked us what our hopes were for that year.]
4. He asked Jane when she usually watched TV.
5. He asked me if[whether] I was for or against dieting.
6. Andy asked me if[whether] I knew how to make a movie clip on my phone.
7. The man asked her if[whether] she could say that again.
8. The gentleman asked the boy what made him think so.
9. I asked James if[whether] he could lend me his bike.
10. Bob asked where he could get the ticket.

PRACTICE 8

1 She advised her neighbor to look on the bright side.
2 Tom told me to bring him a chair.
3 Jim told me to tell him when her birthday was.
4 The police officer ordered him not to move.
5 Mom asked me to pass her the salt.
6 The doctor advised me not to eat too much junk food.
7 Patrick ordered his son to wear a helmet on the bike.
8 Mr. Anderson told us not to be late.

PRACTICE 9

1 mightier than
2 comes a calm
3 Strike, hot
4 Out of, into
5 in need, indeed
6 thicker than
7 speak louder
8 A watched pot
9 a will, a way
10 gathers no moss
11 is worth
12 Better late, never
13 Haste, waste
14 who laughs last
15 before they are hatched

Chapter Review Test 정답 본문 _ p.436

1 ③ 2 ④ 3 ⑤ 4 ①,③ 5 ⑤ 6 ⑤ 7 ①
8 ③ 9 I knew the guy 10 (1) did I see a boring movie like this (2) stood a pretty girl (3) could he ride his bike 11 think → thought
12 ③ 13 ② 14 not to, my 15 ②
16 (1) what I was going (2) he would go to Canada 17 Deborah asked Davis to buy that necklace for her. 18 ③ 19 ② 20 ②,⑤
21 (1) said to (2) said to, Don't (3) said to, Have
22 Jane asked him if[whether] he had enough money. 23 ④ 24 Never has he had any training on the cello. 25 ③

Chapter Review Test 해설

1 주절의 동사 said가 과거로 쓰였으므로 시제 일치 조건에 따라 종속절의 시제도 과거로 바꿔주어야 한다.

2 의문사 뒤의 어순을 「주어＋동사」로 바꾸고 주어를 전달자의 입장에 맞게 I로 바꾼다. 전달 동사의 시제가 과거이므로 의문사절의 시제도 과거로 바꿔야 한다.

3 전달 동사는 said이므로 그대로 두고, 인칭대명사를 전달하는 사람의 입장에 맞게 바꾸며, 주절의 시제와 종속절의 시제를 일치시킨다.

4 ① How come은 '왜?'라는 의미로 의문문에서 사용된다. 하지만 의문문임에도 how come 뒤의 어순은 평서문과 같이 「주어＋동사」로 써 준다.
(did you visit → you visited)
③ 부정어구가 도치될 때는 「부정어＋조동사＋주어＋동사」의 어순으로 도치된다.
(Hardly I met → Hardly did I meet)

5 장군이 군인들에게 명령하는 내용이므로 전달 동사로 order를 쓰고 명령문의 내용은 order의 목적격 보어이므로 to부정사로 바꾼다.

6 전달 동사의 시제가 과거이므로 현재 진행형을 과거 진행형으로 바꾸고, 인칭 대명사를 전달자의 입장에 맞게 바꿔준다.

7 시간이 많이 걸리는 일을 함께 해서 시간을 절약하자는 내용이므로 '백지장도 맞들면 낫다.'라는 뜻의 Many hands make light work.가 적절하다.

8 날 수 없는 거위가 끊임없는 노력과 긍정적인 생각으로 결국 날 수 있게 되었다는 내용이므로 '뜻이 있는 곳에 길이 있다.'라는 뜻의 Where there is a will, there is a way.가 적절하다.

9 의문사 뒤의 어순을 「주어＋동사」로 바꾸고 주어를 전달자의 입장에 맞게 I로 바꾼다. 전달 동사의 시제가 과거이므로 의문사절의 시제도 과거로 바꿔야 한다.

10 (1), (3) 부정어구가 도치될 때는 「부정어＋조동사＋주어＋동사」의 어순으로 써준다.
(2) 장소나 방향을 나타내는 부사(구)가 도치될 때는 「부사구＋동사＋주어」의 어순으로 써준다.

11 주절의 동사가 과거이므로 시제 일치 조건에 따라 종속절의 시제도 과거로 바꿔주어야 한다.

12 의문문의 전달 동사는 asked로 바꾸고, 의문사가 없기 때문에 if[whether]로 문장을 연결한다. 인칭 대명사는 전달자가 I이므로 그대로 두고, 시제는 과거시제로, 부사구 here는 there로 바꾼다.

13 도로에서 자전거를 타는 것에 여러 번 위험을 느낀 Emily가 필요에 의해서 보호 장치를 발명했다는 내용이므로 '필요는 발명의 어머니이다.'라는 뜻의 Necessity is the mother of invention.이 적절하다.

14 부정 명령문이므로 not to를, 인칭대명사는 전달하는 사람의 입장으로 고쳐야 하므로 my를 쓴다.

15 (a) 부정어(Rarely)가 문장의 맨 앞으로 나오면, 「부정어(Rarely)+조동사(does)+주어(Wendy)+동사(offer)」의 어순으로 도치된다.
(b) 장소를 나타내는 부사구(In the parking lot)가 앞으로 나오면, 「부사구+동사+주어」의 어순으로 도치된다.
(c) 주어 people이 복수명사이므로 동사도 복수인 are로 써주어야 한다. (is → are)
(d) 장소를 나타내는 부사구(Under the bridge)가 문장의 앞으로 나오면, 「부사구+동사+주어」의 어순으로 도치된다. (does the stream flow → flows the stream)
(e) Here이 문장의 앞으로 나오면, 「Here+동사+주어」의 어순으로 도치된다.

16 (1) 의문사가 있는 의문문의 간접화법은 「주어+ask+목적어+의문사+주어+동사」로 쓴다.
(2) 평서문의 간접화법에서 간접화법 부분의 시제는 주절의 시제에 일치시킨다.

17 please가 쓰인 명령문은 간접화법으로 고칠 때 '부탁하다'의 ask를 써서 「ask+목적어+to부정사」로 표현한다.

18 「ask+목적어+to부정사」는 '~에게 …해달라고 부탁하다'라는 뜻이고, help는 준사역동사로 목적격보어 자리에 동사원형과 to부정사가 올 수 있다.

19 그 모임에서 Tim을 만난 지 10년이 흘렀다는 게 믿기지 않고 어제 서로 본 것 같다고 하였으므로 '시간은 쏜살같이 지나간다.'는 의미의 time flies like an arrow가 알맞다.

20 ① '내가 너에게 말한 것을 듣지 못했니?'라고 묻고 있으므로 선행사를 포함한 관계대명사 what(~하는 것)의 쓰임은 적절하다.
② to부정사의 부정형은 「not to+동사원형」의 어순으로 쓴다. (to not → not to)
③ '같이 농구를 하기 위해서'라는 목적을 나타내는 to부정사의 부사적 용법으로 알맞게 쓰였다.
④ 목적격 명사절을 이끄는 접속사 that이 적절하게 쓰였다.
⑤ 주절의 동사가 said로 과거시제이므로, 종속절의 시제도 과거나 과거완료를 써야 한다. will의 과거형인 would로 고쳐야 한다. (will → would)

21 (1) tell을 say to로 바꾸고 시제를 과거로 일치시킨다.
(2) tell을 say to로 바꾸고 과거형으로 시제를 일치시킨 뒤 부정명령문이므로 Don't를 쓴다.
(3) ask를 say to로 바꾸어 과거시제로 일치시킨 뒤 의문사가 없는 의문문이므로 Have를 쓴다.

22 의문사가 없는 의문문에서 if[whether]는 '~인지 아닌지'의 뜻을 갖는다.

23 ④ 모든 구름의 뒷편은 은빛으로 빛난다. (괴로움 뒤에는 기쁨이 있다.)

24 부정어구가 도치될 때는 「부정어+조동사+주어+동사」의 어순으로 써준다.

25 ③ 부정어가 문장의 맨 앞으로 나오면, 「부정어+조동사+주어+동사원형」의 어순으로 도치된다. 동사가 과거형이므로, 과거시제를 만들어주는 조동사 did를 주어 I의 앞에 써야 한다. (I did → did I)
①⑤ 부정어가 문장의 맨 앞으로 나오면, 「부정어+조동사+주어+동사」의 어순으로 도치된다.
②④ 장소를 나타내는 부사(구)가 문장의 맨 앞으로 나오면, 「부사구+동사+주어」의 어순으로 도치된다. 단, 주어가 대명사일 경우에는 주어와 동사의 순서가 바뀌지 않는다.

탄탄한 영어 실력을 위한 영문법의 시작

토익·토플
TEPS
공무원영어
대비

마더텅 영문법 3800제
단어·표현 암기장

INTERMEDIATE 2

마더텅 영문법 3800제 단어·표현 암기장 활용법

1. 마더텅 영문법 3800제 단어·표현 암기장은 한 달 학습 계획(총 31일)으로 구성되어 있습니다.
2. 오늘 외울 단어를 원어민 녹음 MP3파일을 활용하여 암기합니다.
3. 세트로 구성된 Word Test를 스스로 풀어 본 후 단어·표현 암기장을 확인하며 채점합니다.
   (정답표가 필요하신 경우 마더텅 홈페이지를 통해 다운로드 받으실 수 있습니다.
   www.toptutor.co.kr)
4. [오늘 외울 단어]로 제공되는 단어들은 마더텅 영문법 3800제 본문에서 선정된
   필수 암기 영단어입니다.
5. 교재와 함께 시작하여 매일 학습 단어를 암기해 나가면, 한 달(31일)이면 주요 단어를 모두
   학습할 수 있습니다.

마더텅 영문법 3800제 2
INTERMEDIATE
단어·표현 암기장
Problem Solving Skill

마더텅

Day 01

오늘 외울 단어 **35**개

Chapter 1 문장의 기초

PSS & PRACTICE

- 001 **finish** [fíniʃ] 동 끝내다, 끝나다
- 002 **homework** [hóumwə̀ːrk] 명 숙제
- 003 **on time** 시간에 맞게, 정각에
- 004 **pass** [pæs] 동 통과하다, 지나가다
- 005 **exam** [igzǽm] 명 시험
- 006 **draw** [drɔː] 동 그리다, 당기다
- 007 **true** [truː] 형 진실인, 사실인
- 008 **classmate** [klǽsmèit] 명 동급생, 반 친구
- 009 **win** [win] 동 이기다
- 010 **race** [reis] 명 경주
- 011 **feel** [fiːl] 동 (~하다고) 느끼다, (~한) 기분이다
- 012 **during** [djúriŋ] 전 ~ 동안에
- 013 **meeting** [míːtiŋ] 명 회의
- 014 **be good at** ~을 잘하다
- 015 **arrive** [əráiv] 동 도착하다
- 016 **vacation** [veikéiʃən] 명 방학, 휴가
- 017 **exercise** [éksərsàiz] 동 운동하다 명 운동, 연습
- 018 **favorite** [féivərit] 형 가장 좋아하는
- 019 **leave** [liːv] 동 떠나다
- 020 **return** [ritə́ːrn] 동 돌아오다
- 021 **without** [wiðáut] 전 ~ 없이
- 022 **taste** [teist] 동 (~한) 맛이 나다, 맛보다
- 023 **prize** [praiz] 명 상
- 024 **guy** [gai] 명 사람, 녀석
- 025 **enter** [éntər] 동 ~에 들어가다
- 026 **take a rest** 휴식을 취하다
- 027 **puppy** [pʌ́pi] 명 강아지
- 028 **healthy** [hélθi] 형 건강한
- 029 **go for a movie** 영화를 보러 가다
- 030 **pay** [pei] 동 지불하다
- 031 **cash** [kæʃ] 명 현금, 돈
- 032 **credit card** [krédit kàːrd] 명 신용카드
- 033 **steak** [steik] 명 스테이크
- 034 **buy** [bai] 동 사다, 구입하다
- 035 **noodle** [núːdl] 명 국수, 면류

Day 02

오늘 외울 단어 **36개**

- ☐ 036 **wonder** [wʌ́ndər] 동 궁금해하다, ~이 아닐까 생각하다
- ☐ 037 **mean** [miːn] 동 의미하다, 의도하다
- ☐ 038 **important** [impɔ́ːrtnt] 형 중요한
- ☐ 039 **break** [breik] 동 깨뜨리다, 부수다
- ☐ 040 **date** [deit] 동 데이트하다 명 날짜
- ☐ 041 **yesterday** [jéstərdèi] 부 명 어제
- ☐ 042 **think** [θiŋk] 동 (~라고) 생각하다
- ☐ 043 **believe** [bilíːv] 동 믿다
- ☐ 044 **right** [rait] 형 바른, 옳은
- ☐ 045 **solve** [sɑlv] 동 풀다, 해결하다
- ☐ 046 **problem** [prɑ́bləm] 명 문제
- ☐ 047 **lose** [luːz] 동 잃다, (게임, 경기에) 지다
- ☐ 048 **creative** [kriéitiv] 형 창조적인, 독창적인
- ☐ 049 **patient** [péiʃənt] 형 참을성 있는, 끈기 있는
- ☐ 050 **humid** [hjúːmid] 형 습기 있는
- ☐ 051 **terrible** [térəbl] 형 끔찍한, 서투른
- ☐ 052 **friendly** [fréndli] 형 정다운, 친절한
- ☐ 053 **polite** [pəláit] 형 예의 바른, 공손한
- ☐ 054 **advice** [ədváis] 명 조언, 충고
- ☐ 055 **ask** [æsk] 동 묻다, 요청하다
- ☐ 056 **question** [kwéstʃən] 명 질문, 문제
- ☐ 057 **interesting** [íntərèstiŋ] 형 흥미 있는, 재미있는
- ☐ 058 **suddenly** [sʌ́dnli] 부 갑자기
- ☐ 059 **quiet** [kwaiət] 형 조용한
- ☐ 060 **turn** [təːrn] 동 ~로 바뀌다, 돌리다
- ☐ 061 **grow** [grou] 동 ~하게 되다, 자라다
- ☐ 062 **special** [spéʃəl] 형 특별한, 특수한
- ☐ 063 **rest** [rest] 명 휴식, 안정 동 쉬다
- ☐ 064 **seem** [siːm] 동 ~처럼 보이다
- ☐ 065 **carry** [kǽri] 동 나르다, 운반하다
- ☐ 066 **appear** [əpíər] 동 ~인 듯하다, 나타나다
- ☐ 067 **treat** [triːt] 동 대우하다, 다루다
- ☐ 068 **sour** [sáuər] 형 신, 시큼한
- ☐ 069 **strange** [streindʒ] 형 이상한
- ☐ 070 **lend** [lend] 동 빌려주다
- ☐ 071 **bring** [briŋ] 동 가져오다

Day 03

오늘 외울 단어 **35개**

- 072 **history** [hístəri] 명 역사
- 073 **surprising** [sərpráiziŋ] 형 놀라운
- 074 **price** [prais] 명 가격
- 075 **difficult** [dífikʌlt] 형 어려운, 곤란한
- 076 **dictionary** [díkʃənèri] 명 사전
- 077 **regularly** [régjələrli] 부 규칙적으로, 정기적으로
- 078 **temperature** [témpərətʃər] 명 온도
- 079 **rule** [ru:l] 명 규칙
- 080 **shake** [ʃeik] 동 흔들리다, 흔들다
- 081 **bark** [ba:rk] 동 짖다
- 082 **shout** [ʃaut] 동 소리치다, 외치다
- 083 **remember** [rimémbər] 동 기억하다
- 084 **consider** [kənsídər] 동 고려하다
- 085 **touch** [tʌtʃ] 동 건드리다, 만지다
- 086 **dimple** [dímpl] 명 보조개

Chapter Review Test

- 087 **prefer** [prifə́:r] 동 ~을 (더) 좋아하다
- 088 **laptop** [lǽptap] 명 휴대용 컴퓨터, 노트북 컴퓨터
- 089 **happen** [hǽpən] 동 (일이) 발생하다
- 090 **unkind** [ʌnkáind] 형 불쾌한, 불친절한
- 091 **awesome** [ɔ́:səm] 형 경탄할 만한
- 092 **famous** [féiməs] 형 유명한
- 093 **inventor** [invéntər] 명 발명가
- 094 **invent** [invént] 동 발명하다
- 095 **include** [inklú:d] 동 포함하다
- 096 **bulb** [bʌlb] 명 전구
- 097 **typewriter** [táipràitər] 명 타자기
- 098 **phonograph** [fóunəgræf] 명 축음기
- 099 **iron** [áiərn] 명 철, 쇠, 다리미
- 100 **smile at** ~에게 미소를 짓다
- 101 **fall on the ground** 땅에 떨어지다
- 102 **grade** [greid] 명 성적, 학년, 등급
- 103 **look like** ~처럼 보이다[생기다]
- 104 **upset** [ʌpsét] 형 속상한, 화가 난
- 105 **throw** [θrou] 동 던지다
- 106 **bullet** [búlit] 명 총알

Day 04

오늘 외울 단어 **34**개

- ☐ 107 **sleepy** [slíːpi] — 형 졸린
- ☐ 108 **warm** [wɔːrm] — 형 따뜻한
- ☐ 109 **bitter** [bítər] — 형 맛이 쓴
- ☐ 110 **diligent** [dílidʒənt] — 형 성실한
- ☐ 111 **semester** [siméstər] — 명 학기
- ☐ 112 **physics** [fíziks] — 명 물리학
- ☐ 113 **chemistry** [kémistri] — 명 화학
- ☐ 114 **funny** [fʌ́ni] — 형 재미있는, 우스운
- ☐ 115 **lonely** [lóunli] — 형 외로운
- ☐ 116 **scream** [skriːm] — 동 소리 지르다
- ☐ 117 **delicious** [dilíʃəs] — 형 맛있는
- ☐ 118 **realistic** [rìː(ː)əlístik] — 형 현실적인
- ☐ 119 **neat** [niːt] — 형 정돈된
- ☐ 120 **all the time** — 항상
- ☐ 121 **spotlessly** [spátlisli] — 부 아주 깨끗하게
- ☐ 122 **big hand** [big hænd] — 큰 박수
- ☐ 123 **cheerful** [tʃíərfəl] — 형 발랄한
- ☐ 124 **inside** [insáid] — 전 ~의 안[속/내부]에
- ☐ 125 **mine** [main] — 명 광산
- ☐ 126 **serious** [síː(ː)əriəs] — 형 심각한, 진지한

Chapter 2 시제

PSS & PRACTICE

- ☐ 127 **relax** [riléks] — 동 휴식을 취하다, 느긋하게 쉬다
- ☐ 128 **copy** [kápi] — 동 복사하다
- ☐ 129 **depart** [dipáːrt] — 동 출발하다
- ☐ 130 **reward** [riwɔ́ːrd] — 동 보답하다, 보상하다
- ☐ 131 **bite** [bait] — 동 물다
- ☐ 132 **breathe** [briːð] — 동 숨 쉬다, 호흡하다
- ☐ 133 **destroy** [distrɔ́i] — 동 파괴하다
- ☐ 134 **prove** [pruːv] — 동 입증하다, 증명하다
- ☐ 135 **reduce** [ridúːs] — 동 줄이다
- ☐ 136 **complain** [kəmpléin] — 동 불평하다
- ☐ 137 **raise** [reiz] — 동 올리다, 기르다
- ☐ 138 **shoot** [ʃuːt] — 동 (총, 화살을) 쏘다
- ☐ 139 **lift** [lift] — 동 들어 올리다
- ☐ 140 **bear** [bɛər] — 동 (아이를) 낳다, 견디다

Day 05

오늘 외울 단어 **36**개

- ☐ 141 **elect** [ilékt] 동 선출하다
- ☐ 142 **recycle** [ri:sáikl] 동 재활용하다
- ☐ 143 **recommend** [rèkəménd] 동 추천하다
- ☐ 144 **exchange** [ikstʃéindʒ] 동 교환하다
- ☐ 145 **interview** [íntərvjù:] 동 면접을 보다 명 면접
- ☐ 146 **allow** [əláu] 동 허락하다
- ☐ 147 **marry** [mǽri] 동 ~와 결혼하다
- ☐ 148 **pray** [prei] 동 기원하다, 기도하다
- ☐ 149 **rescue** [réskju:] 동 구조하다, 구하다
- ☐ 150 **vow** [vau] 동 맹세하다
- ☐ 151 **mention** [ménʃən] 동 언급하다
- ☐ 152 **imagine** [imǽdʒin] 동 상상하다
- ☐ 153 **lead** [li:d] 동 인도하다, 안내하다
- ☐ 154 **fight** [fait] 동 싸우다
- ☐ 155 **wrap** [ræp] 동 싸다, 포장하다
- ☐ 156 **flow** [flou] 동 (액체, 기체, 전류가) 흐르다
- ☐ 157 **argue** [á:rgju:] 동 논하다, 언쟁하다
- ☐ 158 **produce** [prədjú:s] 동 생산하다
- ☐ 159 **serve** [sə:rv] 동 제공하다, 차려 주다
- ☐ 160 **add** [æd] 동 더하다
- ☐ 161 **discover** [diskʌ́vər] 동 발견하다
- ☐ 162 **admire** [ədmáiər] 동 감탄하다, 존경하다
- ☐ 163 **sink** [siŋk] 동 가라앉다
- ☐ 164 **quit** [kwit] 동 그만두다
- ☐ 165 **stretch** [stretʃ] 동 늘이다, 늘어나다
- ☐ 166 **suppose** [səpóuz] 동 ~라고 가정하다
- ☐ 167 **beat** [bi:t] 동 치다, 두드리다
- ☐ 168 **hatch** [hætʃ] 동 (알을) 까다, 부화하다
- ☐ 169 **describe** [diskráib] 동 묘사하다
- ☐ 170 **appreciate** [əprí:ʃieit] 동 고마워하다
- ☐ 171 **close** [klouz] 동 닫다
- ☐ 172 **in need** 어려움에 처한
- ☐ 173 **pick** [pik] 동 따다, 고르다
- ☐ 174 **dig** [dig] 동 (땅을) 파다
- ☐ 175 **push** [puʃ] 동 밀다
- ☐ 176 **spill** [spil] 동 엎지르다, 쏟다

Day 06

오늘 외울 단어 36개

- 177 **publish** [pʌ́bliʃ] 동 공표하다, 출판하다
- 178 **select** [silékt] 동 고르다, 선택하다
- 179 **dictate** [díkteit] 동 받아쓰게 하다
- 180 **consist** [kənsíst] 동 ~로 이루어져 있다
- 181 **drop** [drɑp] 동 떨어뜨리다, 떨어지다
- 182 **fix** [fiks] 동 수리하다
- 183 **tease** [tiːz] 동 괴롭히다, 놀리다
- 184 **rise** [raiz] 동 (해, 달이) 뜨다, 오르다
- 185 **indeed** [indíːd] 부 실로, 참으로
- 186 **around** [əráund] 전 ~의 주위에
- 187 **blame** [bleim] 동 비난하다
- 188 **tool** [tuːl] 명 연장, 도구
- 189 **pull** [pul] 동 당기다
- 190 **delay** [diléi] 동 늦추다, 미루다
- 191 **pop** [pɑp] 동 튀어나오다
- 192 **offer** [ɔ́ːfər] 동 제공하다, 제안하다
- 193 **rip** [rip] 동 찢다
- 194 **judge** [dʒʌdʒ] 동 재판하다, 판단하다
- 195 **notice** [nóutis] 동 주의하다, 인지하다
- 196 **rush** [rʌʃ] 동 돌진하다, 서두르다
- 197 **kick** [kik] 동 발로 차다
- 198 **collect** [kəlékt] 동 모으다, 수집하다
- 199 **practice** [prǽktis] 동 연습하다, 실행하다
- 200 **waste** [weist] 동 낭비하다
- 201 **worry** [wə́ːri] 동 걱정하다, 걱정하게 만들다
- 202 **form** [fɔːrm] 동 형성하다
- 203 **disappear** [dìsəpíər] 동 사라지다
- 204 **chat** [tʃæt] 동 수다를 떨다
- 205 **realize** [ríːəlàiz] 동 깨닫다
- 206 **bow** [bau] 동 숙이다, 절하다
- 207 **reply** [riplái] 동 대답하다 명 대답
- 208 **observe** [əbzə́ːrv] 동 관찰하다
- 209 **cause** [kɔːz] 동 초래하다, 야기하다
- 210 **operate** [ɑ́pərèit] 동 작동하다, 수술을 하다
- 211 **control** [kəntróul] 동 통제하다, 제어하다
- 212 **die** [dai] 동 죽다

Day 07

오늘 외울 단어 36개

- ²¹³ **report** [ripɔ́ːrt] 동 보고하다 명 보고서
- ²¹⁴ **blow** [blou] 동 (입으로/바람이) 불다
- ²¹⁵ **hide** [haid] 동 숨기다
- ²¹⁶ **hold** [hould] 동 (손에) 들다, 잡다
- ²¹⁷ **lay** [lei] 동 놓다, (알을) 낳다
- ²¹⁸ **lie** [lai] 동 눕다, 놓여 있다
- ²¹⁹ **steal** [stiːl] 동 훔치다
- ²²⁰ **overcome** [òuvərkʌ́m] 동 극복하다
- ²²¹ **build** [bild] 동 짓다, 건설하다
- ²²² **shut** [ʃʌt] 동 닫다
- ²²³ **sweep** [swiːp] 동 (빗자루로) 쓸다, 털다
- ²²⁴ **be born** 태어나다
- ²²⁵ **fall down** 넘어지다, 떨어지다
- ²²⁶ **speech** [spiːtʃ] 명 말하기, 연설
- ²²⁷ **contest** [kántest] 명 대회, 시합
- ²²⁸ **show** [ʃou] 동 보여주다
- ²²⁹ **painting** [péintiŋ] 명 그림, 회화
- ²³⁰ **housework** [háuswəːrk] 명 집안일
- ²³¹ **midnight** [mídnait] 명 한밤중, 자정
- ²³² **follow** [fálou] 동 따라가다, 따르다
- ²³³ **face** [feis] 동 직면하다, 마주하다
- ²³⁴ **tumble** [tʌ́mbl] 동 넘어지다, 굴러 떨어지다
- ²³⁵ **join** [dʒɔin] 동 결합하다, 가입하다, 참여하다
- ²³⁶ **encourage** [inkə́ːridʒ] 동 격려하다, 장려하다
- ²³⁷ **burn** [bəːrn] 동 불에 태우다
- ²³⁸ **act** [ækt] 동 행동하다
- ²³⁹ **celebrate** [sélibreit] 동 기념하다, 축하하다
- ²⁴⁰ **deny** [dinái] 동 부인하다
- ²⁴¹ **repeat** [ripíːt] 동 되풀이하다
- ²⁴² **hit** [hit] 동 때리다, 치다
- ²⁴³ **shine** [ʃain] 동 빛나다
- ²⁴⁴ **roll** [roul] 동 구르다
- ²⁴⁵ **share** [ʃɛər] 동 함께 나누다, 공유하다
- ²⁴⁶ **fill** [fil] 동 채우다
- ²⁴⁷ **cheat** [tʃiːt] 동 속이다
- ²⁴⁸ **remove** [rimúːv] 동 제거하다

Day 08

오늘 외울 단어 **35**개

- ☐ 249 **take a shower** — 샤워를 하다
- ☐ 250 **on one's way to** — ~로 가는 도중에
- ☐ 251 **stand** [stænd] — 동 서 있다, 일어서다
- ☐ 252 **actor** [ǽktər] — 명 배우
- ☐ 253 **parent** [pɛ́(:)ərənt] — 명 부모
- ☐ 254 **pass away** — 사망하다
- ☐ 255 **hen** [hen] — 명 암탉
- ☐ 256 **plant** [plænt] — 명 식물, 초목
- ☐ 257 **set up** — 설비하다, 설치하다
- ☐ 258 **several** [sévrəl] — 형 몇몇의
- ☐ 259 **popular** [pápjulər] — 형 인기 있는
- ☐ 260 **a lot** — 훨씬, 많이
- ☐ 261 **fable** [féibl] — 명 우화
- ☐ 262 **empty** [émpti] — 형 비어 있는
- ☐ 263 **lately** [léitli] — 부 요즘에, 최근에
- ☐ 264 **pride** [praid] — 명 자부심, 자만, 긍지
- ☐ 265 **prejudice** [prédʒudis] — 명 편견, 선입관
- ☐ 266 **sure** [ʃuər] — 형 확신하는, 확실히 아는
- ☐ 267 **recently** [rí:səntli] — 부 최근에
- ☐ 268 **nervous** [nə́:rvəs] — 형 불안한, 신경과민의
- ☐ 269 **useful** [jú:sfəl] — 형 쓸모 있는, 유용한
- ☐ 270 **heavily** [hévili] — 부 심하게, 대량으로, 무겁게

Chapter Review Test

- ☐ 271 **send** [send] — 동 보내다
- ☐ 272 **spend** [spend] — 동 (돈, 시간을) 쓰다
- ☐ 273 **hurt** [hə:rt] — 동 다치다, 아프다
- ☐ 274 **leave for** — ~를 향해 떠나다
- ☐ 275 **flight** [flait] — 명 항공편, 항공기
- ☐ 276 **climbing** [kláimiŋ] — 명 등산, 등반
- ☐ 277 **theater** [θí(:)ətər] — 명 극장
- ☐ 278 **depart from** — ~에서 출발하다
- ☐ 279 **vase** [veis] — 명 꽃병
- ☐ 280 **captain** [kǽptin] — 명 선장
- ☐ 281 **wallet** [wάlit] — 명 지갑, (서류를 넣는 납작한) 가방
- ☐ 282 **keep a diary** — 일기를 쓰다
- ☐ 283 **take a nap** — 낮잠을 자다

Day 09

오늘 외울 단어 **34**개

- 284 **take care of** ~를 돌보다
- 285 **seed** [siːd] 명 씨앗
- 286 **bud** [bʌd] 명 싹, 꽃봉오리
- 287 **mobile phone** [móubəl foun] 명 휴대 전화기
- 288 **bleed** [bliːd] 동 피를 흘리다
- 289 **thief** [θiːf] 명 도둑, 절도범
- 290 **escalator** [éskəlèitər] 명 에스컬레이터
- 291 **department store** [dipáːrtmənt stɔːr] 명 백화점
- 292 **break into** 몰래 잠입하다
- 293 **statue** [stǽtʃuː] 명 조각상
- 294 **liberty** [líbərti] 명 자유

Chapter 3 조동사

PSS & PRACTICE

- 295 **take off** (옷 등을) 벗다, 벗기다
- 296 **go for a walk** 산책 가다
- 297 **give an answer** 대답하다
- 298 **horror** [hɔ́ːrər] 명 공포
- 299 **truth** [truːθ] 명 진실
- 300 **go on a diet** 다이어트를 하다
- 301 **safe** [seif] 형 안전한
- 302 **hang** [hæŋ] 동 걸다
- 303 **cross** [krɔːs] 동 횡단하다
- 304 **first** [fəːrst] 형 첫 번째의
- 305 **notebook** [nóutbùk] 명 공책
- 306 **language** [lǽŋgwidʒ] 명 언어
- 307 **find** [faind] 동 찾다
- 308 **exit** [égzit] 명 출구
- 309 **pick up** 태우러 가다, 태우다
- 310 **carefully** [kɛ́ərfəli] 부 조심스럽게, 신중하게
- 311 **feed** [fiːd] 동 먹이를 주다
- 312 **walk** [wɔːk] 동 산책시키다, 걷다
- 313 **park** [paːrk] 동 주차하다
- 314 **elderly** [éldərli] 명 중장년층, 어르신
- 315 **zoo** [zuː] 명 동물원
- 316 **university** [jùːnəvə́ːrsəti] 명 대학교
- 317 **dish** [diʃ] 명 요리, 접시

Day 10

오늘 외울 단어 **35**개

- ☐ 318 **possible** [pásəbl] 형 가능한
- ☐ 319 **unbelievable** [ʌ̀nbilíːvəbl] 형 믿을 수 없는
- ☐ 320 **second** [sékənd] 명 (시간 단위의) 초
- ☐ 321 **memory** [méməri] 명 기억
- ☐ 322 **certain** [sə́ːrtn] 형 확신하는, 확실한
- ☐ 323 **bright** [brait] 형 빛나는, 밝은
- ☐ 324 **future** [fjúːtʃər] 명 미래
- ☐ 325 **again** [əgén] 부 이번에도, 다시 한 번
- ☐ 326 **stadium** [stéidiəm] 명 경기장
- ☐ 327 **kind** [kaind] 명 유형, 종류
- ☐ 328 **make a noise** 시끄럽게 하다
- ☐ 329 **school uniform** [skuːl júːnəfɔ̀ːrm] 명 교복
- ☐ 330 **sore** [sɔːr] 형 아픈, 쓰린
- ☐ 331 **throat** [θrout] 명 목
- ☐ 332 **midterm** [mídtə̀ːrm] 명 중간고사
- ☐ 333 **accident** [ǽksidənt] 명 사고
- ☐ 334 **favor** [féivər] 명 호의, 친절
- ☐ 335 **do someone a favor** ~의 부탁을 들어주다
- ☐ 336 **living** [líviŋ] 명 생계 수단, 생활
- ☐ 337 **turn down** (소리, 온도 등을) 낮추다
- ☐ 338 **sell** [sel] 동 팔다
- ☐ 339 **by oneself** 혼자
- ☐ 340 **salty** [sɔ́ːlti] 형 짠, 짭짤한

Chapter Review Test

- ☐ 341 **look around** 주위를 둘러보다
- ☐ 342 **do one's best** 최선을 다하다
- ☐ 343 **do well** 잘하다, 성공하다
- ☐ 344 **near** [niər] 형 가까운, 근처의
- ☐ 345 **handicapped** [hǽndikæ̀pt] 형 장애를 가진
- ☐ 346 **koala** [kouáːlə] 명 코알라
- ☐ 347 **get lost** 길을 잃다
- ☐ 348 **go out** 외출하다, 나가다
- ☐ 349 **shopper** [ʃápər] 명 쇼핑객
- ☐ 350 **errand** [érənd] 명 심부름
- ☐ 351 **win a prize** 상을 받다
- ☐ 352 **competition** [kàmpitíʃən] 명 대회, 경쟁

Day 11

오늘 외울 단어 **34**개

- 353 **turn right** — 우회전하다

Chapter 4 수동태

👤 PSS & PRACTICE

- 354 **catch** [kætʃ] — 동 잡다
- 355 **change** [tʃeindʒ] — 동 바꾸다, 변화시키다
- 356 **keep** [kiːp] — 동 가지다, 유지하다
- 357 **understand** [ʌndərstǽnd] — 동 이해하다
- 358 **bottle** [bátl] — 명 (물체를 담는) 병
- 359 **hunter** [hʌ́ntər] — 명 사냥꾼
- 360 **hold** [hóuld] — 동 개최하다
- 361 **president** [prézidənt] — 명 대통령, 회장
- 362 **play** [plei] — 명 연극
- 363 **respect** [rispékt] — 동 존경하다
- 364 **bill** [bil] — 명 계산서, 청구서
- 365 **deliver** [dilívər] — 동 배달하다
- 366 **magazine** [mæ̀gəzíːn] — 명 잡지
- 367 **cut down** — 베어내다
- 368 **lie** [lai] — 명 거짓말 동 거짓말하다
- 369 **director** [diréktər] — 명 감독
- 370 **forgive** [fərgív] — 동 용서하다
- 371 **pollute** [pəlúːt] — 동 오염시키다
- 372 **obey** [əbéi] — 동 복종하다, 준수하다
- 373 **plan** [plæn] — 명 계획
- 374 **prepare** [pripɛ́ər] — 동 준비하다
- 375 **task** [tæsk] — 명 직무, 과제
- 376 **view** [vjuː] — 명 경치
- 377 **resource** [ríːsɔːrs] — 명 자원, 물자
- 378 **call** [kɔːl] — 동 ~라고 부르다
- 379 **lovely** [lʌ́vli] — 형 사랑스러운, 아름다운
- 380 **tear** [tiər] — 명 눈물
- 381 **result** [rizʌ́lt] — 명 결과
- 382 **joy** [dʒɔi] — 명 기쁨
- 383 **word** [wəːrd] — 명 말, 단어
- 384 **postpone** [poustpóun] — 동 연기하다, 미루다
- 385 **information** [ìnfərméiʃən] — 명 정보
- 386 **photocopier** [fóutoukàːpiər] — 명 복사기

Day 12

오늘 외울 단어 **33**개

- ☐ 387 **name** [neim] 동 ~에 이름을 지어주다

Chapter Review Test

- ☐ 388 **principal** [prínsəpəl] 명 학장, 교장
- ☐ 389 **rubber** [rʌ́bər] 명 고무
- ☐ 390 **release** [rilíːs] 동 발표하다, 공개하다
- ☐ 391 **poem** [póuəm] 명 시
- ☐ 392 **classroom** [klǽsrùːm] 명 교실
- ☐ 393 **ring** [riŋ] 명 반지
- ☐ 394 **be held** 열리다, 개최되다
- ☐ 395 **experiment** [ikspérəmənt] 명 실험 동 실험하다
- ☐ 396 **ruin** [rúːin] 동 망치다
- ☐ 397 **neighbor** [néibər] 명 이웃
- ☐ 398 **surround** [səráund] 동 둘러싸다
- ☐ 399 **stamp** [stæmp] 명 우표
- ☐ 400 **resemble** [rizémbl] 동 닮다
- ☐ 401 **a bunch of** 다수의, 한 묶음의
- ☐ 402 **suit** [sjuːt] 동 ~에게 맞다, 어울리다
- ☐ 403 **rob** [rɑb] 동 도둑질하다
- ☐ 404 **personal** [pə́rsənəl] 형 개인의, 개인적인
- ☐ 405 **mystery** [místəri] 명 수수께끼, 불가사의
- ☐ 406 **canned** [kænd] 형 통조림으로 된
- ☐ 407 **conference** [kɑ́nfərəns] 명 회의, 학회
- ☐ 408 **firefighter** [fáiərfàitər] 명 소방관
- ☐ 409 **theory** [θíː(ː)əri] 명 이론
- ☐ 410 **mayor** [méiər] 명 시장, 군수

Chapter 5 명사와 관사

PSS & PRACTICE

- ☐ 411 **custom** [kʌ́stəm] 명 관습, 풍습
- ☐ 412 **match** [mætʃ] 명 성냥, 경기, 시합
- ☐ 413 **penny** [péni] 명 잔돈, 1페니
- ☐ 414 **couch** [kautʃ] 명 긴 의자, 소파
- ☐ 415 **activity** [æktívəti] 명 활동
- ☐ 416 **donkey** [dɑ́ŋki] 명 당나귀
- ☐ 417 **culture** [kʌ́ltʃər] 명 문화
- ☐ 418 **factory** [fǽktəri] 명 공장
- ☐ 419 **ferry** [féri] 명 나룻배, 여객선

Day 13

오늘 외울 단어 **36**개

- ⬜ 420 **community** [kəmjú:nəti] 명 공동체, 지역사회
- ⬜ 421 **hero** [hí:rou] 명 영웅
- ⬜ 422 **mosquito** [məskí:tou] 명 모기
- ⬜ 423 **calf** [kæf] 명 송아지
- ⬜ 424 **safe** [seif] 명 금고 형 안전한
- ⬜ 425 **belief** [bilí:f] 명 믿음, 신조
- ⬜ 426 **chief** [tʃi:f] 명 장(長), 상사
- ⬜ 427 **sheep** [ʃi:p] 명 양
- ⬜ 428 **ox** [ɑks] 명 황소
- ⬜ 429 **emergency** [imə́:rdʒənsi] 명 비상사태
- ⬜ 430 **audience** [ɔ́:diəns] 명 청중
- ⬜ 431 **furniture** [fə́:rnitʃər] 명 가구
- ⬜ 432 **knowledge** [nɑ́lidʒ] 명 지식
- ⬜ 433 **kindness** [káindnis] 명 친절, 호의
- ⬜ 434 **across** [əkrɔ́:s] 전 ~을 가로질러
- ⬜ 435 **while** [wail] 접 ~하는 동안
- ⬜ 436 **express** [iksprés] 동 표현하다
- ⬜ 437 **beauty** [bjú:ti] 명 아름다움
- ⬜ 438 **subject** [sʌ́bdʒikt] 명 주제
- ⬜ 439 **support** [səpɔ́:rt] 동 후원하다, 지탱하다
- ⬜ 440 **take part in** 참여하다
- ⬜ 441 **go on a trip** 여행을 가다
- ⬜ 442 **cheerful** [tʃíərfəl] 형 쾌활한
- ⬜ 443 **autumn** [ɔ́:təm] 명 가을
- ⬜ 444 **downtown** [dàuntáun] 형 도심지의 명 도심지
- ⬜ 445 **honesty** [ɑ́nisti] 명 정직
- ⬜ 446 **policy** [pɑ́ləsi] 명 정책
- ⬜ 447 **death** [deθ] 명 죽음
- ⬜ 448 **look forward to** ~을 고대하다
- ⬜ 449 **economics** [ì:kənɑ́miks] 명 경제학
- ⬜ 450 **politics** [pɑ́litiks] 명 정치학, 정치
- ⬜ 451 **customs** [kʌ́stəmz] 명 세관
- ⬜ 452 **means** [mi:nz] 명 수단, 방법
- ⬜ 453 **earthquake** [ə́:rθkwèik] 명 지진
- ⬜ 454 **shocking** [ʃɑ́kiŋ] 형 충격적인
- ⬜ 455 **tax** [tæks] 명 세금

Day 14

오늘 외울 단어 **35**개

- ☐ 456 **goods** [gudz] 명 상품, 물품
- ☐ 457 **foreign** [fɔ́:rən] 형 외국의
- ☐ 458 **government** [gʌ́vərnmənt] 명 정부
- ☐ 459 **interest** [íntrest] 동 흥미를 끌다 / 명 흥미, 관심
- ☐ 460 **handmade** [hǽndméid] 형 손으로 만든
- ☐ 461 **walk** [wɔːk] 명 산책
- ☐ 462 **niece** [niːs] 명 여자 조카
- ☐ 463 **bottom** [bátəm] 명 바닥
- ☐ 464 **report card** [ripɔ́ːrt kàːrd] 명 성적표
- ☐ 465 **blanket** [blǽŋkit] 명 담요
- ☐ 466 **fact** [fækt] 명 사실
- ☐ 467 **borrow** [bárou] 동 빌리다
- ☐ 468 **impossible** [impásəbl] 형 불가능한
- ☐ 469 **unique** [juːníːk] 형 독특한
- ☐ 470 **in a moment** 곧, 바로
- ☐ 471 **feather** [féðər] 명 깃털
- ☐ 472 **flock** [flɑk] 명 떼, 무리 / 동 모이다
- ☐ 473 **whale** [hweil] 명 고래
- ☐ 474 **capital** [kǽpitl] 명 (국가의) 수도
- ☐ 475 **flat** [flæt] 형 평평한
- ☐ 476 **spaceship** [spéisʃip] 명 우주선
- ☐ 477 **psychology** [saikálədʒi] 명 심리학, 심리
- ☐ 478 **very** [véri] 부 매우
- ☐ 479 **row** [rou] 명 열, 줄
- ☐ 480 **the other day** 일전에, 며칠 전에
- ☐ 481 **stranger** [stréindʒər] 명 낯선 사람
- ☐ 482 **sailor** [séilər] 명 선원, 뱃사람
- ☐ 483 **carelessly** [kɛ́ərlisli] 부 부주의하게, 무심코
- ☐ 484 **comfortable** [kʌ́mfərtəbl] 형 편안한
- ☐ 485 **retire** [ritáiər] 동 퇴직하다
- ☐ 486 **scenery** [síːnəri] 명 풍경
- ☐ 487 **professor** [prəfésər] 명 교수
- ☐ 488 **lesson** [lésn] 명 수업, 교훈
- ☐ 489 **tend to** ~하는 경향이 있다

Chapter Review Test

- ☐ 490 **toast** [toust] 동 (빵을) 노르스름하게 굽다

Day 15

오늘 외울 단어 **34**개

- □ 491 **piece** [piːs] 명 조각
- □ 492 **title** [táitl] 명 제목
- □ 493 **faithful** [féiθfəl] 형 충성스러운
- □ 494 **slice** [slais] 명 (얇게 썬) 조각
- □ 495 **bowl** [boul] 명 사발, 공기
- □ 496 **loaf** [louf] 명 (빵의) 덩어리
- □ 497 **pound** [paund] 명 (중량의 단위) 파운드
- □ 498 **pork** [pɔːrk] 명 돼지고기
- □ 499 **master** [mǽstər] 동 ~에 통달하다
- □ 500 **set foot on** ~에 발을 딛다
- □ 501 **spoonful** [spúːnfùl] 명 숟가락으로 하나
- □ 502 **honest** [ánist] 형 정직한
- □ 503 **noisy** [nɔ́izi] 형 시끄러운
- □ 504 **loudly** [láudli] 부 큰소리로, 소란스럽게
- □ 505 **fail** [feil] 동 실패하다
- □ 506 **plain** [plein] 형 있는 그대로의
- □ 507 **black pepper** [blǽk pépər] 명 (검은) 후추
- □ 508 **cucumber** [kjúːkʌmbər] 명 오이
- □ 509 **grind** [graind] 동 (잘게) 갈다
- □ 510 **stir** [stəːr] 동 젓다, 섞다
- □ 511 **season** [síːzən] 동 양념하다
- □ 512 **refrigerate** [rifrídʒərèit] 동 냉장하다
- □ 513 **at least** 적어도
- □ 514 **marathon** [mǽrəθàn] 명 마라톤
- □ 515 **ignore** [ignɔ́ːr] 동 무시하다
- □ 516 **innocent** [ínəsənt] 형 순수한, 순결한, 결백한

Chapter 6 대명사

👤 **PSS & PRACTICE**

- □ 517 **lawyer** [lɔ́ːjər] 명 변호사
- □ 518 **through** [θruː] 전 ~을 통하여
- □ 519 **musical instrument** [mjúːzikl ínstrəmənt] 명 악기
- □ 520 **cover** [kʌ́vər] 명 표지
- □ 521 **importance** [impɔ́ːrtns] 명 중요성
- □ 522 **be proud of** ~을 자랑스러워하다
- □ 523 **come true** 실현되다
- □ 524 **by accident** 우연히

Day 16

오늘 외울 단어 **35개**

- 525 **make oneself at home** — 편하게 있다
- 526 **introduce** [ìntrədjúːs] — 동 소개하다
- 527 **mirror** [mírər] — 명 거울
- 528 **degree** [digríː] — 명 (온도, 각도 단위) 도, 정도
- 529 **fiction** [fíkʃən] — 명 소설, 허구
- 530 **disappointing** [dìsəpɔ́intiŋ] — 형 실망스러운
- 531 **expensive** [ikspénsiv] — 형 비싼
- 532 **smoke** [smouk] — 동 흡연하다
- 533 **population** [pὰpjuléiʃən] — 명 인구
- 534 **succeed** [səksíːd] — 동 성공하다
- 535 **employee** [implɔ́iiː] — 명 피고용자, 종업원
- 536 **balloon** [bəlúːn] — 명 풍선
- 537 **friendship** [fréndʃip] — 명 우정
- 538 **throw away** — 내다 버리다
- 539 **twin** [twin] — 명 쌍둥이 중 한 명 / 형 쌍둥이의
- 540 **chance** [tʃæns] — 명 기회
- 541 **care** [kɛər] — 동 신경 쓰다
- 542 **dozen** [dʌ́zn] — 명 12개, 12개짜리 한 묶음
- 543 **cloth** [klɔːθ] — 명 천, 옷감
- 544 **passenger** [pǽsəndʒər] — 명 승객
- 545 **performance** [pərfɔ́ːrməns] — 명 공연, 연주
- 546 **all of a sudden** — 갑자기
- 547 **correctly** [kəréktli] — 부 정확하게, 바르게
- 548 **wait for** — ~를 기다리다
- 549 **suggestion** [sədʒéstʃən] — 명 제안, 의견
- 550 **drop by** — 방문하다, ~에 들르다

Chapter Review Test

- 551 **astronomer** [əstrάnəmər] — 명 천문학자
- 552 **author** [ɔ́ːθər] — 명 저자, 작가
- 553 **be known for** — ~로 알려지다
- 554 **club** [klʌb] — 명 동호회
- 555 **logo** [lɔ́(ː)gou] — 명 상징, 로고
- 556 **closet** [klάzit] — 명 옷장
- 557 **treasure** [tréʒər] — 명 보물
- 558 **example** [igzǽmpl] — 명 예, 예시
- 559 **always** [ɔ́ːlweiz] — 부 항상, 늘

Day 17

오늘 외울 단어 **36**개

- 560 **save** [seiv] — 동 구하다, 안전하게 하다
- 561 **for sale** — 팔려고 내놓은, 판매 중인
- 562 **own** [oun] — 형 자기 자신의, 자기 소유의
- 563 **umbrella** [ʌmbrélə] — 명 우산
- 564 **spicy** [spáisi] — 형 양념 맛이 강한, 매콤한
- 565 **minute** [mínit] — 명 (시간 단위의) 분
- 566 **astronaut** [ǽstrənɔ̀ːt] — 명 우주비행사
- 567 **space** [speis] — 명 우주, 공간
- 568 **dentist** [déntist] — 명 치과의사
- 569 **lily** [líli] — 명 백합
- 570 **fluently** [flúːəntli] — 부 유창하게
- 571 **topic** [tápik] — 명 주제, 화제
- 572 **same** [seim] — 형 같은
- 573 **divide up** — 분배하다, 나눠 갖다
- 574 **homeroom** [hóumrùː(ː)m] — 명 (미국의) 교실
- 575 **climate** [kláimit] — 명 기후
- 576 **pollution** [pəlúːʃən] — 명 오염
- 577 **opinion** [əpínjən] — 명 의견
- 578 **stare at** — 빤히 쳐다보다
- 579 **break down** — 고장 나다
- 580 **purple** [pə́ːrpl] — 형 자주색의, 보라색의
- 581 **be afraid of** — ~을 두려워하다
- 582 **tiny** [táini] — 형 아주 작은
- 583 **blind** [blaind] — 명 (창문에 치는) 블라인드
- 584 **glove** [glʌv] — 명 장갑
- 585 **entertainer** [èntərtéinər] — 명 연예인
- 586 **look after** — ~을 맡다[돌보다]
- 587 **set up the tent** — 텐트를 치다
- 588 **live with** — ~와 함께 살다
- 589 **boil** [bɔil] — 동 끓이다, 끓다
- 590 **teapot** [tíːpàːt] — 명 찻주전자
- 591 **burn** [bəːrn] — 동 타오르다, 타다
- 592 **Halloween** [hæ̀ləwíːn] — 명 할로윈
- 593 **used to** — ~하곤 했다
- 594 **comic book** [kámik bùk] — 명 만화책
- 595 **violin** [vàiəlín] — 명 바이올린

Day 18

오늘 외울 단어 **34개**

- 596 **decide** [disáid] 동 결심하다
- 597 **matter** [mǽtər] 명 문제, 일
- 598 **jacket** [dʒǽkit] 명 재킷, 상의
- 599 **cheap** [tʃi:p] 형 저렴한, 싼

Chapter 7 부정사

PSS & PRACTICE

- 600 **clearly** [klíərli] 부 또렷하게
- 601 **jog** [dʒɑg] 동 조깅하다
- 602 **eyesight** [áisàit] 명 시력
- 603 **expect** [ikspékt] 동 기대하다, 예상하다
- 604 **refuse** [rifjú:z] 동 거절하다, 거부하다
- 605 **musician** [mju:zíʃən] 명 음악가
- 606 **protect** [prətékt] 동 보호하다
- 607 **garage sale** [gərá:dʒ seil] 명 차고에서 하는 중고품 세일
- 608 **repair** [ripéər] 동 수리하다
- 609 **explain** [ikspléin] 동 설명하다
- 610 **crop** [krɑp] 명 농작물
- 611 **enough** [inʌ́f] 형 충분한
- 612 **final exam** [fáinəl igzǽm] 명 기말고사
- 613 **surf the Internet** 인터넷 서핑을 하다
- 614 **windshield** [wíndʃì:ld] 명 (자동차의) 앞 유리
- 615 **nod** [nɑd] 동 (고개를) 끄덕이다
- 616 **lucky** [lʌ́ki] 형 운 좋은
- 617 **pleased** [pli:zd] 형 기쁜
- 618 **surprised** [sərpráizd] 형 놀란
- 619 **disappointed** [dìsəpɔ́intid] 형 실망한
- 620 **essential** [isénʃl] 형 필수적인, 없어서는 안 될
- 621 **trust** [trʌst] 동 믿다, 신뢰하다
- 622 **college** [kɑ́lidʒ] 명 대학, 단과대학
- 623 **reach** [ri:tʃ] 동 도달하다, 도착하다
- 624 **shelf** [ʃelf] 명 선반
- 625 **attract** [ətrǽkt] 동 유인하다, 끌어당기다
- 626 **butterfly** [bʌ́tərflài] 명 나비
- 627 **generous** [dʒénərəs] 형 관대한
- 628 **confusing** [kənfjú:ziŋ] 형 혼란시키는
- 629 **upstairs** [ʌ́pstéərz] 부 위층으로, 위층에(서)

Day 19

오늘 외울 단어 **33**개

- ⬜ 630 **ring** 동 (벨, 종이) 울리다
  [riŋ]

Chapter Review Test

- ⬜ 631 **library** 명 도서관
  [láibrèri]
- ⬜ 632 **post office** 명 우체국
  [poust ɔ́(:)fis]
- ⬜ 633 **pass the exam** 시험을 통과하다
- ⬜ 634 **business** 명 사업, 업무
  [bíznis]
- ⬜ 635 **course** 명 강의, 강좌
  [kɔːrs]
- ⬜ 636 **have dinner** 저녁 식사를 하다
- ⬜ 637 **get up early** 일찍 일어나다
- ⬜ 638 **table tennis** 명 탁구
  [téibl ténis]
- ⬜ 639 **dangerous** 형 위험한
  [déindʒərəs]
- ⬜ 640 **deep** 형 깊은
  [diːp]
- ⬜ 641 **helpful** 형 도움이 되는
  [hélpfəl]
- ⬜ 642 **mask** 명 가면, 복면
  [mæsk]
- ⬜ 643 **apologize** 동 사과하다
  [əpálədʒàiz]
- ⬜ 644 **proud** 형 거만한, 자랑스러워하는
  [praud]
- ⬜ 645 **end** 동 끝나다, 끝내다
  [end]
- ⬜ 646 **license** 명 면허증
  [láisəns]
- ⬜ 647 **saving** 명 예금, 저금, 절약
  [séiviŋ]

Chapter 8 동명사

PSS & PRACTICE

- ⬜ 648 **depress** 동 우울하게 하다
  [diprés]
- ⬜ 649 **design** 동 디자인하다 명 디자인
  [dizáin]
- ⬜ 650 **refresh** 동 상쾌하게 하다
  [rifréʃ]
- ⬜ 651 **effort** 명 노력
  [éfərt]
- ⬜ 652 **outside** 부 밖에서, 옥외로
  [áutsàid]
- ⬜ 653 **countryside** 명 시골, 지방
  [kʌ́ntrisàid]
- ⬜ 654 **mind** 동 신경 쓰다, 꺼려하다
  [maind]
- ⬜ 655 **put off** 연기하다, 미루다
- ⬜ 656 **dislike** 동 싫어하다
  [disláik]
- ⬜ 657 **dolphin** 명 돌고래
  [dálfin]
- ⬜ 658 **skip** 동 거르다, 건너뛰다
  [skip]
- ⬜ 659 **continue** 동 계속하다
  [kəntínjuː]
- ⬜ 660 **chairman** 명 의장, 회장
  [tʃɛ́ərmən]
- ⬜ 661 **trash** 명 쓰레기
  [træʃ]
- ⬜ 662 **for a while** 잠시 동안

Day 20

오늘 외울 단어 33개

- 663 **fill up** — (~로) 가득 차다, 채우다
- 664 **gas station** [gǽs stèiʃən] — 명 주유소
- 665 **in the end** — 결국에
- 666 **responsible** [rispánsəbl] — 형 책임이 있는
- 667 **care for** — ~을 돌보다
- 668 **prevent** [privént] — 동 막다, 방해하다
- 669 **illness** [ílnis] — 명 병, 질환
- 670 **ignorant** [ígnərənt] — 형 무식한, 무지한
- 671 **major** [méidʒər] — 명 전공, 전공자 / 동 전공하다
- 672 **laugh** [læf] — 동 (소리 내어) 웃다

Chapter Review Test

- 673 **usually** [júːʒuəli] — 부 보통, 대개
- 674 **interrupt** [ìntərʌ́pt] — 동 ~을 방해하다
- 675 **grow up** — 자라다, 성장하다
- 676 **plant** [plænt] — 동 (나무, 씨앗 등을) 심다
- 677 **recent** [ríːsnt] — 형 최근의
- 678 **turn on** — (전등, 기계 등을) 켜다
- 679 **schedule** [skédʒuːl] — 명 일정, 스케줄
- 680 **fall in love** — 사랑에 빠지다
- 681 **upgrade** [ʌ́pgrèid] — 동 (기계 등을) 개선하다
- 682 **postcard** [póustkàːrd] — 명 엽서
- 683 **difficulty** [dífikʌ̀lti] — 명 어려움, 곤경
- 684 **take a walk** — 산책하다
- 685 **dessert** [dizə́ːrt] — 명 디저트, 후식
- 686 **violate** [váiəlèit] — 동 위반하다, 어기다
- 687 **traffic** [trǽfik] — 명 교통
- 688 **regulation** [règjuléiʃən] — 명 규정
- 689 **balanced** [bǽlənst] — 형 균형 잡힌
- 690 **debate** [dibéit] — 명 토론, 토의
- 691 **pocket money** [pákit mʌ́ni] — 명 용돈
- 692 **package** [pǽkidʒ] — 명 소포, 포장물

Chapter 9 분사

PSS & PRACTICE

- 693 **fall** [fɔːl] — 동 떨어지다
- 694 **depressing** [diprésiŋ] — 형 우울하게 하는
- 695 **boiled** [bɔild] — 형 삶은, 끓은

Day 21

오늘 외울 단어 **33**개

- ☐ 696 **be filled with** ~로 가득 차다
- ☐ 697 **gym** [dʒim] 명 체육관
- ☐ 698 **stage** [steidʒ] 명 무대, 단계
- ☐ 699 **run away** 도망치다
- ☐ 700 **frying pan** [fráiŋ pæn] 명 후라이팬
- ☐ 701 **drinking water** [dríŋkiŋ wɔ́ːtər] 명 식수
- ☐ 702 **satisfy** [sǽtisfài] 동 만족시키다
- ☐ 703 **embarrass** [imbǽrəs] 동 당황스럽게 하다
- ☐ 704 **move** [muːv] 동 감동시키다
- ☐ 705 **amaze** [əméiz] 동 놀라게 하다
- ☐ 706 **puzzle** [pʌ́zl] 동 곤혹하게 하다, 어리둥절하게 하다
- ☐ 707 **essay** [ései] 명 에세이, 수필
- ☐ 708 **public** [pʌ́blik] 명 대중 형 공공의
- ☐ 709 **festival** [féstivl] 명 축제
- ☐ 710 **by mistake** 실수로
- ☐ 711 **beside** [bisáid] 전 ~ 곁[옆]에
- ☐ 712 **cross** [krɔːs] 동 교차시키다, 건너다, 가로지르다
- ☐ 713 **clean up** ~을 치우다, 청소하다
- ☐ 714 **tie** [tai] 동 묶다, 매다

Chapter Review Test

- ☐ 715 **excited** [iksáitid] 형 신이 난, 들뜬
- ☐ 716 **beach** [biːtʃ] 명 해변, 바닷가
- ☐ 717 **shed** [ʃed] 동 (피, 눈물 등을) 흘리다
- ☐ 718 **pot** [pɑt] 명 냄비, 솥
- ☐ 719 **restroom** [réstrùm] 명 화장실
- ☐ 720 **grass** [græs] 명 잔디, 풀
- ☐ 721 **fantastic** [fæntǽstik] 형 환상적인
- ☐ 722 **fall asleep** 잠들다
- ☐ 723 **owner** [óunər] 명 주인, 소유주
- ☐ 724 **after all** 결국에는
- ☐ 725 **holiday** [hálədèi] 명 휴가, 방학
- ☐ 726 **amusement park** [əmjúːzmənt pɑːrk] 명 놀이공원
- ☐ 727 **type** [taip] 명 유형, 종류
- ☐ 728 **cartoon** [kɑːrtúːn] 명 (시사 풍자) 만화

Chapter 10 형용사

PSS & PRACTICE

Day 22

오늘 외울 단어 **33**개

- ☐ 729 **alive** [əláiv] — 형 살아 있는
- ☐ 730 **ashamed** [əʃéimd] — 형 부끄러워하는, 수치스러운
- ☐ 731 **necklace** [nékləs] — 명 목걸이
- ☐ 732 **intelligent** [intélidʒənt] — 형 지적인, 총명한
- ☐ 733 **impressive** [imprésiv] — 형 인상적인, 인상 깊은
- ☐ 734 **starfish** [stáːrfiʃ] — 명 불가사리
- ☐ 735 **scared** [skɛərd] — 형 겁에 질린
- ☐ 736 **handsome** [hǽnsəm] — 형 잘생긴
- ☐ 737 **familiar** [fəmíljər] — 형 잘 아는, 익숙한
- ☐ 738 **rich** [ritʃ] — 형 부유한, 돈 많은
- ☐ 739 **blind** [blaind] — 형 눈이 먼
- ☐ 740 **deaf** [def] — 형 귀가 먼
- ☐ 741 **brave** [breiv] — 형 용감한
- ☐ 742 **intonation** [ìntənéiʃən] — 명 억양
- ☐ 743 **metal** [métl] — 명 금속
- ☐ 744 **million** [míljən] — 형 100만의 명 100만
- ☐ 745 **plenty** [plénti] — 명 많음, 풍부
- ☐ 746 **chapter** [tʃǽptər] — 명 (책의) 장
- ☐ 747 **except** [iksépt] — 전 ~을 제외하고
- ☐ 748 **unpleasant** [ʌnpléznt] — 형 불쾌한

Chapter Review Test

- ☐ 749 **fitness center** [fítnəs sèntər] — 명 피트니스 센터, 헬스클럽
- ☐ 750 **trendy** [tréndi] — 형 최신 유행의
- ☐ 751 **refrigerator** [rifrídʒərèitər] — 명 냉장고
- ☐ 752 **daughter** [dɔ́ːtər] — 명 딸
- ☐ 753 **collection** [kəlékʃən] — 명 수집품, 소장품
- ☐ 754 **proverb** [právəːrb] — 명 속담
- ☐ 755 **wrong** [rɔ(ː)ŋ] — 형 틀린, 잘못된
- ☐ 756 **gain weight** — 체중이 증가하다
- ☐ 757 **get stressed** — 스트레스를 받다
- ☐ 758 **asleep** [əslíːp] — 형 잠이 든
- ☐ 759 **alike** [əláik] — 형 비슷한
- ☐ 760 **experience** [ikspíriəns] — 명 경험
- ☐ 761 **depressed** [diprést] — 형 우울한

Chapter 11 부사

PSS & PRACTICE

Day 23

오늘 외울 단어 **35**개

- ☐ 762 **sudden** [sʌ́dn] — 형 갑작스러운, 뜻밖의
- ☐ 763 **final** [fáinl] — 형 마지막의, 결정적인
- ☐ 764 **sincere** [sinsíər] — 형 진실한, 진심의
- ☐ 765 **slight** [slait] — 형 약간의, 근소한
- ☐ 766 **gentle** [dʒéntl] — 형 온화한, 친절한
- ☐ 767 **simple** [símpl] — 형 간단한, 단순한
- ☐ 768 **reasonable** [ríːznəbl] — 형 합리적인, 타당한
- ☐ 769 **visible** [vízəbl] — 형 눈에 보이는
- ☐ 770 **anxious** [ǽŋkʃəs] — 형 불안해하는, 염려하는
- ☐ 771 **last** [læst] — 동 지속되다
- ☐ 772 **closely** [klóusli] — 부 주의 깊게, 면밀히
- ☐ 773 **hardly** [háːrdli] — 부 거의 ~ 않다
- ☐ 774 **highly** [háili] — 부 높이 평가하여
- ☐ 775 **nearly** [níərli] — 부 거의, 대략
- ☐ 776 **shake hands** — 악수를 하다
- ☐ 777 **greet** [griːt] — 동 인사하다, 환영하다
- ☐ 778 **graduate** [grǽdʒuèit] — 동 졸업하다
- ☐ 779 **attend** [əténd] — 동 참석하다, 출석하다
- ☐ 780 **cool** [kuːl] — 형 시원한, 서늘한
- ☐ 781 **mean** [miːn] — 형 짓궂은, 비열한
- ☐ 782 **try on** — 입어 보다
- ☐ 783 **give up** — 포기하다
- ☐ 784 **look for** — ~을 찾다
- ☐ 785 **check out** — (책 등을) 대출하다
- ☐ 786 **call off** — 취소하다
- ☐ 787 **admission** [ædmíʃən] — 명 입장(료)

Chapter Review Test

- ☐ 788 **slow** [slou] — 형 느린, 더딘
- ☐ 789 **easily** [íːzəli] — 부 쉽게, 용이하게
- ☐ 790 **take out** — (안에서 밖으로) 꺼내다
- ☐ 791 **still** [stil] — 부 여전히
- ☐ 792 **deeply** [díːpli] — 부 깊게
- ☐ 793 **impressed** [imprést] — 형 감명을 받은
- ☐ 794 **such** [sʌtʃ] — 대 앞에 이미 언급한, 그런[그러한]
- ☐ 795 **intention** [inténʃən] — 명 의도, 목적
- ☐ 796 **alcohol** [ǽlkəhɔ̀ːl] — 명 술, 알코올

Day 24

오늘 외울 단어 **33개**

- 797 **interview** [íntərvjùː] 명 면접, 인터뷰
- 798 **successful** [səksésfəl] 형 (어떤 일에) 성공한, 성공적인
- 799 **station** [stéiʃn] 명 (기차)역, (버스) 정류장
- 800 **firework** [fáiərwə̀ːrk] 명 불꽃놀이, 폭죽
- 801 **display** [displéi] 명 전시, 표현
- 802 **cherry blossom** [tʃéri blásəm] 명 벚꽃
- 803 **bloom** [bluːm] 동 꽃을 피우다
- 804 **visit** [vízit] 동 방문하다, 찾아가다
- 805 **pile** [pail] 동 (물건을) 쌓다
- 806 **bomb** [bɑm] 명 폭탄
- 807 **explode** [iksplóud] 동 폭발하다
- 808 **skin** [skin] 명 피부
- 809 **set up** 건립하다, 수립하다
- 810 **church** [tʃəːrtʃ] 명 교회
- 811 **hard** [hɑːrd] 형 열심히 하는, 단단한, 어려운
- 812 **quickly** [kwíkli] 부 빨리, 빠르게

Chapter 12 가정법

PSS & PRACTICE

- 813 **be in danger** 위험에 처하다
- 814 **for free** 공짜로, 무료로
- 815 **discuss** [diskʌ́s] 동 토론하다, 논의하다
- 816 **cell phone** [sél fòun] 명 휴대폰
- 817 **in fact** 실은, 사실
- 818 **give someone a ride** ~를 태워주다
- 819 **youth** [juːθ] 명 청년 시절, 젊음, 젊은이
- 820 **lecture** [léktʃər] 명 강의, 강연

Chapter Review Test

- 821 **be able to** ~을 할 수 있다
- 822 **pass the test** 시험에 통과하다
- 823 **lose weight** 살이 빠지다
- 824 **as if** 마치 ~인 듯이
- 825 **fly** [flai] 동 날다
- 826 **item** [áitem] 명 항목, 품목
- 827 **invite** [inváit] 동 초대하다
- 828 **let someone know** ~에게 알리다
- 829 **do the dishes** 설거지하다

Day 25

오늘 외울 단어 **33**개

Chapter 13 비교구문

PSS & PRACTICE

- ☐ 830 **thin** [θin] 혱 얇은, 가는
- ☐ 831 **tasty** [téisti] 혱 맛있는
- ☐ 832 **useless** [júːslis] 혱 쓸모없는
- ☐ 833 **exactly** [igzǽktli] 부 정확히, 엄밀하게는
- ☐ 834 **wet** [wet] 혱 젖은
- ☐ 835 **scary** [skɛ́əri] 혱 무서운, 두려운
- ☐ 836 **curious** [kjúəriəs] 혱 호기심이 많은, 호기심을 돋우는
- ☐ 837 **convenient** [kənvíːniənt] 혱 편리한, 사용하기 좋은
- ☐ 838 **foolish** [fúːliʃ] 혱 바보 같은
- ☐ 839 **write back to** ~에게 답장을 쓰다
- ☐ 840 **mild** [maild] 혱 온화한, 순한, 따뜻한
- ☐ 841 **kindly** [káindli] 부 친절하게
- ☐ 842 **count** [kaunt] 동 세다, 계산하다
- ☐ 843 **weigh** [wei] 동 무게가 ~ 나가다
- ☐ 844 **per** [pəːr] 전 ~마다, ~당
- ☐ 845 **active** [ǽktiv] 혱 활동적인, 적극적인
- ☐ 846 **version** [və́ːrʒən] 명 개작, 각색
- ☐ 847 **article** [áːrtikl] 명 글, 기사
- ☐ 848 **boring** [bɔ́ːriŋ] 혱 재미없는, 지루한
- ☐ 849 **invention** [invénʃən] 명 발명품, 발명
- ☐ 850 **transportation** [trænspərtéiʃn] 명 수송, 운송기관

Chapter Review Test

- ☐ 851 **product** [prádəkt] 명 생산물, 상품
- ☐ 852 **save** [seiv] 동 아끼다, 절약하다
- ☐ 853 **especially** [ispéʃəli] 부 특히
- ☐ 854 **elephant** [éləfənt] 명 코끼리
- ☐ 855 **giraffe** [dʒəræf] 명 기린
- ☐ 856 **turtle** [tə́ːrtl] 명 거북
- ☐ 857 **lifespan** [láifspæn] 명 수명
- ☐ 858 **height** [hait] 명 높이, 키
- ☐ 859 **fame** [feim] 명 명성
- ☐ 860 **wise** [waiz] 혱 현명한
- ☐ 861 **pale** [peil] 혱 창백한
- ☐ 862 **present** [préznt] 명 선물

Day 26

오늘 외울 단어 **34개**

Chapter 14 관계사

PSS & PRACTICE

- 863 **sharp** [ʃɑːrp] 형 날카로운, 예리한
- 864 **belong to** ~에 속하다, ~의 것이다
- 865 **judge** [dʒʌdʒ] 명 판사
- 866 **suggest** [sədʒést] 동 제안하다, 추천하다
- 867 **pocket** [pákit] 명 주머니
- 868 **stove** [stouv] 명 가스레인지, 화로
- 869 **disappoint** [dìsəpɔ́int] 동 실망시키다
- 870 **on sale** 할인 중인
- 871 **reason** [ríːzn] 명 이유, 동기
- 872 **chopstick** [tʃápstìk] 명 젓가락
- 873 **cancel** [kǽnsəl] 동 취소하다

Chapter Review Test

- 874 **person** [pə́ːrsn] 명 사람, 개인
- 875 **teach** [tiːtʃ] 동 가르치다
- 876 **eat up** ~을 다 먹다
- 877 **police officer** [pəlíːs ɔ́(ː)fisər] 명 경찰관
- 878 **street** [striːt] 명 거리, 도로
- 879 **award** [əwɔ́ːrd] 동 수여하다
- 880 **table** [téibl] 명 탁자
- 881 **technique** [tekníːk] 명 기법, 기술
- 882 **magic** [mǽdʒik] 명 마술
- 883 **stone** [stoun] 명 돌, 비석
- 884 **tomb** [tuːm] 명 무덤
- 885 **site** [sait] 명 장소, 부지
- 886 **heritage** [héritidʒ] 명 (국가의) 유산
- 887 **ginseng** [dʒínseŋ] 명 인삼
- 888 **environment** [inváiərənmənt] 명 환경
- 889 **leader** [líːdər] 명 지도자
- 890 **put out** (불을) 끄다
- 891 **do harm** 해를 끼치다
- 892 **painter** [péintər] 명 화가
- 893 **focus on** ~에 주력하다, 초점을 맞추다
- 894 **village** [vílidʒ] 명 마을, 촌락
- 895 **documentary** [dàkjəméntəri] 명 다큐멘터리, 기록물
- 896 **project** [prádʒekt] 명 과제, 연구

Day 27

오늘 외울 단어 33개

- 897 **bake** [beik] 동 (빵 등을) 굽다
- 898 **earn** [əːrn] 동 (돈을) 벌다, (자질이 되어 무엇을) 받다
- 899 **BA degree** [biːei digríː] 명 학사 학위
- 900 **communicate** [kəmjúːnəkèit] 동 의사소통을 하다
- 901 **political** [pəlítikəl] 형 정치적인
- 902 **activist** [æktəvist] 명 운동가, 활동가
- 903 **lecturer** [léktʃərər] 명 강연가, 강사
- 904 **advertiser** [ædvərtàizər] 명 광고인, 광고회사
- 905 **trick** [trik] 명 속임수, 장난
- 906 **dump** [dʌmp] 동 버리다
- 907 **garbage** [gáːrbidʒ] 명 쓰레기

Chapter 15 접속사

PSS & PRACTICE

- 908 **talk on the phone** 전화로 얘기하다
- 909 **hurry up** 서두르다
- 910 **tonight** [tənáit] 부 오늘밤에
- 911 **heavy snow** [hévi snòu] 명 폭설
- 912 **do the laundry** 빨래를 하다
- 913 **be in trouble** 곤란한 상황에 있다
- 914 **pool** [puːl] 명 수영장, 웅덩이
- 915 **unhappy** [ʌnhǽpi] 형 불행한
- 916 **pity** [píti] 명 유감, 연민
- 917 **customer** [kʌ́stəmər] 명 손님, 고객
- 918 **quite** [kwait] 부 아주, 꽤, 제법
- 919 **successfully** [səksésfəli] 부 성공적으로
- 920 **instead of** ~ 대신에
- 921 **absent** [ǽbsnt] 형 결석의, 결근의
- 922 **traffic jam** [trǽfik dʒæm] 명 교통 정체

Chapter Review Test

- 923 **in order to** ~하기 위해
- 924 **nutritious** [njuːtríʃəs] 형 영양가 높은
- 925 **ride** [raid] 동 (차량을) 타다
- 926 **roller coaster** [róulər kòustər] 명 롤러코스터
- 927 **wear** [wɛər] 동 입다
- 928 **breakfast** [brékfəst] 명 아침 식사
- 929 **wash one's hair** 머리를 감다

Day 28

오늘 외울 단어 **34**개

- ☐ 930 **be compared to** ~와 비교되다
- ☐ 931 **western** [wéstərn] 형 서부의, 서쪽에 위치한
- ☐ 932 **pass by** 지나다, 지나치다
- ☐ 933 **in addition** 게다가
- ☐ 934 **luckily** [lʌ́kili] 부 운 좋게, 다행히도
- ☐ 935 **concentrate** [kánsəntrèit] 동 집중하다
- ☐ 936 **boss** [bɑs] 명 상사
- ☐ 937 **error** [érər] 명 오류, 실수
- ☐ 938 **second place** [sékənd pleis] 명 2등, 준우승
- ☐ 939 **feeling** [fíːliŋ] 명 감정, 기분
- ☐ 940 **eventually** [ivéntʃuəli] 부 결국
- ☐ 941 **attain** [ətéin] 동 이루다, 획득하다
- ☐ 942 **aim** [eim] 명 목적, 목표
- ☐ 943 **order** [ɔ́ːrdər] 동 주문하다
- ☐ 944 **substance** [sʌ́bstəns] 명 물질
- ☐ 945 **unusual** [ʌnjúːʒuəl] 형 특이한, 흔치 않은
- ☐ 946 **adopt** [ədápt] 동 입양하다
- ☐ 947 **resign** [rizáin] 동 사임하다
- ☐ 948 **amount** [əmáunt] 명 양, 액수

Chapter 16 전치사

👤 PSS & PRACTICE

- ☐ 949 **modern** [mádərn] 형 현대적인, 현대의
- ☐ 950 **sunset** [sʌ́nsèt] 명 해질녘, 일몰
- ☐ 951 **discovery** [diskʌ́vəri] 명 발견, 발견물
- ☐ 952 **coin** [kɔin] 명 동전, 주화
- ☐ 953 **floor** [flɔːr] 명 마루, 층
- ☐ 954 **at work** 일하는 중인, 직장에서
- ☐ 955 **prison** [prízn] 명 감옥, 교도소
- ☐ 956 **middle** [mídl] 명 중앙 형 한가운데의, 중앙의
- ☐ 957 **plane** [plein] 명 비행기
- ☐ 958 **island** [áilənd] 명 섬
- ☐ 959 **look up** (사전에서) 찾아보다
- ☐ 960 **welcome** [wélkəm] 동 환영하다 명 환영
- ☐ 961 **bridge** [bridʒ] 명 다리
- ☐ 962 **get out of** ~에서 나가다, ~에서 내리다
- ☐ 963 **stair** [stɛər] 명 계단, 층계

Day 29

오늘 외울 단어 **35**개

- ☐ 964 **ladder** [lǽdər] 명 사다리
- ☐ 965 **row** [rou] 동 노를 젓다
- ☐ 966 **serve** [sə:rv] 동 공을 서브하다
- ☐ 967 **jump** [dʒʌmp] 동 뛰다, 뛰어오르다
- ☐ 968 **rock** [rɑk] 명 바위
- ☐ 969 **streetlight** [strí:tlàit] 명 가로등
- ☐ 970 **forest** [fɔ́:rist] 명 숲
- ☐ 971 **postbox** [póustbɑ̀ks] 명 우체통
- ☐ 972 **corner** [kɔ́:rnər] 명 모퉁이, 구석
- ☐ 973 **tower** [tauər] 명 탑
- ☐ 974 **time difference** [taim dífərəns] 명 시차
- ☐ 975 **relationship** [riléiʃənʃip] 명 관계
- ☐ 976 **start** [stɑ:rt] 동 출발하다, 떠나다
- ☐ 977 **be on board** (배, 비행기 등에) 승선하다, 탑승하다
- ☐ 978 **flour** [flauər] 명 밀가루
- ☐ 979 **traditional** [trədíʃənl] 형 전통의, 전통적인
- ☐ 980 **be supposed to** ~하기로 되어 있다
- ☐ 981 **unlock** [ʌnlɑ́k] 동 (자물쇠를) 열다
- ☐ 982 **keep in touch** 연락하다
- ☐ 983 **novel** [nɑ́vəl] 명 소설
- ☐ 984 **in half** 반으로
- ☐ 985 **manager** [mǽnidʒər] 명 경영자, 관리자
- ☐ 986 **sketch** [sketʃ] 동 스케치하다
- ☐ 987 **romantic** [roumǽntik] 형 낭만적인
- ☐ 988 **manner** [mǽnər] 명 태도, 몸가짐
- ☐ 989 **cancer** [kǽnsər] 명 암
- ☐ 990 **response** [rispɑ́ns] 명 응답, 반응
- ☐ 991 **folk music** [fóuk mjú:zik] 명 민속 음악
- ☐ 992 **clown** [klaun] 명 어릿광대
- ☐ 993 **hunger** [hʌ́ŋgər] 명 굶주림, 기아
- ☐ 994 **dressed** [drest] 형 옷을 입은, 치장한
- ☐ 995 **in a hurry** 급히, 서둘러

Chapter Review Test

- ☐ 996 **address** [ǽdres] 명 주소
- ☐ 997 **stick** [stik] 동 찌르다, (풀 따위로) 붙이다
- ☐ 998 **envelope** [énvəlòup] 명 봉투

Day 30

오늘 외울 단어 **34**개

- 999 **first language** [fə:rst læŋgwidʒ] 명 모국어
- 1000 **wild** [waild] 형 야생의
- 1001 **bead** [bi:d] 명 구슬, 염주
- 1002 **frame** [freim] 명 액자, 틀
- 1003 **entrance** [éntrəns] 명 입장, 입학
- 1004 **federal** [fédərəl] 형 연방 정부의
- 1005 **patent** [pǽtnt] 명 특허권
- 1006 **emigration** [èməgréiʃən] 명 이민, 이주
- 1007 **atomic** [ətámik] 형 원자의, 원자력의
- 1008 **participate** [pɑ:rtísəpèit] 동 참가하다, 참여하다
- 1009 **ahead** [əhéd] 부 앞으로, 앞에
- 1010 **anti** [ǽnti] 전 반대하는, 좋아하지 않는
- 1011 **utopian** [ju:tóupiən] 형 유토피아적인, 이상적인
- 1012 **ideal** [aidí(:)əl] 형 이상적인, 완벽한
- 1013 **existence** [igzístəns] 명 존재, 실재
- 1014 **passport** [pǽspɔ:rt] 명 여권
- 1015 **construct** [kənstrʌ́kt] 동 건설하다
- 1016 **flood** [flʌd] 명 홍수
- 1017 **due** [dju:] 형 ~하기로 예정된

Chapter 17 일치·도치·화법&속담

PSS & PRACTICE

- 1018 **grateful for** ~를 감사히 여기는
- 1019 **learn** [lə:rn] 동 배우다
- 1020 **member** [mémbər] 명 회원, 구성원
- 1021 **raise** [reiz] 동 모으다
- 1022 **donation** [dounéiʃən] 명 기부
- 1023 **be ready to** ~할 준비가 되다
- 1024 **hope** [houp] 명 희망 동 바라다
- 1025 **against** [əgénst] 전 ~에 반대하여
- 1026 **watch out** 주의하다, 조심하다
- 1027 **junk food** [dʒʌŋk fù:d] 명 즉석식품, 정크푸드
- 1028 **haste** [heist] 명 서두름
- 1029 **waste** [weist] 명 낭비
- 1030 **command** [kəmǽnd] 동 명령하다
- 1031 **calm** [kɑ:m] 명 평온함 형 차분한
- 1032 **thick** [θik] 형 진한, 두꺼운

Day 31

오늘 외울 단어 35개

1033	**strike** [straik]	동 치다, 때리다	1050	**data** [déitə]	명 자료, 정보
1034	**candle** [kǽndl]	명 양초	1051	**take up one's time**	~의 시간을 빼앗다
1035	**fear** [fíər]	명 두려움, 공포	1052	**goose** [guːs]	명 거위
1036	**worth** [wəːrθ]	형 ~의 가치가 있는	1053	**fool** [fuːl]	명 바보
1037	**gather** [gǽðər]	동 모이다, 모으다	1054	**roof** [ruːf]	명 지붕
1038	**moss** [mɔːs]	명 이끼	1055	**envious** [énviəs]	형 부러워하는
1039	**mighty** [máiti]	형 강력한	1056	**come close to**	거의 ~하게 되다
1040	**sword** [sɔːrd]	명 검, 칼	1057	**safely** [séifli]	부 무사히
1041	**will** [wil]	명 의지	1058	**device** [diváis]	명 장치
1042	**bush** [buʃ]	명 덤불	1059	**laser** [léizər]	명 레이저

Chapter Review Test

			1060	**image** [ímidʒ]	명 영상, 이미지
1043	**wrath** [ræθ]	명 분노, 노여움	1061	**purpose** [pə́ːrpəs]	명 목적
1044	**keep one's mouth closed**	비밀을 지키다	1062	**alert** [əláːrt]	동 (위험을) 알리다, 경보를 발하다
1045	**give away**	거저 주다, 수여하다	1063	**nearby** [níərbài]	형 인근의, 가까운 곳의
1046	**turn up**	나타나다, (소리·온도 등을) 올리다	1064	**lessen** [lésn]	동 줄이다
1047	**turn away**	물리치다, 외면하다	1065	**silver lining** [sílvər láiniŋ]	명 구름의 흰 가장자리, 밝은 희망
1048	**general** [dʒénərəl]	명 장군	1066	**cloudy** [kláudi]	형 날이 흐린
1049	**invitation** [ìnvitéiʃən]	명 초대, 초대장	1067	**cheer up**	격려하다, 힘을 불러일으키다

마더텅 영문법 3800제 2
INTERMEDIATE

Word Test

Problem Solving Skill

마 더 텅

Word Test 001 - 035

Day 01

날짜:　　　　　　점수　　/ 35

● 영어를 우리말로 쓰세요.

01	pay
02	homework
03	pass
04	be good at
05	draw
06	leave
07	meeting
08	exam
09	guy
10	vacation
11	favorite
12	during
13	prize
14	arrive
15	take a rest
16	finish
17	cash
18	buy

● 우리말을 영어로 쓰세요.

19	진실인, 사실인
20	스테이크
21	시간에 맞게, 정각에
22	건강한
23	~ 없이
24	(~하다고) 느끼다, (~한) 기분이다
25	운동하다, 운동, 연습
26	돌아오다
27	이기다
28	(~한) 맛이 나다, 맛보다
29	~에 들어가다
30	강아지
31	경주
32	영화를 보러 가다
33	신용카드
34	동급생, 반 친구
35	국수, 면류

Word Test 036-071　　　　Day 02

날짜:　　　　점수　　/36

● 영어를 우리말로 쓰세요.

01 | wonder
02 | important
03 | think
04 | right
05 | friendly
06 | problem
07 | mean
08 | patient
09 | terrible
10 | solve
11 | polite
12 | ask
13 | interesting
14 | turn
15 | special
16 | appear
17 | strange
18 | bring

● 우리말을 영어로 쓰세요.

19 | 창조적인, 독창적인
20 | 깨뜨리다, 부수다
21 | 대우하다, 다루다
22 | 어제
23 | 믿다
24 | ~처럼 보이다
25 | 데이트하다, 날짜
26 | 신, 시큼한
27 | 빌려주다
28 | 휴식, 안정, 쉬다
29 | 잃다, (게임, 경기에) 지다
30 | 갑자기
31 | 질문, 문제
32 | 조언, 충고
33 | 조용한
34 | 나르다, 운반하다
35 | ~하게 되다, 자라다
36 | 습기 있는

Word Test 072-106

Day 03

날짜: 점수 / 35

● 영어를 우리말로 쓰세요.

01 | inventor
02 | surprising
03 | grade
04 | regularly
05 | include
06 | bullet
07 | shake
08 | shout
09 | throw
10 | laptop
11 | consider
12 | bulb
13 | typewriter
14 | rule
15 | iron
16 | unkind
17 | upset

● 우리말을 영어로 쓰세요.

18 | 유명한
19 | 가격
20 | ~에게 미소를 짓다
21 | 온도
22 | 경탄할 만한
23 | 기억하다
24 | 어려운, 곤란한
25 | 보조개
26 | 축음기
27 | 역사
28 | ~처럼 보이다[생기다]
29 | ~을 (더) 좋아하다
30 | 짖다
31 | 발명하다
32 | 사전
33 | (일이) 발생하다
34 | 건드리다, 만지다
35 | 땅에 떨어지다

Word Test 107-140

Day 04

날짜:　　　　　　점수　　/34

● 영어를 우리말로 쓰세요.

01 | serious
02 | all the time
03 | neat
04 | spotlessly
05 | depart
06 | lonely
07 | chemistry
08 | semester
09 | bitter
10 | inside
11 | warm
12 | diligent
13 | scream
14 | reward
15 | relax
16 | sleepy

● 우리말을 영어로 쓰세요.

17 | 광산
18 | 물리학
19 | 입증하다, 증명하다
20 | 들어 올리다
21 | 줄이다
22 | 맛있는
23 | 현실적인
24 | (아이를) 낳다, 견디다
25 | 재미있는, 우스운
26 | 큰 박수
27 | 발랄한
28 | 복사하다
29 | 파괴하다
30 | (총, 화살을) 쏘다
31 | 물다
32 | 불평하다
33 | 올리다, 기르다
34 | 숨 쉬다, 호흡하다

Word Test 141-176 — Day 05

● 영어를 우리말로 쓰세요.

01 | recommend
02 | serve
03 | allow
04 | vow
05 | discover
06 | imagine
07 | close
08 | wrap
09 | suppose
10 | exchange
11 | add
12 | mention
13 | admire
14 | quit
15 | argue
16 | appreciate
17 | lead
18 | in need

● 우리말을 영어로 쓰세요.

19 | 묘사하다
20 | 재활용하다
21 | 늘이다, 늘어나다
22 | ~와 결혼하다
23 | (땅을) 파다
24 | 구조하다, 구하다
25 | 밀다
26 | 생산하다
27 | (액체, 기체, 전류가) 흐르다
28 | 엎지르다, 쏟다
29 | 선출하다
30 | (알을) 까다, 부화하다
31 | 면접을 보다, 면접
32 | 치다, 두드리다
33 | 기원하다, 기도하다
34 | 따다, 고르다
35 | 싸우다
36 | 가라앉다

Word Test 177-212　　　　　　　　　　Day 06

날짜:　　　　　　점수　　/36

● 영어를 우리말로 쓰세요.

01 | control
02 | consist
03 | reply
04 | indeed
05 | chat
06 | blame
07 | practice
08 | offer
09 | notice
10 | rip
11 | rush
12 | delay
13 | worry
14 | around
15 | realize
16 | fix
17 | cause
18 | select

● 우리말을 영어로 쓰세요.

19 | 공표하다, 출판하다
20 | 관찰하다
21 | 떨어뜨리다, 떨어지다
22 | (해, 달이) 뜨다, 오르다
23 | 발로 차다
24 | 연장, 도구
25 | 튀어나오다
26 | 작동하다, 수술을 하다
27 | 사라지다
28 | 숙이다, 절하다
29 | 받아쓰게 하다
30 | 죽다
31 | 형성하다
32 | 당기다
33 | 낭비하다
34 | 재판하다, 판단하다
35 | 모으다, 수집하다
36 | 괴롭히다, 놀리다

Word Test 213-248 — Day 07

날짜:　　　　점수　　/36

● 영어를 우리말로 쓰세요.

01 | contest
02 | blow
03 | burn
04 | lay
05 | share
06 | sweep
07 | be born
08 | join
09 | show
10 | tumble
11 | painting
12 | report
13 | deny
14 | fill
15 | build
16 | roll
17 | cheat
18 | remove

● 우리말을 영어로 쓰세요.

19 | 훔치다
20 | 닫다
21 | 직면하다, 마주하다
22 | 극복하다
23 | 따라가다, 따르다
24 | 한밤중, 자정
25 | 집안일
26 | 말하기, 연설
27 | 넘어지다, 떨어지다
28 | 빛나다
29 | 행동하다
30 | 되풀이하다
31 | 기념하다, 축하하다
32 | 때리다, 치다
33 | 숨기다
34 | 격려하다, 장려하다
35 | 눕다, 놓여 있다
36 | (손에) 들다, 잡다

Word Test 249-283

Day 08

날짜:　　　　　점수　　/35

● 영어를 우리말로 쓰세요.

01 | a lot
02 | send
03 | nervous
04 | spend
05 | prejudice
06 | flight
07 | pass away
08 | stand
09 | hurt
10 | recently
11 | sure
12 | climbing
13 | empty
14 | fable
15 | parent
16 | several
17 | set up
18 | leave for

● 우리말을 영어로 쓰세요.

19 | 일기를 쓰다
20 | ~로 가는 도중에
21 | 암탉
22 | 식물, 초목
23 | 선장
24 | 쓸모 있는, 유용한
25 | 자부심, 자만, 긍지
26 | 극장
27 | 샤워를 하다
28 | 심하게, 대량으로, 무겁게
29 | 낮잠을 자다
30 | 배우
31 | 인기 있는
32 | 꽃병
33 | 요즘에, 최근에
34 | ~에서 출발하다
35 | 지갑, (서류를 넣는 납작한) 가방

Word Test 284-317 — Day 09

● 영어를 우리말로 쓰세요.

01 | elderly
02 | feed
03 | language
04 | exit
05 | bud
06 | notebook
07 | statue
08 | hang
09 | zoo
10 | horror
11 | seed
12 | thief
13 | give an answer
14 | liberty
15 | take off
16 | mobile phone
17 | take care of

● 우리말을 영어로 쓰세요.

18 | 몰래 잠입하다
19 | 산책 가다
20 | 조심스럽게, 신중하게
21 | 태우러 가다, 태우다
22 | 대학교
23 | 찾다
24 | 산책시키다, 걷다
25 | 에스컬레이터
26 | 주차하다
27 | 횡단하다
28 | 첫 번째의
29 | 요리, 접시
30 | 안전한
31 | 백화점
32 | 다이어트를 하다
33 | 진실
34 | 피를 흘리다

Word Test 318-352　　　　Day 10

날짜:　　　　점수:　　/35

● 영어를 우리말로 쓰세요.

01 | unbelievable
02 | kind
03 | get lost
04 | possible
05 | accident
06 | stadium
07 | look around
08 | koala
09 | competition
10 | bright
11 | handicapped
12 | favor
13 | midterm
14 | shopper
15 | school uniform
16 | throat
17 | by oneself
18 | go out

● 우리말을 영어로 쓰세요.

19 | 시끄럽게 하다
20 | 잘하다, 성공하다
21 | 아픈, 쓰린
22 | 가까운, 근처의
23 | 심부름
24 | 최선을 다하다
25 | 미래
26 | 짠, 짭짤한
27 | ~의 부탁을 들어주다
28 | 상을 받다
29 | (소리, 온도 등을) 낮추다
30 | 생계 수단, 생활
31 | (시간 단위의) 초
32 | 확신하는, 확실한
33 | 이번에도, 다시 한 번
34 | 팔다
35 | 기억

Word Test 353 - 386 — Day 11

● 영어를 우리말로 쓰세요.

01 | turn right
02 | call
03 | plan
04 | prepare
05 | keep
06 | joy
07 | hold
08 | play
09 | director
10 | bottle
11 | obey
12 | change
13 | resource
14 | catch
15 | result
16 | understand
17 | postpone

● 우리말을 영어로 쓰세요.

18 | 거짓말, 거짓말하다
19 | 말, 단어
20 | 잡지
21 | 복사기
22 | 사랑스러운, 아름다운
23 | 대통령, 회장
24 | 존경하다
25 | 경치
26 | 배달하다
27 | 정보
28 | 베어내다
29 | 용서하다
30 | 사냥꾼
31 | 오염시키다
32 | 직무, 과제
33 | 계산서, 청구서
34 | 눈물

Word Test 387 - 419

Day 12

날짜: 점수   /33

● 영어를 우리말로 쓰세요.

01	canned
02	resemble
03	experiment
04	rob
05	mystery
06	conference
07	surround
08	activity
09	neighbor
10	ferry
11	ruin
12	penny
13	custom
14	classroom
15	firefighter
16	poem

● 우리말을 영어로 쓰세요.

17	다수의, 한 묶음의
18	~에게 맞다, 어울리다
19	당나귀
20	문화
21	시장, 군수
22	이론
23	긴 의자, 소파
24	성냥, 경기, 시합
25	발표하다, 공개하다
26	반지
27	공장
28	고무
29	우표
30	~에 이름을 지어주다
31	개인의, 개인적인
32	열리다, 개최되다
33	학장, 교장

Word Test 420 - 455

Day 13

● 영어를 우리말로 쓰세요.

01 | cheerful
02 | furniture
03 | policy
04 | across
05 | look forward to
06 | express
07 | sheep
08 | beauty
09 | tax
10 | take part in
11 | audience
12 | autumn
13 | knowledge
14 | death
15 | while
16 | politics
17 | shocking
18 | support

● 우리말을 영어로 쓰세요.

19 | 모기
20 | 수단, 방법
21 | 공동체, 지역사회
22 | 경제학
23 | 금고, 안전한
24 | 주제
25 | 장(長), 상사
26 | 친절, 호의
27 | 비상사태
28 | 지진
29 | 영웅
30 | 세관
31 | 송아지
32 | 도심지의, 도심지
33 | 정직
34 | 여행을 가다
35 | 황소
36 | 믿음, 신조

Word Test 456-490 — Day 14

날짜: 점수   / 35

● 영어를 우리말로 쓰세요.

01 | feather
02 | toast
03 | carelessly
04 | interest
05 | walk
06 | bottom
07 | comfortable
08 | borrow
09 | tend to
10 | in a moment
11 | goods
12 | very
13 | the other day
14 | government
15 | fact
16 | scenery
17 | impossible

● 우리말을 영어로 쓰세요.

18 | 외국의
19 | 평평한
20 | 고래
21 | 심리학, 심리
22 | 독특한
23 | 낯선 사람
24 | 담요
25 | 교수
26 | 퇴직하다
27 | 수업, 교훈
28 | (국가의) 수도
29 | 떼, 무리, 모이다
30 | 우주선
31 | 여자 조카
32 | 손으로 만든
33 | 성적표
34 | 열, 줄
35 | 선원, 뱃사람

Word Test 491-524   Day 15

날짜:　　　　　점수　　/34

● 영어를 우리말로 쓰세요.

01 | lawyer
02 | piece
03 | title
04 | innocent
05 | spoonful
06 | noisy
07 | loaf
08 | cucumber
09 | musical instrument
10 | fail
11 | slice
12 | marathon
13 | pork
14 | loudly
15 | bowl
16 | plain
17 | pound

● 우리말을 영어로 쓰세요.

18 | ~을 통하여
19 | 무시하다
20 | 적어도
21 | 중요성
22 | 냉장하다
23 | 표지
24 | 젓다, 섞다
25 | 양념하다
26 | (검은) 후추
27 | 우연히
28 | ~에 발을 딛다
29 | ~을 자랑스러워하다
30 | 충성스러운
31 | ~에 통달하다
32 | 정직한
33 | 실현되다
34 | (잘게) 갈다

Word Test 525 - 559 Day 16

날짜:　　　　점수　　/ 35

● 영어를 우리말로 쓰세요.

01 | make oneself at home
02 | wait for
03 | disappointing
04 | throw away
05 | club
06 | care
07 | all of a sudden
08 | correctly
09 | fiction
10 | suggestion
11 | always
12 | treasure
13 | be known for
14 | chance
15 | logo
16 | author
17 | drop by

● 우리말을 영어로 쓰세요.

18 | 천, 옷감
19 | 거울
20 | 우정
21 | 비싼
22 | 예, 예시
23 | 인구
24 | 옷장
25 | 피고용자, 종업원
26 | 승객
27 | (온도, 각도 단위) 도, 정도
28 | 쌍둥이 중 한 명, 쌍둥이의
29 | 12개, 12개짜리 한 묶음
30 | 소개하다
31 | 풍선
32 | 천문학자
33 | 성공하다
34 | 공연, 연주
35 | 흡연하다

Word Test 560-595 — Day 17

● 영어를 우리말로 쓰세요.

01 | be afraid of
02 | astronaut
03 | fluently
04 | climate
05 | tiny
06 | look after
07 | boil
08 | spicy
09 | same
10 | save
11 | pollution
12 | minute
13 | burn
14 | divide up
15 | homeroom
16 | for sale
17 | own
18 | dentist

● 우리말을 영어로 쓰세요.

19 | 빤히 쳐다보다
20 | 바이올린
21 | 고장 나다
22 | 할로윈
23 | 자주색의, 보라색의
24 | 연예인
25 | 우산
26 | (창문에 치는) 블라인드
27 | 만화책
28 | 우주, 공간
29 | 장갑
30 | ~하곤 했다
31 | ~와 함께 살다
32 | 주제, 화제
33 | 의견
34 | 텐트를 치다
35 | 백합
36 | 찻주전자

Word Test 596-629　　Day 18

날짜:　　　　점수　/34

● 영어를 우리말로 쓰세요.

01 | enough
02 | cheap
03 | confusing
04 | expect
05 | reach
06 | explain
07 | disappointed
08 | repair
09 | protect
10 | jacket
11 | pleased
12 | surprised
13 | garage sale
14 | trust
15 | refuse
16 | generous
17 | clearly

● 우리말을 영어로 쓰세요.

18 | 운 좋은
19 | 시력
20 | 나비
21 | 농작물
22 | 선반
23 | 인터넷 서핑을 하다
24 | (고개를) 끄덕이다
25 | 대학, 단과대학
26 | 기말고사
27 | 음악가
28 | 위층으로, 위층에(서)
29 | 결심하다
30 | (자동차의) 앞 유리
31 | 문제, 일
32 | 필수적인, 없어서는 안 될
33 | 유인하다, 끌어당기다
34 | 조깅하다

Word Test 630 - 662 — Day 19

날짜: 점수   / 33

● 영어를 우리말로 쓰세요.

01 | continue
02 | depress
03 | refresh
04 | put off
05 | dangerous
06 | design
07 | chairman
08 | skip
09 | saving
10 | license
11 | dislike
12 | course
13 | business
14 | apologize
15 | have dinner
16 | pass the exam

● 우리말을 영어로 쓰세요.

17 | 시골, 지방
18 | 쓰레기
19 | 잠시 동안
20 | 일찍 일어나다
21 | 신경 쓰다, 꺼려하다
22 | 돌고래
23 | 밖에서, 옥외로
24 | 가면, 복면
25 | 도움이 되는
26 | 도서관
27 | 노력
28 | 우체국
29 | 거만한, 자랑스러워하는
30 | 끝나다, 끝내다
31 | 깊은
32 | 탁구
33 | (벨, 종이) 울리다

Word Test 663-695 — Day 20

날짜:　　　　점수　　/33

● 영어를 우리말로 쓰세요.

01 | debate
02 | prevent
03 | violate
04 | usually
05 | interrupt
06 | plant
07 | responsible
08 | regulation
09 | package
10 | depressing
11 | recent
12 | difficulty
13 | postcard
14 | grow up
15 | major
16 | illness

● 우리말을 영어로 쓰세요.

17 | 결국에
18 | 디저트, 후식
19 | ~을 돌보다
20 | 교통
21 | 용돈
22 | (소리 내어) 웃다
23 | 삶은, 끓은
24 | 무식한, 무지한
25 | 떨어지다
26 | (전등, 기계 등을) 켜다
27 | 산책하다
28 | 주유소
29 | 균형 잡힌
30 | 일정, 스케줄
31 | (기계 등을) 개선하다
32 | 사랑에 빠지다
33 | (~로) 가득 차다, 채우다

Word Test 696-728 — Day 21

● 영어를 우리말로 쓰세요.

01 | restroom
02 | cross
03 | shed
04 | excited
05 | pot
06 | puzzle
07 | beside
08 | amaze
09 | amusement park
10 | festival
11 | embarrass
12 | public
13 | cartoon
14 | gym
15 | fall asleep
16 | satisfy
17 | fantastic

● 우리말을 영어로 쓰세요.

18 | 결국에는
19 | 식수
20 | ~을 치우다, 청소하다
21 | 해변, 바닷가
22 | 유형, 종류
23 | 에세이, 수필
24 | 도망치다
25 | 주인, 소유주
26 | 잔디, 풀
27 | 무대, 단계
28 | 묶다, 매다
29 | 실수로
30 | 감동시키다
31 | 후라이팬
32 | 휴가, 방학
33 | ~로 가득 차다

Word Test 729-761 — Day 22

날짜:　　　　　점수　　/33

● 영어를 우리말로 쓰세요.

01 | experience
02 | intonation
03 | collection
04 | proverb
05 | asleep
06 | rich
07 | unpleasant
08 | familiar
09 | trendy
10 | depressed
11 | brave
12 | refrigerator
13 | blind
14 | alike
15 | wrong
16 | daughter
17 | fitness center

● 우리말을 영어로 쓰세요.

18 | 부끄러워하는, 수치스러운
19 | 살아 있는
20 | 100만의, 100만
21 | 많음, 풍부
22 | 체중이 증가하다
23 | 지적인, 총명한
24 | 겁에 질린
25 | 잘생긴
26 | ~을 제외하고
27 | 귀가 먼
28 | 불가사리
29 | 스트레스를 받다
30 | 목걸이
31 | (책의) 장
32 | 금속
33 | 인상적인, 인상 깊은

Word Test 762-796　　Day 23

날짜:　　　　　점수　　/ 35

● 영어를 우리말로 쓰세요.

01 | shake hands
02 | sincere
03 | impressed
04 | closely
05 | still
06 | highly
07 | admission
08 | final
09 | look for
10 | slow
11 | call off
12 | nearly
13 | take out
14 | hardly
15 | deeply
16 | anxious
17 | such
18 | check out

● 우리말을 영어로 쓰세요.

19 | 간단한, 단순한
20 | 짓궂은, 비열한
21 | 지속되다
22 | 시원한, 서늘한
23 | 쉽게, 용이하게
24 | 의도, 목적
25 | 약간의, 근소한
26 | 졸업하다
27 | 참석하다, 출석하다
28 | 인사하다, 환영하다
29 | 입어 보다
30 | 눈에 보이는
31 | 합리적인, 타당한
32 | 갑작스러운, 뜻밖의
33 | 술, 알코올
34 | 온화한, 친절한
35 | 포기하다

Word Test 797-829　　　Day 24

●영어를 우리말로 쓰세요.

01 | be able to
02 | interview
03 | quickly
04 | set up
05 | discuss
06 | youth
07 | as if
08 | lecture
09 | fly
10 | visit
11 | item
12 | be in danger
13 | bomb
14 | cell phone
15 | successful
16 | invite
17 | station

●우리말을 영어로 쓰세요.

18 | 실은, 사실
19 | 공짜로, 무료로
20 | ~를 태워주다
21 | 열심히 하는, 단단한, 어려운
22 | 폭발하다
23 | 꽃을 피우다
24 | 전시, 표현
25 | 시험에 통과하다
26 | 교회
27 | ~에게 알리다
28 | 피부
29 | 설거지하다
30 | 살이 빠지다
31 | (물건을) 쌓다
32 | 불꽃놀이, 폭죽
33 | 벚꽃

Word Test 830 - 862 — Day 25

날짜: 점수   / 33

● 영어를 우리말로 쓰세요.

01 | present
02 | tasty
03 | especially
04 | curious
05 | transportation
06 | write back to
07 | boring
08 | kindly
09 | per
10 | count
11 | version
12 | mild
13 | convenient
14 | save
15 | exactly
16 | wise
17 | thin

● 우리말을 영어로 쓰세요.

18 | 무게가 ~ 나가다
19 | 무서운, 두려운
20 | 활동적인, 적극적인
21 | 기린
22 | 거북
23 | 수명
24 | 창백한
25 | 생산물, 상품
26 | 코끼리
27 | 명성
28 | 높이, 키
29 | 쓸모없는
30 | 젖은
31 | 글, 기사
32 | 발명품, 발명
33 | 바보 같은

Word Test 863-896 Day 26

날짜:　　　　　점수　　/34

● 영어를 우리말로 쓰세요.

01 | technique
02 | cancel
03 | village
04 | disappoint
05 | stove
06 | judge
07 | suggest
08 | do harm
09 | eat up
10 | heritage
11 | pocket
12 | environment
13 | focus on
14 | site
15 | sharp
16 | magic
17 | project

● 우리말을 영어로 쓰세요.

18 | ~에 속하다, ~의 것이다
19 | 가르치다
20 | 거리, 도로
21 | 탁자
22 | 돌, 비석
23 | (불을) 끄다
24 | 화가
25 | 젓가락
26 | 지도자
27 | 이유, 동기
28 | 다큐멘터리, 기록물
29 | 수여하다
30 | 경찰관
31 | 인삼
32 | 무덤
33 | 사람, 개인
34 | 할인 중인

Word Test 897-929 — Day 27

● 영어를 우리말로 쓰세요.

01 | advertiser
02 | communicate
03 | pity
04 | absent
05 | unhappy
06 | garbage
07 | customer
08 | lecturer
09 | trick
10 | successfully
11 | instead of
12 | quite
13 | pool
14 | earn
15 | political
16 | activist
17 | dump

● 우리말을 영어로 쓰세요.

18 | 학사 학위
19 | 폭설
20 | ~하기 위해
21 | 입다
22 | 아침 식사
23 | 머리를 감다
24 | (빵 등을) 굽다
25 | 롤러코스터
26 | 교통 정체
27 | (차량을) 타다
28 | 영양가 높은
29 | 곤란한 상황에 있다
30 | 전화로 얘기하다
31 | 오늘밤에
32 | 빨래를 하다
33 | 서두르다

Word Test 930-963　　Day 28

날짜:　　　　점수　　/34

● 영어를 우리말로 쓰세요.

01 | amount
02 | unusual
03 | resign
04 | eventually
05 | discovery
06 | look up
07 | bridge
08 | attain
09 | western
10 | luckily
11 | concentrate
12 | adopt
13 | feeling
14 | order
15 | in addition
16 | substance
17 | be compared to

● 우리말을 영어로 쓰세요.

18 | ~에서 나가다, ~에서 내리다
19 | 계단, 층계
20 | 현대적인, 현대의
21 | 중앙, 한가운데의, 중앙의
22 | 환영하다, 환영
23 | 지나다, 지나치다
24 | 감옥, 교도소
25 | 섬
26 | 동전, 주화
27 | 목적, 목표
28 | 비행기
29 | 상사
30 | 마루, 층
31 | 2등, 준우승
32 | 일하는 중인, 직장에서
33 | 해질녘, 일몰
34 | 오류, 실수

Word Test 964 - 998 Day 29

●영어를 우리말로 쓰세요.

01 | row
02 | in a hurry
03 | corner
04 | response
05 | relationship
06 | in half
07 | flour
08 | keep in touch
09 | unlock
10 | be supposed to
11 | novel
12 | start
13 | manner
14 | tower
15 | dressed
16 | serve
17 | stick

●우리말을 영어로 쓰세요.

18 | 시차
19 | 봉투
20 | 전통의, 전통적인
21 | 굶주림, 기아
22 | 스케치하다
23 | 바위
24 | 암
25 | 숲
26 | 민속 음악
27 | 경영자, 관리자
28 | 우체통
29 | 낭만적인
30 | 가로등
31 | 어릿광대
32 | 뛰다, 뛰어오르다
33 | 사다리
34 | (배, 비행기 등에) 승선하다, 탑승하다
35 | 주소

Word Test 999-1032　　Day 30

날짜:　　　점수　　/34

● 영어를 우리말로 쓰세요.

01 | donation
02 | frame
03 | hope
04 | haste
05 | patent
06 | against
07 | raise
08 | existence
09 | emigration
10 | entrance
11 | due
12 | bead
13 | ideal
14 | participate
15 | utopian
16 | anti
17 | construct

● 우리말을 영어로 쓰세요.

18 | 명령하다
19 | 회원, 구성원
20 | 홍수
21 | 낭비
22 | 평온함, 차분한
23 | 진한, 두꺼운
24 | 즉석식품, 정크푸드
25 | ~를 감사히 여기는
26 | 야생의
27 | 앞으로, 앞에
28 | 연방 정부의
29 | ~할 준비가 되다
30 | 배우다
31 | 주의하다, 조심하다
32 | 모국어
33 | 여권
34 | 원자의, 원자력의

Word Test 1033-1067　　Day 31

● 영어를 우리말로 쓰세요.

01 | purpose
02 | invitation
03 | lessen
04 | take up one's time
05 | turn up
06 | device
07 | turn away
08 | alert
09 | sword
10 | roof
11 | give away
12 | fool
13 | general
14 | envious
15 | keep one's mouth closed
16 | nearby
17 | safely

● 우리말을 영어로 쓰세요.

18 | 두려움, 공포
19 | 분노, 노여움
20 | 강력한
21 | 의지
22 | 자료, 정보
23 | 영상, 이미지
24 | 날이 흐린
25 | 구름의 흰 가장자리, 밝은 희망
26 | ~의 가치가 있는
27 | 레이저
28 | 격려하다, 힘을 불러일으키다
29 | 모이다, 모으다
30 | 양초
31 | 거의 ~하게 되다
32 | 덤불
33 | 이끼
34 | 거위
35 | 치다, 때리다

마더텅 영문법 3800제 2 INTERMEDIATE 학습계획표

DAY	Ch	학습내용	학습날짜
DAY 1	1	PSS 1-1 ~ 1-4	월 일
DAY 2		PSS 1-5 ~ 1-8	월 일
DAY 3		PSS 2-1 ~ 2-6	월 일
DAY 4		Chapter Review Test	월 일
DAY 5	2	PSS 1-1 ~ 2-4	월 일
DAY 6		PSS 3 ~ 4-2	월 일
DAY 7		PSS 5-1 ~ 5-5	월 일
DAY 8		Chapter Review Test	월 일
DAY 9	3	PSS 1 ~ 4-4	월 일
DAY 10		PSS 4-5 ~ 4-9	월 일
DAY 11		Chapter Review Test	월 일
DAY 12	4	PSS 1 ~ 2	월 일
DAY 13		PSS 3 ~ 4	월 일
DAY 14		PSS 5 ~ 7	월 일
DAY 15		Chapter Review Test	월 일
DAY 16	5	PSS 1-1 ~ 1-3	월 일
DAY 17		PSS 2-1 ~ 2-7	월 일
DAY 18		PSS 3-1 ~ 5	월 일
DAY 19		Chapter Review Test	월 일
DAY 20	6	PSS 1-1 ~ 2-3	월 일
DAY 21		PSS 3-1 ~ 4-3	월 일
DAY 22		PSS 4-4 ~ 5-2	월 일
DAY 23		Chapter Review Test	월 일
DAY 24	7	PSS 1-1 ~ 1-4	월 일
DAY 25		PSS 2 ~ 3-2	월 일
DAY 26		PSS 4 ~ 6	월 일
DAY 27		Chapter Review Test	월 일
DAY 28	8	PSS 1 ~ 2-3	월 일
DAY 29		PSS 3 ~ 4	월 일
DAY 30		Chapter Review Test	월 일
DAY 31	9	PSS 1 ~ 3	월 일
DAY 32		PSS 4 ~ 5-2	월 일
DAY 33		Chapter Review Test	월 일
DAY 34	10	PSS 1 ~ 4	월 일
DAY 35		PSS 5-1 ~ 5-4	월 일
DAY 36		PSS 6-1 ~ 6-3	월 일
DAY 37		Chapter Review Test	월 일
DAY 38	11	PSS 1-1 ~ 1-4	월 일
DAY 39		PSS 2-1 ~ 2-7	월 일
DAY 40		Chapter Review Test	월 일
DAY 41	12	PSS 1 ~ 2-3	월 일
DAY 42		PSS 3-1 ~ 3-3	월 일
DAY 43		Chapter Review Test	월 일
DAY 44	13	PSS 1-1 ~ 1-4	월 일
DAY 45		PSS 2-1 ~ 3-6	월 일
DAY 46		PSS 4-1 ~ 4-3	월 일
DAY 47		Chapter Review Test	월 일
DAY 48	14	PSS 1-1 ~ 1-4	월 일
DAY 49		PSS 1-5 ~ 2-2	월 일
DAY 50		Chapter Review Test	월 일
DAY 51	15	PSS 1 ~ 5	월 일
DAY 52		PSS 6 ~ 10	월 일
DAY 53		Chapter Review Test	월 일
DAY 54	16	PSS 1-1 ~ 1-6	월 일
DAY 55		PSS 2-1 ~ 2-6	월 일
DAY 56		PSS 2-7 ~ 3-4	월 일
DAY 57		Chapter Review Test	월 일
DAY 58	17	PSS 1-1 ~ 3	월 일
DAY 59		PSS 4 ~ 6	월 일
DAY 60		Chapter Review Test	월 일

학습계획표 작성하고, 선물 받으세요! 참여해 주신 모든 분께 선물을 드립니다.

책을 다 풀고, SNS 또는 온라인 커뮤니티에 작성한 학습계획표 사진을 업로드

좌측 QR코드를 스캔하여 작성한 게시물의 URL 인증

참여자 전원 증정!

1천 원권   2천 점

필수 태그 #마더텅 #마더텅영문법3800제 #학습계획표 #공스타그램
SNS / 온라인 커뮤니티 페이스북, 인스타그램, 블로그, 네이버/다음 카페 등

※ 상품은 이벤트 참여일로부터 2~3일(영업일 기준) 내에 발송됩니다.
※ 동일한 교재의 학습계획표로 중복 참여 시, 이벤트 대상에서 제외됩니다.
※ 자세한 사항은 왼쪽 QR 코드를 스캔하거나 또는 홈페이지 이벤트 공지글을 참고해 주세요.
※ 만 14세 미만은 부모님께서 신청해 주셔야 합니다.
※ 이벤트 기간: 2023년 12월 31일까지 (※해당 이벤트는 당사 사정에 따라 조기 종료될 수 있습니다.)

⑧ Book 포인트란? 마더텅 인터넷 서점(http://book.toptutor.co.kr)에서 교재 구매 시 현금처럼 사용할 수 있는 포인트입니다.

필수암기 동사구

단어	뜻	예시
bring up	~을 기르다, 양육하다	She brought up five children. 그녀는 다섯 명의 아이를 길렀다.
carry out	~을 수행하다	They will carry out their duties. 그들은 그들의 임무를 수행할 것이다.
catch up with	~을 따라잡다	James started pedalling faster, and within seconds caught up with her. James는 더 빨리 페달을 밟기 시작했고, 수 초 이내에 그녀를 따라잡았다.
call off	~을 취소하다	I have to call off the meeting. 나는 회의를 취소해야겠어요.
deal with	~을 처리하다	There are important matters to deal with. 처리해야 할 중요한 사안들이 있다.
get rid of	~을 없애다, 처분하다	I am going to get rid of my old car. 나는 낡은 차를 처분하려고 한다.
knock down	~을 치다, 때려눕히다	He knocked his opponent down three times. 그는 상대를 세 번 때려눕혔다.
laugh at	~을 비웃다	Amy thinks people will laugh at her if she sings. Amy는 만약 그녀가 노래를 한다면 사람들이 그녀를 비웃을 것이라고 생각한다.
look after	~을 돌보다	I need someone to look after my dog. 내 애완견을 돌봐줄 사람이 필요하다.
look down on	~을 낮춰보다(얕보다)	Don't look down on me because I'm young. 내가 어리다고 얕보지 마세요.
look up to	~을 존경하다	I look up to my parents. 나는 우리 부모님을 존경한다.
take advantage of	~을 이용하다	We took full advantage of the school facilities. 우리는 학교 시설을 최대한 이용했다.
pay attention to	~에 주의를 기울이다	Pay attention to what I'm saying! 제 말에 귀 기울여 주세요!
pick up	~을 줍다/(차에) 태우다	They picked up garbage on the street. 그들은 거리에서 쓰레기를 주웠다.
put off	~을 연기하다	Never put off till tomorrow what you can do today. 오늘 할 수 있는 일을 내일로 미루지 마라.
refer to A as B	A를 B라고 부르다/일컫다	Mark refers to him as a dear friend. Mark는 그를 소중한 친구라고 부른다.
speak ill of	~에 대해 안 좋게 말하다	Don't speak ill of others behind their backs. 뒤에서 남의 욕을 하지 마라.
take care of	~을 돌보다/처리하다	Please take care of my son. 제 아들을 돌봐 주세요.
throw away	~을 버리다	We throw away paper and plastic. 우리는 종이와 플라스틱을 버린다.
turn down	~을 거절하다	He asked her to marry him but she turned him down. 그가 그녀에게 청혼을 했지만 그녀가 거절했다.
turn off	~을 끄다	Please turn the television off before you go to bed. 잠자리에 들기 전에 텔레비전을 꺼 주세요.
turn on	~을 켜다	I'll turn on the air conditioner. 제가 에어컨을 켤게요.

필수문법용어

		예문
동명사	동사를 동사원형+~ing의 형태로 변형하여 명사처럼 쓸 수 있도록 한 말 문장에서 주어, 보어, 목적어의 역할을 함	I enjoyed **playing** baseball last summer. 나는 지난여름 야구 하는 것을 즐겼다.
분사	동사가 변형되어 형용사 역할을 하는 말 예) 현재분사, 과거분사	I found a big **melting** ice. 나는 녹고 있는 큰 얼음을 찾았다. There were a lot of **fallen** leaves. 떨어진 잎이 많이 있었다.
현재분사	'~하고 있는, ~하는'의 의미로 진행이나 능동을 나타내는 분사	It is an **interesting** story. 그것은 흥미로운 이야기이다.
과거분사	'~한, ~된, ~당한'의 의미로 완료나 수동을 나타내는 분사	It was just a **broken** radio. 그것은 단지 고장 난 라디오였다.
가정법	실제로 일어나지 않은 상황을 가정할 때 쓰는 동사의 형태	If I **were** rich, I **could buy** the house. 내가 부자라면, 그 집을 살 수 있을 텐데.
관계대명사 관계부사	두 개의 문장을 연결하여 두 문장의 관계를 나타내는 말 접속사+대명사[부사]의 역할을 함	This is the letter **which** was written by her. 이것은 그녀에 의해 쓰여진 편지다. I remember the day **when** he left. 나는 그가 떠났던 날을 기억한다.
선행사	관계사 앞에 오는 말로 관계사가 수식하는 명사, 구, 절을 의미함	Once there lived **a farmer** who was diligent. 옛날에 부지런한 한 농부가 살았다.

필수문법용어

		예문
직접목적어	4형식 문장에서 **동작의 대상**이 되는 목적어 '~을[를]'이라고 해석	I gave him a piece of advice. 나는 그에게 조언을 해 주었다.
간접목적어	4형식 문장에서 직접목적어를 받는 사람(사물) '~에게'라고 해석	I gave him a piece of advice. 나는 그에게 조언을 해 주었다.
대과거	과거 시점보다 **더 앞선 과거**, had+과거분사의 형태로 나타냄	He lost the pen he had bought the day before. 그는 전날 산 펜을 잃어버렸다.
시제	사건이나 사실이 **언제 일어난** 것인지 표시하는 문법 요소 현재, 과거, 미래, 진행 시제, 완료 시제 등을 포함한 12시제가 있음	He teaches English to us. 그는 우리에게 영어를 가르친다. World War II ended in 1945. 세계 2차 대전은 1945년에 끝났다.
격	명사, 대명사가 문장 안에서 갖는 자격 예) 주격, 목적격, 소유격	I know a girl. Her eyes are very big. 나는 한 소녀를 안다. 그녀의 눈은 매우 크다.
조동사	동사 앞에서 의무, 추측, 가능, 요청, 허가, 제안 등의 의미를 더하는 말	You must stay awake. 너는 깨어 있어야 한다.
태	주어와 동사와의 관계 - 능동태: 주어가 동작을 스스로 할 경우 - 수동태: 주어가 동작을 받는 경우	She built this house. 그녀는 이 집을 지었다. This house was built by her. 이 집은 그녀에 의해 지어졌다.